MUSEUM MEDIA

T0338050

Museum Media

Edited by
Michelle Henning

General Editors
Sharon Macdonald and Helen Rees Leahy

WILEY Blackwell

This paperback edition first published 2020
© 2015 John Wiley & Sons Ltd

Edition history: John Wiley and Sons Ltd (hardback, 2015)

All rights reserved. No part of this publication may be reproduced, stored in a retrieval system, or transmitted, in any form or by any means, electronic, mechanical, photocopying, recording or otherwise, except as permitted by law. Advice on how to obtain permission to reuse material from this title is available at http://www.wiley.com/go/permissions.

The right of Michelle Henning, Sharon Macdonald, and Helen Rees Leahy to be identified as the authors of the editorial material in this work has been asserted in accordance with law.

Registered Offices
John Wiley & Sons, Inc., 111 River Street, Hoboken, NJ 07030, USA
John Wiley & Sons Ltd, The Atrium, Southern Gate, Chichester, West Sussex, PO19 8SQ, UK

Editorial Office
The Atrium, Southern Gate, Chichester, West Sussex, PO19 8SQ, UK

For details of our global editorial offices, customer services, and more information about Wiley products visit us at www.wiley.com.

Wiley also publishes its books in a variety of electronic formats and by print-on-demand. Some content that appears in standard print versions of this book may not be available in other formats.

Limit of Liability/Disclaimer of Warranty
While the publisher and authors have used their best efforts in preparing this work, they make no representations or warranties with respect to the accuracy or completeness of the contents of this work and specifically disclaim all warranties, including without limitation any implied warranties of merchantability or fitness for a particular purpose. No warranty may be created or extended by sales representatives, written sales materials or promotional statements for this work. The fact that an organization, website, or product is referred to in this work as a citation and/or potential source of further information does not mean that the publisher and authors endorse the information or services the organization, website, or product may provide or recommendations it may make. This work is sold with the understanding that the publisher is not engaged in rendering professional services. The advice and strategies contained herein may not be suitable for your situation. You should consult with a specialist where appropriate. Further, readers should be aware that websites listed in this work may have changed or disappeared between when this work was written and when it is read. Neither the publisher nor authors shall be liable for any loss of profit or any other commercial damages, including but not limited to special, incidental, consequential, or other damages.

Library of Congress Cataloging-in-Publication Data

Museum media – The international handbooks of museum studies / edited by Michelle Henning / general editors: Sharon Macdonald, Helen Rees Leahy. – First edition.
    pages   cm
  Includes bibliographical references and index.
  ISBN 978-1-4051-9850-9 (cloth) | ISBN 978-1-119-64202-2 (pbk)
1. Museums.   2. Museum exhibits.   I. Macdonald, Sharon.   II. Leahy, Helen Rees.
  AM5.I565 2015
  069–dc23

2015003407

A catalogue record for this book is available from the British Library

Cover Design: Wiley
Cover Image: Rafael Lozano-Hemmer, Pulse Room, 2010, Manchester Art Gallery, Manchester, UK. © DACS 2014 / VEGAP. Photo by Peter Mallet.

Set in 11/13pt Dante by SPi Global, Pondicherry, India

Printed and bound by CPI Group (UK) Ltd, Croydon, CR0 4YY

10 9 8 7 6 5 4 3 2 1

CONTENTS

LIST OF ILLUSTRATIONS

Color plate section

Chapter illustrations

EDITOR

Michelle Henning is Professor in Photography and Cultural History in the London School of Film, Media and Design at the University of West London. She is a practicing photographer and designer and has written widely on museums, media, and photography in her books *Museums, Media and Cultural Theory* (Open University Press, 2006) and *Photography: The Unfettered Image* (Routledge 2018) as well as in numerous collections.

Michelle Henning
London School of Film, Media and Design
University of West London
London, UK

GENERAL EDITORS

Sharon Macdonald is Alexander van Humboldt Professor in Social Anthropology at the Humboldt University Berlin where she directs the Centre for Anthropological Research on Museums and Heritage – CARMAH. The centre works closely with a wide range of museums. Sharon's edited and coedited volumes include the *Companion to Museum Studies* (Blackwell, 2006), *Exhibition Experiments* (with Paul Basu; Blackwell, 2007), and *Theorizing Museums* (with Gordon Fyfe; Blackwell, 1996). Her authored books include *Behind the Scenes at the Science Museum* (Berg, 2002), *Difficult Heritage: Negotiating the Nazi Past in Nuremberg and Beyond* (Routledge, 2009), and *Memorylands: Heritage and Identity in Europe Today* (Routledge, 2013). Her current projects include *Making Differences: Transforming Museums and Heritage in the 21st Century.*

Professor Sharon Macdonald
Alexander van Humboldt Professor in Social Anthropology
Institute for European Ethnology
Humboldt University of Berlin
Berlin, Germany

Helen Rees Leahy is Professor Emerita of Museology at the University of Manchester, where, between 2002 and 2017 she directed the Centre for Museology. Previously, Helen held a variety of senior posts in UK museums, including the Design Museum, Eureka! The Museum for Children, and the National Art Collections Fund. She has also worked as an independent consultant and curator, and has organized numerous exhibitions of art and design. She has published widely on practices of individual and institutional collecting, in both historical and contemporary contexts, including issues of patronage, display and interpretation. Her *Museum Bodies: The Politics and Practices of Visiting and Viewing* was published by Ashgate in 2012.

Professor Emerita Helen Rees Leahy
Centre for Museology
School of Arts, Languages and Cultures
University of Manchester
Manchester, UK

CONTRIBUTORS

Alice Barnaby, University of Bedfordshire, UK

John Bell, University of Maine, USA

Brigitte Biehl-Missal, BSP Business School Berlin Potsdam, Germany

Fiona Candlin, Birkbeck, University of London, UK

Jenny Chamarette, Queen Mary, University of London, UK

Luigina Ciolfi, Sheffield Hallam University, UK

Maeve Connolly, Dún Laoghaire Institute of Art, Design and Technology, Ireland

Rupert Cox, University of Manchester, UK

Steffi de Jong, University of Cologne, Germany

Wolfgang Ernst, Humboldt University, Berlin, Germany

Ivan Gaskell, Bard Graduate Center, New York City, USA

Seth Giddings, Winchester School of Art, University of Southampton, UK

Beryl Graham, University of Sunderland, UK

Bettina Habsburg-Lothringen, Universalmuseum Joanneum, Austria

Beat Hächler, Swiss Alpine Museum, Switzerland

Karin Harrasser, University of Art and Design Linz, Austria

Michelle Henning, University of West London, UK

Peter Higgins, Land Design Studio, UK

Amy Holdsworth, University of Glasgow, UK

Andrew Hoskins, University of Glasgow, UK

Erkki Huhtamo, University of California, Los Angeles, USA

Jon Ippolito, University of Maine, USA

Petra Tjitske Kalshoven, University of Manchester, UK

Nils Lindahl Elliot, independent scholar, UK

Sue Perks, Perks Willis Design, UK

Nancy Proctor, Baltimore Museum of Art, USA

Mark W. Rectanus, Iowa State University, USA

Dirk vom Lehn, King's College London, UK

Haidee Wasson, Concordia University, Canada

ACKNOWLEDGMENTS

This volume of the *International Handbooks of Museum Studies* could not have been compiled without the extensive help of Gill Whitley, project manager for Wiley Blackwell, the copy-editor Jacqueline Harvey, and the *Handbooks'* editors Sharon Macdonald and Helen Rees Leahy. I would also like to thank Jen Rhodes who was an invaluable research assistant during the early development of the project, and Niall Hoskins, who translated Beat Hächler's chapter. Both Jen and Niall were funded by the Digital Cultures Research Centre at the University of the West of England, Bristol, and I would like to thank the then director of the center, Professor Jon Dovey, and especially the research administrator, Nick Triggs, for making this possible. The project was also made possible by the research leave I received from the faculty of Arts, Creative Industries and Education at the University of the West of England, and by the support of my ex-colleagues in Media and Cultural Studies. For a long time, this was a wonderfully diverse research and teaching environment in which it was possible to teach classes such as "The Politics of Collecting and Display" along side the history and practice of photography and new media, and to follow the most unusual research paths with encouragement. Although many of us have now gone on to other places and roles, and this tolerant and stimulating environment has changed, it strongly informed my view that museum studies and media studies have interesting things to say to each other. My work on this book was facilitated by the support, understanding, and intellectual companionship of Jane Arthurs, Helen Kennedy, Gillian Swanson, Richard Hornsey, and Rehan Hyder. Above all, this book would have been impossible without the many kindnesses of my partner John Parish, and of my daughters Honor and Hopey Parish. Finally, I am immeasurably grateful to all the contributors, many of whom must have wondered at times if this book would ever actually materialize, for their patience with my editorial lapses and nitpicking, and for their generosity in the production of these chapters. They are academics, artists, curators, exhibition designers, and museum directors, and their chapters are very different but all, I believe, offer fascinating insights into media in the museum, museums' relationship to different media, and how media concepts inform museum practice.

GENERAL EDITORS' PREFACE TO *MUSEUM MEDIA* AND *THE INTERNATIONAL HANDBOOKS IN MUSEUM STUDIES*

Museum Media

As general editors of *The International Handbooks in Museum Studies*, we – Sharon Macdonald and Helen Rees Leahy – are delighted that *Museum Media* is now appearing in paperback, as a self-standing volume. So too are the other volumes, which is testament to the strength of these volumes individually, as well as collectively, and to the importance of the issues that they each address. *Museum Media* clearly concerns a fundamental area of museum studies – museums can be said to in a sense *be* media, as well as to deploy a wide range of different forms of media. Despite the fact that media are fundamental to museums – and thus to museum studies – there is not, however, an established consensus on precisely what might be covered under the label "museum media". One reason for this is the relative recency of museum studies as a field. A second reason is that museum studies draws on a wide range of disciplines, each themselves renewing their toolkits in various ways, resulting in new impulses for thinking about the media in museums. In addition, and perhaps of most significance, is the fact of change in the media available for use in museums. This results in fresh thinking about the possibilities for deploying such media, as well as for consideration of its potential consequences not only for engaging new audiences but also for rethinking what the museum already does, as well as what it might do in new ways.

Confronted by the fast-changing world of new media, as well as fascinating redeployments of older media, the editor of *Museum Media*, Michelle Henning, in consultation with us as general editors, faced a task of how to achieve a volume that would cover approaches that have become central to consideration of museum media, while also being sure to include as much as possible of the new directions and ideas that have been emerging in recent years. That this was achieved so well is evident from the resulting volume. The range of topics included and the ways in which they are tackled, provide a sound and also cutting-edge coverage of museum media.

The International Handbooks in Museum Studies

Collectively, *The International Handbooks in Museum Studies* include over a hundred original, state-of-the-art chapters on museums and museum studies. As such, they are the most comprehensive review to date of the lively and expanding field of museum studies. Written by a wide range of scholars and practitioners – newer voices as well as those already widely esteemed – *The International Handbooks* provide not only extensive coverage of key topics and debates in the museum field, but also make a productive contribution to emerging debates and areas, as well as to suggest how museum studies – and museums – might develop in the future.

The number of excellent contributors able and willing to write on museum topics is itself testimony to the state of the field, as was recognition by the publishers that the field warranted such a substantial work. Bringing together such a range and quantity of new writing about museums was accomplished through the deep knowledge, extensive networks, and sheer labour of the volume editors – Andrea Witcomb and Kylie Message, *Museum Theory*; Conal McCarthy, *Museum Practice*; Michelle Henning, *Museum Media*; and Annie E. Coombes and Ruth B. Phillips, *Museum Transformations*. All enthusiastically took up the mandate to go out and recruit those they thought would be best able to write useful and timely essays on what they defined as the most important topics within their area of remit. Their brief was to look widely for potential contributors, including unfamiliar, as well as familiar, names. We – and they – were especially interested in perspectives from people whose voices have not always been heard within the international museum studies conversation thus far. This breadth is also a feature of the expanded and expanding field itself, as we explain further below.

Diversification and democratization

The editors of the four volumes that constitute *The International Handbooks* are based in four different countries – Australia, New Zealand, the United Kingdom, and Canada; and contributors have their institutional homes in over a dozen more. Yet these numbers alone do not fully convey the trend to diversification that we see in these volumes, and in museum studies more widely. "Internationalization" is a term that might be used but does not, we think, adequately characterize what is involved. Certainly, there is more traffic between nations of ideas about museums and about how to study them. Debates travel from one part of the globe to another, with museums and exhibitions in one location being used as models for emulation or avoidance in another. The massive expansion of professional training in museum studies that has taken place over the past three decades helps establish a shared discourse, not least as many students study away from their home countries or those in which they will later work. So too do texts in and about the field, certain key ones often being found on reading lists in numerous countries and also republished in successive readers. Such developments establish the basis for a conversation capable of transcending borders.

It is evident from the contents of *The International Handbooks of Museum Studies*, however, that the democratization runs deeper than the traffic of discourse and practice across national borders, and, in particular, that the traffic is more multi-directional than it was previously. Not only do contributors have their primary work bases in a range of different countries, and not only do many have experience of training or working in others, they also often give attention – sometimes through the direct engagement of collaborative work or study – to a wide range of groups and populations in a variety of countries, including their own. In doing so, they strive not merely to incorporate but also to learn from and be challenged by people and perspectives that have not been part of mainstream museological debate. The attention to the (not unproblematic) category of the indigenous is especially marked in these *International Handbooks*, most notably in the *Transformations* volume, although it also finds its way into the others. Like attention to other forms of absence from the existing mainstream museum conversation, this is symptomatic of a broader move toward finding alternative ways of seeing and doing, ways that both add to the range of existing possibilities and also, sometimes, unsettle these by showing how, say, particular theorizing or practice relies on unspoken or previously unrecognized assumptions.

Diversification takes other forms too. These volumes are not organized by type of museum – a format that we think restrictive in its lack of recognition of so many shared features and concerns of museums – and do not use this as a classification of content. Nevertheless, it is easy to see that the volumes include a great range of museum kinds, and even of forms that might not always be considered museums, or that challenge the idea of the museum as a physical space. Museums of art, history, and ethnography – and also those more general and eclectic museums that have sometimes been described as encyclopedic – have powered a good deal of museum theorizing and debate, and they are amply represented here. But they are accompanied also by examples from museums of natural history, science, technology, and medicine, as well as heritage sites and out-of-gallery installations. Alongside national museums, which were the backbone of much important theorizing of the role of museums in the making of national identity and citizenship, are numerous examples of smaller museums, some of which are devoted to a specific topic and others of which have a regional or local foundation and focus. These museums may be less well endowed with staff, buildings, or funds, but are nevertheless doing important, even pioneering, work that deserves attention from museum studies. That attention contributes not only to extending the range of types and cases but also helps to illuminate the variety of specific features of museums that need to be taken into account in formulating more comprehensive approaches. As many chapters across the volumes show, one size does not fit all – or, to put it better perhaps, one theoretical perspective or set of guidelines for practice, one apt choice of media or transformative activity, does not fit all types and sizes of museums. Adding more to the mix does not just provide greater coverage or choice but also helps to identify better what is at stake and what might be possible in different kinds of situations, constellations, or conjunctures (to use a word favored in *Museum Theory*). As such, it helps those of us engaged in and with museums to get a better grasp on what is and what might be shared, as well as on what is distinctive and needs to be understood in more fine-grained ways.

Another feature of diversification that deserves comment here is the temporal. There has been a considerable amount of outstanding historical research undertaken in museum studies and the *International Handbooks* both review some of this and contribute further to it. Such work is important in its own terms, helping us to understand better the contexts in which museums emerged and have operated, and the concerns, constraints, personalities, and opportunities in evidence in particular times and places. It also contributes in vital ways to contemporary understandings, both by adding to the range of cases available for analysis and by showing the longer historical trajectories out of which various current approaches and practices emerged. Sometimes – and there are examples in all of the volumes here – their message is salutary, showing that what seemed like an innovation has been tried before, and perhaps with the distance of time allowing a more critical perspective than might feel comfortable today. The past shows change but also continuities and the re-emergence, or even repackaging, of what has gone before.

Disciplinarity and methodology

Research on past museum innovation and practice shows the importance of historical method, and of history as a discipline, within museum studies. This brings us to the wider issue of disciplinarity and methodology. To talk of museum studies as interdisciplinary has become a truism. The volumes here are a clear illustration that those involved in museum studies have been trained in and may have primary institutional locations in a wide range of disciplines and areas of study, including anthropology, archaeology, architecture, area studies, cultural studies, economics, education, geography, literature, management, media studies, political science, and sociology, as well as history and art history. Beyond that, however, they are also carving out new niches, sometimes institutionally recognized, sometimes not, in areas such as digital curation and creative technologies, as well as in art gallery, museum, and heritage studies, in various combinations or alone. Moreover, in addition to disciplines and a multitude of academic specialisms, practitioner contributors bring diverse professional expertise in areas including exhibition design, community engagement, conservation, interpretation, and management.

Alongside the diversity of concepts and methodologies offered by various disciplines and diverse forms of practical expertise, is also the distinctive feature of museum studies – its engagement with the past, present, and future world of museums. Such work, to varying extents, confronts researchers and academics with the actual concerns, predicaments, objects, spaces, media, and people all, in various ways, involved in museum collections and exhibitions. Increasingly, this means actual collaboration, and the development of methodological approaches to enable this. Examples in these volumes include those who consider themselves to be primarily academics, artists, or activists being directly involved in the production of collections, media (e.g., new media apps or forms of display), and exhibitions. The nature of museum work is, inevitably, collaborative, but in some cases it also involves more explicit attempts to work with those who have had little previous engagement in museum worlds and draws on methodology and ethical insight from disciplines such as social and cultural anthropology to do so. Such actual engagement – coupled with what we see as more fluid traffic between academia and museums also powers new forms of theorizing and practice. This productive mobility affords museum studies its characteristic – and, in our view, especially exciting – dynamic.

Organization of the *International Handbooks*

As we originally planned these *International Handbooks*, dividing their coverage into the four volumes of Theory, Practice, Media, and Transformations made good sense as a way of grouping key areas of work within the field. Our idea was that *Theory* would bring together work that showed central areas of theorizing that have shaped museum studies so far, together with those that might do so in the future. We envisaged *Practice* as attending especially to areas of actual museum work, especially those that have tended to be ignored in past theorizing, not in order to try to reinstate a theory/practice division but, rather, to take the opportunity to transcend it through theorizing these too. We saw *Media* as the appropriate label to cover the crucially important area for museums of their architecture, spaces, and uses of diverse media primarily, though not exclusively, for display. *Transformations* was intended to direct its attention especially to some of the most important social, cultural, political, and economic developments that are shaping and look likely to reshape museums in the future.

In many ways, what has resulted fits this original remit. We always knew that there would inevitably be areas of convergence: in particular, that theory can derive from practice, and vice versa; that the development and expansion of social media is propelling some of the most significant transformations in museums, and so forth. Yet it is probably true to say that there are more synergies than we had imagined, perhaps because museum work has itself become more open to change, new ideas and practice, and unconventional practitioners and participants, from what would previously have been considered outside. To make distinctions between practitioners and theorists continues to make sense in some contexts. What we see, however, is an increasing band of critical practitioners and practice-based researchers – those who operate in both worlds, drawing inspiration for new practice from areas of theorizing as well as from adaptations of cases from elsewhere. Equally they use practice to think through issues such as the nature of objects, the role of media, or sensory potentials.

It is interesting to note that at an analytical level, the volumes all contain chapters that give emphasis to specific cases and argue for the importance of paying close attention to grounded process – what actually happens, where, who, and what is involved. Although not all are informed by theoretical perspectives of actor network theory or assemblage theory, there is much here that recognizes the significance of material forms not just as objects of analysis but as agents in processes themselves. There is also much work across the volumes that gives explicit attention to the affective dimensions of museums, exploring, for example, how different media or spaces might afford certain emotional engagements. The sensory is also given new levels of consideration in what we see as, collectively, a more extensive attempt to really get to grips with the distinctiveness of museums as a medium, as well as with their sheer variety.

Various forms of collaborative engagement with specific groups – sometimes called communities – as well as with individual visitors, is also a notable theme cutting across the various volumes. Certainly, the idea of a generic "audience" or "public" seems to be less present as a central but abstract focus than in the past. Divisions along lines of gender or class are made less frequently than they might have been in earlier critical perspectives – though when they are, this is often done especially well and powerfully, as, for example, in some contributions to the discussion of museum media. Interestingly, and this is a comment on our times as well as on social and political developments in which museums are embroiled, the work with "communities" is framed less in terms of identity politics than would probably have been the case previously. No longer, perhaps, is the issue so much about making presence seen in a museum, increasingly it is more about mutually enriching ways of working together, and about pursuing particular areas or issues of concern, such as those of the environment or future generations. Yet politics is certainly not absent. Not only is the fundamental question about whose voice is represented in the museum a thoroughly political one, the chapters also show political concerns over relatively subtle matters such as methodology and reformulations of intimacy, as well as over questions of sponsorship, money-flow in the art world, the development of mega-museums in Gulf states, environmental destruction, and so forth. Indeed, there is a strong current of work that positions the museum as an activist institution and that shows its potential as such – something perhaps indicative of at least one future direction that more museums might take.

One thing that is clear from these volumes, however, is that there is no single trajectory that museums have taken in the past. Neither is there a single track along which they are all heading, nor one that those of us who have contributed would agree that they should necessarily all take. The diversity of museums themselves, as well as of those who work in, on, and with them, and of the perspectives that these volumes show can be brought to bear upon them – as well as their very various histories, collections, contexts, personnel, publics, and ambitions – has inspired the diversified museum studies represented in these *International*

Handbooks. Our hope is that this more diversified museum studies can contribute not only to new ways of understanding museums but also to new, and more varied, forms of practice within them – and to exciting, challenging futures, whatever these might be.

Acknowledgments

Producing these *International Handbooks of Museum Studies* has probably been a bigger and more demanding project than any of us had anticipated at the outset. Assembling together so many authors across four different volumes, and accommodating so many different timetables, work dynamics, styles, and sensitivities has been a major task over more years than we like to recall for both us as general editors, and even more especially for the editors of our four volumes: Andrea Witcomb, Kylie Message, Conal McCarthy, Michelle Henning, Annie E. Coombes, and Ruth B. Phillips. As general editors, our first thanks must be to the volume editors, who have done a remarkable task of identifying and eliciting so many insightful and illuminating contributions from such a wide field, and of working with authors – not all of whom were experienced in academic writing and many of whom were already grappling with hectic schedules – to coax the best possible chapters from them. We thank our volume editors too for working with us and what may sometimes have seemed overly interventionist assistance on our part in our push to make the volumes work together, as well as individually, and for all contributions, as well as the *International Handbooks* as a whole, to be a substantial contribution to the field. We also thank our volume editors for sharing so much good humor and so many cheering messages along the way, turning what sometimes felt like relentless chasing and head-aching over deadlines into something much more human and enjoyable. All of the contributors also deserve immense thanks too, of course, for joining the convoy and staying the journey. We hope that it feels well worth it for all concerned. Without you – editors and contributors – it couldn't have happened.

There is also somebody else without whom it couldn't have happened. This is Gill Whitley. Gill joined the project in 2012 as Project Editor. In short, she transformed our lives through her impeccable organization and skillful diplomacy, directly contacting contributors to extract chapters from them, setting up systems to keep us all on track with where things were up to, and securing many of the picture permissions. She has been a pleasure to work with and we are immensely grateful to her.

The idea for a series of *International Handbooks of Museum Studies* came from Jayne Fargnoli at Wiley Blackwell and we are grateful to her for this and being such a great cheerleader for the project. She read a good deal of the work as it came in and knowing that this only increased her enthusiasm for the project boosted everyone's energy as we chased deadlines. We also thank other staff at Wiley Blackwell for their role in the production processes, including, most recently, Jake Opie, for helping to at last allow us to bring out the individual volumes in paperback format.

Because of its extended nature and because things don't always happen according to initial timetables, editorial work like this often has to be fitted into what might otherwise be leisure time or time allocated for other things. Luckily, both of our Mikes (Mike Beaney and Mike Leahy) were sympathetic, not least as both have deeply occupying work of their own; and we thank them for being there for us when we needed them.

Lastly, we would like to thank each other. We have each benefited from the other's complementary expertise and networks, from the confidence of having that insightful second opinion, and from the sharing of the load. Having somebody else with whom to experience the frustrations and joys, the tribulations and amusements, has made it so much more fun. Not only has this helped to keep us relatively sane, but it has also made *The International Handbooks of Museum Studies* so much better than they would otherwise have been.

Sharon Macdonald and Helen Rees Leahy
August 2014 and July 2019

MUSEUM MEDIA
An Introduction

Michelle Henning

On January 2, 2014 the award-winning journalist John Pilger presented a segment on the BBC Radio 4 *Today* program entitled "Is Media Just Another Word for Control?" He succinctly articulated two familiar analyses of the media: first, that media institutions serve the powerful by assuming consensus and by producing "censorship by omission" ("we in Britain have been misled by those whose job is to keep the record straight"); second, that media forms and technologies distract us from what is actually happening in the world, not just through their content but through the affective relationship we have with them, particularly our smartphones, which we "caress … like rosary beads" (Pilger 2014).[1]

The reaction to the program by right-wing British newspapers was rapid and hostile. In articles based almost entirely on harvesting selected "tweets" from the social media platform Twitter, they were quick to claim there was a consensus among listeners that the program was unbalanced, biased, and "unfairly left-wing" (Chorley and Robinson 2014; Marsden 2014). Pilger argued that the media are "hijacked" rather than inherently and inevitably repressive, and the press reaction suggests that control is not impenetrable or infallible, that this program was a rupture in the fabric, something that needed to be quickly contained and disarmed. The reaction was what Edward S. Herman and Noam Chomsky describe as "flak" – "a means of disciplining the media" – here, almost entirely contrived by the press (Herman and Chomsky 1988, 2).

As an illustration of Chomskian media theory, this argument and the reaction to it are almost perfect, but they also point to a new complexity when "media" refers to powerful corporations like the BBC, CNN, Reuters; the institutions of the press, television, and radio broadcasting; and also to Twitter and smartphones. "The media" are now providers of content to be consumed on different digital "platforms," or media, via computers, smartphones, and tablets, as well as television, radio, and the press. This complex material and technical infrastructure does not leave content unchanged: as Seth Giddings puts it in in this volume, "media are not simply conduits or channels … through which messages and meanings flow, more or less effectively" (Chapter 7).

In media studies, the recent revival of interest in the 1960s Canadian media theorist Marshall McLuhan and his maxim "The medium is the message" has been meant as a corrective to analyses that treat media technologies as mere platforms for content. Museum studies can also benefit from this shift toward an emphasis on the mode of communication. Like media, museums are powerful institutions involved in producing and keeping the historical record, establishing "what really happened" and communicating it to a public. While, as Wolfgang Ernst points out in Chapter 1, it makes sense to clearly distinguish museums from electronic media, since they are not technical devices, in museums and exhibitions the medium – including exhibition design, architecture, and atmosphere, as well as technical infrastructure – is all the more powerful because it addresses visitors in a bodily, felt way. These are the things that pull on our emotions, alter our behavior, influence the ways in which we socialize with one another.

McLuhan was interested in how the technical design and structure of the media imposes certain dispositions or orientation even before any specific content is encountered. In 1964 he stated: "the 'message' of any medium or technology is the change of scale or pace or pattern that it introduces into human affairs" (McLuhan [1964] 2001, 8). This statement shows the influence of the political economist Harold Innis, who emphasized the material or technical "staples" that shape nations economically, politically, and culturally.[2] In 1951 Innis wrote that the material basis of communication has a bias or orientation determined by its "relative emphasis on time or space" (Innis [1951] 2008, 33). Heavy, durable media disseminate knowledge across time; light, transportable media facilitate societies that need their communication to have a wide geographic reach.[3] Understanding media bias, for Innis, means seeing different media as favoring different kinds of action and forms of social organization. Nancy Proctor gives an example in this volume: in museum tours, the shift from the tape-based audio tour to smartphones and interactives means a shift in museum and audience behaviors. The broadcast model is increasingly replaced by a distributed network model that connects people and "facilitate[s] conversations" (Proctor, Chapter 22). These technologies provide new opportunities for museums to engage with their audiences differently.

However, the smartphones that the majority of visitors carry are intimate, attention-seeking devices, which have arguably produced rapid and unanticipated changes in behavior that we are still seeking to understand. Pilger views people's behavior with their smartphones as cementing the insidious power of the media; we are addicted, attached. A related argument is made by Sherry Turkle in her book *Alone Together* (2011). Turkle's social-psychological research into people's engagement with technology, from computational toys to smartphones and robots, is concerned with what these technologies do to our relationships with one another. Such arguments emphasize nonhuman agency – the ability of our technologies to act on us – but are pessimistic regarding the ability of media users and audiences to renegotiate or resist the behaviors hardwired into the technology. For them, the media bias is not facilitating conversation but closing it down.

This volume sets out to understand the uses of contemporary media in museum contexts, and also to understand the ways museums have taken shape in relation to different media and technologies. This means paying attention not only to technologies, forms, genres, and so on, but also to what we do with different media, how we engage with them, and what they do to us. Understanding people's relationships with media technologies and display techniques in museum contexts requires research methodologies sensitive to both the nuances and diversity of display media and of visitor behaviors. One way in which museums researchers have attempted to understand visitor experience is through ethnographic studies, such as those carried out by Karin Harrasser and her colleagues, and described in Chapter 17 here. These complement a semiotic analysis of how museum narratives and "museum messages" are constructed and communicated, "encoded" within the museum and "decoded" by visitors (see Hooper-Greenhill 1995, 16–17; Hall [1973] 1980).[4]

Another approach is the method Erkki Huhtamo calls "exhibition anthropology," an observational approach to the minute details of visitor activity within exhibitions, which involves treating the museum as "a kind of experience apparatus" (Huhtamo, Chapter 12). While Huhtamo observes visitor and museum behaviors, Giddings has proposed "microethology" as a more intimate and participative methodology, which attends to both human and nonhuman agency in "everyday technoculture." Microethology uses participant observation to investigate "the everyday and habitual coming-together of human bodies and technologies" (Giddings 2009). For Harrasser, these encounters need to be understood in terms of performance: contemporary immersive exhibitions and interactive science centers "offer beautiful and effective 'stages' for both the training and transgression of culturally coded identities" (Harrasser, Chapter 17).

Where does this leave a politics of media and of museums? Pilger's central (and most controversial) point on the *Today* program was that the British media had misrepresented and underrepresented the Iraq war, leaving the British public largely ignorant of the scale of civilian deaths. Similar critiques have been directed at museums and this is what is generally understood as a political critique within museum studies – one which focuses on the museum's role in power and governance, its constructions of canons and dominant narratives.

It might seem, therefore, like a depoliticizing move to pay close attention, as this volume does, to the formal and technical aspects of exhibition practice (and to a lesser extent the collection, research, and conservation practices of museums), since (to some extent) it brackets off questions of representation, relationships to stakeholder communities, and institutional politics. However, just as there is another politics of media, there is another politics of museums, and there is a different political urgency to attending to museum media. This is related to, for example, questions of the transformation of history and memory by new media; the ways in which media habits and expectations are imported into museums; and the insertion of museums into a wider commercial and corporate landscape.

The present volume is divided into four parts. Part I, "The Museum as Medium," focuses primarily on the question of how museums draw on other media, and also introduces some key approaches from media studies (such as media archaeology). Part II, "Mediation and Immersion," centers around the pervasive and often intangible ways in which exhibitions mediate visitor experience, and also around the question of how material objects in particular are experienced and encountered. Part III, "Design and Curating in the Media Age," looks at museums and media primarily from the perspective of the designer and curator, and at new kinds of relationships with visitors. Part IV, "Extending the Museum," is particularly concerned with how media enable the museum to go beyond its walls and spill out into the world.

The structure of the volume is intended to highlight some connections between the chapters. However, the following discussion offers some other ways of thinking about the thematic connections between chapters, linking them to a wider literature. I explore questions of temporality, museums' relationships to various media and genres, attachment to objects, atmospheric and immersive exhibition design, the reinvention of the exhibition medium, the rise of scenography, new roles for audiences and for museum makers, and, finally, the collection and display of media objects.

Changing times

As Wolfgang Ernst explains, in the interview that opens Part I, our cultural objects are increasingly "digitally born" and the dominance of time-based, pervasive digital media means that material experience is neglected or underplayed. In contemporary culture, the emphasis on liveness and high-speed transmission poses a challenge to the traditional collection-based museum (Chapter 1). Andrew Hoskins and Amy Holdsworth use the term "post-scarcity culture" to describe the massive and simultaneous availability of images, footage, text, and data. This new media environment appears to be transforming cultural memory and crushing historical distance by making the past available on demand, producing a "smooth and smothering immediacy" (Chapter 2). This is something museums are forced to engage with because it is reconfiguring their role. How museums engage with this media environment, whether they embrace it, attempt to reconfigure or shape it, or stolidly continue to pursue their own goals regardless, are politicized issues.

In the past, museums have been criticized for their irrelevance to the present. In my own chapter, I give the example of a 1920s dispute in which museum director Alexander Dornor advocated facsimiles as a means of bringing museums into "the stream of contemporary life" (Dorner, cited in Chapter 25). The way in which museums construct the past has also come under critical scrutiny: the myth of history as progress is reinforced and naturalized by linear evolutionary arrangements that marshal objects into an "encyclopedic overview" (Habsburg-Lothringen,

Chapter 15). The chronological display that invites the visitor to walk through time naturalizes the timeline, creating the sense that this is actually how history unravels (Lubar 2013). Meanwhile, the contemporary art world, now dominated by large private contemporary art galleries, has been characterized as locked in a kind of "presentism" in which fashion and the market rule (Bishop 2013, 12–23). Art historian Claire Bishop suggests that "the permanent collection can be a museum's greatest weapon in breaking the stasis of presentism," to create new forms of historical awareness, new ways of mobilizing the past in the present, in displays that go far beyond the chronological (Bishop 2013, 24, 61–62).

In the present volume, several contributors see museums as able to provide alternatives to the historical flattening produced by digital networked media. New approaches in display design, open storage, and collection management can provide counterstrategies to a dominant understanding of history (Ernst, Chapter 1). Some museums seem to fully embrace the new digital immediacy, opening themselves up to the onslaught of images in a new, networked culture. Others try to reveal the discontinuities and gaps in both traditional narratives of smooth progress and the contemporary sense of complete and simultaneous availability of history (Hoskins and Holdsworth, Chapter 2). This is not so far removed from the aims of 1980s museum designers and curators such as Gottfried Korff. Bettina Habsburg-Lothringen, head of the Museumsakademie Joanneum in Graz, writes in Chapter 15 of the ways Korff wanted to challenge the sense of an accessible, unmediated historical past that folk museum reconstructions and period rooms seemed to promote.

Arguably, these changes in the cultural relationship to the past began as early as the mid-nineteenth century when photographic, telegraphic, and phonographic media made it possible to see and hear the faces and voices of the dead. As writers such as John Durham Peters have shown, this was especially poignant in wartime and in an era of high child mortality (Peters 1999). In 1936 Walter Benjamin wrote about an increasing inability in the modern period to make experiences – the things that happen to us – into experience, in the sense of a deeply embedded and practical understanding. He connected this to media via the example of the newspaper, with its fragmented and disconnected articles, but also more widely to modernity, an era of rapid and accelerating social and technological change in which an onslaught of stimuli combines with the absence of any stable, unchanging position from which to view the world (Benjamin [1936] 2002, 146). Swiss curator Beat Hächler, in Chapter 16, considers this decay of experience as offering a new remit to museums to transform themselves into spaces that enable people to experience and reflect on their collective present.

One way in which stable and coherent historical accounts have traditionally been ensured is via a strict separation between individual memory (understood as unreliable, narrowly specific, and subjective) and official history (underpinned by documentary evidence and the authority of academic expertise and research). In Chapter 4, Steffi de Jong argues that the video testimonies now commonly used in historical museums overturn this old hierarchy of historical transmission and memory. Personal, individual memory is now an acceptable part of the historical narrative and a museum object. Indeed, the medium of video has been a key tool in prioritizing individual memory and personal experience. In the 1980s video enabled home movies to move out of the living room and innovative television makers used the video camcorder to make first-person experiences a part of broadcast television through genres such as "video diaries" (Rose 1994–95; Dovey [1995] 2004). De Jong sees the rise of video testimonies as symptomatic of the "era of the witness" (Wieviorka 2006). In this context, remembering is not simply a matter of reporting but of bearing witness, giving testimony. The media coverage of the 1961 trial of Adolf Eichmann, one of the first televised trials, boosted the visibility of the witness to history. Television enabled testimony to be made public; video enabled it to be gathered and stored en masse.

Mediazation and transmediation

De Jong's account shows how video testimonies have developed a specific aesthetic: framing, location, and lighting prioritize emotional, extra-verbal expression and create the impression of direct eye contact between interviewee and viewer, an illusion of conversational directness. At the same time, these aesthetic conventions reinforce the museum's traditional role: to transmit historical information and moral messages, to produce a self-disciplining form of citizenship (Bennett 1995; de Jong, Chapter 4). Video testimony is a powerful tool for this purpose, because it is affective (communicating feeling via facial expression and nonverbal signals) yet its aesthetic and methodology imply objectivity, neutrality, and a documentary status.

The potential of media to bring new kinds of authority and new forms of audience address make them attractive to museums and galleries, which not only incorporate different media in their exhibition spaces, but frequently invoke or engage with other media by adapting and quoting media genres and formats. One issue discussed in Chapter 1 is how museums tend to mirror the media of their time, emulating cinema, for example, through displays such as the period room or the diorama. In fact, it is hard to imagine a museum remaining unchanged by media: my own chapter (25) relates how photography has dramatically altered the ways in which museum visitors see and understand art, so that the art museum, without even rehanging its collections, is subjected to altered modes of attention. Haidee Wasson's chapter shows that American museums became closely involved with media as technologies and institutions from a very early date: museums' "early experiments with television" began almost as soon as television was launched at the 1939 New York World's Fair (Wasson, Chapter 26).

Sometimes museums and exhibitions explicitly use media formats in order to comment critically on them or to reflect on the museum as institution.

For instance, in her chapter in Part I, Maeve Connolly discusses how contemporary art exhibitions that explore television as a cultural form have used design techniques to evoke television studios and the living room as a television viewing space. Design elements such as the choice of monitor, seating, and lighting have been used to evoke different relationships to television, the social and pedagogic role of the medium, and TV's changing status. TV formats are also used to reflect on the art institution and art market itself, from the use of reality TV references and modes, to close collaborations with broadcasters (Connolly, Chapter 6).

Elsewhere, museums' attempts to embrace contemporary media are not intended to produce commentary or reflection on either institution, but rather to reinvent the museum as medium. In Chapter 3, Nils Lindahl Elliot describes Wildwalk in Bristol, UK (a futuristic attraction that closed only seven years after opening), as an attempt to "transmediate" the wildlife documentary in the form of a museum/zoo. Zoos had already attempted to transmediate wildlife television – giving visitors the sense that they were visiting animals in their habitats – and attempting to make the whole experience more cinematic. Using C. S. Peirce's semeiotics (as distinguished from the more familiar post-Saussurean "semiotics"), Lindahl Elliot shows the complex and contradictory character of transmediation and "mediazation" (Thompson 1990, 11). He concludes that while transmediation can happen between museums and media genres, the effects can be unforeseen and problematic, producing inadvertent pedagogic effects.

Seth Giddings's chapter also touches on the ways in which museums' incorporation of other media forms can contradict or give a very different message from that intended. He acknowledges the limitations of certain museum videogames, in which what is learnt is mainly "knowledge of the game itself, its structures and puzzles" (Giddings, Chapter 7). Rather than see this as a consequence of transmediation, Giddings sees it as related to expectations of "what kinds of knowledge – or knowledge of what kind of object" museum games and interactives might produce. He argues that simulations produce knowledge not of objects but of systems, also using an example from Wildwalk, where artificial life (Alife) flocking simulations were used to produce the experience of walking through water among schools of fish. For Giddings, "attention to the machinery of display" is not necessarily at odds with processes of learning and the generating of knowledges, while even the simulation designer cannot always constrain the possibilities opened up by a playful simulation.

Part of the problem for Wildwalk, Lindahl Elliot argues, was that genres "involve not just techniques and technologies of communication, but also a horizon of expectation shared by the audience" (Chapter 3). Such horizons of expectation may remain invisible and unspoken, but they determine the form of visitors engagement with displays. In Chapter 5, Jenny Chamarette starts from the premise that the museum itself does a similar disappearing act. Yet, by bringing cinema into the museum, Chamarette argues, the museum (as well as cinema) is put on display. This idea, that cinema can work critically to make the museum's framing visible, recalls a point made by Alexander Horwath, director of the Austrian Film Museum in Vienna, that the detachment of artists' film from both commercial cinema and the art museum enables it to reflect critically on both institutions (Sperlinger and White 2008, 119). Chamarette focuses on the Pompidou Center in Paris, where, she suggests, filmmakers have challenged the status of the museum as the protector of cultural heritage or patrimony. She gives the example of Roberto Rossellini's 1977 film *Le Centre Georges Pompidou* which, she argues, subtly critiqued the ideas of high culture and democratization that underpinned the new museum, as did the sociological analysis of the center, undertaken at the same time under the direction of Pierre Bourdieu (Fabiani and Menger 1979; Heinich 2003).

For Horwath, the film museum is the in-between space that artists' film can occupy (and has occupied in the past), an institution closely related to *cinémathèques* and film libraries, and one that has marginal status compared to the art museum (Sperlinger and White 2008, 120). The Pompidou both collects and shows moving image work within an art museum context. But, according to Chamarette, the meeting of cinema and museum at the Pompidou is not a tale of the incorporation of one by the other but of a clash of spaces, conventions, and expectations; a relationship of mutual suspicion as well as interdependence. That this is not always the case is suggested by Wasson's account of the "harmonious and mutually interdependent" historical relationship between the two institutions in the United States (Chapter 26). Even at the Pompidou, Chamarette suggests, the relationship has ultimately been productive: faced with the resistance and challenges of film, the Pompidou Center has been able to renegotiate itself and to challenge what a museum can be and do (Chapter 5).

"Mediazation" can involve a closer relationship with commercial environments than some public museums are used to. Maeve Connolly discusses how, initially, experimental art projects in television were made possible by television broadcasters themselves, but these declined with the development of a deregulated neoliberal and commercialized media environment. New "participatory and discursive activities" have flourished, and art projects continue to reflect critically on both television and art institutions and practices. However, some museums and galleries adopt broadcast formats or collaborate with broadcasters, not in order to reflect on these, but simply to try to engage a broader public, and in the process become full participants in a "celebrity-driven cultural economy" (Connolly, Chapter 6).

Bringing things to life

In Chapter 1, Ernst suggests that museums need to focus on their own specificity, particularly the strengths that result from the presence of the material object. In my own chapter, I recount how museums have a history of being hospitable to reproductions and facsimiles, and argue that the value attached to direct experiences of authentic, original artifacts is associated with the notion that they are under threat from mediation (Henning, Chapter 25). The physical, material qualities of museum artworks became all the more vivid when they could be used to set the art object apart from the media object or photographic facsimile. While mediation in the form of information, context, and framing is necessary to make objects meaningful, it also appears to put a distance between visitors and the artifact, to diminish the potential for wonder, to "kill" the object.

The rhetoric of "bringing objects to life" is commonly used, even though most Western museums subscribe to the Western scientific view that the objects in their collections do not have life in any real sense. In her chapter, Fiona Candlin addresses this notion, asking "why museum exhibits are commonly perceived to be in need of resuscitation" (Chapter 13). She sees the use of the terms "live" and "dead" to describe museum objects as metaphoric (except where talking about living animals or animal and human remains). The dead object is one where "the practices and responses associated with its former functions have been sidelined and ... scholarly and aesthetic responses dominate." A live object, by contrast, continues to elicit responses related to its previous role. Candlin is using a distinction derived from the early nineteenth century argument of Quatremère de Quincy, who saw museums as destroying artworks by removing them from their previous contexts and uses. Barbara Kirschenblatt-Gimblett, in her writing on anthropological displays, suggests that the question of how much context is brought with an object into the display is really a question of where to make the "cut" (Kirshenblatt-Gimblett 1998; see also Henning, Chapter 25). This cut not only produces the object as object by severing it from the world of which it was a part, but also destroys its use value.

The metaphoric sense of animate, lively things predominates in the anthropological concept of the "social life of things," and in actor network theory where "nonhumans" (often, but not exclusively, technical objects) are understood as "actants" able to take on "delegated" human actions and capacities as if alive (Appadurai 1986; Latour 1992). However, Ivan Gaskell argues in his chapter that "to use a thing as though it were alive is not the same ontologically as for it to be alive" (Chapter 8). Some societies and cultures do hold certain objects to be sacred, numinous, or alive: and many such objects reside in museum collections. As Gaskell explains, both "life" and "things" are unstable concepts that are not settled even within a Western philosophical or scientific framework. Yet, many Western museums assume that the things in their collection are not alive in any meaningful sense. Gaskell argues that museums that hold objects in their collections that are sacred objects of veneration, or considered as living by their originating communities, need to begin from the premise that the Western biological sense of life is not the only valid one. He concludes that we need to consider "variable worlds" in which the quality that is "life" itself varies, and to understand museums as the mediators between these worlds (Chapter 8). Museums that facilitate acts of veneration such as smudging with smoke and touching, enable sacred objects to be returned to communities for rituals, or participate in reciprocal exchange carry out this mediating role more equitably than those "encyclopedic museums" that claim to be cosmopolitan yet refuse to countenance such exchanges.

While Gaskell is interested in the treatment by museums of sacred or numinous objects, Candlin is interested in the ways in which small, informal museums avoid the sense of deadened or impotent objects by not separating objects from the originating community, by being situated in an environment "broadly consonant with its interests" and by mediating its objects in such a way that they seem more immediate and "alive" (Chapter 13). The notion of liveness as something that is produced through display practices also resonates in anthropologist Petra Tjitske Kalshoven's chapter. She writes about living history and re-enactment practices that animate museum objects, bringing them to life through replication and performance in ways that "both defy and celebrate the sanctity of the museum space" (Chapter 24). She sees this in terms of play, which, following Johan Huizinga's famous study *Homo Ludens* ([1950] 1967), she describes in terms of the construction of temporary "worlds apart." In Kalshoven's account, museum objects are given back their usefulness, but as replicas, miniatures, and in the context of the intense experience of historical re-enactment. For her, the liveliness of objects comes in their integration into play, or via the careful staging of objects in exhibition giving them the opportunity to "perform."

Fiona Candlin's account gives the sense that it can be a certain *carelessness* of staging that enlivens objects, producing a powerful sense of the "having been there" of past occupants, through used objects that metonymically suggest their presence: shoes "molded to the shape" of the owner's feet, "half-used" soap, doors "stained with the grease of repeated touch" (Chapter 13). A more chaotic, unregulated appearance might actually add to a sense of unmediated presence. Yet legibility depends on staging: as Caroline Morris has said about Charles Darwin's study at Down House, the visitor's ability to read the room as narrating the presence of Darwin and his activities within the study is enhanced by the careful placing of objects: "the cluttered table and carefully positioned stool narrate the chair's use" (Morris 2013).

Ivan Gaskell argues that museums mediate not only through exhibitions, but also in their other practices, in laboratories and storage rooms. He shows how mediation occurs through conservation practices, and through prohibitions and rules: such as those preventing the touching of objects and the application of other substances such as incense or smoke, which are part of acts of veneration. Rules against handling of collections not only prevent "ritual interactions" but sometimes "appear to protect the power privileges of museum staff rather than serve demonstrable utilitarian purposes." Even the most practical regulations can also operate symbolically, as "a way of establishing, enforcing, or contesting power hierarchies" (Chapter 8).

Touch prohibitions arrived both with the development of the museum as a disciplinary institution and as an imperial institution. According to Erkki Huhtamo, prohibitions on touching in art museums arrived with the nineteenth-century public museum. Visitors to early museums expected to be able to touch artworks. However, the new *déclassé* audiences of the public museum were not trusted to behave appropriately (Chapter 12). Today, Huhtamo suggests, museums can no longer rely on shared ideas about acceptable behavior in a museum context, and it is increasingly difficult to enforce touch prohibitions. He attributes this to a combination of the juxtaposition of touchable and untouchable works in the same spaces, and the growing tactility of a society acculturated to touch screens and push buttons. This notion – that visitors import into the museum behaviors and ways of seeing that are associated with other media or other exhibitions contexts – has had a long circulation: for instance, Sue Perks, in her chapter later in the volume, refers to 1970s discussions in which museum professionals diagnosed a new kind of inattentiveness in visitors, attributing this to the negative influence of television (Chapter 18).

Atmospheres of display

In many museums, intangible qualities, such as light, smell, sound, and climate, are very carefully controlled. Museums and galleries mediate objects through environmental technologies. Systems necessary for preservation purposes also affect visitor experience: displaying the watercolors of William Blake in a dimly lit room prevents them from fading, but it can also produce a sense of intimacy and add to the dreamlike, almost hallucinatory, quality of the pictures, reinforcing the narrative of Blake as a visionary. Light is a particularly powerful mediating tool because, while it renders things visible, it often passes unnoticed. Alice Barnaby's chapter shows how light has a role in producing certain kinds of valued aesthetic experiences, by charting changes in exhibition lighting in Britain over a 100 year period, from 1750 to 1850 (Chapter 9).

The idea of lighting as a media technology is not new. McLuhan used the example of the electric light bulb to explain the concept that "the medium is the message" in his book *Understanding Media* ([1964] 2001). For McLuhan the light bulb is a medium without any content, which nevertheless makes possible certain kinds of social practice and experiences.[5] By contrast, Alice Barnaby sees light as having a symbolic content that is closely tied to its technical form. In 1961 the exhibition designer Herbert Bayer listed light among the "combined means of visual communication" that made exhibition design "an intensified and new language" (quoted in Staniszewski 1998, 3). In fact, Barnaby shows that this language was already being developed by means of new lighting technologies in the early nineteenth century, when light was used for "the staging of statements about wealth, power, and taste" (Chapter 9). Cultural trends in art gallery lighting were linked to ideas about who should have access to public art collections, and what they ought to get from the experience, with different lighting styles seeming to produce "civilizing effects" associated with rationality and civic virtue or producing a sensuality and poetic quality that confirmed an aristocratic sensibility.

Barnaby's discussion of the nuances of different approaches to lighting in this period provides a different perspective from accounts of museums as "hegemonic disciplinary structures," instead making vivid the "multiple and seemingly contradictory agendas" which produced and popularized a wide range of different lighting practices (Chapter 9). Nevertheless, Barnaby shares with these accounts an emphasis on the visual and visibility. Rupert Cox's chapter challenges this emphasis, offering sound and aurality as a means to rethink social relations in art museum and gallery contexts. He suggests we think of museum space in terms of acoustics and address "listening as part of the sensorium through which museum visitors engage with artworks" (Chapter 10). The materials used in new museum interiors are chosen with acoustics in mind: to dampen or muffle the sound of footsteps or of visitors talking, for instance. At the same time, there are various uncontrolled sounds – air conditioning and heating systems – or sounds from nearby displays. Inviting visitors to attend to such sounds means inviting them to think differently about the museum space. This attentiveness to sound is something that has been encouraged by the sound art installations and projects Cox discusses.

Cox argues that sound can be experienced by visitors as ambiguous and dispersed, bodily felt rather than cerebrally interpreted (Chapter 10). While he discusses sound art in terms of "affective space" – with "the absence of a fixed viewing perspective," Brigitte Biehl-Missal and Dirk vom Lehn point to how atmosphere in general is experienced bodily as "indeterminate, a spatially extended quality of feeling" (Chapter 11). The construction of atmospheres in museums and retail environments involves architecture, lighting, color, sound, electronic media, and even the behavior and speech of staff. Biehl-Missal and vom Lehn see atmospherics as a means of ideological manipulation because it includes intangible aspects which nevertheless impact on the museum experience. Designed or manufactured atmospheres appear to bypass symbolic communication altogether, working directly on feelings – Bettina Habsburg-Lothringen refers to the discipline of constructing atmosphere as "emotional design" (Chapter 15).

In highly staged environments, meaning appears to emanate from the atmosphere itself. Atmospherics welds feeling and affect to the museum narrative. This can be understood as a variation of the "reality effect": in literature, the way in which an accumulation of apparently insignificant details (details that don't appear to be "signs" within the larger text) combine to produce a strong sense of realism (Barthes 1986). Hilde Hein sees immersive exhibitions as potentially creating "a public reality that passes for knowledge" (2000, 80). But this assumes that all exhibitions must be first and foremost factual representations. Yet, reality effects are part of the pleasures of fiction (which is never entirely invention), and in exhibition contexts they arguably help to construct temporary and playful worlds apart, rather than insidious substitutes for fact.

Reinventing exhibition space

Biehl-Missal and vom Lehm look at the development of atmospherics as a retail marketing tool in the context of the "experience economy" (Chapter 11). They suggest that the production of staged atmospheres is about the production of value. In a time of corporate sponsorship and private–public partnerships, high-profile and often spectacular museums have become integral parts of new planned urban environments, alongside shopping centers, travel hubs, and other "cultural assets." In his chapter, museum designer Peter Higgins lists some of the elements of increasingly vigorous attempts to market museums as destinations alongside other attractions and family days out: "including high-quality food and beverage, sophisticated retail, profitable temporary exhibitions, and corporate out-of-hours events" (Chapter 14).

The global spread of neoliberal economics and ideology is particularly evident in the contemporary art world; as Mark Rectanus points out, art museums are entangled with private agencies, large-scale commercial events, and global art markets. Rectanus gives the example of corporate museums such as the BMW complex in Munich, and the Leeum Samsung Museum of Art in Seoul, South Korea, which combine educational, consumption, and entertainment facilities to reshape, not just the museum, but the urban environment (Chapter 23). In the late 1980s the majority of commercial art galleries in London were to be found in Cork Street, Piccadilly, and had relatively small exhibition spaces. During the 1990s wealthy collectors and art patrons started to develop their own large exhibition spaces that could compete with museums (such as the Saatchi Gallery in St. John's Wood). Today, London is full of museum-standard, huge white cube spaces which are privately owned and which sell contemporary art rather than collect it, such as the Gagosian, the Lisson Gallery, and Hauser & Wirth's large Savile Row galleries. These private museums reconfigure social space more widely: in summer 2014 Hauser & Wirth opened another large-scale institution on a rural farm in the southwest of England with five galleries covering 2483 square meters, which will turn the small town in which it is situated into a key destination for contemporary art tourism (Shalam 2014).[6]

Designing retail environments and designing museums involve different constraints and priorities: in the United Kingdom, Peter Higgins finds that National Lottery funding makes it difficult to adopt a holistic, integrated approach to the architecture and the interior, which is often "retro-fitted" into a spectacular but perhaps impractical building (Chapter 14). In the case of the contemporary art museum, the competition for iconic buildings has been understood as the "visual expression" of an increased privatization in which "a collection, a history, a position or a mission" are demoted in favor of "cool" and "photogenic" environments (Bishop 2013, 11–12). Concerns about illusionistic environments and manipulative atmosphere implicitly suggest that there might be such a thing as a neutral exhibition space. Yet, even the white cube art gallery is a designed space, intended to facilitate particular understandings of the autonomy of modern or contemporary art.

Exhibitions choreograph visitors; they produce a certain kind of social space. Herbert Bayer, quoted earlier, suggested that exhibitions were and are exciting to design because they could involve so many different media and materials in the production of new kinds of experience. Higgins, whose company, Land Design

Studio, has designed many major museums and exhibitions, calls his chapter (14) "Total Media" as an appeal for a more collaborative, holistic approach to museum-making, but also in recognition of the complex, multisensory, multimedia aspects of exhibition design involving the use of light, sound, and the "tactile and olfactory" alongside audiovisual and graphic elements.

Discussing the practices of the Stapferhaus in Lenzburg, Switzerland, Beat Hächler writes that space can be understood not as a container but as an arrangement of relationships, as a means of engineering certain performative possibilities. Indeed, since the 1920s, artists and designers have conceived of the exhibition space as an environment that changes as visitors move around it. It was a means of creating new experiences, new ways of seeing and exploring space, that corresponded with artistic practices aimed at transforming perception. Some of these exhibition experiments can be viewed today. For example, at the Muzeum Sztuki in Łódz in Poland, Wladysław Strzeminski's Neoplastic Room has been restored. The gallery, which originally opened in June 1948, is both a container for various works of art by Strzeminski and his contemporaries, and an immersive abstract artwork itself. The paintings and sculptural constructions within it are not simply the subject of the exhibition but are part of the same field of practice: like many avant-garde artists, Strzeminski worked in design and architecture as well as painting (Szczerski 2012, 237).[7]

The Van Abbemuseum in Eindhoven in the Netherlands has made a point of collecting, or reconstructing, historically important exhibition spaces and multimedia installations such as Aleksandr Rodchenko's *Workers' Reading Room* of 1925; El Lissitzky's *Abstract Cabinet*, originally commissioned in 1927 for the Landesmuseum in Hanover, Germany, by Alexander Dorner and destroyed in 1936; and László Moholy Nagy's *Room of Our Time* (1930), which was never constructed in its entirety until its (re)construction in 2009 (see Elcott 2010). Haidee Wasson situates the avant-garde's reinvention of exhibition space in relation to film and in the context of trying to "defy the static models that dominated in established museums" (Chapter 26). The artists themselves often expressed the aims of these innovative installations in more explicitly political terms, wanting to jolt the visitor from "passivity" into (implicitly revolutionary) "activity."

This idea of using installation to reinvent visitor activity also informed British pop artist Richard Hamilton's pioneering exhibitions from the 1950s. The Institute of Contemporary Arts (ICA) in London recently exhibited a reconstruction of *an Exhibit* (1957), the result of his collaboration with another artist, Victor Pasmore, and the critic Laurence Alloway. It consists of a room full of rectangular sheets of Perspex, suspended at different heights and angles and ranging in color and translucency from completely transparent to semitransparent coffee brown, dark red, yellow, and opaque black. Hamilton and his collaborators described *an Exhibit* as a game for the artists, who construct it improvisationally on site, according to predecided rules but without rehearsal: "Once the rules were settled, a high number of moves was possible … *an Exhibit* as it stands, records one set of possible moves."

They suggest that, by entering the exhibit, visitors also participate in a game.[8] Conceived in this way, the exhibition still has a structure, and its explicit content becomes something that is an implicit content of every exhibition: the moves and decisions of the visitors. This is the exhibition medium stripped down to its bare minimum. Nevertheless, visitors to the ICA in 2014 played a different game from visitors in 1957: armed with camera phones, many (including myself) photographed and videoed the installation.

Today, exhibition designers tend to think in terms of narrative as the key element that gives an exhibition coherence. For designer Frank den Oudsten, the spectator, the audience, "completes the narrative environment" (2012, 21). This emphasis on the exhibition narrative is connected to the influence of film and theater. Since the 1970s, exhibitions have increasingly used techniques from these fields. In his chapter here, Higgins refers to his own career trajectory, "shifting from architecture to work in TV, film and theater" before establishing himself as a designer of exhibitions (Chapter 14). However, he sees "limited crossover" both in the organization of the production and division of labor, and in the different and medium-specific qualities of exhibitions, film, and theater. Unlike in film and theater, the exhibition designer must plan for the "personalized sequence" visitor experience.

For Higgins, the concept of scenography is very much associated with film and theater; in German-speaking countries, however, the term *Szenographie* has a wider meaning, although it has been applied to museums only since the millennium, according to Habsburg-Lothringen. Generally it tends to call to mind simulated, immersive environments along the lines of naturalistic film and theater sets – the highly atmospheric, immersive spaces described earlier. In Part III, Habsburg-Lothringen describes contemporary scenography in terms of the construction of "flexible, atmospherically dense, and interactive illusory spaces, in which the viewer is immersed temporarily" (Chapter 15).

Such "illusory spaces" might seem to be a logical, even inevitable, progression from displays such as dioramas and period rooms. However, Habsburg-Lothringen also discusses the 1980s rejection of this kind of naturalism or illusionism among German-speaking curators and designers of historical exhibitions who turned instead to a kind of Brechtian realism in which "alienating effects and distortions" disrupt the illusion of the exhibition and expose it as a construction (Chapter 15). A new critical and poetic approach to exhibition making led in the direction of more aesthetic, sensual, and atmospheric environments. From a present-day perspective, and in relation to the earlier discussion of atmospherics, this is perhaps unexpected: it suggests that, far from always being a tool for the construction of illusions or for the manipulation of visitors/consumers, atmospheric media could be used to produce what Habsburg-Lothringen refers to as a "productive shock" in visitors. In the context of a historical exhibition, this shock serves to disrupt any assumption of an objectively knowable past, seamlessly connected to the present, and unfiltered by present values and understandings.

For den Oudsten (2012), scenography doesn't refer only to thematic, highly designed environments, but to a dramaturgy that takes place within a space between observer and observed. The idea that scenography does not have to describe only immersive exhibits is made clear in Beat Hächler's chapter. Hächler refers to his practice at the Stapferhaus in Lenzburg as "social scenography," a concept intended to capture "the performative aspect of exhibitions" (Chapter 16). In a social scenographic exhibition, the exhibition space is conceived of as a dynamic space, a space produced by action, by the activity of visitors. This requires rethinking the museum as "a space of the present," which produces reflection in visitors because "what museum visitors are confronted with above all is themselves."

Audience participation

New media curator and writer Beryl Graham notes that participation is challenging to some art curators, critics, and institutions because it is associated with a loss of curatorial control and with inciting disorderly audience behavior – notoriously in installations like Cyprien Gaillard's *The Recovery of Discovery* (2011) discussed by Rectanus in Chapter 23, or Robert Morris's 1971 *Bodyspacemotionthings* discussed by Graham in Chapter 20. Huhtamo characterizes visitor engagement with interactives as often chaotic, impulsive, and depthless: "momentary acts of punching and tapping, pushing and pulling" (Chapter 12). Yet, Luigina Ciolfi, who designs interactives for heritage sites, shows how the design process is increasingly rooted in a "rich view of human interaction and experience" and how point-and-click technologies are being replaced with multisensory forms of engagement, and site-specific designs (Chapter 19). For John Bell and Jon Ippolito, as for Ciolfi, digital technologies can actually enhance the sensual, emotional experience of place (Chapter 21).

Hands-on participatory exhibits have often led to accusations that the museum is treading too closely to other nonserious popular contexts such as the circus, the dime museum, and the fairground (see Goodman 1990, Giddings, Chapter 7). I have written elsewhere about how the pioneering exhibition *Cybernetic Serendipity* at London's ICA attracted this kind of criticism (Henning 2006, 88). Sue Perks cites the critics of the *Human Biology* exhibition at the Natural History Museum, London, which opened in 1977: they referred to the exhibition variously as a "cheap disco," a "lewd offal-shop nightmare," "tasteless," and like a "fairground 'tunnel of love'" (Chapter 18). These are associated with fears about populism and "dumbing down"; anxieties about the working class are not far from the surface in this discourse. In this context, the most interesting (and, as Perks points out, "scathing") critique came from Patrick Boylan who "considered *Human Biology* to be self-consciously 'modern tasteful' in style – 'pure Middle Class "Habitat"'… reinforcing 'fashionable, mildly liberal, educational and social theory and practice'" (quoted in Chapter 18). By associating the visual style of the exhibition with the homes of middle-class liberals (who shopped at Terence Conran's fashionable Habitat store), Boylan manages to imply that, far from making the museum more accessible, the Human Biology Hall was actually speaking to a narrow self-congratulatory elite.

Boylan was right to recognize that the *Human Biology* exhibits owed at least as much to liberal educational theory as they did to the inspiration of popular entertainment and commerce. In fact, while they are heavily associated with entertainment contexts, interactives actually developed in the context of the museum's educational remit. Perks recounts how the Natural History Museum, in planning its innovative New Exhibition Scheme in the 1970s, drew on the influence of the Exploratorium in San Francisco, the work of the Open University, and the Isotype method of the 1920s and 1930s (Chapter 18). These shaped a new emphasis on visitor participation, well-defined learning objectives, and techniques to evaluate effectiveness. At the Exploratorium, interactives and hands-on exhibits were intended to communicate abstract scientific concepts in an enjoyable and accessible way, and to enable visitors to understand the workings of technologies that appeared to them in everyday life as mysterious "black boxes." However, as interactives have become more widely used, their use has changed: in heritage contexts, for example, the priority is not an understanding of technology; rather, the technology is there to enhance a sense of place and to embody the kinds of interactions associated with the place (Ciolfi, Chapter 19). This is facilitated by technologies disguised as mock-historical artifacts, which record and respond to visitors' locations, including motion sensors, GPS (satellite-based navigation), and geotagging (using geographical metadata attached to images, video, or objects).

Instead of increasing accessibility, Karin Harrasser argues, hands-on learning in museums can stand in the way of deeper learning and reproduce existing educational inequalities (Chapter 17). In their research on hands-on displays in children's museums, Harrasser and her colleagues focused on observing children using them. Their research confirmed Pierre Bourdieu's observations in the 1970s that "open learning" through interaction privileges the already privileged, while other children struggle, being "unfamiliar with the whole environment" and lacking a sense of entitlement. The irony (or tragedy) here is that the development of interaction and visitor participation in museums was a genuine attempt to expand the audience across social classes and to increase accessibility.

Other devices intended to enrich visitor experience can also have unintended effects. Biehl-Missal and vom Lehn find that information kiosks and handheld devices can mean that visitors spend more time with the technology than with the objects it is intended to support, and that groups either separate and take in the exhibition individually, or "become frustrated with the systems and abandon them" (Chapter 11). In other words, these media can have the same effect of individuation that has been observed with the older audio guides. Yet we should differentiate between these media and their effects: as Proctor suggests (quoting Laura Mann), the linear audio tour had an ability to immerse visitors in the experience that later interactive, or personalized, digital tours lost (Chapter 22). Reduced sociability is not an inevitable effect of interactives: Higgins points to ways in which they can provide a social experience where "one person, the avatar, is able to operate the system of behalf of much larger user groups who may be engaged with the learning process" (Chapter 14). Similarly, Graham observes that the audience for one augmented reality-based artwork "even went so far as to loan that most intimate and covetable of devices, the mobile phone, to strangers without a camera, in order to pass on the experience" (Chapter 20).

Graham suggests that new media art can offer "critical tools" for understanding audience participation and interaction with artworks, beyond the traditional model of aesthetic contemplation. Participation and interaction include the audience's role in documenting and archiving the experience of the artwork: so for example, in the case of audience photography, museums have tended to move away from seeing it as a threat to copyright and ownership, to viewing it as (variously or simultaneously) documentation, publicity, and participation (Graham, Chapter 20; Henning, Chapter 25). Networked media also allow for "art projects which are distributed coproductions," with the audience as coproducer, and for audiences to become involved in curating. This can include the online tagging and annotation of artworks and collections, as well as collaborative curating using live online chat and discussion boards (Graham, Chapter 20).

The audience role is diversifying. Rectanus argues that "museums increasingly position audiences in multiple roles as viewers, spectators, performers, and consumers" (Chapter 23). Networked audiences have different expectations, different ways of engaging with museums, and, according to Proctor, "the potential to transform the museum, the way it works, its structures of power, and even its mission" (Chapter 22). As Proctor describes in her chapter, mobile media used for interpretation "can capture data (metrics) and feedback from these visitors on where they go, what they do, and what questions they ask of the museum's content and collections, events, and so on." Museums increasingly "data-mine" social media, but must be wary that they do not "violate the public trust" (Proctor, Chapter 22). From an exhibition design perspective, the potential of new media seems very exciting, with "individual profiling" increasing the possibility of personalized content (Higgins, Chapter 14).[9] On a larger scale, violating trust is perhaps less of a concern than the ways in which institutions play an uncritical role in an increasingly standard practice of audiences voluntarily (and often unwittingly) supplying large amounts of data about themselves. This kind of audience participation has worrying political implications.

New roles

Graham claims that "the behaviors of new media affect how curators and other museum workers work in time and space, online and offline" (Chapter 20). She explains that the overlap and blurring of boundaries between new media art and new media as interactives, as interpretation, as promotional tools for the museum, and as part of our everyday experience make new media art particularly difficult for museums and galleries to deal with. Proctor too sees mobile digital media as having a great deal of impact on museum professionals, who now have to take mobile access into account when planning, who have limited editorial control on the information being circulated about the museum, its events and exhibitions, and who are now responsible to people who may never actually visit the museum itself (Chapter 22).

In their chapter, John Bell and Jon Ippolito address ways in which new media art has challenged curatorial control, such as augmented reality projects that use the technology to invade and take over existing museum exhibitions – in ways that are perceivable only to those in the know and with the appropriate app on their mobile phone (Chapter 21). They understand this in terms of an expansion or "diffusion" of the museum into virtual space. They are interested in the ways in which museums have attempted to control and delimit the curatorial space, and set down boundary markers online. Bell and Ippolito concur with Graham when they say that "Even the brick-and-mortar museum has to accept that they are no longer singular authoritative voices on the artifacts they exhibit and that the voices of outside experts are at the fingertips of anyone with a smartphone." Citing commentators who view the stretching of the term "curating" to include online curating as an insult to the profession, they celebrate this expansion of "vernacular curating." In the attempt to restrict the title to "museum-appointed staff," they perceive a certain anxiety about feminized, and consequently devalued, labor.

However, it is clear that neither the museum's relationship with its audience nor the professional division of labor within museums and related institutions have been completely stable for a long time. Studies of audience attention in museums go back to the 1920s and 1930s. Wasson discusses how the use of Taylorist time–motion studies in that early period informed the exhibition strategies of the Philadelphia Museum of Art in Pennsylvania in the United States, and also how "museum fatigue" became increasingly something museums attempted to address, or allay (Chapter 26). Perks's study of the New Exhibition Scheme focuses on the collaborative relationship between scientists and designers at the Natural History Museum and the intermediary role of the "transformer," invented in 1920s Vienna (Chapter 18). Her archival research shows how British Museum conferences in the early 1970s devoted much discussion to the difficult relationship between designers and curators, and the need for better communication with audiences. While designers tended to "neglect intellectual content," scholarly curators seemed overly obsessed with it (Wade, quoted in Chapter 18).

Even today, the separation of curator and designer can be an inhibiting and problematic one: these are disciplines with their own discrete curricula, conferences, festivals, and professional bodies (den Oudsten 2012, 9). In addition, the field of exhibition design has opened up to include "representatives from the fields of art, film, comics, costume design, music, and dance" (Habsburg-Lothringen,

Chapter 15). While "transformers" as such have disappeared, a whole host of new roles have sprung up to cater for the expanded field of museum and curatorial practice – from the independent "critical" curator and the scenographer, to the citizen curator mentioned earlier, to what Bell and Ippolito call vernacular curators, to new media strategists and new media curators. While writers such as Harrasser (Chapter 17) and Huhtamo (Chapter 12) argue for the need to observe visitor interaction as part of a critical methodology for analyzing exhibitions, Luigina Ciolfi's chapter shows that a similar methodology is in use in design processes. At Bunratty Folk Park in Ireland, Ciolfi's research involved "documenting the visitors' relationships to the place and how they experienced it in terms of physical accommodation, cultural understandings, social interaction, and personal and emotional connections" (Chapter 19). Ethnographic, observational, and interview techniques were used as a basis for developing "design scenarios" and ultimately prototype interactive artifacts, which were then piloted and tested with visitors.

The museum has recast itself as a commissioner and/or collaborator in new forms of social activism involved in "increasingly complex constellations of media use" and the "deterritorialization of museum contents and programming" (Rectanus, Chapter 23). In many cases, museums have been quick to respond to new media environments and are not as wary of media as they are sometimes portrayed. Proctor observes that they were "early adopters of personal handheld devices" (Chapter 22) while Wasson writes of the wide range of ways in which museums have engaged with modern media over a long period, "effectively participating in a vast media ecology" (Chapter 26). The Metropolitan Museum, New York, had an early film program in the 1920s, that sent films out "like mobile, mechanical docents," producing "satellite museums out of ad hoc, often impromptu, spaces" (Wasson, Chapter 26). Images traveled too: in my chapter, I discuss André Malraux's notion of the "museum without walls": a world of mass reproduction that was connected to, but not entirely controlled by, museums (Chapter 25). The new context for museum artworks is nicely evoked by Wasson when she talks of how reproductions "shared space with pictures of fashion contestants, bathing beauties, coronations, and presidential speeches" in the newspapers (Chapter 26). While Ernst sees museums' media specificity as residing in the material object (Chapter 1), several contributors emphasize museums' long-term engagement with media.

Media objects

This deep and historical involvement with different kinds of electronic media has involved museums reinventing themselves, no longer to be understood as "a permanent, unmoving, physical structure but as a kind of tentacular hub for a range of circulating things and ways of presenting those things" (Wasson, Chapter 26).

However, both electronic media and the museum as medium have a tendency to efface themselves, to conceal or naturalize their own technologies. For this reason, it is important to preserve older museum arrangements (such as dioramas or the avant-garde installations discussed earlier), and also to archive and collect media as objects.

However, because museum displays tend to center around visibility, media objects prove problematic to collect and display. Even visual electronic media such as television need to be operational to be understood as more than a piece of product design, and often the core similarities and differences between media as technological objects are not visible. Ernst indicates that electronic media raise all sorts of questions about how you display dynamic objects, operational machines, and software. Displaying media objects often requires the creative reinvention of exhibition space. The blackbox space is an invention necessary for the increasing number of film and media projections, especially in art contexts. Chamarette (Chapter 5) and Graham (Chapter 20) mention some of the difficulties of engaging with such exhibits, from the "bleeding" of sound, to the problems of visitors' time commitment.

Media also raise difficulties in terms of where to make the "cut." Arguably, they are cultural phenomena that need to be understood in relation to an audience, to certain kinds of social spaces, professions, and practices. Do television and computers make sense when removed from their living room and office habitats; or the newspaper from the cafe or the train? Can film be understood without cinema, and do film collections need to also include the ephemera of cinema and cinema-going? There are also, inevitably, complex conservation and archival issues: for filmic culture to be preserved, the museum has to develop techniques to preserve its material, but Chamarette argues that there is a too common tendency in museums and museum studies to ignore film's materiality and to treat it as a mode of transmission whose contents might therefore simply be translated across to magnetic tape or as digital data (Chapter 5). Cox, in Chapter 10, notes that scientific and anthropological recordings have a place in museums, but sound art proves difficult for art museums to conserve and classify. Indeed, sound art is often a live event and therefore poses problems for archivists and conservationists similar to those posed by performance art (on which see Clarke and Warren 2009). Similarly, Internet art has proved challenging for a number of reasons including the difficulties of classification and a lack of clarity over issues of conservation and display. New media curators have consequently found institutional support for the collection and display of Internet art to be somewhat shaky and variable (Vershooren 2010). In the face of poor institutional support and rapidly changing digital formats, many curators and scholars fear that early new media art and documentation is disappearing or already lost. An "international declaration" drawn up in 2011 called for sustainable funding structures and global collaboration to halt this process.[10]

Media collections are important because they offer the possibility for reflection and analysis of media worlds that otherwise appear to us as very natural and normal, since they are so integrated into our everyday lives. In this volume, Huhtamo argues that the widespread use of interactivity, not just in the form of museum interactives but also in everyday life, contributes to a normalization or naturalization of it that makes it harder to ask questions about it, and that embeds it as involuntary reflex, mere habit (Chapter 12). Harrasser expresses concern that the close coupling of museum interactives and visitors' wider media environment may not be a good thing, making rarer "the moment when the medium creeps into perception that triggers complex learning processes" (Chapter 17). Rectanus also warns that the audience's deep and proliferating involvement in media production and use can eat away at the space for critical reflection, challenging museums to find ways to provide that reflective space in a media-saturated world (Chapter 23).

The museum as reflective space is a model that is frequently invoked, but it does not take account of the possibility that the tradition of silent, receptive, critical contemplation, especially in the art museum, is itself the product of a particular culture, social class, and set of priorities. In my chapter, I refer to play as the name for another kind of aesthetic experience (Chapter 25). Kalshoven sees play as a means to enable a deep engagement with historical objects (Chapter 24). And, while Huhtamo questions the impact of an increasingly tactile emphasis in museum contexts (Chapter 12), Ciolfi affirms the value of tangibility for keeping visitors focused on the site and on the material, sensual aspects of their experience (Chapter 19). I draw on Jacques Rancière's notion of a "[re]distribution of the sensible," arguing that the present all-pervasive image culture, the product of an increasingly mobile, networked digital photography, can offer new models of attention and aesthetic experience for art museums (Chapter 25). Rectanus refers to turning the museum "inside out," to museums becoming increasingly flexible, mobile, and connected with a wider "commons," both geographically and online (Chapter 23). Graham argues that the incorporation of new media art in the museum has involved a "rethinking of the role of the visitor, the artist, and the curator," and leads us to the notion of the "open" participatory museum (Chapter 20; see also Simon 2010). Museums continue to "keep the record," to enable people to reflect on and attend to their present as well as the past, but, as the diverse essays in this volume suggest, changes in media bring with them changed forms of attention that require new strategies for museum-making, and new kinds of research and analysis.

Notes

1 "We all live in an information age – or so we tell each other as we caress our smart phones like rosary beads, heads down, checking, monitoring, tweeting. We're wired; we're on message; and the dominant theme of the message is ourselves. Identity is the zeitgeist. A lifetime ago in 'Brave New World,' Aldous Huxley predicted this as the ultimate means of social control because it was voluntary, addictive and shrouded in illusions of personal freedom" (Pilger 2014).

2   In his introduction to the 1964 edition of Innis's book *The Bias of Communication* (originally published in 1951), McLuhan wrote: "I am pleased to think of my own book *The Gutenberg Galaxy* as a footnote to the observations of Innis on the subject of the psychic and social consequences, first of writing then of printing" (McLuhan 2005, 8).

3   In his essay "The Bias of Communication" Innis argued that different historical technologies of communication (stone and hieroglyphics; clay and cuneiform script; papyrus and alphabet; paper and printed gothic script) favored or hindered different kinds of social organization – from centralized absolute monarchies to oligarchies, to complexly administered empires. In Innis's terms, radio itself already carries a specific and undemocratic bias toward "centralization" and "a concern with continuity" (Innis [1951] 2008, 33).

4   The research conducted by Karin Harrasser and her colleagues makes use of Stuart Hall's semiotic encoding–decoding model, but while Hall tended to view oppositional, or resistant, readings as empowering, Harrasser found that the process of negotiating such readings can actually be stressful and difficult (Harrasser, Chapter 17).

5   "Whether the light is being used for brain surgery or night baseball is a matter of indifference. It could be argued that these activities are in some way the 'content' of the electric light, since they could not exist without the electric light. This fact merely underlines the point that 'the medium is the message' because it is the medium that shapes and controls the scale and form of human association and action. The content or uses of such media are as diverse as they are ineffectual in shaping the form of human association" (McLuhan [1964] 2001, 23–24).

6   See http://www.hauserwirthsomerset.com/about (accessed September 2, 2014).

7   Like the natural history dioramas in the American Museum of Natural History, New York, it raises interesting questions about how an exhibition design can itself become an artifact, worthy of conservation. To recognize the dioramas as aesthetic objects worth preserving means acknowledging a change in function: these are no longer just preserved moments and spaces from nature, intended to educate and inspire visitors about the natural world; they are also time capsules of exhibition design, a specific moment in the history of the craft.

8   Visitors are asked "to inhabit, for the duration of the game, a real environment. The meaning of an Exhibit is now dependent on the decisions of the visitors, just as, at an earlier stage, it was dependent on the artists who were the players. It is a game, a maze, a ceremony completed by the participation of the visitors. Which routes will they take, will they *move* through narrow or wide spaces, where will they decide to stop and assess the whole" (poster for *an Exhibit*, displayed at the ICA, February 2014; emphasis original).

9   These are concerns heightened by early twenty-first-century scandals regarding data-gathering by both commercial organizations and security and surveillance agencies such as the National Security Agency (NSA) in the United States, and Government Communications Headquarters (GCHQ) in the United Kingdom.

10 This international declaration can be found at http://www.mediaarthistory.org/declaration (accessed July 17, 2014).

References

Appadurai, Arjun, ed. 1986. *The Social Life of Things: Commodities in Cultural Perspective.* Cambridge: Cambridge University Press.

Barthes, Roland. 1986. "The *Reality Effect.*" In *The Rustle of Language*, translated by Richard Howard, 141–48. Oxford: Blackwell.

Benjamin, Walter. (1936) 2002. "The Storyteller: Observations on the Works of Nikolai Leskov." In *Selected Writings, vol. 3, 1935–1938*, translated by Edmynd Jephcott, Howard Eiland et al.; edited by Howard Eiland and Michael W. Jennings, 143–66. Cambridge, MA: Belknap.

Bennett, Tony. 1995. *The Birth of the Museum: History, Theory, Politics.* London: Routledge.

Bishop, Claire. 2013. *Radical Museology; or, What's "Contemporary" in Museums of Contemporary Art?* London: Koenig.

Chorley, Matt, and Martin Robinson. 2014. "Radio 4's 'Worst Ever' Today Programme Edited by PJ Harvey Slammed by Listeners, MPs and even BBC Staff over Left-Wing Rants." *Daily Mail*, January 2.

Clarke, Paul, and Julian Warren. 2009. "Ephemera: Between Archival Objects and Events." *Journal of the Society of Archivists* 30(1): 45–66.

den Oudsten, Frank. 2012. "The Poetry of Place." In Herman Kossmann, Suzanne Mulder, Frank den Oudsten, and Pieter Kiewiet de Jonge, *Narrative Spaces: On the Art of Exhibiting*, 8–45. Rotterdam: 010.

Dovey, Jon. (1995) 2004. "Camcorder Cults." In *The Television Studies Reader*, edited by R. C. Allen and A. Hill, 557–68. London: Routledge.

Elcott, Noam M. 2010. Review of *Raum der Gegenwart (Room of Our Time). Journal of the Society of Architectural Historians* 69(2): 265–269.

Fabiani, J. L., and P. M. Menger. 1979. "Études sur le Public du Centre." Archives of the Centre Pompidou.

Giddings, Seth. 2009. "Events and Collusions: A Glossary for the Microethnography of Videogame Play." *Games and Culture* 4(2): 144–57.

Goodman, David, 1990. "Fear of Circuses: Founding the National Museum of Victoria." *Continuum: Australian Journal of Media and Culture* 3(1): 18–34.

Hall, Stuart. (1973) 1980. "Encoding/Decoding." In *Culture, Media, Language: Working Papers in Cultural Studies, 1972–79*, edited by the Centre for Contemporary Cultural Studies, 128–138. London: Hutchinson.

Hein, Hilde. 2000. *The Museum in Transition: A Philosophical Perspective.* Washington, DC: Smithsonian Institution.

Heinich, Nathalie. 2003. "The Pompidou Centre and Its Public: The Limits of a Utopian Site." In *The Museum Time Machine: Putting Cultures on Display*, edited by Robert Lumley, 197–210. London: Routledge.

Henning, Michelle. 2006. *Museums, Media and Cultural Theory.* Maidenhead, UK: Open University Press.

Herman, Edward S., and Noam Chomsky. 1988. *Manufacturing Consent: The Political Economy of the Media.* New York: Pantheon.

Hooper-Greenhill, Eilean. 1995. *Museum Media Message*. London: Routledge.

Huizinga, Johan. (1950) 1967. *Homo Ludens: A Study of the Play Element in Culture*. Boston: Beacon.

Innis, Harold. (1951) 2008. *The Bias of Communication*, 2nd ed. Toronto: University of Toronto Press.

Kirschenblatt-Gimblett, Barbara. 1998. *Destination Culture: Tourism, Museums, and Heritage*. Berkeley: University of California Press.

Latour, Bruno. 1992. "Where Are the Missing Masses: The Sociology of a Few Mundane Artefacts." In *Shaping Technology/Building Society: Studies in Sociotechnical Change*, edited by Wiebe E. Bijker and John Law, 225–258. Cambridge, MA: MIT Press.

Lubar, Steven. 2013. "Timelines in Exhibitions." *Curator: The Museum Journal* 56(2): 169–88.

Marsden, Sam. 2014. "BBC Radio 4 Today Criticised for 'Left-Wing Tosh' Chosen by Guest Editor PJ Harvey." *Telegraph, January 2*.

McLuhan, Marshall. (1964) 2001. *Understanding Media: The Extensions of Man*. London: Routledge.

McLuhan, Marshall. 2005. *Marshall McLuhan Unbound, vol. 8, The Bias of Communication*. Corte Madera, CA: Gingko.

Morris, Caroline. 2013. "Biographical Objects and the Changing Rhetoric of Display in the Nineteenth and Early Twentieth Century." Paper presented to the Long Nineteenth Century Network, University of the West of England, Bristol, May 9. Accessed July 16, 2014. http://www.academia.edu/4028565/Biographical_objects_and_the_changing_rhetoric_of_display_in_the_Nineteenth_and_early_Twentieth_Century.

Peters, John Durham. 1999. *Speaking into the Air: A History of the Idea of Communication*. Chicago: University of Chicago Press.

Pilger, John. 2014. "Is Media Just Another Word for Control?" Accessed July 16, 2014. http://johnpilger.com/articles/is-media-just-another-word-for-control.

Rose, Mandy. 1994–95. "Real Lives: Video Nation." *Vertigo Magazine* 1(4). Accessed September 2, 2014. http://www.closeupfilmcentre.com/vertigo_magazine/volume-1-issue-4-winter-1994-5/real-lives-video-nation/.

Shalam, Sally. 2014. "Hauser & Wirth Somerset the Next Guggenheim?" *Guardian*, March 21. Accessed July 16, 2014. http://www.theguardian.com/travel/2014/mar/21/hauser-and-wirth-somerset-art-gallery-next-guggenheim?INTCMP=ILCNE TTXT3487.

Simon, Nina. 2010. *The Participatory Museum*. Santa Cruz, CA: Museum 2.0. Accessed September 2, 2014. http://www.participatorymuseum.org/read/.

Sperlinger, Mike, and Ian White. 2008. *Kinomuseum: Towards an Artists Cinema*. Cologne: Walther König.

Staniszewski, Mary Anne. 1998. *The Power of Display: A History of Exhibition Installations at the Museum of Modern Art*. Cambridge, MA: MIT Press.

Szczerski, Andrzej. 2012. "Strzemiński – The Moderniser." In *Afterimages of Life: Władysław Strzemiński and Rights for Art*, edited by Jarosław Lubiak. Łódz: Muzeum Sztuki.

Thompson, John B. 1990. *Ideology and Modern Culture*. Cambridge: Polity.

Turkle, Sherry. 2011. *Alone Together: Why We Expect More from Technology and Less from Each Other*. New York: Basic Books.

Vershooren, Karen. 2010. "Art – A Place for Internet Art in the Museum of Contemporary Art." In *The Weight of Photography: Photography History, Theory and Criticism*, edited by Johan Swinnen and Luc Deneulin. Brussels: Academic and Scientific.

Wieviorka, Annette. 2006. *The Era of the Witness*. Ithaca, NY: Cornell University Press.

PART I

The Museum as Medium

1 MUSEUMS AND MEDIA ARCHAEOLOGY

An Interview with Wolfgang Ernst

Michelle Henning

Professor Wolfgang Ernst is Chair of Media Theories at the Institute of Musicology and Media Studies at Humboldt University in Berlin, where he also runs the Media Archaeological Fundus, a collection of historical technical media artifacts. The collection is intended to support media studies teaching and research by grounding it in the material history of developments in electronic media hardware, through the examination of working media technologies (as opposed to "dead," unworkable radios, televisions, etc.). Ernst has written several books (in German): *M.edium F.oucault* (2000), *Das Rumoren der Archive* (The rumbling of the archives, 2002), *Im Namen von Geschichte* (In the name of history, 2003), and *Das Gesetz des Gedächtnisses* (The law of memory, 2007), and many articles and book chapters, including several English-language articles, which outline his approach to media theory. An English-language collection of his writings, entitled *Digital Memory and the Archive*, was published by the University of Minnesota Press in 2013 (Ernst 2013a).

My own interest in Ernst's work came out of a broader interest in German media theory, particularly the work of the late Friedrich Kittler, who held a chair in media aesthetics and history at Humboldt from 1993, and Siegfried Zielinski, currently chair in Media Theory: Archaeology and Varientology of the Media at Berlin University of the Arts: both of these writers, though their approaches are quite distinctive, are influenced by the French historian Michel Foucault, especially his notion of history as "archaeology," as outlined in *The Archaeology of Knowledge* ([1969] 2002). Kittler, in particular, was also influenced by the Canadian media theorist Harold Innis, who distinguished between media according to how their material properties oriented them in terms of time and space, and attempted to trace the impact of this on the social and political development of different societies (Innis [1951] 2008). Kittler has become well known in anglophone media studies for

The International Handbooks of Museum Studies: Museum Media, First Edition.
Edited by Michelle Henning.
© 2015 John Wiley & Sons Ltd. Published 2020 by John Wiley & Sons Ltd.

his materialist approach to media, emphasizing the significance of the forms and technology of media over questions of representation.

Ernst also engages with Foucault's ideas in his books and through the practice of a distinctive kind of "media archaeology" which addresses questions relating to archives and museums. Like Kittler, Ernst emphasizes not just the transmission and broadcast aspects of media, but data storage and machine memory, media as recording devices. His English-language writings include a chapter in Susan Crane's anthology *Museums and Memory* (2000), in which he noted the ways in which information-processing technologies are reshaping museums, and also the ways in which museum display and collection management techniques follow the logic of database technologies in doing away with the separation between storage and display and replacing it with a model of data processing and retrieval (Ernst 2000, 25–26). German media archaeology is usually characterized as focusing on hardware over symbolic meaning, on machinic agency over human agency (Winthrop-Young 2006; Parikka 2011, 54). In Ernst's case there is also a strong emphasis on temporal media processes, on data flows and electrical signals (Parikka 2011, 54). For me, Ernst's writing on museums and history suggested new ways of thinking about museums. Media become more than objects for the media archaeologist to research, they are themselves machinic "techniques of remembering" that are very different from the practice and discourse of history (Ernst 2005, 595). This machinic memory nevertheless has cultural implications, reconfiguring the very cultural constructions on which museums depend, as in the case of photography: "the improved technologies of visual reproduction led to the availability of arts and artefacts which André Malraux praised as a condition for the thinkability of notions such as a cross artistic 'style' in his celebrated photo-based *musée imaginaire* of 1947" (Ernst 2005, 599). Media archaeologist Jussi Parikka summarizes the relevance of Ernst's work for museums as follows:

> The implications for the wider set of cultural institutions and museums are radical: the need to think museums and archives as nonplaces, and as addresses and hence as modes of management of protocols, software structures and patterns of retrieval which potentially can open up new ways of user-engagement as well, and where data storage cannot be detached from its continuous searchability and distribution. (Parikka 2011, 58).

However, this corresponds more to Ernst's understanding of the archive (which becomes transformed into software structures) rather than of the museum, which he views as quite distinct. In the following interview, conducted in his office in Humboldt University in February 2011, Ernst's materialist approach to media leads him to insist on the resistance of the material object (which cannot be completely absorbed by digitalization). Thus, he envisages the museum as something that cannot be understood along the lines of electronic media, as something that is not immune to the effects of technological change, but that needs to maintain its own distinctive quality, centered around the thing that sets it apart from electronic media: the physical presentation of material objects.[1]

MH: *Could you explain what media archaeology is, in your version of it?*

WE: Media archaeology refers to the well-known discipline of archaeology in the sense that it takes the media first of all as material objects, even in our so-called virtual world and information society. All this information flow is still based on real cables, real transmitters, real technologies. So media archaeology tries to take the point of view of the media as technological object, which means, for example, to look at what a television image *is*, not in terms of content. The question of what the political or whatever manipulated message of the video or the television image is has been taken care of by communication studies and other related disciplines – and it has to be done – and, to a certain degree, cultural studies interprets this semiotics and coding and decoding of the television image. Media archaeology is in this respect closer to Marshall McLuhan's approach and looks at what the television image means, which makes it different from the cinematographic image, or the photographic image, or the digital image (McLuhan [1964] 2003).

Now, how is the electronic image different from the digital image, what difference does it make? First of all, one has to look at it technically, and techno-mathematically, to know how it is made, for example, what the electronic image does to our eyes, which is of a completely different nature to the projected screen image of cinema. How does it subconsciously influence our perception? The cathode ray, the light, the speed of lines of television: these are processes where the medium works on our perception although we are not conscious of it.

So media archaeology tries to uncover or discover these processes. In order to discover it, media archaeology has to know how your own perception works in terms of neuro-biology and physiology, and at the same time how the medium actually works, because it makes such a big difference whether it is electronically driven or driven by software, which has a completely different cultural power and mechanism and technique behind it. So, to take the example of the most popular medium of today, which would be the computer as laptop (most people now have computers as laptops or similar devices): whereas most people know the computer from the interface, media archaeology looks behind the interface. Like the open software movement, it asks: What are the driving mechanisms behind the interface? What is the software behind the interface? How can we actually gain control of the computer ourselves? This means, not just being a user – using, clicking icons, or using apps, which is the most popular way now to use these devices – but analyzing who decides and what decides what can be used, what can't be used, and how can we use that in different ways. In order to know that, we have to look to what is behind the interface, which today would be software, and in the old media would be electronic technology (Figure 1.1).

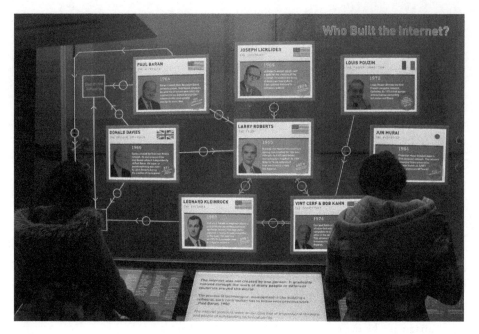

FIGURE 1.1 "Who Built the Internet?" display at the National Media Museum, Bradford, UK.

Photo: Michelle Henning. Reproduced by kind permission of the National Media Museum.

MH: *How do you then go from looking at media, such as the examples you gave of the computer, the television, software, etc. to thinking about museums and exhibitions? What's the connection there? How does that relate?*

WE: Well, first of all, the relationship between media and museums, of course, is a manifold one. The traditional approach would ask for media as objects of museum display. Science museums and technology museums do this, they show old media on display as part of cultural history. That's the most natural relation between media and museums – they become museum objects. Already, at that point, the problem starts. In Berlin, for example, you can go to the Museum of Technology and you see old televisions of the late 1950s – you see them as an object like any other object displayed by the museum.

Now as a media theorist I would say that a medium that is not performing in its medium state is just a piece of furniture. A television on display in a museum which does not show the screen working is not shown as a medium; it's just a piece of hardware, a design object. And most people actually look at old TVs and radios like a piece of furniture: they recognize the style of the fifties and sixties and they become nostalgic about it, and see it as a piece of furniture, not attending to it as a medium. And that's a big challenge for museums because, if they want to show the medium, they somehow need to show it running. Now, this is a big problem for museum conservators: it's not easy to get those old media working again. If you have to replace parts of the medium, then it's not original anymore – little condensers have to be exchanged. When you show it running, do you show historical footage from the period of the television or do you show up-to-date programs? So it undermines already the idea of the museum object. Since media are so process-oriented, they are only media when they are in operation. They somehow are a challenge to the idea of a museum as a place to present objects, material objects.

MH: *But in science and technology museums you often have steam engines, don't you, or that kind of thing, actually running?*

WE: They definitely have to be shown working, which is suddenly the dynamic object, and this becomes a new genre of museum display. This is a challenge, of course, for museums to manage to keep it running and conservators to allow it to run, because one should have it as an original running or a replica at least. Museums are progressing to this but already it shows the challenge. The mobile object, the cultural artifact, which is also a dynamic object, is a challenge to museums.

New media are defined by the fact that they are not primarily the technology but formats. Television or radio or the book – these are all being perceived more on more on the computer screen. And behind them is the software which defines these objects and enables these old media to return. Now how do you display software? As a cultural good which needs to be preserved as a document of our time, it's very difficult. How you preserve software? Doron Swade – the former curator of the computer department at the London Science museum who has now moved to the United States to run the Computer History Museum – has said this is now a challenge for curators (Swade 2002). It's very complex to preserve software on the original hardware or to emulate software. How do you display it? It has to do something and then again you need the running system to operate this software. It's very immaterial: you cannot touch software as such. This is a big challenge for the traditional object-/artifact-oriented museum. In this respect, the relation between media and museum becomes more complicated.

The next step, and the most complicated, is, of course, asking whether the museum itself is a medium. I would always try to emphasize that it makes sense to keep the difference. There is a broad sense of the term "medium," which even covers the human body as a medium. Luckily there is no master definition of media but, if it becomes too broadly defined, the strength of the museum would be lost; it would lose its specificity if you just call it a medium. I would say the museum is not a technical medium because it's not able to operate itself. It needs to be run by the museum people – which differentiates it from the first medium in the technical sense, the photographic camera. The camera can actually produce a picture without human intervention. It needs a human to start it, but the rest of it can be done using the apparatus. An electronic camera can produce a live transmission from Cairo to our living room on the television screen. This is done by the medium: the medium is operative. But the museum in itself does not move and operate – it depends on humans as the processor. That is why I couldn't call it medium in the strict sense.

Since when did "media" become a popular word? Let's take Marshall McLuhan's influential book from 1964, *Understanding Media*, where the word "media" became part of a book title that wasn't just for the physical sciences. He meant the mass medium, the electronic mass media. They are based on an electric current, on signal processing, on all kinds of electrical engineering which are completely different from how a museum works, how an archive works, or how a library works (which are the old memory institutions).

These are institutions, they are memory agencies; I would say they are symbolic systems for sure. A lot of work in museums is coded by symbolic systems, by inventories, by labeling and moving real objects. But this is different from the way a medium would be defined. And, since the word "medium" as a discursive term only emerged in coexistence with the modern apparatus-based or even electricity-based systems, it makes sense to limit the word "medium" to those systems and not to use it too broadly for everything that is somehow doing something.

MH: *Nevertheless, as a media archaeologist you've written quite a bit about museums and exhibitions. So, given that you're saying that the museum isn't a medium, what can media archaeology tell us? How can it give us a different perspective from conventional museum studies?*

WE: By discovering similarities and differences. A lot of archaeologists now are interested in how cultural memory works. A lot of studies have been done on how memory is being created in societies. What are the institutions, the agencies, the places where memory takes place? And how and where does cultural transmission take place? How is tradition made? How does tradition actually work? Now both media in the technical sense, and museums and other agencies in the traditional sense, are transferring information from one point to another, or from one point in time to another. One of the main tasks of the museum has been how to transmit information over time. Time is the channel. Doing media studies, I am sensitive in terms of being aware of how to analyze this: How does it work? Where is the sender? Where is the channel? Where is the receiver? How are things coded? How is this done? So, media studies creates the kinds of questions which I readdress to previous agencies of memory transmission. Media studies provides me with a vocabulary and the questions through which I look at something like tradition in a more differentiated way, maybe even a bit more technical way. Then the notion of tradition loses a bit of its metaphysical, culturally somehow cloudy, quality and can be more precisely analyzed: Who has the power? What technology do we need for transmission? What is the institutional part? What is the technical part? To what degree is memory a social event, a technical event, a storage event? Since technical media are always based on processes of transmission and storage, the study of them provides me with a vocabulary to ask how the museum works.

The next step would then be to find out how the museum is different from technical media. For example, the museum has a strength that so far no other medium is able to provide, and that is the material object. We still can't send material objects over the Internet. We can order objects but they still have to be sent by traditional mail. Also, think about the preservation of information. This is an ever growing problem for electronic media starting from old photographs, which have a surprising endurance over 150 years, although they become yellow, but film is more difficult. The early films, with their chemical material that tends to burn when stored somewhere too hot, or the color films where the colors fade – now this is a big problem for film restorers. So there is physical entropy, the tendency to decay in the material. We have the video tape and magnetic audio tape … one can say, "Well, I can listen to a 50-year-old magnetic tape and still hear a lot" – which is a positive surprise, but at the same time there are dropouts. As for digital tapes, as almost everyone knows now from their own experience, these are more efficient than ever, can be faster transmitters and processors than ever, but they are not long-lasting. The CD-ROM will not last – in itself, it will not keep its data intact for a long time – but the machines themselves will also become dated and be replaced by other systems and faster rhythms. So we have a big technical problem.

Compared to that, if we consider the museum in terms of its objects (the thing that differentiates the museum from the library and the archive is the collection of material artifacts), these objects are surprisingly enduring. This quality of the museum should not be lost when museums are trying to be immaterial themselves. The discussion of the immaterial museum has been a media and cultural studies project starting with photography and with André Malraux and others, and to a certain degree Walter Benjamin, who were already concerned with the question whether or not the photograph-based image collection could be called the imaginary museum (Malraux [1947] 1967; Benjamin [1936] 2002a). This is fine: it's opening the museum, extending the museum, but it loses the museum's material basis. The basis of the museum is the material object, the picture which is actually, in its physicality, there, and this is completely different from the photographic or the electronic image reproduction.

MH: *I am almost going to reverse my earlier question, because I asked how media archaeology likes to think about museums. In reverse, it seems that thinking museologically, as well, actually helps you to understand about media. That orientation toward preservation, toward storage, and so on, which is very familiar within the museum context, is quite new to thinking about media, isn't it? It seems that you're doing both, examining the productive differences between the two things.*

WE: Yeah, it's trying to take both sides. On the one hand, one can look at how computer architecture works and then one discovers that a lot of the storage mechanisms sound familiar if one has done museum studies or archive studies or library studies. Even down to the terms that we are using, terms like "memory" in the computer, which is actually a metaphor because technically the computer does not have a memory. We call it a memory because our culture tends to address even technology in terms that have been created in previous agencies of tradition, such as the museum or library or archive.

But, on the other hand, one reason to call what we do "media archaeology" is, of course, that one is concentrating on the material object, which sounds like traditional archaeology which has always been object-oriented. But then the other use of the word "archaeology" comes from Michel Foucault's nonmetaphorical use of "archaeology," meaning analyzing the hidden mechanisms which create knowledge or evidence and through that term, and in his book *The Archaeology of Knowledge* Foucault said, let us look at the discontinuities ([1969] 2002). That's what makes his archaeology different from "history," and media archaeology different from media history. Media archaeology looks at discontinuity. What difference do media make to previous cultural mechanisms of memory and tradition? Now, what this emphasis on discontinuity, rupture, and difference does is sharpen analysis. It may be a bit one-sided overall; maybe in the end there are many more continuities. But historians would always tend to emphasize the continuities. Our traditional cultural model emphasizes continuities, from the ancient Greek temple to today. Learning from Foucault, let's look at the discontinuities – that's how to look archaeologically. Then we can decide how, when we talk about computer architecture with words such as "memory," how far it is a metaphor, which in a way makes the discontinuity oblique, which harms the discontinuity. Let's look at where the discontinuity is and name it, in order to make our contemporaries realize that it makes a difference.

MH: *When you talk about how metaphors might harm the discontinuities, I remember Walter Benjamin writing about iron architecture in the nineteenth century being covered by a veil of stone, so that the newness of the thing was concealed, and that was a problem: the radically new disguised as tradition (Benjamin [1935] 2002b). Is that the kind of thing you're talking about?*

WE: Yes, yes. Once again I would quote Marshall McLuhan, who said that, very quickly, the content of the new medium tends to become the older medium (McLuhan [1964] 2003, 8). Like in early films that took a lot of theater plays as their content, or how television shows a lot of films even today. It's true for the computer. In a way, we use the computer like an extended book when it comes to texts. We use it now to listen to radio formats or to look at various kinds of media movies. Media archaeology tries to uncover the media and to lay their structure bare.

MH: *And so, by doing that, reveal the discontinuities that are concealed by that continuity of content?*

WE: For example, to come back to what happens if media are objects in museums. We have the radio of the 1940s which, stylistically, looks like it is part of the design of that era but, if we take off this external appearance and look at the technological structure, it looks almost ahistorical. As a technological object, it principally works as a radio from much later. The electronic tubes (or valves) have been replaced by transistors, but functionally it works in exactly the same way, amplitude motivated (AM) or frequency motivated (FM) radio – which some people still remember! It's still working on the same principle. Considered in this way, suddenly there are objects that, from the archaeological point of view, are structurally not that historical: they are invariant against temporal change until they are completely displaced or replaced by a completely new system. It's another temporal rhythm. Now, to show this is a challenge to the idea of display: What do I display if I display media? If I display them on the surface, then I miss their essence, but it's more difficult for visitors to have a medium opened and to understand what's going on. It's a big challenge to museum education and didactics to explain what's really happening there. That's a challenge to the design-oriented, surface-oriented display.

MH: *Coming back to the museum being a medium or not a medium – one of the things you talk about in your writing is the time–space structure of exhibitions and museums. By which I mean, the ways in which museums or exhibitions are experienced by visitors in terms of how they control their time by pausing in front of an exhibit or moving on, whether they are linear in design, and so on. One of the things that interests me in your writing is that, although you're not saying that the museum is a medium, at the same time you are drawing parallels between some of the technical structures, between the experiences of the contemporary computer-based media and the experience of moving around an exhibition space, in particular the spaces of contemporary art exhibitions.*

WE: With interactive media, we come back closer to the museum than we did with earlier mass media. But, first of all, let me quote the German museologist Heinz Ladendorf who said the museum is not a medium but a collection, which makes it very clear that the basic function of the traditional museum is a very different one (Ladendorf 1973, 23). It has to collect a choice of objects, not everything, unlike in an archive, which normally gets from its administration, first of all, all the files and then they can make a selection. Whereas a library or a museum is a selection, they can select objects from the beginning. In most cases, it's their duty to preserve the choice of objects; officially, even legally, they are there for protecting certain types of objects. It's different from data processing; it's different from the archive; it's a collection. Museums are therefore differentiated from the medium in its technical and other senses.

Now, for a long time media was meant to be mass media which means broadcasting, you know, radio, television and so on, which had no feedback channel, which could only be consumed in a way. At that time, how we experienced images, on television or in cinemas, was not directed by the viewer. The cuts, the speed, the change of perspective – all of these were done by the camera and we were just subjected to them as viewers. That differentiated the experience of objects and images from the museum, where the visitor is free to move, usually at their own speed, and to make a choice where to stand or view an image more closely. Now this self-autonomous, sovereign time of information processing used to be a quality of the museum against the dictatorship of time in the mass media. This has now changed, with interactive media, with the Internet. Again, the user decides to a large degree how long to stay at an object, to choose whether to get it replayed, like with a video as opposed to a television image. You could look at it in your own time; you can see it several times; you can even cut it, manipulate it, and appropriate it. For a long time the medium had a time dominance over the viewer, whereas in the museum the visitor could be in control of their own time of information processing, so this was a virtue of the museum against this dominating of time.

MH: *One thing I have noticed, though, and this is just speculative, if you look at the halls of dioramas in the American Museum of Natural History, or any number of American exhibits from the 1920s to the 1940s, what you see is something incredibly cinematic. Alison Griffiths pointed to this when she linked early twentieth-century museum curators' anxieties about museum life groups to anxieties about motion pictures and spectacle, and I mention it in an essay on new media in museums (Griffiths 2002, 24–30; Henning 2006a, 304). You know: the darkened hall, the lit-up windows, the scene that you watch from the outside. It is immersive but cinematic: your presence isn't acknowledged; it's going to unravel without you. And I really noticed, particularly in the American Museum of Natural History in New York, that when you came to present-day exhibits of natural history they were much more inviting you to look over here, then look over there – they were much more dispersed or networked in their structure (Henning 2006b, 145–146). So I wonder if another tendency is for museums to actually mimic the popular media of their time, whether that's something that also happened so that they conceal their own medium specificity.*

WE: There has always been a sort of mirroring of the new media in museum practices. It started with photography, when suddenly the period rooms started appearing in museums. That's the idea that a historical museum might create a room which recreates the historical atmosphere of the period of the time. This is certainly an effect of the photographic medium which could preserve a coherent image of a moment in time. The art historian Stephen Bann, for example, has shown that the idea of a period room was contemporary to the emergence of photography (Bann 1984; Ernst 2005). And, of course, with cinematography, the museum tried to emulate moving parts, even moving images and that happened until today as if the museum always had to rival the prospective new media. I would almost say that the museum misses its own quality and its strength. I would propose a counterstrategy: What can the museum do that new media cannot do?

It might sound very conservative if I return to the material object but materiality is the blind spot of the information age. Because, first of all, digital media cannot provide materiality, the resistance of the object, which is not the same as the information of the object. The object has more information in it than a recording or a scan of an object would be able to provide. Then we have things that have been discussed again and again, things like the aura which Walter Benjamin has described: to what degree does the aura depend on the materiality? For Walter Benjamin, any reproduction of the material object makes it lose its aura, which is its quality of being here and now (Benjamin [1936] 2002a). The idea of presence which is created by a material object is not easily mimicked by electronic media. This is true even of virtual spaces that you are immersed in, three-dimensional spaces, because human perception can clearly work out the difference as to whether you're really hitting a rock or whether this is something that is happening in a data glove space. So there is a quality of the museum there.

MH: *And that's something that media are constantly trying to mimic, and so, if the museum were trying to mimic the media, the media are also trying to mimic the museum by constantly trying to simulate an experience of the thing itself.*

WE: Yes, that is why the relationship is dynamic. I would not categorically say that the museum is completely and categorically different from media. To a high degree, it is different, but there is a dynamic relationship of course: the modes of perception of the visitors are dominated by media perception and museums have to react to it. And the other way round: museum aesthetics has an influence on media interface display. Brenda Laurel in her book *Computers as Theater* (1991) has shown how much our aesthetics of the interface of the computer is dominated by cultural ways of looking which come from theater, from the drama of the theatrical space, and in a way this is true of museum space as well. Still, the media archaeological analysis would like to emphasize the discontinuity because otherwise it looks as if culture was a friendly, coexistent, and homogeneous and harmonious play between different agencies. I think the challenge is much much bigger, to be aware of what really changes now and what has changed.

MH: *You mentioned that you took from Foucault the concept of rupture and historical discontinuity, as opposed to a kind of narrative progression that you have in traditional history, but presumably you also took from Foucault that concept of power as something that's not centralized or held, that's dispersed …?*

WE: Yes, and both the critique of the narrative progression and the analysis of power mechanisms are essential parts of media archaeology, even in the analysis of the museum. For example, the museum includes not just the public display parts of the museum; the real powerful side of the museum is in the parts which are hidden to the normal visitor, the offices where the inventories are being created, even the storage spaces where a lot of objects are being stored which are never on display. It is only recently that museums have started to open these spaces. Spaces which are not normally ordered, they are just open shelves (Figure 1.2).

MH: *And you're quite in favor of that aren't you?*

WE: I am in favor of that – it's like opening a medium and looking at how it works. One does not have the offer of an interpreted presentation already. But we have a data bank, one that we could now call the aesthetics of the data bank itself, now that we live in a media culture where the user is much more able than we used to be before to handle a data bank itself. Not to get it translated into a narrative, but to work with the databank itself, to get access to the information in the data bank itself, even to demand open source, to get access to the source codes: this is the equivalent of getting access to the nonprefigured, nonordered spaces of the museum.

FIGURE 1.2   8 mm film cameras in storage at the National Media Museum.
Photo: Michelle Henning. Reproduced by kind permission of the National Media Museum.

MH: *To me, one of the ironies of the use of new media interactive booths or touch screens in museums is that they seem to be based in a desire to increase access to all the information that maybe would be too much to put on a written label, to the detailed context or the provenance of the object, all the stuff that the museum knows and can now share. But, for me, the experience is the other way: what actually happens is that it's just more interpretation, instead of opening up to the concealed parts of the museum or to information you couldn't otherwise normally have on display. Instead of opening and expanding the display, it just seems to put more layers of interpretation between you and the experience of really going down into the basement, unlocking the doors, and having a poke around.*

WE: There was, of course, always a debate within museums studies itself as to how much text should be provided in a museum. Was the strength of the museum the material object or do we urgently need contextualization? – which was, of course, a very enlightened attitude. But to what degree can the museum then be replaced by just reading the texts? I can get a lot of information on museum objects online, but it cannot replace my confrontation with the objects as long as we are confronted with traditional objects. However, it all changes now with a culture that not only produces pieces of art as objects, but also as digitally born objects, as they are called. Then the difference is that it is not *that* book anymore. A book that is produced and published only online … I don't have to go to a library to borrow a book; I can download it at home and it's as authentic as ever. And digital art, for example, which is digitally born, there is good reason to say it is the original which I experience if I download it online. I don't have to go to an art museum to see that. So that changes.

   For the traditional culture, which is object-oriented to a high degree, we need the traditional museum, which displays the real object, and so far the difference works. But it becomes different now – the museum loses it and becomes itself changed from an institution, a place, or an agency to a format. When it comes to truly digital culture, then the museum is a format. It's a way of ordering information, ordering images, offering a guided tour. Once the museum is a format, it's not an institution anymore. I would make a difference between a format, which is a sort of technical term, and a real institution. The real place, which is based on material objects, exists on two different levels. Of course we can make it as complicated as we like. If we look at the history of the term "museum" or the history of the museum itself, we find it was not always the object-based rooms and places. In the early Renaissance, it could be the name for an empty room where you think: this was a museum as well – a cognitive space.

MH: *You have that in contemporary holocaust museums sometimes – contemplative spaces.*

WE: Yes, but this example shows that the very word "museum" was not bound strictly to the object base; it could mean arranging things in your head only, and for that you only needed a quiet and empty space – we call it the museum. So even that was genealogically more thinkable already but, as we know, the museum is an institution. It's an object-bound institution and the strength is its object-basedness. It's not like time-based media – that's not the strength. Its resistance against time, that's the incredible power of the museum – the resistance against time.

MH: *You mentioned this earlier and you used a phrase that reminded me of Harold Innis,*
     the transmitting through time, the museum as something that transmits through time but
     at the same time resists the passing of time (Innis [1951] 2008).

WE: Yes, the objects of the museum by their very presence resist the passing of
     time. We can see Roman inscriptions in the Vatican Museum, and it's not that self-
     evident that for 2000 years we would still be able to decipher the letters inscribed in
     stone, so in a way it resists time. Actually one of the allegories of the paintings on
     the ceiling that connects the Vatican Museum to the Vatican Library, painted by
     Anton Raphael Mengs, who was a friend of Johann Joachim Winckelmann in the
     eighteenth century, shows how the Vatican Museum was actually founded on the
     idea that there are long-lasting values. The Catholic Church was very interested in
     claiming its authority as not changing with history [this painting is known in
     English as *The Triumph of History over Time*, or *The Allegory of History*, and is in the
     Camera dei Papiri]. There is an authority which traverses history and which resists
     time, which we can see by this allegorical painting which nicely shows the
     mechanism of tradition.

     We now live in a media culture that is now very much real time-oriented, in
     which fast transmission is the most valuable quality. The almost immediate transfer
     of information which was already present in the transmission of live radio and live
     television is now referred to as real time processing. This traversing of space almost
     immediately started with the age of telegraphy and other information media
     communication. The virtue of the museum is completely different: to traverse long
     distances of time, to transfer objects in a time channel which lasts for several
     thousand years in the case of ancient Egypt and several other civilizations. This is a
     completely different channel of transmission, to use this media technical term. And
     it's even a challenge to the idea of history, the museum, because it's based on the
     invariance of the object. We can see an object of the eighteenth century, a painting
     for example, and still be touched by it. That's a very strange thing, because we don't
     dress like people of that age, we don't think like them anymore … Or take Greek
     objects: something happens – something interacts between our perception and this
     object. This undercuts the idea of history which emphasizes the difference, the
     change, the transformation.

MH: *Yes, in your writing on "media tempor(e)alities" you quoted Heidegger's* Being and
     Time *on the question of the extent to which the object is historical (Ernst 2008; 2012;*
     Heidegger [1927] 1962). There is a tendency to assume that the traces of use make an object
     historical.

WE: That's the way Heidegger tries to answer it, but the question he poses, I think,
     is still open to discussion because we know most of the objects in a museum are
     traditionally understood as historical objects but they are present and they have a
     present impression on us. So there is dissonance, a cognitive dissonance: cognitively
     we know they are past but we are affected by the object as present. Now this is a big
     paradox, and this is a productive paradox actually, which shows that the museum is
     not just part of cultural history or an agency of cultural history. And even the idea
     of history is challenged: for a long time the museum tour or narrative would start in
     early times and end in the present, although they could be arranged in a completely

different way. The archaeological reading would be to take objects which traverse this seemingly historical sequence. For a long time the museum as a history machine produced history by the illusion that things progress, so that we begin by experiencing rough or crude objects and then end up with the most elaborate versions, as in technical museums which show technological progress. A lot of nineteenth- and twentieth-century museums were built on this model, or rather they were not only built on the historical model but they helped to build the historical model. Because, by physically wandering through these museums, we got this idea of history as progress which was based on the Hegelian idea of progress.

MH: *Yes it's interesting that in the art historical museum you have this Hegelian notion of the progress of art, and yet at the same time it was punctuated by these masterpieces that were supposed to transcend time and that you were supposed to almost sit in front of and commune with in some transhistorical way.*

WE: Yes, this was the aesthetics of the art museum, of the art piece in the collection, until the age of Winckelmann and others when suddenly art itself became historicized. It's fascinating to see how, for a long time, art from antiquity would have a metahistorical perfection. There was no historical distance to it; there was just a perfection which to later generations was the guideline. And one was confronted with it in private collections or in public museums or collections. Then there were figures like Winckelmann in 1764, writing *History of the Art of Antiquity*, where he said that art is dependent on its historical contexts (Winckelmann [1764] 2006). Suddenly art itself became historicized. Museums like the Berlin Altes Museum, built by Schinkel, reacted to it by arranging pieces of art in a historical sequence. It's a spatial sequence, because all the museum rooms coexist spatially, but it was arranged in a way that we get the idea of a historical progress. And Hegel, who was living near the museum, built a lot of his ideas influenced by this arrangement of a gallery of pictures in a historical way. We can take it very literally, this phenomenology of mind – he in the end writes how the world and spirit progress through a gallery of pictures. We can take it very literally and visit the Altes Museum in Berlin: he was living just a few hundred yards away, and so was very much influenced by the new way of arranging museums.

MH: *Something else you said that really resonated with me was in your chapter in the Susan Crane book – it was where you are writing about archives and you say the "true tragic archive is the soil" (Ernst 2000, 28). And, while I suppose I think of archives as things that have been authored, things that have been put together and ordered, collections that have been cataloged, at the same time it's interesting to think of soil as an archive; it is an interesting way to think of power and the museum and what museums occlude or cover up. It reminded me of when I was researching whaling museums: there's always some display of whaling equipment and a couple of whales, but then I read how the blood and oil from each sperm whale soaked into the earth – an extreme amount so that the whole port stank and the ground was full of the oil (Henning 2011). Similarly, what you said about the tragic archive being the soil made me think of the way in which history materially embeds itself. The effects of human activity on the earth and so on are constructing an inadvertent record, an archaeological record, and that sometimes conflicts with the version of events the authored museum wants to present.*

WE: Yes, and this again depends first of all on the physical evidence, those traces you can smell: with the old machines, if they are not cleaned too much in the museum, you can smell the oil. Now this is what physically would be the entropy of the material, the decay – the decay which physically provides the time era. In physics there is the law of thermodynamics which says there is a tendency from order to disorder: this is a law of nature which gives time an arrow at all in a physical sense. Now you can only experience this with physical objects. It might be the soil or a videotape: there is history at work in the physical sense and for that you need the real object. We need this experience and this again is a virtue of the museum as opposed to the experience which we make now. Because, for everything that is digitally there and you copy it, there is no decay; the information can be copied without loss.

MH: *But the museum tries to halt decay sometimes and sanitizes things.*

WE: Yes, and it erases history. I would almost say that the strengths of the museum now would be counterstrategies to this to the new negentropic virtue of the information society,[2] where you cannot make a distinction between the original and its copy anymore: for a digital copy this is true. The copy is not a copy anymore; it's a second version of the original. Then you lose any trace of history. The negentropic material almost is not at work; it's just very marginally at work – but that's another discussion.

Now this creates a different sense of culture, of time, all those emphatic notions that are now in our cultural discourse. This opens a big gap between the old culture, which is dominated by the experience of entropy, and the new culture, which creates the illusion that there is lossless tradition. Now this is fascinating and worrying at the same time, this idea of lossless tradition. Where is the authority which can decide which is original and which is not? Is our authority within the material or is it just metadata providing the authority? Now, these are all questions the museum, if it's clever, can address. The museum could be the place where those new semiological challenges are being reflected because the new media themselves have no place where they can reflect this. The Internet itself has no place where it can reflect itself. But the museum is a space and a place and a time; when you visit a museum you reserve some time to be open to reflection and contemplation. Now museums could be used to reflect cultural mechanisms or cultural technologies as they take place in the contemporary media world. Because we need another place, in the Foucauldian sense, we need a place which is different from the media in order to reflect on the media. You cannot reflect on a medium within the same medium – according to the system theory of the position of the observer, you have to create a difference. And, by proudly not being a medium in the modern sense, the museum could say exactly, "This is a place where we can reflect about media," because it introduces a distance, a distance which is a precondition for reflection.

MH: *Do you think there are any museums or exhibits that are already doing that, or starting to do that, in an interesting way?*

WE: Yes there are museums which are starting to do that. For example, of recent experience the National Museum of Photography, Film and Television in Bradford in England.

MH: *It's now the National Media Museum.*

WE: Which is in itself interesting. It started out as a history museum of television and photography and is now called the National Media Museum. This change is significant: it says that we don't just want to be known as some nostalgic place of the old electronic or electromechanical television but we use it as a place to reflect on the new media, the new audiovisual media. And then suddenly there is the whole message – that the museum is not about cultural history but a dynamic place of reflection; it's a completely different function from that of the museum – it becomes in itself a flexible institution. This is, of course, losing a bit of its strong read-only memory-oriented function, which it used to have for a long time. There are maybe other museums which are stronger when they are just proudly keeping the read-only memory because they have pieces of art or so which derive their authority and aura exactly from not being replaced by contemporary versions. So different museums should have different strategies – it depends on if it's a museum of technology or a museum of art. I think even the museum itself should be differentiated and should develop different strategies for the different types of objects it has.

MH: *I was very interested when I visited the Darwin Centre in the Natural History Museum in London because they had that. I went on a tour where you could see the research collection and the scientists at work. So it's like a behind-the-scenes tour but it's actually part of the design of it.*

WE: Yes, the archaeological aesthetic has already been opening up the museums. It's because they are used to gaining and organizing information themselves. You can now open the archive. For a long time we needed historians to work in the archive, but then to write it for us in the form of a big narrative that produces history. Now, more and more as a product of information, the user wants to use the archive material directly themselves. It doesn't mean it's not interesting to have a plausible interpretation offered by historians in a plausible museum exhibition which arranges objects in a way that is convincing, but at the same time there is a chance to rearrange it in accordance with different criteria. This aesthetic has opened the museum through access to the shelves or the tendency to replace the long-term exhibition with more temporary exhibitions. It's more dynamic – like the tendency to have more short-term memories being a product of our media age, which means that the idea of the emphatic long-term memory is being replaced by the idea of short-term memories which are more functionally reusable by the present but which won't last long. Once more, museum people have to decide to choose a precise counterstrategy, to say we are one of the only few places where there is a resistance to this acceleration of short-term memory.

MH: *But, by doing that, they risk situating themselves as reactionary?*

WE: In the Jean Baudrillard way: not reactionary, but rather retroactive. Exactly because museums are challenged by new media, they can develop counterstrategies. Let's look at the opera house and other cultural institutions. The idea was that the gramophone would kill opera. No, it didn't; that never happened – it just displaced that institution. These institutions did not win by trying to rival the new media. A theater can never be as good as a cinema when it comes to bringing together different places in one, or a montage, or jumping back and forth between times. Every film can do that which a theater cannot easily do. But the theater has the real presence, the authority of the real actor, and the accidents of the actor. Every performance is live, so if something goes wrong it actually goes wrong – it's not recorded on tape. So there are virtues or qualities which are preserved in the opera house, in the theater, and I would say in the museum, like the material object as a counterstrategy. Not completely separate from the new media, always playing with the critical dialogue, playing with it dynamically, critically, or adopting a bit but still caring about the difference.

MH: *But you mentioned earlier, I think, that visitors arrive with their senses adjusted to the different media with which they live. I was thinking of taking my daughter when she was very young to the theater for the first time. She shouted, cried, hid under the chairs, and then stood up on them and clapped, completely responding to what was happening and all the other children were sat there blank-faced as if it were a screen. She had never been to the theater or cinema and so I did wonder if she was out of sync with them in terms of how her mode of attention had been adjusted.*

WE: Yes but that shows that the strength of the real theater would be to make us aware of the difference. There are qualities which cannot be covered by the cinema, although the cinema has opened marvelous new cultural options and, as a media theorist, I am fascinated by what media can do. But there are things which media cannot do and there are at least interesting differences in perception, in aesthetics, in information, so that's why I come back to this counterstrategy again and again.

MH: *But I suppose what I'm getting at is that, if you arrive at the museum with a cinema-adjusted brain, you're going to look at the same displays very differently than if you had arrived before the age of cinema.*

WE: Yes, and that's why museum people cannot simply proudly ignore the new media. That's not what counterstrategy is. Counterstrategy means paying attention to what is part of a discursive field, and this is a media-dominated cultural field. Now that's why museum people have to know other ways of looking, of hearing, of moving, of interacting. Now people want to interact in museums naturally because of the use of the Internet, and so on. So all of this has to be known by the museum people, calculated by them, in order to then create their aesthetic strategies of the museum. But, then in the next step, not by trying to imitate and mimic this or say that we've fulfilled this expectation as well, but maybe by cleverly showing them the difference that is the unique strength of the museum. Just as you could show a unique strength of what the archive is as opposed to other memory agencies. This archive could well be separated and differentiated from the old world collective memory agencies by saying this is a completely different kind of authority which the archive has. It's not just a memory. The archive has to do with the power of having access to things like that. The museum has material properties which are its unique feature. Lyotard made that the topic of his big exhibition *Les immatériaux* in Paris in 1985: to what degree does the material physical world count in our immaterial media culture? Those are the questions to which the museum can really respond – which is more difficult for libraries, which consist mainly of printed symbols in books that are still material.

MH: *In Britain at the moment the government is trying to close libraries, and it seems there is a very strong countercampaign because libraries have become the place where people who don't have much money have access to the new media as well. So they're not just the preserve of the book. The destruction of the library is about the destruction of public space and a kind of attack on the public sphere.*

WE: Whereas, for the library, the situation is really different. First of all, it's symbolic. It's based on symbols, the printed object. Although the material object is there, and a lot of conservative librarians will always trust the material object of the book, now e-books can imitate even the turning of the page and things like that. Since the central quality of the postmedieval book is the printed letter, which can be reproduced on a symbolic level, this can be adopted by new media to a high degree. But I will say it again: The structure of the archive cannot be adopted because it's an authoritative space which is, first of all, not about memory. The museum, with its quality of being out of time for the moment, creating a space out of time, based on the metareality or the physicality of objects, is a quality that so far can in no way be replaced by any other reproduction media, not photography, nor television, nor film, nor the digital computer. And from that it can derive a lot of energy as a counterenergy, a reflective, dynamic counterenergy. Not a conservative counterenergy, but a dynamic counterenergy.

Acknowledgments

This interview was transcribed by Jen Rhodes. My thanks to her and to Wolfgang Ernst for all their help in the production of this chapter.

Notes

1   See also Ernst 1994; 2013b; Emerson 2013.
2   Negentropy is a scientific term meaning "negative entropy." While, in thermodynamics, entropy refers to a tendency toward equilibrium in thermodynamic systems, which involves the dissipation or loss of useful energy, the term is more generally used to refer to a tendency to increased disorder and loss. Negentropy therefore has become associated with the idea that information processing produces order from chaos, with data appearing to become increasingly ordered and "lossless."

References

Bann, Stephen. 1984. "The Poetics of the Museum." In *The Clothing of Clio: A Study in the Representation of History in Nineteenth-Century Britain and France*, 77–92. Cambridge: Cambridge University Press.

Benjamin, Walter. (1936) 2002a. "The Work of Art in the Age of Its Technological Reproducibility," 2nd version. In *Walter Benjamin: Selected Writings*, vol. 3, edited by Michael W. Jennings, 101–133. Cambridge, MA: Harvard University Press.

Benjamin, Walter. (1935) 2002b. "Paris: Capital of the Nineteenth Century." In *Walter Benjamin: Selected Writings*, vol. 3, edited by Michael W. Jennings, 33–34. Cambridge, MA: Harvard University Press.

Emerson, Lori. 2013. "Archives, Materiality and the 'Agency of the Machine': An Interview with Wolfgang Ernst." National Digital Stewardship Alliance Innovation. Accessed July 18, 2014. http://blogs.loc.gov/digitalpreservation/2013/02/archives-materiality-and-agency-of-the-machine-an-interview-with-wolfgang-ernst/.

Ernst, Wolfgang. 1994. "Arsenals of Memory: The Archi(ve)texture of the Museum." *Mediamatic* 8(1). Accessed July 18, 2014. http://www.mediamatic.net/5884/en/arsenals-of-memory (in English/Dutch).

Ernst, Wolfgang. 2000. "Archi(ve)textures of Museology." In *Museums and Memory*, edited by Susan A. Crane, 17–34. Stanford: Stanford University Press.

Ernst, Wolfgang. 2005. "Let There Be Irony: Cultural History and Media Archaeology in Parallel Lines." *Art History* 28(5): 582–603.

Ernst, Wolfgang. 2008. "DISTORY: 100 Years of Electron Tubes: Media-Archaeologically Interpreted vis-à-vis 100 Years of Radio." In *Re-inventing Radio: Aspects of Radio as Art*, edited by Heidi Grundmann et al., 415–430. Frankfurt: Revolver.

Ernst, Wolfgang. 2012. *Gleichursprünglichkeit: Zeitwesen und Zeitgegebenheit technischer Medien* [Equiprimoridality: The temporal being and the being-in-time of technical media]. Berlin: Kulturverlag Kadmos.

Ernst, Wolfgang. 2013a. *Digital Memory and the Archive*, edited with an introduction by Jussi Parikka. Minneapolis: University of Minnesota Press.

Ernst, Wolfgang. 2013b. "From Media History to *Zeitkritik*." *Theory, Culture & Society* 30: 132–146.

Foucault, Michel. (1969) 2002. *The Archaeology of Knowledge*. Translated by A. M. Sheridan Smith. London: Routledge.

Griffiths, Alison. 2002. *Wondrous Difference: Cinema, Anthropology, and Turn-of-the-Century Visual Culture*. New York: Columbia University Press.

Heidegger, Martin. (1927) 1962. *Being and Time*. Translated by John Macquarrie and Edward Robinson. Oxford: Blackwell. Originally published as *Sein und Zeit* (Tübingen: Niemeyer, 1927).

Henning, Michelle. 2006a. "New Media." In *A Companion to Museum Studies*, edited by Sharon Macdonald, 302–318. Oxford: Blackwell.

Henning, Michelle. 2006b. *Museums, Media and Cultural Theory*. Maidenhead, UK: Open University Press.

Henning, Michelle. 2011. "Neurath's Whale." In *The Afterlives of Animals*, edited by Sam Alberti, 151–168. Charlottesville: University of Virginia Press.

Innis, Harold. (1951) 2008. *The Bias of Communication*, 2nd ed. Toronto: University of Toronto Press.

Ladendorf, Heinz. 1973. "Das Museum – Geschichte, Aufgaben, Probleme" [The museum – History, tasks, issues]. In *Museologie: Bericht über ein internationales Symposium* [Museology: Report on an international symposium], edited by International Council of Museums/Deutsches Nationalkomitee, 14–28. Pullach, Germany: Dokumentation.

Laurel, Brenda. 1991. *Computers as Theater*. Reading, MA: Addison-Wesley.

Malraux, André. (1947) 1967. *Museum Without Walls*. London: Secker & Warburg.

McLuhan, Marshall. (1964) 2003. *Understanding Media: The Extensions of Man.* Berkeley, CA: Gingko.

Parikka, Jussi. 2011 "Operative Media Archaeology: Wolfgang Ernst's Materialist Media Diagrammatics." *Theory Culture & Society* 28(5): 52–74.

Swade, Doron. 2002. "Collecting Software: Preserving Information in an Object-Centered Culture." In *History of Computing: Software Issues*, edited by U. Hashagen, Reinhard Keil-Slawik, and Arthur L. Norberg, 227–235. Berlin: Springer.

Winckelmann, Johann Joachim. (1764) 2006. *History of the Art of Antiquity.* Translated by Harry Mallgrave. Los Angeles: Getty Research Institute.

Winthrop-Young, Geoffrey. 2006. "Cultural Studies and German Media Theory." In *New Cultural Studies: Adventures in Theory*, edited by G. Hall and C. Birchall, 88–104. Edinburgh: Edinburgh University Press.

Wolfgang Ernst has been Full Professor for Media Theories at the Institute of Musicology and Media Studies, Humboldt University, Berlin, since 2003. He studied history, classics, and archaeology; in the 1980s and 1990s his academic focus was the theory of history, museology, and the archive. His current research fields embrace time-based and time-critical media, their chrono-poetical capacities and implicit sonicity. He has published many books in German, including, recently, *Chronopoetik: Zeitweisen und Zeitgaben technischer Medien* (Chrono-poetics: Time in and of technological media; Kulturverlag Kadmos, 2012), *Gleichursprünglichkeit. Zeitwesen und Zeitgegebenheit technischer Medien* (Equiprimoridality: The temporal being and the being-in-time of technical media; Kulturverlag Kadmos, 2012), and *Signale aus der Vergangenheit: Eine kleine Geschichtskritik* (Signals from the past: A small historical critique; Wilhelm Fink, 2013). In English he has most recently published *Digital Memory and the Archive*, edited and with an introduction by Jussi Parikka (University of Minnesota Press, 2013).

Michelle Henning is Senior Lecturer in Photography and Visual Culture in the Media Department, College of Arts and Humanities at the University of Brighton. She is also a Visiting Senior Research Fellow in the Digital Cultures Research Centre at the University of the West of England, Bristol. Prior to this she was Associate Professor of Media and Culture at the University of the West of England, Bristol. She is a practicing photographer and designer and has written widely on museums, media, and display techniques in her book *Museums, Media and Cultural Theory* (Open University Press, 2006), as well as in numerous collections.

2 MEDIA ARCHAEOLOGY OF/IN THE MUSEUM

Andrew Hoskins and Amy Holdsworth

The connective turn has threatened the scarcity value of museal media culture (Hoskins 2011a; 2011b). This "turn" is the sudden abundance, pervasiveness, and immediacy of communication networks, nodes, and digital media content which opens up new histories: new ways of sorting, sifting, and seeing the past. The past, which was once scarce and relatively inaccessible from the present, is suddenly and inexorably visible and accessible in an emergent "post-scarcity" culture. But the connective turn is far from being some benign phase in the evolution of media and memory; rather, it devalues scarcity as the once universal currency of museum culture. Museum content, simply put, is everywhere.

But how museums use or can use media to represent the past and shape memory of media and media's pasts – the subject of this chapter – has been deeply affected, and indeed infiltrated, by the media of the day. Media have long entwined the personal and the public, locating the unfolding details of everyday life in terms of the events of the larger society. But the difference today is that digital connecting, networking, and archiving is a qualitatively different force of media memory from previous transformative media in that it simultaneously makes present multiple pasts, while captivating the present.

As the key dynamic of the shifting relationship between media and memory, digital connectivity offers an immediacy and fluidity, ushering in a new set of opportunities and challenges to how the past is represented and representable through contemporary media forms. Databases organize, classify, and make accessible the past in new configurations that transcend and translate time and space. For example, the *Crimes against Humanity* exhibition at the Imperial War Museum, London, does not contain a single artifact or museal object. Instead it uses a 30 minute

The International Handbooks of Museum Studies: Museum Media, First Edition.
Edited by Michelle Henning.
© 2015 John Wiley & Sons Ltd. Published 2020 by John Wiley & Sons Ltd.

documentary film projection onto a large screen and six touch-screen consoles which provide database access. And it is here that the database, which is updated with ongoing and emergent crimes against humanity, is open to reflect the incoming present. Thus it is as much future as past oriented.

It is through this open and continuous connectivity that Peter Lunenfeld sees cultural memory as "warped": "When image, text, photo, graphic, and all manner of audiovisual records are available at the touch of a button anywhere in the unimodern wired world, the ordered progression through time is replaced by a blended presentness" (2011, 46).

An influential factor here is the impact of different media in shaping an experience of proximity (in time and space) to events deemed "historical." For example, "historical distance," according to Mark Salber Phillips, is manifested "along a gradient of distances, including proximity or immediacy as well as remoteness or detachment" (2004, 89). But digital devices and networks have seized and short-circuited precisely these "manifestations" of distance and not least in their deliverance of immediacy as one of the defining – and compulsive – experiences of their use. And the conditions of remoteness or detachment seem inexorably dissolvable through the equivocations of the digital: the reduction and reproduction of all-things-past in the fluidity of digital data. Digital networks and databases don't just bridge historical distance: they crush it. And yet these are precisely the media that are being brought in to represent, organize, and manage the organizational, archival, and official memory of museums.

How then to respond to these transformations, in terms both of the uses of media in the museum and of a theoretical framework that can best interrogate the warping of cultural memory, in Lunenfeld's terms? To both these ends, we offer media archaeology. *Media archaeology* is an emerging approach that departs from traditional methods of media history. It implicitly opposes the simple construction of linear narratives that follow the history of specific forms and their economic, political, and social developments. Instead, media archaeology reconsiders objects, technologies, media, techniques, and processes in their historical specificity and singularity. According to Bolter, media archaeologists "examine earlier media and media forms in both their technical and their cultural contexts. They are particularly concerned to get behind the ossified narratives that are told about the development of such media" (2007, 108). So, media archaeology looks for discontinuities and disruptions while also considering nonlinear lines of descent. This entails interrogating the forms, processes, and phenomena of media, especially how they are rediscovered, remade, and reappear in later eras and media. However, within media archaeology there are different strands of emphasis. For example, Wolfgang Ernst (see Chapter 1 in this volume) sees media as process rather than as object or design oriented, and thus the challenge for museums is how to show media in operation rather than merely as a display object. More broadly, Erkki Huhtamo and Jussi Parikka encapsulate the work of media archaeology as "a cruise in time." They explain: "The past is brought to the present, and the present to the past; both inform and explain each other, raising questions and pointing to futures that may or may not be" (2011, 15). While Ernst and others employ media archaeology as an analytical model, here we want to propose it as a model for museum practice.

The museum then is inevitably caught up in media archaeology, both as a version or form from a macro-historical (or antihistorical) perspective, and in the uses of media archaeology as a curatorial strategy in responding to not only the transformations of the digital outlined above but, at the same time, a deep dissatisfaction with the novelty from which discourses on the digital are frequently hung. Furthermore, it is precisely in this space and time that artists have flourished, intervening to construct alternative or hypothetical media histories to challenge both the inexorable immediacy of the present and its post-scarcity digital futures.[1]

In what follows we explore some cases of media archaeology in practice – both implicit and explicit – and consider their effectiveness in offering alternative medial times and spaces amid the onslaught of the connective turn.

Media archaeology and the memory booms

The *Memorial to the Iraq War* exhibition, which ran at London's Institute for Contemporary Arts (ICA) in the spring of 2007, was composed of the work of 26 artists from Europe, North America, and the Middle East who were each asked to imagine what a memorial to the Iraq War might look like. Amid the frustration and exhaustion of the seemingly perpetual flux of news images that characterized much Western mainstream coverage of this war, the exhibition sought to dig into an alternative future. This future is one in which the traditional forms of memorialization seem more uncertain, given the current era in which wars and conflicts deemed to "need" memorials appear perpetual and horizonless rather than of fixed duration and of unambiguous conclusion. The exhibit shown in Figure 2.1, Roman Ondák's *Snapshots from Baghdad, 2007*, is a disposable black camera on a white plinth. Notably, this camera is a one-off: it is already antithetical to the insatiable appetite and seeming perpetual reproducibility of digital photography today as an unsatisfactory basis for remembrance.

The camera supposedly contains an undeveloped film of shots from present-day Baghdad. The unexposed images trapped inside permit a future that is both imaginable, in relation to what the photographs may contain and their impact, and unimaginable, with regard to the contingency of the indeterminable moment of their exposure. In this way the intact camera challenges the highly media-saturated imagination of the 2007 aftermath of war in Baghdad, instead making it contingent on the moment and context – the emergence – of the exposure and mediation of the unseen images.

But the camera, placed as it is in a cabinet on a pedestal, "evokes the eventual ossification of the circulation of both people and images" (Galerie Martin Janda 2008). In this way, *Snapshots from Baghdad, 2007* speaks to James E. Young's notion

FIGURE 2.1   Roman Ondák, *Snapshots from Baghdad*, 2007. Single use camera with undeveloped film. Installation Institute of Contemporary Arts, London. Private collection, Mexico City.

of a "countermonument" (1992; 2000). Notably, it simultaneously draws attention to both the possibilities and the limitations of the traditional memorial. It challenges the notion of the monumentality of images in the unknowable future and the content of the photographs inside the camera; in other words, it reflects a profound uncertainty of future media memory. At the same time, the exhibit is ossified both in its truncation of the process of photographic recording, exposure, circulation, and through its form of display. The temporal delay of the analogue photographic process is stalled and that "spark of contingency" (Benjamin 1999, 150) characteristic of the photographic image is arrested and preserved within the plastic shell of the camera. It is doubly sealed, first within the plain black plastic case and then within a glass display cabinet, the latter fetishizing and emphasizing the sculptural qualities of the throwaway monument.

Furthermore, Ondák's work and the wider ICA *Memorial to the Iraq War* can be seen to counter traditional memorial culture through a strategy of "premediation" (Grusin 2004; 2010; Erll 2009; Hoskins and O'Loughlin 2010). That is, efforts to try to imagine, shape or challenge, future (as well as current) memorial cultures through imaging, conceptualizing, representing what a future memorial might or should look like. What is striking about this collapse of the future into the present is that the events that are subject to premediation or "prememorialization" are not only recent in living memory – compared to the more common length of passage of time between, particularly, twentieth-century nodal events and their memorializations – but in the case of twenty-first-century warfare in Iraq and Afghanistan, for example, public memorialization becomes synchronous with the event itself. It is precisely this synchronicity that is denied by Ondák's exhibit.

So, a new immediacy of memorialization is caught up in the politics of memory of the twenty-first century, in legitimizing or delegitimizing ongoing warfare. These memorializations include the potential continuousness afforded by digital memorial networks, archives, and databases, which set out the potential trajectories of future memory of present and recent past warfare and other catastrophes. For example, the artist Joseph DeLappe's iraqimemorial.org project aims to commemorate civilian deaths since the onset of the 2003 Iraq War and its bloody aftermath (www.iraqimemorial.org). Its stated aims include: to "mobilize an international community of artists to contribute proposals that will represent a collective expression of memory, unity and peace" and to "create a context for the initiation of a process of symbolic, creative atonement." The site lists over 150 artists' works under "Exhibition of Memorial Concepts." This includes diagrams, gallery plans, photographs, videos, and mixed media exhibits. The site is also open to public views and ratings of entries in addition to those made by "internationally based curators and scholars." To these ends, the web provides a memorial platform that is dynamic, apparently democratic, and potentially highly expansionist. In this way, the project probes and extends the concept and practices of memorialization, affording the memorial new immediacy and an "extended present" (Nowotny 1994).

Welcome, then, to the "third memory boom" (Hoskins and O'Loughlin 2010). The first memory boom, set out by Jay Winter, is marked by the formation of national identities around the memorialization of the victims of the Great War after 1914 (2006, 18). And, for Winter, remembrance of World War II and the Holocaust in the 1960s and 1970s is indicative of a second memory boom. It is this latter era that is most often seen as the modern memory boom in the field of memory studies, most influentially by Andreas Huyssen (2003). This includes significant developments in the role of technologies and media in facilitating the reflexive audiovisual capture and representation of personal testimony, namely the mediatization of oral history.

Although the third memory boom overlaps with the second, it is the connective turn that makes it distinctive in shaping an inexorable media present and presence. Under these conditions, the museum can survive only if it becomes media archaeological, if it can offer new value amid the flattening of post-scarcity culture.

The connective turn has dislocated the memorial connection between the medium of the time of an event's first mass mediation and its later representation (in museums and exhibitions). How an event is later represented, seen, and understood has always been to some extent determined by the medium through which it first entered into a collective or cultural imagination. As Lisa Gitelman argues, media, no matter how "old" or "new," are "functionally integral to a sense of pastness" through the "implicit encounters" we have with the past via the media responsible for producing that past (2006, 5).

For example, the audio of radio and the audio/visual of television have become increasingly defining of the second memory boom, particularly with such media entangled in the actual production of the events they record, in which process they alter the moment-by-moment trajectory of events and so become inseparable from those events. But these (traditionally, at least) "punctual" media have always sat uncertainly in the museum space in terms of the curatorial organization required to shepherd the highly mobile and distracted visitor-as-audience. The common looping of audio and video content (unless prescheduled and advertised) inevitably finds the wandering visitor arriving (and departing) out of sync with the beginning and end, respectively, of the recording being reproduced. Here the visitor becomes, according to Jessica Morgan, "victims of its timing" (quoted in Cowie 2009, 127).

Digital media that have ushered in the third memory boom, however, effect a continuous time through mobile and pervasive connectivity (including the remediation of traditionally more punctual and cyclical media – radio, TV, press). And it is this greater connectivity of past with present that requires new kinds of excavation and interrogation. Whereas media history privileges continuities over discontinuities, "media-archaeology replaces the concept of a historical development, from writing to printing to digital data processing, through a concept of mediatic short-circuits" (Ernst 2006, 111). So, despite the seeming digital crushing of historical distance, the media archaeological museum has to reveal and interrogate the fissures, the unintended, and the gaps, against the apparent smooth and smothering immediacy and pervasiveness of memory forged amid and from post-scarcity culture.

"The persistence of vision"

In 2010–11 a major artistic media archaeological intervention entitled *Persistence of Vision* was exhibited at FACT (Foundation for Art and Creative Technology, Liverpool, UK) and at Nikolaj Kunsthal (Nikolaj Contemporary Art Center, Copenhagen, Denmark). This exhibition explored the interplay of media, vision, and memory, and included the repurposing of a range of current and past image technologies – camera obscura, slide projectors, 16 mm cameras – to revisit and reimagine the media and technologies through which memory is mediated.

The potential scarcity of film (at least in the era of the second memory boom) is explored by Melik Ohanian in his *Invisible Film* video projection, a media archaeology of the controversial 1971 docu-fiction film *Punishment Park*, written and directed by Peter Watkins, and not officially distributed in the United Kingdom and United States for over 20 years. This pseudo-documentary is set amid the escalation of the Vietnam War and is seen by some as a landmark work on US political repression. It follows an assortment of 1960s counterculture detainees who, opting to avoid long prison sentences, embark on an attempt to reach an American flag planted many miles into the inhospitable Southern Californian desert, pursued by a bunch of gung-ho law enforcement types: their three days in "Punishment Park."

FIGURE 2.2   Melik Ohanian, *Invisible Film*, 2005, video projection, 90 minutes. (For a color version of this figure, please see the color plate section.)
Courtesy of the artist and Galerie Chantal Crousel, Paris.

Ohanian's work is encountered through hearing the audio track and seeing the film's subtitles on the screen, synchronized to the video projection. On entering the exhibition space (hidden by curved screens), the visitor is confronted with a video projection of a 35 mm projector (Figure 2.2) beaming the film *Punishment Park* into thin air in the same desert landscape the original film was shot in: there is no surface on which to project the film. So, the absence of the film offers reflection on the relative absence and suppression of the antiwar movement – not least over the 20 years or so during which *Punishment Park* was banned.

Invisible Film marks the significant interruption in time of the distribution of *Punishment Park* (now widely available) and the suspension of media history. But it also challenges the notion of cinematic space, of the copresence of projector and screen or other surface through the invisibility of the displaced projection. The film is reduced to the form of the projector.

At the same time, the idea of an invisible film is a very useful metaphor for reflection on the suppression of antiwar discourses and a kind of underground countermemory which, despite its repression, has a certain residual presence that is always with us. As with the ICA's *Memorial to the Iraq War* exhibition, Ohanian's work can be seen as antithetical to the overexposure associated with the televisual excess of the coverage of warfare, especially since the 1991 Gulf War. Indeed, it is precisely the stream of images of conflict and warfare that is said to have driven what many see as today's memory boom. Ohanian's *Invisible Film* offers us countermodalities of memory – in terms both of the closure of the visual mode of engagement and of the absence over time that this represents (see McLuhan 1964).

FIGURE 2.3   Julien Maire, *Exploding Camera*, 2007, exhibited in the *Persistence of Vision* exhibition, Foundation for Art and Creative Technology (FACT), Liverpool. (For a color version of this figure, please see the color plate section.)
Photo: Brian Slater.

The medium is privileged over content in another striking piece from the same exhibition in Julien Maire's *Exploding Camera* (2007) (Figure 2.3). Two days before September 11, 2001, an exploding camera killed the most senior anti-Taliban Afghan war commander Massoud in his camp in Afghanistan. The use of a camera by terrorists inspired this exhibit – for Maire, it is as though the camera has continued to work to film a war film ever since. So, according to Maire, through this destroyed medium, a new live experimental historical film is rendered as a means of reinterpreting the events of the war. In this way, he implicates the camera as a new form of eyewitness both in relation to historical fact and through its process of image production.

The work consists of a still functional dissected video camera on a table which has had its lens removed. Video images are produced on a nearby monitor through direct illumination of the camera's CCD (light sensor) through LEDs and a laser as well as external light. The images are sourced from photographic positives on a transparent disk placed between the lights and the CCD. Explosion sound effects are triggered by lights and the laser (Maire 2007).

Through constructing the camera as weapon, Maire also highlights the media as an object inextricably bound up in the conflict it purports to report on. The exploding camera is thus the ultimate realization of the weaponization of the media, and offers a kind of dystopian vision of the relationship between media and warfare. The installation thus prompts us to think about this relationship at a visceral and machinic level, making the media form centrifugal both as medium and as weapon.

However, Maire's work is not only media archaeological in teasing with form, content, and history; it is also performative: "The lights that produce the 'explosions' not only illuminate the frame for the video image but also the exhibition space and spectators at the same time" (Maire 2007). In this way, according to Maire, the exhibition space becomes an "experimental film studio," invoking the battlefield as theater. The battlefield theatricality of *Exploding Camera* is also emphasized by the very limited light in this space, so that spectators are almost wholly reliant on the lights from the exhibit itself and they – and the exhibit – are often plunged into darkness. Furthermore, there is no easily discernible beginning or end to the performance, and there is an absence of a chronology to disturb or to miss. In this way, the exhibit is not constrained by a punctuality, which so often makes museum media awkward for visitor navigation.

Maire's work is an instructive case of media archaeology in affording the camera a new technological beginning. He offers material emergence from a destroyed medium in that, instead of reproducing (again) the already overfamiliar and saturative images of twenty-first-century warfare, he makes them experimental – affording them new life, history, and meaning.

An unexposed film entombed within plastic and glass, the projection of an invisible projection, an undead camera: what links these works and what more might they tell us about the uses and potentials of media archaeology in the museum? Each emphasizes and fetishizes the materiality of media hardware – the plain black camera on a white pedestal, the lone projector against a desert landscape, the deconstructed video camera, illuminated by its own explosions. The sculptural qualities of each technology is insisted on. But so is the potentiality of the image. Our expectations of media processes – production, exhibition, distribution – are frozen, denied, or disrupted. What remains are spaces of anticipation, where the spark of contingency keeps firing but never catches light. They challenge the immediacy of post-scarcity culture and the digital archival myth of total access and accumulation. While constructing alternative or hypothetical media histories, they should also be seen as part of a new set of opportunities and challenges that open up the time, space, and memory of the museum.

The "Big Picture Show," Imperial War Museum North

In the main exhibition hall of the Imperial War Museum North (IWM North), in Manchester, UK, visitors are immersed every hour in the images and sounds of the "Big Picture Show" (see Figure 2.4). Designed as a showcase for the museum's audiovisual collections of photography, art, archival footage, oral history, and testimony, the "Big Picture Show" consists of eight distinctive shows that focus predominantly on conflicts from World War I until the present day. The original three are themed around weaponry, the home front, and children's experiences of war (*Weapons of War*, *Children and War*, and the *War at Home*, respectively). More recent

FIGURE 2.4   A precursor to the "Big Picture Show," main exhibition hall, Imperial War Museum North, Manchester, UK.
Photo: Andrew Hoskins, December 22, 2011.

commissions offer a focus on the memorialization of war (*Remembrance*), conflict resolution (*Build the Truce*), the experiences of a nurse in Afghanistan (*Service and Separation*), a creative response to a street bombing in Baghdad in 2007 (*Al-Mutanabbi Street: A Reaction*), and a Horrible Histories take on rationing during World War II (*Rotten Rationing*). Each foregrounds specific curatorial themes and emphasizes the museum's remit as a war museum rather than as a military museum.[2] This distinction highlights the museum's specific focus on people's experience of war, for example, as the male British voice that speaks out of the darkness at the beginning of *Al-Mutanabbi Street: A Reaction*, makes evident: "Every image, every document, every voice is part of someone's story." The museum website describes the "Big Picture Show" as

> an award-winning 360-degree experience unique to IWM North. Using surround sound, projected digital moving images and photographs, the show brings to life

people's experiences of war. It immerses you in the heart of the action, creating a complete sensory experience which is totally involving, and often very moving.[3]

Enabled by developments in digital sound and image projection, and certainly a distinctive exhibition strategy, the "Big Picture Show" must also be placed within a longer history of the relationship between the museum artifact and the moving image. The use of screen media in museum exhibitions is commonplace. Often acting as a supplement to object displays – documentary footage, archive film, or television operates as an additional layer of contextualization and narrativization, animating and bearing witness to the images, objects, and stories recounted. The work of Alison Griffiths (2002), Haidee Wasson (2005), and Michelle Henning (2006) reminds us that this use of moving images to supplement artifact-based exhibits dates back to the 1920s and 1930s.

Henning has also usefully sought to connect and establish continuities between "new media" and earlier technologies of visual display. She writes of the parallel between the organization and modes of address of analogue and digital media, employing an example from the American Museum of Natural History in New York where the

> famous halls of dioramas, dating from the 1920s to the 1940s, the darkened spaces recall cinema auditoriums. The backlit habitat dioramas are breathtakingly naturalistic. Taxidermy, painted backdrops, and wax modeling, through "multimedia," are combined to give the organic coherence of narrative cinema, inviting us to momentarily forget their status as representations and imagine they are more than skin deep. (Henning 2006, 304)

Here the "spectacular mise-en-scene" of the museum and the cinema coalesce and both must be seen as part of an "exhibitionary complex" where technologies of display developed in circulation across a number of exhibitionary sites and institutions (Huyssen 1995, 34; Bennett 1995, ch. 2).[4] The "Big Picture Show" is part of a continuing relationship between the museum and the moving image that evokes persistent tensions between the stillness and movement of artifacts, images, technologies, and bodies.[5] These tensions reveal the temporal and spatial characteristics of the "Big Picture Show" exhibition strategy as a media archaelogical intervention.

On every hour the exhibition hall of IWM North plunges into near darkness to be lit only by the bright red lights illuminating the bases of the static exhibits (a theatrical flourish that is no doubt a product of health and safety regulations). The visitor is enclosed within the darkness, to some extent hostage to the sights and sounds of the film. The six architectural silos which intersect this permanent exhibition space are independent of the "Big Picture Show" and are still navigable during each performance. The projection itself is not cast on one fluid 360 degree screen but is pieced together over a series of disjointed walls that fragment the large cavernous space of the main hall. The experience is spectacular, cine-matic, yet verisimilitude is not its aim. It neither evokes the naturalistic dioramas of Henning's description nor the simulation of "total cinema" (Bazin 1967) offered by the IMAX experience (which accompanies many contemporary science muse-ums). It is an example of an immersive exhibition strategy, as discussed by Habsburg-Lothringen in this volume (see Chapter 15), in both its scale and the ways in which it organizes the movement and attention of the visitor.

We have already seen the tension between stasis and movement at play in the interruptive nature of the works previously discussed. However, in contrast to the temporal uncertainty of these artworks, the "Big Picture Show" returns us to the "punctual" media of the second memory boom, programmed to "interrupt" the visitor's time with a different film on each hour of the museum's day (the schedule itself is projected onto one of the white walls of the main exhibition space). While the visitor is perhaps less likely to become a victim of its timing, the "Big Picture Show" is still a time-based installation with distinctive temporal and spatial characteristics. Elizabeth Cowie, while arguing for the specificity of digital media in the gallery, writes that "each place of viewing a time-based installation is not only a context – geographical and social, public or private – but also an architec-tural place, organizing the spectator's access to mobility and stillness" (2009, 124). Here, the stillness of the museal artifact and the movement of the film are reflected by the spatial configurations of stillness and movement enacted by the visitor.

Whether the visitor has planned the show into their visit or are taken by sur-prise, the temporal darkness of the exhibition hall necessitates the interruption of movement. Most sit against the walls / screens or stand still; a few others continue moving through the space with added care. Architectural and space syntax approaches to museum studies remind us how, "like any spatial layout, a museum or gallery will generate and sustain a certain pattern of co-presence and encounter amongst visitors through the way it shapes movement" (Hillier and Tzortzi 2006, 299). The Daniel Libeskind-designed architecture of IWM North already affords the exhibition space a fragmentary and chaotic character within and onto which the "Big Picture Show" is projected. Jonathan Shaw, Ben Squire Scholes, and Christopher Thurgood, for instance, writing on space and place at IWM North, argue: "As an example of deconstructivist architecture, which is a subset or devel-opment of post-industrial architecture, a sense of controlled chaos is conveyed through architectural forms" (2008, 227). Here then, the combined temporal-spatial ecology of the museum mediates visitor experience to a unique event.[6] The deconstructivist architecture and scattered artifacts produce a fragmented screen, but one which is further disjointed by the movement of visitors onto whom the film also projects and distorts, affording another level of random mobility to the "Big Picture Show." In this latter instance, there is a certain media-visitor coconstruction in that media interrupt the churn of visitor patterns to produce a time-based "integration core, where congregation takes place" (Hillier and Tzortzi, 2006, 299).[7] These congregations, however, are relatively dispersed and not really crowd-like: affected through the location of the seating and visitors' sense of the best advantage points for viewing and being immersed in the spectacle.

There is another temporal element to this experience and that is duration. If visitors are patient enough (and/or aware of the schedule) then they will experience the full 25 minutes of each performance. Otherwise, they will be subject to the same temporal uncertainty of beginning, end and duration, of looped and other video/filmic screenings in museum spaces.

So, the space and time of the museum is wrapped in the immersive strategies of the projection. In its play with the built environment, and its kinesthetic and sensory staging of bodies, to what extent does immersion, as Margaret Morse (1990) and Elizabeth Cowie (2009) have argued, give way to reflection? Once again, the organization of stillness and movement is central and draws on the performative characteristics of commemorative practices.

In their introduction to the edited collection *Still Moving*, an interrogation of the relationship between photography and cinema, Karen Beckman and Jean Ma argue that "the hesitation between stasis and motion actually produces an interval in which rigorous thinking can emerge" (2008, 5). In contrast, social psychologist Steven Brown's discussion of the two-minute silence as a commemorative practice offers an alternative perspective. Brown usefully challenges some of the assumptions about the commemorative or reflective functions/experiences of silence and, by extension, stillness, as he questions the "modes of access to the past [that] are opened up through public silence and the forms of experience that are thereby afforded" (2012, 239). Here, public silence becomes a spectacle, a performance of empathy and sorrow where those commemorated are doubly absent. But the commemorative silence remains a particularly powerful social force, dictated by an enactment of remembrance and dominated instead by particular behavioral expectations around the stillness and silence of our bodies. As an experiential form it evokes the "scopic reciprocity" (Bennett 1995) of the museum. While the behavioral expectations of visitors within this hybrid museum/cinema space are arguably less clear, the sense of copresence maintained throughout the "Big Picture Show" insists on a peripheral awareness of the bodies of the other visitors.

Sat against screens, or moving through the projectile stream, bodies, disruptive or compliant, also become part of the surface of the projection, made over as "temporary monuments" and integrated into the exhibition space. Brown argues that

> to stand still, to make oneself into a temporary monument, is to have accomplished the act of making the past relevant without words. Again this is not so much as "overmastering of self" as allowing one's own bodily substrate to temporarily become a vehicle for the performance of the past in the present. (2012, 248)

And, when the show is over, the congregation departs, as the "instant community" dissipates throughout the museum and the museum reverts to its recognizable self.

While the "Big Picture Show" can be seen to choreograph bodies and a performance of remembrance in a similar vein to Brown's argument, the interruption of time and the transformation of space in it invite reflection in specific ways: on the curatorial themes and messages, on the films as memorials and the experience as commemorative, and also on the different and various strategies of mediation and the use of media within the museum. Morse, writing on video installation in the gallery, argues that "installation art in this setting reinvigorates all the spaces-in-between, so that the museum visitor becomes aware of the museum itself as a mega-installation, even to the point of self-critique" (1990, 166).

The collection, Susan Stewart writes, is often about containment as a mode of control and confinement in which it strives for the closure of all space and temporality (1993, 151). While this is perhaps not a fair interpretation of all contemporary curatorial practices, it is precisely through an aesthetics of immersion and enclosure that the world of the exhibition at IWM North is self-reflexively thrown open. The curators and visitors' mastery over the world of the collection is tested by both the dramatically shifting scales of the exhibition and the challenges of an emergent post-scarcity culture.

The nature and development of the "Big Picture Show," projected against and on the artifacts and the architecture housed in and constitutive of the space, reveals the upgradable form of this kind of intervention. For example, this exhibition strategy was originally composed of 60 slide projectors to showcase the museum's photographic archive; digital projectors were installed in 2011, allowing greater flexibility and creativity in the commissioning of audiovisual presentations. The "Big Picture Show" has also upgraded from an original three to its current eight shows. This, as we have already observed, reflects IWM North's focus on people's experience of war. However, the increased flexibility that came with the projection of media content into the void, so to speak, enables the museum to be more responsive to understandings and representations of more recent conflicts (e.g., *Al-Mutanabbi Street: A Reaction*). But this also opens the potential for the museum space to become more of a mutable medium in its own right, being liberated "from archival space into archival time" (Ernst 2004; see also Hoskins 2009). This is how even static architecture and artifacts – and their impression of permanence – suddenly seem vulnerable to the more fluid temporalities and dynamics of "permanent data transfer" (Ernst 2004, 46) as their surfaces and fissures are increasingly employed as, and connected to, screens. In this way, IWM North reveals its media archaeological tensions. Although IWM North is an artifactually and architecturally determined space, it is also fundamentally mediated through the smothering immediacy and pervasiveness of post-scarcity media.

Whereas the ICA's *Memorial to the Iraq War* exhibition, discussed above, sought (in part at least) to wrest a separate and distinct time and space in contradistinction to the flux of the new media ecology, IWM North exposes itself to the data-driven extended and immersive present of post-scarcity culture. While the aesthetics of immersion in the "Big Picture Show" operate as a particular exhibition strategy, the space and times of IWM North and other museums are being more radically thrown open and diffused through the inexorable penetration of digital and social media. For example, Huhtamo (Chapter 12 in this volume) argues that an "exhibition anthropology" approach is needed to take account of the new permeability of the museum's walls, while other contributions to this volume envisage the museum as "diffused" (Bell and Ippolito, Chapter 21) and "elastic" (Wasson, Chapter 26). As an example of this, as part of a Social Interpretation project, IWM London and IWM North have developed mobile applications through which visitors can scan objects' Quick Response (QR) codes to access the "story" of each. This enables the visitor-as-curator to "share stories of their own memories and experiences about War and the IWM collections."[8] And the IWM blog claims that, via the IWM website, they have "added social interpretation elements to over 750,000 collection objects!"[9] This development is part of the "Internet of Things" linking the material and the Internet, whereby objects are embedded with sensors to produce a sophisticated network of traceable items. In this context, the museum is newly extended, networked and diffused, plugged in to a distributed sociality of its objects and their ongoing trajectories of connections. This challenges its principal authority of containment and closure (in Stewart's terms: see above) but also gives its objects new temporal momentum and new status as media archaeology.

Conclusion

Media archaeology is inexorably an effect and a strategy of/in the museum, subject to a post-scarcity culture which is ushering in both a digital revelation/revolution of the past and an astonishing connectivity in and of the present. The post-scarcity museum offers a new archival regime that can more easily track the history of events that are still unfolding, as part of a longer trajectory of time.

Yet, the museum's increased capacity to be responsive to the events of the day, as well as recent and more distant histories, presents both a media archaeological tension and an opportunity. Technologies and media of the day have long developed modes of representation and mediation. But the advantage and the challenge of pervasive digital media networks and connectivities is their terrific temporal force. Connective culture fundamentally reconstitutes the past but digitally bleeds more of the present into all of the museum's fissures. The result is a pressure pot in which the media of this day have not only become irresistible to shaping curatorial strategies but inexorable in pushing a connective present into representational spaces, and in pushing the museum's objects and artifacts outward as part of the emergent "Internet of Things." In these circumstances, containment and scarcity are no longer workable as curatorial strategies: cultural memory is well and truly out of its metaphorical box made transparent through post-scarcity culture. The digital present inexorably disinters the past of, and the past in, museums, and new curatorial imaginations are required to make a greater play for the memory of the future (as with the ICA's *Memorial to the Iraq War*).

And yet the very challenges of the temporality and pervasiveness of museum and media content can be seized and reimagined as strategy: to redeploy and reimagine museum artifacts as part of the "Internet of Things," for example, makes the museum a centrifugal dynamic of the connective turn, rather than being merely its subject, and in effect networks the "canon" and the "archive" in Aleida Assmann's (2008) terms.[10] The new temporal and memorial paradigm of the third memory boom can be harnessed as a rampant media archaeology which turns the museum inside out and (re)creates it anew.

Notes

1   The work of contemporary media artists and their media archaeological approach can be seen in part as a continuation of the strategies of artists such as Nam June Paik and Wolf Vostell. Their play with, and configurations of, television hardware were in part an effort to defamiliarize the medium and to interrogate and critique commercial television.

2   Imperial Imperial War Museum Acquisition and Disposal Policy, March 2011, http://www.iwm.org.uk/sites/default/files/public-document/A%26D_Policy_March_2011.pdf (accessed July 24, 2014). This policy is due for review in March 2016.

3   See http://www.iwm.org.uk/exhibitions/iwm-north/big-picture-show (accessed July 22, 2014).

4   For example, between the 1880s and the 1940s, architects and designers in the United States worked on and with technologies of display across a series of sites including theaters, department stores, and museums (Leach 1989, quoted in Henning 2006, 304).

5   The relationship between vision and movement within the museum and its influence on the development of cinema in the nineteenth century have been well traced. For an excellent overview see Eleftheriotis's *Cinematic Journeys* (2010).

6   See also Peter Higgins's concept of "total media" in Chapter 14 in this volume.

7   With reference to the work of Hsu Huang (2001), Hillier and Tzortzi emphasize "two key themes embodied in the spatial layout of the modern museum: organized walking and the congregation of visitors. The former is realized by the organization of spaces into visitable sequences so as to map knowledge, and the latter is manifested by the creation of gathering spaces, the integration core, where the congregation takes place" (2006, 292).

8   Claire, "Roll Up and Roll Out: The Final Push for SI," Imperial War Museums Social Interpretation Blog. Accessed July 22, 2014. http://blogs.iwm.org.uk/social-interpretation/category/qr-codes/.

9   Claire, "Roll Up and Roll Out" (see n. 8).

10   Assmann (2008, 98) sees the "canon" as an "active" mode of cultural memory in the museum in terms of that which is on show and visible to visitors, whereas the "archive" is a "passively stored memory" comprising objects stored and out of sight.

References

Assmann, Aleida. 2008. "Canon and Archive." In *Cultural Memory Studies: An International and Interdisciplinary Handbook*, edited by Astrid Erll and Ansgar Nünning with Sara B. Young, 97–107. Berlin: De Gruyter.

Bazin, André. 1967. *What Is Cinema?*, vol. 1. Translated by Hugh Gray. Berkeley: University of California Press.

Beckman, Karen, and Jean Ma, eds. 2008. *Still Moving: Between Cinema and Photography*. Durham, NC: Duke University Press.

Benjamin, Walter. 1999. *Selected Writings*, vol. 2, *1927–1934*. Translated by Rodney Livingstone. Cambridge, MA: Harvard University Press.

Bennett, Tony. 1995. *The Birth of the Museum*. London: Routledge.

Bolter, Jay. D. 2007. "Digital Media and Art: Always Already Complicit?" *Criticism* 49(1): 107–118.

Brown, Steven. D. 2012. "Two Minutes of Silence: Social Technologies of Public Commemoration." *Theory & Psychology* 22(2): 234–252.

Cowie, Elizabeth. 2009. "On Documentary Sounds and Images in the Gallery." *Screen* 50(1): 124–134.

Eleftheriotis, Dimitris. 2010 .*Cinematic Journeys*. Edinburgh: Edinburgh University Press.

Erll, Astrid. 2009. "Remembering across Time, Space and Cultures." In *Mediation, Remediation, and the Dynamics of Cultural Memory*, edited by Astrid Erll and Ann Rigney, 109–138. Berlin: De Gruyter.

Ernst, Wolfgang. 2004. "The Archive as Metaphor." *Open* 7: 46–53.

Ernst, Wolfgang. 2006. "Dis/continuities: Does the Archive Become Metaphorical in Multi-Media Space?" In *New Media, Old Media: A History and Theory Reader*, edited by Wendy Hui Kyong Chun and Thomas Keenan, 105–123. New York: Routledge.

Galerie Martin Janda. 2008. "Roman Ondák." Accessed July 21, 2014. http://www.mutualart. com/OpenArticle/Roman-Ondak/3E35E1DEE8531FFA.

Gitelman, Lisa. 2006. *Always Already New: Media, History and the Data of Culture*. Cambridge, MA: MIT Press.

Griffiths, Alison. 2002. *Wondrous Difference: Cinema, Anthropology and Turn of the Century Visual Culture*. New York: Columbia University Press.

Grusin, Richard. 2004. "Premediation." *Criticism* 46(1): 17–39.

Grusin, Richard. 2010. *Premediation: Affect and Mediality After 9/11*. Basingstoke, UK: Palgrave Macmillan.

Henning, Michelle. 2006. "New Media." In *A Companion to Museum Studies*, edited by Sharon Macdonald, 302–318. Oxford: Blackwell.

Hillier, Bill, and Kali Tzortzi. 2006. "Space Syntax: The Language of Museum Space." In *A Companion to Museum Studies*, edited by Sharon Macdonald, 282–301. Oxford: Blackwell.

Hoskins, Andrew. 2009. "Digital Network Memory." In *Mediation, Remediation, and the Dynamics of Cultural Memory*, edited by Astrid Erll and Ann Rigney, 91–106. Berlin: De Gruyter.

Hoskins, Andrew. 2011a. "Media, Memory, Metaphor: Remembering and the Connective Turn." *Parallax* 17(4): 19–31.

Hoskins, Andrew. 2011b. "7/7 and Connective Memory: Interactional Trajectories of Remembering in Post-Scarcity Culture." *Memory Studies* 4(3): 269–280.

Hoskins, Andrew, and B. O'Loughlin. 2010. *War and Media: The Emergence of Diffused War.* Cambridge: Polity.

Huang, Hsu. 2001. "The Spatialization of Knowledge and Social Relationships." In *Proceedings of the Third International Space Syntax Symposium*, 43.1–43.14. Accessed July 21, 2014. http://www.ucl.ac.uk/bartlett/3sss/papers_pdf/43_huang.pdf.

Huhtamo, Erkki, and Jussi Parikka. 2011. *Media Archaeology: Approaches, Applications, and Implications.* Berkeley: University of California Press.

Huyssen, Andreas. 1995. *Twilight Memories: Marking Time in a Culture of Amnesia.* London: Routledge.

Huyssen, Andreas. 2003. *Present Pasts: Urban Palimpsests and the Politics of Memory.* Stanford: Stanford University Press.

Leach, William. R. 1989. "Strategies of Display and the Production of Desire." In *Consuming Visions: Accumulation and Display of Goods in America 1880–1920*, edited by Simon J. Bronner, 99–132. New York: Norton.

Lunenfeld, Peter. 2011. *The Secret War between Downloading and Uploading: Tales of the Computer as Culture Machine.* Cambridge, MA: MIT Press.

Maire, Julien. 2007. *Exploding Camera, 2007.* Accessed July 21, 2014. http://julienmaire.ideenshop.net/project5.shtml.

McLuhan, Marshall. 1964. *Understanding Media: The Extensions of Man.* London: Routledge.

Morse, Margaret. 1990. "Video Installation Art: The Body, the Image, and the Space-in-Between." In *Illuminating Video: An Essential Guide to Video Art*, edited by Doug Hall and Sally Jo Fifer, 153–167. New York: Aperture/Bay Area Video Coalition.

Nowotny, Helga. 1994. *Time: The Modern and Postmodern Experience.* Cambridge: Polity.

Phillips, Mark S. 2004. "History, Memory, and Historical Distance." In *Theorizing Historical Consciousness*, edited by Peter Seixas, 86–108. Toronto: University of Toronto Press.

Shaw, Jonathan, Ben Squire Scholes, and Christopher Thurgood. 2008. "Space and Place – Imperial War Museum North." *Journal of Place Management and Development* 1(2): 227–231.

Stewart, Susan. 1993. *On Longing.* Durham, NC: Duke University Press.

Wasson, Haidee. 2005. *Museum Movies: The Museum of Modern Art and the Birth of Art Cinema.* Los Angeles: University of California Press.

Winter, Jay. 2006. *Remembering War: The Great War between Memory and History in the Twentieth Century.* New Haven: Yale University Press.

Young, James E. 1992. "The Counter-Monument: Memory against Itself in Germany Today." *Critical Inquiry* 18(2): 267–296.

Young, James E. 2000. *At Memory's Edge: After Images of the Holocaust in Contemporary Art and Architecture.* New Haven: Yale University Press.

Andrew Hoskins is Interdisciplinary Research Professor at the University of Glasgow. His research focuses on digital memory Studies, (hyper)connectivity theory, media/memory ecologies, and diffused war. He is founding editor-in-chief of the Sage journal *Memory Studies*, founding coeditor of the Palgrave Macmillan book series Memory Studies, and founding coeditor of the Routledge book series Media, War and Security. He holds an AHRC Research Fellowship (2014–15) for "Technologies of Memory and Archival Regimes: War Diaries Before and After the Connective Turn," and leads the ESRC Google Data Analytics Project, "The Role of Internet Search in Elections in Established and Challenged Democracies" (http://voterecology.com). His latest book, *Risk and Hyperconnectivity: Media, Memory, Uncertainty*, coauthored with John Tulloch, is forthcoming from Oxford University Press.

Amy Holdsworth is Lecturer in Film and Television Studies in the School of Culture and Creative Arts at the University of Glasgow. She is the author of *Television, Memory and Nostalgia* (Palgrave Macmillan, 2011) and has contributed articles to *Screen, Cinema Journal, Journal of British Cinema and Television*, and *Critical Studies in Television*.

3 MUSEUMS AND THE CHALLENGE OF TRANSMEDIATION
The Case of Bristol's Wildwalk

Nils Lindahl Elliot

Can the design of a museum so blur the boundaries between its own genre and those of other media – for example, the media of mass communication, or indeed the newer digital media – so as to transform the museum into something akin to a peripatetic version of those media? Is such a transformation not only feasible but desirable? And if it is, what challenges do designers face in the quest for what can be termed the "mediazation" of museums?

I understand mediazation in much the same way as John B. Thompson (1990), that is, as the process by which a growing number of spheres of modern culture have come to be affected directly and indirectly by the media of mass communication and, more recently, by the technologies associated with the so-called digital culture. While the political sphere offers perhaps the most obvious example of the process in question, mediazation has affected countless other fields, ranging from everyday consumption and lifestyle choices to the structuring of the leisure industry itself.

Museums are no exception. Museum designers have long sought to find ways of incorporating changing techniques and technologies of mediated representation within existing genres of display. In one recent intervention, the director of the Clevedon Museum of Art put mediazation in dramatic focus when he suggested that "Every museum is searching for this holy grail, this blending of technology and art." He did so in reference to his own institution's much celebrated incorporation of tablet computers as a means by which visitors could locate artworks within the institution and engage in a variety of interactive practices (Bernstein 2013).

For every generation of museum designers, and for every generation of new technologies, different design challenges may be identified which appear to be

The International Handbooks of Museum Studies: Museum Media, First Edition.
Edited by Michelle Henning.
© 2015 John Wiley & Sons Ltd. Published 2020 by John Wiley & Sons Ltd.

FIGURE 3.1   Wildwalk, Bristol, UK.
Photo: Mark Boyce, February 3, 2007.

prompted by the latest innovations. In fact, the innovations at once reflect and affect social semiotic ecologies whose delicate interrelations go far beyond technology in any narrowly instrumental sense of the term. In this chapter I illustrate this point by engaging in a case study of a museum that was conceived at the crossover of the so-called electronic and digital revolutions. Wildscreen opened in July 2000 in Bristol, England, as part of an all-new £94 million complex of technology, science, and nature-related visitor attractions. The complex, initially known as @Bristol, was built at Canon's Marsh, in Bristol's harborside: it included Explore, a hands-on science center; an IMAX cinema, the first of its kind in the west of England; and Wildscreen itself, a science museum with a focus on natural history and biodiversity.

Wildscreen was very much a hybrid science museum, combining modes of representation and display typically found in natural history museums – for example, fossil casts and accounts of the nature of the evolutionary process – with consoles of the kind associated with science centers and participatory science museums (Figure 3.1). At the same time, Wildscreen had numerous living animals on display, and included a walk-through botanical house, one part of which evoked the kind of immersive simulacra of tropical forests often found in the newest generations of zoos.

The most radical aspect of the attraction was its least obvious one to the visiting public: it was conceived as a walk-through version of a wildlife documentary.

The museum's originator, the late Christopher Parsons, was an internationally acclaimed wildlife documentary producer, and he proposed to create what he called an "electronic zoo," in a reference to the changes made possible in part by the incorporation of charge-coupled devices (CCDs) in video and television. Wildscreen's architects later described the attraction as "the museum counterpart to the BBC's Natural History Unit" (Hopkins Architects 2000), which Parsons himself led between 1979 and 1983. This unit, known by its acronym as the NHU, is the BBC department responsible for the production of BBC wildlife documentaries, including the blockbuster documentaries presented by Sir David Attenborough from 1979 onward.

In the year it opened, large numbers of visitors traveled to see @Bristol thanks to a massive publicity campaign and the project's association with Britain's millennium celebrations. However, after the first year, it became clear that @Bristol would fail to attract the required number of visitors – a number which Gillian Thomas, @Bristol's chief executive during the building and opening phase, described as a "modest" 200,000 visitors per attraction per year.[1] A name change from Wildscreen to Wildwalk and a shift in emphasis from the then futuristic "@Bristol" to the almost pleonastic "At-Bristol" failed to improve attendance levels. By 2006, Wildwalk was attracting fewer than 150,000 visitors, and a significant proportion of these visitors were school groups.[2] While this was by no means an insignificant figure, it was financially unsustainable for an institution whose running costs were comparatively high thanks to the display of living animals and a climate-controlled botanical house.

The IMAX theater also failed to produce the required attendance level. Once the start-up funds for the overall complex were used up, At-Bristol was forced to carry two underperforming attractions. Its classification as a science center meant that the complex could not benefit from the state subsidies given in the United Kingdom to museums, and so, in early 2007, the trustees of the charity that ran At-Bristol decided to sacrifice Wildwalk and the IMAX and to focus all available resources on the Explore science center.

It seems likely that, if there had been a different funding regime for science centers, Wildwalk would have managed to survive. In this chapter I will nonetheless argue that the attraction failed to fulfill the expected potential for reasons to do with the overall design of the complex and with Wildwalk's own characteristic form of mediazation. At-Bristol effectively pitted two relatively expensive and science-based attractions against each other. This problem was compounded by the fact that Bristol City Council had contradictory aims for the regeneration of the Canon's Marsh district. The overall site was forced to be at once a futuristic showcase for the city's reputation for high-tech science and technology, and a historic harborside designed to attract heritage tourism. This meant that, even as Wildwalk was fronted by a late nineteenth-century leadworks made with the rubble of gray Pennant sandstone and quaintly decorated with Bath stone quoins and dressings, there stood just behind this building an impressive ethylene tetrafluoroethylene (ETFE) roof which covered the attraction's tropical house. This dramatic contrast was a visible mani-festation of an architectural formalism that undermined several aspects of the building's function, a factor which itself may have weakened the attraction.[3]

Problems like these notwithstanding, I shall make the case that perhaps the main reason why Wildwalk failed to fulfill its potential was that its exhibits engaged in problematic dynamics of transmediation (Lindahl Elliot 2006a, 47). Such dynam-ics are a key aspect of mediazation, and involve the transposition of aspects of a mode of representation or display from one context to another. As I began to note above, Wildwalk attempted to recombine elements of various genres in order to create a *peripatetic* version of a wildlife TV documentary. I use "peripatetic" in ref-erence to the walked nature of the attraction, but also to refer to the original ety-mology of the word, which invokes the legend of Aristotle teaching while walking around the colonnaded Lyceum in Athens. Wildwalk was designed to teach visi-tors about the evolution of life on earth, and more specifically, about the evolution of biodiversity on the planet. It is on this level that it is possible to identify and analyze what were at once the most provocative, and arguably the most problem-atic, aspects of Wildwalk's design.

The analysis I offer will intertwine two methodologies. The first, a social semei-otic[4] approach drawing on the work of Charles Sanders Peirce, will identify the characteristic signs employed by each of the different modes of representation and/or display, and will chart the changes produced by their transmediation within Wildwalk. The second methodology will employ a genealogical mode of inquiry to at once problematize and historicize those same modes (Foucault 1984).

Wildwalk and the NHU's blue-chip wildlife documentaries

The overall At-Bristol complex reflected Bristol's political and economic elites' aspirations to consolidate the city's reputation as the high-tech regional capital of England's West Country (Bassett, Griffiths, and Smith 2002a). However, Wildwalk's actual exhibits were more of an expression of Bristol's growing *cultural* industry, in and for which the BBC's NHU was to play a leading role. By the 1990s, Bristol had become a world center for the making of wildlife and natural history firms, some-thing akin to a "Green Hollywood" (Bassett, Griffiths, and Smith 2002b, 167).

Christopher Parsons was a leading figure in the field, a founding member of the NHU who rose through the ranks to become executive producer and who, together with Sir David Attenborough, effectively put the NHU on the world map of wild-life TV production. As I noted earlier, it was Parsons who proposed and then pro-moted Wildwalk. This being so, a genealogical link between Wildwalk and the NHU may be established via his career, and via the series and genre that earned him global recognition: *Life on Earth*, widely regarded as the first of the "blue-chip" wildlife documentary blockbusters (the expression "blue chip" is used within the wildlife TV industry to refer to the documentaries with the highest production values).

Parsons joined the BBC in 1955 as an apprentice film editor. In the two decades that followed, he rose to become first a producer, and then an executive producer of BBC wildlife programs. Like Attenborough before him, part of Parsons's early reputation was built via TV shows based on expeditions to collect wild animals for zoos. Parsons worked with Gerald Durrell, the wild animal trader turned world-renowned conservationist. With Durrell, Parsons traveled to Malaysia, Australia, New Zealand, and Sierra Leone to produce two series, *Two in the Bush* (1963) and *Catch me a Colubus* (1966). As I will explain in the next section, these and much later interactions with zoos would have their own impact on Wildwalk.

While Parsons's early career included a number of successful series, he is best known as the executive producer of *Life on Earth* (1979). Parsons referred to the program as the first of the BBC's wildlife "megaseries" (Parsons 1982, 308). Years later, a time line by the BBC of major events in the corporation's history suggested that "Although natural history programmes had been seen on BBC TV before, it wasn't until David Attenborough started this epic series that the genre really took off. Revealing life around the globe through beautiful photography and compelling and intimate commentary …"[5] Thanks in no small part to the series' success, the NHU nearly doubled in size and was granted status as a BBC department (as opposed to a unit), with Parsons as the department's first director from 1979 (Parsons 1982, 351).

Although the opening titles of *Life on Earth* called it "A Natural History by David Attenborough," an idea echoed by the quote above, Parsons played a key role in designing the program. He also proposed that Attenborough be the presenter of the new series, and by so doing effectively launched the latter's career as the face of BBC wildlife television. Twenty years after it was first broadcast, Parsons's series would also constitute part of the template for Wildwalk.

Life on Earth traced the rise of life on the planet, beginning with the simplest single-celled organisms and finishing with the most complex ecosystems. Together with *The Living Planet* (1984) and *Trials of Life* (1990), the series produced a virtual version of what can be described as a heterotopia of nature (Lindahl Elliot 2006a, 47–49). Michel Foucault conceived heterotopias as real places that act like "counter-sites":

> a kind of effectively enacted utopia in which the real sites, all the other real sites that can be found within the culture, are simultaneously represented, contested, and inverted. Places of this kind are outside of all places, even though it may be possible to indicate their location in reality. (Foucault 1986, 24)

As examples of such sites, Foucault referred to holiday villages and gardens, but also to brothels, cemeteries, museums, prisons, and even ships.

The concept of heterotopia can be extended to include what can be termed heterotopic practices (Alfonso and Lindahl Elliot 2002). In contrast to Foucault,

I regard both heterotopias and heterotopic practices as being culturally specific: they involve a comparatively recent form of globalization, and constitute a central aspect of the mass mediation of nature (Lindahl Elliot 2006a, 48–49). Heterotopic practices work to produce heterotopias in virtual sites, as opposed to the "physical" geography of an actual place envisaged by Foucault. News genres are perhaps the most obvious example of such sites; however, a case can be made that the media of mass communication as a whole are premised on a heterotopic spatiality.

I describe as heterotopias of nature all those sites which ostensibly bring together in one place the natural worlds, or at any rate, "representative samples" of such worlds (Lindahl Elliot 2006a, 129). Two examples of such heterotopias are zoological gardens (an institution included by Foucault in his own typology of heterotopias) and natural history museums. If there are heterotopias of nature, there are also heterotopic *practices* that specialize in the virtual representation of nature. One way of thinking about *Life on Earth*'s innovative qualities is that its different episodes took the spatiality of heterotopias of nature to wildlife television in a single series – one that boldly set out to represent, as the title itself proclaimed, "life on earth."

By the mid-1970s, wildlife documentary production techniques had long incorporated the techniques of observation associated with realist cinema. Such techniques included what the film theorist Noël Burch has described as the "ubiquitisation" of the cinematic observer and, with it, the "centring of the subject" (1990, 202–233). Simplifying somewhat, the former aspect gives the illusion that the camera narrator can travel, indeed can simply *be*, anywhere; the latter encourages spectators to at once project themselves into, and identify with, the world shown on the screen.

By deploying such techniques as part of a heterotopic practice, *Life on Earth* appeared to give television viewers the capacity not just to travel to any part of the natural world in the proverbial blink of an eye, but to travel across time. As Attenborough put it in his memoirs, "Sometimes I came back having been filmed speaking the first half of a sentence that fitted neatly on to a second half that we had filmed on another continent two years earlier" (2002, 294).

If ubiquitization enabled such seamless transcontinental narrative displacements, it also allowed the series to reveal, equally effortlessly, the most recondite "secrets" of nature (for the gender politics of this discourse in wildlife documentary, see Barbara Crowther 1995). The audiovisual narrator took its cotravelers, which is really to say covoyeurs into all manner of natural spaces never before seen on television and, in some cases, never even studied by scientists: a Kowari (*Dasyuroides byrnei*) giving birth to her pups is one example highlighted by Parsons himself in his memoirs, *True to Nature* (1982, 319–322). These and other innovations were highly acclaimed; if Parsons and the NHU had already produced a number of well-received series, *Life on Earth* inaugurated a period during which the BBC came to be regarded as the world's premier natural history broadcaster.

Now the burgeoning cultural authority of the BBC's blue-chip wildlife documentaries was undoubtedly bolstered by the remarkable technical ingenuity of the programs, the beauty of their images, and indeed Attenborough's oft-celebrated style of presentation. It is, however, clear that this authority also relied on a problematic form of naturalism. To explain how and why this is the case, a somewhat detailed excursus on the blue-chip documentaries' characteristic naturalism is now required.

The naturalism in question has often been conceived as a form of representation that is, as the title of Parsons's (1982) memoirs says, "true to nature." Within the wildlife filmmaking industry, such a truth has often been portrayed as being both "science-based" (Davies 2000) and the outcome of the exploitation of the ostensibly objective qualities of cinematographic technologies – qualities thought to be capable of revealing "nature itself." As Colin Willock, the head of Anglia Television's competing Natural History Unit once put it in his own memoirs, "Nature as it really exists is our line of business" (1978, 41).

Aspects of this understanding of the cinematographic/televisual process go at least as far back as the emergence of photography, and involve the myth of the pencil of nature (Lindahl Elliot 2008, 11; see also Lindahl Elliot 2006a, 145). I refer to Henry Fox Talbot's term for the new art form whose execution took place "without any aid whatever from the artist's pencil" (1844, 1). Versions of this discourse continue to this day and cannot be entirely dismissed. From the perspective of Peirce's semeiotic theory, a case can be made that blue-chip wildlife documentaries do have an indexical dimension. Indexes are signs that, in Peirce's vocabulary, refer to an object "by virtue of being really affected by that Object" (Peirce 1998, 291). Peirce explains that indexes are actually modified by the object; as such, they can be said to characterize the semeiotics of documentary films, which ostensibly involve a natural process: light reflects off the surface of an object, and makes its way into a lens which refracts it onto a photosensitive surface which is transformed accordingly. Thus, it can be argued that there clearly *is* an indexical relation between the cinematographic image, and whatever object(s) it represents.

It would, however, be a mistake to reduce documentary films to a matter of indexes. In the case of the natural history documentary, at least four levels of the filmmaking process work to embed any indexes within cultural forms, or what Peirce calls *symbols* – signs which refer to the objects that they denote by virtue of a "law" or "rule," or a social convention (Peirce 1998, 292). I have described the four levels in some detail elsewhere (Lindahl Elliot 2008); here it suffices to list them. The levels in question build on the work of Gilles Deleuze (1986) and are the *frame*, or a single image captured by cinematographic means; the *shot*, in the sense of multiple frames giving rise to movement; the *montage*, the linking of two or more shots; and the *narrativization*, which is to say the forms used to organize frames, shots, and montage into a story.

For each of these levels, it is possible to claim that wildlife documentaries of the kind produced on film by the BBC (and indeed other organizations such as the National Geographic) are purely indexical. However, on each of the levels, it is the symbol that arguably prevails: for example, even if what is "in" the frame interacts with what is beyond the frame – the "out of field" – framing is always partial insofar as it involves not only selection, but also a symbolism in the Peircean sense of a convention. There is, for instance, a relatively restricted menu of subjects thought to be worthy of a wildlife documentary; over the decades, megafauna and apex predators have been represented out of all proportion to their numbers relative to the earth's biodiversity.

On the level of the shot, the cinematographic *management* of movement is also the outcome of a selective and a symbolic process: the filmmaker chooses some movements and not others, and engages in a variety of practices that work to relate those movements to a "whole" in accordance with particular conventions. The trailers for the BBC's major documentary series are a particularly good example of this relativity, revealing the extent to which the genre privileges what I term a *hyperkinetic* nature (Lindahl Elliot 2008), that is, a nature that is not only dynamic (as any natural phenomenon invariably is) but appears to be engaged in a constant process of visible physical displacement. Hyperkinesis works to intensify the natural world for a TV world that demands this kind of intensification. But, in so doing, it transforms the character of objects not otherwise associated with hyperkinesis: for example, *The Private Life of Plants* (1995), one of the BBC's very few series concerned mainly with plants, used time-lapse photography again and again to make plants fit the generic requirement for hyperkinesis, and, in so doing, arguably made them "behave" more like animals (Lindahl Elliot 2001).

What is true of frame and shot is also true of montage and narrativization. Much of the narrative logic of blue-chip wildlife documentaries rests on the production of "Hey Mays." Unlike, say, a fictional film that has been minutely scripted far in advance of the actual filming, blue-chip wildlife films tend to involve a tactical editing process. The editors must build a story, or rather a string of "mini-stories," constructed around whatever shots the wildlife cinematographers have been able to obtain. Such mini-stories must be compelling in the context of a TV medium where a ruthless competition for audiences prevails. Over the years, this has meant that the editing has often been structured as strings of scenes designed to provoke responses of the kind "Hey May, come and look at this," and these have been achieved via anthropomorphic narratives of predation, familial relations, or humor (Lindahl Elliot 2001; 2006a).

By anthropomorphism, I do not mean the common sense understanding of the term which suggests that it occurs only when someone explicitly projects human values onto nature. Instead, the etymology of the word (*anthropo*, "man" or human; *morph*, shape) suggests that, despite its indexical qualities, *any* aspect of a wildlife film as film *must* be anthropomorphic if only because it involves human-made technology that imposes not just a story but humanized forms by way of the levels of frame, shot, and montage onto whatever nature is represented. From this perspective, the problem is not to find ways of avoiding anthropomorphism, but to consider what forms of anthropomorphism do a better job of representing nature for a given context (Lindahl Elliot 2001).

The more general point I am leading to is this: the paradigmatic technique of observation employed by the BBC's blue-chip wildlife documentaries revolves not around the index, but around what Peirce terms the *dicent symbol*: a representation which is really affected by what it represents but which, at one and the same time, projects onto the object of representation a conventional association of ideas (Peirce 1998, 295). While the NHU's wildlife documentaries are celebrated for their indexical qualities, their success was also a matter of their symbolism, and with it the manifold anthropomorphic transformations imposed on the natural world. Such transformations have ranged from relatively subtle semeiotic refigurations of the kind just outlined on the levels of shot and frame, to the construction via audiovisual montages of what can be described as the blue-chip narratives' leitmotif: a sublime, sublimated nature apparently devoid of any modern human intervention – not least that of the filmmakers themselves.[6]

It is on this level that the documentaries' heterotopic function becomes fully evident. As noted earlier, for Foucault heterotopias involve the juxtaposition of worlds, but this in a manner that simultaneously represents, contests, or inverts what is juxtaposed. Series such as *Life on Earth* not only appeared to bring together all the "real sites" of nature, but did so in a manner that involved an *ideological* inversion: more often than not, the filmmakers went to extraordinarily lengths to eliminate any evidence of modern human intervention in habitats which had in fact been modified, however subtly, by such intervention.

This inversion has nevertheless gone largely unnoticed. Even today, criticism of the genre tends to be centered on the numerous "fake" zoo scenes introduced by the filmmakers to scenes ostensibly shot in the wild (see, e.g., Singh 2011). In the late 1980s, when Parsons's idea for Wildwalk started to come to fruition, even these relatively crude interventions were generally not acknowledged or debated. In the United Kingdom, the BBC's blue-chip wildlife documentaries commanded not just a remarkable cultural authority but huge audiences. Overseas, the success of the NHU's output translated into a significant profit for the BBC via series that were often coproduced with US organizations. In 1996 a new joint venture with Discovery Communications (*Animal Planet*) generated wall-to-wall wildlife TV (Cottle 2004).

In this context, it is hardly surprising that Parsons's proposals were well received by Bristol City Council. If Parsons could bank on the global success of series such *Life on Earth*, he could also bank on the success of his ventures within Bristol itself, including the Wildscreen Festival, which he cofounded with World Wildlife Fund founder Peter Scott in 1982. This festival doubled up as an international trade show, complete with its own version of wildlife film Oscars, the "Pandas." It also gave Wildwalk its first, and somewhat misleading, name (Wildscreen@Bristol).

While the NHU's cultural authority in Bristol generated goodwill for Parsons's project, its blue-chip documentaries' characteristic naturalism may have led to a fundamental misunderstanding of the challenges of transmediating the blue-chip documentary mode of representation to a museum. As I explained earlier, the documentaries suggested an effortless representation of "nature itself." To anyone not familiar with the extent of the transformations produced by the programs, or indeed the unique mobilities afforded by the medium, the idea of a "museum counterpart" of series such as *Life on Earth* might well have seemed not just desirable, but eminently plausible, with its success virtually guaranteed. If so, the very naturalism that was such an integral part of the success of the blue-chip genre may well have been the beginning of the undoing of Wildwalk.

Wildwalk and the "new zoos"

In 1983 health problems forced Parsons to step down as head of the NHU, but he continued at the BBC until 1988 as head of Natural History Development, a position that involved searching for new commercial possibilities for the NHU and BBC Enterprises. In an interview that Parsons gave Attenborough a couple of years before he died, he suggested that it was during this period that he had the idea of a new kind of visitor attraction:

> while I was head of development, I'd, one of the ideas which I tried to get [BBC] [E]nterprises involved with was a rather different type of visitor attraction, which I called the Electronic Zoo. The reason for this was that, that I'd become very disenchanted with existing zoos. I'd become rung up, during the years that I was Head of Development, I was constantly being rung up by Natural History Museums and Zoos, and, who were really sort of begging for bits of film, and for advice on how to run bits of audio-visual exhibits. And I just felt, well this, we shouldn't be gluing on audio-visual exhibits onto existing zoos and museums, it's not going to be very successful. But there is a good case for actually using the resources of our industry, and creating a different type of attraction, which is going to be much more holistic. (Parsons 2001)

In the same interview, Parsons also noted that he'd attended a meeting in the United States with several leading zoologists, which clearly marked a key point in the development of his ideas. At this meeting there was a sense of growing environmental crisis that needed to be urgently addressed. The meeting was attended by Paul Erhlich, Peter Raven, and Tom Lovejoy, and so it may be deduced that one of its central concerns was the promotion of the then new concept of biodiversity as a cornerstone of a new ethic of conservationism. Henceforth, biodiversity would become a key theme in Parson's plans for Wildwalk.[7]

After 1988, Parsons set up a company devoted to making natural history documentaries for IMAX-affiliated theaters around the world. This company brought him into contact with museums associated with such theaters. Equally, the new business generated profits that Parsons devoted entirely to the promotion of the Wildwalk idea (Parsons 2001), which he conceived as an "electronic zoo." Today, such a zoo might be described as a "virtual zoo"; Parsons's choice of words reflected the vocabulary of his time: at a time when the Internet had not yet materialized, he anticipated that the "electronic revolution," which had been "made possible by the development of micro-chips," "would undoubtedly have a profound effect on wildlife television as well as the rest of the industry" (Parsons 1982, 361).

In fact, zoos had already been transformed, at least partly by the success of older forms of TV production. During the 1980s zoos had begun their own far-reaching dynamic of transmediation, a dynamic which would in some respects influence the design of Wildwalk itself. An account of the changes in zoos is thus required in order to explain this influence, and also to explain how Wildwalk in turn translated the transformations.

When Parsons began his career in television, zoos played a key role in natural history television. During the 1950s television producers regularly transmediated the zoos' modes of representation and their characteristic techniques of display to the context of early broadcast television. They borrowed zoo animals and their curators to make programs that were little more than televised keeper talks. As Attenborough put it in his memoirs, "The most successful animal programme on television in the early 1950s was a series in which George Cansdale, then Curator of Mammals in the London Zoo, exhibited his charges on a large table covered by a door mat" (2002, 31).

The programs were, if anything, a poor version of a zoo naturalism which, until the early 1960s if not much later, was usually based on three main criteria: guaranteeing the visibility of animals to visitors; keeping animals in (and visitors out of) enclosures; and maintaining asepsis. In practice this meant that animals were often displayed in relatively small displays with hard surfaces. These displays prevailed because the popular appeal of zoos for most visitors continued to rest on two contradictory pleasures: first, experiencing in close proximity the sheer living presence of what were thought to be wild animals; and, second, experiencing the character of zoos as the "original" heterotopias of nature, understood in quasi-encyclopedic terms, as a kind of tour of all the major animal classes, or later as something akin to an ABC book of nature for children.

The underlying semeiotics of this naturalism can be clarified by returning to Peirce. Insofar as each specimen in a zoo is an actual occurrence of a species, it is not just an index, but what Peirce terms a *sinsign*. As he puts it, "A Sinsign (where the syllable *sin* is taken as meaning 'being only once,' as in *single*, *simple*, Latin *semel*, etc.) is an actual existent thing or event which is a sign. It can only be so through its qualities": a sinsign forms a sign "through being actually embodied" (Peirce 1998, 291). A banal but good example is a buzzer that makes itself known by the actual event of buzzing.

Despite being almost literally framed by zoo displays (in enclosures with bars, or indeed other less obvious barriers), zoo animals have traditionally been displayed as if they were no more (and no less) than iconic sinsigns, that is, as if they were simply themselves, which is to say "wild animals," albeit "in captivity."

As such, their presence in zoos has more often than not been interpreted as *rhemes*: a rheme, Peirce proposed, is "a sign which is understood to represent its Object in its characters merely" (1998, 291). From the perspective of his baroque vocabulary, zoo animals may thus be regarded as *rhematic indexical sinsigns* (1998, 294): the actual occurrence of so many types (sinsign), but where each occurrence is "really affected" by its object (index), and where the object in effect points at, or appears to point at, nothing other than itself (rheme): "See me, I am an Alligator"; "See me, I am a Bear"; "See me, I am a Camel"; and so forth.

So long as this "rhematism" was unquestioned, zoos were safe. However, the late 1950s and the 1960s saw the beginning of two social changes which were to generate a crisis for zoos. The first of these changes is widely recognized, and involves the rise of what became known eventually as the animal rights movement. At first, this movement entailed a relatively gentle and romantic criticism, of the kind found in books and films like Joy Adamson's *Born Free* (1960 and 1966, respectively). By the 1970s, it had become a determined attack on the speciesist ethics of zoos. Animal rights activists sought not just to close down specific zoos with poor animal welfare records but to end the very *genre* of the zoo.

A second, often overlooked, change involved natural history television. Even as the BBC employed zoos and curators for its natural history television, some of its programs started to employ footage shot by amateurs and a few professionals beyond zoos. Eventually, the amateurs were replaced by professional BBC production teams that traveled further and further afield, making programs which might still be linked to zoos (as in the case of Attenborough's *Zoo Quest*, or indeed Parsons's work with Gerald Durrell), but which foreshadowed the development of genres that would become almost entirely independent of zoos. While zoo shows continued, by the early 1960s a growing number of wildlife TV programs were organized around footage obtained in natural reserves and other areas of outstanding ecological interest. These areas now became the symbols, which is to say the convention, the symbolic measure, of "nature itself."

These changes meant that, during the 1970s, zoos were increasingly forced to fight a battle for survival on two fronts: even as the fundamental ethos of the zoological gardens was questioned, its underlying semeiotic was undermined by new, media-based forms of naturalism of the kind I described earlier. The most forward-thinking zoos responded in two ways.

First, they attempted to recast zoos as Noah's arks in waiting, a reservoir of animals which might one day save whole species from extinction. In the first two or so decades, only a handful of zoos could back up such claims with bona fide *ex situ* and/or *in situ* conservation projects, and even now the validity of this kind of claim continues to be disputed (see, e.g., the PETA website or, for a more sustained analysis, Margodt 2000). Parsons himself was highly critical of the claims; as he put it in the interview with Attenborough, "I felt that zoos were making this big thing about you know, being, you know great for conservation and education. [But] apart from Gerry Durrell I thought it was a load of baloney quite frankly" (Parsons 2001).

Second, zoos transformed their displays to transmediate aspects of the wildlife documentaries' techniques of observation. New "naturalistic" displays were ostensively "closer to nature," while later, "immersive" displays referred to the idea that visitors might in effect break the traditional boundaries between the observer and the observed in order to actually enter the display space itself.

I have made the case elsewhere that, rather than being "closer to nature," naturalistic exhibits actually engaged in new forms of transmediation (Lindahl Elliot 2005a). Aspects of this change have a long history, and go back at least as far as the late nineteenth century, to figures such as William T. Hornaday, who revolutionized natural history museum displays and then attempted, paradoxically, to extend the three-dimensional diorama principles from the Smithsonian's National Museum to the future Bronx Zoo (Hanson 2002).

By the time that plans for Wildwalk were being drawn up, the "source" of transmediation for zoos was arguably wildlife documentaries on television, and other nature media such as wildlife photography in nature magazines and coffee table books. In the new technologies of exhibition, the apparent rhematism of zoo displays tacitly invoked the naturalism of the nature media, creating what I describe as *hypernaturalistic* modes of display. The evidence for this change can be found not just in the displays themselves, but in a variety of literatures. First, zoo leaflets, guides, and other promotional materials began to present zoo animals much as wildlife photography and filmmaking did their wild cousins. Additionally, a new generation of zoo designers employed not just the vocabulary of landscape painting (McClintock 2005), but actual photographic media as part of the process of recreating habitats (Malmberg 1998). In zoo design forums, some observers even began to directly propose the need to transform the zoo visiting experience into a cinematographic one (Maier 2005).

Thanks no doubt to a much broader cultural logic of mediazation, the strategy appears to have worked: zoo attendance levels, which had undergone a long period of decline since the 1960s, began to attain new records in some zoos with the new generation of displays.[8] The 1990s and 2000s witnessed an extraordinary investment in new displays and, in some cases, in all-new zoos such as Disney's Animal Kingdom, an $800 million, 500 acre facility in Florida. My own research into zoo visitors suggested that, by the early 2000s, many visitors were interpreting displays with reference to a variety of media representations. For example, visitors to one zoo complained that the lions were unhappy because they were "inactive" (arguably a tacit incorporation of the hyperkinesis analyzed earlier); and, after Pixar premiered *Finding Nemo*, clownfish not only became a star attraction in zoos with aquariums, but were interpreted with reference to the film's narrative (Lindahl Elliot 2005b).

It would, however, be a mistake to deduce from this remarkable turnaround that the "new zoos" succeeded simply by emulating the naturalism of wildlife documentaries on television. While the zoos sought to elide the visiting experience with viewing experiences of the kind associated with films and wildlife documentaries on television, their displays continued to be grounded in what, with Peirce, we might describe as *dynamical* objects. For Peirce, a dynamical object is one that exists independently of an act of representation, and which can generate signs in its own right. It contrasts with *immediate* objects, which are the objects generated by way of the act of representation, or to simplify it, the object that a sign *conjures*.[9]

This semeiotic difference is key to the difference between zoos and wildlife documentaries. In the case of wildlife documentaries, wild animals are necessarily reduced to immediate objects, however lifelike the audiovisual representation might seem. Put more simply, the represented animals are physically absent from the audiences at the moment of being seen. It might be suggested, in this sense, that zoo animals "correct" this "problem" by presenting the "real McCoy." In fact, zoo animals are simultaneously dynamical and immediate objects: living, breathing creatures with a real, if drastically limited, capacity to determine their own presentation (by way of their sheer sinsignal presence, by way of their "antics," or indeed simply by disappearing into the furthest corner of the enclosure); and the imagined creatures that visitors and the zoos themselves represent by way of additional signs (what Peirce called "interpretants") and, by so doing, anthropomorphicize with reference to concurrent display practices and a myriad of prior experiences. Zoo animals might, in this sense, be described as "re/presentations," where the oblique is meant to highlight the ontological ambiguity of the displays.

While Parsons was very critical of most zoos' conservationist claims, he was undoubtedly aware of their success in attracting new generations of visitors. For Wildwalk, he sought to borrow from their semeiotic when he conceived a museum which included many living animals and immersive exhibits. By 2002, Wildwalk had one mammal species, five bird species, two species of reptiles, four species of amphibians, 80 species of fish, and 29 species of invertebrates. Including the ants in a leafcutter colony, Wildwalk had on display over 80,000 specimens of living creatures. Wildwalk's botanical house was divided into two halves: the first described the rise of the plant kingdom, and the second was an immersive, walk-through "tropical forest" with live birds, leafcutter ants, and an aquarium with tropical fish.

As I shall explain below, in Wildwalk these aspects were nevertheless recontextualized in a manner that sought to link them to the symbolism of a science museum specializing in teaching about evolution and the rise of biodiversity. If Parsons was critical of zoos' conservationist claims, he was equally critical of most zoos' focus on the megafauna. In his words, the zoos

> concentrated mainly on big vertebrates, they do very little on invertebrates. And if you actually look at biodiversity, you suddenly realise that it's actually a very small segment of the world's biodiversity. And their education was very much tied to this, and at a time when I just felt people should just be much more aware of the true extent of biodiversity and how the planet was being worked by animals; run by wildlife, by nature, it was actually not very constructive. (Parsons 2001)

As this quote makes clear, Parsons objected not to zoos per se, but to the limitations of most zoos' heterotopic "menu." This objection seems contradictory when it is considered that the heterotopic practice of natural history documentaries had itself privileged megafauna, apex predators, and a highly restricted selection of "charismatic" animals. The limited nature of Parsons's zoo critique, and his awareness of the pedagogic potential of zoo animals as dynamical objects, doubtless explains why he was happy for Wildwalk to include live animals – albeit a collection of "minifauna" as opposed to the more traditional zoos' "megafauna."

Wildwalk as a hybrid museum

By now it will be clear that Wildwalk made its own classification complex by transmediating several very different traditions of representation and display. It is no coincidence that, during its lifetime, the attraction was characterized by its designers, architects, and promoters in a variety of ways: as a "multimedia wildlife center," a "natural history exhibition," a "natural history center," an "ecology science center," and as I noted above, an "electronic zoo" by Parsons himself.

The At-Bristol charity itself classified the overall At-Bristol complex as a *science center*, thereby defining Wildwalk as a science center as well. This is ironic given the disastrous implication from the point of view of state funding. It is also peculiar given the fact that, in the early 1990s, John Durant, At-Bristol's first chief executive after the complex opened and a leading figure in Britain's Public Understanding of Science (PUS) movement, offered a characterization of science museums and centers which located Wildwalk firmly in the former type. He characterized science centers as generally consisting of one or more relatively open spaces with freestanding interactive exhibits which visitors play with in order to arrive at an understanding of a scientific or technological principle. By contrast, he characterized science museums as having smaller, relatively closed spaces with a mixture of permanent and temporary exhibitions which are scripted around a "story" about a particular area of science and technology. Such a story, he suggested, is told by way of a variety of objects, captions, interactives, and audiovisual/electronic media (Durant 1992).

This account notwithstanding, a case can also be made that Wildwalk was a "participatory" museum, an instance of the genre that San Francisco's Exploratorium has often been credited with having started in 1969, and which has an explicitly pedagogical and even emancipatory function (Hein 1990). The Exploratorium made use of the theories of Richard Gregory (Henning 2006, 85), a Bristol-based psychologist of perception who, in 1978, opened up his own science center in Bristol known as Exploratory. Exploratory was the first British science center, and At-Bristol was designed to replace it. Central to both institutions' approach was the idea of constructing exhibits that not only gave visitors center stage, but enabled them to "have fun exploring their own sensory and cognitive responses" (Henning 2006, 85).

In Wildwalk, such explorations were not an end in themselves, but part of an effort to render intelligible scientific knowledge, a key function of the new kind of science museum/center (Hein 1990). Perhaps the most obvious manifestation of this was the hands-on character of the displays and the attraction's many audio-visual consoles, which used games to teach about individual species (or ecological phenomena) even as they attempted to make tangible a broader theory of evolution. More than evolution per se, Wildwalk sought to illustrate the principle of a growing (evolutionary) biodiversity via a peripatetic narrative about the origin and growing complexity of life on earth.

Architecturally speaking, it did so via a "black box," with a botanical house at the front and an IMAX theater at the back. Its entrance prefigured the aforementioned narrative by way of a curving corridor that began with four large photographs showing different biomes, and then moved on to smaller and smaller images of particular life forms: the photographic building blocks, as it were, of nature. These were followed by a time line that started with a straight line representing the present but ended up spiraling "back" (in walked direction, forward) to the emergence of life on the planet. Quoted along the top of this time line was a famous fragment of *On the Origin of Species*: "endless forms most beautiful and most wonderful." The quote was taken from the last sentence of *On the Origin of Species*, which stated in its modified version (which added "by the Creator") that

> There is grandeur in this view of life, with its several powers, having been originally breathed by the Creator into a few forms or into one; and that, whilst this planet has gone cycling on according to the fixed law of gravity, from so simple a beginning endless forms most beautiful and most wonderful have been, and are being, evolved. (Darwin [1872] 1994, 428–429)

And "cycling," or circling, was what Wildwalk required its visitors to do: the attraction set out a route which spiraled across the building and over two floors. This route was divided up into several distinct spaces and galleries. The first space, on the ground floor, comprised two galleries, "A Simple Beginning" and "Building Bodies." Offset to one side was a dark atrium spanning the entire height of the black box, whose main feature was an abstract light sculpture, superimposed on large screens with images. As the lights came on and off, they interacted with the screens, representing the progression in time from the simplest to the most complex life forms. In this, as in the rest of the interior spaces of the museum, an overall chiaroscuro but futuristic lighting effect was combined with the gaudy, almost cartoonesque colors associated with the work of John Czáky Associates, one of Britain's leading interior design companies for museums and exhibitions.

As in the first episodes of *Life on Earth*, the first half of Wildwalk's ground floor was devoted to the beginning of life in the oceans. "A Simple Beginning" described the start of life via single-celled organisms, primarily via screens with looping montages, and via simple touch screens. *Building Bodies* – the same title as that of the second episode of *Life on Earth* – then explained how single-celled organisms evolved to become complex multicellular organisms. This space combined casts of fossils, which visitors could see and touch, and aquariums with live invertebrates and fish.

After observing the aquariums, visitors crossed a threshold in the form of a doorway between the relative darkness of the first two galleries and the daylight of the first of two immersive exhibits ("Plants on Land") situated in the botanical house. This threshold – and three later ones involving similar passages from dark to light/light to dark – was the closest that the peripatetic narrative came to having an "edit point" of the kind that allowed *Life on Earth* to engage in the forms of ubiquitization that it pioneered. In Wildwalk such a transition took visitors not so much from one era to another, but to different life forms.

In some respects this space contradicted the *raison d'être* of the kind of immersion found in the more spectacular zoo displays. On the one hand, the ETFE "tent" used to allow sunlight into the botanical house meant that visitors could look out of the attraction, and see the utilitarian buildings of the Canon's Marsh regeneration. On the other hand, the plants in the exhibit were meant to re/present not an existing biome (as was often the case in zoos), but the evolution and growing complexity of plants on land: visitors made their way up a serpentine walkway that took them from simple mosses and liverworts, horsetails, ferns, and conifers to the flowering plants. This meant, first, that the narrative appeal was based on a theory about the likely origins of plant life on land and, second, that this part of the botanical house was closer to a botanic garden than to a zoo display. The only concession to a zoo-like rhematism was the inclusion of live butterflies, which flew above the eons represented by the different kinds of plants.

At the end of the serpentine walkway, visitors reached a second threshold that took them back to the first floor of the black box. Immediately to the left of the entry point, visitors encountered an ironically tiny gallery – really only a recess – about the "Forgotten Kingdom": fungi. The rest of the first floor was divided into two galleries: "Land Legs," and "Living Planet." The former gallery was, like "Plants on Land," meant to trace the evolutionary shift from sea to land – but this time with respect to the animal kingdom. It also offered a tour of the major classes of land-based fauna, with much of the space devoted to invertebrates, as per Parsons's critique of zoos' emphasis on megafauna. Consequently, all of the animals on display were relatively small, and they were re/presented in relatively modest enclosures with little or no landscaping. Indeed, far from being instances of the newer zoos' *tableaux vivants* or indeed the almost alive *nature morte* of the dioramas of natural history museums, many of these displays were "jewel box" or terrarium-like displays of the kind that zoos often intersperse in indoor exhibits.

Where zoos might accompany such displays with a printed sign with the name of the species and limited information about its natural history, Wildwalk's living animals were meant to be viewed in association with interactive consoles which used video segments to show aspects of the displayed creatures' ecology. The audiovisual elements had a certain independence, and so could be viewed on their own or in tandem with the exhibits of live animals. But the consoles' footage, an instance of transmediation in its own right, was devoid of the kind of narratives found in actual TV wildlife documentaries; it followed a logic of frame, shot, and montage, but was shorn of the kind of narrativization found in the TV programs.

The peripatetic nature of the viewing experience, and the need for brevity in order to maximize throughput presumably precluded the type of storytelling found in the documentaries. However, deprived of this narrative structuring, much of the footage provided by the consoles arguably lost a key element of the appeal of the documentaries. More importantly, the absence of this narrativization also limited the genre's characteristic use of ellipses, the out-of-field and voice-over narration as a way of linking up the various parts to a broader pedagogic message of the kind featured in *Life on Earth*.

In this context, one risk from the point of view of Wildwalk's pedagogic ambition was that the combination of live and audiovisual displays might fail to produce a more meaningful whole. At the same time, the conjunction of live and audiovisual displays might imply an equivalence, or perhaps even a hierarchy between the dynamical and the immediate objects, with the latter taking precedence in the design if not in the actual observation of the displays.

This issue was particularly evident in a display innovation with a small video camera installed in one of the terrarium-like tanks. The camera could be manipulated by visitors to take shots of a living insect. At a time when consumer video cameras were still not as ubiquitous as they are now, the possibility of just playing with a miniature video camera might well lead to unexpected discoveries of the kind promoted by participatory science museums. It nonetheless raised the question: why this exception to consoles otherwise driven by relatively mechanistic and closed software? Was this not simply a celebration of video technology for its own sake?

As is so often the case in participatory science museums, Wildwalk had numerous consoles and exhibits which were organized around a ludic logic. This logic was evident throughout the museum thanks to the playful, cartoonesque qualities of the colors and frames mentioned earlier. But, in many cases, playfulness was also evident in consoles and larger exhibits organized around actual games. The implicit, or as I call it the "nonformal" (Lindahl Elliot 2006a) pedagogic dimension of some of the games was not always sufficiently thought through; for example, a display called "The Hunting Gallery" used mock rifles, of the kind normally found in shooting arcades, to invite visitors to "shoot" species on the verge of extinction. A screen next to the arcade then explained what threats faced the species being targeted. It seems that Wildwalk's designers were entirely unaware of the irony of this pedagogic choice.

Where "Land Legs" focused on the natural history of particular taxa, the second gallery, "Living Planet," attempted to engage in more ecosystematic representations, framed as simulations of particular biomes. As described by the attraction's promotional literature, these simulations were designed to be immersive in their own right; in the words of At-Bristol's description of one such simulation, they should allow visitors to "experience what it is like to join an Antarctic penguin colony, without freezing to death."

An exit at the end of this display, another edit point between dark and light allowed visitors to enter the second half of the botanical house, which had an exhibit called "Tropical Forests." Here, too, there was a serpentine walkway, which this time led down to a simulation of a rainforest. This was, however, a hetero-topic, and indeed *hyperreal*, rainforest in the sense of the term used by Jean Baudrillard (1994): the display was not an effort to represent a particular forest, but all tropical forests "in general." As Wildwalk's promotional literature put it, the display had plants "from all tropical continents," and hence it echoed the placeless-ness that has arguably haunted many blue-chip documentary representations of tropical forests. While the documentaries usually identify the general geographical location of the forests, they often overlook the geographical and botanical particu-larities of forest structures in favor of representations of idealized "jungles," densely vegetated and "teeming with wildlife."

Alas, this exhibit was not as densely planted as those in many equivalent zoo displays, and here again the transparency of the ETFE panes that covered the botanical house limited the extent of the immersion: the "view" this time was north, to a busy thoroughfare (Anchor Road) and the buildings alongside it. Nor was it "teeming with wildlife"; while it included a living colony of leafcutter ants, an aquarium representing the "flooded forest," and several species of birds, a visitor might wander through this display and not notice any "wildlife" until s/he reached the aquarium at the very end of the walkway. Despite this, the display did make use of zoo-like techniques to recreate ambient sounds, and to instrumentalize them by way of devices designed to produce the kind of pedagogy of the senses which I have described in the context of the newer zoos (see Lindahl Elliot 2006b), and which Henning (2006) notes is central to the hands-on science education move-ment. In the case of "Tropical Forests," devices along the walkway invited visitors to press buttons in order to "call up your own sounds of the forest."

The exit from this last quasi-exterior space took visitors into the final space. Early in the attraction's life, this was known as "People and the Planet," and there was an "environmental news room" with a series of workstations where visitors were invited to explore a variety of environmental issues. In some respects, this room was a prefiguration of ARKive, a web-based archive of wildlife footage which Parsons conceived as a separate project, and which came to fruition in 2003, a year after he died (see www.arkive.org). However, this section was eventually replaced by a walk-through "coral reef" with an acrylic tunnel of the kind that has become de rigueur in major aquariums, designed to give visitors an almost literal sense of immersion. This addition was to foreshadow the future of the building, which in 2009 was transformed – indeed, transmediated in its entirety – to make way for an aquarium run by the Blue Reef chain.

After walking through this part of the final space, visitors entered a gallery that represented various ways of recycling the by-products of consumer culture's excesses. Ironically, thereafter visitors departed via a final "gallery," the museum's shop, itself a traditional citadel of consumption.

Science centers have generally contributed to the move away from the object-centered museum (Henning 2006, 85). In Wildwalk's case, this movement was at once confirmed and contradicted by the transmediations I have just outlined. Wildwalk's overall organization as a peripatetic narrative about the evolution and growing complexity of life on earth was clearly meant to be grounded in theory. In a science museum, objects – in Peirce's sense of dynamical and immediate objects – are typically employed at once as an observational hook, and as an illustration of a phenomenon, be it a scientific principle, a natural law, or a technological procedure or practice. The illustration hinges on a multimodal form of communication, which itself typically involves text on walls, display surfaces close to the object or, more recently, in screens or consoles. While the object may be what initially engages the visitor, the hierarchy of the display and its characteristic naturalism generally privilege the communication of *arguments* via linguistic symbols, numbers, diagrams, or other similarly abstract signs. For Peirce, arguments are conventional signs which "tend to the truth" via symbols and "legisigns" (1998, 296). Legisigns are general types, or "laws," which is to say conventions, established by people (291). Symbols, Peirce noted, "afford the means of thinking about thoughts in ways in which we could not otherwise think of them. They enable us, for example, to create Abstractions, without which we should lack a great engine of discovery" (1931–1958, vol. 4, para. 531). From this perspective, in Wildwalk the mixture of multimediated consoles, inanimate objects such as fossil casts, and living beings such as plants and animals were the narrative vehicles of an overarching "plot" that was itself abstract.

A case can nonetheless be made that the kind of transmediation that took place in the attraction actually undermined this semeiotic and its corresponding pedagogic function. As has long been true in zoos themselves, the rhematism, or what Peirce himself would also describe as the "firstness" of live animals, might actually work against the kind of abstraction required by Wildwalk's pedagogic function. When confronted with living, breathing creatures, visitors might do no more (and no less) than focus on the creatures themselves, which is to say, the sheer presence of their shapes, their movements, and so forth.

Of course, this tendency might be controlled, or redirected by way of texts, graphics, and interactives. But such a strategy was vulnerable to a rather more grievous problem: that in the effort to promote the transition from iconic sinsign to argument (in Peirce's sense of the term), the museum might end up using living creatures as little more than a prop, an instrumental means to an end of the kind that animal rights protestors have rightly critiqued in the context of zoos.

There was, finally, also the risk that the numerous audiovisual consoles in Wildwalk, unaccompanied by explanations of their workings or of the manner in which their footage was acquired, might well be reduced to black boxes in their own right: black boxes not in the architectural, but in the engineering or cybernetic, sense of the term, which is to say, devices that might be viewed only in terms of the output – in this case, machine-like representations whose provenance and characteristic semeiotic remained unknown and unquestioned. In this context, the absence of reflection on the *making* of wildlife representations (in TV and elsewhere) meant that Wildwalk lost an opportunity to become an emancipatory space of the kind associated with the most critical participatory science museums.

Conclusions

In *True to Nature*, Parsons explained that when he first proposed a "definitive natural history series" to the BBC's senior management, his series was to be "the television equivalent of all the glossy Time-Life nature books and other noted coffee table volumes rolled up into 20 programmes" (1982, 310). If, in the early 1970s, Parsons proposed to engage in the transmediation of the then prominent genre of the nature coffee table books, in the late 1980s he proposed to engage in an analogous translation: to revolutionize zoos and museums by creating an "electronic" zoo – or what might equally be described as an electronic *science museum*.

That he could gather the resources to build it suggests an affirmative answer to the first question that I posed in the introduction to this chapter: a museum, or rather a museum designer, *can* so blur the boundaries between the museum genre and a medium of mass communication as to transform the museum into what I have described as a peripatetic version of whatever medium is transmediated. There is, however, always a gap between what is said and what is done, and indeed between what is said and what is done *in* saying. It is clear that Wildwalk was no more a peripatetic version of a wildlife documentary than *Life on Earth* was itself an audiovisual version of Time-Life coffee table books. Both were *sui generis* media which might be linked in various ways to earlier media, but which had a semeiotic logic completely different from that of their ostensive predecessors.

What was true for Wildwalk is bound to be true for any such attempt in any other context: the genres of wildlife documentaries, zoological gardens, and science museums have intricate and subtle cultural ecologies; while it might seem that success in one medium, one technology may provide a springboard for success in another, this chapter has made clear that decontexualizing aspects of any one mode or genre, let alone several, and then transposing them to another, is likely to lead to semeiotic transformation – at times, completely unforeseen transformation.

Such change is more likely if one takes for granted that any one genre's techniques of observation are inherently superior to those of another. It seems clear, for example, that Parsons assumed that the mobility afforded by a cinematographic observer was necessarily a good thing; the same was true of his attempt to build on the apparent rhematism of living plants and animals in zoos. But in the context of participatory science museums, Exploratorium founder and physicist Frank Oppenheimer once explained why the opposite might be true:

> Sightseeing through these media [classrooms and television films] resembles sightings from the windows of trains that are unstoppable, irreversible, and dominated more by the smells, sounds, and motions of the train than by the landscape. Sightseeing is invariably unsatisfactory where the main concern is a rush toward a destination or a need to catch the next train. The best kind of sightseeing involves some exploration and the freedom to decide what not to investigate and where to linger. The more one can become involved with the sights through touching, feeling, smelling, and activity, the more rewarding it can be. It is nice to be able to linger and backtrack. (Oppenheimer 1972, 980)

Unforeseen semeiotic dynamics are also more likely if it is assumed that modes of representation are automatically amenable to recombination. Wildwalk illustrated this problem insofar as it did what Parsons himself criticized in museums and zoos, namely, at times it simply "glued on" audiovisual images to object-based displays. Worse, the attraction's black box, in both the architectural and cybernetic senses described earlier, at times seemed to "glue" *real animals* to the visitor attraction, with little more than a superficial regard for the pedagogic consequences of this remarkable inversion.

The reference to pedagogy leads me to a final point. In environmental education it is common to make a distinction between formal and informal modes of pedagogic communication. Less acknowledged is something akin to the "shadow" of both of those modes, a *nonformal* mode, for which something may be taught without being taught, and something may be learned without being learned (Lindahl Elliot 2006a, 4). Neither the science educator nor the museum attendee set out to teach or learn something deliberately, but something is nevertheless taught and learned unselfconsciously.

In Wildwalk's case, Parsons wished not only to promote a better understanding of biodiversity, but to convey the beauty and sheer magnificence of the evolutionary process. However, anecdotic evidence gathered by staff at Wildwalk and during my own observations at the museum suggested that many visitors failed to perceive the overarching narrative about growing evolutionary complexity. On the contrary, many thronged around either the exhibits that were more zoo-like (e.g., the aquariums or the tropical house), or those that offered opportunities for instrumentalizing relations with nature (e.g., "The Hunting Gallery"), and did so oblivious of questions of evolution, biodiversity, let alone growing complexity.

The last point returns us to the issue I raised at the outset about technological determinism. Genres involve not just techniques and technologies of communication, but also a horizon of expectation shared by the audience. The lived logic of this generic "inertia" may ultimately escape even the most carefully planned transmediations. This is a problem that was reflected in Wildwalk's struggle not just to achieve higher attendance levels, but to find an appropriate name and description for itself. The attraction's changing names may be taken as an index, in Peirce's sense of the term, of the challenges of transmediation.

Notes

1   Select Committee on Culture, Media and Sport, Minutes of Evidence, Examination of Witnesses, June 15, 2000, Question 134, http://www.publications.parliament.uk/pa/cm199900/cmselect/cmcumeds/578/0061521.htm (accessed July 22, 2014).

2   Statistic provided in 2006 to the author by Marie Orchard, the manager of Wildwalk at the time of its closure.

3   An article in the *Architects' Journal* referred to Wildscreen director Anne Finnie's sense that the building's entrance had stressed the entrance to the IMAX to the disadvantage of Wildwalk's displays (Melvin 2000). The Wildwalk foyer also had such bad acoustics that two school groups together created an unacceptable level of noise. Moreover, the main access to an education suite on the top floor was by a lift which was unsuitable for use by all but very small groups (Rogers 2004). Catherine Aldridge, the director of learning of At-Bristol, summed up the problems politely when she noted in 2004 that the design of Wildwalk was more "architecture-led than looking at day-to-day practicalities" (quoted in Rogers 2004, 24).

4   The extra *e* is added to "semiotics" to highlight the fact that my approach is based on the work of Peirce (1931–1958), as opposed to poststructuralist approaches based on the work of Ferdinand de Saussure.

5   "January 1979 – Life on Earth – The Nation Is Hooked," http://www.bbc.co.uk/programmes/p0166zhl (accessed July 22, 2014).

6   Filmmakers have on occasion been caught transporting specimens illegally across national borders for the purpose of "studio-based" filming. For example, in 2003 there was a scandal when an award-winning British filmmaker and conservationist, Michael Linley, pleaded guilty in a court in Western Australia to a series of charges involving animal smuggling. See "Briton Admits Animal Smuggling," BBC News, October 30, 2003, http://news.bbc.co.uk/1/hi/uk/3227433.stm (accessed July 22, 2014). Parsons himself hinted at this kind of practice in *True to Nature* (1982).

7   An account of the history of the concept of biodiversity, and its impact on Wildwalk, is beyond the scope of this chapter. For an account of how biodiversity was launched as a key theme in modern conservationism, see Wilson 1988.

8   For example, in the United States zoos in locations as diverse as Minnesota, Houston, and Oregon reported record attendance levels in 2007–2008.

9   As Peirce himself put it, "we have to distinguish the Immediate Object, which is the Object as the Sign itself represents it, and whose Being is thus dependent upon the Representation of it in the Sign, from the Dynamical Object, which is the Reality which by some means contrives to determine the Sign to its Representation" (1931–1958, vol. 4, para. 536).

References

Alfonso, Carmen, and Nils Lindahl Elliot. 2002. "Of Hallowed Spacings: Diana's Crash as Heterotopia." In *Crash Cultures: Modernity, Mediation and the Material*, edited by J. Arthurs and I. Grant, 153–174. London: Free Association.

Attenborough, David. 2002. *Life on Air*. London: BBC.

Bassett, Keith, Ron Griffiths, and Ian Smith. 2002a. "Testing Governance: Partnerships, Planning and Conflict in Waterfront Regeneration." *Urban Studies* 39(10): 1757–1775.

Bassett, Keith, Ron Griffiths, and Ian Smith. 2002b. "Cultural Industries, Cultural Clusters and the City: The Example of Natural History Film-Making in Bristol." *Geoforum* 33: 165–177.

Baudrillard, Jean. 1994. *Simulacra and Simulation*. Translated by S. F. Glaser. Ann Arbor: University of Michigan Press.

Bernstein, Fred A. 2013. "Technology That Serves to Enhance, Not to Distract." *New York Times*, March 20. Accessed July 22, 2014. http://www.nytimes.com/2013/03/21/arts/artsspecial/at-cleveland-museum-of-art-the-ipad-enhances.html.

Burch, Noël. 1990. *Life to Those Shadows*. London: BFI.

Cottle, Simon. 2004. "Producing Nature(s): On the Changing Production Ecology of Natural History TV." *Media, Culture & Society* 26(1): 81–101.

Crowther, Barbara. 1995. "Towards a Feminist Critique of Natural History Programmes." In *Feminist Subjects, Multimedia: Cultural Methodologies*, edited by P. Florence and D. Reynolds. Manchester: Manchester University Press.

Darwin, Charles. (1872) 1994. *On the Origin of Species*. London: Senate.

Davies, Gail. 2000. "Science, Observation and Entertainment: Competing Visions of Postwar British Natural History Television, 1946–1967." *Cultural Geographies* 7(4): 432–460.

Deleuze, Gilles. 1986. *Cinema 1: The Movement-Image*. Translated by Hugh Tomlinson and Barbara Habberjam. London: Athlone.

Durant, John. 1992. "Introduction." In *Museums and the Public Understanding of Science*, edited by J. Durant, 7–11. London: Science Museum.

Foucault, Michel. 1984. "Le souci de la verite" [Concern for the truth]. *Magazine Littéraire* 207(May): 18–23.

Foucault, Michel. 1986. "Of Other Spaces." *Diacritics* 16(2): 22–27.

Hanson, Elizabeth. 2002. *Animal Attractions: Nature on Display in American Zoos*. Princeton: Princeton University Press.

Hein, Hilde. 1990. *The Exploratorium: The Museum as Laboratory*. Washington, DC: Smithsonian Institution.

Henning, Michelle. 2006. *Museums, Media and Cultural Theory*. New York: McGraw-Hill.

Hopkins Architects. 2000. "Wildscreen, Bristol, United Kingdom 2000." Accessed July 22, 2014. http://www.hopkins.co.uk/projects/3/110/.

Lindahl Elliot, Nils. 2001. "Signs of Anthropomorphism: The Case of Natural History Television Documentaries." *Social Semiotics* 11(3): 289–305.

Lindahl Elliot, Nils. 2005a. "The Natures of Naturalistic Enclosures." In *Innovation or Replication? Proceedings of the 6th International Symposium of Zoo Design*, edited by A. B. Plowman and S. Tongue, 87–99. Paignton, UK: Whitley Wildlife Conservation Trust.

Lindahl Elliot, Nils. 2005b. "The New Zoos: Science, Media and Culture." Award Report, Economic and Social Research Council. Accessed July 22, 2014. http://www.esrc. ac.uk/my-esrc/grants/L144250052/read/reports.

Lindahl Elliot, Nils. 2006a. *Mediating Nature*. London: Routledge.

Lindahl Elliot, Nils. 2006b. "See it, Sense it, Save it: Economies of Multisensuality in Contemporary Zoos." *Senses and Society* 1(2): 203–224.

Lindahl Elliot, Nils. 2008. "Esittää suojellakseen? Television luontodokumenttien kritiikki" [Showing to save? A critique of wildlife documentaries on television], translated by Ville V. Lahde. *Journal of the European Society of Philosophy* (Finland) 57(2): 10–15.

Maier, Gerhard. 2005. "Brad Pitt is a Monkey: How a Zoo Works Like a Movie." In *Innovation or Replication? Proceedings of the 6th International Symposium of Zoo Design*, edited by A. B. Plowman and S. Tongue, 43–48. Paignton, UK: Whitley Wildlife Conservation Trust.

Malmberg, Melody. 1998. *The Making of Disney's Animal Kingdom Theme Park*. New York: Hyperion.

Margodt, Koen. 2000. *The Welfare Ark: Suggestions for a Renewed Policy in Zoos*. Brussels: VUB University Press.

McClintock, Keith. 2005. "Constructed Realism: Incorporating the Principles of Art and Perception to Communicate Realistic Natural Habitats." In *Innovation or Replication? Proceedings of the 6th International Symposium of Zoo Design*, edited by A. B. Plowman and S. Tongue, 37–42. Paignton, UK: Whitley Wildlife Conservation Trust.

Melvin, Jeremy. 2000. "Wildscreen@Bristol by Michael Hopkins." *Architects Journal*, November 30. Accessed July 22, 2014. http://www.architectsjournal.co.uk/%20 wildscreenbristol-by-michael-hopkins/194694.article#.

Oppenheimer, Frank. 1972. "The Exploratorium: A Playful Museum Combines Perception and Art in Science Education." *American Journal of Physics* 40(7): 978–982.

Parsons, Christopher. 1982. *True to Nature*. Cambridge: Patrick Stevens.

Parsons, Christopher. 2001. "Christopher Parsons: Oral History Transcription." Interview by David Attenborough, July 26. *Wild Film History*. Accessed July 22, 2014. file:///C:/ Users/owner/Downloads/Christopher_Parsons%20(2).pdf.

Peirce, Charles Sanders. 1931–1958. *Collected Papers*. 8 vols. Edited by C. Hartshorne, P. Weiss and A. Burks. Cambridge, MA: Harvard University Press.

Peirce, Charles Sanders. 1998. *The Essential Peirce*, vol. 2. Edited by N. Houser et al. Bloomington: Indiana University Press.

Rogers, Rick. 2004. *Space for Learning: A Handbook for Education Spaces in Museums, Heritage Sites and Discovery Centres*. London: Space for Learning Partners.

Singh, Anita. 2011. "Frozen Planet: BBC 'Faked' Polar Bear Birth." *Daily Telegraph*, December 12. Accessed July 22, 2014. http://www.telegraph.co.uk/culture/tvandradio/ bbc/8950070/Frozen-Planet-BBC-faked-polar-bear-birth.html.

Talbot, Henry Fox. 1844. *The Pencil of Nature*. London: Longman.

Thompson, John B. 1990. *Ideology and Modern Culture*. Cambridge: Polity.

Willock, Colin. 1978. *The World of Survival*. London: Deutsch.

Wilson, E. O., ed. 1988. *Biodiversity*. Washington, DC: National Academy of Sciences.

Nils Lindahl Elliot is author of *Mediating Nature* (Routledge 2006). His most recent project, *Observing Wildlife in a Tropical Forest*, develops a genealogy of the pedagogy of wildlife observation among guides and tourists on Barro Colorado Island, Panama.

4 MEDIATIZED MEMORY
Video Testimonies in Museums

Steffi de Jong

Within its exhibition section on World War II, the Royal Army Museum in Brussels shows a rather peculiar oil painting by the Russian artists Pavel Boyko and Arkadi Lebedev (Figure 4.1). The picture is called *The Battle of Kursk: A History Lesson* and was offered to the museum in 2001 by the Russian embassy. It shows the interior of a museum with a large painting of the battle. Before the painting, a Russian colonel gives a history lesson to representatives of the allied forces: a French lieutenant-colonel, a British navy lieutenant, and an American major. A German Bundeswehr soldier is shown at some distance from the group looking at the painting, his back turned toward the viewer. Behind the group of younger soldiers being given the history lesson, a Russian veteran in a wheelchair is pushed toward the painting by his daughter, who is also dressed in an army uniform. His granddaughter is lagging behind, contemplating the statue of a Russian hero. A Red Army flag and some photographs can be seen in the back in another exhibition room.

Here, I will not go into the rather blatant memory-political message of the painting. What interests me are the different forms of transmission of history that are shown. Such a transmission happens on a first level through the exhibited objects, documents, and artworks. The latter are, on a second level, interpreted and explained by the guide – in this case the Russian colonel. On a third level, we see a transmission of memory from one generation to another in the veteran's family. The veteran in the painting does not talk, nor does he seem to listen to the Russian colonel's history lesson. The official transmission of history is therefore shown as separate from individual memory. In this, the painting contrasts with the Royal Army Museum's own representation of World War II. In the same exhibition section, the museum makes veterans – and other witnesses of the war – speak:

The International Handbooks of Museum Studies: Museum Media, First Edition.
Edited by Michelle Henning.
© 2015 John Wiley & Sons Ltd. Published 2020 by John Wiley & Sons Ltd.

FIGURE 4.1   Pavel Boyko and Arkadi Lebedev, *The Battle of Kursk: A History Lesson.*
(For a color version of this figure, please see the color plate section.)
© Royal Museum of the Army and of Military History, Brussels.

in video testimonies. Their individual memory is part of the exhibition, and thus of the first level of transmission of history.

Like the Royal Army Museum, more and more museums integrate video testimonies into their permanent exhibitions. This is especially but not only the case in Holocaust and World War II museums such as Yad Vashem in Jerusalem, the Holocaust Exhibition at the Imperial War Museum in London, or the Bergen-Belsen and the Neuengamme Memorials. The Haus der Geschichte der Bundesrepublik Deutschland in Bonn (literally, House of the History of the Federal Republic of Germany, but known as the German National Museum of Contemporary History), a state-run museum on the post-1945 history of Germany, has renewed its exhibition in 2011 to include, among other things, more video testimonies. The Villa Schöningen, Haus an der Glienicker Brücke, a museum in Potsdam positioned on one of the bordering bridges between East and West Berlin, has based its exhibition primarily on video testimonies. Video testimonies were also given a prominent role in the Museum of Europe's exhibition on European integration *It's Our History!* (De Jong 2011a).

This use of video testimonies in museum exhibitions raises the question of their musealization. How are video testimonies turned into museum objects? What functions are video testimonies given in museums? In order to answer those questions,

I will draw on my research into the collection and exhibition of video testimonies, as well as on their didactic uses, in Holocaust and World War II museums in Europe and Israel (De Jong 2011a; 2012; 2013). I will also take a look at the Haus der Geschichte, mentioned above, which deals with more recent historical events. I will consider the collection of video testimonies, their use as exhibition items, and the didactic functions that they are given. I will show how personal memory has become part of the official transmission of history – and thereby been put on one footing with the first and second levels of transmission of history in museums as shown on the oil painting in the Royal Army Museum in Brussels: material remains and museum guides. Referring to Jan and Aleida Assmann's theory of collective memory, I argue that the musealization of video testimonies is postmodern society's attempt to turn communicative memory into cultural memory.

Video testimonies: Communicative memory as cultural memory

The Egyptologist Jan Assmann, in what has by now become a classic of memory studies, *Cultural Memory and Early Civilization: Writing, Remembrance, and Political Imagination* (2011, first published in German in 1992), differentiates between two modes of collectively remembering the past: communicative memory and cultural memory. Communicative memory is "based exclusively on everyday communications" and "characterized by a high degree of non-specialization, reciprocity of roles, thematic instability, and disorganization" (J. Assmann and Czaplicka 1995, 126). Communicative memory concerns events in a recent past that some of the participants of the conversations can still remember. It lasts at the most 80 to 100 years, or three to four generations. Cultural memory on the other hand, "has its fixed points; its horizon does not change with the passing of time. These fixed points are fateful events of the past, whose memory is maintained through cultural formation (texts, rites, monuments) and institutional communication (recitation, practice, observance)" (J. Assmann and Czaplicka 1995, 129). Cultural memory concerns events in a distant past that are reconstructed according to a contemporary context (J. Assmann and Czaplicka 1995, 130). Both modes of remembering the past are linked by a time of transition, a floating gap (J. Assmann 1992, 48).

The Anglicist Aleida Assmann has further developed Jan Assmann's theory and divided cultural memory into storage memory and functional memory (2006, 54–58). Storage memory refers to those carriers of cultural memory that are stored in archives, magazines, libraries, and so on, but are not actively used at the present moment. Functional memory, on the other hand, concerns those carriers that are of direct relevance for a contemporary memorial culture. Aleida Assmann uses the art museum as an example to illustrate the difference between functional memory and storage memory, but any historically oriented museum would have done really. Generally, only a fraction of the objects in a museum's storerooms, the museum's storage memory, are actually exhibited in the galleries, the museum's functional memory. Carriers of cultural memory that have once been part of storage memory can of course be rediscovered and become functional memory, while carriers of functional memory, after some time in the limelight, can end up in museum storerooms, archives, or libraries.

For Jan and Aleida Assmann, the transition between communicative memory and cultural memory is rather schematic. Although Jan Assmann accounts for a "floating gap," this time of transition appears only at the end of the time of communicative memory and the beginning of its transformation into cultural memory. The theory does not account for the coexistence of cultural and communicative memory – or for the use of communicative memory as cultural memory. I argue that exactly the latter is happening right now: the musealization of video testimonies is an endeavor to turn communicative memory itself into cultural memory and to save it from oblivion.

The mediatization of the witness to history

In 2008 a conference in Jena analyzed "The Birth of the Witness after 1945" ("Die Geburt des Zeitzeugen nach 1945") (Sabrow and Frei 2012). Ten years earlier, the French historian Annette Wieviorka had already observed that we are living in the "era of the witness" (2006, first published in French in 1998). Wieviorka concentrated on the memory of the Holocaust while the conference took postwar memory in its entirety into consideration. Both, however, argued that a proliferation of personal testimonies in public representations of contemporary history can currently be observed. In German, a new word even appeared in the 1970s and 1980s that denotes people who have witnessed an event of historical importance: *Zeitzeuge* (Sabrow and Frei 2012, 14–15). The word is now used ubiquitously, but no English equivalent has yet been coined. I therefore propose the concept of "witness to history" as an analytical concept in English. I understand the "witness to history" in a more narrow sense than the German *Zeitzeuge*, which basically denotes anybody who has witnessed historical events. I use the concept of "witness to history" to denote a person who has witnessed the past *and* gives testimony to this past in a public sphere. With his or her testimony, the witness to history constructs a certain narrative of the past – a certain history – and at the same time testifies to this narrative. The medium for the transmission of this testimony that I will analyze here is video. The term "video testimony" was first used by the collaborators of the Fortunoff Video Archive for Holocaust Testimonies (hereafter Fortunoff Archive), a project that systematically records on video and collects interviews with Holocaust survivors.[1] By using the term "video testimony" instead of "video interview," I want to underline the fact that, in these videos, witnesses to history do not only report on the past but also testify to this past.

Studies on the figure of the witness to history observe that, over the last 40-odd years, witnesses to history have become ever more mediatized and ever more prominent in public representations of the past (Wieviorka [1998] 2006; Bösch 2008; Elm 2008; Fischer 2008; Keilbach 2008; De Jong 2011b, 250–256; 2012, 299–301; Sabrow and Frei 2012). Events that can here be named and that appear again and again in the literature are: the Eichmann trial in 1961, the foundation of the Fortunoff Archive in 1979, the (re)discovery of oral history as a research method in the 1980s, and the individualization of TV documentaries especially since the 1990s. It is this mediatization that provides the foundation for the musealization of video testimonies.

Only a few survivors had appeared as witnesses in the trials against the National Socialist elite that took place before the trial of Adolf Eichmann, notably during the Nuremberg trials, when documents were used as the main evidence (Wieviorka [1998] 2006, 67; Keilbach 2008, 144; Yablonka 2012, 177). The Eichmann trial now put the survivors center stage. The trial was in fact as much about giving a history lesson to Israel and the world as it was about convicting Eichmann. "We want the nations of the world to know ... and they should be ashamed," declared Prime Minister David Ben Gurion at the time (quoted in Arendt 1994, 10). For this purpose, 110 witnesses were invited to give testimony. The role of those witnesses was less to attest to Eichmann's guilt than to embody history. They were supposed to give "a phantom a dimension of reality," as the attorney general Guideon Hausner declared (Wieviorka [1998] 2006, 70). What the witnesses said was therefore of lesser importance than the fact that they said it. The trial was a media event. Four cameras had been installed in the courtroom and the trial was broadcast on TV and radio. The plan to educate the world by affecting the audience of the trial worked. International TV stations soon started to request only pictures of the witnesses. Caught on camera, the witnesses' bodies and their voice became part of their testimony – and were often considered of a higher value than their actual words. With the Eichmann trial, the Holocaust was given a voice and a face. It was not just the six million anymore. Ordinary men and women were accepted as witnesses to history and first steps toward their mediatization were undertaken.

Such an acceptance and mediatization gained further relevance when the Fortunoff Archive started its work in 1979. It started as a small-scale community project at Yale University when the television journalist Laurel F. Vlock and the child survivor and psychiatrist Dori Laub interviewed Holocaust survivors for a documentary produced for the opening of a Holocaust monument in New Haven. The project soon grew in size and importance, and affiliated projects were created all over the world. The Fortunoff Archive was the first large-scale project to systematically collect video testimonies with Holocaust survivors. To date 4400 videos have been amassed. Other projects have followed this example, the most well-known probably being the Survivors of the Shoah Visual History Foundation (hereafter Shoah Foundation), founded by Steven Spielberg after the filming of *Schindler's List* (1993). By 2003, when the collection period ended, the Shoah

Foundation had exceeded its goal of recording fifty thousand video testimonies within 10–15 years and collected 51,700 testimonies (Jungblut 2005, 509).

Oral history as a research method has risen in popularity since the 1980s – especially in circles of lay historians (Wierling 2003). Many of the interview projects that are being carried out have World War II and the Holocaust as their object. While the first interviews were recorded on audio files, more and more interviews are being recorded on video – a consequence of the drop in the cost of the technology. What is more, although there had been groundbreaking uses of witnesses to history in TV documentaries before, for instance in the BBC documentary *The World at War* (1973) and in Claude Lanzmann's *Shoah* (1985), witnesses to history have also started to be ever more frequently used in history documentaries since the 1990s. It has now become customary to include short clips from video testimonies on all kinds of events in documentaries (Bösch 2008; Elm 2008; Fischer 2008; Keilbach 2008; Kansteiner 2012). In those documentaries, an aesthetics was developed that was later to be used in museums as well.

With the popularization of oral history and the frequent use of video testimonies in documentaries, video testimonies have gained in acceptance and popularity both as objects of research and within public history. The musealization of video testimonies has to be seen against this background of a gradual mediatization and popularization of witnesses to history. Video testimonies were introduced into museums only after they had become popular as means to transmit history in other media.

Turning video testimonies into museum objects

As the examples of the Fortunoff Archive and the Shoah Foundation show, video testimonies were collected long before they were used as exhibition items. Video testimonies from those collections are now also shown in museums and exhibitions. Clips from the video testimonies of the Shoah Foundation are part of the permanent exhibition of the Museum of Jewish Heritage in New York, for example. As well as drawing on already existing collections, many museums started to collect video testimonies before they decided to present them in their exhibitions. In the Neuengamme Memorial the first major interview project was carried out in the early 1990s. First, audio technology was used, but video recordings soon replaced it. Both have been included in the new permanent exhibition which opened its doors in 2005. In the Bergen-Belsen Memorial, where the first oral history interviews were carried out in the early 1990s as well, a large-scale video interview project was initiated in 1999. When the memorial decided to design a new permanent exhibition (which opened in 2007) the video testimonies were included in the plans for the new exhibition. Yad Vashem has carried out interviews since its beginnings in 1953. Today around 60 percent of the collected ten thousand testimonies are in video format.[2] Some clips from those video testimonies have entered the permanent exhibition which was inaugurated in 2005.

Video testimonies were, and are, collected to bridge collection gaps, to complement other sources with the voices and faces of the witnesses to history and for research purposes. In the case of video survivor testimonies, for example, the director of the Neuengamme Memorial, Detelf Garbe, observes that information on "the prisoner's multi-layered 'everyday life,' the inner structures of the camp society, the conditions for survival and the perspectives of the different prisoner groups" could be extracted only from the memory of the survivors (1994, 35).[3] With the advent of oral history and social history in the 1980s, such questions gained more and more research interest. Especially in the case of video testimonies from Holocaust survivors, collections were also motivated by a desire to give a voice back to the victims and by a sense of duty to preserve their testimonies for future audiences (De Jong 2011b, 248; 2012, 298). At least since the broadcast of Marvin J. Chomsky's mini-series *Holocaust* in 1979, there has been a demand that the victims themselves be heard. Their voices and faces should be contrasted to the fictionalized representations of the Holocaust – but also to the archival pictures showing starved prisoners and heaps of corpses (see Young 1988, 163; Hartman 1996, 143).

Collecting can be considered the first step of the musealization of an object. Being collected, an object is taken out of its original context to enter the realm of signification. In the words of the Polish historian Krzysztof Pomian (1990), the object becomes a "semiophore"; its primary function becomes a semiotic one. The collected object represents an event, a time period, a style school, a person, and so on. What sounds fairly straightforward in the case of objects and artworks – a Greek vase comes to represent Greek antiquity, a painting by Umberto Boccioni represents Futurism, and so on – raises some ethical questions in the case of video testimonies. Video testimonies are representations of remembering individuals. Collecting video testimonies means – as macabre as this might sound – storing for the future aging bodies and voices that will inevitably die. Especially in the case of the Holocaust and World War II, where we are facing the disappearance of the last witnesses to history, video testimony appears as a medium that allows us to save communicative memory for future generations. As I will show in what follows, in video testimonies a conversation between a future audience and the witnesses to history is therefore staged. The methodologies that are used for the production of this medium, in turn, are supposed to show a pristine representation of the individual memory of the witness to history.

Turning communicative memory into cultural memory

For most video testimonies, the method of the so-called narrative interview or biographical interview is deployed. This interview method is meant to give the witness to history the greatest possible freedom to relate their story in their own way. The interviews generally start with the interviewer asking the interviewees to tell their life story. Only in a second stage do the interviewers ask direct questions. In general, the interviewer is supposed to refrain from interfering too much in the interviewee's narrative (Jureit 1999; Wierling 2003, 110; Gring and Theilen 2007, 175). The social psychologist Harald Welzer has pointed out that the narrative interview is based on a model of the natural sciences according to which "a specific methodology can be used in order to 'extract' 'data' from the context of every day life that can be 'interpreted' for research purposes" (2000, 53). Through the "neutral" behavior of the interviewer, an untainted individual memory is supposed to be captured. Welzer observes that, rather than capturing memory, the situation of the interview creates this memory. He points out that "first, we cannot not communicate and ... secondly, we speak in such a way as we think that our interlocutor expects us to talk" (2000, 52). The interview is an asymmetrical conversation in which one of the parties mainly asks questions and the other one mainly answers those questions:

> A biographical narrative is therefore rather determined by the normative requirements and the cultural criteria for a good story on the one hand and by the conditions of its performance on the other hand than by something like a really lived life. (Welzer 2000, 55)

Video testimonies, in other words, are representations of a highly structured conversation taking place at a certain point in time and at a certain place.

In their interviews for video testimonies, witnesses to history do in fact generally try to give a logical structure to their memory. In general, weeks, often months, of preparation in which the witnesses can reflect on what to say and how to say it precede the actual interview. There will have been phone calls and informal meetings between the interviewers and the witnesses before the actual recording takes place. The Shoah Foundation even used a preinterview questionnaire, thereby helping the witnesses to history to structure their testimony.

What is said in an oral history interview, and how it is said, are also dependent on the identity of the interviewer and the chemistry between the interviewer and the witness. Some things we will say only to a person of the same gender or of a similar age, to somebody who has experienced something similar, or – quite to the contrary – to a complete stranger. For all witnesses to history, the interview is moreover undoubtedly an important event. The invisible future audience is thereby always present. There are things that witnesses to history will not reveal in front of a camera. Maximilian Preisler, who has carried out interviews with Holocaust survivors, observes: "The imagined audience is present. And what will those future listeners think? For the sake of creating a meaningful narrative, the witnesses might feel under pressure to put coincidences and experiences into a non-existent rational framework" (1998, 197). Rather than extracting individual memory, the narrative interview thus constructs a particular memorial narrative. This narrative would sound different at any other moment in time, at any other location, and with any other interviewer.

An untainted individual memory, of course, does not even exist outside of the interview process, as Welzer is also eager to point out. Neurological studies have shown that, when we recall an event, millions of brain cells interact so that our memory is a "continuous reactivation of neuronal networks" (Thießen 2008, 610). Individual memory is at best a "representation of past impressions" cued by the present (Erll 2005, 82) – and we might actually never have lived through some of those impressions. Individual memory is influenced by the sociocultural context that we live in and by the cultural memory that is practiced at the time. In early interviews with Holocaust survivors, such as those carried out by the American psychologist David Boder, for example, "references to Jewish violence and revenge, as well as expressions of personal depravity" (Deblinger 2012, 121), were frequent. Such stories can hardly ever be found in testimonies today – they do not fit a contemporary memorial culture that focuses on victimhood and the figure of the survivor (see Jureit and Schneider 2010; Welzer 2011). In 1946 "it was not clear that any one part of a survivor's wartime experience should be either highlighted or minimized"; the survivors therefore "openly shared stories that later became shameful or controversial" (Deblinger 2012, 121).

As the above quote from Maximilian Preisler shows, many interviewers are now aware of the limitations of the medium of video testimony to represent an untainted memory. Nevertheless, the precarious character of individual memory and the methodology used to produce the video testimonies are hardly ever made apparent in the video testimonies themselves. On the contrary, the aesthetics used for video testimonies highlight an "authentic" individual memory, while at the same time staging a conversation between the represented witness to history and the future viewers (De Jong 2013, 22–26). Several practitioners and scholars have considered video testimony to be the most adequate medium to represent the coming about of individual memory. "In video testimonies ... there is nothing between us and the survivor; nor when the interview gets going between the survivor and his/her recollections," writes Geoffrey Hartman (1996, 140) of the Fortunoff Insitute. James E. Young observes:

> It is not merely a story or narrative being recorded in cinematographic and video testimony, but the literal making of it: the painful and deliberate choice of words, selection of details and memories, the effect of these details on the speaker, and then the effect of these details on the narrative itself. We watch as experiences enter speech: that point at which memory is transformed into language, often for the first time. (1988, 161)

For both Young and Hartman, the real testimony happens somewhere beyond the oral narrative. According to Young,

FIGURE 4.2   A still from the video testimony of Ulrike Poppe from 2010 in the Haus der Geschichte, Bonn.
© Haus der Geschichte der Bundesrepublik Deutschland.

> In the testimonial image, we also perceive traces of a story the survivor is not telling; these traces are in his eyes, his movements, his expressions – all of which become part of the overall text of video testimony, suggesting much more than we are hearing or seeing. (1988, 162)

For Hartman, "the embodiment of the survivor, their gestures and bearing is part of the testimony" (1996, 144). Those extra-verbal expressions of testimony tend in fact to appear as more "real," more "authentic," than the oral narrative. Young (1988) acknowledges that the medium of video has an ordering effect on the testimony and that camera position and lighting have an impact on the representation of the object on film. He fails, however, to acknowledge the full impact of the aesthetics of video testimonies on both the representation of the witnesses to history's individual memory and the viewers' reception thereof.

Video testimonies have been dubbed rather derogatively as "talking heads": the camera focus is generally on the face of the witnesses to history or their upper body. Occasionally the hands are also shown. In this way, the emphasis is placed on those parts of the body that are generally considered to represent the extra-verbal expressions of individual memory particularly well. The choice of background and lighting techniques further highlight those expressions. Early video testimonies were generally recorded in a private environment, often in the witnesses' living room and sometimes at the location of the event that the witness testifies to. The camera angle and lightening were often rather arbitrary. Lately, however, an aesthetics that was developed for TV documentaries (see Bösch 2008; Keilbach 2008) has been adopted for most video testimonies, in particular those shown in museums. The witness's face is illuminated in such a way that all of the emotional expressions are highlighted and a monochromatic, mostly black or gray, background is chosen (see Figure 4.2). Diana Gring and Karin Theilen, who carried out the video testimony project for the Bergen-Belsen Memorial, explain that the neutral background

> is on the one hand beneficial for the editing process; on the other hand, the picture focuses in this way on the witness to history. Recipients can concentrate on the face, the facial expressions and the gestures of the interviewees; this allowed us to mimic a dialogic structure, a "virtual encounter." (2007, 122)

Through the camera focus, the lighting, and the choice of background, a dialogue between the witnesses to history and the viewers is therefore mimicked.

The prerequisite for the construction of such a dialogue is that the interview process that is the origin of the video testimony has to be masked. The interviewer is generally left out of the camera frame. In the extracts that are shown in museums, his or her voice is only rarely heard. While, in normal TV interviews, the interviewee is generally looking at the interviewer, in video testimonies, especially in those shown in museums, the witnesses to history are often asked to look directly into the camera. In this way, the viewer will look the witness directly in the eye when watching the video. The producers of the video testimonies for the interviews in the Imperial War Museum observed that asking the witnesses to history to look into the camera instead of at the interviewer was one of the most difficult things about the interviews.[4] In the Museo Diffuso, a small World War II museum in Turin which has based its exhibition almost exclusively on video testimonies, the sound of the video testimonies, which is transmitted over headphones, works only if visitors stand in front of the video testimonies and look straight at them.

The aesthetics of video testimonies thus construct a representation of individual memory that is supposed to bring viewers particularly close to the individual memory of the witness to history while at the same time engaging them in a virtual conversation. This effect is arrived at by decontextualizing the witnesses to history from the sociocultural context in which they live and their testimony from the situation that brought it about – the narrative interview. This decontextualization in turn allows the musealization of video testimonies and their use as carriers of cultural memory. Like an object when it enters a collection, the memory of witnesses to history is taken out of its original context. Their testimony, a supposed representation of individual memory, is presented as existing outside time and space. The collection of video testimonies also means turning them into storage memory; it is the attempt to turn communicative memory into cultural memory. This, in turn, means detaching the testimonies from the witnesses to the history that uttered them. Neither the interviewers nor the witnesses can fully control how future viewers will receive their testimonies and for what purposes they will be used. Recoded testimonies allow viewers to flick through them, skip parts, and fast-forward. They also allow curators to choose the most appropriate video testimonies for the exhibitions.

Exhibiting video testimonies

Only very few video testimonies from the entire collections enter museums' exhibition halls – and only short clips of those video testimonies. Museum visitors' attention span is short. Multiple objects, texts, and other information sources demand their attention. The video testimonies for museums are, therefore, generally cut to a length of a few minutes or even seconds. Out of the whole collection, the most interesting stories and the best storytellers tend to be chosen. Occasionally, in museums where the video testimonies are produced directly for the exhibitions, interviewers even try to extract the most "exhibitable" stories from the witnesses to history during the interview process itself (De Jong 2011b, 259; 2012, 302–303). In museums, visitors are presented with the highlights, with the most eloquent witnesses to history and with the most interesting or affective stories.

This process of selection is not different from the process of selection of other museum objects. In the case of video testimonies, however, it does raise urgent ethical questions. Is it permissible only to use extracts from entire testimonies and only to present to the visitors some of the witnesses to history? Exhibiting video testimonies always means making a compromise between the needs of the visitors and the video testimonies as ethically fragile sources. Curators are aware of this dilemma. Thus, Suzanne Bardgett of the Imperial War Museum observes that, "to our intense relief, the survivors liked the way their testimonies had been used and understood the reasons for their 'fragmentation'" (Bardgett, n.d.). Exactly because of these ethical questions, the Memorial to the Murdered Jews of Europe in Berlin decided against using video testimonies in its exhibition. Instead, visitors are given the opportunity to watch entire video testimonies from the collection of the Fortunoff Institute in a separate room (Baranowski 2009).

If they are exhibited, video testimonies occupy a rather peculiar position among the things shown in an exhibition. For museum exhibitions, Roger Fayet proposes a distinction between primary, secondary, and tertiary museum objects (2007, 24). Primary museum objects are the things and artworks that are exhibited. Secondary museum objects are the "models, replicas, reconstructions or visual representations as well as textual information" (Fayet 2007, 26) that are used to explain to the visitors how they should read the primary museum objects and what they are supposed to represent. Tertiary museum objects are objects that are in the museum, that do not directly have relevance for the exhibition, but that nevertheless influence the way in which the exhibition is received by the visitors – such as CCTV cameras, signs for emergency exits, or fire extinguishers. Video testimonies are generally used as a combination of the three: they stand for themselves as self-explanatory museum objects; they serve as secondary museum objects for other objects; and the choice of device on which they are shown and their aesthetics have some bearing on the reception of the exhibition by the visitors. Using selected examples, in what follows I will reflect on those three functions of video testimonies in more depth.

So far few museums have decided to base their exhibitions exclusively on video testimonies. An exception is the Museo Diffuso, which has already been mentioned above. In the Museo Diffuso, there is only one museum text – a time line of the war that is barely readable – and two objects – an execution chair and a printing press used by partisan groups. The main exhibition objects are video testimonies and videos with archival footage. In this museum, the video testimonies are exhibited as primary museum objects and carry the exhibition narrative.

In most museums however, video testimonies are shown in conjunction with material objects, documents, and pictures. They are placed in relation to the latter and used to comment on them. For the objects in what he calls "memorial museums," Paul Williams has observed that, "in a sense, it is the story that is the object, insofar as it is not the item itself that is distinctive, but the associated history to which it is attached" (2007, 133).

This accounts for most objects in museums of contemporary history. Video testimonies are a particularly pertinent means to reveal this story. Thus, the Jewish Museum in London, for example, has based its exhibition chapter on the Holocaust almost exclusively on the story of Leon Greenman, a survivor of six concentration camps whose wife and son died in Auschwitz. In the middle of the exhibition, a glass case shows some personal belongings of Greenman and his family such as his son's toy truck, his wife's wedding dress, and his camp uniform. In the film, Greenman talks about these objects. As I have shown elsewhere with reference to examples in Yad Vashem and in the Bergen-Belsen Memorial, the objects and the video testimonies are here placed in a relationship of mutual authentication (De Jong 2011b; 2012; 2013).

As observed above, witnesses to history have been accepted as legitimate carriers of cultural memory. This legitimation is based on the perceived authenticity of their testimonies. Witnesses to history have physically been at the events on which they give testimony. Their presence in time and place authenticates their testimonies given subsequently. In the case of video testimonies with Holocaust survivors such as Leon Greenman, the "authentic" character of the testimonies is reinforced by the extraordinary brutality of their experiences. "While treacherous happiness is easily suspected to be a masquerade, in pain, man appears as an untainted being that is not bound to any rules of orchestration," observes Helmut Lethen (1996, 221). The suffering of Holocaust survivors is supposed to have left uncontrollable traces on their psyche – it is supposed to have traumatized them. The most pertinent extra-verbal expressions of testimony referred to above – such as tears, lapsing into silence, and uncontrollable twitches – are interpreted as an expression of this trauma (De Jong 2013, 23). The juxtaposition of objects and video testimonies in which witnesses to history speak about those objects duplicates the "authentic" character both of the witnesses to history and of the objects. The material reality of the objects and the represented authenticity of the video testimonies meld. We believe Greenman's story because we see the historical objects, while the testimony authenticates the objects as originals.

FIGURE 4.3   View of exhibition section on the beat generation in the Haus der Geschichte.
© Steffi de Jong.

Generally, however, the link between video testimonies and objects is less direct – but no less effective for that. In the Haus der Geschichte in Bonn, visitors are presented with video testimonies on topics like the end of World War II, flight and displacement, the June 17, 1953 uprising in East Germany, or the construction of the Berlin Wall, and also, for example, the foundation of the Green Party or the beat generation. The most prominent object in the exhibition section on the beat generation is a pink VW bus with a rainbow ceiling. On the wall, videos show popular bands of the time, fashion shows, important political events such as the Vietnam War, influential figures like Martin Luther King, Jr., and Che Guevara, as well as student demonstrations (see Figure 4.3). Through different sensory means, the visitor is affectively drawn into the time of the flower-power generation.

A combination of original objects, film footage, and video testimonies is often supposed to create an "authentic" experience for visitors. They are invited to become witnesses to history themselves. Thus, Dorit Harel, who designed the new exhibition in Yad Vashem, writes of one of the many reconstructions in the museum that "authentic cobblestones of Leszno Street in the Warsaw Ghetto, surrounded by its sights and sounds, authentic artefacts, enlarged film-montage from the period, blow-up photographs, and other multidisciplinary means … generate an experience that is close to authentic" (2010, 42).

Such an "authentic" experience, while it might be intended, can never be complete. Visitors are hardly ever made to forget that they are in a museum. Being temporally distant from the events, they never completely fit in. Video testimonies can reinforce this dual character of the visitors' experience. While they link the objects to lived stories, thus facilitating immersion in the period, they also remind the visitors that the time that is represented – whether good or bad – is over. They are often used to offer an interpretation of this time in hindsight. All but one of the witnesses to history in the Haus der Geschichte have cut their long hair and discarded their hippy clothes. The testimonies focus on the political impact of the beat generation, especially in East Germany. For example, East and West German participants of the Youth Meeting in East Berlin in 1963 remember how the youth movements influenced East and West German politics to the point that the Beatles could be played on East German youth radio and the government started to actively target the youth. Many of the witnesses to history romanticize the time when they were young rebels, with long hair and miniskirts, living in communes. Some, however, criticize the relationship between consumption and the beat generation. Thus, Günter Zint, a photographer, observes that everything from long-haired wigs to Indian necklaces was marketed and that the beat generation's incorporation into the capitalist system in fact killed their ideals. Zint unmasks the myth of an alternative lifestyle that surrounds the hippies, of which objects like the VW bus and the bands are symbols. Visitors are, here, turned partly into participants and partly into observers. The VW bus, the music and pictures from the time, and the video testimonies invite the visitors to immerse themselves in the past. At the same time, the video testimonies also serve as critical "museum text" to the other exhibits.

Besides objects, photographs and film documents are the most frequently used exhibits in museums on contemporary history. If objects appear as authentic because they have been involved in events of the past, photographs and film are often perceived as a window onto the past. Paul Williams observes, critically, that "although the camera was undeniably present, it is a notable initial paradox that, in the museum context, photographs are typically viewed as interpretive illustrations rather than as objects that existed in the world at the time" (2007, 51).

Lately there has been some criticism of an undertheorized use of photographs in museums (Brink 1998; Thiemeyer 2010). Nevertheless, photographs are mostly presented as a reproduction of the past rather than as a representation and interpretation based on a particular device – the camera – and on the point of view of a particular individual – the photographer. Video testimonies are often juxtaposed with photographs or film documents from the time. Occasionally, photographs and film documents are included in the video testimonies themselves, mostly to comment on or illustrate what the witnesses are talking about and vice versa. For example, in the Haus der Geschichte the visitor can watch a video testimony from the mason Lothar Wesner, who was ordered to build the Berlin Wall. The video testimony starts with Wesner relating how he was brought to the corner of

Friedrichstraße and Zimmerstraße and started to build under supervision. While Wesner is telling this, the viewer sees some documentary footage, starting with a shot of a soldier and then of some masons building the wall. The origin of the film footage, and whether the mason on the footage is actually Lothar Wesner or the street the Friedrichstraße, is nowhere revealed. Again, the video testimony and the film footage mutually authenticate each other. The film footage serves as an illustration of Wesner's testimony.

However, video testimonies and film and photographs can also be used to critically reflect on one another. In its section on German reunification, the Haus der Geschichte shows, among other things, a video testimony from the German political singer Wolf Biermann, who was stripped of his East German citizenship while on tour in West Germany in 1976. Biermann recalls here how people laughed at Helmut Kohl's metaphor of the "blooming landscapes" that East Germany would be turned into. "That fat Kohl was proved right," he comments; "it took a bit longer, it cost a bit more … So what, that's good. I am glad that we have this problem rather than another." The other witnesses to history that are shown – all of them politicians – agree with Biermann in their positive evaluation of German unification. Right next to the video testimony, the museum shows the cycle of photographs *Unterwegs im Beitrittsgebiet* (En route through the accession region) that the West German photographer Michael Rutschky took during several journeys into East Germany between 1989 and 1993. The photographs show anything but blooming landscapes: factories, desolate houses, desperate graffiti, poverty, and the process of renovation. The testimony and the photographs here have an illustrative, but also a corrective effect on each other. The photographs suggest that it took – and still takes – time to turn East Germany into an economically blooming landscape. The video testimony relativizes the rather negative impression given by the photographs.

The examples that I have given here are, of course, not exhaustive. Each exhibition using video testimonies is different, and so are the epistemological associations that are made with other museum objects. What the examples show, however, is how video testimonies are used as representatives of the past in their own right as well as critical or affirmative comments on other exhibits. Video testimonies are used to place objects within a framework of lived history that illustrates what the object is supposed to represent. The juxtaposition of video testimonies and other museum exhibits can thereby serve a function of mutual authentication. It can also invite critical evaluation. Both uses, as the example of the exhibition section on the beat generation in the Haus der Geschichte shows, are not necessarily mutually exclusive. Video testimonies can be used to illustrate and authenticate, and at the same time to relativize.

I observed earlier that video testimonies can serve as design elements. Video testimonies are still most prominently used in Holocaust and World War II museums. In many Holocaust and World War II museums, an "aesthetic of horror" has been adopted, with the use of dark colors and large bare spaces – often made of concrete. The dark, monochromatic background that is chosen, and the gray or black stelae that the screens are built into, underline these aesthetics. For example in the Museo Diffuso, located in the cellar of an eighteenth-century palazzo, the stelae almost disappear in the darkened space. How much this gloomy atmosphere has become the standard and how much the aesthetics of video testimonies can serve to underline them becomes apparent when looking at counterexamples. In the Neuengamme Memorial, a former concentration camp memorial in northern Germany, the curators have decided against the aesthetic of horror.[5] Consequently, the walls in the old stone barracks in which the exhibitions are located are white and the rooms bright. The video testimonies, many of which were recorded in the 1990s, at a time when a standard aesthetic for video testimonies had not yet been developed, show the witnesses to history in a homely environment such as their living room. The video testimonies therefore underline the comparatively inviting aesthetic of the Neuengamme Memorial. Moreover, while the elaborate video testimonies in museums like the Museo Diffuso tend to make the witnesses to history appear as part of a series, the less sophisticated videos showing them in their home environment further help to present witnesses to history as individuals with a specific history living in a very specific memorial context.[6]

Video testimonies as didactic means

Because of their perceived authenticity and the fact that they combine visual elements with textual elements, video testimonies serve as particularly potent didactic means. The witnesses' testimonies have a bearing on the narrative of the exhibition – or even carry this narrative completely, as in the case of the Museo Diffuso. Through their selection of the particular video testimonies from the collection, and of the extracts from those videos, to include in the exhibition, curators can – and do – structure and model the narrative of the video testimonies and the messages that are transmitted to visitors. Generally speaking, there are three basic messages: video testimonies are used to transmit historical knowledge to visitors, to give them moral lessons, and to affect them. Using the Haus der Geschichte as an example, I will analyze the use of video testimonies as didactic means.

First, since witnesses to history have been physically and temporally part of the events that they testify to, their testimonies are used to transmit historical knowledge to visitors. This is especially the case when alternative documentation is missing. In particular, video testimonies of Holocaust survivors are used to testify to the prisoners' life in the camps, as alternative documents are often missing. However, the teaching of history with the help of video testimonies does not stop here. Through the selection of extracts and the way in which those extracts are arranged, curators also guide visitors' interpretation of historical information. In particular, the last sentences, those that conclude the video testimony, are meticulously chosen. Thus, in the Haus der Geschichte, Carola Stern, who in 1945 was a leader in the League of German Girls and later a journalist, remembers that, when they were told by some soldiers that "the Führer has fallen in the battle of the Reich Chancellery," her mother burst into tears and her cousin cried: "Now there is no sense in life anymore." She, however, told them: "Are you crazy? Do you believe what he is saying? That man has taken his own life. He has left us alone in the dirt and escaped. That's the truth!" It does not matter whether Carola Stern really grasped the situation this well at the time – it seems unlikely, since she was a young girl who obviously believed in the National Socialist project and was surrounded by people who did. What is important is that, with her testimony, Carola Stern both forecloses a heroic interpretation of Hitler's death and interprets her mother's and cousin's behavior as irrational and futile.

In another video the American soldier La Verne Keats relates that, when he first heard about Dachau, he could hardly believe "that a people like the Germans with all of their education, would permit something like this to happen." In order to understand, he and his fellow soldiers started questioning the prisoners. He concludes his testimony with the sentence: "I could hardly sympathize with the German soldiers anymore because with their fighting they had supported this regime." La Verne Keats's testimony corrects the image of the clean Wehrmacht which has for a long time been prominent in Germany. This image was finally challenged in the 1990s by the exhibition *Vernichungskrieg: Verbrechen der Wehrmacht 1941–1944* (War of annihilation: Crimes of the Wehrmacht 1941–1944). The exhibition toured 33 German and Austrian cities between 1995 and 1999 and can be seen as a turning point in German memorial culture. The exhibition, which documented crimes committed by ordinary Wehrmacht soldiers, shattered the ideas that many Germans had about their fathers and grandfathers. It met with protests and vandalism from right-wing extremists and became a subject of political debate in every city where it was shown. In 1999 the exhibition eventually had to close down, because of criticism relating to an incorrect attribution of photographs. A revised version opened again in 2001 under the title *Verbrechen der Wehrmacht: Dimensionen des Vernichtungskrieges 1941–1944* (Crimes of the Wehrmacht: Dimensions of the war of annihilation 1941–1944; see Williams 2007, 59; Musial 2011). La Verne Keats's testimony can be seen as an extension to, and final word on, the debate on the exhibition: he accuses not only those soldiers who actively took part in the crimes, but all soldiers who, in their fighting, all supported a criminal regime.

In a video testimony on the construction of the Berlin Wall, Dorothee Wilms defends then chancellor Konrad Adenauer's much criticized decision not to travel to Berlin. She observes that she understands Adenauer's decision, that he could not have done much, that Berlin was still occupied territory, and that this was a question that had to be resolved by the four victorious powers. Moreover, the situation was so heated that a war seemed imminent. Visitors are, therefore, not only given the information that Hitler committed suicide, that the camps were liberated by the Allies, and that Adenauer did not travel to Berlin, but they are also guided in their evaluation of those events.

Second, because they show individuals who can reflect on the past, video testimonies are used to give moral lessons and to transmit norms and values. In the Haus der Geschichte, again, the German writer Wolfgang Held remembers his visit to Buchenwald concentration camp as a 15-year-old boy. He remembers seeing masses of bodies and fleeing terrified from a barrack where he found people lying on pallets, like corpses, only their eyes revealing that they were alive. When he was standing there, crying, a survivor tapped him on the shoulder and said: "Junge, mit Heulen, das ist zu wenig" (Boy – sniveling is not enough). Everything that he has written since emanates from this sentence, he says. Held's testimony both instructs (German) visitors that nothing can redeem the major crimes of the past and, at the same time, invites them to become active citizens – like Held himself who today acts not only as a writer but also as a kind of professional witness to history.

In a video testimony on European integration, the curators try to transmit some form of European conscience or European identity to their (German) visitors. Here, Hans-Gert Pöttering, former president of the European Parliament reflects on the opening of borders:

> In the past, borders were something that divided and when borders were trespassed it was soldiers who trespassed those borders and the outcome were misery, poverty, death. It was war. And today border controls are abolished. ... It is something wonderful, historically new. And today Czechs and Poles are welcome here and we are welcome in Poland. And this links us Europeans together and this makes us also stronger in a sense. That we are a community of values.

Incidentally, the exhibition does not mention the fact that Germany opted to restrict Polish citizens' access to the German labor market for the maximum period of seven years after Poland joined the European Union. Dorotee Wilms again observes that some things might not please everyone, but that European integration is a historical stroke of luck for Germany. The former German minister Hans-Jochen Vogel advances the eternally repeated argument that young people, used to a united Europe, might take peace for granted, but that for his generation war was the norm. In this way, not only do the witnesses to history serve as history teachers, but the video testimonies are also used to turn the visitors into active members of civil society – and into good Europeans.

Finally, by relating what it felt like to go through certain experiences, video testimonies are used to educate the visitors emotionally. The extracts selected for the exhibitions are not only the most interesting, but often also the most touching. Thus, Lothar Wesner, the mason who helped to build the Berlin Wall, remembers being disturbed and thinking that he was now contributing to something that would prevent him from seeing his family. When he went home at night he would be so distressed that his mother and his wife said to him, "Junge, wie siehst du den aus?!" (Boy, what a sight you are?!). The former minister Rainer Eppelman talks about "wall sickness," a psychological condition that seemingly befell people who were living close to the wall. He observes that the idea that "you can't get out of here" must have been traumatic for many people. Visitors are not only made aware of the psychological consequences of historical events, but also invited to empathize with the witnesses to history. The intention may be to make them evaluate the present positively compared to the past. It may also be to prevent them from doing something similar in the future; this is especially the intention in holocaust museums.

The ultimate goal of most museums of contemporary history today is not only to instruct their visitors on the past, but also to turn them into active citizens. Video testimonies are used as a means toward this goal. In the case of Holocaust survivors, the term "secondary witnessing" has been used to describe the transmission of the testimonies from one generation to another in order to make sure that "we never forget" (Baer 2000). In Holocaust museums which do not function only as historical museums but also as memorials to the victims, survivors make up the largest group of the witnesses to history that are presented. Only occasionally can video testimonies with so-called bystanders be found, while perpetrators never appear. The witnesses to history in Holocaust museums are rarely prominent individuals. They are generally presented as ordinary individuals to whom the average visitor can easily relate. In the Haus der Geschichte, where one of the main goals is to turn visitors into active German citizens, another practice can be observed. The museum presents very few video testimonies with what we would call "ordinary citizens." Most of the witnesses to history here are prominent actors, writers, journalists, and politicians. Those witnesses to history are, because of their status and their proximity to decision centers, particularly authoritative teachers of history and morals. They also serve as role models for visitors, who are invited to become historically interested and politically active citizens.

Conclusion

Video testimonies have thus become the subject of musealization. While they have been collection items for around 35 years, they have recently also been introduced into museum's permanent exhibitions. This process of the musealization of video testimonies represents an attempt to turn communicative memory into cultural memory. While, in past times, communicative memory has been in natural decay, we are now trying to preserve it for the future. The availability of technology to store communicative memory is not the only factor here. How we choose to use the technology is also significant. The interest in recording the memories of individuals is, as I have shown, a consequence of a change in the perception of the individual as an authoritative carrier of memory, which first became evident at the Eichmann trial. For the purpose of storage, communicative memory is standardized – it is put into the format of the narrative interview. The narrative interview is supposed to lead to a particularly pure narration of individual memory.

The methodology of the narrative interview, combined with aesthetic choices highlighting the extra-verbal expressions of memory, leads to a representation of individual memory as existing outside time and space.

While collected video testimonies become storage memory, video testimonies are turned into functional memory once they are used in museums' exhibitions. They are exhibited as testimonies to the past and to illustrate and authenticate, or comment on, other museum exhibits. Documents provide information on what happened. Objects and photographs show what it looked like. Video testimonies simultaneously inform visitors what happened, how it was lived through, what it felt like, and how it is remembered. This combination of different potential narratives makes video testimony a particularly potent didactic means. Video testimonies can be used to transmit historical knowledge, to instruct visitors on how to interpret this knowledge, to give them moral lessons, and to affect them. To come back to the painting described in the introduction: video testimonies have now become an additional or alternative means to material remains, documents, and museum text or museum guides of transmitting history. However, as the painting in Figure 4.1 shows, any transmission of history is embedded in a sociocultural context. Cultural memory is always the expression of a particular time and place. In the painting, the history of the Battle of Kursk is related by a Russian colonel to Allied soldiers only. The German Wehrmacht officer is allowed only to overhear this history lesson, not to take active part in it – let alone to have a say. The same is, of course, true of the use of video testimonies in museums. Only a fraction of the potential witnesses to history are interviewed at all, and the testimonies that those witnesses to history give are tainted by their sociocultural context and guided by the questions of the interviewer. Of all of the possible extracts from those video testimonies, only some meticulously selected stories enter a particular museum's exhibition and are used as functional memory. Which ones are chosen depends on the particular museum and the period in which the exhibition has been designed.

Notes

1 Yale University Library, Fortunoff Video Archive for Holocaust Testimonies, at http://www.library.yale.edu/testimonies/ (accessed August 4, 2014).
2 See the Yad Vashem Archive at http://www.yadvashem.org/yv/en/about/archive/about_archive_whats_in_archive.asp (accessed July 23, 2014).
3 All translations of source material are the author's.
4 Author's interview with James Barker, producer of the video testimonies for the Imperial War Museum's *Holocaust Exhibition*, September 10, 2009.
5 Author's interview with Detlef Garbe, Director, Neuengamme Memorial, December 12, 2009.
6 For a similar argument on video testimonies in TV documentaries, see Bösch (2008, 68), and also De Jong (2013, 37).

References

Arendt, Hannah. 1994. *Eichmann in Jerusalem: A Report on the Banality of Evil.* New York: Penguin.

Assmann, Aleida. 2006. *Der lange Schatten der Vergangenheit: Erinnerungskultur und Geschichtspolitik* [The long shadow of the past: Memory culture and the politics of history]. Munich: C. H. Beck.

Assmann, Jan. 1992. *Das kulturelle Gedächtnis: Schrift, Erinnerung und politische Identität in frühen Hochkulturen.* Munich: C. H. Beck. Translated as *Cultural Memory and Early Civilization: Writing, Remembrance, and Political Imagination.* Cambridge: Cambridge University Press, 2011.

Assmann, Jan, and John Czaplicka. 1995. "Collective Memory and Cultural Identity." *New German Critique* 65: 125–133.

Baer, Ulrich. 2000. "Einleitung" [Introduction]. In *Niemand zeugt für den Zeugen: Erinnerungskultur nach der Shoa* [No one bears witness for the witnesses: Memory culture after the Shoah], edited by Ulrich Baer, 7–31. Frankfurt: Suhrkamp.

Baranowski, Daniel, ed. 2009. *"Ich bin die Stimme der sechs Millionen": Das Videoarchiv im Ort der Information* ["I am the voice of the six milion": The video archive in the place of information]. Berlin: Stiftung Denkmal für die Ermordeten Juden Europas.

Bardgett, Suzanne. n.d. "The Use of Oral History in the Imperial War Museum's Holocaust Exhibition." Unpublished paper, available from the Imperial War Museum.

Bösch, Frank. 2008. "Geschichte mit Gesicht. Zur Genese des Zeitzeugen in Holocaust-Dokumentationen seit den 1950er Jahren" [History with a face: On the evolution of witnesses in Holocaust documentaries since the 1950s]. In *Alles Authentisch? Popularisierung der Geschichte im Fernsehen* [Is it all authentic? The popularization of history on television], edited by Thomas Fischer and Rainer Wirtz, 51–69. Konstanz, Germany: Universitätsverlag Konstanz.

Brink, Cornelia. 1998. *Ikonen der Vernichtung: Öffentlicher Gebrauch von Fotografien aus nationalsozialistischen Konzentrationslagern nach 1945* [Icons of destruction: The public use of photographs of Nazi concentration camps after 1945]. Berlin: Akademie.

Deblinger, Rachel. 2012. "Holocaust Memory in Displaced Persons Camps." In *After the Holocaust: Challenging the Myth of Silence*, edited by David Cesarani and Eric J. Sundquist, 115–126. London: Routledge.

de Jong, Steffi. 2011a. "Is This Us? The Construction of European Woman/Man in the Exhibition *It's Our History!*" *Culture Unbound* 3: 369–383. Accessed July 23, 2014. http://www.cultureunbound.ep.liu.se/v3/a24/.

de Jong, Steffi. 2011b. "Bewegte Objekte: Zur Musealisierung des Zeitzeugen" [Moving objects: On the musealization of the witness]. In *Politik der Zeugenschaft* [The politics of witnessing], edited by Sibylle Schmidt, Sibylle Krämer, and Ramon Voges, 243–264. Bielefeld, Germany: transcript.

de Jong, Steffi. 2012. "Who is History? The Use of Autobiographical Accounts in History Museums." In *Museums and Biographies: Stories, Objects, Identities*, edited by Kate Hill, 295–308. Woodbridge, UK: Boydell & Brewer.

de Jong, Steffi. 2013. "Im Spiegel der Geschichten: Objekte und Zeitzeugenvideos in Museen des Holocaust und des Zweiten Weltkrieges" [In the mirror of stories: Objects and video testimonies in Holocaust and World War II museums]. *Werkstatt Geschichte* 62: 19–41.

Elm, Michael. 2008. *Zeugenschaft im Film: Eine Erinnerungskulturelle Analyse filmischer Erzählungen des Holocaust* [Witnessing in film: A cultural memory analysis of cinematic narratives of the Holocaust]. Berlin: Metropol.

Erll, Astrid. 2005. *Kollektives Gedächtnis und Erinnerungskulturen* [Collective memory and memory cultures]. Stuttgart: J. B. Metzler.

Fayet, Roger. 2007. "Das Vokabular der Dinge" [The vocabulary of things]. *Österreichische Zeitschrift für Geschichtswissenschaften* 18: 7–31.

Fischer, Thomas. 2008. "Erinnern und Erzählen: Zeitzeugen im Geschichts-TV" [Remembering and telling: Witnesses on history television]. In *Alles Authentisch? Popularisierung der Geschichte im Fernsehen* [Is it all authentic? The popularization of history on television], edited by Thomas Fischer and Rainer Wirtz, 33–49. Konstanz, Germany: Universitätsverlag Konstanz.

Garbe, Detlef. 1994. "Das KZ-Neuengamme" [The Neuengamm concentration camp]. In *Überlebensgeschichten, Gespräche mit Überlebenden des KZ-Neuengamme* [Survival stories, talking with survivors of the Neuengamm concentration camp], edited by Ulrike Jureit and Karin Orth, 16–43. Hamburg: Dölling & Galitz.

Gring, Diana, and Karin Theilen. 2007. "Fragmente der Erinnerung" [Fragments of memory]. In *AugenZeugen: Fotos, Filme und Zeitzeugenberichte in der neuen Dauerausstellung der Gedenkstätte Bergen-Belsen: Hintergrund und Kontext* [Eyewitness: Photos, films, and witness testimonies in the new permanent exhibition of the Bergen-Belsen Memorial: Background and context], edited by Rainer Schulze and Wilfried Wiedemann, 153–216. Celle, Germany: Stiftung Niedersächsische Gedenkstätten.

Harel, Dorit. 2010. *Facts and Feelings: Dilemmas in Designing the Yad Vashem Holocaust History Museum.* Jerusalem: Yad Vashem.

Hartman, Geoffrey H. 1996. *The Longest Shadow: In the Aftermath of the Holocaust.* Bloomington: Indiana University Press.

Jungblut, Karen. 2005. "Survivors of the Shoah Visual History Foundation: An Analytical Retrospective of the Foundation's Collection Phase." In *NS-Gewaltherrschaft* [Nazi tyranny], edited by Alfred Gottwald, Norbert Kampe, and Peter Klein, 508–519. Berlin: Hentrich.

Jureit, Ulrike. 1999. *Zur Methodik lebensgeschichtlicher Interviews mit Überlebenden der Konzentrations- und Vernichtungslager* [On the methodology of oral history interviews with survivors of concentration and extermination camps]. Hamburg: Ergebnisse.

Jureit, Ulrike, and Christian Schneider. 2010. *Gefühlte Opfer: Illusionen der Vergangeheitsbewältigung* [Perceived victims: Illusions of coming to terms with the past]. Stuttgart: Klett-Cotta.

Kansteiner, Wulf. 2012. "Aufstieg und Abschied des NS-Zeitzeugen in den Geschichtsdoumentationen des ZDF" [The rise and decline of witnesses of National Socialism in the documentaries of the ZDF]. In *Die Geburt des Zeitzeugen nach 1945*

[The birth of the witness after 1945], edited by Martin Sabrow and Norbert Frei, 320–353. Göttingen, Germany: Wallstein.

Keilbach, Judith. 2008. *Geschichtsbilder und Zeitzeugen: Zur Darstellung des Nationalsozialismus im Bundesdeutschen Fernsehen* [Images of history and witnesses: The representation of National Socialism on federal German television]. Münster, Germany: Lit.

Lethen, Helmut. 1996. "Versionen des Authentischen: sechs Gemeinplätze" [Versions of authenticity: Six truisms]. In *Literatur und Kulturwissenschaften: Positionen, Theorien, Modelle* [Literature and cultural studies: Positions, theories, models], edited by Hartmut Böhme and Klaus R. Scherpe, 205–231. Reinbeck, Germany: Rowohlt.

Musial, Bogdan. 2011. "Der Bildersturm: Aufstieg und Fall der ersten Wehrmachtsausstellung" [Iconoclasm: The rise and fall of the first Wehrmacht exhibition]. *Deutschland Archiv* 1. Accessed July 23, 2014. http://www.bpb.de/geschichte/zeitgeschichte/deutschlandarchiv/53181/die-erste-wehrmachtsausstellung.

Pomian, Krzysztof. 1990. *Collectors and Curiosities: Origins of the Museum.* Oxford: Polity.

Preisler, Maximilian. 1998. "Narrativer Prozess und Subjektkonstruktion in Überlebensgeschichten" [Narrative process and subject construction in survival stories]. In *Archiv der Erinnerung: Interviews mit Überlebenden der Shoah* [Archives of memory: Interviews with survivors of the Shoah], edited by Cathy Gelbin, Eva Lezzi, and Geoffrey Hartman. Potsdam, Germany: Verlag für Berlin-Brandenburg.

Sabrow, Martin, and Norbert Frei, eds. 2012. *Die Geburt des Zeitzeugen nach 1945* [The birth of the witness after 1945]. Göttingen, Germany: Wallstein.

Thiemeyer, Thomas. 2010. *Fortsetzung des Krieges mit anderen Mitteln: Die beiden Weltkriege im Museum* [Continuation of war by other means: The two world wars in the museum]. Paderborn, Germany: Schöningh.

Thießen, Malte. 2008. "Gedächtnisgeschichte: Neue Forschungen zur Entstehung und Tradierung von Erinnerung" [History and memory: New research on the emergence and transmission of memory]. *Archiv für Sozialgeschichte* 48: 607–634.

Welzer, Harald. 2000. "Das Interview als Artefakt: Zur Kritik und Zeitzeugenforschung" [The interview as artifact: Toward a critique of the methods of oral history]. *BIOS: Zeitschrift für Biographieforschung und Oral History* 13: 51–63.

Welzer, Harald. 2011. "Für eine Modernisierung der Erinnerungs- und Gedenkkultur" [For a modernization of remembrance and memorial culture]. *Gedenkstättenrundbrief* 162: 3–9.

Wierling, Dorothée. 2003. "Oral History." In *Aufriss der Historischen Wissenschaft. Neue Themen und Methoden der Geschichtswissenschaft* [The rise of historical science: New themes and methods of historical research], vol. 7, edited by Michael Maurer, 81–151. Stuttgart: Reclam.

Wieviorka, Annette. (1998) 2006. *The Era of the Witness.* Ithaca, NY: Cornell University Press.

Williams, Paul. 2007. *Memorial Museums: The Global Rush to Commemorate Atrocities.* Oxford: Berg.

Yablonka, Hanna. 2012. "Die Bedeutung der Zeugenaussagen im Prozess gegen Adolf Eichmann" [The importance of witness testimonies in the trial of Adolf Eichmann].

In *Die Geburt des Zeitzeugen nach 1945* [The birth of the witness after 1945], edited by Martin Sabrow and Norbert Frei, 176–189. Göttingen, Germany: Wallstein.

Young, James E. 1988. *Writing and Rewriting the Holocaust.* Bloomington: Indiana University Press.

Steffi de Jong works as a research assistant at the Historical Institute of the University of Cologne. Her research interests cover memory studies, museum studies, public history, sound studies, and European cultural politics. She holds a PhD from the Norwegian University of Science and Technology where she was a collaborator in the international research project *Exhibiting Europe.* In her PhD thesis she analyzes the representation of video testimonies in Holocaust and World War II museums.

5 VISIBLE AND INVISIBLE INSTITUTIONS
Cinema in the French Art Museum

Jenny Chamarette

No medium is ever completely replaced by another. Newspapers, radio, television persist in the age of the World Wide Web. Newer, more glamorous technologies still glimmer with mysterious and sensual ancestors. The ghosts lurking even in state-of-the-art devices remind us of the major challenge still confronting the age of trans- everything.

Stafford 2001, 1

Public space [… is a] political present which is constantly transformed, in its structure and its content, by the teletechnology of what is so confusedly called information or communication.

Derrida and Stiegler 2002, 3

[F]rom the inside, the museum effaces itself to become an invisible frame for the art or artifacts it appears merely to house, conserve and exhibit. To recognize that the institution itself produces meaning, we need to widen our focus to see its active framing of its contents and our experience.

Pollock 2007, 1

Cinema and film partake of a curious, sensuous circulation of media: the ghosts of media, past and present, are well documented by museum curators and film archivists. Film technologies make their ghostly presence felt in the proliferation of online, digital moving images that seem to embody our twenty-first-century moment. Technologies of cinema have, in fact, consistently overlapped, since the emergence of highly flammable cellulose nitrate prints, right up to contemporary digital and CGI-enhanced moving images: older optical illusions established in the late nineteenth century are still functional principles in film narratives and

The International Handbooks of Museum Studies: Museum Media, First Edition.
Edited by Michelle Henning.
© 2015 John Wiley & Sons Ltd. Published 2020 by John Wiley & Sons Ltd.

two-dimensional settings. These technological ghosts, together with the ghostly presence of other times and other places so adeptly represented by cinema and film, have a transformative political potential on the present moment, as Jacques Derrida and Bernd Stiegler point out in their volume of televised interviews, *Echographies of Television* (2002).

It is from here that I take the interpretive thread that runs through each of my case studies in this chapter: Derrida and Stiegler's book, a transcript of filmed television interviews, acknowledges that visibility and invisibility are useful and subtle modes of expressing the spectral haunting of moving image media (television) by other moving image media (film). Derrida writes:

> the specter is first and foremost something visible. It is of the visible, but of the invisible visible, it is the visibility of a body which is not present in flesh and blood. It resists the intuition towards which it presents itself, it is not *tangible*. (Derrida and Stiegler 2002, 115)

Derrida and Stiegler discuss visibility and invisibility specifically with relation to the terminology of ghosts and phantoms in contemporary media, drawing attention to the etymological relationship between the ghostly specter and the spectacle, the phantom and the "vision" or "apparition." Here, I argue that if contemporary moving image media technologies, housed and exhibited within museums, contain the ghosts of earlier technologies, then these ghosts also destabilize the position from which it becomes possible to understand their political impact on museums as public spaces.

Moving images are a way of archiving the past, but the media through which these images are transmitted, communicated, publicized, and viewed, are also in themselves objects whose gradual obsolescence affords only a small number of them entry into museum collections. Consequently, the phenomenological appearance of film can become an object worthy of attention within the museum space, or a means of drawing attention to specific elements of the museum space. In other words, film can be exhibited or stored within the museum, or it can itself exhibit or archive the past spaces of the museum (and sometimes it does both). Consequently, film shifts between its "visible" presence as a constitutive element of museums' public spaces, and its "invisible" absence as a provocation or critique of a museum space that seeks to exclude it. Visibility and invisibility are not absolute values in this theoretical sense, but rather they are ways of discussing the dynamics of what is seen within a public space – and, specifically in this instance, the museum space – and by whom. The "invisibility" which Griselda Pollock notes in her assessment of Suzanne Oberhardt's work on the ideologies of museum scholarship and practice (see epigraph above) refers to ideological, political, and contextual framing (Pollock 2007; Oberhardt 2001). In this chapter, I argue the case that both metaphorical and literal shifts of focus and frame created by cinema in the museum eliminate some aspects of the museum from the perceptual field while highlighting others. These aspects are also subject to and affected by changes in the tangible materiality of cinema as an object, an experience, an exhibition space, and a cultural institution.

Through these ideas of ghostly traces, and the framing of visibility and invisibility, this chapter explores the intertwining of the institution of cinema through film technologies, and the institution of the museum through its public spaces and cultural politics. Rather than imagining film as a *medium* in the technological or communicative sense, the chapter examines the politics of film as a mediator, negotiator, or indeed even critic of museum spaces and museum politics. This chapter focuses primarily on film as an exhibition or curatorial practice, to interrogate the ways in which film and cinema usefully explore and contest the spaces of the contemporary art museum. I am interested in issues of institutional visibility and invisibility in the sense in which Derrida and Stiegler explore it: how examples of film exhibition practices *in* museums have exerted political force over public representations *of* museums, and how examples of museum films, and film exhibitions within the museum, have tacitly or explicitly exposed the cultural politics of established institutions, via ongoing and evolving museological critiques.

I draw attention to the ways in which moving images are made present and visible in the contemporary French art museum, with a specific focus on the Centre Georges Pompidou in Paris (known locally as Beaubourg or the Pompidou, and in English as the Pompidou Center), a modern art museum established under the auspices of post-1968 France, which envisaged a museum founded on democratic and egalitarian principles, open (and visible) to all. Via a number of examples from throughout the historical development of the Pompidou, I explore the visibility of film as an exhibited object, and by extension the visibility of the institution of cinema, *within* the institutional housing of the museum. I build on earlier examples of filmmaking in museums, both as conventional film and as film installations for museum exhibition, including the work of Roberto Rossellini and Jean-Luc Godard, to reflect on the cultural dynamics that have brought cinema into the museum. In particular, I consider these issues via films and film exhibitions which have, either directly or indirectly, interrogated the cultural politics of museum institutions in France. I explore the ways in which curatorial politics and cultural policy in France have shaped the orientations of the moving image in the contemporary French museum.

The particular choice of a French context is not incidental: in museum studies, as in art historical studies of the moving image, there has been a tendency in English-speaking research communities to focus predominantly on anglophone contexts, ignoring the richness of material contexts that lie beyond North America, the United Kingdom, and Australia. Furthermore, since France is the historic birthplace of cinema, and its policies of "cultural exception" and cultural diplomacy still promote French cinema as a distinctive and unique contribution to the worldwide moving image, a case study from France reveals in the most concentrated and direct way the political and cultural complexities of the relationship between cinema and the public space of the museum in the twentieth and twenty-first centuries.

Cinema's historical and contemporary privileged position in French cultural heritage also implies that thinking about French museum can inform an understanding of the moving image's conceptual and spatial shift away from "cinema" as such. Cinema as we like to think about it has long since left the auditorium and found itself transmitted across multiple screen media technologies, from the hand-held mobile device to digital streaming, to large-scale screening on tower blocks. Increasingly, cinema, as a mutable institution that defies visible definition, has also made a shift into the "museum": an institution which often courts both physical presence and virtual existence, in add-on digital apps, screen-based interpretation, and online exhibition spaces. Consequently, these case studies become useful opportunities to interrogate the complex political, curatorial, and broader sociocultural concerns with regard to the institutionalized housing of film within the museum, both as a public space and as a political institution. However, before embarking on the particular case studies that inform this chapter, I will first outline the relevant contexts of film beyond the cinema, giving an overview of the significance of film for museum studies, and of the museum for film. In particular, this overview draws attention to the materiality of film as an object, as well as an exhibition mode, an exhibition experience, and a set of cultural values, and the ways in which these might be relevantly discussed in the context of museum studies.

Film studies beyond the cinema, museum studies through the screen: An overview

In addition to temporary exhibitions or even entire museums specifically dedicated to cinema, *cinémathèques*, film archives and libraries, and art museums in particular have explored film's close relationships to other image-making and representational arts. Cinema retains both technological and aesthetic relationships to photography, painting, installation, and performance, and to the modes of exhibition and display through which these works are made visible to the public. Recent global exhibitions have drawn on these relationships in order to explore the contemporary proliferation of the moving image as art, science, and entertainment, as well as its historical and cultural precedents. The *Devices of Wonder* exhibition at the Getty Museum is one example, and the first epigraph of this chapter is drawn from Barbara Maria Stafford's illuminating essay in the exhibition's catalog. Others, such as the *Future Cinema* exhibition at the ZKM (Center for Art and Media) Karlsruhe in 2003 or *Le mouvement des images/The Movement of Images* exhibition at the Pompidou Center in Paris in 2006, explored the complex and multivalent relationships of cinema to technologies, to media, and to art.

There is a growing convergence between, on the one hand, recent curatorial and exhibition practices that have increased the visibility of film and the moving image on display, both within the museum space and as objects in their own right, and, on the other, an evolving interest within film studies in the spaces of film exhibition and preservation, and the futures of cinema. Within these studies, contemporary film scholars and film theorists have sought to respond to material and epistemological claims on the part of conservators and archivists about the "death of cinema": a concept explored and extended by theorists such as Laura Mulvey (2005), and D. N. Rodowick (2007). These responses are shaped by the arguments of film conservators such as Paolo Cherchi Usai, who mourns the loss of recent screen cultures which have disappeared because traditional repositories of rare collections – that is, museums – had failed to support film preservation in a timely manner (Usai 2001).

It is clear that talking about cinema, film, and the museum involves important conceptual, disciplinary, and institutional relationships. This chapter responds to two key questions with regard to these relationships: Why is film relevant to museum studies? And what has propelled film into recent museum contexts? These questions usefully connect the interdisciplinary matrix of concepts that make up contemporary museum studies, to the growing field of research into film archives, preservation, exhibition, and technological multiplicity in film studies.

Several examples of existing research operate effectively in this context, such as the work of Usai, Haidee Wasson (who also contributes to this volume), and Alison Griffiths's fascinating work on immersive spectatorship in cathedrals, planetariums, and natural history museums (Wasson 2005; Griffiths 2008). Broadly speaking, one might categorize the relationships and relevance of film to museums in the following ways:

- film as technology, or archived technologies that mediate moving images;
- film as archive, representation of the past, cultural and historical source;
- film as documentation; social, cultural, or ethnographic study; or anthropological tool;
- film as illustration, education, narrative enhancement of the museum space;
- film as virtual museum (exploring the museum and its objects through film); creating virtual or imaginary museums through film with no brick-and-mortar equivalent;
- film as narrative space; or architectural exploration of the museum's spaces; and
- film as exhibition or curatorial practice.

Inevitably, these relationships overlap with one another, and with other representational media and art forms of the twentieth century. Photography, for example, might well be an equivalent medium that could easily replace the term "film" in some of the categories above.

Just as film is inflected by film cultures, traversed by sociopolitical and cultural currents that shape not only where a film is seen but what visual codes, narratives, and forms inform the public evaluation of a film work, so too are the practices of what kind of cinema goes into museums – what is collected, displayed, exhibited, preserved, archived, and protected – subject to cultural and political histories and ideologies. If it is true that film cultures are migrating, both toward the digital realm and toward the material housing of museums, then the nature of these cultures will also be shaped by the geopolitical and sociocultural conditions of these museums, actual and digital, and their spaces. My analysis of recent and historic examples of cinematic exhibitions and film commissioning in the Pompidou Center probes some of these cultural and sociopolitical specificities. Film becomes a political and ideological object within these contexts, while at the same time being a material, visible *thing* and a form of invisible cultural practice, thus both complicating and concretizing relationships between cinema and the museum in the twenty-first century.

The presence of the moving image as a material object within museum collections and exhibitions continues to be a complex issue in museum studies. One might note a certain tendency to assume that film is illustrative rather than material; that it is a medium-based contextualizer of other objects in collections rather than an object within the collection itself; or that it is a medium of communication and information, its materiality secondary, if acknowledged at all (Sorensen 1989, 71–72; Witcomb 2003, 103–104; 2007). According to some museological trends, then, film is not a material object, but exclusively a mode of transmission. While this tendency very usefully serves a conceptualization of moving image technologies as information-bearing media, it does not deal with the messy, difficult processes of preserving, maintaining, and exhibiting the multifarious, defiantly material historical technologies of the moving image.

Nonetheless, recent scholarship on cinema and the moving image within the museum, archive, and *cinémathèque* is inflected with practical and ontological issues related precisely to the materiality of film as an object. These issues originate in concerns about, for example, the advanced degradation and flammability of improperly washed cellulose nitrate film, or the difficulty of maintaining the technical machinery, and the human expertise, to operate earlier technologies of moving image display.[1] Scholars dealing specifically with film preservation in film archives, rather than in museums as such, initially raised such issues, but their implications have extended even into the most abstract discourses of film theory. For example, Usai's *The Death of Cinema: History, Cultural Memory and the Digital Dark Age* (2001) has become one of the most well-cited texts in the ongoing theoretical debates surrounding the death and/or future of cinema in contemporary film studies. Current debates about the ontological status of film and of cinema have been deeply informed by concerns about the close analysis of the material technologies of filmmaking and film exhibition, the observation of film works currently housed within museum collections or displayed within their permanent and temporary exhibitions, and, more broadly, the role that film archives and film preservation play within the cultural policy of the contemporary museum.

Film studies' concerns with film cultures have also expanded in recent years to address the contexts of film exhibition in museums, relocating histories of film audiences into museum spaces as well as cinema auditoriums. Alongside the work of museums of cinema, film historians and archivists have also sought to reconstruct film-going experience via the paratextual and extra-filmic paraphernalia of film: posters, flyers, merchandising, costumes, and props. The curatorial and archival work, and the preservation of collections at the Cinema Museum in London, the Bill Douglas Centre at the University of Exeter, the National Media Museum in Bradford, the Cinémathèque Française in Paris, and the National Cinema Museum in Turin might be included within this category, as might the Museum of Modern Art in New York, whose particular relationship to film viewing in the twentieth century has been very profitably explored in Haidee Wasson's *Museum Movies: The Museum of Modern Art and the Birth of Art Cinema* (2005). Current thinking about the relationship between cinema and the museum has been informed by recent research on the use of moving image archives for reconstructing cultural history, and their relationships to the museums that house them. Lee Grieveson and Nananda Bose's innovative coedited e-book, *Using Moving Image Archives* (2010), explores this recent resurgent interest in the relationships between film, the archive, and the museum.

Naturally, the interest in audiences, viewing practices, interactivity and engagement that can be found in museum studies scholarship also intersects with concerns about film materials, audiences, and cultures in film studies. Participation is a key concept that crosses boundaries between the cinema and the museum. Thinking about the cultures of viewing and experiencing film, in the museum and in the auditorium, can also help to draw out the links between cinema, on the one hand – a cultural institution, material object, and viewing phenomenon that is barely 120 years old – and the museum, on the other – a cultural history, architectural and structural institution, and politically contested housing of multitudinous objects and interpretations, whose public establishment is centuries old.

The shift toward exhibition practices in film and contemporary art scholarship, in particular in terms of film exhibition in the gallery space, has been described as the "cinematic turn" in art historical research. This cinematic turn is often aligned with theoretical explorations of filmmaking practices outside or beyond the cinema auditorium. Emphasis is placed on the specificity of the gallery space as a site of contemporary art exhibition, as a dynamic and culturally contested environment that sets its own agendas as to how the moving image is experienced. The scholarship of Chrissie Iles, Catherine Fowler, Erika Balsom, and Maeve Connolly has been instrumental in this field, and their focus on the thin line between textual studies of film and art historical studies of moving image installation and artist's cinema has contributed significantly to this emerging area of interest (see Iles 2001; Fowler 2004; Balsom 2009; and Connolly 2009).

However, research in anglophone film studies into "gallery films" has to date focused primarily on an array of English-speaking artists in relation to ostensibly anglophone curatorial practice. Works that fall under such scrutiny often reside in gallery settings in well-known American and British galleries and museums: for instance, Tacita Dean, whose complex and artisanal relationship to film material, and exhibition practices within galleries rather than in conventional cinema theaters is well publicized, or Bill Viola, who has been working with screen practices and exhibition since the 1970s. While much work has been undertaken to date on the intersections between cinema and the museum, there is a risk that the dominant narratives of anglophone scholarship might ignore the cultural specificity of certain kinds of cinema or film cultures in geographically unique museum spaces. By tilting the sphere of inquiry into France, and acknowledging France's very particular cultural history, the focus on the moving image and the museum may take shape rather differently.

Alongside those artists who have always worked with film within the gallery or art space, there are also a demonstrable number of filmmakers best known for their cinema-based works, who have explored screen-based installation both within museums (especially art museums) and within public (and private) art galleries and public art spaces. One such contemporary "movement," if it might be described as such, has taken place in the past decade in public art institutions and spaces in metropolitan France, with works by Jean-Luc Godard, Agnès Varda, Abbas Kiarostami, David Lynch, and Chantal Akerman being exhibited in recent years. The emergence of this phenomenon, and a specific analysis of Godard's exhibition, will be discussed in the later sections of this chapter.

Setting the scene: Cinema and/in the French art museum

In his work on cinema and the museum, *Le temps exposé: Le cinéma de la salle au musée*, Dominique Païni explains:

> The museological act of display produces history in itself. More precisely, methods of display can produce other stories, other historical links, other chains of events; they can reveal other resemblances through connections which do not respect the chronological origins of the works on show.[2] (2002, 15)

By mounting cinema and cinematic objects within museum spaces, the relationships between these objects, and between other objects on display, are transformed. These shifting relationships establish new historical narratives, much like the hanging of paintings within a more conventional museum gallery space. And yet, as Païni explains, cinema was, for many years, set apart from the academic discourses of art history in museums, precisely because of its countercultural, subversive potential in the eyes of the cinephile (2002, 16). We might be reminded at this point that the figure of the *cinéphile* in France is more than simply a film amateur, but rather a complex cultural position from which many of the auteurist New Wave film critics and filmmakers of the 1950s and 1960s emerged. France's particular cinematic heritage is often held to be something that is proudly anti-institutional, and the figure of the *cinéphile* is well documented and critiqued in the work of film theorists such as Christian Metz ([1977] 1982). Filmmakers such as Jean-Luc Godard and François Truffaut received their understanding of and education in film through regular attendance at programmer Henri Langlois's Cinémathèque (predecessor to the Cinémathèque Française, now housed in the 12th arrondissement in Paris) and through their writing for André Bazin's journal, the *Cahiers du Cinema*. Both the Cinémathèque and the *Cahiers du Cinéma* stood as a politically oppositional voices to the French government-backed film industry in the 1940s and 1950s which embodied a closed community of filmmakers with long apprenticeships and closely tied relationships between directors and screenwriters (see Crisp 1993, 147–212). In effect, cinephilia and a love of cinema outside the professional industry was a serious and subversive business. Consequently, the nature of the film amateur, in the etymological sense of the "lover of film" or the cinephile, has a particularly important role in the cultural and cinematic landscape of twentieth- and twenty-first-century France.

For contemporary French cultural institutions, particularly those established after the social and political upheavals of May 1968, film has become part of their history. While it has taken some time for film to enter the museum space as an exhibited and preserved object in its own right, contemporary art museums themselves have emerged in an era of moving image representation. Even if museums have not uniformly demonstrated an interest in preserving or archiving film, filmmakers have certainly demonstrated an interest in representing and contesting museums, often with a critical perspective on the position of the museum as a "protector" or "liberator" of cultural heritage. Roberto Rossellini's film of the Pompidou Center, *Beaubourg, Centre d'art et de culture Georges Pompidou*, commissioned for its opening in 1977, is a rarely screened but extraordinary insight into the troubled politics that brought the Pompidou into being. Some 57 minutes long, the film presents a long perambulation through the museum's modern and contemporary art collection as it was displayed at its opening.[3] The film entirely disregards the curatorial, institutional, and political figures that were crucial to the Pompidou's establishment as a post-1968 museum, offering these figures no screen time at all. By muting the visible manifestations of power – the individuals who had striven to establish the Pompidou itself – Rossellini's film produces a tacit critique of cultural elitism. With the key museum officials out of the frame, and not present even in voice-over, the film wanders almost silently through the collections as if in one long tracking shot and one long take. The camera sets itself at eye height before a Picasso painting, a Brancusi sculpture, or a pop art screen print, recording both ambient sound and the banal, often irreverent, post-produced conversations of visitors to the museum (though the voices' authenticity as unmediated responses to the artworks remains in question). Rossellini's film does not celebrate the museum, as his commissioning body, the French Ministry of Foreign Affairs, might have hoped. Rather, the film mutely identifies with audiences and their freedom to express distaste, confusion, frustration, titillation, and their aleatory passage through the museum space. Perhaps most pertinently, this freedom of the audience also aligns the film with calls for a democratization of the art space. These calls played a significant ideological role in the emergence of the Pompidou in the years following the societal upheavals of May 1968. While Rossellini is clear on his own sentiments about the newly built Pompidou in 1977, the film itself is far more ambiguous. In interview Rossellini stated:

> I personally believe that people confuse culture and refinement. Refinement, for me, has nothing to do with knowledge. But when people speak of "culture," they really mean refinement. But before being refined, we have to be thinking beings, people who understand what it means to be man. We learn to be accountants, doctors, journalists, filmmakers, but who teaches us the principal profession, the profession of being man? Beaubourg is a flagrant thing: it is the exposition of refinement at all costs. (Rossellini 1977, quoted in Brunette 1996, 352)

The banality of the "conversations," which ebb and flow throughout the film, appear to counterbalance the "exposition of refinement" that Rossellini critiques. In the 1960s Pierre Bourdieu and Alain Darbel (1990) produced a scathing, empirically founded critique of the cultural elitism of museums and their tacit, "invisible" practices that effectively excluded from their museum visitors large numbers of socially disadvantaged groups. Rossellini's quiet ethnography of the spaces of the Pompidou in his film offers perhaps a subtler critique of notions of bourgeois high culture than Bourdieu and Darbel's work, and yet it still invokes a politicized "present moment" via the recording of an ostensibly public space – the newly inaugurated Centre Georges Pompidou.

In a sense, Rossellini's film project enacts a critique of public art institutions that the Pompidou itself would be unable to undertake, immersed as it was in a high-level network of past and present governmental politics and cultural policy, espoused via France's historic attitudes to the *patrimoine* (another term for tangible cultural heritage). The film reshapes the cultural politics of the Pompidou's spaces, reinserting dissenting voices and unconditioned wandering into the dominant historical-cultural narratives of the Pompidou. The invisible voices of dissent are made tangible through the film's form, and, in this sense, offer a rejoinder and critique of what Rebecca DeRoo has described as the Pompidou Center's aims, namely to be "the first cultural center to respond to the May '68 demands that the museum be radically transformed … to democratize the museum" (2006, 167). In this sense, Rossellini's film offers perhaps a more radical attempt to "democratize" the public spaces of the Pompidou in the post-1968 period than the building, its advocates, and its collections alone were able to implement. Consequently, this controversial and little-seen film simultaneously extends, critiques, and undermines the cultural-political principles of the Pompidou at the moment of its inception.

As DeRoo has adeptly explored, the emergence of the Pompidou as an art institution in fact shares some of the self-reflexive sentiment, and democratic aspirations for art, of Rossellini's film. In her cultural history of the exhibitions of Christian Boltanski and Annette Messager, DeRoo discusses the emergence of art activism and social politics in 1968, and its influence on the construction of the center, one of the most iconic contemporary art institutions in the world. She argues that the cultural politics involved in the construction of the Pompidou resonated with the post-1968 revolutionary call for democratization and populari-zation of museum spaces:

> The Pompidou Center was the first and most ambitious wide-ranging cultural program that France had undertaken since the *maisons de la culture* [provincial cultural centers] were established under Malraux [the center-right writer, politician, and minister for culture] in the 1960s. Unlike those institutions, which had as their mission the democratization of a restricted vision of French artistic excellence, the Pompidou Center was intended to respond to the 1968 vision of a different kind of democracy, one that engaged with the everyday politics of the street and the people. In its location, architecture, programs, and curatorial mission, the Pompidou was to be a newly vital, democratic kind of cultural institution. (DeRoo 2006, 169)

However, as DeRoo notes, the ostensible aim of the institution, to democratize art, and the implementation of these democratic processes, were often at odds with one another. The Pompidou suffered heavy criticism of its architectural structure, its programming, its expenditure (at the expense of support to regional and provincial museums), its location, and its popularization of museum-going as a leisure attraction and form of mass entertainment (DeRoo 2006, 167–175).

What proves particularly relevant here is the manner in which Rossellini's film, designed to promote the Pompidou Center to audiences outside France, in fact critiques the collision of bourgeois high art values and high-level governmental cultural policy, with the popularization of a museological practice of museum architecture, display, and exhibition that places art exhibition on a level with other forms of mass entertainment. That film itself should also be part of those other forms of mass entertainment, that it illuminates, illustrates, and critiques the space of the "new museum," offers an interesting twist to conceptualizations of the con-temporary art museum in France. *Beaubourg*, directed by one of Europe's most famous modernist filmmakers, very shortly before his death in June 1977, had the potential to make the museum and its works available to film audiences far beyond France. Paradoxically, the film at the same time critiques the bourgeois sentiments that were still working invisibly behind the scenes but within the public spaces of this most popular of contemporary art museums. And, yet, this film is rarely screened and not widely disseminated, no doubt as a result of its tacit political radicalism, which stood at odds with its commissioned role as an inaugural documentary. Rossellini's film played a key role in exploring and critiquing the contested politics of the Pompidou as new cultural institution, from its very begin-nings, revealing and making tangible the older cultural politics of the "new museum." Nonetheless, retrospectively, the very commissioning of Rossellini to make the film also attests the significance of film as a modernist medium; as a significant component of the Pompidou's collections, film played a key role in establishing the image of the Pompidou Center as a museum of modern art. Consequently film, and its relationship to cinema through the auteur figure of Rossellini, were part of the Pompidou Center's concerns from its earliest public moments at its opening in 1977.

Several months after the Pompidou's opening on January 31, 1977, new French laws provided frameworks for the legal deposit of films in an unprecedented manner. Although a legal deposit of film had been established by law in 1943, it took until 1977 to establish a location for such films at the French National Library (the Bibliothèque Nationale, then entirely located at the rue Richelieu in the second arrondissement in Paris), and an institutional body, the National Centre for Cinematography (CNC), that would be responsible for their conservation (see Vignaux 2003). The establishment of this new legislation in France was timely: in the same year that the Pompidou opened its doors, film and the moving image were finally, institutionally recognized as creative works requiring the care and conservation of a trained body of expertise. The cultural politics of preserving and archiving the moving image thus coincided with the emergence of a new cultural institution, whose beginnings had in turn been closely tied up with the national cultural politics of France, marking a new ideology with relation to the moving image and the contemporary art museum.

However, in the case of the Pompidou, the moving image had also been present within its contemporary art collections since its inception (at the Musée National d'Art Moderne (MNAM), installed at the heart of the Pompidou from 1976 onward). The Pompidou's online time line of exhibitions and acquisitions cites the exhibition *Une histoire du cinéma* among its first in 1976–1977 (see Dufrêne 2007). Conceived by the experimental filmmaker Peter Kubelka and co-organized by Alain Sayag, curator at the Musée National d'Art Moderne at the Pompidou from 1972, the retrospective included over 300 films by over 100 filmmakers, and explored the origins of cinema as art up to 1976 (see Kubelka 1976). According to Dominique Païni, who was from 2000 to 2005 the Pompidou's pluridisciplinary curator, its aim was "to design, build and concretely initiate a film collection according to the same principles of enrichment, conservation and display as for the other visual arts"[4] (2007, 403).

After this extensive retrospective, film was placed at the heart of the projects of the Pompidou, not only in its collections and exhibitions, but also in the availability of documentary film material to researchers and to the public, and in the programming of regular film screenings in the center's auditorium. Exhibitions in subsequent years included the work of video and moving image artists from across the world, including Nam June Paik and Michael Snow (1978), Alain Fleischer (1982), Thierry Kuntzel (1984), Andy Warhol (1990), not to mention the diverse and innovative programs of exhibitions curated by the Centre for Industrial

Creation (CCI). These included one of the first co-curated exhibitions between the Pompidou and a philosopher: Jean-François Lyotard's *Les immatériaux* (1985). This exhibition, co-curated with design historian Thierry Chaput, has recently attracted scholarly interest owing to its innovative engagement of a philosopher at its helm, and its exploration of what had been cutting-edge digital and audiovisual technologies, including holograms, music videos, films, and magnetic recording devices for visitors to record their movement through the exhibition (see Lyotard 1996; Hudek 2009; Bamford 2012). The exhibition also innovatively combined the full range of creative practices present within the Pompidou's spaces, including design, architecture, a cinema program, and contemporary musical premières.

It would seem that the moving image had completely saturated this contemporary art space by the 1980s. In turn, the interventions of the moving image, such as those of Rossellini's film, and the introduction of film into the collections of the Musée National d'Art Moderne at its earliest stages, have contributed to shifts in the identity and cultural policies of the Pompidou. Currently, the structural organization of the Pompidou Center and the Musée National d'Art Moderne retains a curator of the museum's experimental cinema collections (currently Philippe-Alain Michaud), as well as a program director for the museum's cinema auditorium (Sylvie Pras), but the moving image is clearly not confined only to these spheres. Film and the moving image have continued to maintain a visible profile, both within the exhibitions held at the Pompidou and within its institutional structures. At times, the moving image has revealed more clearly the cultural and political conflicts within the establishment. Take, for example, the failure of the Pompidou to establish a *cinémathèque* within its walls, in the manner that Henri Langlois, former director of the Cinémathèque Française, might have hoped before he died in January 1977. At other times, such as during the exhibition of *Les immatériaux*, the moving image has become a medium and an object of exhibition and curatorial practice. Combined with other forms of the art object, the moving image is equally subject to the policies and politics of curation and preservation at the heart of the museum's internal operations: operations ostensibly invisible to the public.

Cinema and curatorship: Cinema and the twenty-first-century French art museum

The April 2006 edition of the prestigious film journal *Cahiers du Cinéma* was a special issue dedicated to cinema and the museum. It cited numerous cases across Europe where filmmakers had not only been invited to screen retrospectives of their work within cinema auditoriums embedded within the architecture of contemporary art museums, but where they had also been commissioned to produce moving image media installations in museums such as the Pompidou, and in contemporary and modern art museums in Barcelona and Berlin. Certainly the period between 2001 and 2010 saw a rapid increase in the number of temporary moving image exhibitions by filmmakers and film artists in art institutions in Paris, includ-ing Chantal Akerman (Jeu de Paume, 2001; Pompidou, 2004), Anri Sala (ARC Musée d'Art Moderne, 2004), Jean-Luc Godard, Victor Erice/Abbas Kiarostami (Pompidou, 2006, 2007), Agnès Varda and David Lynch (Fondation Cartier, 2006, 2007), and William Kentridge (Jeu de Paume, 2010). These exhibitions combined aspects of conventional cinema exhibition, video art, and installation, and histori-cally experienced considerable degrees of success. In each case, the exhibitions did not simply transplant the cinema auditorium, and consequently the cinema experience, into a museum setting (although many of these exhibitions did include significant retrospectives of filmmakers' work) but they also employed, challenged, and explored the spaces of the museum itself, radically transforming the experi-ence of the moving image for museum visitors.

The critical coverage of some of these exhibitions in the *Cahiers du Cinéma* spe-cial issue seemed to mark a kind of watershed moment for French museum cul-ture and the moving image. Since the centennial celebrations of cinema's birth in 1995, the moving image in France has established some kind of institutional vali-dation within the art museum, as well as within its own cinema museums. This included the opening of the rehoused Cinémathèque Française in 2005, in a Frank Gehry-designed building on the opposite bank of the Seine to the new Bibliothèque Nationale de France–François Mitterrand. This recently developed cultural sector across the 12th and 13th arrondissements of Paris twinned the largest knowledge repository in France with the Cinémathèque, the two being conjoined across the river Seine by an undulating, architect-designed footbridge, the Passerelle Simone de Beauvoir, in 2006.

This historical narrative of the development and expansion of the moving image as a recognized art form, worthy of its own large-scale traveling exhibitions and retrospectives, is also supported by major figures in the cultural landscape of the moving image in France. In the 2006 issue of the *Cahiers du Cinéma*, in an interview with Jean-Michel Frodon, the Pompidou's film programmer Sylvie Pras, stated his aims regarding the screening and availability of films in their more conventional auditorium settings:

> I wanted to display filmmakers in the same way that painters are shown in the [Pompidou] Centre, with many expectations: exhaustive research, a considerable effort made to present each film using its best existing copy, presenting the largest possible number of audio-visual documents pertaining to the chosen filmmaker. … And also all the accessible elements of the filmmakers work beyond the finished films, in the same way that the sketches of a painter are also displayed.[5] (Pras and Frodon 2006, 21)

This approach to film programming in conventional cinematic exhibition spaces was mirrored more generally by a series of attempts to bring the moving image, and the work of filmmakers, into the art exhibition spaces of museums as a whole. Between 2000 and 2010, cinematic installations had entered into contemporary museum spaces in such volume as to indicate that they were now being considered significant works of art in their own right, and not as adjuncts to artworks or institutions, or as illustrations, documentation, or educational tools to explore the institutions.

Alongside the *Cahiers du Cinéma's* special issue on cinema and the museum in 2006, one of the most pivotal encounters between contemporary art museums and the moving image was the vast exhibition in 2006 at the Pompidou Center, *Le mouvement des images*. Conceived by Philippe-Alain Michaud, curator of experimental cinema within the MNAM at the Pompidou, the exhibition staged a vast series of multiroomed installations, using "black box" exhibition design techniques as an inversion of the contemporary "white cube" gallery form (see O'Doherty [1976] 1999) to isolate and localize sound and light projection, so that individual films could be displayed alongside one another in the exhibition space. This particular exhibition technique evidently resembled more closely the contemporary design of gallery spaces than it did the particular environs of the cinema auditorium. In its totality, *Le mouvement des images* effectively enacted a retrospective of experimental, avant-garde, noncommercial, and multiplatform moving image works, placed specifically within the contexts of museum exhibition and museographical design. However, rather than arranging the displays in chronological order as display conventions might dictate, the exhibition grouped works within formal, generic, and conceptual structures, which included works that might otherwise be considered to fall outside the remit of the "moving image." As Bruno Racine, president of the Pompidou put it:

[the exhibition's] self-appointed aim is to show how the "seventh art" now irreversibly conditions our experience of both artworks and images ... What is thus involved here is to propose new answers to the two questions which are henceforth being raised in each and every institution assigned to modern and contemporary art: how is film to be exhibited? And how is film to attain artwork status? (Racine 2006)

The comprehensive exhibition showcased the extraordinary depth of the MNAM's moving image collections, and included rare film excerpts from 1920s avant-garde filmmaking such as Marcel Duchamp's *Anémic cinéma* (1925), Ferdinand Léger's *Le ballet mécanique* (1923–1924), and May Ray's *Le retour à la raison* (1923), preserved and projected digitally onto the exhibition's walls. It also included large multichannel installations such as the newly acquired installation by Bruce Nauman, *Mapping the Studio II with Color Shift, Flip, Flop & Flip/Flop (Fat Chance John Cage)* (2001), as well as a wide range of American avant-garde video art. Alongside these moving image works were arrange other multimedia artworks, including Robert Rauschenberg's *Oracle* (1962–1965), an assemblage of metal urban fragments designed to evoke urban soundscapes, and Mona Hatoum's *Light Sentence* (1992), a set of wire mesh cages arranged in a U shape with a motor-powered lightbulb rising and falling inside, to arrange and rearrange the projection of shadows outside the cages. Collages by Georges Braque and Pablo Picasso were arranged against those from Barbara Klüger and photographs from Jeff Wall; Andy Warhol's screen print of *Ten Lizes* (1963) and Donald Judd's industrial sculpture of red geometric shapes, *Stack* (1973), were placed thematically in relation to Peter Kubelka's "metric" film *Arnulf Rainer* (1958–1960) and Nan Goldin's *Heartbeat* (2000–2001), a slideshow, with accompanying soundtrack, of her deeply intimate photographs tracking human relationships.

Arranged in four "chapters," and occupying an entire floor of the Pompidou Center, the exhibition was divided into a number of thematic rooms, some of which were divided again by a long corridor of projections. The four themes – *montage*, *récit* (narrative), *projection*, and *défilement* (unwinding) – explored not only the nature of the moving image, but also its complex relationships to other art forms, and to perceiving other art forms: painting, collage, sculpture, digital art, and of course photography. The orientations of display in this space shifted away from chronological narratives: instead, the moving image works, assembled and displayed in the space, encouraged spectators to build formal connections between artworks, both moving image and nonmoving image. *Le mouvement des images* was more than simply an exhibition of moving images: it was a major showcase of the MNAM's collections, moving image and visual art collections, and a curatorial and museological statement in terms of the relationship of this contemporary art museum to the moving image.

The exhibition certainly gave almost simultaneous access to visitors to a huge range of moving image material within one exhibition encounter. The effect was, for a visitor, somewhat overwhelming. I recall my own bewilderment as I shifted from "box" to "box," watching a short film for a brief spell, or on a loop in quick succession, before "grazing" other parts of the exhibition space that contained a vast assemblage of modern and contemporary art from the 1920s to the present day. *Le mouvement des images* was as much a conceptual exhibition as it was an actual one: the limits of time and human endurance stretched the ability of any visitor, even one as obsessively fascinated by cinema as myself, to observe, remember, and engage with each of the exhibits, even if it were possible to view them all. Volker Pantenburg has critiqued the exhibition in slightly different terms, arguing that the presentation of moving images within a gallery setting risks deprivileging the role that sound technologies have played in the histories of cinema: "The desire to establish a simultaneous interaction between different artworks and to make the visitor part of that interaction involuntarily means privileging the loudest, or else it forces the curator to re-establish the unloved cinema-principle via the black box" (2008, 4).

My own critique of the exhibition might be less forceful than Pantenburg's, in that the "noisebleed" he notes as being a problematic aspect of audiovisual installation might also function as an important element of cross-fertilization between works (Pantenburg 2008, 4; see also Holert 2005). The exhibition experience did not isolate moving image works; instead, it created an intermittent set of unexpected dialogues between images and sound. However, one might acknowledge the critical and curatorial disjuncture between the conceptual possibilities of the exhibition – plural dialogues between film and artworks – and spectatorial actuality – the possibilities of being overwhelmed, distracted, and confused by the viewing experience.

Once again, issues of tangible visibility and perceptible invisibility become useful metaphors for examining the complex relationship between cinema, curatorship, and the museum. The installed exhibition of film not only exposed the putative spaces of theatrical, "cinematic" exhibition within the museum, but also made prominent the traces of curatorial intention within the documentation surrounding the exhibition. Curatorial decisions within the exhibition space ultimately privileged some moving image works over others in terms of both their display and their sound levels, creating darkened black box mini auditoriums for key pieces, while allowing noise and light contamination to create very different, perhaps more diffuse, viewing experiences for others. The plentiful documentation that accompanied the exhibition, including its catalog, reveals the exhibition to be a celebration not only of the moving image, but also of the integration of the moving image within contemporary art, and the central role of the Pompidou in establishing this interaction. The ongoing issues of the public museum's responsibilities to public visibility, including the human reach of its exhibitions, have a complex and sometimes antagonistic relationship with the conceptual role that curatorial and cultural practices of the institution have to play in making cinema a tangible, formally recognized, and innovative work of art within its walls.

New art histories of film and the gallery suggest that this type of crossover between cinematic medium and art space is a recent phenomenon (see Balsom 2013), while museological interest in film often returns to tropes of film as a "medium," rather than an object (see Sorensen 1989, 7–72; Witcomb 2003, 103–104). However, a close examination of cultural institutions within France, such as the Pompidou, which integrated the moving image into its operations and collections from its inception, reveal a nuanced consideration of film, cinematic spaces, and museums as politically inflected institutions. If, as scholars examining museum media, we focus too much on the moving image as an information medium or a curatorial object, rather than also as a cultural phenomenon that has permeated all reaches of human cultural activity, and which comments on culture as much as it is commented on, then we risk ignoring the invisible political environments of culture. In this case, that would include the cultural politics of France with regard to film and cinematic heritage, and the institutional politics of France's foremost contemporary art museum, which have played such a pivotal role in the current visibility of the moving image within contemporary art collections and exhibitions. I have explored institutional and political, as well as technical and curatorial, tensions arising from the public exhibition of film within a contemporary French art museum. The next section will explore perhaps the most aggressive example to date of the potential for film and moving image exhibition to subject both the visible, tangible institutional housing of the museum, and the invisible but nonetheless perceptible ideologies of the museum, to radical political and museological critique.

Cinematic rifts: Institutional tensions in the twenty-first-century French art museum

Issues of public visibility, as well as the conceptual and museological clarity of curatorial policy at the Pompidou, have not been the only bones of contention in the influx of cinema into the art museum. In particular, a smaller moving image exhibition that ran concurrent to *Le mouvement des images* was to prove to be one of the most contentious, and arguably "failed," moving image projects that the Pompidou Center had ever known. *Voyage(s) en Utopie* [Travel(s) in Utopia, 2006], conceived by Jean-Luc Godard and Dominique Païni, was the long-awaited result of a lengthy collaboration between the filmmaker and the institution. Païni, whose previous posts at the audiovisual production unit of the Louvre Museum and then as director of the Cinémathèque de Paris had enabled him to establish ongoing dialogues with Godard, was instrumental in the realization of what was hoped to be an institutional *coup de grâce*. Both Antoine de Baecque's account of the contentious politics of the exhibition and the Pompidou's publicity suggest that the initial proposal for the exhibition titled *Collage(s) de France, archéologie du cinéma* [Collage(s) of France: Archaeology of cinema] – a play on words on the famous Collège de France, where some of the most influential French scholars of the twentieth century had delivered lectures – was planned as a blockbuster, high-cost, high-gloss exhibition (see de Baecque 2010). Finally, committing Godard, one of the most canonical and notoriously difficult figures of European art cinema, to produce an exhibition in a contemporary art institution that had striven to incorporate the moving image into its collections and practices for so long, was initially seen as a great achievement on the part of the Pompidou. Certainly such a significant exhibition would have had the potential to confirm the unique position of the Pompidou and the MNAM as one of the foremost museums of the moving image on an international stage.

According to de Baecque's biography, the project had been in discussion since at least 2000, if not earlier (see de Baecque 2004). Godard's encyclopedic video collage work, *Histoire(s) du cinéma* (1988–1998), had visually sedimented his ongoing concerns with conceptualizing and recreating a multilayered set of "histories," archaeologies even, of cinema: histories that would not attempt to recreate a chronology of cinema any more than they would reconstruct a historical narrative of the twentieth century (see also Godard and Ishaghpour 2005). The notion of media archaeology is explored elsewhere in this volume.[6] However, in this instance,

Histoire(s) du cinéma, with its complex layering of the technologies of analogue film, typewriting, subtitling, and video, might also be better conceived as an "archaeological" project, uncovering the sedimented resemblances and resonances between cinematic history and the histories of the twentieth century. As de Baecque wrote in 2004, Godard's videographic histories of cinema take on the proportions of an imaginary museum, first outlined by André Malraux in 1951 in his book *Les voix du silence*:

> This method of creating a tool for comparison, namely video, is also a museographic device, since Godard also takes the liberty of removing paintings or images from traditional museums to "edit" them into film. ... Godard's imaginary museum is not a spiritual flight of fancy; on the contrary, it is a vision of the history of the twentieth century. ... Godard's prophecy, where the cinematic form undertakes to embody the history of the century, is a personal epic, the confession of a child of the century who is also a son of the cinema (*ciné-fils*) and vice versa. It is a prosopopeia: I, the cinema, speak, or more precisely: I, Jean-Luc Godard, who embody cinema, narrate the history of my twentieth century. (de Baecque 2004, 121–122)

This treatment of history as complex artifacts, of cinema as complex histories, indicates an ambivalent relationship to the museum on Godard's part: his previous projects demonstrated a resistance to linear historical narratives about the twentieth century, and a consequent resistance to rhetorics of power frequently associated with museum institutions tasked with amassing and distributing cultural capital.[7] However, the ambivalent fascination with the museum revealed by Godard's works also established a conceptual basis for negotiations between Païni, Godard, and the Pompidou for a museum exhibition. Documentation from de Baecque and Païni suggests that this project would have concretized many of the theoretical concepts explored through Godard's video project (see de Baecque 2010). However, once the significant sum of money had been obtained to commission Godard to make the exhibition, and after *carte blanche* had effectively been given to the filmmaker to conceive of the space, events seemed to swiftly snowball. The costs of the project, together with its design and realization, rapidly spiraled out of control, ultimately straining relations between Godard and Païni to breaking point. This eventually led to a curatorial and political fallout, not only between Godard and Païni, who resigned from his post shortly before the exhibition opened, but also between Godard, a cinematic anti-establishment all of his own, and the Pompidou Center, whose complex political and curatorial relationship with film had some historical precedents. With a matter of months to go before the opening of the exhibition, the project was entirely redesigned and reformulated, newly titled *Voyage(s) en Utopie: Jean-Luc Godard 1946–2006, À la recherche d'un théorème perdu* [Travel(s) in Utopia: Jean-Luc Godard, 1946–2006, In search of a lost theorem].

The exhibition opened to muted acclaim on May 11, 2006. Antoine de Baecque has reconstructed this series of events in painstaking detail, noting in particular the handwritten note pasted on the wall by the entrance to the exhibition:

> The Pompidou Centre has decided not to complete the exhibition project entitled: "Collage(s) of France: Archaeology of Cinema" owing to the artistic, technical and financial difficulties that it presented [the words "technical and financial" are almost entirely scored out], and to replace it by another project entitled *Voyage(s) in Utopia: In Search of a Lost Theorem: JLG 1945–2005*. This second project includes the partial or complete presentation of the maquette of *Collage(s) of France*. Jean-Luc Godard has agreed to the decision of the Pompidou Centre.[8] (de Baecque 2010, 805)

This handwritten note set the scene for the rest of the exhibition, which laid bare the cabling, wall sockets, scaffolding, paint rags, and all manner of other materials that one might more obviously associate with the building of an exhibition and not its completion. The exhibition did include seven new film works produced by Godard, alongside excerpts of others coproduced with Anne-Marie Miéville, and a wide range of excerpts from other films ranging from Ridley Scott's *Black Hawk Down* (2001) to *The Testament of Dr. Mabuse* (dir. Fritz Lang, 1932). Nonetheless, the exhibition made the process of exhibition-making, and the exhibition's failure to meet the ambitions of the Pompidou, painfully visible to the thousand or so visitors who flocked to it each day of its opening (see de Baecque 2010). Resistance to the museum institution was made manifest in the rebarbative, user-unfriendly interfaces of the exhibits: tiny LCD screens were arranged against one another with such extensive sound interference as to make it almost impossible to engage in a sustained manner with them; flat screen televisions were placed face up on a kitchen table, stretching the willingness of an observer to remain hovered over it in order to watch. The distraction of the gallery space, naturally lit as a series of white spaces, rather than subdued dramatically as a black box-style set of rooms, seemed to enact a resistance to the seamless placement of the moving image, indeed of cinema itself, within the institutionalized exhibition space of the Pompidou. While the comprehensive sensory feast of the moving image was underway upstairs in *Le mouvement des images* exhibition within the MNAM, the temporary exhibition space below was displayed as unfinished and leaking into the exterior environment: one "room" in the exhibition was open to the glass outer walls of the Pompidou's building, exposing its unfinished rawness to pedestrians outside, as well as visitors inside.

Concluding thoughts

The institutional, curatorial, and political battles fought over the moving image in the first decade of the twenty-first century might seem surprising, were they not examined in the light of the always contentious position of film and the moving image in the Pompidou Center, and the Pompidou's own contentious history within the cultural politics of France after the social upheavals of 1968. One might consider Godard's "failed" exhibition as a manifestation of the always contested spaces of the museum: in particular, a manifestation of the complex ways in which cinema, via multiple film technologies, can resist and contest historical narratives about the role of art within a museum institution, and about the place of film, as a technological medium, an artifactual object, and a mode of political critique, with regard to national and international policies of cultural heritage.

This chapter has selectively traced some of the phenomena within the Centre Georges Pompidou since its inauguration in 1977, which highlight the historical relationships between the contemporary art institution in France and the moving image. It is clear that the Pompidou Center has played a pivotal role in the shaping of these relationships, not least via its innovations in its curatorial programs and acquisition policies. Nonetheless, by doing so, the museum as a cultural institution and a public space, has shaped the ways in which cinema responds to both cultural institutions and the "political present" of public spaces.

Rossellini's 1977 film and Godard's paradoxically abortive and self-reflexive exhibition project in 2006 share an underlying suspicion of the museum institution. Rossellini's film critiques the traces of bourgeois elitism remaining within the "democratic" spaces of the Pompidou. Godard's exhibition attempted to tear down both the human infrastructures of the Pompidou, simultaneously revealing the cracks, tears, and messiness of exhibition construction, while at the same time displaying a utopian vision of what a museological history of cinema might be. The work of these auteurist filmmakers, which has been elevated to the status of art in contemporary discourses of cinema, offers distinctive case studies. Their canonical status effectively authorized them, as director-curators, to demonstrate resistance to the narratives and histories that the Pompidou, as a contemporary art museum, was itself instrumental in constructing.

And yet, somehow, the Pompidou has, albeit sometimes reluctantly, allowed sufficient flexibility within its curatorial and exhibition practices for those processes and spaces of dissent to be configured within its archives, collections, and exhibition spaces. The Pompidou is also a live space of negotiation between the resistant discourses of avant-garde and experimental moving image art, and the acts of conservation, acquisition, and curation that govern the visibility of such works. As a result, the contemporary history of cinema and the museum is not simply a history of objects or artworks, nor a history of media, but rather a complex negotiation of works, cultures, politics, institutions, exhibition spaces, collections, curators, filmmakers, and people.

Film, as a technological and material artifact, is also a culture, a politics, and a mode of criticism that abuts the institutional politics of contemporary art spaces and theatrical exhibition venues: film in the public space becomes cinema. Within the context of the Pompidou Center, as a world-leading contemporary art museum and exhibition space, these case studies have demonstrated film's capacity to challenge existing discourses of curation, preservation, and display. Consequently, this study of the Pompidou offers the potential to reshape the ways in which other forms of artwork, and other museum objects, are mediated, perceived, and contextualized as "art." The intertwined notions of cinema, film, and the museum sit nested within one another. They are not only housed architecturally within the space of the contemporary art museum, but also reveal the porousness of terms like "curation," "direction," and the "political presence" induced by the moving image.

From the massive public exhibition of avant-garde and experimental moving image works in *Le mouvement des images*, to the curatorial deconstruction of the very notion of the art institution in *Voyage(s) en Utopie*, the spectral traces of cinema and its filmic technologies also make tangible the political dynamics of museums as public spaces. The Pompidou Center, in particular, has effectively become a cultural barometer of the status of cinema within France, while the moving image works that it has housed have brought forth ongoing critical dialogues about the role of the Pompidou as both a cultural center and an art museum. In this sense, the Pompidou Center offers a powerful example of the cultural politics, both visible and invisible, that operate in the dynamic between film and moving image technologies, and the contemporary art museum. Cinema and the moving image are an integral part of contemporary art spaces and their curation and collections, but they are also now irrevocably at the heart of current debates about the politics of contemporary art museums.

Notes

1   See, for example, the United Kingdom Health and Safety Executive's guidelines on the disposal of celluloid film at http://www.hse.gov.uk/pubns/indg469.pdf (accessed August 4, 2014).

2   "Un accrochage muséographique produit de l'histoire. Plus précisément, l'accrochage peut produire d'autres histoires, d'autres liens historiques, d'autres enchaînements, découvrir d'autres ressemblances depuis des rapprochements qui ne respectent pas la chronologie de la création des œuvres montrées." (Païni 2002, 15). All translations are mine except where indicated otherwise.

3   I am very grateful to Antony Hudek for organizing a rare screening of this film at University College London in 2011, where I had the opportunity to view it.

4   "la mission de concevoir et de commencer concrètement une collection de films selon les mêmes principes d'enrichissement, de conservation et de monstration que pour les autres arts visuels" (Païni 2007, 403).

5   "J'ai voulu montrer les cinéastes comme on expose les peintres au Centre, avec plus-ieurs exigences: la recherche de l'exhaustivité, un effort considérable pour présenter chaque film dans la meilleure copie existante, la présentation du plus grand nombre possible de documents audiovisuels relatifs au cinéaste choisi … Et aussi tous les éléments accessibles de son travail en dehors des films achevés, de la même manière qu'on montre aussi les esquisses d'un peintre" (Pras and Frodon 2006, 21).

6   For more on media archaeology, see Michelle Henning's interview with Wolfgang Ernst in Chapter 1 and Chapter 2 by Andrew Hoskins and Amy Holdsworth in this volume.

7   For a detailed discussion of Godard's conceptual relationships to cinema history, see Witt 2013.
8   "Le Centre Pompidou a décidé de ne pas réaliser le projet d'exposition intitulé 'Collage(s) de France. Archéologie du cinéma' en raison de difficultés artistiques, techniques et financières qu'il présentait [les mentions 'techniques et financières' sont ostensiblement rayées], et de le remplacer par un autre projet intitulé Voyage(s) en Utopie. A la recherche d'un théorème perdu. JLG 1945–2005. Ce second projet inclut la présentation partielle ou complète de la maquette de Collage(s) de France. Jean-Luc Godard a agréé la décision du Centre Pompidou."

References

Balsom, E. 2009. "A Cinema in the Gallery, a Cinema in Ruins." *Screen* 50(4): 411–427.

Balsom, E. 2013. *Exhibiting Cinema in Contemporary Art*. Amsterdam: Amsterdam University Press.

Bamford, K. 2012. "Acconci's *Pied à Terre*: Taking the Archive for a Walk." *Performance Research* 17(2): 54–61.

Bourdieu, P., and A. Darbel. 1990. *The Love of Art: European Museums and Their Public*. Cambridge: Polity.

Brunette, P. 1996. *Roberto Rossellini*. Berkeley: University of California Press. Accessed August 4, 2014. http://ark.cdlib.org/ark:/13030/ft709nb48d/.

Connolly, M. 2009. *The Place of Artists' Cinema: Space, Site and Screen*. Bristol: Intellect; Chicago: University of Chicago Press.

Crisp, C. 1993. *The Classic French Cinema, 1930–1960*. Bloomington: Indiana University Press.

de Baecque, A. 2004. "Godard in the Museum." In *For Ever Godard*, edited by M. Temple, J. S. Williams, and M. Witt, 118–125. London: Black Dog.

de Baecque, A. 2010. *Godard: Biographie*. Paris: Grasset.

DeRoo, R. 2006. *The Museum Establishment and Contemporary Art: The Politics of Artistic Display in France after 1968*. Cambridge: Cambridge University Press.

Derrida, J., and B. Stiegler. 2002. *Echographies of Television*. Cambridge: Polity.

Dufrêne, B., ed. 2007. *Centre Pompidou: Trente ans d'histoire* [The Pompidou Center: A 30 year history]. Paris: Centre Pompidou.

Fowler, C. 2004. "Room for Experiment: Gallery Films and Vertical Time from Maya Deren to Eija Liisa Ahtila." *Screen* 45(4): 324–343.

Godard, J.-L., and Y. Ishaghpour. 2005. *Cinema: The Archaeology of Film and the Memory of a Century*. Oxford: Berg.

Grieveson, L., and N. Bose., eds. 2010. *Using Moving Image Archives: A Scope e-Book*. Accessed August 4, 2014. http://www.academia.edu/431435/Using_Moving_Image_Archives.

Griffiths, A. 2008. *Shivers Down Your Spine: Cinema, Museums, and the Immersive View*. New York: Columbia University Press.

Holert, T. 2005. "Noisebleed." *Texte zur Kunst* 15(60): 146–154. Accessed August 4, 2014. http://www.textezurkunst.de/60/noisebleed/.

Hudek, A. 2009. "From Over- to Sub-Exposure: The Anamnesis of *Les immatériaux*." Tate Papers 12. Accessed August 4, 2014. http://www.tate.org.uk/research/publications/tate-papers/over-sub-exposure-anamnesis-les-immateriaux.

Iles, C., ed. 2001. *Into the Light: The Projected Image in American Art 1964–1977*. New York: Whitney Museum.

Kubelka, P. 1976. *Une histoire du cinéma: Exposition* [A history of cinema: The exhibition]. Paris: Centre Pompidou/Musée National d'Art Moderne.

Lyotard, J.-F. 1996. "Les immatériaux." In *Thinking about Exhibitions*, edited by R. Greenberg, B. W. Ferguson, and S. Nairne, 159–173. London: Routledge.

Malraux, A. 1951. *Les voix du silence* [The voices of silence]. Paris: Georges Lang.

Metz, C. (1977) 1982. "The Imaginary and the 'Good Object' in the Cinema and in the Theory of Cinema." In *Psychoanalysis and Cinema: The Imaginary Signifier*, translated by Celia Britton, 1–16. London: Macmillan.

Michaud, P.-A., ed. 2006. *Le mouvement des images/The Movement of Images*. Paris: Centre Pompidou.

Mulvey, L. 2005. *Death 24x a Second*. London: Reaktion.

Oberhardt, S. 2001. *Frames within Frames: The Art Museum as Cultural Artifact*. New York: Peter Lang.

O'Doherty, B. (1976) 1999. *White Cube: The Ideology of the Gallery Space*. Berkeley: University of California Press.

Païni, D. 2002. *Le temps exposé: Le cinéma de la salle au musée* [Time exhibited: Cinema in the museum]. Paris: Cahiers du Cinéma.

Païni, D. 2007. "Exposer le cinéma au Centre Pompidou" [Exhibiting cinema at the Pompidou Center]. In *Centre Pompidou: Trente ans d'histoire* [The Pompidou Center: A 30 year history], edited by B. Dufrêne, 403–409. Paris: Centre Pompidou.

Pantenburg, V. 2008. "'Post Cinema?' Movies, Museums, Mutations." *SITE* 24: 4–5.

Pollock, G. 2007. "Un-framing the Modern: Critical Space/Public Possibility." In *Museums After Modernism: Strategies of Engagement*, edited by G. Pollock and J. Zemans, 1–39. Oxford: Blackwell.

Pras, S., and J.-M. Frodon. 2006. "Montrer les cinéastes comme on expose les peintres" [Exhibiting filmmakers in the same way as painters]. *Cahiers du Cinéma* 611: 21.

Racine, B. 2006. "Foreword." In *Le mouvement des images/The Movement of Images*, edited by P.-A. Michaud, 9. Paris: Centre Pompidou.

Rodowick, D. N. 2007. *The Virtual Life of Film*. Cambridge, MA: London: Harvard University Press.

Rossellini, R. 1977. "Interview." *Écran 77* 60: 46.

Sorensen, C. 1989. "Theme Parks and Time Machines." In *The New Museology*, edited by P. Vergo, 60–73. London: Reaktion.

Stafford, B. M. 2001. "Revealing Technologies/Magical Domains." In *Devices of Wonder: From the World in a Box to Images on a Screen*, edited by B. M. Stafford and F. Terpak, 1–142. Los Angeles: Getty Research Institute.

Usai, P. C. 2001. *The Death of Cinema: History, Cultural Memory and the Digital Dark Age*. London: BFI.

Vignaux, V. 2003. "Archives et histoire: Des archives pour l'histoire – du cinéma?" [Archives and history: some archives for the history - of cinema?] *1895: Revue de l'Association Française de Recherche sur l'Histoire du Cinéma* 40: 107–119. Accessed August 4, 2014. http://1895.revues.org/3532.

Wasson, H. 2005. *Museum Movies: The Museum of Modern Art and the Birth of Art Cinema.* Berkeley: University of California Press.

Witcomb, A. 2003. *Reimagining the Museum: Beyond the Mausoleum.* London: Routledge.

Witcomb, A. 2007. "The Materiality of Virtual Technologies: A New Approach to Thinking about the Impact of Multimedia in Museums." In *Theorizing Digital Cultural Heritage: A Critical Discourse,* edited by F. Cameron and S. Kenderdine, 35–49. Cambridge, MA: MIT University Press.

Witt, M. 2013. *Jean-Luc Godard: Cinema Historian.* Bloomington: Indiana University Press.

Jenny Chamarette is Senior Lecturer in Film at Queen Mary, University of London. She is the author of *Phenomenology and the Future of Film: Rethinking Subjectivity beyond French Cinema* (Palgrave Macmillan, 2012) and has published widely in journals such as *Paragraph, Studies in French Cinema, Studies in European Cinema,* and *Modern and Contemporary France.* Her research examines intermediality, phenomenology, embodiment, and affect in contemporary visual and moving image cultures in Europe, North America, and the Middle East. She has particular interests in the cultural, political, and embodied relations between cinema and the museum, gallery and archive, artist's moving image and curatorial practice.

6 THE MUSEUM AS TV PRODUCER

Televisual Form in Curating, Commissioning, and Public Programming

Maeve Connolly

Art museums and institutions have long sought to find ways of extending their programming through television. This is evidenced by Lynn Spigel's (2008) research on the Television Project, an initiative developed by New York's Museum of Modern Art, with the support of the Rockefeller Brothers Fund, over three years during the early 1950s. Spigel's research demonstrates that art institutions such as the Museum of Modern Art (MoMA) were interested in TV before it had fully emerged as an object of artistic inquiry, and certainly long before artists had begun to incorporate television receivers into sculptural works and performance events. In recent years, art and media scholars have begun to examine histories of art–television exchange more closely, and the result has been a number of important publications (Mehring 2008; Wyver 2009; Sutton 2011). Yet there currently exists no comprehensive account of television as a focus for art institutional practices of curating, commissioning, and public programming. This chapter does not attempt to offer such an account; rather, it looks more closely at a selection of TV-themed projects realized since the 1970s with the involvement of various art institutions, curators, and artists. The institutions include Long Beach Museum of Art in Long Beach, California; the Hammer Museum and the Museum of Contemporary Art, both in Los Angeles; the Brooklyn Museum, New York; the Kunstverein München (Munich); the Contemporary Art Centre in Vilnius, Lithuania; the Rooseum in Malmö; the Institute of Contemporary Arts in London; the Museum d'Art Contemporani de Barcelona, and the Sydney Biennale. Through analysis of these projects, I identify a number of significant shifts in the relationship between television and the art museum, and also consider the role played by artists and curators in articulating television's altered status as a cultural form.[1]

The International Handbooks of Museum Studies: Museum Media, First Edition.
Edited by Michelle Henning.
© 2015 John Wiley & Sons Ltd. Published 2020 by John Wiley & Sons Ltd.

MoMA's Television Project was an attempt to understand, through research, the altered situation and function of the art museum in the "age of television" (Spigel 2008, 151). Its contributors were acutely aware of the growing significance of television in contemporary society, and the attendant changes wrought in practices of leisure and consumption, which would impact on the future of the museum. Two decades later, the programs developed at Long Beach Museum of Art (LBMA) took up the challenge of curating and commissioning within a cultural, economic, and social environment where television continued to occupy a central, even dominant, role. But, unlike their predecessors at MoMA, the curators at LBMA were engaging with television as an established object (and setting) for artistic inquiry. Here I am referring not only to the activities of the first wave of artists working with television as medium and object, including Nam June Paik and Wolf Vostell among others, but also to the expansion of video production by artists and activists in the late 1960s and early 1970s (Huffman 1990). The history of TV-focused activity at LBMA was also directly shaped by changes in the economy and technology of television, since it developed from an initial plan to establish a cable TV studio facility within the museum's new building (Sutton 2011, 122).

By the late 1990s, artists and art institutions were proposing an even more expansive notion of the televisual, sometimes involving the development of TV-themed content for online platforms. I am referring here to GALA Committee's online exploration of television fandom, as part of a project developed for exhibition at the LA Museum of Contemporary Art (MOCA) in 1997, and also to various TV-themed initiatives developed by European art centers in the early 2000s (Farquharson 2006). These projects communicate a fascination with television as a mutable and adaptable form, which can be reconfigured and repurposed to serve the needs of art institutions. By this point, some artists and curators were also beginning to directly address television's displacement by newer media, as evidenced by the online exhibition *TV Swansong* (discussed below), which provocatively announced television's demise in 2002. Yet, even in a definitively "post-broadcast" era, art institutions continue to engage with familiar broadcast formats such as the talk show, as evidenced by exhibitions and public programs developed within such diverse contexts as the Munich Kunstverein and the Hammer Museum (both discussed below). For some artists and curators, appropriations of this type enable a critique of television as a conduit for celebrity-driven entertainment culture. But, in other institutional contexts, the talk show is understood as a platform for political discourse, as evidenced by the Hammer Forum, a current affairs themed program of public debates at the Hammer Museum.

Before they can be analyzed more closely, developments in TV-themed commissioning, curating, and programming need to be situated in relation to broader transformations in practices and processes of television production and reception, occurring within local, national, and supranational contexts that are culturally and historically distinct. In the 1950s and 1960s the television landscape in the United States was dominated by a small number of powerful networks and their affiliates, while the European landscape was largely organized around state-supported and regulated public broadcasters, initially with limited domestic competition. Toward the end of the 1960s, a new political imperative to legitimate television as a public cultural form in the United States contributed to a wave of "guerrilla television" production by artists and activists over the following decade (Boyle 1997). The late 1960s and early 1970s also witnessed a number of important art–television exchanges in Germany and the Netherlands (Wyver 2009), and the intermittent support could be found for artist-produced television in various European contexts during the 1970s and 1980s. For example, formal experimentation in television was actively encouraged in some European socialist states, as evidenced by the television show *TV Gallery* produced by Belgrade Television as a platform for artists from 1984 until 1990 (Ćurčić 2007). In addition, the early 1980s initially witnessed important innovations at the newly established Channel 4 in Britain (Born 2003). For example, the channel's celebrated *Workshop* program supported formally and politically challenging work by groups such as Black Audio Film Collective and Sankofa. But, with the rise of a neoliberal economy, the deregulation of many European broadcasting environments, and increased competition for audiences and advertising since the 1990s, resources for art–television exchanges seemed to decline (Wyver 2009).

Yet, rather than charting the gradual withdrawal of art and artists from television, this chapter identifies an altered context for collaboration between museums and broadcasters, and examines a range of new developments in the commissioning, curating, and programming of TV-themed exhibitions and artworks. The specific examples discussed here should be understood in relation to a broader array of strategic development initiatives that have brought museums and broadcasters – particularly those dependent on public subvention – into closer proximity, creating the conditions to support both long-term alliances and more short-term informal collaborations. Now that broadcasters seek to operate across an array of platforms and contexts, televisual forms are increasingly encountered in environments that have also served as important settings for contemporary art, ranging from galleries and museums to outdoor screens located in urban centers (Mcquire 2010, 572).

As the age of television has given way to the age of convergent media, TV-themed exhibitions and public programs have persisted, perhaps even proliferated, and in many instances they propose new ways of thinking about television's history and future as a cultural form. In the discussion that follows I emphasize the important role played by television in the transformation of organizational and institutional structures developed at the Long Beach Museum of Art during the 1970s and 1980s. Informed by Gloria Sutton's research, I argue that the LBMA's engagement with cable TV production and distribution was animated and shaped by questions over the future of the museum as cultural and social institution, which were posed by artists (such as Nam June Paik) as well as by the museum's own curators. Furthermore, I argue that television returned, during the early 2000s, as an important reference point for a number of smaller, explicitly self-critical European art institutions seeking to reconfigure the social and cultural function and organizational form of the art museum.

The era of expansion: Television at Long Beach Museum of Art

In recent years, LBMA has been recognized as one of the first art institutions to fully embrace the role of the museum as TV producer (Sutton 2011). Founded in the 1950s, and located in a building that was formerly a private home, LBMA's relatively small gallery spaces were well suited to the screening of single-channel monitor works and it was one of the first US museums to establish a video art department (set up in 1974) staffed by specialists such as David A. Ross and, subsequently, Kathy Rae Huffman (1976–1983). The museum's initial involvement with cable television occurred in May 1977, with a performance event called *Douglas Davis: Two Cities, A Text, Flesh, and the Devil*, held simultaneously in Santa Monica and San Francisco. During this period, staff at the museum advised on the development of a new building, which was initially supposed to include a cable television studio facility as part of its infrastructure (Huffman 2011, 13). This facility was partly inspired by Ross's experience of working at the independent video studio Art/Tapes/22 in Florence (Italy), but the plans for a new building at Long Beach were ultimately shelved, prompting his departure as curator.

In 1980 the existing LBMA video studio was upgraded to broadcast quality with assistance from the Rockefeller Foundation and the National Endowment for the Arts (NEA). Two years later, the museum collaborated with various US universities to produce *The Arts for Television*, a three-hour, one-off live cable TV program, linking artists in New York, Long Beach, and Iowa City, and featuring contributions from curators such as John Hanhardt and Barbara London and artists such as Nancy Buchanan, Chris Burden, Jaime Davidovich, Mike Kelley, and Michael Smith. Around this time, the museum also hosted a conference called *Shared Realities*, which brought artists, curators, and the developers of new cable TV services together to explore the future of "art as TV." The conference was followed by the LBMA's first regular cable TV show, also called *Shared Realities* (1983) and, during the 1980s, LBMA also established (with the support of the local cable industry) a television production grant program for California-based video artists called Open Channels. This program ran from 1986 until 1995 and it included cable operators, artists, and curators as jurors (Huffman 2011, 17–18). The museum also produced an 18 part series of short works by video artists called *Video Viewpoints* (1987–1989) and arts television programs such as *Art Off the Wall* and *Arts Revue* for cable. These initiatives were developed alongside a program of exhibitions that often engaged directly with television, including shows such as *Tele-Visions: Channels for Changing TV* (1991), curated by Michael Nash and featuring works by David Lynch and Mark Frost, Martha Rosler and Paper Tiger Television, and Antonio Muntadas.

Reflecting on the significance of LBMA's engagement with television, Gloria Sutton suggests that it was one of several organizations seeking to establish "new institutional models for the collection, preservation, circulation, and exhibition of visual art during the 1970s and 80s" (2011, 123). But, rather than framing it as "overtly anti-institutional," Sutton notes that the LBMA instead "sought to radically recast the museum itself and expand its reach through television" (123). Sutton also emphasizes that Nam June Paik was a highly influential figure in the development of Ross's concept of the "museum as medium" (Ross, quoted in Sutton 2011, 122).

Television and "new institutions"

David Ross, following Paik, envisaged the museum of the future as a "television channel, among other things" (Sutton 2011, 123), and was interested in television's potential as a means to allow artists to sidestep the infrastructure of the museum and engage with audiences directly. In some respects, this impulse coheres with the wider critique of art institutions advocated by many artists and curators, a critique that has continued to unfold in a variety of forms since at least the 1970s. In a valuable analysis of institutional critique and its legacies, Hito Steyerl (2006) differentiates between various historical moments and theorizes how such strategies might function in relation to a changing conception of the public sphere and altered conditions of labor and production. She argues that the first wave of critique "challenged the authority which had accumulated in cultural institutions within the framework of the nation state." It was, she notes, premised on the view that a cultural institution could operate as a potential public sphere in its own right, a public sphere that was both "implicitly national" and founded on "the model of representative parliamentarism." By the 1990s, however, both the cultural authority vested in the museum and the Fordist economic model on which it had depended could no longer be sustained. Steyerl goes on to chart a subsequent shift in institutional critique, articulated in the symbolic integration of minority constituencies into the museum, through engagement with feminist and postcolonial critiques of representation. Yet she defines this change as primarily symbolic, because social and economic inequalities persisted in the structure and organization of many art institutions.

Paralleling aspects of Steyerl's account, Simon Sheikh has highlighted the fragmentation of public spheres and markets, and the museum's attendant loss of cultural authority, in the late twentieth century. He emphasizes that the bourgeois subject, integral to the concept of the public sphere, was historically constituted through "interlinked process of self-representation and self-authorization" and so cannot be understood in isolation from its "cultural self-representation as a public" (Sheikh 2004). During the eighteenth and nineteenth centuries, museums, academies, newspapers, and journals all played a key role in this process, allowing the bourgeois public to become *visibly* present to itself. In the era of post-public fragmentation, however, these traditional modes of bourgeois self-representation have changed, displaced by what Sheikh (2004) describes as a neoliberal discourse of "consumer groups, as segments of a market with particular demands and desires to be catered to, and to be commodified." Steyerl (2006), who is more specifically focused on practices of artistic production, argues that critique has been symbolically integrated into the institution, or rather "on the surface of the institution without any material consequences within the institution itself or its organisation." Steyerl's point is that, while many art museums began to perform and display criticality, the conditions of labor for those engaged in this performance – such as artists and independent curators – are increasingly precarious. Here she is referring in part to the pervasiveness of commissioning practices that require artists to work very closely with institutions, sometimes operating as designers, facilitators, or mediators of institutional objectives.

Steyerl's third phase of critique coincides with a development in European curatorial and museum practice that has been theorized elsewhere as "new institutionalism" (Doherty 2004). This term is used to describe a move away from the exhibition as the primary medium of curatorial inquiry and practice, and a shift toward participatory and discursive activities, sometimes supported by artistic research in the form of commissions and residencies. Writing in 2004, Claire Doherty identified new institutionalism as "the buzzword of current European curatorial discourse," describing it as "a field of curatorial practice, institutional reform and critical debate concerned with the transformation of art institutions from within." Several of these so-called new institutions relied heavily on publishing and media production (in a variety of physical and virtual forms) to document and disseminate information on their activities. Surveying these publishing initiatives in an article for *Frieze*, Alex Farquharson cites an array of newspapers and magazines, and also identifies three specific examples of "in-house television as art work and curatorial medium" (2006, 157) at various European art institutions. They include Arteleku TV, an online platform developed from 2003 until the late 2000s by the arts center Arteleku in Donostia/San Sebastián, northern Spain, and an array of webcasting projects realized by the Danish artists' group Superflex as part of their Superchannel project, with institutions such as Rooseum in Malmö, Sweden (2001–2002).

Unlike the other examples identified by Farquharson, the CAC TV project produced by the Contemporary Art Centre in Vilnius, Lithuania (2004–2007) was devised not for the web but rather for transmission on commercial television, and developed in response to a proposition from a Lithuanian broadcaster (Figure 6.1). It was led by Contemporary Art Centre (CAC) curator Raimundas Malasauskas, whose approach was informed by the earlier work of artists such as Andy Warhol and Chris Burden, among others (CAC TV 2004). CAC TV programs were transmitted on the Lithuanian commercial channel TV1, at 11 p.m. on Wednesday evenings, over a three-year period, with episodes also available for viewing on the CAC website. In a text titled "Public CAC TV Draft Concept," the producers list a number of goals, which include "creating a TV genre that does not exist yet in Lithuanian television, developing critical skills of [the] TV audience, deconstructing fundamentals of

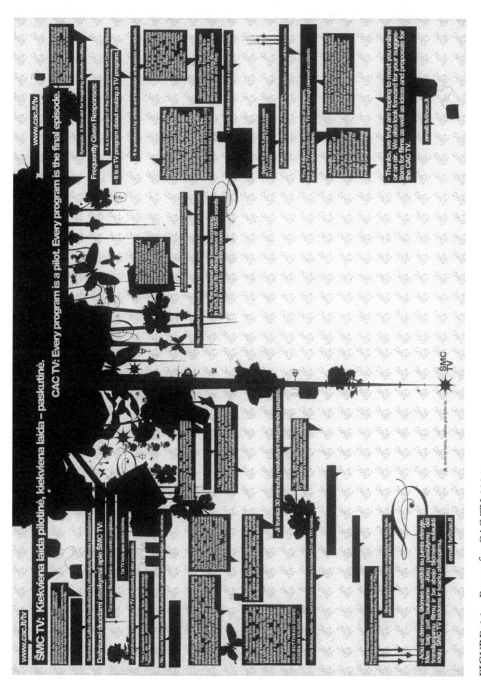

FIGURE 6.1   Poster for CAC TV, 2004.
Courtesy of Contemporary Art Centre (CAC), Vilnius. Designer: Povilas Utovka.

intellectual infotainment, exploring the field of open-source (reality) programming and self-regulation [through the] genre of the Reality meta-show" (CAC TV 2004). This "meta-show" was to be broadcast monthly, with more frequent transmissions of artists' film and video.

In addition to these web and broadcast projects, some of the so-called new institutions explored aspects of televisual form in exhibition-making. *Telling Histories: An Archive and Three Case Studies* (October 11–November 23, 2003), curated by Maria Lind, Søren Grammel, and Ana Paula Cohen at Kunstverein München, set out to examine three highly controversial exhibitions presented at the Kunstverein since 1970: *Poetry Must Be Made by All! Transform the World!* (1970), *Dove Sta Memoria* (Where is memory) by Gerhard Merz (1986), and *Eine Gessellschaft des geschmacks* (A society of taste) by Andrea Fraser (1993). The *Telling Histories* show featured an archive of material relating to these three "case studies," assembled and presented by artist Mabe Bethonico, and included catalogs, press clippings, and exhibition files, with contracts, lists of works, and letters accessible via a computer. This archival material also formed the basis for three public discussions staged in the manner of a television talk show, within an environment designed by Liam Gillick. As evidenced by the video documentation, the set was relatively simple, with the guests seated on either side of the host, on a raised platform facing the audience.

Grammel, who originated the talk show component of *Telling Histories*, selected all the guests and also took on the role of host. Several cameras were used, enabling close-ups and reaction shots of guests, and edited video recordings of the "show" were subsequently presented for viewing on monitors installed in the gallery. Reflecting on this project some years later, Grammel (2011) argued that the talk show format was especially relevant to the Munich context, because of "its saturated TV- and tabloid-based boulevard mentality," noting that he "chose the talk show as a metaphor for the phantom of mediation in general – or, to put it differently – a metaphor for the promises of the mediation industry." Implicitly, the exhibition is framed by Grammel as space in which visitors can perform and display their awareness of the constructedness of television and what he terms the "mediation industry." So, while the producers of CAC TV specifically sought to pose questions about practices of television production and consumption in Lithuania, the curators of the *Telling History* used the talk show format as a way to comment self-reflexively on the Kunstverein's exploration – and mediation – of its own history.

Art museums after the age of television

Just as art institutions were finding new ways to engage with broadcast structures and formats in the early 2000s, artists and independent curators were beginning to contest television's status as a dominant cultural form, as evidenced by the online project *TV Swansong*. Curated by UK-based artists Nina Pope and Karen Guthrie in

2002, *TV Swansong* consisted entirely of newly commissioned works – including one by Pope and Guthrie – devised to be experienced as a live webcast on a specific date (Graham and Cook 2010, 225). Reviewing *TV Swansong* for *Frieze* magazine, Dan Fox (2002) interpreted the title as a somewhat grandiose reference to "television's last gasp, a final act set in the digital heartland of its nemesis, the Internet," before going on to list numerous technical hiccups, suggesting that *TV Swansong*'s embrace of the Internet might have been somewhat premature. Noting that the project was promoted as a critical reflection on "the current state of television," Fox identifies "nostalgia" as pervasive in early 2000s television production and reception, and concludes that many of the artists involved in *TV Swansong* failed to offer a meaningful counterpoint to this dominant mode. Significantly, Fox also questions the notion, reiterated in publicity for *TV Swansong*, that web-based and TV-themed artist-curated projects are inherently more "democratic" or "accessible" than those realized by conventional art institutions. His analysis suggests that, for Pope and Guthrie, television remained strongly linked to notions of public service and access, which continue to be symbolically potent even in the post-broadcast era.

TV Swansong was also revisited in a subsequent exhibition, *Broadcast Yourself*, co-curated by Sarah Cook and Kathy Rae Huffman, and first presented at the Hatton Gallery in Newcastle upon Tyne, UK, within the context of the city's annual AV Festival, which explores intersections between art, society, and technology. The 2008 edition of the festival engaged directly with the spread of Web 2.0 technologies, including social media that enable a form of "self-broadcasting" such as YouTube and Facebook. Although interested in contemporary social practices of media sharing, Cook and Huffman specifically aimed to situate these practices in relation to histories of artistic production and activism, by drawing attention to a range of artworks from the 1970s and 1980s devised for broadcast contexts, including a number of canonical works. They included Chris Burden's *TV Commercials* (1973–1977), a series of four separately realized video works featuring the artist as performer and broadcast during commercial breaks (following the artist's purchase of airtime), and Bill Viola's *Reverse Television* (1983–1984), which depicts individual TV viewers apparently "looking back" at television. The exhibition also featured newly commissioned works, including several that explored self-promotional practices typically associated with social media, such as *The Fantasy A-List Generator* (2008) by Active Ingredient (Rachel Jacobs / Matt Watkins), which consisted of a video booth in which members of the public took on the personality of a celebrity and were interviewed in this role in a live webcast.

By including documentation of earlier TV-themed curatorial projects such as *TV Swansong*, *Broadcast Yourself* underscored the continued significance of the gallery as a site for the ordering of relations between art and television, most notably through material strategies of exhibition design and display. The show included a viewing environment, which was described in documentation as the "living room installation," featuring a patterned rug, curtains, electrical fire, potted plant, coffee table, couch, and CRT (cathode ray tube) television. This environment was used to display several single-channel works, including Burden's *TV Commercials*. Cook and Huffman also drew attention to the social and material architecture of the TV studio through their installation of *The Amarillo News Tapes* (1980) by Doug Hall, Chip Lord, and Jody Procter, a work produced during a residency undertaken by the artists and organized by Hall at KVII-TV (Channel 7) in Amarillo, Texas, in 1979. The three artists worked in collaboration with local news reporters and anchorman Dan Garcia to explore forms of news gathering and presentation practices, with a particular emphasis on theatrical style and ritual. In addition to displaying the video documentation of this project, Cook and Huffman worked with the AV Festival and Cornerhouse to produce a full-size replica of the KVII-TV news desk, which was spot-lit and raised above floor level on a low, carpeted dais. This replica underscored the theatrical quality of the news production and presentation environment, while at the same time clearly differentiating the gallery from the web as an exhibition space.

Since the mid-2000s, curators have continued to explore the history and significance of television as a cultural form, as evidenced by exhibitions such as *Are You Ready for TV?*, curated by Chus Martinez at MACBA, Barcelona (2010–2011), and *Remote Control* at the ICA, London (2011) (Figure 6.2). *Are You Ready for TV?* was

FIGURE 6.2   Installation view of *Remote Control*, Institute of Contemporary Arts, London, 2012. (For a color version of this figure, please see the color plate section.)
Photo: Mark Blower.

structured around a series of 10 thematic selections, including "The Empty Podium," exploring the presence of philosophy on French television; "Dead Air: That Dreaded Silence," featuring works that show aspects of television usually hidden such as *TVTV Looks at the Oscars* (TVTV, 1976); "Site-Specific Television," featuring canonical broadcast artworks by David Hall, among others; and "What's My Line?," dealing with themes of mediated identity through reference to the work of Warhol, Judith Barry, and Chip Lord. Each thematic selection proposed a conceptual framework that might be used to understand the changing relationship between art and television. The vast majority of works included in the show were produced before 2000, but the project did encompass a new multipart commission by Albert Serra entitled *Els noms de Crist* (2010), shot in the spaces of the museum, exhibited as an installation, and made temporarily accessible online.

Within the gallery spaces, each of the 10 selections was assigned its own specific environment, and video works were displayed on huge glass-fronted television monitors; on smaller, flat and touch screen monitors, with headphones attached; or on monitors embedded in the gallery walls. Lighting and seating arrangements were used in some of these environments to suggest specific modes of sociality, which are variously associated with the classroom, the television studio, and (less obviously) the private home. The overall aesthetic was much more clinical than that of *Broadcast Yourself*, with extensive use of white plastic chairs throughout. At MACBA, the "TV studio" environment was also quite different from the replica presented in *Broadcast Yourself*, both because it lacked a retro aesthetic and because it did not actually incorporate a studio set. Instead, at MACBA the banks of raked seating facing the large screen and the prominent suspended lighting alluded more generally to the physical and social architecture of the studio, as a setting in which TV production processes could potentially be observed by an audience.

The large television monitors used throughout *Are You Ready for TV?* also tended to dominate the galleries, and the combination of reflective surfaces and high contrast lighting found in several environments created significant barriers to viewing, so that visitors seated in front of these screens were often confronted with their own reflected images. This does not mean that the exhibition design asserted a traditional hierarchical relation between art and television, framing the museum as a site of order and critique. Instead, the evocation of the classroom in the design of the MACBA show seemed highly self-conscious, almost parodic, as though questioning whether the museum could legitimately fulfill a pedagogical role in relation to television, while at the same time fully acknowledging television's *own* neglected history of critique and experimentation.

While the MACBA show highlighted the *cultural* specificity of television as a context and setting for artistic exploration, the ICA show focused attention on technological, infrastructural, and material aspects of broadcasting. Even though *Remote Control* was considerably smaller in scale than *Are You Ready for TV?*, in terms of the number of works exhibited, it nonetheless incorporated an expansive program of performances and talks, entitled "Television Delivers People," including several events devised for web streaming. In addition, the ICA show was specifically scheduled to coincide with a significant moment in the history of British television broadcasting: the commencement in the London region of the United Kingdom's switchover from an analogue to a digital signal. Perhaps as a consequence of this context, *Remote Control* was also distinguished by a particularly strong emphasis on technological obsolescence and televisual materiality, in relation to both broadcast infrastructure and TV as a consumer object.

This emphasis was especially apparent in the lower gallery, a section of the exhibition designed and curated by the artist Simon Denny in collaboration with ICA curator Matt Williams. This space featured Denny's installation *Channel 4 Analogue Broadcasting Hardware from Arqiva's Sudbury Transmitter* (2012). This hardware installation did not bear an obvious relationship to "television" in its consumer form, consisting instead of a large bank of machinery incorporating dials, gauges, and other analogue display devices, contained in various equipment cabinets placed in a row, with several doors opened to reveal circuitry. A gallery information sheet framed this installation as an exploration of "questions surrounding spatial distribution and ecology," while also noting a visual resemblance between the older hardware and newer technologies that will "ultimately replace it – namely the vast data storage stacks owned by companies such as Google and Facebook." Denny also contributed a wall-mounted sculpture, *Analogue/Digital Transmission Switchover: London* (2012), incorporating a 3D flat screen television and artificial eyeballs, comically alluding to "advancements" in television technology.

The lower gallery also featured a series of 18 identical wall-mounted video monitors, each displaying a single-channel work produced since the late 1960s. Several of these works were originally devised for broadcast, including Gerry Schum's *Fernsehgalerie/TV Gallery: Land Art* (1968–1969), David Hall's *TV Interruptions* (1971) and *This Is a Television Receiver* (1976), and Dara Birnbaum and Dan Graham's *Local TV News Analysis* (1980). Many of these videos are well known – even iconic – examples of artists' television, which also featured in several of the exhibitions already cited. But, placed in proximity to Denny's hardware installation and sculpture, the display proved especially effective in highlighting television's mutable materiality.

Hall's *This Is a Television Receiver* (1976), one of the iconic videos shown at *Remote Control*, was originally commissioned by the BBC as an unannounced opening work for their special *Arena* video art program, first transmitted on March 10, 1976. At the outset, BBC news presenter Richard Baker delivers a didactic text on illusionism in television production, culminating in the statement "This is a television receiver." Using analogue means, the statement was rerecorded several times, so that the image is progressively distorted. Since the curvature of the television screen also becomes more apparent (Cubitt 2006), Hall's work emphasizes both the material properties of the receiver and its function within a larger institutional formation. Although devised to be viewed on a domestic television receiver, Hall's work is conventionally exhibited in gallery spaces on a museum-standard Hantarex or Sony "cube" monitor with CRT. The wall-mounted monitors used at the ICA to display video works such as *This Is a Television Receiver* were, however, much smaller than standard museum cube monitors and, although they incorporated CRTs, they also loosely resembled computer screens commonly used in office environments. Consequently they did not physically resemble the type of "receiver" actually used by Hall in the production of his video work, lacking the subtle curvature integral to his progressive distortion of the image. Through the presentation of *This Is a Television Receiver* on this nonstandard monitor, in proximity to the display of obsolete hardware, *Remote Control* drew attention to television's complex (and continually shifting) status as commodity object, medium, and institution.

Remote Control also highlighted interdependencies between art and media economies, with regard to the generation of publicity. The exhibition's event program, titled "Television Delivers People," included a project by London-based art group LuckyPDF (James Early, John Hill, Ollie Hogan, and Yuri Pattison), known for their use of television formats to explore, and sometimes amplify, the promotional character of art discourse. Their previous works include a "TV show" produced for the Frieze Art Fair in 2011, featuring 50 artists who were invited to show and produce new work. More recently, LuckyPDF have developed the parodic "School of Global Art," which promises (according to the project website) to take students "on a journey to the cusp of a new era in learning." "School of Global Art" was launched during a program of talks and events accompanying *Remote Control*. An "enrolment booth" in the ICA gallery offered membership and a "welcome pack of essays" to prospective students in exchange for their personal data.

The event also included a publicity stunt organized by LuckyPDF and involving reality TV star Chloe Sims, from *The Only Way Is Essex* (2010), famous for her plastic surgery and extravagant lifestyle (Figure 6.3). Sims was led on a tour of the *Remote Control* show, and her response to works by artists such as Michelangelo Pistoletto were duly reported in promotional coverage of the event:

> It's something that I'm interested in as in my day-to-day work I have to negotiate reality and created fictions. [The Pistoletto work] is also a mirror, both for the viewer and as a metaphor, it's both art and I can check my make-up in it, and that is very practical. (Phaidon 2012)

The exhibition tour with Sims should not be interpreted as a critique of reality TV or of celebrity culture in general. Instead, it functions more specifically as a commentary on the changing form and function of publicity within the contemporary art economy. LuckyPDF does not distinguish between art fairs and publicly funded art galleries as institutional sites, or seek to operate "outside" publicity-driven media industries. Instead its work is concerned with practices of symbolic exchange between art and media economies, and with changing modes of publicity. In an analysis of the relationship between the art market and celebrity culture, Isabelle

FIGURE 6.3   LuckyPDF's James Early and Chloe Sims at *Remote Control*, Institute of Contemporary Arts, London, 2012. (For a color version of this figure, please see the color plate section.)
Photo: Victoria Erdelevskaya. Courtesy of LuckyPDF and Institute of Contemporary Arts.

Graw (2009, 32) notes the historically important role played by "symbol-bearers" such as art historians, critics, and curators. These privileged producers of knowledge contribute to the generation of symbolic – and consequently market – value (Graw 2009, 23). According to Graw, however, lifestyle and fashion magazines have begun, in recent decades, to rival established symbol-bearers in the designation of contemporary art's symbolic value. She finds evidence of this in the prevalence of lists in art and lifestyle publications, in which critics rank their favorite artists or exhibitions (2009, 43). These modes of publicity meet the demand for clear hierarchies, but rarely offer any reflection on criteria for inclusion or exclusion. As her analysis makes clear, value is not simply bestowed by museums, but rather produced through a complex and fluid exchange of publicities, involving art institutions and lifestyle-oriented media.

Broadcast form in public programming

Some art institutions have, however, deliberately sought to dissociate themselves from celebrity- and lifestyle-oriented culture by appropriating modes of rational-critical discourse that are historically associated with current affairs and news media. These discursive modes are routinely valorized and defended by some theorists of media and culture because they are thought to play an important role in the ongoing formation of the public sphere, while others entirely reject the notion that television audiences can ever function as a public. According to Sonia Livingstone, value-laden distinctions tend to persist between televisual audiences and publics, despite significant changes in technologies and practices of media consumption. Livingstone notes that publics and audiences are often thought to be "mutually opposed," in part because "'public' implies an orientation to collective and consensual action, perhaps even requires that action to be effective for a public to be valued" (2005, 17). She notes that "in both popular and elite discourses, audiences are denigrated as trivial, passive, individualized, while publics are valued as active, critically engaged and politically significant," with face-to-face communication often judged as inferior to mediated communication (2005, 18).

Livingstone argues for a rethinking of the distinction between audience and public, within a "media and communications environment characterized both by the mediation of publics and the participation of audiences" (2005, 17). For example, she identifies talk shows as especially ambiguous objects, because they often involve expert discussion of topical issues in public, yet "is often taken as representing the antithesis of rational public debate" (2005, 20). An opposition between audience and public also finds expression in curatorial projects such as *Telling Histories* and in more recent public programming initiatives developed by the Hammer Museum in Los Angeles. While it is not a new institution in the sense already discussed, the Hammer Museum has nonetheless sought to review and revise aspects of its institutional structure during the 2000s, and to reconfigure its relationship to its audience, which includes a considerable number of local residents.

I am especially interested in the role played by broadcasting in the museum's ongoing series of current affairs themed talks entitled the Hammer Forum, which consists of a series of public discussions, usually held monthly in the museum's Billy Wilder Theater, focusing on topical issues such as environmental concerns, gay marriage, and the role of commercial media in the democratic political process.[2] Admission is free and the discussions (which are also webcast and archived online) typically involve presentations by one or two speakers, followed by questions from the audience. The Forum is moderated by the journalist and broadcaster Ian Masters, host of the radio show *Background Briefing*, which deals primarily with political issues and is broadcast on KPFK 90.7 FM. It is a listener-supported (as opposed to advertising-dependent) radio station that forms part of the left-leaning California-based Pacifica Radio network. Masters' long-standing experience as a radio host is strongly emphasized in the Hammer Museum's publicity for the Forum, and he is often introduced at the start of the discussions as a BBC-trained journalist, an association that seems symbolically as well as professionally significant because of the BBC's history and international prominence as a public service broadcaster. Masters and Claudia Bestor (Director of Public Programs at the Hammer) work together on the identification of possible speakers, who are usually confirmed several months in advance of the Forum event, and a news-related theme is often explored over a series of public sessions.

It is worth noting that the origins of the Hammer Forum lie partly in the huge public attention generated by a public talk delivered by Gore Vidal in March 2003, prior to the US bombing of Iraq (Sheets 2004). Following this event, museum staff recognized that there was a local interest in discursive events focusing explicitly on politics. But, as the museum is not a broadcaster or social media website, newsworthy material can actually result in costs to the institution, since they are charged by their server for very large volumes of downloading prompted by events dealing with controversial or highly topical issues. So the program promotes in-depth exploration of issues that fall within the territory of current affairs but are not necessarily headline news. The 2011–2012 program, for example, included several sessions on the theme of the "American Dream" as well as a session on November 19, 2011, entitled "Political Persuasion," addressing the role of demographic research in the 2012 US presidential election campaign. It featured two "veteran campaign strategists," both of whom critiqued the divisive, and often highly emotive, use of television advertising in recent election campaigns.

The Hammer Museum does not currently gather detailed demographic information on the Forum attendees, but anecdotal evidence offered by museum staff suggests that events attract a mix of museum members, listeners to Ian Masters' radio show, UCLA students, and also specific interest groups targeted by the Public Program staff in relation to specific issues. Forum events are ticketed but free and attendees receive a calendar detailing forthcoming exhibitions and public programs. Since 2011, the Hammer's communications department has also produced a short presentation about the museum's activities, which plays in the theater before the discussion begins. Surprisingly, however, there is no attempt to directly link the Forum topics with the exhibition or event calendar. Instead, Bestor emphasizes that the aim of the event is to offer a physical space for audiences, most of them LA residents, to engage with each other and to pose unscripted questions on current issues to experts, such as policymakers. So, even though Forum events are webcast, and legitimated through reference to internationally situated broadcast institutions (such as the BBC), the Hammer Forum clearly reiterates the significance of the museum as a localized space of social gathering and public visibility. In terms of its content, the Hammer Forum seems to address directly many of the problems of social and political participation posed by the fragmentation and segmentation of the bourgeois public sphere, also highlighted in exhibitions such as *Telling Histories*. But, rather than engaging with the form of the entertainment TV talk show, the Hammer Forum invokes the authority and seriousness of a current affairs public radio show, a form of broadcasting that enjoys a relatively high cultural status and legitimacy within the United States.

Television production and contemporary art commissioning

In addition to curatorially led projects and public programming initiatives engaging with televisual form, art institutions have also played host in recent decades to numerous commissioned works realized through collaborations between artists and TV producers. In some instances these collaborations have resulted in works intended exclusively for gallery exhibition but others have extended into broadcast and online platforms. For example, the props and sets of the primetime television soap *Melrose Place* served as the focus of a three-year (1995–1998) art project realized by GALA Committee, the name given to a collaboration between the artist Mel Chin, students and faculty at the University of Athens, Georgia ("GA") and the California Institute of the Arts ("LA"), and the show's producers and set decorator. Reflecting on this project in 2000, Yilmaz Dziewior notes that Chin worked with a network of 102 artists and "persuaded Spelling Entertainment Group … to grant them a contract to provide the program with more than 150 props over the course of two seasons" (2000, 193). These prop objects often included imagery or textual material relating to social or political themes raised obliquely (but rarely addressed directly) in *Melrose Place* plotlines, including environmental concerns, global conflict, crime and violence, and gender and sexual health issues.

This project was not initiated as a critique of *Melrose Place* but rather devised as a more open-ended exploration of television culture and discourse. Unlike an earlier generation of artists seeking to present themselves as innovators or critics, Chin and the GALA Committee did not frame their project as an attempt to question or to reform established modes of television production. Instead, the artists, students, and television workers involved in this collaboration were motivated by a shared interest in a range of social and political causes, which they perceived as highly significant. Although the additions and alterations to the show's sets were intended to be unobtrusive, the project was premised on the notion that some viewers would become curious about the unusual objects visible on screen. Perhaps recognizing the limitations of this approach, GALA Committee members also experimented with mediation strategies that could operate in tandem with the existing *Melrose Place* fan culture. In 1996 the project expanded to include an online component – a website designed around a fictional fan called "Eliza," whose homepage included speculative commentary about the odd objects appearing on the show, with the aim of arousing the interest of real fans. It is not clear, however, if this strategy succeeded, and the online archive of the GALA Committee websites (initially maintained by the Carsey-Wolf Center at the University of California, Santa Barbara) is no longer active.

It is important to note that the GALA Committee project developed as the result of a museum commission. The collaboration was initiated by Chin in response to an invitation extended in 1995 by curators at the Geffen Contemporary, MOCA,

Los Angeles, to produce work for the exhibition *Uncommon Sense*, planned for 1997. The exhibition focused on the theme of social interaction and consisted of six newly commissioned works by artists committed to engaging public interaction. At MOCA, the GALA Committee presented *In the Name of the Place*, an installation featuring a Melrose-style set complete with a selection of objects and videos of several episodes. These works were subsequently auctioned with the aim of generating funds (and publicity) for nonprofit organizations associated with the various social issues highlighted by the project. According to Dziewior, "GALA Committee not only influenced the design of the props but also, over time, had a subtle effect on aspects of the series' plot development," as both the auction and the *Uncommon Sense* opening at MOCA were incorporated into the TV show (2000, 193–194).

While the GALA Committee project remains distinctive, as a long-term collaboration between artists and television workers elaborated across the contexts of museum, broadcast TV series, and Internet, several other artists have collaborated with television producers on the realization of installation works for specific exhibition contexts, including Katya Sander, *Televised I: The Anchor, the I and the Studio* (2006); Liz Magic Laser, *In Camera* (2012); and Gerard Byrne, *A Man and a Woman Make Love* (2012). My next example involves a collaboration between an artist and the entire cast and crew of a telenovela produced by the Mexican commercial broadcaster Televisa. Christian Jankowski's *Crying for the March of Humanity* is a reproduction of an episode of the Televisa show *La que no podía amar* (The one who could not love) shot side by side with the original, using the same actors, crew, locations, sets, and scenarios, and adhering to the standard production and post-production approaches. The only difference between the production of the original episode and Jankowski's version is that the artist instructed the actors not to speak any of their lines, but rather to remain mute and communicate only by means of dramatic emotional outbursts, primarily crying. During filming, the actors could hear the script through hidden earphones,[3] so they could synchronize the timing of their tears with the dialogue in the original episode.

The end result is at times comical but also emotionally engaging, largely on account of the performances. Many of the actors visibly struggle to hold back their words and to "speak" with their eyes and their tears, and the episode includes a large number of close-ups (using the standard techniques of shot reverse shot, with careful eyeline matches), underscoring the importance of gesture in melodrama. Even though the episode is drawn from the midpoint of the telenovela serial, and is presented without contextualizing information about characters or the storyline, it is possible to speculate with some degree of certainty on the main aspects of the plot. The setting is a lavishly furnished villa, and the narrative appears to revolve around a wealthy man, a husband and father, who is so traumatized by his inability to walk (he is pictured in a wheelchair) that he cannot love his wife and child. The video was produced for exhibition in the Sala de Arte Público Siqueiros, a museum located in the former home and studio of the artist David

Alfaro Siqueiros (1896–1974) in Mexico City. Its title refers specifically to the latter's monumental mural work *La marcha de la humanidad* (The march of humanity, 1965–1971), proposing a relationship between the telenovela and mural forms in terms of the use of gesture.

Crying for the March of Humanity is not the first work by Jankowski to borrow from commercial television, and he has often utilized reality TV formats (particularly the makeover genre) to structure scenarios in which art world conventions are observed by outsiders, sometimes to comic effect. Jankowski has also devised makeover projects that require the participation of art workers as well as TV performers. In *The Perfect Gallery* (2010), for example, he "hired" interior designer Gordon Whistance, known for appearances on the home improvement show *Changing Rooms* (1996–2004), to speedily renovate the Pump House Gallery in South London, in preparation for his forthcoming solo show. The exchanges between the designer and the gallery director suggest (somewhat unconvincingly) that Whistance is unaware of the fact that the empty gallery will be the artwork and the video is structured so as to resemble a conventional makeover show, following the designer as he conducts perfunctory research on galleries and agonizes over his miniscule budget and impending deadline.

Jankowski has also produced works that involve a broadcast component, such as *Tableaux Vivant TV* (2010), which consists of a series of short location reports conducted by television journalists covering preparations for the Sydney Biennale. These reports functioned as publicity for the exhibition but, instead of featuring the usual TV-friendly action shots, they incorporated live *tableaux vivants*, in which key players in the Biennale, such as the artist, the administrative team, and the artistic director David Elliot, were depicted in a moment of artificial stillness. As their cameras move around these highly theatrical scenes, the TV presenters attempt to verbally inject a sense of excitement and animation that is entirely absent from the on-screen image.

In one sequence Jankowski is depicted sitting alone looking out to sea, frozen in a moment of highly choreographed reflection, while the cameras look on and the TV presenter speculates about his innermost thoughts and hopes. At another moment, the television cameras move through a production office in which the administrators and curators involved in the realization of the Biennale are also frozen in motion. This sequence is particularly significant in that it requires the (presumably already overworked) production staff to perform in yet another capacity, helping to realize an artwork by pausing their usual activity. So the project offered a view of action behind the scenes, in keeping with the conventions of news coverage of major cultural events, but presented these scenes as highly choreographed. In contrast to *The Perfect Gallery*, which closely follows the conventions of reality TV transformation-themed shows, *Tableaux Vivant TV* is both unsettling and formally distinctive. By choreographing and artificially pausing the action that serves as the content of each reportage sequences, Jankowski both makes explicit and subtly confounds the conventional strategies used to publicize artistic and curatorial work.

Conclusion: Coproduction, partnership, and publicity

Jankowski's work, like that of LuckyPDF, utilizes televisual modes of production and publicity to articulate a position within, rather than outside, the celebrity-driven cultural economy that is analyzed by Isabelle Graw. Art institutions such as the Hammer Museum seem to articulate a different position in relation to this economy, through initiatives such as the Hammer Forum, which appropriate the self-consciously rational discursive form of current affairs journalism. In conjunction with its public programs, however, the Hammer has also commissioned artworks that are more obviously indebted to celebrity- and lifestyle-oriented culture, as evidenced by the exhibition *Hammer Projects: My Barbarian* in 2010–2011. This show featured a six-part video work, *The Night Epi$ode* (2010), commissioned from the artists' group My Barbarian. It was inspired by the 1970s anthology series *Rod Serling's Night Gallery*, which opened each week with the host wandering through a museum at night. In *The Night Epi$ode*, My Barbarian explore a variety of surreal and supernatural situations loosely linked by a focus on labor, exploitation, economic marginalization, and competition. The pilot episode, for example, features a group of "curators" locked inside a room, evaluating a succession of works in which artists seek to attract attention through bizarre and self-destructive strategies. According to the press release, in this work "the arts become a stand-in for the equalizing force of a bad economy. Everyone is struggling, has been violated, or has sacrificed … artists have vanished, imprisoned themselves, become vampires" (Hammer Museum 2010).

Clearly, television's current and historical forms now serve as an important resource, even a repertoire, for artists seeking to articulate and analyze their position within the contemporary economy of self-exploitation. Yet it would be a mistake to categorize museums and art institutions exclusively as spaces for the interrogation of this economy. Instead, it might be more accurate to position the art museum within an economy of commercial coproduction, in which art institutions are often the weaker partner. Here I am thinking of the role played by Brooklyn Museum in the production and promotion of the art-themed reality TV show broadcast by the US cable and satellite channel Bravo, *Work of Art: The Next Great Artist*. Launched in 2010, and developed by the actress Sarah Jessica Parker's production company Pretty Matches, in conjunction with the reality TV producer Magical Elves, *Work of Art* focuses on the "discovery" and promotion of artists in the early stages of their careers. Unlike music- or dance-based reality TV contests, art-themed shows tend *not* to be organized around viewer participation and voting. Instead, the focus is primarily on judgments and evaluations performed by art world insiders, and on endorsements by established art institutions such as museums or auction houses.

Presenting its participants (a mix of graduates and artists without formal qualifications) with tasks that are vaguely reminiscent of art school projects, *Work of Art* involves the participation of powerful art world "mentors" such as Simon de Pury, the chair of Phillips de Pury auction house, with equally prominent figures as "judges," such as the influential art critic Jerry Saltz. Participants compete for

$100,000 in prize money and a solo exhibition at the Brooklyn Museum, with the winner selected by a panel that includes the museum's curator. While this association has generated controversy, it has also undoubtedly raised the Brooklyn Museum's profile, and has been defended by the institution's director as the continuation of a venerable tradition of juried competition in the arts (Rosenberg 2010). In the long term, however, this partnership signals a troubling move away from the institutional self-questioning that characterized earlier forays into TV production by publicly funded art institutions and commercial television, extending from the work of the LBMA in the 1970s and 1980s to more recent initiatives. Rather than enabling critical exploration of the Brooklyn Museum's function and future in a celebrity-driven cultural economy, *Work of Art: The Next Great Artist* both exploits and undermines its credibility as a public institution.

As evidenced by this selection of TV-themed art projects, television no longer functions as an emblem of contemporary popular culture. Nonetheless, "television" persists as an object of fascination for artists, curators, and art institutions, perhaps because of its status as (simultaneously) commodity object, medium, and cultural institution. This complexity, or indeterminacy, may help to explain why television has proved important for those seeking to question the traditional function of the museum, whether as a site for the classification and categorization of objects, or as an institution devoted to the narration of history, and to the formation of citizens and publics. Ultimately, the examples drawn together in this chapter demonstrate that television in the museum is very often the focus of contradictory associations and claims, particularly regarding the differences between audiences and publics. Consequently, when transposed to the art institution, TV formats such as talk shows can function as a means to bolster the status of the museum as a public sphere, or as a way to expose the very dissolution of the ideals underpinning this notion of publicness. Even though television has relinquished its cultural dominance to the Internet and social media, it seems likely that these contradictory associations and claims will persist, and continue to shape the relationship between museums and media.

Acknowledgments

My research was supported by a fellowship from the International Research Institute for Cultural Technologies and Media Philosophy, Bauhaus-Universität Weimar.

Notes

1   This chapter incorporates material revised from my *TV Museum: Contemporary Art and the Age of Television* (Bristol, UK: Intellect; Chicago: University of Chicago Press, 2014), and also from "Televisual Objects: Props, Relics and Prosthetics," *Afterall* 33 (2013): 66–77.

2   My discussion is informed by interviews conducted at the Hammer Museum with Claudia Bestor, Director of Public Programs, and her colleague Camille Thoma, on February 22, 2013.

3   Production details provided by Christian Jankowski in a personal interview on September 12, 2012, during the preview of his exhibition *Monument to the Bourgeois Working Class*, Kosterfelde Gallery, Berlin, September 13–November 3, 2012.

References

Born, Georgina. 2003. "Strategy, Positioning and Projection in Digital Television: Channel Four and the Commercialization of Public Service Broadcasting in the UK." *Media, Culture & Society* 25: 773–799.

Boyle, Deirdre. 1997. *Subject to Change: Guerrilla Television Revisited.* New York: Oxford University Press.

CAC TV. 2004. "Public CAC TV Draft Concept." Centre for Contemporary Art, October 20. Accessed August 4, 2014. http://www.cac.lt/tv/movies.php?_id=2330.

Cubitt, Sean. 2006. "Grayscale Video and the Shift to Color." *Art Journal* 65(3): 46–49.

Ćurčić, Branka. 2007. "Television as a Symbol of Lost Public Space." European Institute for Progressive Cultural Policies, December 12. Accessed August 4, 2014. http://transform.eipcp.net/correspondence/1197491434#redir#redir.

Doherty, Claire. 2004. "The Institution Is Dead! Long Live the Institution! Contemporary Art and New Institutionalism." *Art of Encounter: Engage* 15. Accessed August 4, 2014. http://www.engage.org/seebook.aspx?id=697.

Dziewior, Yilmaz. 2000. "GALA Committee." *Artforum* 33(10): 193–194.

Farquharson, Alex. 2006. "Bureaux de Change." *Frieze* 101: 156–159.

Fox, Dan. 2002. "TV Swansong." *Frieze* 68: 124.

Graham, Beryl, and Sarah Cook. 2010. *Rethinking Curating: Art after New Media.* Cambridge, MA: MIT Press.

Grammel, Søren. 2011. "A Series of Acts and Spaces." *On Curating* 8: 33–38. Accessed August 4, 2014. http://www.fridericianum-kassel.de/fileadmin/Fotos/Symposium/oncurating_issue_0811.pdf.

Graw, Isabelle. 2009. *High Price: Art between the Market and Celebrity Culture.* Berlin: Sternberg.

Hammer Museum. 2010. "My Barbarian, October 23, 2010–January 23, 2011." Accessed August 4, 2014. http://hammer.ucla.edu/exhibitions/detail/exhibition_id/188.

Huffman, Kathy Rae. 1990. "Video Art: What's TV Got to Do with It?" In *Illuminating Video: An Essential Guide to Video Art*, edited by Doug Hall and Sally Jo Fifer, 81–90. New York: Aperture Foundation with Bay Area Video Coalition.

Huffman, Kathy Rae. 2011. "Exchange and Evolution: Worldwide Video Long Beach 1974–1999." *Exchange and Evolution: Worldwide Video Long Beach 1974–1999*, edited by Kathy Rae Huffman, 10–25. Long Beach, CA: Long Beach Museum of Art.

Livingstone, Sonia. 2005. "On the Relation between Audiences and Publics." In *Audiences and Publics: When Cultural Engagement Matters for the Public Sphere*, edited by Sonia Livingstone, 17–41. Bristol, UK: Intellect.

Mcquire, Scott. 2010. "Rethinking Media Events: Large Screens, Public Space Broadcasting and Beyond." *New Media Society* 12: 567–582. doi:10.1177/1461444809342764.

Mehring, Christine. 2008. "Television Art's Abstract Starts: Europe circa 1944–1969." *October* 125: 29–64.

Phaidon. 2012. "LuckyPDF Invite Reality TV Star to Critique ICA Show." Accessed August 4,2014.http://de.phaidon.com/agenda/art/events/2012/april/03/luckypdf-invite-reality-tv-star-to-critique-ica-show/.

Rosenberg, Karen. 2010. "A Museum Show as a TV Contest Prize." New York Times, August 18.

Sheets, Hilarie M. 2004. "Armand Hammer's Orphan Museum Turns into Cinderella in Los Angeles." New York Times, October 6.

Sheikh, Simon. 2004. "In the Place of the Public Sphere? Or, The World in Fragments." European Institute for Progressive Cultural Policies. Accessed August 4, 2014. http://republicart.net/disc/publicum/sheikh03_en.htm.

Spigel, Lynn. 2008. *TV by Design: Modern Art and the Rise of Network Television*. Chicago: University of Chicago Press.

Steyerl, Hito. 2006. "The Institution of Critique." European Institute for Progressive Cultural Policies, January. EIPCP Transversal Project. Accessed August 4, 2014. http://eipcp.net/transversal/0106/steyerl/en.

Sutton, Gloria. 2011. "Playback: Reconsidering the Long Beach Museum of Art as a Media Art Center." In *Exchange and Evolution: Worldwide Video Long Beach 1974–1999*, edited by Kathy Rae Huffman, 120–129. Long Beach, CA: Long Beach Museum of Art.

Wyver, John. 2009. "TV against TV: Video Art on Television." In *Film and Video Art*, edited by Stuart Comer, 122–131. London: Tate.

Maeve Connolly is a lecturer in the Faculty of Film, Art and Creative Technologies at Dún Laoghaire Institute of Art, Design and Technology, Ireland. Her books include *TV Museum: Contemporary Art and the Age of Television* (Intellect/University of Chicago Press, 2014), which charts television's changing status as cultural form, object of critique, and site of artistic invention; *The Place of Artists' Cinema: Space, Site and Screen* (Intellect/University of Chicago Press, 2009), a critical history of the cinematic turn in contemporary art since the 1990s; and *The Glass Eye: Artists and Television* (Project, 2000), a collection of artists' projects and texts coedited with Orla Ryan. She has contributed to journals such as *Afterall, Artforum, Art Monthly, Frieze, Journal of Curatorial Studies, MIRAJ, Mousse, Screen*, and the *Velvet Light Trap*, and curated screenings at venues such as Darklight Film Festival, the Irish Film Institute, LUX, Picture This, and Project Arts Centre.

7 SIMKNOWLEDGE
What Museums Can Learn from Video Games

Seth Giddings

The museum looked familiar yet strangely different. The floor and pillars too shiny, the paintings and sculptures dotted along the walls of the rooms and halls bland and generic, like the sketched-in background to a dream. My companion led me into a spacious gallery, past an information desk empty except for lamps and computer screens, past vitrines holding suspiciously modern-looking automatic weaponry, and up to one of the half dozen or so tableaux on display. Within an unglazed diorama, against the illusionistic perspective of its painted backdrop, five animatronic figures in combat fatigues moved slightly yet fluidly. As we approached, they shifted into a prescripted routine, pointing, nodding, checking weaponry, sketching out a dramatic vignette from some war or war film. After a few seconds they froze, mannequins again. We circled the room, each display vivified in animatronic precision as we approached, before lapsing again into motionlessness.

"Watch this," said my companion, and opened fire with his M9. The nearest mannequin flew back, jerking, as the bullets hit, and fell to the floor crumpled – I realized with horror that it was a human body, not a mechanical device. My companion laughed and we moved, running now, to the information desk. He hit a large red button on the desk and immediately the room erupted into violent action. The mannequins leapt from their displays and headed straight for us, guns blazing. We smashed the nearest vitrine, grabbed its guns and ammunition, and dashed for cover ...

This nightmarish museum is a bonus level in the popular video game *Call of Duty: Modern Warfare 2*. Playing it evoked in me an ironic vision of dire predictions of a future in which culture and science have been swallowed up by technologies of entertainment, distraction, and spectacle: an age of spectacular digital effects and interactive networked entertainment; a virtual world of shiny surface

The International Handbooks of Museum Studies: Museum Media, First Edition.
Edited by Michelle Henning.
© 2015 John Wiley & Sons Ltd. Published 2020 by John Wiley & Sons Ltd.

spectacle, filled with empty signs of cultural and scientific heritage, which have become mere tokens or props for apparently mindless violent action; intellectual or aesthetic reflection, learning, study, the communication or transmission of *meaning* all exploding in bursts of computer-driven violence. It is one vivid example of what Andrew Darley has called "digital visual culture," a culture characterized by a waning, or loss, of meaning, driven by new aesthetic forms of computer-generated imagery (CGI) in cinema and television and video games. This chapter will explore some of the implications of an emergent visual culture of digital media for museum education, and especially the popular communication of scientific ideas to a youthful audience. It will look at some examples from science museums and centers, at popular science media forms, most notably the use of CGI in science documentaries, and at computer applications, both in entertainment and in an educational context.

A key concept will be that of *simulation*. This term addresses both the pervasive sense of an emerging culture of the fake or illusory (e.g., Eco 1986; Jameson 1991; Cubitt 2001), and – in computer simulation – new modes of exploring and modeling complex natural systems. Simulation, I will argue, goes to the heart of the anxieties about, and possibilities for, new modes of communication today.

> [These visual digital forms] lack the symbolic depth and representational complexity of earlier forms, appearing by contrast to operate within a drastically reduced field of meaning. They are direct and one-dimensional, about little, other than their ability to commandeer the sight and the senses. Popular forms of diversion and amusement, these new technological entertainments are, perhaps, the clearest manifestation of the advance of the culture of the "depthless image." (Darley 2000, 76)

As we'll see, these worries are not unique to recent technological developments, and anxieties about contemporary changes in public communication of science through museums and TV documentaries are widespread, if not always expressed in the apocalyptic terms of the "loss of meaning." In both academic and popular discourse, computer-generated effects in television and cinema are generally considered as, at best, eye-catching and entertaining, but superficial, an aesthetic of the surface and depthlessness, always threatening to overwhelm the true mission of popular screen media to tell a story or transmit knowledge. From this anxious viewpoint, the potential of CGI to distract, dazzle, and seduce has to be monitored carefully: these images seem to blur carefully drawn and redrawn borders between entertainment and knowledge, running the risk of turning flagship programs and important exhibits into commercial, Disneyfied distractions. At worst, they seem dissimulating and illusory, symptomatic of a dangerous cultural trajectory toward the emptying of meaning and the waning of affect through hyperrealist aesthetics. Of particular relevance to this chapter is the often explicit insistence in theories of popular visual culture on a binary opposition between "spectacle" and "knowledge" (e.g., Jameson 1991; Mulvey 1996; Darley 2000).

This unhelpful hierarchy hides the possibility that new forms of knowledge are made possible by digital media, across science and popular screen media. This chapter will argue that the genealogy of simulation in the computer modeling of complex systems, the spectacular techniques and aesthetics of animation, and the relationships between these technocultural forms and the televisual medium of the video game suggests a more nuanced and productive way of thinking about technology, entertainment, spectacle, and knowledge in museums and science centers.

There is a rich literature on the historical precedents for recent debates and concerns about the tensions between attracting visitors' attention to museums and exhibits through novel techniques of display and the serious educational and research aims of public museums. Barbara Stafford (1994) has charted the interplay between science education and the spectacular presentation of technologies and scientific phenomena back to the eighteenth century, and other writers have discussed how new media technologies such as photography and cinema have been both embraced and resisted by museums since the mid-nineteenth century (Griffiths 2003).

A key moment was the end of the nineteenth century, when a significant shift occurred in the focus of museums in the United States from public education to popular spectacle. As the museum's role as a research institution largely shifted to the university, there was an "increasing pressure to turn museums into sites of mass popular appeal … at the expense of the notion of the museum as a research institution for everyone" (Henning 2006, 46). This shift was typified by the widespread adoption in American museums of the diorama as an exhibition technique for anthropological or natural history displays. Though familiar, even quaint, today (indeed, as our *Modern Warfare 2* example shows, it can easily serve as an archetypal signifier of museumness), at its inception the diorama was controversial. Though it addressed the problem of how to attract and keep a visitor's attention among the bewildering accumulation of artifacts in museum halls and display cases, and offered a visual cue as to the environment in which the artifact or creature originated, for some critics and curators its aesthetic and technical characteristics were too closely connected with the emergent commercial spectacle of shop window displays and arcades, as well as popular attractions such as panoramas. As Alison Griffiths puts it, the display of natural history and anthropology has always been a "site [of] complex negotiations … between anthropology, popular culture and commerce in attempting to strike the right balance between education, spectacle and profit" (2002, 47). This negotiation of the competing motives of edification and commercialism in display techniques continues today. Griffiths notes that contemporary concerns about "Disneyfication" in natural history museums echo debates in professional museum journals and popular science publications at the end of the nineteenth century on new visual technologies such as lantern slides and cinema, technologies that required "careful supervision, lest their associations with popular culture contaminate the scientific seriousness of the exhibit and institution," blurring the museums' distinction from the nickelodeon and the sensationalist dime museum (Griffiths 2003, 376). Today, the threat of distraction from eye-catching new techniques is still felt. Chandler Screven argues that the three-dimensionality and novelty of museum "gadgetry," while offering some interest, risks "distract[ing] viewers from the main ideas, distinctions, or story line," whereas Lisa C. Roberts fears these display technologies may "overshadow the objects they were designed to set off," competing for both space and attention (quoted in Griffiths 2003, 384).

So, prefiguring more recent display technologies, the dioramas were, as Michelle Henning notes, "increasingly illusionistic," "using technical devices and three-dimensional objects." With clear resonances with contemporary displays and attractions, the aim was "to envelop the spectator, giving them the sensation of being in the scene" (Henning 2006, 47), but always running the risk of overplaying spectacle at the expense of knowledge. Visitors might, it was feared, pay attention only to the technical devices and a presentation of simplified or preformed knowledge rather than to the artifacts themselves, the intended knowledge transfer short-circuited.

Drawing on Mark Sandberg's (2003) work on tableaux in nineteenth-century Scandinavian folk museums, Henning connects these concerns to the simulational digital technologies of today:

> While the museum founders were looking for immediacy, a sense of unmediated contact with the past, many visitors seemed to enjoy the simulation *as* simulation, finding pleasure in the to-and-fro between deception and recognition. Instead of desiring an older and lost (or rapidly disappearing) reality, a good number of visitors took pleasure in that in-betweenness, a pleasure that was possible through modern spectator positions, and that dispensed with the priority of the original over the copy, reality over the representation. (Henning 2006, 57)

Concerns about visitor attention were evident across the range of museums and instructional institutions, from folk museums to zoological gardens. It is significant for my argument here to note the precise terms of these anxieties that visitors might be distracted by the techniques and apparatus of display, interaction, and illusion. There is knowledge transmission here, but it is misdirected, wrong – we learn of the devices of simulation, not of the primary object of study whether that be an animal, a people, a natural phenomenon, or an artifact. It is worth noting, however, that the science center as a distinct institution has always – since its inception in the 1960s with the Exploratorium in San Francisco – been characterized by novel interactive displays (see Pedretti 2002).

Attention to the historical precedents for the negotiation of attraction and contemplation, spectacle and knowledge, commerce and research, helps us to understand contemporary concerns about public engagement with science and natural history through museums and science centers. However, there are significant material and industrial differences attendant on the emergence of digital media, and in their effects on exhibition design and visitor behavior. As we'll see, some of these characteristics and effects are not separable from early moments of spectacle and interaction – fears of the merging of the museum with the theme park and the retail outlet are only intensified in the vivid glare and eye-catching effects of digital media – but they do offer or promise new possibilities for engagement and interaction. Again, these innovations have been viewed with distrust as well as excitement.

Prehistoric simulation: The case of *Walking with Dinosaurs*

In this era of digital technology and connectivity, access to heritage is increasingly mediated through the consumption of signs, electronic images, and simulacra. In virtual heritage, an algorithmically accurate large-scale 3D model of a cathedral or castle is taken as the hallmark of authenticity

Flynn 2007, 349

In an interesting article on the implications of digital media for the modeling and display of heritage sites and museums, Bernadette Flynn identifies the processes of virtualization as a fundamental challenge to the truth status of museums, in particular the ambiguity of an artifact's historical significance when rendered as a virtual presence. The modeling of heritage sites and objects in 3D software, for example, the virtual reconstruction of a ruined cathedral, or the presentation of remote objects held in storage or at other institutions, raises important questions not only about the authenticity of any particular display for both the curator and the visitor, but also perhaps the nature of authenticity itself: "As the significance of digital images has grown, the form of the factual has become increasingly virtualized – that is to say, it has become separated from any real object" (Flynn 2007, 349).

What does it mean to have an experience of a virtual object rather than its original? Particularly if, unlike the earlier removes of photography, that experience might be more vivid, offering the reconstruction of details and luster lost over centuries? Though Flynn notes a longer historical process of mediation or separation of the artifact from its authentic context – from its isolation through vitrines, labels, new forms of lighting, through to the replacement of the artifact with its photographic depiction – digital simulation marks a new phase in this dematerialization and dehistoricization: "However, the reduction of the monument or artifact to visual simulation disrupts its connection to material evidence and thus to history" (Flynn 2007, 349–350).

We'll see later that Flynn goes on to argue that video games, rather than fully instantiating this dematerializing, virtualizing trajectory, actually offer significant ways to reconnect to the social, the cultural environments of the artifacts. The terms "virtual" and "simulation" are key here, and while they are often used interchangeably in the context of digital media, they have distinct conceptual implications.

First, however, I will explore how the historical anxieties in popular and academic discourses around museums, science, and spectacle have been evident in reactions to specifically digital media. I will take the BBC television series *Walking with Dinosaurs* (first screened 1999), along with subsequent series that built on its success, as an extended case study. *Walking with Dinosaurs* epitomizes these anxieties and has generated intense debate among academics, broadcasters, museums curators, and scientists – and, interestingly, sustained discussion by public contributors to BBC online forums (Jeffries 2003). Criticisms of the program tended to fall into three categories that overlap in ways that go to the heart of the popular presentation and communication of knowledge in an era of digital simulation and spectacle.

The series featured cutting-edge CGI to render the appearance, movement, and behavior of dinosaurs in convincing detail. The program makers used conventional photographic media to film diverse environments, with the synthetic prehistoric animals composited into the scenes. The scenes were presented to viewers framed by familiar conventions of the television genre of the natural history documentary, complete with authoritative voice-over. The conceit of the series was not that the viewer was watching a reconstruction of, or set of speculations about, the lives of long extinct creatures, but rather that they were watching actual animals and their behavior just as if the program were about, say, zebras in Africa today. This hybrid of digital spectacle and natural history documentary proved deeply worrying for some critics and scientists for a number of reasons. Much of the criticism was expressed through interrogation of the accuracy of the scientific information, for example, the depiction of a dinosaur urinating was particularly controversial, as Michael Benton (2001), a paleontologist who acted as a consultant for the series, explained. However, it is clear that it was not so much its *accuracy* that concerned the critics as the convincing way the series presented conjecture about dinosaur behavior as fact. Or, rather, its convincing simulation of dinosaur appearance and behavior seemed to render conjecture and speculation as convincing fact through the deployment of a combination of established natural history documentary conventions and the verisimilitude of computer animation. The biologist Steven Rose, for instance, argued that

> the main problem is the inability of the programmes to distinguish known fact from interpretation and sheer speculation. These mini-sagas are presented as life stories without a shadow of uncertainty ... the borderlines between fact and fiction become even more blurred. (2001, 116)

Scientists and media critics alike were suspicious of its synthetic imagery – it was a "High-tech Sooty Show" for one TV reviewer (Scott and White 2003, 317) – in particular, its obvious (and deliberate) resonance with the recent blockbuster film

Jurassic Park. The series epitomized Andrew Darley's view that spectacular entertainment and technology have a powerful tendency to override or distract from any educational or informational potential. Darley usefully sets the series within the context of the history and conventions of natural history broadcasting but, less helpfully, interprets its significance in the postmodernist binaries of surface versus depth, style versus content, and spectacle versus narrative. *Walking with Dinosaurs*, then, "falls prey to contemporary aesthetic strategies that tend to negate representation and meaning (content), promoting instead the fascinations of spectacle and form (style)" (Darley 2003, 229). For Darley, the series was a "fake documentary," a key example of a "digital visual culture" in which scientific, cultural, and historical meaning and knowledge wane with the emergence of simulational and photorealistic screen media. However, as argued throughout this chapter, the relationships between new technologies of display and the popular communication of science do not divide so neatly into a binary opposition between spectacle and knowledge, and cannot be reduced to a narrative of the waning of meaning.

A persistent criticism of the computer-generated dinosaurs in *Walking with Dinosaurs* was that the details – color, sound, feeding, speed, and so on – were speculative. The programs did not present their images as sketches, artists' impressions, or suggestions – and the natural history generic conventions of continuity editing and voice-over added to this false confidence. However, I would argue that, in the face of the convincing virtual images, the extent to which science is often always already a speculative practice is forgotten. Michael Benton countered these criticisms by pointing out the extent to which science has always relied on speculation, particularly when attending to intangible or invisible phenomena, whether these absences are due to cosmological or microscopic scale or to extinction:

> Science would be rather dull if we had to restrict ourselves to what we could see and touch, to 100% certainty. It's extraordinary that some professional paleontologists were unable to understand that reconstructing the bodily appearance and behaviour of an extinct animal is identical in scientific terms to any other normal activity in science, such as reconstructing the atmosphere on Saturn. The sequence of observations and conjectures that stand between the bones of Brachiosaurus lying in the ground and its moving image in WWD is identical to the sequence of observations and conjectures that lie between the biochemical and crystallographic observations on chromosomes and the creation of the model of the structure of DNA … in both cases, the models reflect the best fit to the facts. (Benton 2001)

While accepting the spirit of Benton's argument, I would note that the modes of visualization and speculation he refers to are not exactly the same as those deployed in popular television series. At the very least, a television program will select the behaviors and appearances about which to speculate according to their fit with its underlying narrative structure and organization, and no doubt with an eye to their attention-grabbing and spectacular appeal. As James Moran puts it, there is a gap between the documentary's need for empirical evidence and the necessity to *recon-struct* evidence for prehistoric phenomena, a gap that "can be bridged only by spec-ulation, a form of interpretation whose historiographic and scientific ends must be compromised by fictive means" (Moran 1999, 259). The notion of *speculation* itself is key to a full understanding of the potential of simulational media for museums, but speculation in the context of simulational media is a more compli-cated process – we'll return to it later.

For now, there are other processes at work, in particular the emergence of new hybrids of knowledge and popular entertainment. Debates on the mediation of historical, anthropological, or scientific knowledge on television and through new technologies in museums tend to regard the particular knowledge as quite distinct from the media technology deployed to convey it. As we have seen, new media of display generate fears that they might distract viewers or visitors from the phe-nomena or artifacts, whether they be dinosaurs or cathedrals, or anxieties that the focusing, editing, or selection of aspects of these phenomena and artifacts is accu-rate or misleading. Or, as Flynn notes and Darley fears, whether the processes of mediation and virtualization simply elide the original, authentic phenomenon altogether. But media are not simply conduits or channels (sometimes blocked) through which messages and meanings flow, more or less effectively. If, in the assessment of computer simulation and video games as new media for museums, we are to avoid assumptions of either the apocalyptic threat of virtualization and the overly simplistic thesis that in their appeal and familiarity these playful media will attract audiences and surreptitiously feed them the same old "content," then we need to draw on an approach to studying the media epitomized by Marshall McLuhan's dictum "The medium is the message." That is, at the very least, a new medium reshapes its message or, taken more literally, the message has never been separable from its mode of communication. As José van Dijck argues:

> The popularity of scientific claims is inevitably defined by the available technology and preferred aesthetics of contemporary media – media that enabled the construc-tion of these claims in the first place. From Galileo's telescope to Etienne-Jules Marey's stereoscope, tools of visualization have moved easily between scientific investigation and entertainment … We do not illustrate science with images, we construct images and deploy media technologies to "think" science (Burnett 2004). Computer graphics and animatronics are to 21st Century physicists and paleontolo-gists what the microscope was to 19th Century biologists: new instruments allowing for new claims, but also for a retooling of the imagination. Animated dinosaurs … are not illustrations of science – they are part of science in action. (van Dijck 2006, 20)

This last observation confirms Benton's argument that simulation and modeling is a necessary part of science, not merely the communication of its findings. However, again, the medium itself must be factored in. Here van Dijck is alluding to an important moment in the production of *Walking with Dinosaurs* that I will use to illustrate and explore this second process. As recounted in the documentary "The Making of *Walking with Dinosaurs*," paleontologists and animators worked alongside each other to establish plausible movements for the computer-generated creatures (see Henderson 1999 for a detailed account of this process). As such, the technicians and animators, whose expertise was developed entirely within the world of media entertainment and production, collaborated in scientific work. The animators worked with paleontological models of dinosaur skeletons and physiology, but their rendering of visually convincing on-screen movement was drawn directly from the techniques of popular animation. The simulated dinosaurs moved to a sense of weight and rhythm honed in the industry of drawn animation and cartoons, yet these aesthetics actually informed scientific understanding, resonating with the paleontologists' modeling of possible planes of movement based on the mechanical affordances of fossil bones:

> Technicians sometimes refuted accepted knowledge in paleontology because their models showed a specific locomotion to be impossible. As one scientist comments in the programme, paleontologists actually learned from animation programmers because they helped "prove" how the Diplodocus walked, how it moved its arms and legs, how the animals grazed and fought … technicians help scientists establish their claims by using the very tools that turn them into attractive spectacle. (van Dijck 2006, 14)

So here we see the specific operations and implications of the overlap between animation and simulation. Animation is generally regarded as an entertainment form associated with the whimsical and fantastical, though it has a parallel history in the visualization of natural phenomena in scientific research and communication. Simulation has an analogous genealogy in scientific research and entertainment applications. *Walking with Dinosaurs* brings together CGI as animation and visual simulation with the computer modeling of complex systems and bodies – generating a new kind of hybrid or monstrous knowledge.

Significantly, both animator and scientist study the movement and behavior of living creatures as sources for their respective speculations on the movement and behavior of nonliving creatures (whether dinosaurs or monsters). At the very least, this example demonstrates that scientific knowledge and entertainment spectacle (here specifically bound up with computer simulation) are not inevitable opposites in some Manichaean cultural universe.

Video games: Beyond the interactive database

This hybridized or monstrous knowledge will be a key theme for the rest of this chapter. Before I return to it, however, some explanation of the specificity of the video game as an informational medium is needed. I will posit two main, but overlapping, ways in which the video game as a medium becomes the message with relevance to its relationship to museums and science centers: first, in their construction and navigation of virtual space and, second, the generative operations of computer simulation.

Popular and academic attention has been focused on the spatial and navigational possibilities of digital networks and virtual media from their inception. The sense of space beyond the screen and within networks has characterized responses to Internet media and virtual reality applications. Computer and video games, in particular, have proved to be the most innovative hothouse of new forms of depiction of virtual space and new modes of interactive engagement with, or navigation of, these spaces (Manovich 2001). For museums, the virtual space of the computer game has suggested new ways of simulating inaccessible or vanished places, not only by picturing a building or an environment, but by offering the visitor/player the ability to move through the simulation and to explore it. Flynn (2007) also points out that key conventions and gameplay features from video games are very useful in managing this movement, in making it engaging. These devices include challenges and puzzles, inventories and artificial intelligence, as well as navigation:

> In entertainment-based computer games, agency or the act of doing is constituted through diverse modes of spatiality. These modes of spatiality contribute to gameplay through such strategies as constraint and concealment, challenging the player to negotiate terrain to access objects, meet avatars, find portals, and do battle … Through these sets of spatial negotiations, players become involved in the sequential unfolding of a record of signposts and metaphors embedded in the landscape. (Flynn 2007, 355)

For Flynn, this spatial negotiation provides an essential counter to the dematerializations and decontextualization of museum media, not least the most recent virtual media. The navigation of virtual space offers the opportunity to "re-enchant" the artifact or building, she suggests, as it is once more surrounded by a dynamic environment with the possibility for the visitor/player to engage with it in a simulation of the ritual or cultural dimensions initially stripped away by the museum, to feel a sense of immersion or presence: "Virtual movement has the potential to create a simulated spatiality that extends the real to a more imaginative, enchanted, lyrical relationship with spatial immersion" (Flynn 2007, 363).

Thus, the virtual spaces emerging from the commercial popular media culture of the video game offer new ways for museum-goers to commune with the absent worlds that shaped these artifacts, rituals, and processes, echoing the motives for earlier contextualizing modes of display in museums such as dioramas.

Games might be thought of as a set of media rather than as one medium. They offer a diverse range of modes of engagement, and hence of engaging with and communicating a range of different knowledges. To illustrate the significance of this for the concerns of this chapter, I'll take two examples, one that simulates the anthropological museum and one that mediates knowledge of natural history.

At the time of writing, the British Museum's website featured a game called *Time Explorer*, an "ultimate adventure"[1] (2010). The game interface is an isometric and stylized rendering of the British Museum, similar in appearance to the popular social website for children, HabboHotel. It draws on familiar conventions of the computer game, from the initial choice of avatar to exploration of the virtual space, the accumulation of virtual objects and solving of puzzles, and the given health and time constraints. The backstory establishes the player as a "gifted young curator" setting out to "identify the exact time when natural disasters struck four great ancient civilisations," using time travel and the collection of treasure. Scores are increased by picking up "knowledge points by collecting bonus objects and facts about the civilisation." Each level is a small, highly stylized virtual architecture with emblems, characters, and puzzles denoting a particular civilization (Aztec Mexico, ancient Egypt, etc.). The Aztec level, for instance, sets a simple puzzle to construct a statue from a small number of elements, while talking to a character in the temple reveals a "bonus fact" about Aztec warriors, and – perhaps more importantly – a number of "fact points."

As a conduit for, or introduction to, anthropological knowledge, this game is limited. The stylized and abstracted environments are more akin to theme park architectonics than any reconstruction of past cultures, and the knowledge attained through playing the game would seem primarily to be knowledge of the game itself, its structure and puzzles, rather than of the civilization (knowledge is quantified and accumulated as points). At best, perhaps, we see a dynamic event in which different knowledges are woven together, even if the most salient and persistent of these might be the player's understanding and experience of computer games themselves. Moreover, *Time Explorer*, while it presents a series of virtual buildings and environments, is not a simulation in the sense of a dynamic model. Instead, its structure is closer to that of an interface/database (Manovich 2001). The player navigates a static virtual space, accessing puzzles and facts and accumulating points. This, I would argue, is a significant distinction within the broad general category of "interactives" in museum and science center display, and most of these displays, from the early CD-ROM-based applications to current touch screen interfaces, fall within the database model as they offer only a selection of text extracts or images, accessed through static menus or a simple quiz structure (see also Taylor 2010 and Witcomb 2011). Though some video games, particularly those with educational aims, have an interface/database structure, most are dynamic in their offering of nonlinear interaction with navigable spaces, more or less artificially intelligent computer-controlled characters, and simulation of environmental factors from light to the physics of friction and gravity.

Close attention to the forms of media deployed – particularly new media – is crucial for any critical understanding of their potential for museums, and the communication of knowledge is inseparable from the media of communication themselves. However, this analysis does not in itself question the pessimistic arguments of the triumph of spectacle over knowledge. To pursue my argument in more detail, and to suggest new ways of thinking about the generative (albeit hybrid) potential of video game forms for science museums and centers, I will return to the distinction I made earlier between virtual space (now supplemented by the navigation/database form) and simulation. I will now concentrate on simulation in its more specific sense as the modeling of complex and dynamic environments or systems.

Simulation is a complex and often contradictory term (see Lister et al. 2009 for a critical account of its use in the study of new media). It is important to distinguish between two key uses of the term while noting their overlap. We have already seen how cultural and media forms characterized as diverting, commodified, or spectacular have informed debates on museums, media, and technologies of display. In this sense, video games are part of what is perceived to be a recent, digital iteration of a visual culture that revels in surface effects at the expense of meaning and "depth." However, video games are also computer media, and as such are all simulations in the computing sense of the word. Games, like other computer software such as weather or economic simulations, *model* worlds or systems – from the complexities of urban development in the *SimCity* series of games to the dynamic artificial ecologies of *Creatures* or *Spore*.

> To simulate is to model a (source) system through a different system which maintains to somebody some of the behaviors of the original system. The key term here is "behavior." Simulation does not simply retain the – generally audiovisual– characteristics of the object but it also includes a model of its behaviors. This model reacts to certain stimuli (input data, pushing buttons, joystick movements), according to a set of conditions. (Frasca 2003, 223)

It is this specific computer form of the simulation, or modeling, of dynamic systems that is of central significance here, a form that originates from scientific imperatives to model complex systems and predict a range of possible outcomes from a set of dynamic variables. These systems might be meteorological (as in weather forecasting), demographical (modeling population growth or urban development), ecological (testing the relationships between predator and prey species), or economical (predicting market growth or collapse). An early example would be the prediction, in World War I, of missile trajectories given prevailing wind speeds, a process mapped out on graph paper and informed by a printed table of ballistic variables (Woolley 1993). Simulations as informational and procedural systems offer new ways of exploring aspects of physical and cultural worlds, whether existing or speculative.

To illustrate this, we can compare *Time Explorer* with another game designed for a museum, *Be a Merchant*.[2] Playing the role of a merchant in fifteenth-century York, players start with £50 and, through a series of straightforward choices, proceed to buy and sell goods across medieval Europe. The game's interface is engaging but simple, with predominantly still images and intermittent audio clips. Its game mechanic simulates trade, as the player buys and sells commodities at varying prices by sailing to different ports. If the player buys cheaper products and sells where they fetch a higher price, money is accumulated. The game's designer, Joe Cutting, points out the possibilities for games as simulation in this context. For him, games are great at "describing systems: a situation where one element or decision affects another. So the *Merchants* game shows a simple economic system … Games are really good at letting players explore systems and getting [*sic*] an understanding of how they work" (2013, 42).

Computer and video games have brought the scientific tools of simulation into the realm of everyday popular media, albeit repurposed for entertainment. Within computer game studies, the distinction is made between narrative and simulation as overarching media forms for explaining and exploring the world – from literature and poetry to journalism and cinema, stories have been dominant:

> unlike traditional media, video games are not just based on representation but on an alternative semiotical structure known as simulation. Even if simulations and narrative do share some common elements – character, settings, events – their mechanics are essentially different. More importantly, they also offer distinct rhetorical possibilities. (Frasca 2003, 222)

Frasca's observations open up wide conceptual terrain on the rhetorical possibilities of simulation as media, a terrain too broad to map in full here (see Aarseth 2004). I will concentrate on the questions that simulation media, such as games, raise for the popular engagement with science and technology through digital media, not least in the setting of the museum or science center. I will argue that we need to rethink the modes and possibilities of popular scientific knowledge and its objects, and acknowledge new forms of speculative and hybrid knowledge.

For Mark J. P. Wolf simulation is "subjunctive documentary," "concerned with what *could be, would be,* or *might have been* … the simulation documents possibilities or probabilities instead of actualities" (1999, 281).

> A simulation is certainly artificial, synthetic and fabricated, but it is not "false" or "illusory." Processes of fabrication, synthesis and artifice are real and all produce new real objects. A videogame world does not necessarily imitate an original space or existing creatures, but it exists … a simulation is real *before* it imitates or represents anything. (Lister et al. 2009, 38)

So, against the prevailing notion of simulation as inherently illusory, artificial, and fake, computer science (and some game scholars) understands the term in quite different terms. A computer model can explore, analyze, and test aspects of real – but intangible or invisible – systems in ways inaccessible to the written word, the photograph, or the video image. However, complex systems such as climate change, demographics, or economies (like prehistoric ecologies, phenomena that cannot be seen, touched, or photographed) are simulated not to predict their future behaviors directly or absolutely, but rather to offer a field of possibilities for their future states, a field that can be manipulated by adjusting variables. There are clear connections with the debates around *Walking with Dinosaurs* in this regard (though the dynamic operations of simulation were deployed in the *making* of the programs, not – as is the case of video games – in their *consumption*). Simulation in this sense can be *speculative*; numerous variables can be adjusted to test their effect on the working of the system as a whole. A simulation can be regarded as prosthetic imagination, testing complex possibilities in what Mizuko Ito, referring to *SimCity 2000*, calls "a structured space of possibility" (1998, 303). A computer science definition of the term resonates with Ito's understanding of the popular digital media form: "a simulation produces a synthetic history of the process. Beginning with a set of initial conditions, the simulation plays through the various kinds of events which might occur."[3]

Simulacral knowledge

Before I return to the museum to make some specific observations on the relevance of this conceptual discussion for thinking knowledge communication, there is one more process that needs to be opened up. So far we have acknowledged the new (though not without precedent) hybridities of knowledge that emerge with digital media, which are exemplified by the cross-fertilization of paleontology and entertainment in the animation of *Walking with Dinosaurs*. It has been suggested that computer simulation facilitates new speculative modes of inquiry and brings to our attention intangible phenomena and behaviors. Yet it should not be assumed that computer simulation is then leading us, incrementally, through advances in programming and visualization, closer and closer to the real world. Even the most detailed and complex simulation remains a set of algorithms, a mathematical and synthetic construction, that – like Zeno's arrow – appears to get closer and closer to its target but can never reach it. Actual systems and computer models are not, as has been suggested, on a continuum, with the (achievable) goal of simulation the "actual 100 per cent implementation of the referent system" (Järvinen 2003).

Again McLuhan's assertion that the medium is the message is apposite. Computer simulation underpins a distinct set of media, with both realist (pace Järvinen) and phantasmagorical trajectories. There are serious simulations and ludicrous ones, and their open-ended structure often offers possibilities for both within the same system (Giddings 2007). Whether playful or practical, an implicit knowledge of the system is essential to play a computer game or engage with a simulational museum exhibit, but more wayward systemic knowledges also emerge. Indeed the interactive possibilities of digital media seem almost to demand a playful testing of their capabilities, a ludic tendency that can only be encouraged by young visitors' own experience of video and computer games. The "space of possibilities" cannot always be constrained or contained by the simulation designer's intentions, and the question of what kinds of knowledge – or knowledge of what kind of object – returns.

At its simplest, this means that that images, symbols, or narrative framing of a computer simulation may not – in any particular event of play or engagement – remain as closely tied to the source system as intended. Media studies has explored countless detachments of signifier from signified in the consumption of television, cinema, magazines, and so on, but simulations add new possibilities for arbitrary semiotic and behavioral trajectories. I will explore this through an example of science education software, Mitchell Resnick's *StarLogo* program. Resnick's own analysis of the workings of *StarLogo* illustrates these operations of simulation beautifully. The program allows children to experiment with various kinds of bottom-up emergent behaviors. Drawing on techniques developed in artificial life (Alife) research, the program presents a microworld of cellular automata. Cellular automata, first developed in the translation of a paper simulation of cell colony growth (John Conway's *Game of Life*) to a computer program, are simple entities (initially a single point or cell on a screen) whose behavior is determined by a set of rules which, though simple, generate complicated and unpredictable development or behavior, analogous to cell growth, evolution, or (as we'll see later) the complex movement of animal groups. Alife and cellular automata principles underpin games such as *SimCity* (Ito 1998), to war simulations (Giddings 2007), and games featuring biological evolution itself, notably *Creatures* (Kember 2003).

StarLogo allows its young programmers to manipulate the starting positions or organization of these automata (playfully called "turtles") and then, through the program's application of simple rules of behavior, the players can watch their world unfold. The turtles are polysemic, figured as traffic jams, slime molds, or termite colonies depending on the intentions of any particular iteration of use/play. Importantly, Resnick is not concerned with exploring slime molds, traffic, and so on in and of themselves; rather, his intention is to facilitate exploration of the systems and dynamic behaviors at a more abstract level. These "microworlds are always manipulable: they encourage users to explore, experiment, invent, and revise." *StarLogo* offers "system science" microworlds, "worlds where systems thinking can hatch and grow" (Resnick 1997, 50). The knowledge generated by *StarLogo* play is not *representational* (players learn nothing specific about a termite colony or a particular city's traffic flows) but *simulational*. It is knowledge about dynamic nonlinear systems in general:

> The real world serves only as an inspiration, a departure point for thinking about decentralized systems ... I am more interested in investigating antlike behaviors than the behaviors of real ants ... The goal is not to simulate particular systems and processes in the world. The goal is to probe, challenge and disrupt the way people think about systems and processes in general. (Resnick 1997, 49–50)

There are echoes here of a longer, predigital philosophy of simulation, of concepts that date back to thinking about the nature of reality and artifice in classical antiquity, which were revived in the media culture of modern times, with simulation understood as "a copy without an original" (Baudrillard 1983). So the challenge for science communication here is significant: the turtles demonstrate that a simulation can explore the complexity of the world in powerful new ways, without actually simulating *anything*, or, perhaps more accurately, without reliably or closely modeling particular natural objects or phenomena. As Wolf points out, simulations can be "used to image real or *imaginary* constructs, or some *combination* of the two" (1999, 280).

A final example will, hopefully, demonstrate the relevance of this discussion for museum and science center exhibits. It is another interactive computer-based game, this time designed for the educational setting of Wildwalk, a science center in Bristol which closed in 2007.[4] Visitors would enter the installation, which was located in the final room of the center, after walking through a range of natural history and ecological displays, from living animals in vitrines to interactive screens and videos. In this smallish dark room, a data projector suspended from the ceiling projects directly down onto the floor, which is transformed into a shallow rock pool or river bed. As visitors walk across it, they can see the clear blue water around their feet. It quickly becomes apparent that this virtual water responds to the visitors'/players' footsteps, rippling and bubbling in a simulation of turbulence. The overall experience is effective, the simple device of rotating the conventional vertical orientation of the screen 90 degrees transforming the now familiar experience of the museum interactive screen into something different – a playful augmented reality in which the visitors inhabit a space that is consistent with the virtual shallows through which they paddle.

Stand still for a moment and small schools of computer-generated fish flit out from the edges of the projection. As with the rippling water, it takes a minute or so to realize that they too are responding to the movements of the visitors. They swim toward a visitor's feet, but any bodily movement sends them flitting away again. A relatively simple mechanic of motion detection and Alife algorithms – of "flocking" this time, the simulation of the complexity of flocks of birds or schools of fish – coupled with the orientation of the projection apparatus and with a playful exploratory willingness on the part of the visitors, and a simple yet dynamic virtual–actual environment is generated.

The fundamental ambiguity of computer simulation is apparent here, as the Alife processes of flocking are practically identical whether the interface is depicting a fish or birds. The general term for this particular type of automata is "boids," a thoroughly simulacral term – these are birdlike but not birds, neither fish nor fowl. Moreover, once this interactive installation enters the museum, and is entered by the museum's visitors, its communicative ambitions are not so smoothly realized. Children run through, "splashing" the virtual water and chasing the fish. Some adults, while their children play, develop their own little games, testing the type and degree of expression needed to send the inquisitive fish darting away again beyond the edges of the microworld. Rhythms are established, the gentle swinging of arms and wiggling of fingers synchronized with the computer-generated responses of the automata as they swim in, react to the visitor, and move away again.[5] Whatever individual visitors to Wildwalk learned from this playful virtual system, it was unlikely to be any straightforward grasp of a marine environment or animal behavior, though the installation may well have been able to "probe, challenge and disrupt" the way they thought about (or perhaps perceived) natural systems and processes. They certainly responded to it as a game, engaging with the mobile entities as abstract elements, testing the system's interactivity and parameters just as a video game player must.

On the one hand then, this simulation/game is a recent example of the potential of all innovative and technically sophisticated museum displays (from dioramas onward) to distract visitors away from the "substance" of the collection and toward the novelty, mechanics, and devices of the display itself. On the other hand, like *StarLogo*'s turtles, it suggests that attention to the machinery of display is not necessarily the flattening out of meaning or knowledge by spectacular screens and surfaces. Simulation media require their own new "literacies" and, while they are not necessarily a superior way to grasp the real world's complexity compared to the more familiar linear narratives of scientific papers and television documentaries, an implicit understanding of them as media and technologies is inseparable from engaging with their rhetorical possibilities.

Moreover, both video games and interactive installations are predicated on what Flynn, referring to the video game *Grand Theft Auto* calls "a mobile and a thinking body" (2007, 359). The potential of video games is not (only) their popular appeal and engagement – it is their simulational form in and of itself as generative of emergent speculation and knowledge, and their potential for articulating bodies, minds, knowledge, and play in new, unpredictable encounters.

Notes

1 At http://www.britishmuseum.org/explore/young_explorers/play/time_explorer. aspx (accessed August 6, 2014).

2 http://www.joecutting.com/work.php?type=history (accessed August 11, 2014).

3 Definition of "simulation," Principia Cybernetica Web, at http://pespmc1.vub.ac.be/ ASC/SIMULATION.html (accessed August 6, 2014).

4 For a detailed discussion of Wildwalk see Chapter 3 by Nils Lindahl Elliot in this volume.

5 For a demonstration, see http://vimeo.com/64221493 (accessed August 6, 2014).

References

Aarseth, Espen. 2004. "Genre Trouble." *Electronic Book Review*. Accessed August 5, 2014. http://www.electronicbookreview.com/thread/firstperson/vigilant.

Baudrillard, Jean. 1983. *Simulations*. New York: Semiotext(e).

Benton, Michael J. 2001. "The Science of *Walking with Dinosaurs*." *Teaching Earth Sciences* 24: 371–400. Accessed August 11, 2014. http://palaeo.gly.bris.ac.uk/Essays/WWD/default.html.

Burnett, Ron. 2004. *How Images Think*. Cambridge, MA: MIT Press.

Cubitt, Sean. 2001. *Simulation and Social Theory*. London: Sage.

Cutting, Joe. 2013. "Telling Stories with Games." In *The Innovative Museum: It's Up to You*, 34–51. Edinburgh: MuseumsEtc.

Darley, Andrew. 2000. *Visual Digital Culture: Surface Play and Spectacle in New Media Genres*. London: Routledge.

Darley, Andrew. 2003. "Simulating Natural History: *Walking with Dinosaurs* as Hyper-real Edutainment." *Science as Culture* 12(2): 227–255.

Eco, Umberto. 1986. *Travels in Hyper-Reality*. London: Minerva.

Flynn, Bernadette. 2007. "The Morphology of Space in Virtual Heritage." In *Theorizing Digital Heritage: A Critical Discourse*, edited by Fiona Cameron and Sarah Kenderdine, 349–368. Cambridge, MA: MIT Press.

Frasca, Gonzalo. 2003. "Simulation versus Narrative." In *The Video Game Theory Reader*, edited by Mark J. P. Wolf and Bernard Perron, 221–235. New York: Routledge.

Giddings, Seth. 2007. "Dionysiac Machines: Videogames and the Triumph of the Simulacra." *Convergence: The International Journal of Research into New Media Technologies* 13(4): 417–431.

Griffiths, Alison. 2002. *Wondrous Difference: Cinema, Anthropology, and Turn-of-the-Century Visual Culture*. New York: Columbia University Press.

Griffiths, Alison. 2003. "Media Technology and Museum Display: A Century of Accommodation and Conflict." In *Rethinking Media Change: The Aesthetics of Transition*, edited by David Thorburn and Henry Jenkins, 375–389. Cambridge, MA: MIT Press.

Henderson, D. M. 1999. "Estimating the Masses and Centers of Mass of Extinct Animals by 3-D Mathematical Slicing." *Paleobiology* 25: 88–106.

Henning, Michelle. 2006. *Museums, Media and Cultural Theory*. Maidenhead, UK: Open University Press.

Ito, Mizuko. 1998. "Inhabiting Multiple Worlds: Making Sense of SimCity 2000 in the Fifth Dimension." In *Cyborg Babies: From Techno-Sex to Techno-Tots*, edited by Robbie Davis-Floyd and Joseph Dumit, 301–316. London: Routledge.

Jameson, Fredric. 1991. *Postmodernism; or, The Cultural Logic of Late Capitalism*. London: Verso.

Järvinen, Aki. 2003. "The Elements of Simulation in Digital Games: System, Representation and Interface in *Grand Theft Auto: Vice City*." *Dichtung-Digital* 4. Accessed August 5, 2014. http://www.dichtung-digital.org/2003/issue/4/jaervinen/index.htm.

Jeffries, Michael. 2003. "BBC Natural History versus Science Paradigms." *Science as Culture* 12(4): 527–545.

Kember, Sarah. 2003. *Cyberfeminism and Artificial Life*. London: Routledge.

Lister, Martin, Jon Dovey, Seth Giddings, Iain Grant, and Kieran Kelly. 2009. *New Media: A Critical Introduction*, 2nd ed. London: Routledge.

Manovich, Lev. 2001. *The Language of New Media*. Cambridge, MA: MIT Press.

Moran, James M. 1999. "A Bone of Contention: Documenting the Prehistoric Subject." In *Collecting Visible Evidence*, edited by Jane M. Gaines and Michael Renov, 255–273. Minneapolis: University of Minnesota Press.

Mulvey, Laura. 1996. *Fetishism and Curiosity*. London: BFI.

Pedretti, Erminia. 2002. "T. Kuhn meet T. Rex: Critical Conversations and New Directions in Science Centres and Science Museums." *Studies in Science Education* 37(1): 1–41.

Resnick, Mitchell. 1997. *Turtles, Termites, and Traffic Jams*. Cambridge, MA: MIT Press.

Rose, Steven. 2001. "What Sort of Science Broadcasting Do We Want for the 21st Century?" *Science as Culture* 10(1): 113–119.

Sandberg, Mark. 2003. *Living Pictures, Missing Persons: Mannequins, Museums and Modernity*. Princeton: Princeton University Press.

Scott, Karen D., and Anne M. White. 2003. "Unnatural History? Deconstructing the Walking with Dinosaurs Phenomenon." *Media, Culture & Society* 25(3): 315–332.

Stafford, Barbara M. 1994. *Artful Science: Enlightenment Education and the Eclipse of Visual Education*. Cambridge, MA: MIT Press.

Taylor, Bradley L. 2010. "Reconsidering Digital Surrogates: Toward a Viewer-Orientated Model of the Gallery Experience." In *Museum Materialities: Objects, Engagements, Interpretations*, edited by Sandra H. Dudley, 175–184. London: Routledge.

van Dijck, José. 2006. "Picturizing Science: The Science Documentary as Multimedia Spectacle." *International Journal of Cultural Studies* 9(1): 5–24.

Witcomb, Andrea. 2011. "Interactivity: Thinking Beyond." In *A Companion to Museum Studies*, edited by Sharon Macdonald, 353–361. Oxford: Wiley-Blackwell.

Wolf, Mark J. P. 1999. "Subjunctive Documentary: Computer Imaging and Simulation." In *Collecting Visible Evidence*, edited by Jane M. Gaines and Michael Renov, 274–291. Minneapolis: University of Minnesota Press.

Woolley, Benjamin. 2003. *Virtual Worlds: A Journey in Hype and Hyperreality*. Harmondsworth, UK: Penguin.

Further Reading

Barry, Andrew. 1998. "On Interactivity: Consumers, Citizens and Culture." In *The Politics of Display: Museums, Science, Culture*, edited by Sharon Macdonald, 98–117. London: Routledge.

Bennett, James. 2007. "From Museum to Interactive Television: Organising the Navigable Space of Natural History Display." In *Multimedia Histories: From the Magic Lantern to the Internet*, edited by James Lyons and James Plunkett, 148–192. Exeter, UK: University of Exeter Press.

Benton, M. J. 2000. *Walking with Dinosaurs: The Facts*. London: BBC Worldwide.

Cottle, Simon. 2004. "Producing Nature(s): On the Changing Production Ecology of Natural History TV." *Media, Culture & Society* 26(1): 81–101.

Franklin, Sarah, Celia Lury, and Jackie Stacey. 2000. *Global Nature, Global Culture*. London: Sage.

Henning, Michelle. 2011. "New Media." In *A Companion to Museum Studies*, edited by Sharon Macdonald, 302–318. Oxford: Wiley-Blackwell.

Moseley, Alex. 2013. "Immersive Games: An Alternative Reality for Museums." In *The Innovative Museum: It's Up to You*. Edinburgh: MuseumsEtc.

Silverstone, Roger. 1984. "Narrative Strategies in Television Science: A Case Study." *Media, Culture & Society* 6: 337–410.

Wills, John. 2002. "Digital Dinosaurs and Artificial Life: Exploring the Culture of Nature in Computer and Video Games." *Cultural Values* 6(4): 395–417.

Seth Giddings is Associate Professor in Digital Culture and Design at Winchester School of Art, University of Southampton. His research tackles the theory and practice of experimental and everyday media technoculture, particularly games, social media, and the moving image. His book *Gameworlds: Virtual Media and Children's Everyday Play* is published by Bloomsbury (2014). He is also the editor of *The New Media and Technocultures Reader* (Routledge, 2011) and a coauthor of *New Media: A Critical Introduction* (Routledge, 2009).

PART II

Mediation and Immersion

8 THE LIFE OF THINGS

Ivan Gaskell

While with an eye made quiet by the power
Of harmony, and the deep power of joy,
We see into the life of things.

Wordsworth [1798] 1974

How might human beings see into the life of things? The things to which William Wordsworth refers in his "Lines Composed a Few Miles above Tintern Abbey" (1798) are not solely material things and, insofar as he was concerned with material things, it was with things in nature, things that exercise "no slight or trivial influence" on those who behold them, as he asserts in this poem, and in others (Wordsworth [1798] 1974, 163–165). Material things are evidently not confined to those in nature, for humans make things: artifacts. But any such firm distinction between things in nature and artificial things has become increasingly problematic in Western thought, as it has long been in various other traditions, so the distinction between things that are natural and things that are artificial has assumed new urgency, both for philosophical reflection and for historical understanding. Nonetheless, whether one accepts or rejects a firm distinction between natural and artificial things, all material things share the characteristic of being "things in this world that have a material aspect usually apprehensible through the senses." (For an attempt at a definition of "tangible things," see Gaskell, forthcoming, and Ulrich et al., forthcoming).

If the term "things" poses a host of puzzles, no less does "life." Indeed, the term "life" in the phrase "the life of things" might assume a more than metaphorical or catachrestic weight as the puzzles of what things have life, and in what that life consists confront thinkers anew.

The International Handbooks of Museum Studies: Museum Media, First Edition.
Edited by Michelle Henning.
© 2015 John Wiley & Sons Ltd. Published 2020 by John Wiley & Sons Ltd.

Among contemporary Western thinkers, the definition of life remains elusive. The *Catalogue of Life* claims to be "the most comprehensive and authoritative global index of species currently available."[1] Annually revised, in 2013 it listed approximately 1,350,000 species of plants, animals, fungi, and micro-organisms. Yet it offers no definition of what constitutes life or living things. Similarly, the online *Encyclopedia of Life*, described on its website as "information and pictures of all species known to science," does not pause to define its subject.[2] This is hardly surprising, as the definition of life is a vexed and contentious topic.

In an influential 2002 article, the biochemist Daniel E. Koshland, Jr., defined life under seven principles or conditions: program, improvisation, compartmentaliza-tion, energy, regeneration, adaptability, and seclusion (Koshland 2002, 2215–2216). The biologist Radu Popa contended with some 300 definitions of life in his book on the subject published in 2004 (Popa 2004). Another biologist, Edward Trifonov (2012), analyzed the language used by scientists in discussing the issue, and offered a simple descriptive phrase: life is the capacity for "self-reproduction with varia-tions." Popa epitomizes the widespread bewilderment in the Western scientific community regarding the definition of life by placing a quotation attributed to the Stoic Roman emperor Marcus Aurelius (121–180 CE) prominently on the landing page of his research group's website: "Everything we hear is an opinion not the fact. Everything we see is a perspective not the truth."[3] However, the opinion and perspective in all these cases are those of Western scientists working within a bio-logical paradigm.

Is that biological paradigm universally applicable when considering what con-stitutes life? Clearly not. There are Western thinkers other than biologists, let alone thinkers in other traditions, who attribute life – admittedly in nonbiologi-cal senses – to things not susceptible of biological speciation. That is, they dis-cuss things other than self-sustaining organisms in terms of life. Some scholars in the social and human sciences, such as Bruno Latour (sociology), and Alfred Gell (anthropology), have discussed attributing agency to inanimate things, but the assumption that a capacity for exercising agency is a characteristic of life remains questionable. Some thinkers refer to the numinous or sacred realm in which things that, in other circumstances, might be considered inanimate acquire properties associated with life. Some subscribe to a belief system in which such exceptions are miraculous rather than magical. Roman Catholic ecclesiastical authorities count as miraculous some images to which animation is sometimes ascribed, and sanction their veneration, but only after thorough investigation (I discuss several instances of this phenomenon in Gaskell 2010a, 60–75). We should recall that the transubstantiation of the host – the bread and wine becom-ing the body and blood of Christ in the Roman Catholic mass – is one such investment of seemingly inanimate things with sacred life, no less miraculous for being a frequent occurrence.

Go beyond Western tradition, and ascriptions of life to things few Westerners would acknowledge as animate proliferate. Even if one objects that life in such circumstances is a metaphor or, at best, catachresis, such use of the term would nonetheless seem to imply that organisms and miraculous things, if not identical to life, at least share characteristics – even if inadequately defined – that are necessary for life to be ascribed to them. Those who would see into the life of things cannot confine themselves to the taxonomic domains of biology, for there is life, in senses numinous or sacred, well beyond their confines.

In this chapter, I am concerned with how people might see into the life of particular kinds of things, specifically some of the particular kinds of things that are collected and categorized in museums. Some of these things are valued for their unique qualities, others as representative specimens. In what sense or senses can Western thinkers associate any or perhaps all such things in museum collections with life? It seems likely that many such things are imbued with life in one sense or another. Some may be currently alive in some sense; others may once have been alive but are now dead. Some things that were formerly alive in a biological sense may remain so in another. How are museum scholars, and others in a wide variety of fields, to make sense of these sometimes apparently contradictory conditions of things? How are they, and how are museum visitors who scrutinize their work, to make sense of the life of things in museums?

People experience things in museums through mediation of one kind or another. By far the most common for most museum visitors is the mediation of gallery display. Indeed, the only way most people experience the life of things in museums is when they are on display in galleries. There are exceptions, and, before turning to the mediation offered by galleries, it is worth noting some of them. Several times a day visitors can take 30 minute tours of the zoological specimens preserved in liquids stored in the Darwin Centre Spirit Collection of the Natural History Museum, London.[4] Some art museums still operate facilities known as print or study rooms where visitors can request works on paper (prints and drawings) to be brought to them at a table for close study. A few – such as the study room of the Department of Prints and Drawings of the British Museum, London – do not require appointments. Various museums have introduced public access to collections known as study storage. For example, the Henry Luce III Center for the Study of American Culture at the New-York Historical Society, New York City, makes thousands of historical objects of many kinds previously kept in off-site storage visually accessible to the public by means of relatively informal, densely packed, large-scale glass-fronted shelving, behind which more things are stored on further shelves or in closed cabinets.

In spite of these and other forms of access, most museum visitors rely on formal gallery exhibits, whether long-term (often misleadingly called permanent) or temporary, to see things in museum collections. Indeed, so prominent are exhibits in museums of all kinds that many people – including scholars who study museums – believe that museums exist only to exhibit, and that exhibitions account for the work museums do in its entirety. While most museums certainly emphasize their exhibits, nothing can be – nor ought to be – further from the truth.

Visitors to the Darwin Centre learn that there are scientists at the Natural History Museum, London, researching the collections in laboratories. They would see similar sights in the research and conservation laboratories of many anthropology, archaeology, and art museums, where scientists and conservators not only conserve and restore fragile items of all kinds, but develop and conduct scientific analyses of their materials. Occasionally, museums contrive conditions in which such work is publicly visible, by temporarily adapting a gallery so that conservators and scientists can work in public view. For instance, the Museum of Fine Arts, Boston, has embraced the idea of making conservation work publicly visible through its Conservation in Action program. Its seven laboratories and studios participate in the public presentation of analytical and conservation projects in various curatorial departments, several projects being visible to visitors in galleries temporarily adapted to be conservation laboratories at any one time. Across the Charles River in Cambridge, between 2011 and 2013, Harvard University's Peabody Museum of Archaeology and Ethnology studied and conserved five Alutiiq kayaks from Alaska. "Conservators at Work: Alaska's Historic Kayaks Renewed" was a collaboration between the Peabody Museum, the Alutiiq Museum and Archaeological Repository in Kodiak, and the last traditionally trained Kodiak Alutiiq kayak maker. Three times a week conservators and scientists worked on the items in a public gallery and answered visitors' questions.[5] Before considering in a little more detail the place of the values of originating communities in museums' strategies for dealing with things imbued with life in some sense, we might acknowledge that the term "life" covers a variety of often puzzling characteristics, whether biological or numinous. Museums can explore these in various ways, some but not all of which involve exhibiting.

The values of originating communities

Projects such as "Conservators at Work: Alaska's Historic Kayaks Renewed" have consequences beyond making behind-the-scenes work known and, to an extent, visible to museum visitors. Collaborations between Western museums and Native representatives and organizations have led Western institutions, such as museums that hold material of great social, cultural, symbolic, and often religious significance to indigenous communities, to realize that dominant Western modes of collection care and exhibition are often at odds with the values of those communities. Some Western collecting institutions reject or ignore claims regarding the life of things, that is, that certain things regarded in Western terms as inanimate are imbued with life. Such rejection leads to what members of originating communities regard as the improper treatment of numinous or living things by some museums, to the extent of causing distress and profound offense (Young 2005, 135–146).

Many Western collecting institutions now take the values of indigenous communities into account in the care of things that originated in those communities. This can have a positive effect on modes of exhibiting. In institutions that are attempting to work sensitively, certain things that would once have been revealed to the public gaze remain concealed, such as the contents of Plains Indians' medicine bundles, and the dangerous medicinal designs on warriors' shields. Certain powerful items are stored and displayed with small offerings of tobacco, sweetgrass, or sage. Various museums in Aotearoa New Zealand and Australia honor prohibitions and obligations associated with Indigenous items. Yet, in most Western museums, fundamental assumptions regarding the treatment of things in their collections often remain at odds with fundamental assumptions regarding their treatment held by the communities from which they originated. This concerns not only precautions in view of their latent powers, but obligations to sustain their health and efficacy.

In the United States, the Native American Graves Protection and Repatriation Act (NAGPRA) of 1990 has led to the return to source communities of considerable numbers of items in certain categories – human remains, grave goods, things required for religious purposes, objects of cultural patrimony – often, though far from invariably, with the enthusiastic collaboration of the institutions concerned. That enthusiasm springs not only from a recognition of moral obligations, but from the prospect of long-term collaborative relationships for research, exhibition, and publication between Indigenous communities and museum scholars. Some inhibitions inevitably remain. Certain items repatriated under the terms of NAGPRA cannot be used in accordance with their religious functions owing to inexpungible contamination with pesticides while in museum care in attempts to protect them from destructive infestation. Thus dance regalia repatriated in 1998 from the Peabody Museum at Harvard to the Hoopa Valley Tribe in northwest California present an acute danger to celebrants from arsenic and mercury poisons applied in the museum in the early twentieth century (Gaskell 2003). The items are taken from the Hoopa Tribal Museum to the dance sites to be present, though, in their poisoned state, they cannot be used.

Many items invested with sacred significance remain in American museums. Museum rules governing the handling of collection objects can interfere with ritual interactions between such sacred items and Native visitors. Some of these rules, such as those designed to protect people from pesticides or to protect items from destructive secretions on human hands, are practically motivated. Others appear to protect the power privileges of museum staff rather than serve demonstrable utilitarian purposes. It is not easy to override some of these Western prohibitions – whether practical or themselves symbolic – in accordance with a conviction that present use can trump the ideal of infinite preservation. Yet some institutions have moved in this direction. For instance, in 2010 five men's shirts of the Niitsítapi (Blackfoot Confederacy), acquired in 1841 by Sir George Simpson, governor of the Hudson's Bay Company, and in the Pitt Rivers Museum of the University of Oxford since 1893, were exhibited at the Glenbow Museum, Calgary, and the Galt Museum, Lethbridge, Alberta, under the title, *Kaahsinnooniksi Ao'toksisawooyawa: Our Ancestors Have Come to Visit: Reconnections with Historic*

Blackfoot Shirts. The exhibitions were preceded by workshops for members of the Kainai, Piikani, and Siksika nations to "examine the shirts, research how to preserve the shirts physically and spiritually, and discuss how the Blackfoot people can further access the shirts once they return to Oxford, England."[6] Three of the shirts and their 2010 visit to the Niitsítapi formed the subject of a further exhibition at the Pitt Rivers Museum in 2013 entitled *Visiting with the Ancestors: The Blackfoot Shirts Project.*[7] The organizers of the exhibition in Calgary and Lethbridge sincerely attempted to overcome the barriers to appropriate interaction between members of Indigenous communities and the shirts as living sacralia.

Although it is a matter of great urgency in settler societies with Native populations worldwide, such as those studied by James Belich (2009), considerations regarding the proper treatment and exhibition – if appropriate – of indigenous things of animate or sacred status far from exhaust the obligations of museums. Certain things from hegemonic, as well as from subaltern, societies retain their sacred status, no matter what.[8] These include Christian Orthodox icons (for a case study in the perpetuity of the sacredness of a Russian Orthodox icon, see Gaskell 2003). The same principle applies to Ethiopian, Greek, Syriac, and other Orthodox icons, and icons of the Armenian Apostolic Church. Many Orthodox icons in museum collections, private collections, and the art trade are treated in a purely secular manner. However, unlike Roman Catholic images, which, if not declared miraculous, lose any sacred status they may once have had during use in devotional settings when they are removed, Orthodox icons remain numinous items of veneration for members of Orthodox communities in perpetuity.

Although most Western museums make no special provision for the veneration of Orthodox icons, on occasion they accommodate these needs. For instance, monks from the Monastery of St. Catherine, the Holy Mountain of God-Trodden Mount Sinai, Egypt, were always present when items from the monastery, founded by the Byzantine emperor Justinian I (r. 527–565), were exhibited at the Metropolitan Museum of Art, New York, in 1997 and 2004, and at the J. Paul Getty Museum, Los Angeles, in 2006–2007.[9] These museums made special provisions to honor the status of the items borrowed from the monastery and to respect the sensibilities of the lenders and of other Orthodox adherents. The Metropolitan Museum hosted a blessing of the gallery of items from St. Catherine's Monastery in the 2004 exhibition. It was conferred by Archbishop Damianos of Sinai, Faran and Raitho, the abbot of the monastery, and echoed the blessing he had offered at the reopening of the monastery treasury, for the installation of which the Metropolitan Museum had provided extensive expertise (Helen Evans, curator of the exhibition, email, August 4 2013).[10] The website of the J. Paul Getty Museum states:

> Couriers from the lending museum travel with the artwork, watching it from the moment it leaves home to the moment it is installed in the galleries of the borrowing museum. But while most couriers go home when the artwork is delivered, monks from Saint Catherine's will stay in Los Angeles for the duration of the exhibition.

They are seen in the galleries, overseeing the holy objects that are in their charge. The monks' presence serves to remind us that these objects are not only art objects, but a living part of the practice of Eastern Orthodox Christianity.[11]

Given the extraordinary survival of early Byzantine icons at the Monastery of St. Catherine, and their immense significance for cultural continuity from classical antiquity, it might be objected that these museums were making exceptions to their ordinary secular practice solely in order to procure the loan of unique materials. Even if this were so, the curators' exposure to devotions in their galleries may have encouraged them to acquiesce favorably in such behavior subsequently. The curator of Byzantine art at the Metropolitan Museum of Art, New York, Helen Evans, notes that "priests do often bring groups to the Museum's Byzantine Galleries and individuals have been seen venerating works in the cases."[12]

The case of the Museum of Russian Icons in Clinton, Massachusetts, is subtly different. Founded in 2006 by Gordon B. Lankton, the museum is based on his private collection. According to the Museum of Russian Icons website, "Gordon approached several local museums to determine their interest. Though the icons were well received, only a few icons would be exhibited at a time, and the remainder would be placed in storage."[13] Containing "more than 500 Russian icons and artifacts," Lankton's museum is billed as the largest collection of Russian icons in North America. The chair of the board of the plastics manufacturer Nypro, Inc., Lankton developed an enthusiasm for Russian icons during his regular business visits to Russia where Nypro had acquired a factory. In a relatively short time, he built a large icon collection, which the museum makes available to his local community. As for the status of the icons, the museum's website is somewhat disingenuous. In response to the frequently asked question: "Are we viewing original icons?" it states:

> In the Orthodox tradition, icons were produced by monks. Icons were, and still are, hand-painted using ancient methods and symbolically significant materials. The monks often recreated important, miracle-working icons and disseminated them across Russia. While monks used the format of specific icons, some details were altered. The icons you see before you are not the original painting. All original icons are kept in sacred spaces, or have been lost during the 2000 year history of icon painting.
>
> Nonetheless, the icons in the Museum collection are quite old and created by monks who studied the craft and perfected the technique of icon writing. Also, though monks recreated the format of specific icons, many details were altered to balance personal taste, region, and styles of the day. While these are not the original, miracle-working icons from the legends, they are considered to be original art.[14]

This explanation implies that the icons in the museum, while original art, are no more than that. This is not strictly accurate. Respect for the prototype of an icon as a particular iconographic model is an important element in the creation of a new icon. Therefore, even if that new icon does not partake of the specifically miraculous quality of the prototype – the particular icon known as the *Virgin of Vladimir*, for instance – such derivatives, if properly made as acts of devotion ("written" is the usual term) are themselves ineluctably sacred items. That is, they are more than "original art" (see Gaskell 2003; Cormack 2007). Although the exhibits in the museum address the making of icons by monks "using ancient methods and symbolically significant materials," as the website states, treating them as art alone appears to be an attempt to absolve the collector and the museum staff from having to directly address the sacred status of the greater part of the collection. Interestingly, the "Museum Vision Statement" makes no mention of the religious status or even function of Russian icons, stressing international relations, implicitly as a condition for the sustained successful conduct of business. It states simply: "The Museum of Russian Icons enhances relations between Russia and the United States through the medium of art, especially Russian icons."[15]

The Museum of Russian Icons is just one of many Western institutions – both museums and commercial organizations – that choose to treat Orthodox icons in a predominantly, or in some cases exclusively, secular manner. To many non-Orthodox adherents they are works of art on a par with Roman Catholic religious paintings that are no longer displayed in sacred settings. Yet, in terms of perceived status among any community of makers and original users, there is a category difference between perpetually sacred icons and Catholic religious paintings (and sculptures) removed from devotional settings, despite their physical similarity. Similarly, for its community of makers and original users, a Plains Indian medicine bundle is far more than the ethnographic item it may be for museum anthropologists.

The British Museum, London, chooses to address Orthodox icons in a slightly different way from the Museum of Russian Icons in Clinton, Massachusetts. If the latter has the largest such collection in North America, the former has the largest collection – numbering 100, of which 72 are Russian – in the United Kingdom. The British Museum is an encyclopedic museum of human history, not an art museum, although it contains and deploys many things amenable to consideration and use as art.[16] Orthodox icons are among those things. Although there is no gallery dedicated to Orthodox icons, 11 are on view with other works from various parts of Europe in two galleries. Five Byzantine icons dating from the mid-thirteenth to the early fifteenth centuries are on view in the "Medieval Europe A.D. 1050–1500" gallery, together with one Russian example, the *Miracle of St. George and the Dragon*, made in Novgorod province in the late fourteenth century. Five Cretan icons from between the fifteenth and the seventeenth centuries are on display in the gallery devoted to "Europe 1400–1800," one of which is on loan from a private collection. This means that only 10 percent of the museum's icon holdings are on view – a rather more generous proportion than in many Western museums with icons in their collections, but indicative of the state of affairs that Lankton specifically sought to avoid by founding his own museum rather than donate his collection to an existing museum.

That 90 percent of the icons in the British Museum are in storage does not mean that they are neglected or ignored: far from it. In a systematic online catalog edited by British Museum curator Chris Entwistle, and launched in 2008, Yuri Bobrov discusses the 72 Russian icons in the collection (Bobrov 2008). A similar online catalog of the Byzantine, Cretan, and post-Byzantine icons by Robin Cormack and Maria Vassilaki is in preparation. Between 2005 and 2007 the Department of Conservation and Scientific Research collaborated with the curatorial department responsible for the icons, Prehistory and Europe, to understand their condition and history of use in preparation for a methodical conservation campaign. This acknowledged that icons are "tools of worship in the Orthodox Church," and that they "become worn and damaged through acts of worship by kissing, handling and exposure to incense and candles." The web page on this project continues: "Repeated cleaning and re-painting for continued use in the church are part of their normal history. It is common to find icons structurally and visually altered."[17] The authors of the account of the treatment of two of the icons acknowledged that the icons had migrated from a liturgical to a secular setting where "different priorities apply" (Harrison et al. 2006). They acknowledge, though, that "although no longer used in liturgy, they retain an intangible spiritual function" in consequence of which,

> It is therefore essential to document fully, through scientific examination and art historical research, their complex technical and cultural history to inform an ethical conservation strategy that addresses the physical, visual, and spiritual integrity of the icons. (Harrison, et al. 2006)

I infer that, although the British Museum curators, conservators, and scientists believe that secular museum considerations should take priority in the care of the icons, they nonetheless sought to honor their perceived moral obligation to do nothing to the icons that might compromise their ability to function as devotional objects. The curator responsible for the icons, Chris Entwistle, acknowledged that no special provision is in place for Orthodox adherents but would welcome the provision of a "small discrete gallery in which they could be shown in a more contemplative context." He pointed out that "visitors are always welcome to come and view (and worship) any of the icons in the reserve collections."[18]

Although Orthodox adherents, and members of other belief communities, will adapt to the circumstances of museum galleries to venerate the things they value and which, for them, are imbued with numinous qualities, some of which might be expressed by the term "life," such galleries are scarcely ideal for such purposes. Their mediation serves other purposes: making things visible, certainly, but preventing or inhibiting touch, which can damage items of many kinds, as the oils from human skin can be deleterious to many substances. Yet touching is an inevasible part of satisfactory devotional encounters with many kinds of numinous things, from the kissing of an icon to the manipulation of the contents of a Native American medicine bundle or the shaking of a sacred rattle. Touch is a matter in exhibition mediation to which I shall return.[19]

In addition to touch, certain kinds of veneration require rendering offerings. Few, if any, Western museums permit the devotional application of substances to things in their collections – foods and liquids – such as occurs in many societies, from sub-Saharan Africa, to subcontinental India, and Andean South America. Bathing in incense, or smudging, with the smoke of burning dried plants or resins is generally prohibited in galleries. However, some museums have recently introduced special provisions to accommodate devotion employing offerings. An example is the change in treatment of the spectacular early nineteenth-century Hawaiian *heiau* (temple) figure of the deity associated with warfare, Kū, or Kūka'ilimoku, in the Peabody Essex Museum in Salem, Massachusetts. Press speculation in 2006 prompted the museum to acknowledge that "groups have made planned offerings at PEM" (Edgers 2006). In 2010 the three surviving large-scale figures of Kūka'ilimoku (Peabody Essex Museum; British Museum, London; Bishop Museum, Honolulu) were united at the Bernice Pauahi Bishop Museum, Honolulu, in an exhibition, *E Kū Ana Ka Paia: Unification, Responsibility and the Kū Images*. The museum website noted:

> Coinciding with the bicentennial of the unification of the Hawaiian Kingdom, the unification of these Kū images provides an unprecedented opportunity to explore issues such as cultural identity, family and community responsibility, political sovereignty, and the role of museums in fostering cross-cultural dialogue. The images will be on display during the season of Kauwela, a time traditionally associated with Kū.[20]

On its return to the Peabody Essex Museum in October 2010, the figure of Kū was ritually honored by a Native Hawaiian delegation, including staff from the Bishop Museum. Since then, the museum has accommodated the devotions and offerings of Native Hawaiian visitors more openly than previously. The figure is shown in a prominent gallery, but away from other items, emphasizing its special status, and secluding any ritual attention or offerings paid to it.

Such changes are not the initiatives of individual museums alone. In August 2006 the Association of Art Museum Directors (an influential body in the American museum world) posted the "Report of the AAMD Subcommittee on the Acquisition and Stewardship of Sacred Objects" on its website. This describes museums' obligations to indigenous sacred things, including their ritual servicing (AAMD 2006). It can scarcely be coincidental that one of the authors of the report was Dan L. Monroe, the director of the Peabody Essex Museum.

As Chris Entwistle indicated in the case of the Orthodox icons in the British Museum, some museums accommodate devotional attention by visitors beyond the exhibition galleries. The Division of Anthropology of the American Museum of Natural History (AMNH), New York, used to welcome those who wished to interact ritually or devotionally with things in the collection to do so in the office of the curator of North American ethnology. Recently, however, a room has been exclusively dedicated to just these occasions, and the museum's safety regulations have even been modified to permit ritual acts such as smudging (the application of smoke from dried plant materials including sage and sweetgrass). Most members of Indigenous communities understand the need for restrictions, such as the prohibition of burning materials in public galleries, but, by making provision for such actions in a dedicated space, museums such as the AMNH demonstrate that they take the needs of originating communities seriously, thereby helping to foster improved long-term relations.

A second means of building improved relations between originating communities and Western museums is to question the institutional assumption that the flow of items for mediated exhibition is naturally and inevitably one way, that is, from originating communities to metropolitan institutions, many of which are encyclopedic museums. The attitude that such institutions are unequivocally beneficial is immensely destructive of trust, for their proponents take for granted the inequitable distribution of collected things, all encyclopedic museums being Western or so-called First World.[21] A pair of exemplary exhibitions in 2011 demonstrated that there is no reason whatsoever that materials should not be exchanged reciprocally. While the Kunsthalle im Lipsiusbau, Dresden, hosted an exhibition of 67 masks, vessels, and items of regalia from the Kwakwaka'wakw peoples preserved in the U'Mista Cultural Centre, the center in Alert Bay, Vancouver Island, British Columbia, hosted an exhibition of 61 mostly European diplomatic and princely gifts, including ceremonial weapons and porcelain from the collections of the Staatliche Kunstsammlungen Dresden. This equal exchange conforms with the cultural conventions of the Kwakwaka'wakw peoples, while also conforming to the conventions of Western museum practice of loan reciprocity, though in a novel form.[22]

The power of touch

All these types of mediation – accommodating offerings, the provision of secluded spaces, loans at appropriate calendar times, equitably reciprocal exchanges – skirt the huge mediational issue that arises when it comes to addressing devotional attention to numinously charged material things – how to satisfy the sense of touch. Not every form of devotional encounter entails physical contact between devotee and the object of veneration, but many do, and – as we have seen – museums generally hedge touching things in their collections with a variety of restrictions. There are exceptions – some museums exhibit objects ranging from sculptures and decorative arts objects to natural specimens, such as mammal pelts, with specific invitations to visitors to touch them, to enhance the sensory engagement of visually impaired visitors or of visitors generally. But usually, restrictions on touch range from absolute prohibition in most museum galleries to qualified prohibitions in museum storage and study areas, where in many instances gloves appropriate to the material of the things concerned must be worn, and only those who have received training in object handling – curators, conservators, scientists, registrars, preparators, installers – may touch the things concerned. On the face of it, this would seem to be a reasonable precaution. Inept handling can cause serious damage, and even careful handling without adequate precautions can result in incremental harm. Yet prohibitions for practical reasons can also be symbolic: a way of establishing, enforcing, or contesting power hierarchies. A university scholar visiting a museum storage area, study room, or conservation laboratory, intent on closely examining material in the collection, is usually wholly dependent on a curator, collections manager, or conservator to move those things at each and every turn. Those museum personnel privileged to handle collection items are truly hierophantic: like priests, they are the indispensable mediators. By contrast, the helpless university scholar – like any other visitor – is a mere member of the laity.

Power assertions expressed by means of access to, and handling of, collection items can take place within the museum hierarchy no less than between museum personnel and outsiders. Some museums in the United States are promoting the rise of collections managers, also known as registrars – employees who physically track and store all collection items. This is an indispensable responsibility, requiring considerable professional skill in the higher positions, but it is not a scholarly role. Increasingly, collections managers are gaining the upper hand in a variety of American museums. In some, they have asserted their claims to power even to the extent of persuading museum directors – who should know better – that only *they* should have access to museum collection storage areas.

The heart of every museum is not its galleries but its collection storage. This is where, in most museums, the majority of their collections is to be found. The conditions of mediation in museum storage are quite different from in exhibition galleries. Regardless of whether any given museum covers many fields or is specialized, collection items occupy case on case of shelving – sometimes movable compact shelving – in seemingly endless ranks; sliding racks on which pictures hang; solander box after solander box, each containing a stack of mounted and matted prints or drawings; drawer on drawer containing small items, from beetles to bird skins, snuff boxes to bladder stones. All these things are sorted – by culture, material, size, type – but so crowded as to produce a sense in the viewer of limitless profusion.

In these circumstances, juxtapositions of seemingly scarcely related things occur unpredictably and serendipitously, suggesting relationships and affinities that no computer database could ever provide. The practiced curatorial eye can scan the contents of a large drawer of ancient Roman miniature terracotta votive models of body parts – arms, eyes, wombs – and discern qualities comparatively with a speed, accuracy, and acuity impossible when consulting images of the same things – however high in quality – in a computer database. Access to such stored materials is indispensable for curatorial scholarship. However, in museum after museum, at least in the United States, collections managers, citing security concerns, are successfully claiming exclusive privilege of access. Curators and conservators – who equally require access to collections in storage to discharge their responsibility of alertness and care – are all too frequently reduced to requesting specific items identified by means of an inevitably inadequate database, which are then brought to them, one at a time or in small groups, in a study room. This exclusionary move is an internal assertion of power, and threatens the end of scholarship in the museums affected. Yet even in such attenuated circumstances, curators and conservators can still touch: something that visitors to study rooms usually cannot do (again, there are exceptions; for instance, some art museums arrange special handling sessions in study rooms for groups – college classes or members of societies dedicated to silver, furniture, or ceramics, for example).

People generally want to touch the things they are examining. One of the lesser known facts about museums is that, in spite of notices urging visitors not to touch objects, they surreptitiously touch exhibits not covered by glass or plexiglass, not once in a while but constantly. Some items are seemingly irresistible. Visitors constantly want to touch the casts after Edgar Degas's two-thirds life-size wax sculpture *Little Dancer of Fourteen Years* (ca. 1881), each of which wears a real fabric hair ribbon and tutu (at least 30 examples of the sculpture were cast posthumously in plaster and bronze, most of which are in museums: see Kendall 1998). Just as common a motive as prurience may be curiosity about the character of the fabric. A visitor may wonder: is it actually real or a representation? This supposition is suggested by a comparison with the surreptitious actions of visitors, to be described below, to an exhibition of Spanish art, *Time to Hope*, held at the Episcopal Cathedral of St. John the Divine, New York, in the fall of 2002.

The power of touch exemplified: *Time to Hope*

While the forms of mediation in museum galleries tend to inhibit rather than encourage devotional attention to the things exhibited, the same cannot be said of Christian churches, where ecclesiastical authorities usually recognize that visitors attend to items displayed in a variety of not necessarily mutually exclusive ways, including devotionally and aesthetically. In addition to sites of worship, ecclesiastical authorities may also set aside spaces for predominantly aesthetic engagement with objects, as in treasuries and ecclesiastical museums. The result is that, within sacred spaces, as opposed to secular museums, viewers in aggregate almost inevitably engage in a broad range of forms of attention to religious artifacts, from the overtly devotional to the wholly secular. Yet, interestingly, ecclesiastical authorities do not inevitably acquiesce in accepting secular aesthetic attention to objects within their precincts. Ecclesiastical authorities sometimes articulate the hope that vestigially religious or wholly secular aesthetic contemplation of such objects might inadvertently lead viewers to the sacred dimension of those same objects, whether by stimulating feelings already present within them but dormant or subordinate, or as a new realization or intuition. This was the organizers' explicit aim in producing the exhibition *Time to Hope*, held at the Episcopal Cathedral of St. John the Divine, New York, in the fall of 2002.

Time to Hope was an exhibition of 101 religious objects from churches throughout the Spanish province of Castilla y León. The exhibition was organized for New York in response to the terrorist outrage there on September 11, 2001. While it sought to provide consolation to the inhabitants of New York, the aim of the Spanish Las Edades del Hombre foundation, which organized it, was frankly evangelical. That purpose was complicated by the confessional difference between the foundation itself, as a Roman Catholic entity, and its Episcopalian host. The ecumenical magnanimity of St. John the Divine is of long standing. The cathedral chapter, headed by the dean, James Kowalski, hoped that the exhibition would serve a spiritual purpose more broadly encompassing than that envisaged by the foundation. As long as visitors attended, both foundation and cathedral chapter could feel vindicated, for spiritual solace in viewers of artworks is impossible to quantify, or even detect reliably. Some may have been spiritually affected without realizing it. Some may have been aware of the purposes of the organizers and consciously resisted them. Some of these may have been among those affected spiritually despite themselves. It is impossible to ascertain whether any of the many visitors were actually affected in the way the organizers intended, and equally impossible to assert whether anyone was affected at all. Rather than dispute imponderables, it would seem more directly informative to look at actual responses to objects as they were occurring, especially as they relate to touch.

Time to Hope was installed in the ambulatory and apse chapels of the cathedral. The entire area was transformed from sacred space into an exhibition space by indicators at once practical and symbolic. These included close-fitting red carpeting, and elaborately designed wall paneling colored a mottled gold. The same mottled gold was used for the bases of the cases that contained many of the objects displayed. These display cases themselves signaled that this was, for now, exhibition space rather than devotional space.

The illuminated manuscripts, paintings, vestments, and polychrome sculpture were arranged in seven thematic sections: "According to the Scriptures," "The Illusion of Happiness," "At the Right Time, God and Man," "Solidarity in Pain and Death," "The Sculpture of Man," "Ecstasy and Emotion," and "Finally Hope." The penultimate in the sequence, "Ecstasy and Emotion," was in some respects its discursive climax. The evangelical rhetoric suggested that the temptation to despair in the face of terrible events, including Christ's Passion, might be countered by considering the emotive and at times mystical responses of the Virgin Mary and the saints. The abused dead body of Christ is a particular focus of fervid emotional meditation and devotion, particularly in this context. The center of the apse chapel devoted to "Ecstasy and Emotion" was occupied by an arresting likeness of Christ's dead body, reclining in an open shallow box on elaborately carved and gilded feet placed on a low, mottled gold plinth. The strikingly lifelike polychrome figure was naked but for a green perizonium (loin cloth) draped across its groin, leaving its right hip exposed. The figure lay on its back on an elaborately edged white shroud, shoulders and head turned slightly to the right, supported by an intricately patterned pillow. Because of its position in the chapel, entering visitors approached the ensemble from the direction of the figure's feet. The figure appeared to have been contrived so that the wounds – notably that in the Christ's side – should be prominently visible from this viewpoint. A small label was attached to the horizontal lower right corner of the plinth stating that this *Reclining Christ* was by Gregorio Fernández (1576–1636), and came from the Museo del Convento de Santa Clara, Medina del Pomar (Burgos). Most visitors, perhaps drawn by the Christ's face, turned to its right, moved up the left side of the box.

Even the most acute observer cannot read the thoughts of those who saw this thing, and thereby learn their reactions. No one could draw more than the grossest inferences from watching visitors' behavior toward it. Yet even these indicate a variety of responses from which the observer can deduce a variety of uses. Many visitors were in all likelihood drawn from a wide range of Christian convictions. Some would, therefore, have been predisposed to find such an object devotionally valid and even welcome, while to others it might have been repugnant. Yet other visitors – adherents of religions other than Christianity, and atheists – might have regarded such a representation as marginal to, or beyond, what they might care about from a religious standpoint.

As an observer of visitors to this chapel, I distinguished four types of behavior toward the *Reclining Christ*: (1) cursory viewing without reading the label, and swift turning away (dismissal); (2) viewing – whether brief or lingering – that sometimes but not invariably included perusal of the label (inspection); (3) engagement that progressed to the tactile realm, as viewers touched the object (engagement); and (4) overt devotional attention to the object made manifest by gestures of prayer (devotion). This order of description does not imply a hierarchy of quality of attention. Touching in itself does not necessarily imply a deeper level of engagement than mere visual inspection, though it can. Furthermore, some viewers touch such an item out of curiosity; others are motivated by a devotional urge to secure a spiritual benefit.

One of the first questions an observer might ask when confronted with this ensemble is: How is such lifelikeness achieved? Most would realize that the figure is painted to render a corpse whose appearance physically registers the abuses inflicted on Christ in the course of the Passion. Similarly, the pillow supporting Christ's head and shoulders is elaborately painted so as to render an intricately woven fabric. Most viewers, presumably, almost instantaneously deduced that the body itself is an artful depiction. Those with previous experience of similar figures must have realized that it is made of painted wood.

The fabric, though, is another matter. The white cloth or shroud on which Christ lies appears to be edged with actual braid, and indeed may not be a depiction but real cloth stiffened with some once liquid agent. The green brocade fabric covering the exterior of the box is even less ambiguously real cloth edged with gold braid, and is clearly not a depiction. It is a real presence within the fictive world of the sculpture, and as such enhances the reality effect of the purely depictive elements by encouraging the viewer to elide the distinction between reality and artifice. This fabric was the object of several visitors' tactile curiosity. They did not touch the figure but rather what appeared to be fabric, presumably because so much in a perceptual sense depends on being able to distinguish between the real and the illusory. Other elements enhance the reality effect, and the uncertainty of the place of this ensemble between reality and artifice. The half-closed eyes of the figure enhance the reality effect by artificial means, for they are made of glass, which gives them a translucent depth unavailable on a painted surface. The teeth, on the other hand, though fashioned by human hand, are ivory – the material of actual teeth – so, like the real fabric, they blur the boundary between depiction and actuality.

What can be established about viewers' uses of this artifact? The observer can infer nothing specific about the use that visitors who either dismiss, or visually inspect, or tactilely engage with the *Reclining Christ* are making of it. One can only surmise that those who inspect it are doing so according to the familiar range of terms available to more or less practiced exhibition visitors. Whatever else they may also be doing, they are using it as an exhibit. What does it mean for a viewer to use an artifact as an exhibit? One element is surely an attempt to satisfy curiosity about the physical composition of the object. Indeed, this curiosity can be prompted by the mode of display that allows close, all round access, as was the case with the *Reclining Christ*. Such inspection can take place adequately only in circumstances unregulated by ceremony (though still regulated by the decorum of exhibition visiting). "How does it work?" is presumably not a question usually in the forefront of the minds of most people while they are using such a thing devotionally. This question characterizes – though it far from exhausts – exhibit use. The physical circumstances contrived in the *Time to Hope* exhibition, while not determining this use, sanctioned it.

However, while there may have been no ceremony enveloping the *Reclining Christ* while displayed in this exhibition, its placement purposefully evoked the physical circumstance of ceremony, for its position in the chapel determined that the visitor's angle of approach to it would be identical with that of a worshipper using it ceremonially. That is, visitors were obliged to approach its feet. This was just how worshippers approached a very similar realistic sculpture of the dead Christ in the Cathedral of St. Mary of Toledo, Spain (as observed by the author, December 14, 1987). They had been engaged in formal devotional attention to the sculpture in a church that was in its ceremonial mode. They stood in line, approached the figure singly in turn, knelt before it, and kissed a foot. Anyone wishing to inspect that figure as though it were an exhibit had to do so from a distance. Was the mediational choice of the curators of the *Time to Hope* exhibition to evoke such devotional use by means of the specific placement of the *Reclining Christ* no more than an attempt to honor the teleology of the artifact for museological reasons – this is how it is meant to be seen and is best seen – or was it, rather, a surreptitious attempt to trigger a devotional response dormant in some viewers in pursuance of the avowed evangelical aim of the exhibition? The physical consequences of both aims for the display of the object are identical, so there is no way to be sure. Yet, in the circumstances, it seems reasonable to infer that the organizers intended a calculated ambiguity such as might stand the best possible chance of evoking a religious response. The circumstances may not have directly encouraged devotion in response to the object, but that use was certainly not only possible – in part owing to subtle curatorial encouragement – but demonstrably occurred. I observed a woman approach the ensemble, move to the left (the side that allowed the better view of Christ's face), cross herself, whisper what was presumably a prayer, cross herself again, and move on. She was clearly using the object devotionally, albeit informally, and not necessarily to the exclusion of other forms of attention to it. What might the character of that prayerful response to the *Reclining Christ* have been? One purpose of such figures was vividly to evoke the ultimate consequence of Christ's sacrifice prior to the miracle of the resurrection in the hearts and minds of devotees. The devout and practiced exponent of meditation and prayer might visualize a saint who imagined union with Christ in this condition, and seek to emulate, or at least identify with that saint. Obviously, one cannot tell whether or not some such notion was a component of the thoughts passing through the mind of the woman in prayer before the *Reclining Christ* in the *Time to Hope* exhibition, but her attention to it was clearly devotional.

Although such a devotional use might – and does – occur in front of Christian artifacts in museums, it is unusual to witness it so overtly, for museum settings, and those who contrive them, generally encourage other forms of attention and, for the most part, while not prohibiting devotional attention in public galleries, seek to accommodate it in storage areas, study rooms, or even – as in the case of the AMNH – in a room set aside for the purpose. The peculiar ambiguity of the setting and circumstances of the *Time to Hope* exhibition would seem to have allowed a greater play between the various possible uses of the objects displayed than might normally be the case, either in an uncompromisingly ecclesiastical setting (at least when worship is in progress) or in a secular museum. One might therefore conclude that the particular setting of this exhibition in part of a church temporarily adapted for a museum-style display, but retaining aspects of its purely ecclesiastical ambiance, and the choice of objects displayed – all directly associated with the practice of Roman Catholic Christianity – combined to promote a variety of uses of those objects on the part of visitors. In particular, some inhibitions – against touching, against informal devotion – appear to have been relatively relaxed in comparison to customary visitor behavior in museums, while inhibitions governing secular curiosity and inquiry that might have been strong in a purely devotional setting were also relatively relaxed. The ambiguity of the setting was in part unavoidable given its character, but was also enhanced by subtle curatorial decisions concerning mediation. This ambiguity appears to have offered visitors opportunities for a wider range of uninhibited response than in either an unmodified church or a museum.

To emphasize this conclusion, it is worth comparing how visitors engaged with Gregorio Fernández's *Reclining Christ* in the *Time for Hope* exhibition with how visitors engaged with another work of the same kind in an exhibition in an art museum. The curator Ronda Kasl included a *Reclining Christ*, dated 1652, attributed to Juan Sánchez Barba, in her exhibition, *Sacred Spain: Art and Belief in the Spanish World* at the Indianapolis Museum of Art in 2009–2010. This work had never previously been loaned from the church of the Hermitage of la Veracruz, Navalcarnero, near Madrid, so in this exhibition it was subject to museum mediation for the first time in its existence. Kasl contrived a kind of Spanish devotional *paragone* (competition between the claims of sculpture and painting) by juxtaposing this sculpture with a painting by Mateo Cerezo of a life-size *Entombed Christ* of about 1659 from the church of Nuestra Señora de San Lorenzo, Valladolid. Although the format and frame of the painting appear to have been altered, the bottom edge of the frame has peg holes so that it could be supported as a freestanding object. As such, in appropriate lighting, the painting, like the sculpture, would have appeared strikingly lifelike (Gaskell 2010b, 263–265). Kasl was making a point about the means whereby artists and ecclesiastical authorities in seventeenth-century Spain attempted to create the conditions for devotional attention through the verisimilitude of representations of – in these instances – the dead and as yet unrisen Christ. In doing so, they exploited the particular qualities of both polychrome sculpture and illusionistic paintings, implying that artists in these respective media might compete for effectiveness. Both works that Kasl used to this end in the museum had come from unequivocally devotional settings in Spanish churches. As far as I could tell from discreetly observing visitors in the same way as I had done in the *Time for Hope* exhibition, the circumstances – institutional setting, mediation of presentation, and discursive juxtaposition – in the *Sacred Spain* exhibition neither encouraged nor sanctioned devotional attention to these items. Again, although it was equally impossible to read the minds of visitors in the Indianapolis Museum of Art as it had been in the Cathedral of St. John the Divine, I observed no explicit devotional attention to either the *Risen Christ* sculpture or the *Entombed Christ* painting. Although both are properly devotional items – sacred items – in their usual ecclesiastical settings, they appear to have been devotionally neutralized by the secular and scholarly setting of the exhibition in the museum.

Variable lives

The life of things – the things discussed in this chapter – is inordinately complicated, and, as in the case of all things that in some sense live – including human beings – they undergo changes throughout their lives. Some of these things retain their living qualities no matter what their circumstances may be, whether recognized or honored, or not. These include Christian Orthodox icons, and Hawaiian *heiau* figures of Kūka'ilimoku, or Kū. Others can alternate between the sacred and secular realms according to circumstance, such as the figure of the *Reclining Christ* by Gregorio Fernández and the similar figure attributed to Juan Sánchez Barba. Exhibition mediation, whether in museums or elsewhere, can do much to inhibit or to encourage specific forms of attention – devotional, aesthetic, historical – selectively, though mediation can never entirely expunge sacredness, where it exists. Further, museum mediation does not only take place in exhibition galleries. It occurs just as importantly in storage areas, laboratories, study rooms, and, in some instances, in rooms set aside for devotion.

Is any aspect of the character of a tangible thing inalienable? I conclude by returning to consider the one Russian Orthodox icon currently exhibited in the British Museum: the late fourteenth-century *Miracle of St. George and the Dragon*, also know as *The Black George* because of the color of the horse ridden by the red-mantled saint as he transfixes the dragon with his spear. The icon has an unusual recent history. The British Museum acquired it in 1986 from the dealers then trading as Axia Art Islamique et Byzantin (now Axia Art Etablissement, a Lichtenstein company, with a subsidiary trading as Axia Art Consultants Ltd in London). The previous owner listed was Maria Vasilievna Rozanova. Rozanova left the Soviet Union with her husband, the prominent dissident writer Andrei Donatovich Sinyavsky in 1973, following his release from the gulag two years earlier. They settled in Paris, where they cofounded, and Rozanova edited, the émigré journal, *Sintaksis* between 1978 and 2001. This icon of St. George, then, has had a life as a witness of the early Soviet dissident movement which attracted international attention in 1966 with the trial and conviction of Sinyavsky and his friend and fellow writer Yuli Markovich Daniel for anti-Soviet activity, both of whom published satirical works in France under pseudonyms.

No owner prior to Rozanova is listed in Bobrov's catalog, but he gives a very brief account of its unusual discovery in 1959 in a small village, Il'inski Pogost, in the Arkhangel'skaya oblast in northern Russia. It was reportedly being used as a window shutter (Bobrov 2008). Bobrov further reports that the icon was conserved by Adolf Ovchinnikov at the I. E. Grabar State Restoration Workshops in Moscow in 1960.

This case is eerily similar to that of a fourteenth-century panel painting, acquired by the Fogg Art Museum of Harvard University in two halves, reportedly retrieved from a barn window near Siena in or before 1920. When juxtaposed, a standing figure of a female saint can be discerned on the dismembered and battered panel. The unique character of the punch marks in the halo indicates that it was made in the workshop of the Sienese painter Pietro Lorenzetti (ca. 1280–1348). Although on long-term loan to the Fogg Art Museum, the upper and lower halves remained the property of its onetime director, Edward Forbes, until his death in 1969. He bequeathed them to the museum. Superseded as part of an altarpiece, this panel, and another representing St. John the Baptist (now untraced) were adapted to board up a barn window, presumably much as the late fourteenth-century icon of the *Miracle of St. George* was adapted for use as a window shutter.

In an earlier study, I used the case of the Sienese panel to propose a modification to Nelson Goodman's contention that the question "What is art?" is a poor one and better replaced by "When is art?" (Gaskell 2007). Here one might ask the same question of the sacred. That is to say, might not "When is (something) sacred?" be a more fruitful question than "What is [the] sacred?" Yet, to suggest that this is so would be to imply that sacredness is a quality dependent on human use. This is tempting, but, just as Goodman's brilliant suggestion is, at base, an ontological evasion – he carefully never claims that to use something as art is to make it into art – so is its analogue in the case of the sacred. Those ontological evasions may indeed lead to useful realms of thought – ontology is not a precondition for all useful thinking, and its pursuit may be at times a distraction – but it is an evasion nonetheless. This becomes clear if one seeks to apply the analogy to life: a pressing issue in the circumstances of this chapter, which seeks to address the life of things. The viability of the question "When is life?" in the sense of ascribing life to things on the basis of human use – as in the cases of art and sacredness – is certainly open to doubt. The quality of animation, whether biological or in the extended terms discussed here, is not dependent on human use, for, clearly, to use a thing as though it were alive is not the same ontologically as for it to be alive.

For things to have lives, then, implies variable worlds in which that quality – life – itself varies. A Niitsítapi world in which an ancestor shirt has life, a Hawaiian world in which a figure of Kūka'ilimoku has life, a Roman Catholic world in which a figure of the dead Christ has life, and a Russian Orthodox world in which an icon of St. George has life can coexist with a Western secular world in which, in a biological sense, they do not. Museums are the sites of mediation between such worlds. That mediation takes place not only in exhibition galleries, but also in other, less generally visible parts of a museum's fabric.

Wherever such mediated encounters occur within a museum, it is that museum's responsibility to foster what Wordsworth termed "the power / Of harmony, and the deep power of joy." This is certainly a strong challenge in the face of the fact that some tangible things evoke the depths of degradation in human behavior, just as others call to mind the heights of human attainment. Yet Wordsworth's insight is that only with the eye made quiet by these powers can human beings see into the life of things. To create the circumstances – in galleries and beyond – in which the eye can thus be quiet is the proper calling of museums.

Acknowledgments

I conducted some of the research for this chapter while simultaneously a senior fellow at the Center for the Study of World Religions, Harvard Divinity School, and visiting curator for research at the Peabody Museum of Archaeology and

Ethnology, Harvard University, in 2003–2004. I am grateful to both for their support, which, in the case of the latter, continues in the form of my appointment as research associate in North American ethnology. I am also grateful to the American Museum of Natural History for support through my appointment as research associate in anthropology.

Philosophical and historical work is incremental, and incurs many debts. While its argument is entirely new, this chapter draws in part on previously published work, and I should like to thank those who sponsored or otherwise enabled those efforts: Akira Akiyama, Conrad Brunk, Sarah Anne Carter, A. W. Eaton, Diana Eck, Alison Edwards, Samantha van Gerbig, Iris Heavy Runner, Sherri Irvin, Ronda Kasl, Laurel Kendall, Andrew McClellan, Brent Rodrigues Plate, John Roe, Sara Schechner, Michele Stanco, Butch Thunder Hawk, Laurel Thatcher Ulrich, Rubie Watson, Peter Whiteley, Alison Wylie, and James O. Young. As always, Jane Whitehead is my most stringent critic, to whom I owe the greatest debt and the most thanks.

Notes

1   http://www.catalogueoflife.org/colwebsite/ (accessed August 6, 2014).
2   http://eol.org/about (accessed August 6, 2014).
3   http://www.rpopa.net/ (accessed August 6, 2014). This widely quoted aphorism appears to be derived from Marcus Aurelius's approbatory attribution of the sentiment "Remember that all is opinion" to the fourth-century BCE Cynic philosopher Monimus of Syracuse.
4   "Spirit Collection Tours," http://www.nhm.ac.uk/visit-us/whats-on/daytime-events/talks-and-tours/spirit-collection-tours/index.html (accessed August 7, 2014).
5   Peabody Museum, "Conserving Alutiiq Cultural Heritage. Conservators at Work: Alaska's Historic Kayaks Renewed," https://www.peabody.harvard.edu/node/747, and "Conserving Alaska Native Kayaks: What We Learned," https://www.peabody.harvard.edu/node/909 (accessed August 6, 2014).
6   http://www.glenbow.org/exhibitions/past/2010-2011/ (accessed August 6, 2014); see also Gaskell (2012, 93).
7   "Visiting with the Ancestors: The Blackfoot Shirts Project," http://www.prm.ox.ac.uk/blackfootexhibition.html (accessed August 7, 2014). See also Chapter 12, "The Blackfoot Shirts Project: 'Our Ancestors Have Come to Visit,'" by Alison K. Brown and Laura Peers, in *Museum Transformations*.
8   I use these terms – "hegemonic" and "subaltern" – in the senses defined in Eaton and Gaskell (2009, 235): "By hegemonic we refer to the values of Western societies that sustain their dominance, especially insofar as they place other societies at a disadvantage; by subaltern, following the usage established by a number of Indian historians, we refer to groups at a disadvantage to those exercising power within a society."

9   *The Glory of Byzantium: Art and Culture in the Middle Byzantine Era*, A.D. *843–1261*,
    Metropolitan Museum of Art, New York, March 11–July 6, 1997; *Byzantium: Faith and
    Power (1261–1557)*, Metropolitan Museum of Art, New York, March 23–July 5, 2004;
    Holy Image, Hallowed Ground: Icons from Sinai, J. Paul Getty Museum, Los Angeles,
    November 2006–March 2007. The curator of both exhibitions in New York, Helen
    Evans, kindly confirmed the presence of monks from St. Catherine's Monastery
    throughout both exhibitions (email comm., August 4, 2013). For the monastery, see,
    in the first instance, the website of the Jerusalem Patriarchate at http://www.
    jerusalem-patriarchate.info/en/oros_sina.htm (accessed August 7, 2014).

10 Helen Evans, curator of the exhibition, email comm., August 4, 2013.

11 "Holy Image, Hallowed Ground – Behind the Scenes of an Exhibition: The Icons'
    Journey from Egypt to Los Angeles," http://www.getty.edu/art/exhibitions/icons_
    sinai/extra_installation.html (accessed August 7, 2014).

12 Helen Evans, email comm., August 4, 2013. I am grateful to Helen Evans for her
    readiness to provide much useful information, and also to Peter Barnet, senior curator
    of the Department of Medieval Art and the Cloisters, Metropolitan Museum of Art,
    New York.

13 http://museumofrussianicons.org/en/about/the-museum/history-of-the-
    museum/ (accessed August 7, 2014).

14 http://museumofrussianicons.org/en/about/the-museum/faq/ (accessed August 7,
    2014).

15 http://museumofrussianicons.org/en/about/the-museum/history-of-the-
    museum/ (accessed August 7, 2014).

16 On the use of things as art, rather than whether or not any given thing is an art-
    work, I follow Nelson Goodman's observations in his *Ways of Worldmaking* (1978,
    57–70, ch. 4, "When Is Art?)," as qualified in my "After Art, Beyond Beauty"
    (Gaskell 2007).

17 "Establishing a Methodology for the Care and Conservation of the Orthodox Icons
    Collection at the British Museum," http://www.britishmuseum.org/research/
    projects/conservation_of_orthodox_icons.aspx (accessed August 7, 2014).

18 Chris Entwistle, email comm., August 4, 2013. I am grateful to Chris Entwistle for his
    generous response to my inquiry.

19 See also Chapters 12, 13, and 16 in this volume by Erkki Huhtamo, Fiona Candlin, and
    Beat Hächler respectively.

20 http://www.bishopmuseum.org/exhibits/pastexhibits.html (accessed August 7,
    2014).

21 A leading proponent of encyclopedic museums is James Cuno, former director of the
    Art Institute of Chicago, now president of the J. Paul Getty Trust (see Cuno 2008;
    2011).

22 The two exhibitions were: in Dresden, *Die Macht des Schenkens: Der Potlatch im Großen
    Haus der Kwakwaka'wakw an der kanadischen Nordwestküste* (The power of giving: The
    potlatch in the big house of the Kwakwaka'wakw on the Canadian Northwest Coast);
    and, in Alert Bay, *The Power of Giving: Gifts at the Saxon Rulers' Court in Dresden and the
    Kwakwaka'wakw Big House*. See, further, Gaskell (2012).

References

AAMD (Association of Art Museum Directors). 2006. "Report of the AAMD Subcommittee on the Acquisition and Stewardship of Sacred Objects." Accessed August 6, 2014. https://aamd.org/document/report-of-the-aamd-subcommittee-on-the-acquisition-and-stewardship-of-sacred-objects.

Belich, James. 2009. *Replenishing the Earth: The Settler Revolution and the Rise of the Anglo-World, 1783–1939*. Oxford: Oxford University Press.

Bobrov, Yuri. 2008. *A Catalogue of the Russian Icons in the British Museum*, edited by Chris Entwistle. Accessed August 6, 2014. http://www.britishmuseum.org/research/publications/online_research_catalogues/russian_icons/catalogue_of_russian_icons.aspx.

Cormack, Robin. 2007. *Icons*. London: British Museum; Cambridge, MA: Harvard University Press.

Cuno, James. 2008. *Who Owns Antiquity? Museums and the Battle over Our Ancient Heritage*. Princeton: Princeton University Press.

Cuno, James. 2011. *Museums Matter: In Praise of the Encyclopedic Museum*. Chicago: University of Chicago Press.

Eaton, A. W., and Ivan Gaskell. 2009. "Do Subaltern Artifacts Belong in Art Museums?" In *The Ethics of Cultural Appropriation*, edited by James O. Young and Conrad Brunk, 235–267. Oxford: Wiley-Blackwell.

Edgers, Geoff. 2006. "Ritual Offerings, Peabody Essex Museum." Boston.com, August 10. Accessed August 6, 2014. http://www.boston.com/ae/theater_arts/exhibitionist/2006/08/ritual_offering_1.html.

Gaskell, Ivan. 2003. "*Sacred to Profane and Back Again.*" In *Art and Its Publics: Museum Studies at the Millennium*, edited by Andrew McClellan, 149–162. Oxford: Blackwell.

Gaskell, Ivan. 2007. "After Art, Beyond Beauty." In *Inspiration and Technique: Theories of Beauty and Art from Antiquity to the Present*, edited by John Roe and Michele Stanco, 311–334. Berne: Peter Lang.

Gaskell, Ivan. 2010a. "In Search of Christian Miraculous Images in the Age of Mechanical Reproduction, and Beyond." In "Death and Life and Visual Culture II: Miraculous Images in Christian and Buddhist Culture," special issue, *Bulletin of Death and Life Studies* (University of Tokyo) 6: 60–75.

Gaskell, Ivan. 2010b. Review of *Sacred Spain: Art and Belief in the Spanish World*, Indianapolis Museum of Art, 2009–2010. *Material Religion* 6(2): 263–265.

Gaskell, Ivan. 2012. "Museums and Philosophy – of Art, and Many Other Things." *Philosophy Compass* 7: 75–76, 93–94.

Gaskell, Ivan. Forthcoming. "The Museum of Big Ideas." In *Philosophy of Museums: Ethics, Aesthetics, Ontology*, edited by Victoria Harrison, Anna Bergqvist, and Gary Kemp. Cambridge: Cambridge University Press.

Goodman, Nelson. 1978. *Ways of Worldmaking*. Indianapolis: Hackett.

Harrison, Lynne, Janet Ambers, Rebecca Stacey, Caroline Cartwright, Duncan Hook, and Chris Entwistle. 2006. "Sacred to Secular: The Care and Conservation of Orthodox Icons at the British Museum." In *The Object in Context: Crossing Conservation Boundaries: Contributions to the Munich Congress, 28 August–1 September, 2006*, edited by David

Saunders, Joyce H. Townsend, and Sally Woodcock, 317. London: International Institute for Conservation of Historic and Artistic Works.

Kendall, Richard, with Douglas W. Druick, Arthur Beale, and the Baltimore Museum of Art. 1998. *Degas and The Little Dancer*. Exhibition catalog, Jocelyn Art Museum, Omaha, NE; Clark Art Institute, Williamstown, MA; New Haven: Yale University Press.

Koshland, Daniel E., Jr. 2002. "The Seven Pillars of Life." *Science* 295(5563): 2215–2216.

Popa, Radu. 2004. *Between Necessity and Probability: Searching for the Origin and Definition of Life*. Berlin: Springer.

Trifonov, Edward N. 2012. "Definition of Life: Navigation through Uncertainties." *Journal of Biomolecular Structure and Dynamics* 29(4): 647–650.

Ulrich, Laurel Thatcher, Sarah Anne Carter, Ivan Gaskell, Sara Schechner, and Samantha van Gerbig. Forthcoming. *Tangible Things*. Oxford: Oxford University Press.

Wordsworth, William. (1798) 1974. "Lines Composed a Few Miles above Tintern Abbey." In *Wordsworth: Poetical Works*, edited by Thomas Hutchinson (1904), rev. ed. by Ernest de Selincourt (1936), 163–165. Oxford: Oxford University Press.

Young, James O. 2005. "'Profound Offence and Cultural Appropriation.'" *Journal of Aesthetics and Art Criticism* 63: 135–146.

Ivan Gaskell is Professor of Cultural History and Museum Studies at the Bard Graduate Center, New York City. Mobilizing nonwritten traces of the past, he addresses intersections between history, art history, anthropology, and philosophy. As well as writing case studies ranging from seventeenth-century Dutch and Flemish paintings, Native American baskets, and Congo textiles, he works on underlying philosophical questions. While at Cambridge University, he edited a 10 book series of multiauthor volumes, Cambridge Studies in Philosophy and the Arts, with the late Salim Kemal. He organized numerous experimental exhibitions at Harvard University, where he taught and curated between 1991 and 2011. At the Bard Graduate Center, Gaskell runs the Focus Project, an ongoing series of experimental exhibitions and publications emerging from faculty research and teaching. Gaskell is the author, editor, or coeditor of 11 books, and has contributed to numerous journals and edited volumes on history, art history, and philosophy.

9 LIGHTING PRACTICES IN ART GALLERIES AND EXHIBITION SPACES, 1750–1850

Alice Barnaby

Light is the unsung hero in the world of galleries, exhibitions, and museums. It is the transparent medium through which we encounter representations of our selves, yet it is rarely the subject of our attention. It is a key atmospheric constituent for the experience of aesthetic contemplation but, more often than not, its qualities remain unevaluated by many. Light guides, informs, and in some cases determines our assessment and interpretation of art – but we are often unaware of the extent to which it is used to manipulate our perceptions. While light is the pre-eminent medium of visuality, it nevertheless evades our focus, and it is this peculiar quality of semivisibility that has proved to be such a powerful tool in shaping taste at both individual and cultural levels.

Fluctuating tastes in lighting designs for galleries emphasize the historical contingency of culture on display. Some of the greatest fluctuations in styles of lighting occurred in the transition from late eighteenth-century to early nineteenth-century culture, and it is for this reason that the scope of this chapter falls roughly between the 1750s and 1850s. It was during this period that what we recognize today as the modern public gallery or museum became a dominant feature of urban topography and national identity. Here, discussion of lighting strategies is centered specifically on sites of artistic display rather than, for example, museums of natural history or science and technology. Light is, after all, of central importance within the visual arts, and in the art gallery it has an emphatically aesthetic role to play in addition to the functional role of making objects visible. How objects are lit defines the quality and meaning of aesthetic experience; therefore, the production of cultural capital is at stake when shifts occur in styles of lighting art. What these alterations in lighting strategies were and what caused some methods to be favored over others is the subject of this chapter. While the cultural landscape of Britain is the focus, many of

The International Handbooks of Museum Studies: Museum Media, First Edition.
Edited by Michelle Henning.
© 2015 John Wiley & Sons Ltd. Published 2020 by John Wiley & Sons Ltd.

the themes discussed resonate with lighting practices in Europe and further afield. Throughout, the aim is to interpret the cultural and aesthetic rather than technical significance of these shifts in lighting practices.

Across this 100 year span the manipulation of light in exhibition spaces was surprisingly varied. Vertical window arrangements; top lighting from skylights, filters of tissue paper, cloth, and colored glass; and the reflecting and refracting qualities of mirrors were all used to varying extents until the middle of the nineteenth century. Of course this was also the period which saw great advances in artificial lighting technologies. The invention of the Argand lamp (1780–1783) and the increasing use of gas lighting in the early decades of the nineteenth century offered new possibilities for viewing collections in the evening. These were the years in which light became so much more than a mere functional necessity. Debates about the advantages and disadvantages of these options preoccupied those with vested interests in the formation of cultural taste. Artists, architects, private collectors, public philanthropists, political legislators, social reformers, museum professionals, and members of the public all contributed a range of political, technical, and aesthetic perspectives to the question of what constituted appropriate viewing conditions. Criticisms of too much light, too little light, the wrong angle of light, or the wrong color of light were frequently expressed about exhibition spaces in this period.

It is no coincidence that different lighting preferences accompanied the proliferation of exhibition spaces during this period. Where once the ownership and appreciation of art had been royal, aristocratic, or religious activities, by the eighteenth century the consumption of art had expanded to include a rising middle class eager to assert its cultural authority. Public and private, permanent and temporary, exhibitions grew, appearing as statements of individual and national wealth. Therefore, in this chapter I trace the significance of the correlation between specific lighting techniques and types of venue, be it private collection, temporary exhibition space, or national museum. Through this mapping of light on display it becomes evident that critical tensions existed in the staging of statements about wealth, power, and taste.

In essence this was a debate about the cultural status and purpose of art. Broadly speaking, lighting styles during this period expressed four perspectives about the purpose of displaying art and cultural artifacts. Natural, unadorned top lighting through skylights was favored by those who, like Charles Eastlake, keeper of the National Gallery, believed that the nation's cultural assets should be preserved and reserved for genteel public appreciation. In this context the lighting technique, referred to here as patrician top lighting, was born out of display practices associated with large eighteenth-century private collections and supported a distinctly cerebral mode of viewing informed by a commitment to Enlightenment principles of reason and rationality. However, Henry Cole, commissioner of the Great Exhibition of 1851 and director of the South Kensington Museum (1854), favored lighting that supported wider principles of accessibility and social improvement. Cole's belief in accessibility is particularly evident in his support for the introduction of artificial lighting in the latter venue. Such a move enabled the working classes to visit public collections for evening viewing. Eastlake was decidedly nervous about this precedent and believed that evening opening for the masses would jeopardize the safety of the nation's collection (House of Commons 1850, 23–36; Swinney 1999).

The third position took a more commercially motivated view of display practices: lighting techniques were used to frame art as entertainment in venues such as the Regent's Park Colosseum (1827–1874), where velvet drapes, mirrors, cut glass, and artificial lighting created a richly sensual atmosphere of theatrical spectacle in the sculpture gallery. The fourth and final mode of exhibition lighting shared some of the lighting techniques used in the commercial entertainment venues, but employed them in venues where private collections were on display. The collections of Sir Thomas Hope, Sir Leicester Fleming, and Sir John Soane are three important examples where a dynamic and dramatic handling of light was used to transform aesthetic contemplation into an event. In these elite spaces a subjective, romantic impression was preferred to the more objective and neutral setting of public collections. In addition, many artists also displayed their own work to members of the public, and the lighting arrangements for the studios and galleries of Thomas Gainsborough, Sir Benjamin West, and J. M. W. Turner will also be briefly considered. Of course, by identifying these categories I am not suggesting that they are fixed or exhaustive but rather that they indicate patterns of cultural trends and pressures. During the first half of the nineteenth century these lighting practices existed simultaneously, but as we discuss them in turn we will see that, as the century progressed, some prospered and thrived, achieving a status of institutionalization whereas others faded into obscurity.

Patrician top lighting and sculpture galleries

An aperture in a building's roof creates a very specific viewing experience that is referred to here as "patrician lighting." The term identifies a style of lighting that dominated many elite eighteenth-century spaces of display across Europe. It evoked powerful Enlightenment principles of civic humanism, rational thought, and intellectual endeavor. The architectural heritage for this mode of lighting can be traced back to antiquity and is best exemplified in the central oculus, or eye, cut into the apex of the Roman Pantheon's domed roof (ca. AD 126). Open to the heavens, the sole source of light within the rotunda provided a rarefied atmosphere in which to venerate the gods and elite of the Roman republic. Many subsequent buildings of spiritual contemplation also favored the use of an oculus design. The church of San Lorenzo in Turin (1687), built by Guarino Guarini, and the church of San Andrea al Quirinale in Rome built by Gian Lorenzo Bernini between 1658 and 1678, are two examples among many which used top lighting to symbolize supernatural presence and support the belief of the faithful. However, a significant process of aesthetic and functional transference occurred in the use of this mode of top lighting during the eighteenth century. British aristocrats returning from the Grand Tour appropriated the feature of the oculus and commissioned a series of neoclassical architectural projects for their private residences. The earlier state or religious use of top lighting was domesticated, adapted for a British climate, and incorporated into elite dwellings to showcase the valuable collections of paintings and sculptures acquired on aristocratic travels. Associations of Roman republicanism and civic virtue were kept alive while activities of ritualistic worship were abandoned in a commitment to the new authority of Enlightenment rationality. The historian E. P. Thompson accounts for this reliance on antiquity, explaining that "it is no accident that the rulers turned back to ancient Rome for a model of their own sociological order" in order to produce a "calculated paternalist style of the gentry as a whole" (1974, 395, 403).

A mid-eighteenth-century example of the elitist desire to import and incorporate Roman republican architecture into a private, landscaped, and aristocratic environment is demonstrated by the activities of the banker and garden designer Henry Hoare II, who owned the Stourhead estate in Wiltshire, England, between 1741 and 1780. After the requisite educational Grand Tour, Hoare erected a number of neoclassical buildings to complete his vision of an Arcadian idyll. The principal lakeside view was reserved for an architecture of top lighting, a version of the Roman Pantheon which Hoare commissioned from the architect Henry Flitcroft in 1753. The pantheon was used as a sculpture gallery and contained "an antique statue of Livia Augusta, in the character of Ceres, and statues of Flora and of Hercules by Rysbrach" (Jones 1829, 3).

In the new context of an eighteenth-century English landscaped garden the replica pantheon "signalled the patrons' acquisition of a good taste and their embrace of a 'modern Augustanism'" (Dixon 2004, 60), but the ancient and double meaning of a pantheon as "a gathering of numerous gods, or a temple to celebrate their powers" (Craske and Wrigley 2004, 1) was only heard as a faint echo from the past. In the English country house, powers were certainly being celebrated, but they were humanly immanent rather than divinely transcendental, and the architecture, as Dana Arnold argues, was "an essential vehicle through which a patrician culture could express its values" (1998, 116).

Ten years after Flitcroft built Hoare's pantheon at Stourhead, Robert Adam completed the interior design for two major rooms at Kedleston Hall in Derbyshire, home of Lord Scarsdale. The hall and sculpture gallery of the saloon are a further example of how top-lit neoclassical architecture was used by the aristocracy to legitimate its claim to cultural authority. Sixty-two feet above the antique statuary a sunken paneled dome and oculus hung over the sculpture collection, creating an atmosphere which, according to the art historian Peter De Bolla, presented the owner "as a cultured man, infused with civic virtue, good taste." De Bolla goes on to emphasize: "it is important to remember that this taste is an invention, a fantasy, a cultural imaginary that reflects self-image back to this elite class" (2003, 208).

By the turn of the century, the English appropriation of the Roman pantheon had evolved from Hoare's garden feature, via the grandeur of Kedleston Hall, into a fashion within numerous elite and genteel residences, many of which used top lighting to exhibit possessions of cultural capital (Beard 1990, 221). The architects Robert Taylor, Henry Holland, John Nash, Benjamin Dean Wyatt, C. R. Cockerell, and John Soane all favored this mode of interior day lighting within their designs.[1] A particularly strong example of the transformation of pagan worship into the secular practice of aesthetic veneration within a pantheon is seen in the semiprivate art gallery of Henry Blundell's home, Ince Blundell Hall in Lancashire. As an art collector, Blundell commissioned a now unknown architect to construct a pantheon (ca. 1802) (Pollard and Pevsner 2006, 47) which, like Kedleston Hall, was designed specifically for the display of art, in particular Blundell's collection of over 400 pieces of antique statuary (Pearce, Bounia, and Martin 2001, 207). By the turn of the nineteenth century the private taste for neoclassical structures and classical artifacts illuminated by a direct top-lit source of daylight had become the preferred formula through which to lay claim to cultural authority. It is perhaps then no surprise that, with the nineteenth-century transference of private collections into the public domain, patrician top lighting, with its civilizing associations of Enlightenment values, continued to be widely used as a display option.

Patrician top lighting and picture galleries

So far discussion has focused on patrician top lighting in sculpture galleries, but top lighting also came to be a preferred option for illuminating many picture galleries (Compton 1991; Giebelhausen 2006, 229). This section identifies new trends in lighting techniques for viewing paintings by briefly examining the shift from pre-eighteenth-century display arrangements to the rise of the modern picture gallery in the eighteenth and nineteenth centuries. Lighting for four British public institutions – the Coram Foundling Hospital (founded 1739), the Royal Academy of Art (founded 1768), the Dulwich Picture Gallery (opened in 1817), and the National Gallery (1838) – will be considered in turn, accompanied by references to European developments in museum lighting practices.

Prior to the eighteenth century, paintings were rarely displayed in purpose-built galleries. Organized groupings occurred either in the long galleries of stately homes such as the fifteenth-century properties of Knole in Kent and Hardwick Hall in Derbyshire, or in cabinets of curiosity. The long gallery arrangement displayed paintings, primarily portraits, along side-lit walls, but these images were never intended to act as the sole focus because the spaces were also designed for residents to socially mingle and exercise (Coope 1986, 60, 61). Cabinets of curiosity, also known variously as *Kunstkammers* (art rooms) and *Wunderkammers* (wonder rooms), were fashionable across Europe in the sixteenth and seventeenth centuries. These elite, private spaces contained a heterogeneous array of natural, man-made, two- and three-dimensional objects. The appreciation of these items was not limited to purely aesthetic qualities; artifacts were also valued for their unique or intriguing properties, and the extent to which they signaled the owner's power and worldly knowledge. While the origin of major nineteenth-century public collections, such as the British Museum, can be traced back to private cabinets of curiosities, the lighting conditions of these public spaces of exhibition bear very little similarity to their earlier versions. The illumination of artifacts did not play a central role in the design of long galleries or cabinets of curiosity. It was only when a distinctly aesthetic mode of appreciation emerged in the eighteenth century that lighting came to be thought of as a significant issue.

During the eighteenth century increased social mobility meant that a powerful and complex cultural bond emerged between the elite sections of society and the nascent, aspirational middle classes. As with sculpture, commissioning, collecting, and displaying paintings was an effective method of signaling cultural authority because these activities transformed new, commercial wealth into aesthetic taste and a refined moral disposition – sensibilities traditionally associated with inherited aristocratic status. In *The Discovery of Painting: The Growth of Interest in the Arts in England, 1680–1768*, Iain Pears charts the rise of this relationship between taste and morality and explains that the act of "collection was not only a visible symbol of wealth and social hierarchy, it was also one of its justifications, metamorphosing wealth into the discharge of a duty and an altruistic act" (1988, 180).

Performing acts of altruism through making, viewing, and purchasing art was part of the agenda of the innovative Foundling Hospital project. Captain Thomas Coram founded this charitable hospital in London for orphans and abandoned children; from the outset, art and artists were involved. In his capacity as one of the original governors, the artist William Hogarth conceived of a scheme to benefit both the foundlings and professional artists. By 1746 Hogarth had successfully persuaded Sir Joshua Reynolds, Thomas Gainsborough, and Francis Hayman to contribute artworks to the organization. The artists benefited from this arrangement because their work received exposure in the morally respectable environment of the hospital's public rooms. For Thomas Coram the presence of art framed his charitable project with an identity of aesthetic as well as moral worth – a mutually beneficial and socially powerful combination. The art historian David Solkin imagines "the overall effect of the ensemble being not unlike that produced by the saloon of an expensive and fashionable country house" (1992, 162). The elite and private spaces of long galleries and cabinets of curiosity were gradually opening out into the public sphere, yet still no additional measures or adjustments in lighting these works were taken into consideration.

By the middle of the century, new class identities asserted their legitimacy to social power through the public institutionalization and professionalization of cultural taste (Bermingham and Brewer 1997). Culture had become a commodity, marketed and consumed by those who wished to claim a place of authority in civil society. Three examples from the middle decades exemplify this trend: the founding of the Society for the Encouragement of Arts, Manufacturers and Commerce (also known as the Society of Arts) in 1754; the transformation of Sir Hans Sloane's private collection, or cabinet of curiosity, into the world's first publicly accessible collection, the British Museum, which opened in 1759; and the inauguration of the Royal Academy of Art in 1768. These institutions exhibited art and artifacts where quality was assessed, prizes awarded, standards established, and prices set. Solkin describes this period as the "watershed" moment for artistic production and consumption in Britain (1992, 247; see also Pears 1988, 127). It was also a watershed moment for the new alliance between light and the display of art.

Royal Academy

The Royal Academy offers the clearest indication of the increasing importance that light played in the aesthetic experience of viewing art. Initially the Academy was based in Pall Mall (1768), but the conditions were found to be too cramped for exhibitions and arrangements were made for a move to William Chambers's redesign of Somerset House on the Strand in 1780.[2] In this purpose-built setting Chambers paid careful attention to both the metaphorical and practical role of light in the production and consumption of art and, in so doing, signaled the more prominent position light would take in nineteenth-century museums and art galleries. The presence of painted light in the Great Room of the Royal Academy is particularly noteworthy. John Murdoch, former director of the Courtauld Institute Galleries, describes how the building's most significant space was accessed via the main staircase, an impressive spiraling curve, which culminates in a painted "blaze of light at the top, forming an allegory of enlightenment suitable for an educational institution" (2001, 14). Murdoch's reference to the Enlightenment and the institutionalization of education is significant as it emphasizes lighting's role in efforts to systematize viewing practices. He describes how the Great Room was presented as "the very temple of art, the roof of which, as if it were that of the Pantheon in Rome, was fictively open at its centre" (2001, 15).

Where in the original Pantheon light flooded in, here the *trompe l'oeil* oculus, a simulacrum of skylight, demonstrated the artistic talent of the institution's members. Real as opposed to painted daylight was provided by four semicircular thermal windows, which provided "an even wash of light across the walls" (Murdoch 2001, 15). However, this mode of lighting caused certain problems when viewing the paintings. In order to avoid light from the windows causing distracting reflections on the canvases, the paintings were hung with their tops at a slight angle from the wall (17). This adjustment suggests that, while the Great Room was notable for the impressive size and quantity of light, it was, nevertheless, not ideally suited for purposes of viewing. In spite of the necessity to tilt paintings away from the wall of the Great Room, Chambers's roof design still proved to be the "most influential innovation," which had a strong impact on the "future design of picture galleries"

(Murdoch 2001, 15). The institution's architectural self-representation was designed to symbolically embed art practice within the respected field of intellectual endeavor, thereby giving equal weight to artists' mental as well physical skills.

In addition to the public exhibitions of the Royal Academy, owners of private collections were beginning to open up their collections to the public, and here top lighting emerged as the preferred lighting choice (Compton 1991).[3] Nowhere is this more clearly seen than in Dulwich Picture Gallery, which opened to the public in 1817. The collectors Sir Peter Francis Bourgeois and Noel Desenfans bequeathed their seventeenth- and eighteenth-century paintings to the nation in 1811 and commissioned the architect Sir John Soane to design the first purpose-built public gallery. By creating a series of elevated roof lanterns rather than horizontal skylights, Soane developed his own highly influential style of top lighting (Stroud 1971, 162). The technique provided dispersed ambient light for viewing, thereby avoiding the problem of direct light falling on the paintings' surfaces and producing glare and distortion for the viewer. However, while groundbreaking, Soane's design was not universally popular and was criticized by some for being too gloomy. For example, in 1836 the *Penny Cyclopaedia of the Society for the Diffusion of Useful Knowledge* referred to the gallery as "dim" and warned readers that the paintings were therefore not "seen to the best advantage" (Knight 1836, 282).

National Gallery

In the years following the opening of the Dulwich Picture Gallery the appetite for publically accessible art gathered momentum and plans for a National Gallery began to take shape. A provisional gallery space was secured at 100 Pall Mall in 1824 but, according to a complaint from a correspondent to the *Times* in 1826 ("National Gallery, Pall Mall"), this space proved to be inadequate, "one is stewed to death and half suffocated for want of space and fresh air", and in Anthony Trollope's opinion the space was "dingy" and "dull" (1861, 166). Therefore a new location for the nation's art collection was secured, and in 1838 the architect William Wilkins completed his commission in Trafalgar Square to design an improved space more suitable for displaying the nation's art collection in the center of the capital (Martin 1971; Taylor 1999; Conlin 2006).

Gallery lighting was now of such cultural importance that it was discussed, in detail, by the government Select Committee on Arts and Manufacture led by the reformer William Ewart, member of parliament for Liverpool. In 1836 the committee consulted Baron von Klenze, the architect of the Pinakothek in Munich, for his views on principles of correct lighting. Unlike the Royal Academy's practice of tilting pictures away from the wall, Klenze maintained that, with careful management, "the large pictures are in very large rooms lighted from above … the rooms are so arranged that the spectator is not annoyed by reflected light; but wherever he stands he sees the pictures without any reflection" (Klenze, quoted in Taylor

1999, 47). The new keeper, Charles Eastlake (1843–1847), and architect James Pennethorne, a pupil of Nash who was influenced by Soane, followed the German model and recommended that the lighting of galleries

> should be high, that the light should be admitted through very thick glass, free of colour, so as to be as much diffused as possible; that the gallery should be a mass of light, and not lighted by only rays of light. The Pantheon at Rome … lighted only from an aperture in the crown of the dome, I have been told by artists is a most excellent place for exhibiting pictures. (House of Commons 1850, 3)

As a museum professional, Eastlake particularly liked Klenze's nuanced approach to lighting design because it accommodated small paintings, which Klenze believed should be lit from side windows, and large works that were better suited to top lighting. Klenze and Eastlake's belief that only precisely manipulated natural lighting was capable of providing superior viewing conditions remains the dominant principle of museum lighting practice today. Eastlake's vision for an ordered display of art arranged in a "scenario of adequate light and uninterrupted attention from a distance stands at the foundation of modern curatorial practice" (Taylor 1999, 47). The work of the architect Louis Kahn, for example, relies on a highly nuanced sensitivity to the effects of light on perception seen in buildings such as the Yale Center for British Art (1977) in New Haven, and the Kimbell Art Museum (1967–1972) in Fort Worth, Texas.

For the new body of nineteenth-century museum professionals, constructing and implementing ideal viewing conditions for aesthetic consumption belonged to the wider project of social improvement through rational recreations. As the art historian Charlotte Klonk argues, art, architecture, and the right kind of light had the capacity to intellectually and morally nurture the life of the individual, lifting them up above the dangerous anonymity of the crowd and shaping them into a valued citizen (2009, 19–47). The convergence of certain qualities of light, acts of looking, and social behavior in the gallery space was very much part of an increasingly pervasive emphasis on the role of inspection as a means of moving toward increased regulation of both public and private life in the nineteenth-century city. The political historian Chris Otter (2008) talks about this shift in terms of a legislative drive to instate a new kind of urban legibility. He suggests that modern governmental practices of inspection, combined with developments in lighting technologies, produced new perceptual expectations about the degree to which the city could actually be seen in detail. Government inspectors who were responsible for assessing conditions such as cleanliness and sanitation visited houses, factories, workshops, and hospitals. The inspectors observed, measured, and recorded conditions of what they saw and in so doing effected a new, politically informed, visual knowledge of the city and its citizens. Otter argues that the principle of authorized inspection produced a form of subjectivity characterized by autonomous and internalized self-inspection (2008, 99–134). Although he does not discuss them, art galleries, and in particular the National Gallery, are striking examples of spaces where this is put to work. Here the task of observation is of the utmost importance, but crucially it is transformed into a pleasurable pastime rather than an administrative procedure. Looking outward to the carefully curated displays and inward to their own responses, gallery visitors passed aesthetic judgment on both the collection and themselves.

Artificial light: Education in museums and galleries

By the middle decades of the nineteenth century the new technology of gas lighting was increasingly being used in public and private buildings (O'Dea 1958; Schivelbusch 1995; Otter 2008). Museum professionals and commercial exhibition managers recognized gas lighting's potential to increase visitor numbers by extending opening hours into the evening – the main period of free time for the working classes. But the possibility of extending opening hours to sections of the population who had not previously been recognized as legitimate consumers of art collections carried with it a range of conflicting agendas. On the one hand, many social reformers, such as the journalist and publisher George Godwin and the MP Thomas Wyse, believed that art education would have an improving effect on the masses (Trodd 1994, 39). This belief in the civilizing benefits of culture was to have its most articulate advocate in the figure of Matthew Arnold, poet, cultural critic, and, it is interesting to note, school inspector. Arnold's essay "Culture and Anarchy" (1869) persuasively lobbied for the moral worth and civilizing influence of culture, and in particular its capacity to produce social cohesion. Yet, on the other hand, the prospect of practicing widening public access to priceless art collections was for some arbiters of taste a dangerous notion. With the rise of industrialized technologies, population growth, and social mobility came attendant anxieties about urbanization, class distinctions, and political unrest.

Many of these anxieties were articulated through debates surrounding the governance of the National Gallery due its high-profile public status. Thomas Uwins, the keeper of the gallery between 1847 and 1855, regularly witnessed visitor behavior that he felt to be improper and took offense at working-class groups who were eating, drinking, and socializing in the gallery rather than quietly and reverently contemplating the displays (Whitehead 2005, 59–68). For Uwins, opening up the gallery space to crowds of working-class spectators jeopardized the fragile moment of encounter between art and the individual. He believed that part of the aesthetic experience was corrupted because the collection was detrimentally affected by dust and dirt brought into the gallery by lower-class multitudes (House of Commons 1850, 18). Uwins was not alone in his reluctance to open the building to a socially diverse audience. In 1853 the art historian G. F. Waagen, an influential voice in the capital's art scene, expressed revulsion toward certain National Gallery visitors "whose filthy dress tainted the atmosphere with a most disagreeable smell" (quoted in Whitehead 2005, 61). In his capacity as director of the National Gallery (1855–1865), Charles Eastlake was sympathetic to such sentiments and therefore maintained that opening the gallery up at night by installing gas lighting would only exacerbate this problem. He was not prepared to risk exposing the collection to what he perceived to be the dangerous combination of gas lighting and the masses (Swinney 1999; 2003).

However, other museum directors embraced the new technology and the new audience. Such a division emphasizes how light was co-opted to either promote or exclude the acquisition of cultural knowledge. Perhaps, as mentioned earlier, the strongest advocate for artificial lighting was Henry Cole, a commissioner for the Great Exhibition and the first director of the South Kensington Museum. George Swinney, a curator and historian of museum lighting, draws attention to the sociopolitical agenda at stake here when he says that "in fostering and promoting the concept of self-improvement through education Cole was in tune with a general movement to make collections more accessible to the public" (Swinney 1999, 118). This desire for accessibility is evident in the collection of British paintings displayed in the Sheepshanks Gallery designed by Francis Fowke and opened in 1857 at the South Kensington Museum. Fowke made use of the by now standard top lighting techniques and, in addition, installed gas lighting: Swinney identifies this as the first instance of gas lighting in a public gallery (1999, 118). The precedent was partially successful for, while the National Gallery resisted gas lighting, other public museums such as the Oxford University Museum and the Walker Art Gallery in Liverpool followed Cole's example in 1860 and 1877 respectively. In these spaces lighting practices framed art as an improving agent for the nation en masse while daylight remained the preserve of a more elite form of individual art appreciation.

Artificial light in commercial exhibition spaces

Alongside the rise of the public art gallery and museum, with their agendas of individual and collective social improvement, the nineteenth century also witnessed a new form of cultural consumption in which exhibitions were commercially motivated and staged as forms of entertainment. The eidophusikon (Baugh 1987), phantasmagoria (Mannoni [1994] 2000; Heard 2006), panorama, and diorama (Altick 1978; Hyde 1988; Plunkett, Sullivan, and Kember 2012) are well-known examples of a Europe-wide fashion for painted displays of high visual drama. The manipulation of artificial light played a central role in the sensory appeal of these spectacles and belonged to a distinctly modern way of perceptually understanding the world and one's place in it through practices of illumination.

A less well-known, but for our purposes more significant, example of the distinction between commercial and noncommercial lighting techniques in public exhibition spaces is the Glyptotheca, or Museum of Sculpture, in the Regent's Park

Colosseum, London. Visitors to the Colosseum, which was in many ways akin to a pleasure garden such as Vauxhall, paid an entrance fee, starting at a shilling, to engage in sociable activities of eating, drinking, and conversing in a fashionable setting that offered various forms of entertainment. The Colosseum was unusual for the range and scale of spectacles on offer. The most well known of these was Thomas Horner's impressive "Panoramic View of London" (1827) (Hyde 1988); other attractions included a Swiss Cottage, a gothic aviary, fountains, tearooms, and the aforementioned Glyptotheca, which opened in 1845. This gallery was located in a rotunda underneath the main attraction of the panorama and was illuminated by an internal domed "ribbed roof being filled with embossed glass" (Timbs 1855, 223). The sparkling effect was enhanced further by artificial light, cut glass chandeliers, candelabras, mirrors, and gilt frames. A selection of over 100 sculptures, including plaster casts of the Elgin Marbles, were placed in recesses around the room and frescos decorated portions of the wall (Saunders 1847, 335). Velvet drapes and upholstery completed the rich effect.

The quantity and diversity of decorative, reflective, and transparent materials, combined with artificial lighting, produced a viewing experience far removed from that seen in the nation's public museums and galleries. The cause of this strikingly different *mise-en-scène* was due to the Regent's Park rotunda being designed not by an architect or museum professional, but by William Bradwell, a former "chief machinist of Covent Garden Theatre" (Timbs 1855, 224). The aristocratic heritage of patrician lighting had been supplemented with a display style that resembled a theatrical set. The Glyptotheca was innovative in its exploitation of popular and elite cultural registers that produced hybrid lighting effects for viewing works of art. In this atmosphere of pleasurable entertainment the relationship between spectator and artwork was radically altered. The purpose of, for example, exhibiting the cast of the Elgin Marbles was not to form morally and aesthetically knowledgeable citizens through the act of quiet contemplation, or to culturally educate the masses. Instead the ambience of display was transformed by the twin imperatives of financial profit and sensory pleasure. Yet, for all its efforts to attract and please, this hybrid attraction was not long-lived and closed in 1874 while publically funded institutions such as the National Gallery endured.

Artificial illumination in private collections

Commercial spaces of exhibition were not the only venues to display works of art in ways that diverged from the increasingly standardized practice of patrician top lighting. In the early years of the nineteenth century a number of significant private collections displayed works of art quite differently to public institutions such as the Royal Academy and the National Gallery. Three noteworthy examples are the collections belonging to Thomas Hope, Sir John Soane, and Sir John Fleming Leicester. These private art collectors favored artificial lighting techniques coupled with the use of mirrors, drapes, and colored glass to create an entirely different viewing experience.

Thomas Hope

Thomas Hope was a neoclassical designer, novelist, and art collector. His groundbreaking text *Household Furniture and Interior Decorations* (1807) gave rise to the discipline of interior design, for it was the first time that the practice of interior design appeared as a fully articulated mode of aesthetic expression. In his house at Duchess Street, London, Hope brought fabrics, furniture, fixtures and fittings, lighting, wall colors, artworks, and room layouts together in a vision of coherent and continuous design, transforming his residence into a semipublic museum for his collections. The architectural historian David Watkin explains that "the house was conceived almost like a theatre in which every room evoked different and appropriate sensations, with light and illusion used to create mood" (2008, xiii).

One particularly striking curatorial arrangement was the display surrounding John Flaxman's sculpture *Aurora Abducting Cephalus* in the Aurora Room. An abundant quantity of black, orange, blue, and purple colored velvet and satin drapes framed this and other smaller sculptures in the room. When drawn back the drapes revealed not windows, but mirrors along the walls. The combination of sparkling mirrors, light-absorbent velvet, gleaming satin, and stark white marble would have produced a viewing atmosphere inflected with a complex and dynamic interplay of ambient lighting effects. Effects such as these were strikingly different from the simple decoration and lighting seen in eighteenth-century sculpture galleries. However, in Hope's house dramatic reflections and shadows would have been registered on and by the sculpture and the viewer's own body. In fact the foregrounding of the viewer's presence through light effects would complete or at least significantly contribute to the overall artistry of the scene. Watkin's reference to the theatricality of Hope's vision hints at the way light was being used to create an alternative to the standard configuration of viewing subject and art object. Hope's curatorial style positioned art as event, where aesthetic experience was understood as a more embodied and somewhat unpredictable process, so that, rather than passively observing from a distance a neutrally lit and therefore seemingly unchanging object, the viewer was, through the drama of illumination, active and implicated in the encounter.

Illumination, for Hope, was never merely a neutral prop. He used it to manipulate the viewer's experience of his collection by ensuring that lighting effects directly corresponded to the arrangement of objects and modes of aesthetic appreciation that varied throughout the rooms. When Hope added a picture gallery to his London house to accommodate his newly acquired collection of Flemish art in 1819 he employed quite different lighting techniques to those seen in the Aurora Room. The nineteenth-century journalist Charles M. Westmacott describes the top-lit room:

> The centre of the ceiling which is divided into sunk pannels [*sic*] with gold pateras in the centre, rises from a gallery of circular headed lights, which are continued on the four sides of a quadrangle, with very slight divisions ... [O]n each side of the screen, ten of the choicest paintings are arranged, and hung on centres, *so that the connoisseur may turn them to obtain a suitable light*. (Westmacott 1824, 230; emphasis added)

Two things are particularly interesting here – the style of top lighting, and the innovative method of hanging pictures. The ceiling was designed in such a way that, as daylight fell through the skylights, the light was animated by the surface design of shallow saucer-like indentations covered in gold which produced an unusual punctuated rhythm of golden decorative reflection. The second portion of the quotation describes how viewers were able to closely appreciate the formal qualities of paint on canvas by turning hinged pictures into or away from the room's available lighting. Viewers were called on to approach, touch, and move both their bodies and the picture frame to secure the optimum viewing position. Again Hope understood aesthetic contemplation to be an active and physically involved process. By adjusting vision according to the vagaries of weather conditions and times of day that affected the quality of daylight, he displayed a highly nuanced sensitivity to the importance of lighting in the aesthetic act of connoisseurship. Many of these features anticipate Soane's own house and museum and the Gainsborough tent room in Leicester's gallery.

Sir John Soane

Soane's exploration of light's aesthetic qualities was both professional and personal; it extended beyond commissions such as the Dulwich Picture Gallery and reached into the more intimate environment of his own home. It is here, at 12–14 Lincoln's Inn Field, London, that Soane expressed most fully his creative vision in which architecture, sculpture, and painting were united through the medium of light.[4] In 1792 Soane purchased number 12 and over the next three decades he acquired numbers 13 and 14, which allowed him to merge and radically alter the internal structure of the three buildings. During Soane's lifetime the building functioned as his domestic house and his office, and as an educational resource for his students; on his death in 1837 he bequeathed the building and its collection to the nation. Perhaps the most suitable way of understanding the structure, which was neither an entirely public nor a private building, is as the embodiment of Soane's idealized public persona and bid for immortality. His collection of artifacts ranged from classical architectural fragments and medieval stained glass to eighteenth-century paintings, and occupied considerable wall, floor, and ceiling space throughout the house. The most explicit and experimental display of manipulated space and light began in 1809 when Soane built a tribuna, a centrally placed, top-lit circular display space. Like many artists and aristocrats, Soane had made his own Grand Tour in 1777 and it is in the structure and decoration of the tribuna that he asserted his cultured status through the exhibition of original and reproduced antique sculptures and architectural fragments. This space is Soane's attempt to unite two languages of light: the patrician light of rationality and reason, and a light which evoked the creative romantic imagination.[5]

At the base of the tribuna Soane positioned the prize of his collection, the Belzoni sarcophagus of Seti I, so called because the archaeologist and entrepreneur Giovanni Battista Belzoni discovered it in Egypt in 1817 (Soane and Hofland 1835, xvii). Soane purchased the alabaster sarcophagus of Seti I from Belzoni in 1824, and in March of the following year invited paying guests to a carefully choreographed event to admire his new and expensive acquisition. He chose to exhibit the stone coffin at night surrounded by strategically placed candelabras, lamps, and mirrors (Dorey 1991). Sensitive to the translucent qualities of the stone, he also placed a light source inside the sarcophagus, which must have produced an uncanny effect of lifelike animation in the otherwise deathly object. This spectacle of light was a performance of the romantic sensibilities expressed in sources such as Gottfried Herder's treatise on sculpture ([1778] 2002) and Goethe's *Roman Elegies* ([1795] 1999). Soane's stylized use of lighting enacted Goethe's aesthetic encounter with sculpture in which "Marble comes doubly alive for me then, as I ponder, comparing / Seeing with vision that feels, feeling with fingers that see" (Goethe [1795] 1999, 15). Yet the event also indicates that Soane's inspiration was not limited to elite spheres of reference but also called on the exhibitionary techniques of artificial lighting used in London's popular illuminated entertainments mentioned in the section on commercial exhibition spaces (see earlier).

In addition to the top-lit tribuna, Soane deployed variously sized and strategically located convex and flat mirrors along the surfaces of walls and ceilings, augmenting and directing the daylight, which penetrated the spaces through a range of apertures, vertical windows, skylights, and lanterns. He further finessed the appearance of light through the interjection of numerous stained glass panels (Coley 2003, 10). The unique styling of light and artifacts in the building caught the eye of a writer for the *Penny Magazine* who, in 1836, reported that "the beams of sun … playing through the coloured glass light up every object with gorgeous hues" (Knight 1836, 458). Soane's familiarity with Hope's exhibitionary experiments is evident throughout all of these spaces and includes the picture gallery where his collection of Hogarth paintings are, like Hope's pictures, displayed on hinged wall brackets.

However, for some critics the merging of patrician and poetic lighting pushed affect and effect too far, threatening standards of taste. An article in the *Civil Engineer and Architect's Journal* of 1837 was of the opinion that at Lincoln's Inn "not a few effects partake of far too much of the petty and the peep-show" (quoted in Watkin 1996, 57). Perhaps the writer had good grounds for this anxiety given that two years prior to this article, the *Satirist, and the Censor of the Time* had referred to the same building as "the gingerbread mansion" with its collections reduced to "absurdities" followed by accusations of the architect's vanity (*Satirist, and the*

Censor of the Time 1835). Fairy stories, confectionary, irrationality, and narcissism were hardly the types of associations an architect of public institutions such as the Bank of England and the Dulwich Picture Gallery would have sought to attract.

Sir John Fleming Leicester's gallery and Thomas Gainsborough's *Cottage Door*

The final example of elite alternatives to the lighting strategies used in public collections is found in the gallery of Sir John Fleming Leicester (1762–1827), an influential patron and collector of British art. Leicester expressed his commitment to artists such as J. M. W. Turner by transforming his private collection into a public resource and securing, in the art historian's Dongho Chun's phrase, "private glory" (2001, 175). Leicester acquired a house at 24 Hill Street, Berkeley Square, London, in 1805 and converted the top-floor library, probably designed by Thomas Cundy senior, into a picture gallery (1818). While the principal gallery was top-lit "through a shallow dome on the roof" (Chun 2001, 177) the area that is of particular interest to us is the space created specifically for the display of Thomas Gainsborough's *Cottage Door* (1780). The room was darkened by sealing off the penetration of external daylight with a comprehensive fabric canopy which hung from the ceiling and produced the effect of a "tent room," a style which both Chun and Ann Bermingham identify as French in influence (Chun 2001, 180; Bermingham 2005, 145). Artificial light was favored over daylight, and lamps and mirrors were introduced into the space so that, as Bermingham notes, any available light was dispersed and multiple views of the painting could be enjoyed. An account from the *Parthenon* in 1825 reported that a visit to the gallery was

> heightened by the judicious arrangement of the light and surrounding accompaniments, the "Cottage Door" of Gainsborough possesses a perfectly magical effect. Glowing with the richest and most voluptuous, yet subdued and mellow tones, it meets the eye with that peculiar charm which is yielded by the mild splendour of the evening sun, tinging the harmonious surface of the autumnal landscape with a still more luxuriant hue. (*Parthenon* 1825, 231)

The "magical effect" implied a type of theatrical staging similar to the work of William Bradwell at the Colosseum's Glypotheca or the more sensational dark shows of the phantasmagoria. However, the review also signals the appreciation of a different aesthetic register that evoked a poetic and romantic set of perceptual values that drew on the tradition of Richard Payne Knight's treatise of the picturesque (1805), Philippe De Loutherbourg's eidophusikon, and Gainsborough's own experiments with transparent painting (Mayne 1965). Sir Leicester's gallery augmented these effects by incorporating them into the exhibition space. The immersive act of viewing produced an embodied and romanticized experience of art consumption that, as Bermingham (2005) points out, was a late articulation of the aristocratic cult of sensibility. This combination of Gainsborough's rural idyll and the carefully lit atmosphere produced an elite and fashionable form of escapism or refuge from experiences of urban modernity (Brewer 2007, 248). By excluding the reality of daylight, a more intense and intimate dynamic was created between viewer and artwork in order to stimulate and refine a viewer's capacity for emotional, physiological, and intellectual responses to art inherent in the discourse of sensibility. An experience such as this was a distinctly elite pastime and was not available in the nation's large public collections.

Artists' studios and galleries

It is no coincidence that the heightened attention to lighting in Sir Leicester's gallery was directly connected to the display of Gainsborough's work, for Gainsborough was intensely attentive to the agency of light in the aesthetic act. He believed the issue of light's suitability for both painting and viewing was of such importance that it caused strained negotiations with the committee of the Royal Academy and resulted in the artist terminating his relationship with the Academy in 1784. The incident centered on a difference of opinion about how his work should be positioned within the space of the Great Room:

> To the Gentlemen of the Hanging Committee of the Royal Academy.
>
> Mr Gainsborough's Compls to the Gentlemen of the Committee, and begs pardon for giving them so much trouble; but as he painted the Picture of the Princess, in so tender a light, that notwithstanding he approves very much of the established line for strong Effects, he cannot possibly consent to have it placed higher that five feet & a half, because, the likeness & Work of the Picture will not be seen any higher; therefore at a word, he will not trouble the Gentleman against their Inclination, but will beg the rest of his Pictures back again. (Gainsborough, quoted in Hutchison 1986, 50)

Gainsborough's concern about precise lighting conditions indicates his perceptual sensitivity about the extent to which context could affect the quality of a viewer's aesthetic experience. From this point on he exhibited his work in a purpose-built studio space in his garden at Schomberg House, Pall Mall, London. Gainsborough was not alone in his preference for specifically designed studio lighting: J. M. W. Turner and Benjamin West also made their own personalized arrangements.

West's gallery at 14 Newman Street, London, which he occupied from the 1780s until his death in 1820, used a combination of light, architecture, and interior design to produce very specific perceptual conditions in which to experience his work. A first-hand account describes the gallery:

> A canopy resting on slender pillars stood in the middle of the room, its opaque roof concealing the skylight from the spectator, who stood thus in a sort of half-obscure

dimness, while both pictures received the full flood of light. The effect was very fine and at that time novel. (Anon., quoted in Waterfield 1992, 78)

A piece from 1822 in the *Examiner* provides a fuller sense of the space and effects of lighting:

The New Gallery is a noble, lofty, and spacious room, or rather a double apartment, connected by a grand arch with a narrow gallery of approach. The two rooms measure nearly 100 feet in length, by 40 in breadth, and 26 in height: the roof is supported by eight lofty columns: the spaces between the columns and the walls is filled with glass, which is sloped in an angle of about 45 degrees; thus a broad and uninterrupted volume of light is shed directly on the Pictures, which displays them to the greatest advantage. The rooms were erected under the direction of Mr Nash, who has constructed a building which far surpasses we believe any other Picture Gallery in England. (*Examiner* 1822, n.p.)

In a painting of West's gallery by J. Pasmore the Younger the dominant visual action takes place above the spectators, even above the paintings. The dynamic thrust of the dark swagged central area of the ceiling is offset by a strip of skylights that run along the edge, creating a pronounced depth of field which provides a large, relatively blank surface against which everything else is defined. Flat, hard surfaces of the structure are disrupted through the repeated use of vertical and horizontal fabrics, which then complicate the behavior of light within the space. Diffusing filters of fabric, nets, and tissue paper were also used by Turner who opened his centrally skylit studio gallery in 1804 at 64 Harley Street.

Unlike the functional and educational gas lighting in the South Kensington Museum or the National Gallery's aesthetic privileging of top lighting, these alternative lighting treatments defy a neat categorization of stylistic principles precisely because they were not attempting to systematically establish a collective consensus. The theatricality and heightened sensory experience of illuminated environments such as Bradwell's sculpture hall in the Colosseum, Fleming's Gainsborough tent room, and Soane's evening exhibition of Belzoni's sarcophagus indicate that, in the opening decades of the nineteenth century, encountering art was a varied and dynamic experience.

The diverse approaches to lighting in this period suggest a different interpretation of museum and art gallery spaces from the museum studies notion of them as hegemonic disciplinary structures designed to deliver a top-down relationship to cultural and/or aesthetic consumption (see, for example, Hooper-Greenhill 1992; Bennett 1995). As Colin Trodd has argued, efforts to control the popular audience and frame cultural knowledge were far from successful. The gallery authorities' reported anxieties about the behavior of working-class visitors exemplify this. Trodd describes the gallery's "endlessly aberrant nature as a social space locked into the perpetual, yet unresolved, mingling of pleasure, hygiene, history, taste, miasma, leisure, work, display, learning, instruction, culture and pollution" (2003, 28).

I would argue that Trodd's case for multiple and seemingly contradictory agendas and viewing experiences at institutions such as the National Gallery was a considerably wider phenomenon, in which boundaries between popular and elite sites of display were blurred across the urban environment in the first half of the nineteenth century, and that this blurring was often articulated through lighting practices. We have seen how drapes, mirrors, and artificial lighting were used at both the popular venue of the Colosseum and at Hope's private house. We have also seen how the aesthetic potential of darkness exploited by the entertainment format of the phantasmagoria was appropriated and repurposed in Sir Fleming Leicester's tent room and Sir John Soane's evening spectacle of the sarcophagus. In these examples light created a form of perceptual dialogue between artwork, viewer, and viewing environment. In effect, the manipulation of light enlarged the aesthetic encounter, filling the space beyond the picture frame, enveloping the viewer in an atmosphere mediated by heightened contrasts, textures, and surfaces that appealed to a more than purely visual experience. In contrast, when art was institutionalized in, for example, the Royal Academy and National Gallery, lighting strategies defined aesthetic experience as a more cerebral activity, in line with gallery administrators' resistance to the embodied reality of lower-class visitors. If these visitors were to attend, and many social reformers believed they should, it needed to be with the aim of enlightenment rather than enjoyment. In this context light was diffuse, shadows were absent and the space between subject and object was rendered immaterial. In these ways the diverse lighting practices invented during this period helped to define the extent to which art was experienced as a sensory pleasure or a cerebral exercise in social reform.

Notes

1   Other examples of elite spaces of private top lighting can be found in a wide number of locations: at Sharpham House, Devon, the architect Robert Taylor designed a top-lit dome ca. 1770; at Newby Hall, Yorkshire, Robert Adam designed the top-lit rotunda for the sculpture gallery between 1767 and 1772; at Carlton House, London, Henry Holland's top-lit room dates from 1781; Attingham Park in Shropshire boasts oval cast iron monitor lights by John Nash from ca. 1807; Willey Hall, Shropshire, has a clerestory lantern by architect Lewis from 1812; Oakley Park, also in Shropshire, acquired a glazed dome in 1819 by C. R. Cockerell; for Waterloo Palace in Hampshire, between 1814 and 1818 Benjamin Dean Wyatt designed, but never built, a top-lit windowless pantheon, for the Duke of Wellington.

2   The Royal Academy remained at Somerset House until it moved to temporary accommodation at the National Gallery in 1837. The Royal Academy then moved to Burlington House, Piccadilly, in 1868.

3   In 1806 George Leveson-Gower, the second marquess of Stafford opened his collection to the public at Cleveland House, London. Stafford had commissioned C. H. Tatham to design a new gallery for the purpose. The curator and historian of museums Giles

Waterfield points out that, "Architecturally, a distinction was made between Tatham's new galleries, dedicated to pictures and top-lit in the style increasingly regarded as obligatory, and the other rooms," which were used for domestic purposes and lit from side windows (1995, 58).

4   In *The Union of Architecture, Sculpture and Painting* (1827) John Britton, Soane's contemporary and eulogist, foregrounded the architect's desire to promote the sensory as well as the intellectual life of the aesthetic imagination.

5   The desire to unite the intellect and the imagination is emphatically articulated in Soane's VIII Royal Academy lecture (Watkin 1996).

References

Altick, Richard. 1978. *The Shows of London*. Cambridge, MA: Harvard University Press.

Arnold, Dana, ed. 1998. *The Georgian Country House: Architecture, Landscape and Society*. Stroud, UK: Sutton.

Baugh, Christopher. 1987. "Loutherbourg and the Early Pictorial Theatre." In *The Theatrical Space*, edited by James Redmond, 99–128. Cambridge: Cambridge University Press.

Beard, Geoffrey. 1990. *The National Trust Book of the English House Interior*. London: Viking.

Bennett, Tony. 1995. *The Birth of the Museum: History, Theory, Politics*. Abingdon, UK: Routledge.

Bermingham, Ann, ed. 2005. *Sensation and Sensibility: Viewing Gainsborough's Cottage Door*. New Haven: Yale University Press.

Bermingham, Ann, and John Brewer, eds. 1997. *The Consumption of Culture, 1600–1800: Image, Object, Text*. Abingdon, UK: Routledge.

Brewer, John. 2007. "Sensibility and the Urban Panorama." *Huntingdon Library Quarterly* 70(2): 229–249.

Britton, John. 1827. *The Union of Architecture, Sculpture and Painting*. London: Longman.

Chun, Dongho. 2001. "Public Display, Private Glory: Sir John Fleming Leicester's Gallery of British Art in Early Nineteenth-Century England." *Journal of Historical Collections* 13(2): 175–189.

Coley, Sandra, ed. 2003. "The Stained Glass Collection of Sir John Soane's Museum." Special issue, *Journal of Stained Glass* 27.

Compton, M. 1991. "The Architecture of Daylight." In *Palaces of Art: Art Galleries in Britain, 1790–1990*, edited by Giles Waterfield, 37–47. London: Dulwich Picture Gallery.

Conlin, Jonathan. 2006. *The Nation's Mantelpiece: A History of the National Gallery*. London: Pallas Athene Arts.

Coope, Rosalys. 1986. "The 'Long Gallery': Its Origins, Development, Use and Decoration." *Architectural History* 29, 43–84.

Craske, Matthew, and Richard Wrigley, eds. 2004. *Pantheons: Transformations of a Monumental Idea*. Farnham, UK: Ashgate.

De Bolla, Peter. 2003. *The Education of the Eye: Painting and Architecture in Eighteenth-Century Britain*. Stanford: Stanford University Press.

Dixon, Susan M. 2004. "Piranesi's Pantheon." In *Architecture as Experience: Radical Change in Spatial Practice*, edited by Dana Arnold and Andrew Ballantyne, 57–108. Abingdon, UK: Routledge.

Dorey, Helen. 1991. "Sir John Soane's Acquisition of the Sarcophagus of the Seti I." *Georgian Group Journal* 1: 26–35.

Examiner. 1822. "West's Gallery." September 1.

Giebelhausen, Michaela. 2006. "Museum Architecture: A Brief History." In *A Companion to Museum Studies*, edited by Sharon Macdonald, 223–244. Oxford: Wiley-Blackwell.

Goethe, Johann Wolfgang von. (1795) 1999. "Roman Elegies VII." In *Erotic Poems*, translated by David Luke; introduction by Hans Rudolf Vaget. Oxford: Oxford University Press.

Heard, Mervyn. 2006. *Phantasmagoria: The Secret Life of the Magic Lantern*. Hastings, UK: Projection Box.

Herder, Gottfried. (1778) 2002. *Sculpture: Some Observations on Shape and Form from Pygmalion's Creative Dream*, edited by Jason Gaiger. Chicago: University of Chicago Press.

Hooper-Greenhill, Eilean. 1992. *Museums and the Shaping of Knowledge*. Abingdon, UK: Routledge.

Hope, Thomas. 1807. *Household Furniture and Interior Decorations*. London.

House of Commons. 1850. *Report from the Select Committee on the National Gallery; Together with the Minutes of Evidence, Appendix and Index*. July 25. House of Commons Parliamentary Papers XV.1, no. 612.

Hutchison, Sidney C. 1986. *The History of the Royal Academy, 1768–1986*. London: Robert Royce.

Hyde, R. 1988. *Panoramania! The Art and Entertainment of the "All-Embracing" View*. London: Trefoil, with Barbican Art Gallery.

Jones. 1829. *Jones' Views of the Seats, Mansions, Castles, Etc. Of Noblemen & Gentlemen in England, Wales, Scotland & Ireland: And Other Picturesque Scenery Accompanied with Historical Descriptions of the Mansions, Lists of Pictures, Statues, &C. And Genealogical Sketches of the Families and Their Possessors*, vol. 2. London.

Klonk, Charlotte. 2009. *Spaces of Experience: Art Gallery Interiors from 1800 to 2000*. New Haven: Yale University Press.

Knight, C. 1836. *Penny Cyclopaedia of the Society for the Diffusion of Useful Knowledge*, vol. 5. London.

Knight, Richard Payne. 1805. *An Analytical Inquiry into the Principles of Taste*. London.

Mannoni, Laurent. (1994) 2000. *The Great Art of Light and Shadow: Archaeology of the Cinema*, 2nd ed. Exeter: University of Exeter Press.

Martin, Gregory. 1971. "Wilkins and the National Gallery." *Burlington Magazine* 113(819): 318–329.

Mayne, Jonathan. 1965. "Thomas Gainsborough's Exhibition Box." *Victoria & Albert Museum Bulletin* 1: 17–24.

Murdoch, John. 2001. "Architecture and Experience: The Visitor and the Spaces of Somerset House, 1780–1796." In *Art on the Line: The Royal Academy Exhibtions at Somerset House 1780–1836*, edited by David Solkin, 9–22. New Haven: Yale University Press.

O'Dea, William T. 1958. *The Social History of Lighting*. Abingdon, UK: Routledge.

Otter, Chris. 2008. *The Victorian Eye: A Political History of Light and Vision in Britain, 1800–1910*. Chicago: University of Chicago Press.

Parthenon. 1825. "Sir John Leicester's Gallery." 13: 230–231.

Pearce, Susan M., Alexandra Bounia, and Paul Martin. 2001. *The Collector's Voice: Critical Readings in the Practice of Collecting*. Farnham, UK: Ashgate.

Pears, Iain. 1988. *The Discovery of Painting: The Growth of Interest in the Arts in England, 1680–1768*. New Haven: Yale University Press.

Plunkett, John, Jill Sullivan, and Joe Kember, eds. 2012. *Popular Exhibitions, Science and Showmanship, 1840–1910*. London: Pickering & Chatto.

Pollard, Richard, and Nikolaus Pevsner. 2006. *Lancashire: Liverpool and the Southwest*. *Buildings of England*, rev. ed. New Haven: Yale University Press.

Satirist, and the Censor of the Time. 1835. "Soane's National Museum." March 29, 99.

Saunders, John. 1847. "The Coliseum." *People's & Howitt's Journal: Of Literature, Art, and Popular Progress* 2: 333–336.

Schivelbusch, Wolfgang. 1995. *Disenchanted Night: The Industrialization of Light in the Nineteenth Century*. Berkeley: University of California Press.

Soane, Sir John, and Barbara Hofland. 1835. *Description of House and Museum of Sir John Soane, Architect*. London.

Solkin, David. 1992. *Painting for Money: The Visual Arts and the Public Sphere in Eighteenth Century England*. New Haven: Yale University Press.

Stroud, D. 1971. *George Dance, Architect, 1741–1825*. London: Faber.

Swinney, G. N. 1999. "Gas Lighting in British Museums and Galleries." *Museum Management and Curatorship* 18(2): 113–143.

Swinney, G. N. 2003. "'The Evil of Vitiating and Heating the Air': Artificial Lighting and Public Access to the National Gallery, London." *Journal of the History of Collections* 15(1): 83–112.

Taylor, Brandon. 1999. *Art for the Nation: Exhibitions and the London Public 1747–2001*. Manchester: Manchester University Press.

Thompson, E. P. 1974. "Patrician Society, Plebeian Culture." *Journal of Social History* 7(4): 382–405.

Timbs, J. 1855. *Curiosities of London: Exhibiting the Most Rare and Remarkable Objects of Interest in the Metropolis*. London.

Trodd, Colin. 1994. "Culture, Class, City: The National Gallery and the Spaces of Education, 1822–1857." In *Art Apart*, edited by M. Pointon, 33–49. Manchester: Manchester University Press.

Trodd, Colin. 2003. "The Discipline of Pleasure; or, How Art History Looks at the Art Museum." *Museums and Society* 1(1): 22–40.

Trollope, Anthony. 1861. "The National Gallery." *St James's Magazine* 2: 163–176.

Waterfield, Giles. 1992. *Palaces of Art: New Galleries in Britain 1790–1990*. London: Dulwich Picture Gallery.

Waterfield, Giles. 1995. "The Town House as Gallery of Art." *London Journal* 20(1): 47–66.

Watkin, David. 1996. *Sir John Soane: Enlightenment Thought and the Royal Academy Lectures*. Cambridge: Cambridge University Press.

Watkin, David, ed. 2008. *Thomas Hope Regency Designer*. New Haven: Yale University Press.

Westmacott, Charles M. 1824. *British Galleries of Painting and Sculpture, Comprising a General Historical and Critical Catalogue*. London.

Whitehead, Christopher. 2005. *The Public Art Museum in Nineteenth Century Britain: The Development of the National Gallery*. Aldershot, UK: Ashgate.

Further Reading

Barnaby, Alice. Forthcoming. *Light Touches: Cultural Practices of Illumination, London 1800–1900*. London: Routledge.

Matheson, C. S. 2001. "'A Shilling Well Laid Out': The Royal Academy's Early Public." In *Art on the Line: The Royal Academy Exhibitions at Somerset House 1780–1836*, edited by David Solkin, 39–53. New Haven: Yale University Press.

Neale, John Preston. 1822. *The English Vision: The Picturesque in Architecture, Landscape and Garden Design*, vol. 5. London: Sherwood, Neely & Jones.

Teyssot, Georges. 1990. "'The Simple Day and the Light of the Sun': Lights and Shadows in the Museum." *Assemblage* 12: 58–83.

Tyack, Geoffrey. 1990. "'A Gallery Worthy of the British People': James Pennethorne's Designs for the National Gallery, 1845–1867." *Architectural History* 33: 120–134.

Alice Barnaby is a lecturer in English literature at the University of Bedfordshire, UK. Her publications include *Light Touches: Cultural Practices of Illumination, 1800–1900* (Routledge, forthcoming); "Surface Recognition: Light and Surface in Drawing Rooms, 1800–1850," in *Surface Tensions: Surface, Finish and the Meanings of Objects* (Manchester University Press, 2013); and "Dresses and Drapery: Female Self-Fashioning in Muslin, 1800–50," in *Crafting the Woman Professional in the Long Nineteenth Century* (Ashgate, 2013).

10 THERE'S SOMETHING IN THE AIR
Sound in the Museum

Rupert Cox

We know of the great museums of the world by the sights they offer us but what are their sounds? This is a question the artist Jake Tilson posed by making sound recordings in the spaces of museums with iconic collections – London's British Museum and Tate (Britain) galleries, New York's Metropolitan Museum of Art, and the Musée du Louvre in Paris. The recordings were part of a project titled *City Picture Fiction* (1991–1999) made up of one-take continuous recordings of background sounds of the chatter and movements of visitors in particular galleries such as the Metropolitan's Great Hall. What we hear in these recordings are the resonant qualities of the museum space as it has been designed for viewers and come to be used by them so as to interact with the exhibits. These are sounds such as footsteps reverberating, voices whispering, muttering, and murmuring, and bodies rustling around the space of the museum.

In these sounds we may hear the form of a relationship between the observer and the object that is usually conceived in terms of vision and visuality. This conception derives from the idea of the museum as a viewing mechanism and of the primacy of vision in its institutional rationale and aesthetic value system. The visual imperative in museum spaces is part of a "master narrative" (Sherman and Rogoff 1994, x) and becomes a means of applying power, described by Carol Duncan in formal terms as "civilizing rituals" (1995) and by Eilean Hooper-Greenhill in *Museums and the Shaping of Knowledge* as "apparatuses" for disciplining bodies (1992, 189). This notion of the power of the museum to exert control through vision has been critiqued by the visual studies scholar James Elkins in his book *The Object Stares Back* (1996). Elkins distinguishes various different forms of looking at work in the interaction of the museum visitor and the objects of their

The International Handbooks of Museum Studies: Museum Media, First Edition.
Edited by Michelle Henning.
© 2015 John Wiley & Sons Ltd. Published 2020 by John Wiley & Sons Ltd.

attention. His argument about the multiplicity and interaction of different looks in the museum complicates the notion of the detached, disembodied observer applying a singular gaze to the object and of the museum as a controlled and controlling viewing mechanism. It is a view supported by the arguments made by Bann (1984), Alpers (1991), and Baxandall (1991) about the art museum as generating multiple and complex ways of seeing, and about vision as part of the application and enervation of the senses acting together. The case for approaching museum artworks in terms of the interpolation of vision with the other senses has been developed by Brodsky (2002) with her discussion of the sensory practices of Impressionist artists such as Cezanne and Delacroix and Judith Okely (2001) in her exploration of the phenomenological differences that Impressionist paintings of the Normandy landscape can reveal between looking and seeing. This idea of vision as a sensory formation and of "visual sense" (Edwards and Bhaumik 2008) draws on the growing field of sensory studies and of the museum itself as a "sensescape" (Classen and Howes 2006) wherein the roles of touch and smell can be distinguished as part of a perceptual regime (Bouquet 2001). The recognition of sound as an element of the sensory formation of museum space has been touched on by Emily Thompson (2004) in her architectural study of the ideas of sound and listening that lay behind the design and materials used in the construction of modern public spaces.

The provocation of these arguments and Tilson's recordings is to recognize the aurality of museum spaces and of listening as part of the sensorium through which museum visitors engage with artworks. It is this that I want to explore in this chapter. My interest is in the modes of relational and affective sociality that are engendered by sound in the museum. This is to consider sound as an affective spatial construct of the architecture and materials of museum spaces and the various forms of its electronic mediation that span oral and aural educational media at one end of an aesthetic spectrum and installed sound art at the other. I also want to look at sound as an object of museum interest, and the development of archives of recordings and the way they are made accessible.

This concern for listening and the aurality of museum-exhibited objects is related to the reflections made about our relationship to sound in the visual and literary arts by the anthropologist Tim Ingold (1993) and the musician and author David Toop (2010). Ingold explores the imagined spaces of Pieter Bruegel's painting *The Harvesters* in order to make us listen, as well as look at its composition through the energies and movements of the environment it represents. Toop's thesis is also exploratory, arguing for an auditory response to a variety of paintings, novels, and essays so that we might recognize that listening is a "form of mediumship" taking us beyond the world of forms into the ephemeral and uncanny qualities of these works. Both Ingold's and Toop's writings conceive of acts of perception in the visual and literary arts as multisensory or synaesthetic and show a cultivated sensitivity to the sonorities of the world.

This is an approach I have followed in my own work where I have been concerned to think of the aurality of the objects on display in two museums in Nagasaki, Japan – the Nagasaki Atomic Bomb Museum (also known as the Peace Museum) commemorating the atomic bombing of the city and the Nagasaki Museum of History and Culture, which celebrates the presence of the Portuguese and Dutch settlements from the sixteenth century (R. Cox 2008; 2010). These objects are the painted "golden screens" (*namban byôbu*) in the Nagasaki Museum of History and Culture which depicts the contact between the Portuguese and Japanese residents in the sixteenth century and, in the Nagasaki Peace Museum, the dioramas of ruins and clinical photographs of injuries to victims of the atomic bombing. These exhibits offer contrasting images of the city and depict places that contemporary visitors can explore outside the museum spaces, on guided walking tours. The tours were led by local volunteers who encouraged visitors to engage with more than a view of these places and to listen as well to certain historical features of the environment, notably running water courses and bells. These environmental features linked the historical episodes represented by the two museums and drew attention to the way in which, in contrast to the environments encountered on the walking tours, the two museum displays were able to control the energies of light and air – as heat and sound – and therefore to direct the sensory engagement of visitors to the act of looking.

What I am indicating here is that the architectural construction of gallery space, the curatorial arrangement of displays, and the use of certain materials, such as wooden floors, glass cases, and steel fittings create the conditions for audition. To give you an example, the gallery that exhibited the golden screens created a certain capacity for reverberation and therefore circumscribed conversation and the audible movement of bodies. The sounds of the gallery were constituted by these material features as well as the low hum of the air conditioning system and the residual sounds of the electronic media in a nearby display that played back sounds of lapping water, wind, and sea birds so as to evoke the sixteenth-century arrival scenes of the Portuguese in Nagasaki (Cox 2010, 127). The sounds of the gallery and the sounds of the places represented by its displays intersected in the sensory apperception of visitors as part of their extra-visual, or in this sense auditory, imagination of the exotic past of the city. Thinking about museum spaces in this way is about making a shift that Giuliana Bruno describes in *Atlas of Emotion* (2002) as "from sight to site," meaning a movement away from the ocular framework of the gaze. The gaze Bruno refers to here is specifically the filmic gaze and its affects which, she argues, are not fully explored in a psycho-analytical (Lacanian) framework (2002, 15). Bruno's architectural point of view recognizes the spatial impact of the museum as part of a haptic, auditory, and emotional landscape and allows us to recognize sound as a latent energy of the museum experience that has only really come to the fore through the increasing use of museum space as a site for the installation of sound art.

The mediumship of sound

If we define sound art in narrow but simple terms as Brandon LaBelle suggests, it is an approach to sound as both subject and object, that is to say, it uses sound as a medium in order to address questions about sound (LaBelle 2004; 2006). The admission of sound into the museum gallery can be understood as a way of materially composing the gallery's space and the social relations that adhere within it and, as such, it can be understood in terms of Jacques Attali's (1977) thesis about "noise" as an organization of sounds that is a mechanism for the creation or consolidation of a social formation. For Attali, taking a *longue durée* approach to the "political economy of music" in Europe, the arrangement of sounds as music (or as "noise") is an ordering principle for understanding society and is based on a theory that socioeconomic circumstances determine the meaning of sounds. It is a view which suggests that today, at a time when sound art and electronically generated sound media for educational and entertainment purposes are a commonly installed feature of museum galleries, it may be productive to consider how the introduction of sound media is an affective form of social relations. The question here is what kinds of sounds have pertained to museum spaces in the age of electronic mediation, when it is possible to manipulate the auditory environment of museums in a number of different ways, and how they have changed the way that visitors and museum professionals relate to the museum.

The works of Alison Griffiths (2003; 2008) and Haidee Wasson (2005) have tracked the introduction of a wide range of media devices and technologies into museums, particularly since the end of the nineteenth century. Most of these media have been visual in design and function, aimed at enhancing the museum experience through dioramas, lantern slides, photographs, guidebooks, pamphlets, postcards, and books. Driven by an educational imperative and an understanding of the museum visitor as being led by the desire to see and to read in order to make sense of what is exhibited, the first recorded uses of aural media were in this pedagogical vein. Alison Griffiths (2008) found that, in 1904, one Dr Ant Frisch recommended that the phonograph be used in exhibitions. Frisch argued that "The time may not be far distant, when we shall be able, by dropping a cent into a phonograph by the side of interesting objects in the museum, secure the pleasure of a short discourse on the exhibit" (quoted in Griffiths 2008, 235).

As Griffiths goes on to state, such an idea had already been incorporated in the displays of the international fairs and great exhibitions in order to get around problems of visibility and access, with too many visitors crowding out the view of exhibits and their contextual information on labels. Besides the utility of the phonograph, the affective spatiality of these recordings was a way of changing relations between visitors whose proximity to others and to the exhibits became a condition not only of what they could more or less see by themselves, but of what they were made to hear all together. When the sounds played out by the phonograph in the museum were musical, this affective spatiality was pronounced and remarked on by contemporary commentators such as the anonymous contributor to the *Museums Journal* in 1931, who described how

> The moment the sound of music reaches the ear the objects of vision seem enveloped in a new architectural form of space and are seen as it were in a different light … aesthetic significance is enormously heightened when the music is so related, and ear and eye walk as it were together through enchanted space. (Griffiths 2008, 242)

The mediumship of sound technology enabled the education of the museum visitor, becoming an established feature of communications between museums and the public through the radio broadcast. For Haidee Wasson, through the radio broadcast, "a new form of virtual museological curation was effected, coordinating airwaves, newspapers, museums, and a geographically expanded audience" (2005, 85). Such "virtual curation" has been a consistent feature of the museum's use of radio since the emergence of the technology in the 1920s, from early initiatives like the Field Museum of Chicago's linking of radio programs with pictures published in the *Chicago Daily News* (Griffiths 2008, 237), right up to the phenomenally successful series of broadcasts on BBC Radio 4 in 2010 titled *A History of the World in 100 Objects* by the director of the British Museum, Neil MacGregor. The educational agenda in radio was somewhat different than it had been for the phonograph, as it allowed for a dialogue to develop between curators and the public that extended and embellished the informational context of exhibits otherwise provided for by labels. Radio broadcasts from inside the museum gave the institution a voice, which while being didactic and authoritative was also a far more discursive and personalized form of knowledge-making than had been the case hitherto. This is what the curator Grace Fisher Ramsey writes about radio broadcast from the museum in 1938: "to depart from visual to aural instruction would be going about as far as possible from the museum idea of objectifying teaching" (1938, 194).

This unease about the misdirection of the museum's knowledge imparting purpose persists in the contemporary debates about the application of more complex electronic media in museum displays. At stake is the authenticity of the museum artifact as a knowledge-bearing object once its meaning has been hived off from the textual forms of the label, pamphlet, and guidebook and presented as a generic form of edutainment, through various kinds of interactive media. As the *New York Times* art critic Virginia Smith wrote in 1993, in response to the refurbished Milstein Hall of Ocean Life at the National Museum of Natural History in Washington, DC, what the new video projectors, interactive computer stations, and playback of recorded whale sounds had achieved was "sounds for silence, information for contemplation, facts for poetry" (quoted in Griffiths 2008, 218). The attitude reflected here is that, through this kind of sonic mediation of visual displays, the forms of sociality that underpin the museum's integrity of purpose as an educational and enlightening institution will be strained and changed as they are dissipated into forms of immersive distraction.

This concern about sound as a means of enabling but also a distracting element in the media of display was not applied to sound as a subject of serious scholarly inquiry and as an element of the collection itself. That is, there is a different attitude in evidence with regard to the illustrative and "edutainment" role of sound in the media of museum display from that pertaining to sound as an element of a museum collection. Such collections were initially created by means of recording technologies such as the phonograph. The phonograph as a technology of sound reproduction allowed for sound to be pieced out into discrete, neat discs, analyzed, and stored as part of museum collections. The technology was utilized by teams of scholars and scientists, among them anthropologists, linguists, and animal behaviorists. Anthropologists used the wax cylinders of the phonographs to "record culture" by capturing the songs and stories of native peoples who were understood to be disappearing (Makagon and Neumann 2009).

The creation of major museum archives of sound recordings such as the Smithsonian's Folkways and the American Folklife Center collections were often the result of sustained, passionate efforts by individuals like Moses Asch and Alan Lomax. Other museum archives were built up from colonial networks and scientific expeditions and in response to major events like World War I, which led to the creation of London's Imperial War Museum's archive of recollections of conflict. The intellectual significance of the recordings, as exercises in salvage, record, and archive-making, often lay in their transcription into textual forms rather than in the sonic qualities of the recordings themselves, and it is only recently, through their digitalization and dissemination, that these recordings have become accessible to the museum public for listening (a notable example of this form of dissemination is the British Library sound archive, which has over 50,000 available recordings). As part of a virtual museum, these recordings, which can be accessed free over the Internet or bought commercially as audio CDs, enable forms of private listening that reduce the affective relations of sound to the configurations of digital space. In this way, listening is imbued with the presence of the museum not as a physical space but as a digital architecture that conveys a sense of the affectivity of sound through the compression parameters of the file format and playback system.

The historical treatment of sound as a recordable, collectible object of museum inquiry has been assessed most recently, in 2011, through an innovative exhibition titled *Noises* at the Museum of Ethnology in Neuchâtel, Switzerland (Gonseth et al. 2011). The exhibition was the outcome of research on intangible cultural heritage and explored how the ideas and practices used to categorize "noise," "sound," "speech," and "music" were also a means of theorizing about culture. The exhibition, which spanned a number of different rooms in the museum, employed a series of metaphors. There was the natural aural metaphor of the seashell as a listening device, and the visitor became their own sound-making mechanism as they were led to walk over a bed of seashells. There was the social metaphor of the "noise" of others, presented as a series of boxes through which different sounds labeled as "noise" were filtered and that the visitor activated as they walked over them.

In a third room, the notion of noise as "music," through its incorporation into the structures of avant-garde composition and folkloric interpretation, was explored through a model of an engine room that referenced the modernist experiments of the Futurist art movement. Finally, there were two spaces that played with the notions of salvaging sound and storing it as data through an analogy with the sirens and echoes of a submarine control room and the instruments that transduce sound as the pressure of air into forms of knowledge. These metaphors and the immersive designs of the display spaces aimed at drawing visitors into the materialities of sound at the same time as they provided a narrative of its academic and artistic deployments. This approach, which uses existing sound archives and the sonic properties of museum objects, including instruments, to embed sound into museum spaces, is one that can be found in museums like the Pitt Rivers anthropology museum in Oxford, UK as a developing strategy for public engagement.

In 2012 the Pitt Rivers Museum employed the sound artist Nathaniel Robin Mann to explore their collection, focusing particularly on their archive of sound recordings and creating recordings that can be played back in the space of the museum. The museum has a relatively small and unknown collection of sound archives which includes recordings of the BayAka communities from the rainforests of the Central African Republic made by the field recorder Louis Sarno. The purpose of the residency is much less an academic investigation of these archives, or about merely finding a means for their dissemination, than about using them as a point of creative departure. For example, one performance during this residency in 2012 involved manipulating and mixing field recordings together with the mechanical sounds of the technologies used to make the recordings. The residency at the Pitt Rivers Museum and the exhibition in Neuchâtel are particular examples, taken from the field of anthropology, but part of a broader and developing interest in taking sound out of the archive and using it to enervate the spaces of the museum. These creative initiatives often look to the field of sound art for inspiration. However, while sound art has a long history of presentation in the museum, this is a complex relationship, with many debates about the viability of sound art performance in spaces designed for the visual arts.

Sound art

The interaction of the visual arts and music can be approached in various ways, as a matter of forms, through the works of well-known figures like Kandinsky and Mondrian (Maur 1999), whose compositions were influenced by modern music, and as a matter of mediumship, indicating an evanescent world of "sinister resonances" beyond forms as David Toop (2010) has done. In the case of sound art as a distinct genre recognized by the art establishment, the interaction is most often traced through the Futurist painter and composer Luigi Russolo and the publication of his musical manifesto *The Art of Noise* (*L'arte dei rumori*) in 1913

(LaBelle 2007). *The Art of Noise* was influential in its day, but it was not until the 1950s and 1960s, with the work of composers of sound like John Cage and Max Neuhaus, Pierre Schafer's *musique concrète* movement, and groups like Fluxus, that sound art properly entered into the exhibition spaces of the contemporary art world, albeit alongside video art, art bands, and performance art (LaBelle 2006). A difficult genre to pin down in museum circles, the art of sound remained part of the art gallery scene, and essentially outside the museum, until relatively recently. With influential exhibitions such as *Sonic Boom* at the Hayward Gallery, London, the Whitney Biennial, and *Sonic Process* at the Centre Pompidou in Paris, all in 2002, the question about how to adapt a visual art environment to a space for sound became a significant curatorial issue. Christine van Assche, the curator of *Sonic Process*, directly addressed the problem of creating a "museum-friendly" work by pairing musicians and sound artists together, with collaborations between artists like Scanner and Mike Kelley, and indirectly by darkening the exhibition space in a manner that a visitor to a visual art exhibit might expect (LaBelle 2007).

Other exhibitions in this vein, which explored the hybridity of sound and vision in electronic art, were *What Sound Does A Colour Make?* (2005), curated by Kathleen Forde and organized by the New York Independent Curators International (iCI), and *Visual Music* (2011), which was organized jointly by the Hirshhorn Museum at the Smithsonian and the Museum of Contemporary Art in Los Angeles. The rapid expansion of sound art into museum spaces in the period since these exhibitions has included old, established institutions like the Victoria and Albert Museum, with *Shhh* in 2004, as well as contemporary art museums like the Tate Modern, which has had numerous sound art installations, from Bruce Nauman in 2004 to Susan Philipsz's Turner Prize-winning work in 2010, when it could be said that there was a benchmark acceptance of sound art into the art world. These artists include Christian Marclay's *Sounds of Christmas* (2004), Marina Rosenfeld's *Emotional Orchestra* (2005) and *Sheer Frost Orchestra* (2006), Bill Fontana's *Harmonic Bridge* (2006), and Electra's *Her Noise* (2012). While recognizing the slipperiness of the demarcation, I am focusing here on what it means for sound art works to be installed in museums rather than art galleries, and there are therefore a large number of works that would otherwise need acknowledging in the recent history of the presentation of sound art such as *Soundworks* at the London ICA gallery and *Urban Sounds* in the House of Electronic Culture in Basle, Switzerland, in 2013.

Brandon LaBelle (2007), drawing on the ideas of Marshall McLuhan (2002), has argued that behind this increasing movement of sound art into the museum is a fundamental paradox expressed as the difference between the "alphabetical" nature of the museum that privileges the use of didactic panels, historical sequencing, fixed meanings, and a static viewers' perspective and the "acoustic" which, in contrast, amplifies meaning and dissipates perspective through sonic immersion. La Belle explains these effects of sonic immersion as follows:

Sound is intrinsically and unignorably relational: it emanates, propagates, communicates, vibrates, and agitates; it leaves a body and enters others; it binds and unhinges, harmonizes and traumatizes; it sends the body moving, the mind dreaming, the air oscillating. It seemingly eludes definition, while having profound effect. (2006, ix)

This problem is reflected in the difficulty of classification of sound art, which resists the categories that have been historically applied to sound recordings in museum archives and must, in contrast, bear the weight of comparison with aesthetic systems of the visual arts. On the level of museum practice, this is about the comparative rarity of sound art works being commissioned and collected by museums. For, while sound art has become a well-established route for bringing audiences into museums as part of live art performances, they are far less likely to become a fixture of the museum's display and are rarely exhibited for more than six to eight weeks. An important practical issue in the length of time sound art exhibitions are on show is the cost and technical complexity of the sound systems required.

On the level of theory, there is a problem about how to interpret sound art which is foregrounded by its relationship with the museum. Christoph Cox describes the issue, drawing on Seth Kim-Cohen's book *In the Blink of an Ear* (2009), as the inclination of composers such as John Cage and Pierre Schafer and sound artists such as Max Neuhaus, Alvin Lucier, Christina Kubisch, Christian Marclay, Francisco Lopez, and Toshiya Tsunoda to resist the reduction of their work to textual representation as part of a signifying discourse and rather to see it in terms of its textural materialities, which is to say, its affective qualities (C. Cox 2011, 146–149). The museum and its critics are often complicit in this recourse to the language of materiality, with Bruce Nauman's 2004 creation of *Raw Materials* in the Tate Modern's Turbine Hall being described as essentially a "sculptural" composition (Searle 2004). The analogy of sound art with sculpture is also present in the ZKM (Center for Art and Media) Karlsruhe's 2012 exhibition *Sound Art: Sound as a Medium of Art*, which refers to loudspeakers as the "building blocks of monumental sculptures"; and in the inaugural exhibition, *Inaudita*, of Rome's new Sound Art Museum, where sculpture is incorporated directly through a light installation by Mario Airo and a giant Styrofoam ear by the Acconci Studio, set amid such compositions as Zelada's *Butterflies on a Rainy Day* and John Bischoff's *Aperture*.

The sculptural references in these museums address the ontological nature of sound art, which resists representation except by itself, and are a way of avoiding sound art's appropriation by wider discourses of art through its incorporation into mainstream modern art museum settings and narratives. An example of this appropriation was the New York Museum of Modern Art's 2011 exhibition *At the Crossroads of Art and Sound*, which described the intersections and borrowings between John Cage's work and the work of Brian Eno, David Byrne, Christian Marclay, and John Zorn as part of the story of modern art that the Museum of Modern Art (MoMA) represents.

Politics of sound

Thus there is a tension – which one may regard as restrictive or productive – between the conceptualization of sound through its medium specificity and the conceptualization of it in terms of its discursive significance in wider cultural fields. This can be seen in exhibitions like *Frequencies*, held in Frankfurt's Kunsthalle in 2002. The exhibition focused on the limits of human audibility through the creation of various acoustic spheres but, alongside these experiments into audiovisual perception, also included the activist group Ultra-red who specialize in political aesthetic projects about issues such as public sex, housing and education, and racism. Their work, which is presented through radio broadcasts, installations, and performances, involves collaborations with social movements and challenges the notion of social relations formulating neatly around the material compositions of sound art, aiming to make the relational process of listening a form of activism. It is a position that effectively subverts the expanded sociality of listening in museum spaces into an interactive process of political agitation.

This possibility of using sound installation and performance as a means of direct interaction and of visitors intervening in the process, potentially for political effect, is one which Paul Moore has explored in his proposal for a soundscape installation in Northern Ireland of the "conflicting sectarian sounds" which visitors would activate by turning the handle of a wind-up radio in a glass box (2003, 274). The visitors would then be asked to confront their political affiliations and cultural assumptions by playing a "green card" or an "orange card" depending on which cultural background they imagined the recorded sounds to be representing (275). This installation was never made, but it is based on an understanding of the interactivity of sound in a museum setting and how, through the rubric of concepts like soundscape, which presuppose the existence of a shared set of commonalities through listening, installations may be used to reflect on ideas about community and memory.

One example of how this idea has been taken up comes from the neighborhood of Hirano in Osaka, Japan, where a soundscape museum was created as a way of encouraging grassroots activity for community development (Nishimura and Hiramatsu 1999). The creators, Atsushi Nishimura and Kozo Hiramatsu, encouraged local residents to be part of the museum through their nomination of important sounds to be recorded and through making oral interviews for incorporation into the collection.

A larger-scale example, also designed around the themes of memory and community and drawing on traditions of oral history, was the *Memory Machine*, created by two composers, Cathy Lane and Nye Parry, and installed at the British Museum's two hundred and fiftieth anniversary exhibition entitled *The Museum of the Mind: Art and Memory in World Cultures* in 2003. Visitors used a 1950s-style telephone in the exhibition area to contribute their own memories to the mix (Lane and Parry 2005, 142). The composers based their work on Francis Yates's thesis *Art of Memory*

(1992), about the history of the spatialization of memory through the creation of mental topographies, and used this concept to play back in the gallery space the memories that visitors and some staff had contributed, in a constantly changing mix of voices. As they describe it:

> This created a collision of words and ideas around the subject of memory and the museum, and provided an aural metaphor for the complex web of inter-relationships of human memory itself. Unlike many interactive exhibits which re-order a given set of materials according to some form of user input, it is the actual content of the Memory Machine that is the subject of the interaction. (Lane and Parry 2005, 142–143)

This staging of interactions between persons and mental and physical space through sound can be understood in anthropological terms as a kind of "encounter." David Tomas has developed this theme in his book *Transcultural Space and Transcultural Beings* (1996), where he describes how encounters governed by misrepresentation or representational excess may generate intercultural spaces and, in one chapter, notes how in this respect it is the ephemerality and voyaging aspects of sound that make it such a powerful cultural agent of encounter between previously unknown or only imagined peoples (1996, 104).

As a traveling emissary between different cultural spaces, sound may be insightful precisely because of its ambiguity. The artist and historian Paul Carter has developed this notion in his sound work *The Calling to Come* (1996), which was a commission of the Museum of Sydney. The work was positioned at the entrance to the museum, itself the former site of the headquarters of British colonial power in New South Wales. The essential material for the sound installation, which played out as a stereo mix, was a script derived from two language books kept at Sydney Cove between 1790 and 1792 by a surgeon named William Dawes. The books recorded his interactions with a young woman named Patyegarang as he tried to compile information about the vocabulary, grammar, and everyday usage of the Sydney language. This script and the sound elements of the environment to which it referred were then composed together into the installation so that the visitor was placed in the midst of an exchange of words in English and Eora. The concept and design of the installation reflected the productive significances of what Carter has called "mishearing" in the auditory spaces of encounters between white settlers and Indigenous peoples, and of how "Immersion in the ambiguities of human communication is not a sign of weakness or self-indulgence: it has a political meaning" (Carter 1996, 96). These political meanings were not lost on the museum and its visitors, for Aboriginal communities were enthusiastic about the work and the installation provoked a lively debate about the legacy of colonialism in Australia.

Another sound artist whose work engages with similarly threatened Indigenous communities and their languages through themes of voice and hearing is John

Wynne. Wynne's collaborations with speakers of the Khoisan and Gitxan languages in South Africa and Gitxsanimaax, an Indigenous language in northern British Columbia, have been exhibited in ways that draw attention to the role of the technologies of recording and playback by constructing a complex multilayered aural space for the encounters between different voices In an earlier exhibition, *Hearing Faces* (2005), Wynne deployed an eight-channel sound mix that spatialized the relationships between the voices with flat screen speaker technology that allowed him to embed the speakers into photographs of Khoisan people shown talking into microphones, but with their faces obscured by the technology. This strategy deliberately problematized the project and the way that the identity of the persons photographed was held to be singularly expressed through their voice recording.

Wynne's installation, *Anspayaxw*, about Gitxsanimaax speakers showed at the Museum of Anthropology in Vancouver for most of 2010 as part of the exhibition *Border Zones: New Art across Cultures*. The sound in this installation, of voices and elements of the natural environment local to the language speakers, was spread across a 12 channel mix, which produced a continuous exchange and flow of voices. It is possible to recognize in the multiple channels deployed in this work a deliberate "mishearing" of fragments of stories and conversations. This can in turn be read as an expression of the history of political and economic relations at stake in this kind of encounter between outsiders such as anthropologists and artists, and Indigenous communities. However, the ambiguity in the multichannel, multivocal mix of many voices intermingled with each other and with the sounds of the environment should not simply be interpreted as a recursive critique of a history of relations with Indigenous communities in northern British Columbia, but rather regarded as productive of a resonantly affective relational space.

Affective spaces

But how should we conceive of the kind of relations that may be produced through the sonic space that Wynne has created in this installation, as well as the other examples that I have been describing in this chapter? Are they a mode of making meaning as some writers such as Hutchison and Collins (2009) have argued? They invite us to think about museum sound installations through the idea of dialogue and its definition by the literary theorist Mikhail Bakhtin, wherein "meaning is made through interaction between 'voices' that are essentially in dialogue" (Hutchison and Collins 2009, 93). This is a useful idea for helping us to understand how the agencies of those involved in sound art installations in museums are enmeshed in a network of institutional relations. The dialogic aspect of these relations, which sound installations may manifest, is linked by Hutchison and Collins to James Clifford's (1997) concept of the

FIGURE 10.1   *Castaways* exhibit, 2007, Whitworth Art Gallery, Manchester, UK.
Photo courtesy of Lorenzo Ferrarini.

museum as a "contact zone" in order to account for the way that a sound installation operates as an affective space. But the notion of a contact zone circum-
scribes museum space in a manner that may not fully accommodate the resonant
properties of sound and the way that its energies reverberate through the materials of bodies and gallery walls. These energies of frequency and vibration
bring us into the materialities of sound that are so difficult to pin down and
make meaningful without recourse to the terms of acoustics. The ambiguity of
sound's meaning in such museum settings stems from the absence of a fixed
viewing perspective and the shift from a spatialization of visitor relations based
on the visual design of a gallery space to a set of relations deriving from the
movements of sounds in space.

The anthropologist and sound artist Steven Feld's work has explored this way of
knowing through listening to recorded sound that he refers to as "acoustemology,"
which is based on the relational ontologies and temporal elements he identifies in
Bakhtin's dialogism (Feld and Brenneis 2004). In his collaborative sound and visual
art exhibition *Castaways* at the Whitworth Art Gallery, Manchester, in 2007, his
starting point was an encounter in an art gallery in Ghana with the "sculptural
paintings" of the artist Virginia Ryan (each sculptural painting is 9×11.5
inches/23 × 29 centimeters) (Figure 10.1). These works were made from discarded

objects collected from Ghana's shorelines at PramPram, Jamestown, Labadi, Anomabo, and Korlegonno, which were the historic sites of the slave trade. Feld found these "castaways" to be

> quite echoic. In their material tactility, color, volume, and assemblage he found them audible as a complete sound environment. Viewing some one hundred Castaways on Ryan's Accra studio floor, he told her that he felt like he was putting an ear to a huge seashell and listening to the detritus of history. (2010, 115)

The ambient sound composition that Feld then went on to make, recorded on Anomabo beach, was a creative response to this way of hearing the "acoustic memory of the Gold Coast becoming the Black Atlantic" (Feld 2010, 115). In the exhibition space, which was a large sculpture court in the Whitworth Art Gallery, the viewer was presented with a wall assembly of 200 or more pieces hung in rows of Ryan's paintings and a 60 minute soundtrack played continuously at ambient volume. The soundtrack was created from eight separate stereo tracks and designed around a watery metaphor of "the washing in and the washing out" of the waves, of people and things. The artist Ryan said of the exhibit: "There was something quite synaesthetic about it in terms of the sensation on the skin; that wetness, that reverberant space, that sense of time being a little more watery or elastic" (Feld 2010, 118). For visitors, there was no particular position from which to view or listen to the installation and they moved around, following the sounds of the waves or to get a different view of the visual work. One of the most interesting expressions of the relational intensity of the sound waves in this space was the choice of some visitors to lie down on the gallery benches. Listening from this position was a spontaneous response to the sonic sense of the space as a shoreline and seemed to reflect a need to find a point of solidity and stillness amid the energy of the waves and the activation of the historical metaphor of the washing in and the washing out of people and things.

In my own sound art collaborations, I have also been interested in finding methods of making sense of the human relationship with forms of sonic energy, and have focused on the impact on everyday life and health of aircraft noise. The project in question, titled *Air Pressure* was a collaboration between an acoustic scientist, a sound artist, and myself as an anthropologist (Figure 10.2). We aimed to bring these perspectives together to tell the story of a farm still located at the end of one of the main runways of Narita, Tokyo's international airport. The acoustic scientist was Professor Hiramatsu, the sound artist was Angus Carlyle, and the project was generously supported by an award from the Wellcome Trust Arts Awards scheme in 2010.

The farm where we worked grows organic vegetables with some livestock, is located some 80 meters or so below the flight path, and belongs to the Shimamura family. As this was a project for the public understanding of the science of

FIGURE 10.2   Rupert Cox and Angus Carlyle, *Air Pressure*, 2012. View of installation at Whitworth Art Gallery, Manchester, UK. (For a color version of this figure, please see the color plate section.)

acoustics and the medical pathologies arising from exposure to noise, we wanted to create a museum installation that would deal with the relationship between the idealized sonic image of noise generated by the paradigms and devices of science and the tragic history of the Narita site which was where the farming community of Sanrizuka had been displaced and protestors and riot police had died in violent confrontations during the 1970s.

We were drawn to the signature sound of the constant aircraft overflights of the farm as it was both a visual and a sonic metaphor for the relations of the family with the airport authorities, and acoustically it was the most intense sound measured on the site. But, while this might have offered a coherent inter-pretation of the unequal encounter between the world of the farm and the world of the airport, it obscured sonic ambiguities like the absence of aircraft taxiing sounds from the acoustic register of "noise" and reduced the complex layers of local and national politics to one sonic rush. Therefore, for the museum installation we created a soundproofed room with a 5.1 surround sound mix and a twin screen film projection in high definition color so that we could con-vey the sense of a multilayered shifting sound world composed of the sonic energies of machines and bodies in motion (Figure 10.3). The spatialities of the sound and visual mix gave an auditory presence to the multiple overlapping energies of weather temperature, wind and rain, the exhaust of burnt jet engine

FIGURE 10.3   Rupert Cox and Angus Carlyle, *Air Pressure*, 2012. Another view of installation at Whitworth Art Gallery, Manchester, UK. (For a color version of this figure, please see the color plate section.)

fuel, and the human and animal rhythms of vegetable and livestock farming. These affective energies were felt by the visitors to the installation through different frequencies and vibrations, as the room itself reverberated. In this sensory design, the meaning was in the materials we assembled and was conveyed jointly by the textures of the sonic and visual elements as well as by the context of wall panels and the museum pamphlet.

The experience this installation offers museum visitors is immersive and yet also ephemeral, as with those of Feld and others mentioned previously. The installations described in this chapter offer an animation of a sense of persons and places by enveloping visitors in sonic space and, while this may be so carefully designed as to constitute a sonic way of knowing the world or "acoustemology" (Feld and Brenneis 2004), it may also be a more prosaic mode of education and diverting entertainment. Perhaps most significant of all, museum sound installations may encourage us to listen more attentively and appreciatively in the rest of the museum. Beyond the exigencies of museum installations as projects of artistic, anthropological, or archival significance, the sonic impression of gallery space may change the way visitors perceive the museum as a place for listening as well as for viewing. This may be a way to think about the museum itself as an affective aggregation of multiple voices and bodies engaged in audible acts of everyday wonder and imagination.

References

Alpers, Svetlana. 1991. "The Museum as a Way of Seeing." In *Exhibiting Cultures*, edited by Ivan Karp and Steven D. Lavine, 344–365. Washington, DC: Smithsonian Institution.

Attali, Jacques. 1977. *Noise: The Political Economy of Music*. Minneapolis: University of Minnesota Press.

Bann, Stephen. 1984. *The Clothing of Clio: A Study of the Representation of History in Nineteenth- Century Britain and France*. Cambridge: Cambridge University Press.

Baxandall, Michael. 1991. "Exhibiting Intention: Some Preconditions of the Visual Display of Culturally Purposeful Objects." In *Exhibiting Cultures*, edited by Ivan Karp and Steven D. Lavine, 33–41. Washington, DC: Smithsonian Institution.

Bouquet, Mary, ed. 2001. *Academic Anthropology and the Museum: Back to the Future*. New York: Berghahn.

Brodsky, Joyce. 2002. "How to 'See' with the Whole Body." *Visual Studies* 17(2): 99–112.

Bruno, Giuliana. 2002. *Atlas of Emotion: Journeys in Art, Architecture, and Film*. New York: Verso.

Carter, Paul. 1996. "Speaking Pantomimes: Notes in 'The Calling to Come.'" *Leonardo Music Journal* 6: 95–98.

Classen, Constance, and David Howes. 2006. "The Sensescape of the Museum: Western Sensibilities and Indigenous Artifacts." In *Sensible Objects: Colonialism, Museums and Material Culture*, edited by Elizabeth Edwards, Chris Gosden, and Ruth B. Phillips, 199–222. Oxford: Berg.

Clifford, James. 1997. *Routes: Travel and Translation in the Late Twentieth Century*. Cambridge, MA: Harvard University Press.

Cox, Christoph. 2011. "Beyond Representation and Signification: Toward a Sonic Materialism." *Journal of Visual Culture* 10: 145–162.

Cox, Rupert. 2008. "Walking without Purpose: Auditory Journeys through History and Memory in Nagasaki." In "Senses of Spatial Equilibrium and the Journey: Confounded, Discomposed, Recomposed," special issue, *Journeys* 9(2): 76–96.

Cox, Rupert. 2010. "Objects that Move: Japanese Namban Screens in Time, Space and the Imagination." *Journal of Instituto de História da Arte – Revista de História da Arte Faculdade de Ciências Sociais e Humanas* (Lisboa) 8: 127–139.

Duncan, Carol. 1995. *Civilizing Rituals: Inside Public Art Museum*. London: Routledge.

Edwards, Elizabeth, and Kaushik Bhaumik, eds. 2008. *Visual Sense: A Cultural Reader*. Oxford: Berg.

Elkins, James. 1996. *The Object Stares Back: On the Nature of Seeing*. New York: Harcourt.

Feld, Steven, in conversation with Virginia Ryan. 2010. "Collaborative Migrations: Contemporary Art in/as Anthropology." In *Between Art and Anthropology: Contemporary Ethnographic Practice*, 109–127. New York: Berg.

Feld, Steven, and Don Brenneis. 2004. "Doing Anthropology in Sound." *American Ethnologist* 31(4): 461–474.

Gonseth, Marc-Olivier, Bernard Knodel, Yann Laville, and Grégoire Mayor, eds. 2011. *Bruits: Échos du patrimoine immatériel*. Neuchâtel, Switzerland: Musée d'Ethnographie de Neuchâtel.

Griffiths, Alison. 2003. "Media Technology and Museum Display: A Century of Accommodation and Conflict." In *Rethinking Media Change: The Aesthetics of Transition*, edited by David Thorburn and Henry Jenkins, 375–389. Cambridge, MA: MIT Press.

Griffiths, Alison. 2008. *Shivers Down Your Spine: Cinema, Museums and the Immersive View*. New York: Columbia University Press.

Hooper-Greenhill, Eilean. 1992. *Museums and the Shaping of Knowledge*. London: Routledge.

Hutchison, Mary, and Lea Collins. 2009. "Translations: Experiments in Dialogic Representation of Cultural Diversity in Three Museum Sound Installations." *Museum and Society* 7(2): 92–109.

Ingold, Tim. 1993. "The Temporality of Landscape." *World Archaeology* 25(2): 152–174.

Kim-Cohen, Seth. 2009. *In the Blink of an Ear: Toward a Non-Cochlear Sonic Art*. New York: Continuum.

LaBelle, Brandon. 2004. *Site Specific Sound*. Los Angeles: Errant Bodies/Selektion.

LaBelle, Brandon. 2006. *Background Noise: Perspectives on Sound Art*. New York: Continuum.

LaBelle, Brandon. 2007. "Short Circuit: Sound Art and the Museum." *BOL Journal of Art* 6. Accessed August 18, 2014. http://www.web.mdx.ac.uk/sonic/research/brandon.html.

Lane, Cathy, and Nye Parry. 2005. "The Memory Machine: Sound and Memory at the British Museum." *Organised Sound* 10(2): 141–148.

Makagon, Daniel, and Mark Neumann, eds. 2009. *Recording Culture, Audio Documentary and the Ethnographic Experience*. London: Sage.

Maur, Karin. 1999. *The Sound of Painting: Music in Modern Art*. London: Prestel.

McLuhan, Marshall. 2002. *Understanding Media*. London: Routledge.

Moore, Paul. 2003. "Sectarian Sound and Cultural Identity in Northern Ireland." In *The Auditory Culture Reader*, edited by Michael Bull and Les Back, 265–279. Oxford: Berg.

Nishimura, Atsushi, and Kozo Hiramatsu. 1999. "Soundscape Museum: A Report on the Method for Sharing and Preserving Soundscapes." *Soundscape* (JSAJ) 1: 99–106 (in Japanese).

Okely, Judith. 2001. "Visualism and Landscape: Looking and Seeing in Normandy." *Ethnos: Journal of Anthropology* 66(1): 99–120.

Ramsey, Grace Fisher. 1938. *Educational Work in Museums of the United States: Development, Methods and Trends*. New York: H. W. Wilson.

Searle, Adrian. 2004. "Inside the Mind of Bruce Nauman." *Guardian*, October 12. Accessed August 11, 2014. http://www.theguardian.com/culture/2004/oct/12/1.

Sherman, Daniel, and Irit Rogoff, eds. 1994. *Museum Culture*. London: Routledge.

Thompson, Emily A. 2004. *The Soundscape of Modernity: Architectural Acoustics and the Culture of Listening in America, 1900–1933*. Cambridge, MA: MIT Press.

Tomas, David. 1996. "Sound and Intercultural Contact Spaces." In *Transcultural Space and Transcultural Beings*, 103–137. Boulder, CO: Westview.

Toop, David. 2010. *Sinister Resonance: The Mediumship of the Listener*. London: Continuum.

Wasson, Haidee. 2005. *Museum Movies: The Museum of Modern Art and the Birth of Art Cinema*. Berkeley: University of California Press.

Further Reading

Bennett, Tony. 2006. "Exhibition, Difference and the Logic of Culture." In *Museum Frictions: Public Cultures/Global Transformations*, edited by Ivan Karp, Corinne A. Kratz, Lynn Szwaja, and Tomas Ybarra-Frausto, 46–69. Durham, NC: Duke University Press.

Biocca, Frank A. 1988. "The Pursuit of Sound: Radio, Perception and Utopia in the Early Twentieth Century." *Media, Culture & Society* 10: 61–79.

Blesser, B., and L. Salter. 2007. *Spaces Speak, Are You Listening? Experiencing Aural Architecture*. Cambridge, MA: MIT Press.

Bull, Michael, and Les Back, eds. 2003. *The Auditory Culture Reader*. Oxford: Berg.

Cage, John. 1973. *Silence: Lectures and Writings*. London: Marion Boyars.

Carter, Paul. 2004. "Ambiguous Traces, Mishearing, and Auditory Space." In *Hearing Cultures*, edited by Erlmann Veit, 43–64. Oxford: Berg.

Carter, Paul. 2004. *Material Thinking*. Melbourne: Melbourne University Press.

Cox, Christoph, ed. 2004. *Audio Culture: Readings In Modern Music*. London: Continuum.

Cox, Rupert, and Angus Carlyle. 2013. "Sky-Larks: An Exploration of a Collaboration between Art, Anthropology and Science." In *Anthropology and Art Practice*, edited by C. Wright and A. Schneider, 157–165. Oxford: Berg.

Daniels, Stephen. 1993. *Fields of Vision: Landscape Imagery and National Identity in England and the United States*. Cambridge: Polity.

Dudley, Sandra, ed. 2010. *Museum Materialities: Objects, Engagements, Interpretations*. London: Routledge.

Fuglerudart, Øivind. 2012. "Art and Ambiguity: An Extended Review of Border Zones at the Museum of Anthropology, British Columbia." *Museum Anthropology* 35(2): 170–184.

Hawkins, Harriet. 2010. "'The Argument of the Eye'? The Cultural Geographies of Installation Art." *Cultural Geographies* 17: 321–342.

Helmreich, Stefan. 2007. "An Anthropologist Underwater: Immersive Soundscapes, Submarine Cyborgs, and Transductive Ethnography." *American Ethnologist* 34: 621–641.

Heon, Laura. 2005. "In Your Ear: Hearing Art in the Twenty-First Century." *Journal of Organised Sound* 10(2): 91–96.

Kahn, Douglas. 1999. *Noise, Water, Meat: A History of Sound in the Arts*. Cambridge, MA: MIT Press.

Kahn, Douglas, and Gregory Whitehead, eds. 1994. *Wireless Imagination: Sound, Radio and the Avant Garde*. Cambridge, MA: MIT Press.

LaBelle, Brandon. 2011. "Sharing Architecture: Space, Time and the Aesthetics of Pressure." *Journal of Visual Culture* 10: 177–189.

Scanner, T. J. 2001. "Remembering How to Forget: An Artist's Exploration of Sound." *Leonardo Music Journal* 11: 65–69.

Sterne, Jonathan. 2012. *MP3: The Meaning of a Format*. Durham, NC: Duke University Press.

Taussig, Michael. 1991. "Tactility and Distraction." *Cultural Anthropology* 6: 147–153.

Tilson, Jake. 1996. *City Picture Fiction*, no. 32. Audio CD. London: Jake Tilson Studio.

Toop, David. 1995. *Ocean of Sound: Aether Talk, Ambient Sound and Imaginary Worlds*. London: Serpent's Tail.

Witcomb, Andrea. 2003. *Re-imagining the Museum: Beyond the Mausoleum*. London: Routledge.

Wynne, John. 2010. "Hearing Faces, Seeing Voices: Sound Art, Experimentalism and the Ethnographic Gaze." In *Between Art and Anthropology: Contemporary Ethnographic Practice*, 49–67. New York: Berg.

Rupert Cox is Senior Lecturer in Visual Anthropology at the University of Manchester, UK. As an anthropologist he has a long-standing interest in Japan and has carried out research on topics including the Zen arts, the idea of Japan as a copying culture, and the environmental politics of military bases. He has developed interests in the intersections between art and science and anthropology that draw on practices from sound art, documentary, and landscape film and are directed toward forms of public engagement. He is currently writing a book about the cultural history of military aircraft noise, *The Sound of the Sky Being Torn*, for Bloomsbury Press.

11 AESTHETICS AND ATMOSPHERE IN MUSEUMS
A Critical Marketing Perspective

Brigitte Biehl-Missal and Dirk vom Lehn

Some of today's retail consumption spaces are sophisticated products of aesthetic work. Museums too are not immune to the changes brought about in contemporary consumption, boasting carefully designed spaces for special visitor experiences. Historically, museums form part of a larger complex of exhibitions that relates to department stores, shopping arcades, trade exhibitions, and world's fairs (Bennett 1995). The aesthetic interchange between museums and department stores dates back to the 1850s, whereby techniques including lighting and commodity and window display were shared between the different settings, and the first stores used museums for inspiration for their interior design (Henning 2006, 30). Today, however, the luxurious setting of nineteenth-century art museums often seems inadequate for the twenty-first century visitor, and museums of all kinds have adapted many experiential strategies from the world of commerce.

Thus, changes in museums from the late twentieth century are closely associated with developments in commodity display, and, as we argue, with the aesthetic economy as such. In order to *realize* rather than *sterilize* objects, history, and culture on display, museums place increasing emphasis on sensual perception or *aesthetic experience*. The notion of aesthetics is used here in the sense of *aisthesis* and is concerned with the sensual perception of reality, not primarily the fine arts – some of these ideas are known from John Dewey's works, which shifted the emphasis from art objects as the focus of traditional aesthetics to the viewer's experience (Dewey 1934). *Aisthesis* opens the broad range of aesthetic reality to analysis. This approach is useful for capturing the aesthetic experience and atmosphere in museums, which

The International Handbooks of Museum Studies: Museum Media, First Edition.
Edited by Michelle Henning.
© 2015 John Wiley & Sons Ltd. Published 2020 by John Wiley & Sons Ltd.

go beyond the mere presentation of artworks or other cultural and technological artifacts, testifying to increased efforts to create memorable experiences for visitors in a context of ubiquitous economic aestheticization.

In this chapter, we apply an interdisciplinary perspective to discuss atmosphere in museums, drawing on Gernot Böhme's aesthetic theory and referring to marketing research, which has been concerned with spaces of consumption since the 1990s. We do not present a conventional marketing approach which is typically focused on improving the efficiency of detailed spatial and atmospheric strategies in order to increase people's inclination to consume, and is often myopic on cultural, social, historic, and artistic issues. Given our occupation as marketing lecturers in business schools, and our backgrounds in theater, film, and media studies and sociology, our research adopts a perspective that is interdisciplinary and often critical of marketing practice and theory. We suggest that, in the context of an aesthetic economy, thorough knowledge of the world of marketing allows comparisons between consumption and museum spaces that can help us better understand aesthetic and spatial practices in the museum. Such practices confirm but also challenge this context of consumption in which museums are socially and economically embedded.

The chapter consists of two main parts. In the first, we discuss the concepts of the "experience economy" and the "aesthetic economy" to show how spatial arrangements are created to influence visitors and consumers by generating specific atmospheres through the use of aesthetic work, with forms, colors, and their specific attributes. We will then present marketing approaches to the design of retail spaces, which, we argue, are not too different from those in contemporary museums. The first part of the chapter concludes by introducing questions of critical marketing and consumer resistance to persuasively styled atmospheres as a means to better understand the contemporary world of museums, which is increasingly oriented toward the marketplace.

The second part of the chapter discusses atmosphere in museums, in a way that is applicable to the broad, but relative, range of museums, including natural history, history, culture, science and technology, and art museums (Waidacher 1996, 299–301). We begin with a discussion of hybrid forms of consumption in museums and consider exterior aesthetics. We consider social interactions in museum space, and end with some critical reflections on atmosphere in museums and the aesthetic economy. Overall, advances in the marketing field, combined with museum studies, provide an interdisciplinary perspective for critically analyzing these contemporary manifestations of the interrelation of culture, education, and marketing.

The aesthetic economy and atmospheres

Museums are not only symbolic or functional ensembles, but they also provide particular aesthetic experiences that are situated in a broader economic and social context. The rise of an aesthetic economy has been identified by philosophers and was discussed in depth in the area of marketing and consumption research. At the turn of the nineteenth century, Thorstein Veblen ([1899] 1953) emphasized the symbolic nature of consumption that extends beyond the fulfillment of direct needs and wants in a marketing context through his work on "conspicuous consumption." This idea links to another classical dichotomy that we find in the Marxian framework of use value and exchange value. Half a century ago, Wolfgang Fritz Haug (1971), in his critique of commodity aesthetics, argued that use value, which is determined by practicality within a particular context of use, has come to be dominated by exchange value, the value that is gained in an exchange process that is typically monetary. Developing this argument, Gernot Böhme suggests as a third value category the concept of the staging value (*Inszenierungswert*):

> In order to raise their exchange value ... commodities are treated in a special way: they are given an appearance, they are aestheticized and staged in the sphere of exchange. These aesthetic qualities of the commodity then develop into an autonomous value, because they play a role for the customer not just in the context of exchange but also in that of use. (2003, 73)

These values, which extend beyond utility and purposiveness are seen as a new type of use value, which derives from exchange value insofar as it is "made of [the objects'] attractiveness, their aura, their atmosphere, [serving] to stage, costume and intensify life" (Böhme 2003, 73). These values do not serve to address and fulfill people's needs and wants, as commonly posited by conventional marketing theory; rather they create and heighten an insatiable desire for ever more consumption (2003, 73). Consequently, a broad range of practices within our society, which may include visual, spatial, and performative elements, are directed toward the creation of value. This notion of aesthetic work "designates the totality of activities which aim to give an appearance to things and people, cities and landscapes, to endow them with an aura, to lend them an atmosphere, or to generate an atmosphere in ensembles" (Böhme 2003, 73).

This concept includes the world of arts, but also extends to contemporary service and design practices and all kinds of production, including architects, marketers, music producers, and people decorating and refurbishing spaces. Our everyday life takes place in many of these atmospheres which are products of aesthetic work. Museums only are one element in this context.

Other writers, including the sociologist Mike Featherstone (1992) and philosopher Wolfgang Welsch (1997), have identified an "aestheticization" of everyday life by which the values of stylization and sensual gratification have come to permeate the economic, social, and personal dimensions of contemporary capitalism. In their work on the "experience economy," Pine and Gilmore (1999) have asserted that work is theater and every business a stage, sketching a concept that resonates with Böhme's ideas of aesthetic and atmospheric work. They argue that businesses must create memorable events for their customers, "experiences" which become the very product that is marketed and consumed. Many of these practices are fueled by strategies from the world of arts, with all kinds of contemporary institutions applying a broad range of aesthetic, visual, and narrative techniques in the attempt to heighten the experience on offer (Biehl-Missal 2011b). In this aesthetic economy, architecture and spaces for aesthetic consumption play a fundamental role and also affect an increasing number of museums of all kinds.

In order to discuss atmospheres and the aesthetic experience in museums from an interdisciplinary marketing perspective, we have chosen an approach to aesthetics that accounts for sensual experience in its relation to actual market developments in the economy. Drawing on the work of Böhme, we follow a concept of the new aesthetics that goes beyond traditional aesthetics developed in the eighteenth century as a theory of art.

In this approach, the notion of "atmosphere" is central. The notion of atmosphere has received some attention in the discipline of aesthetics within philosophy (Schmitz 1964) and links to Benjamin's (1968) idea of the "aura" as an immaterial quality that pertains to or surrounds original works of art but is considered absent in their technical reproductions. With the ready-made in art, aura was extended to everyday objects once they were placed in an art context (Böhme 1993, 116). Today, as art, life, and aesthetic work are increasingly united in product and space design, atmosphere can be encountered in any context. Böhme's concept of the aura also includes Benjamin's observations on "breathing" the aura: the notion that people corporeally perceive and absorb the atmosphere in bodily ways, for example, when they let the impression of a spectacular natural setting "enter" the body to produce effects of relaxation (Böhme 1993, 118). This is echoed in statements such as "As we enter a space, the space enters us," which expresses the idea of people's "innate capacities to internalize abstract emotive structures" (Pallasmaa 2012, 242, 239), and which becomes obvious when we consider odor, which enters the body directly; musical rhythm, which vibrates and affects bodily tensions; or colors that "hurt" the eyes. Atmosphere is something that is, in a certain sense, indeterminate, a spatially extended quality of feeling. Atmospheres are considered spatial bearers of moods, created by a range of different elements: "atmospheres are evidently what are experienced in bodily presence in relation to persons and things or in spaces" (Böhme 1993, 119). Thus the notion of the atmosphere helps us to explain corporeal and emotional responses in carefully designed environments.

So, in this chapter, when we refer to the notion of aesthetic experience, we take into account the entire atmosphere and the sensual perception of people in relation to spaces, objects, and humans. *Aisthesis* refers to the sensual perception of the reality, and focuses on the relation between environmental qualities and human states in actual aesthetic environments (Böhme 1993, 125). Marketing and consumer research also emphasizes experience as the apprehension of something via the sensorial and the corporeal (Biehl-Missal and Saren 2012). This approach is useful in looking at all kinds of museums and allows to take into account their embeddedness in the aesthetic and experience economy.

Marketing research on retail space and atmospheres

In a broader context of the aesthetic economy, research in the area of marketing strongly emphasizes that consumption is more than the acquisition and use of goods in that it includes extraordinary experiences for consumers. Marketing practice, as a melting pot of creative practices that constitute aesthetic work, and marketing research have made some effort to theorize the role and function of architecture and experience. Three decades ago, Holbrook and Hirschman (1982) highlighted the relevance of emotional experiences that are created by and are related to products and services. Consumer experiences are influenced and stimulated by many aspects of the environment in which consumption takes place.

Böhme (2006) refers to the plethora of consumption spaces that include shopping malls, a variety of stores, and locations for services as "architectures of seduction" and as products of aesthetic work that serve to further intensify people's "desire" in a continuous theatrical staging of life through consumption. An example in this endeavor is Louis Vuitton, which cooperates with famous architects such as Jun Aoki, Kumiko Inui, and Peter Marino, and its flagship store, Maison Louis Vuitton, at the Avenue des Champs-Elysées in Paris, France. The strategies applied here are strongly inspired by many artistic and museal concepts (Biehl-Missal 2011b, 63). In the space, the brand is recreated by the visual gestalt and atmosphere: the company's signature LV monogram and historic Damier pattern are used for optical effect and to provide an illusion of height and depth. The presentation of products is reminiscent of the presentation of artifacts in museums, and they are framed by a permeable wall of stainless steel which recreates countless multiples of the signature monogram. The atmosphere is influenced by the density and materiality of expensive fabrics, stimulating the imagination of potential customers and their perception of the commodity's material. Architecture and fashion, two sisters in the art world, reaffirm and reinforce each other, symbolically communicating messages of status and taste, in a three-dimensional total work of art, a commercial *Gesamtkunstwerk*.

As in many museums, the setting is educational and influential. Museums such as Museum of Modern Art (MoMA) in New York have at times explicitly set about this schooling of taste and style (see Staniszewski 1998). One could argue that the commercial "education" received in luxury stores shapes people's perceptions and understanding of the value of things, which is then embodied through behavior and items purchased with staging values (Böhme 2003). This consumer knowledge is then communicated and spread socially.

The Louis Vuitton marketing strategy also involves cooperations with famous artists for the decoration of its shop window. This includes theater director Robert Wilson's colorful outlet in 2002 and the 2006 Danish Icelandic artist Olafur Eliasson's installation of light bulbs, steel, and aluminum in the form of a massive eye, called "Eye See You," which attracted the gaze of shoppers. Many of the strategies observed here situate themselves in a long history of a creative circuit

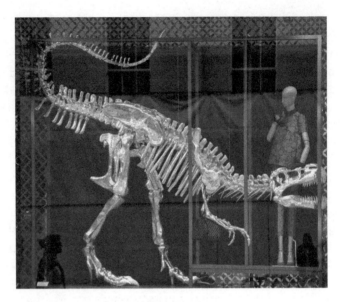

FIGURE 11.1   Louis Vuitton shop window, Paris.
Photo: Georgina Mascolo.

between museums and department stores where the distanced presentation of objects, often behind glass and windows, and the touchable presentation of sensual materials helped to turn goods into a desirable fetish (Henning 2006, 31). In museums, certain display techniques such as, for example, the habitat diorama with taxidermy in naturalistic scenes, closely resemble shop windows and create illusions of a different world (Henning 2006, 44). This creative circuit becomes strikingly obvious when considering a Louis Vuitton shop window design that uses carefully built and spectacularly arranged massive models of dinosaur fossils as a backdrop for its leather products (Figure 11.1).

In a local Paris context, this setting mirrors the history and grandeur of the French Natural History Museum in the city's Les Jardins des Plantes, which may have inspired the design team, although the dinosaurs later appeared at Louis Vuitton's Fifth Avenue store in Manhattan. By evoking the museum, Louis Vuitton stores emphasize the quality of the products. The Cherry Blossom handbag range designed by the artist Takashi Murakami for Louis Vuitton was eventually exhibited in the Guggenheim Museum in Bilbao, Spain, turning the museum itself into an impressive space for the display of luxury consumer goods.

These aesthetic qualities of retail environments have indirect implications for strengthened brand identity, and help to embody the essence and experience that is for sale. Other examples are jewelry stores with imposing doors which create an exclusive atmosphere, discouraging nonserious shoppers from entering and potentially selling the exclusive "fantasy" of the jewelry purchase to women. Other locations, such as Nike stores, try to recreate an atmosphere loaded with sport via imagery, architecture, and features, for example, tartan tracks recreated on the floor.

In the marketing literature, not only the general and brand implications have been analyzed, but research on "atmospherics" (Kotler 1973) has a tradition of four decades, analyzing in detail factors such as interior and exterior elements, layout and decoration, which influence buying behavior (Turley and Milliman 2000). Attention has also been paid to the careful arrangement of window displays (Soto 2002). Stronger competition between retail and consumptions settings has led to the development of ever new creative strategies to provide attractive experiences through store design, events, and entertainment (Fiore and Kim 2007). Researchers find that the constitution of consumer experiences seems to be directly affected by sensory and emotional stimuli from the retail environment to the extent that "where shoppers go, what they see, and how they respond determines the very nature of the shopping experience" (Underhill 1999, 44). In order to create elaborate atmospheres for shopping, marketers employ a diverse range of lighting techniques, staging, and decorating (Dennis and King 2007), which also includes the use of background music that functions as acoustic wallpaper. This genre of music, often referred to as elevator music, easy listening, or Muzak, is intended to be inoffensive but often is received critically by people who bemoan its pervasiveness and insipid content (Lanza 2004). A range of factors is considered to be stimuli which may affect consumers' responses, such as ambient cues (e.g., music, lighting, scent, temperature), design cues (e.g., parking, wall color, size of space), and social cues (e.g., crowding, staff appearance) (Fiore and Kim 2007). An "effective" retail environment has an impact on consumers who approach merchandise more directly and stay longer in the store (Stoel, Wickliffe, and Lee 2004).

These perspectives have led to explicit critique, for example, of contemporary shopping malls that appropriate ideas of utopia and harmony for purely commercial purposes. For instance, Anna-Maria Murtola asserts that people are rendered apathetic and numb, like on the lotus drug which she uses as a comparison: "As long as you stay within this world and keep on shopping, you can feel happy. But the happiness is ephemeral" (2010, 47). In this view, atmospheres in consumption contexts are deemed manipulative and rather restricting to the experience and imagination, while Böhme (2003) at least accords some aesthetic pleasure besides pervasive aesthetic manipulation.

Further analyses have studied exterior and interior design and architecture and its role of creating visual stimuli to affect the customer in a way that is often described as "seduction" (Soto 2002, 24). Experience-oriented strategies have been found to affect fashion shoppers who reported a positive mood and referred to their shopping as more pleasurable (Michon et al. 2007). In order to achieve effective consumer seduction, retail environments must be free of distraction and complications, and unpleasant or disturbing emotions must be avoided, so that the shopper feels "comfortable yet excited" (Jones 1999, 137). Factors such as a restraining layout, unattractive decoration, and badly informed staff have to be avoided as they distract from the shopping experience by creating "negative" atmospheres and emotions. In addition to architectural layout, design cues, and the point of purchase and decoration displays, so-called human variables have been identified as relevant for atmospheric cues in retail settings (Turley and Milliman 2000). In this vein, marketing settings have been likened to a theater where scripted behavior and performances take place to create superior services (Grove and Fisk 1992). Similar observations have been made with regard to museum spaces, as we will discuss.

A critical marketing approach

The idea of pleasant atmospheres may be appropriate for corporate museums, which often have a strong emphasis on a positive message. However, many art and history museums emphasize the controversial potential of their artifacts and the generally challenging potential of art, which allows for unexpected and unpleasant experiences. With regard to this difference, Böhme emphasizes that being in marketing atmospheres differs in several ways from encountering atmospheres in environments devoted to art (Böhme 2003, 79). Art is understood as a special form of aesthetic work, which has its own social function, namely the mediation of the encounter and response to atmospheres in situations such as theaters, museums, and exhibitions *set apart from* action contexts (Böhme 1993, 116). Böhme suggests that the function of art is to develop human sensuality in such atmospheres which he defines as not "seductive" or "obliging," but "liberating" (*handlungsentlastend*) (1995, 16). The purpose in this sense is to provide a space for aesthetic experience, enabling people to dwell on the atmosphere and to emotionally and imaginatively explore and feel moods and moments without being influenced with regard to a specific purpose such as consumption. In this vein, philosopher and museum theorist Hilde Hein suggests that stimulated experiences

> may excite visitors to further inquiry ... Alternatively, the discovery might terminate simply with pleasurable aesthetic enjoyment of the experience as an end in itself – a "wow effect," not unlike that stimulated by the theme park or joy ride. If the experience is complex and transformative, it may even resemble a religious epiphany or the rapture of enjoying art. (2000, 86)

However, museums have been critiqued as fundamentally ideological institutions (Kaplan 1994; Bennett 1995), and atmosphere as a means of manufacturing experience becomes – as in the shopping center – an ideological tool. Hence it seems worth taking a look at critical research on atmospheres in marketing, part of a broader field of "critical marketing," which does not aim to increase marketing efficiency, but rather often draws on critical theory and radical approaches (Saren et al. 2007). A critical marketing approach argues that these atmospheres may provide opportunities for aesthetic pleasure but function as opportunities for aesthetic manipulation as well; they hide a reality of exploitation whereby people's desire to consume is intensified, and thus constitute a real social power (Biehl-Missal and Saren 2012, 168).

Studies of "servicescapes" address the totality of the physical environment in which a service process takes place and also refer to the reactions of people present (Bitner 1992; Grove and Fisk 1992; Turley and Milliman 2000). Researchers have described how people resist, renegotiate, or challenge the atmosphere in servicescapes, in case studies including Nike Town Chicago and the Starbucks coffee chain (Sherry 1998; Kozinets et al. 2004; Thompson and Arsel 2004).

Biehl-Missal and Saren (2012) have used Böhme's concept of atmosphere to critique marketing practices, to explain how they work and why they may be challenged and opposed by activists and consumers. Starbucks is a prominent example because atmosphere is a key strategic tool for the company and its branding, which largely extends beyond the actual coffee products it sells to encompass the overall ambience of its coffee shops. In Starbucks coffee shops, all the elements work together to create the desired atmosphere. The space is framed by high columns, square cut forms, and wide windows which constitute a modern frame, suggesting openness and helping to create the appearance of an accessible, inviting, and friendly place. The space is tinged with a "warm" materiality by the soft furnishings, yellow light, pleasant coffee aroma, discreet rippling of musical sound, and an airy and emotionally relaxing arrangement. These elements are all perceived sensually via synaesthesia, the combination of, for example, the visual and the tactile in the soft sofas and warm light. Behind this aesthetic pleasure there is aesthetic manipulation whereby consumption is encouraged. In addition, the transnational company has also been accused of other actions behind the scenes that are belied by the peaceful atmosphere: Starbucks has been criticized for destroying neighborhoods and offering fake communities in place of locally owned spaces (Thompson and Arsel 2004). Numerous human rights and environmental violations, including the exploitation of workers and rejection of fair trade agreements, have come to public attention. Biehl-Missal and Saren conclude: "Rather than being a truly alternative public sphere open to community and democracy, the atmosphere in the stores veils the reality outside and creates a substitute of peacefulness and any related disturbing and political actions are rapidly ended" (2012, 175).

There is a broad spectrum of consumer resistance that includes approaches that more or less publicly reject certain products for ethical, environmental, or financial reasons. It also includes forms of rebellious activism. The latter, more extreme, actions include, for example, the work of William Talen and the Church of Stop Shopping. Talen has been arrested for his satiric performances as the preacher "Reverend Billy" at Starbucks and other slick retail spaces such as Victoria's Secret, Disney Stores, and several global banks which are involved in unsustainable and unethical business behavior. Resistance can also include tactical, artful techniques of "poaching" (de Certeau 1984). Researchers have studied consumers' use of Starbucks for the production of personally significant experiences that do not correspond to what marketers had envisioned. In Starbucks coffee shops in China, for example, it has been found that consumers who are exposed to spatial arrangements, colors, decoration, and Western cultural elements in the setting create their own personally meaningful aesthetic experiences, for example, using the setting for lengthy private and even romantic meetings or birthday celebrations away from their parents (Venkatraman and Nelson 2008).

In the case of museums, Mark Rectanus (2002) has framed the Western museum as a contested site of commercial branding and privatized cultural funding, where artists collaborate with corporations, merging art, business, and museums, but also challenge and resist these developments. For example, the aforementioned Reverend Billy and the gospel choir Church of Earthalujah, who rally in retail stores, also staged a protest in the sleek, dark Turbine Hall of the Tate Modern in London at the oil giant BP's sponsorship of the art gallery. Other practices of resistance in museum spaces, for example, the three collectives of artists known as Platform, Art Not Oil, and Liberate, who seized the occasion of the Tate's 2010 Summer Party to mark 20 years of BP support to challenge this partnership (Chong 2013). They contended that the ethics of arts sponsorship is compromised by outcomes of multinational capitalism such as the 2010 Gulf of Mexico oil spill. Less explicitly political appropriation of the museum space goes back to the nineteenth century when, as Charlotte Klonk (2009) pointed out, mothers visited the National Gallery in London solely to teach their children to walk, while others used the space for quiet naps, flirtatious encounters, or picnics.

Museums, commerce, and atmosphere

In today's aesthetic economy, the creative circuit between commercial and museum settings seems to run even faster and many other parallels have become obvious. Increasing efforts are being made not to sterilize art by presenting it in a museum, but to realize it. Whereas many nineteenth-century museums were crowded, chaotic, and dark, and remained incomprehensible to many visitors, museums have increasingly become more people-centered, emphasizing visitors' experiences (Henning 2006, 91). Just as marketing and consumption processes have been compared to a theater performance in order to emphasize the emotional and aesthetic experience they create (Pine and Gilmore 1999), museums are now understood as providing a setting for performance, more often in the sense of postmodern or postdramatic theater, where spectators are integrated into a situation of materiality, movement, sound, and atmosphere rather than being exposed to an illusionary dramatic story (Lehmann 2006; Biehl-Missal 2011a). The creative processes that come into play here are historically related to theater scenography, a term increasingly being applied to museums which designates the totality of spatial and material elements including light and also the invisible odor of the space.[1]

Museums can be seen as part of the experience economy in that they not only serve to display art, history, technology, nature, and so on, but also often mimic ubiquitous commercial sites that "mass produce and retail 'unique experiences' that are phenomenologically real" (Hein 2000, 80). It is increasingly difficult to determine what is a museum and what is not. As mentioned earlier, marketing research has provided many examples of museum-like atmospheres from Nike Town Chicago (Sherry 1998) to the Louis Vuitton flagship store (Biehl-Missal 2011b, 62). Economic spaces like the Frankfurt Stock Exchange have been completely refurbished to reflect a dynamic and futuristic face of the financial markets so that they appear attractive and reliable to private investors, and the trading floor also provides a revamped additional exhibition space for visitors where they can soak up the digital-technological atmosphere of contemporary stock market trading (Biehl-Missal 2013).

In many cases, the professionals who design corporate spaces and retail stores also work for museums. Disney is not the only operator which deploys marketing and educational research and uses theatrical action to produce aesthetically gratifying experiences in its theme parks (Hein 2000, 82). Another is Atelier Brückner in Germany, which was involved in the refurbishment of the Frankfurt Stock Exchange, the BMW Museum, and many other corporate museums; has designed technology and nature museums; and has provided scenography for the theater and opera as well. In the United Kingdom, Land Design Studio also creates museum and commercial spaces, integrating architecture and scenography.[2]

These theatrical developments connect to other elements in museums, for example, the hybrid consumption that Bryman describes as part of a "Disneyization" or "Disneyfication" of society (2004, 72). An example of hybrid consumption can be found in the way museum restaurant and shopping opportunities for visitors have become major sources of revenue in larger museums, and are often framed by remarkable architectonic spaces. Museums are also part of general hybrid consumption settings; for example, Manchester United Football Club and Spanish football clubs FC Barcelona and Real Madrid include a museum alongside themed restaurants and shops in their stadiums (Bryman 2004, 72). The pressure to consume by taking the "exit through the gift shop" has been highlighted by artists as well, for example in Banksy's film *Exit through the Gift Shop* (2010).

When discussing museums designed along commercial lines, it needs to be pointed out that the interior atmosphere of the traditional didactic museum space is influenced by the external form and context which are strongly related to retail and consumption culture: cities themselves are being marketed in a competition to attract visitors. While the grandeur of the Louvre situated nineteenth-century Paris in a symbolic context of cultural progress and democracy (Duncan 1999, 306, 307), many of the recent twenty-first-century buildings by "star" architects welcome citizens and tourists in a commercial setting that speaks to the capitalist aesthetic economy. For example, Frank Gehry's Guggenheim Museum Bilbao, Spain, is one expression of the municipal government's effort to attract creative workers, and Daniel Libeskind's Royal Ontario Museum in Toronto, Canada,

FIGURE 11.2   Atelier Brückner, BMW Museum, Munich.
Photo: Marcus Meyer. Reproduced by permission of Atelier Brückner.

enhances the attractiveness of the adjacent retail strip. In this sense, the commercial retail landscape and museums are not two fundamentally different things.

For corporate museums, architects create atmospheres that tell stories and invite visitors to experience the story. An example is the BMW Museum in Munich, Germany, designed by the company, which is a landmark in the city of Munich and materially symbolizes the roots of the Bavarian car company (Figure 11.2).[3]

The BMW Museum brings to life the overarching experience of movement, dynamics, and the pleasure of driving (Biehl-Missal 2011b, 57). The concept is based on theme-specific spaces accessed via connecting ramps that create an experience of mobility and movement: thus the theme is not only symbolized but made accessible, bodily and architectonically. Within the exhibitions, the sleek and polished automobiles are not only rationally perceived as special and valuable, but sensually experienced; this combines with the multimedia-enhanced exhibition architecture to present a joyful, idealized experience of driving.

In other words, according to our aesthetic approach in this chapter, the encounter with artifacts in such museum spaces is understood not primarily as a mental, rational activity, but as including the embodied and lived experiencing of the situation. The concept of atmosphere reflects this emphasis on the interaction between viewer and visual artifact, and supports the argument that aesthetically designed spaces have an affective power which is experienced bodily by the visitor. An artifact does not need to refer to some meaning as a sign, as a BMW model might semiotically refer to "luxury" and "wealth," but in the first instance it has its own presence, reality, and atmosphere. From a marketing and organization studies perspective, it has been acknowledged that artifacts not only are perceived in reaction to signs with reference to semiotic theory, but they also have an effect via the atmosphere they create and the moods which are induced in the perceiver (Gagliardi 1996; Biehl-Missal 2013). This is an idea that also appears in art history and aesthetics, whereby pictures are perceived to have a relatively autonomous reality and presence, "appearing" to people and touching their inner feelings (Schmitz 1964; Klages 1972; Gombrich 1982). Böhme states that, for example, paintings which depict a melancholy scene "are not just signs for this scene but produce this scene itself" (Böhme 1993, 124; 2006, 74). They emanate a specific atmosphere. The technological devices in the example used here also make an impact via the carefully styled aesthetic situation.

This aesthetic perception may be felt but, as we have suggested, it is not ideologically neutral, and extends to history itself, for example, at the Volkswagen Autostadt in Wolfsburg, Germany. On 28 hectares of hills and lakes in a carefully designed park, landscape visitors encounter numerous attractions, including exhibition of classic cars and innovative cars, artworks and films, and interactive stations, and experience the company's view of its brands and values such as safety, sustainability, and service, and its history. In this museum the development of technology very much suggests, in an almost teleological line, the development of the automobile, not illustrating possible alternatives to this form of individual transportation and, in a green setting, not providing space for representation of destructive ecological consequences. The embodied experience promotes acceptance of this belief.

Challenging atmospheres

Aesthetic work in museum architecture can further an embodied historical understanding for quite different purposes. Museums may generate different atmospheres that are not "positive," as they are in marketing environments, and do not stand in any obvious relation to consumption and the industry; rather, they achieve an experience of history that encourages further interpretation in the visitor. An example of this is the building by Daniel Libeskind which forms part of the Jewish Museum in Berlin. Five empty spaces or voids run vertically all the way through from the ground floor of the building up to the roof. They have walls of bare concrete, without heat or air conditioning and largely without artificial light. Libeskind explained that they refer to "that which can never be exhibited when it comes to Jewish Berlin history: Humanity reduced to ashes" (Stiftung Jüdisches Museum Berlin 2013). These spaces are not just symbolically meaningful but create a strong atmosphere that affects visitors.

This approach of affecting people's values and understanding rather than presenting historic objects that tell their story goes along with an increasing appeal to sensory responses, emotions, and feelings in museums. With regard to visual displays and three-dimensional "walk-in" environments, Hein describes how knowledge flows from emotional intensity and subjective feeling:

> If seeing is believing, seeing forcefully may foster a still stronger belief, and a timid or weak presentation can undermine an idea's credibility. Theatricality makes a story more compelling emotively, and so design and the art of spectacle compete with logic and evidence in the inducement of belief. ... The production of shared, powerful experiences becomes a means to create a public reality that passes for knowledge. (2000, 80)

Similarly, the Washington United States Holocaust Memorial Museum does not aim only at rational explanation but uses an exhibit architecture which makes visitors undergo and discover a range of "disorienting feelings" that reveal the architecture's strong didactic function (Hein 2000, 84). Emphasizing the *impression* rather than the *expression* of artifacts and spaces (Böhme 1995, 54), the social character of elements (when, for example, concrete is linked to a certain building tradition, or when the "void" is only symbolically equated with the absence of the deported and murdered Jews) becomes less important. Böhme (2006, 107) emphasizes that architecture is perceived through sensing rather than seeing: space, with its dimensions and perspective, is fundamentally aesthetic. In this perspective what is valued is the synesthetic character of perception, the combined contribution of several different senses, which differs from mechanistic views in which elements are perceived through separate channels: seeing by eye, hearing by ear, and so on (Biehl-Missal 2013, 360). Because of its synaesthetic character, one can describe the atmospheric "coolness" and "emptiness" of both materials and spaces. For example, the visual impression people get from a material results in an atmospheric sensing that is different from the results of a tactile examination (Böhme 1995, 55). When touching a material, iron for example, one does not perceive its actual temperature but its thermal conductivity. Cross-sensory metaphors are indicative of this process, such as when referring to a "warm" material or a "high" tone (Biehl-Missal 2013, 360). The synaesthetic character of a museum space is produced through several factors: coolness in this example via sleek, massive surfaces and the absence of warm light. This perception also derives from earlier bodily encounters with the material. The perception of a material and its imagery depends on the atmosphere. For example, the installation by Menashe Kadishman, *Shalechet* (Fallen leaves) filled one of the voids at the Jewish Museum in Berlin with countless small "screaming" faces made of iron which, via synaesthetic perception, produce a doubly mute situation because of the absence of sound mimetically connotated by open mouths; this produces a solely material echo of the past laments that is as cold and metallic as the iron is for us (Figure 11.3).

When visitors walk on the faces, an extraordinary resonant auditory effect is produced as the void fills with the resulting clanging. The chilly air, the concrete, and the heavy materiality of the iron aesthetically reproduce the weight and misery in history.

Through their acoustic experience, the voids also allow for a synaesthetic perception that in many ways accounts for Jewish history in Germany. They make visitors and the ancestors of victims and assassins experience the nonreversible loss in German society of moral and values in a Christian-humanist ideal and the loss of emancipatory power (Bendt 1992, 25). An additional empty tower ("voided void") situated in the building essentially manifests the void and absence that is continuous in history, the solid built remains of a voided void that can also be aesthetically perceived.

FIGURE 11.3   Menashe Kadishman, *Shalechet*, Libeskind Building, Jewish Museum, Berlin. Donation Dieter and Si Rosenkranz. (For a color version of this figure, please see the color plate section.)
Photo: Jens Ziehe.

The pragmatic aesthetics of museum visiting

Using an atmospheric perspective to make sense of museum exhibitions. Böhme (2006) offers us an interesting starting point for exploring how people co-create atmosphere in response to the aesthetic influence of space, objects, and, more importantly, other visitors. Exhibitions are not only populated by museal objects arranged by curators and museum designers, but they are also explored and examined by museum visitors, and often in very different ways than anticipated by the curators (Baker 1999).

When social theorists and historians describe the museum as ritual (Duncan 1995), they consider the "interaction order" (Goffman 1983) in the galleries as institutionally predefined by the museum, its architecture and layout, as well as by the social conventions and rules that govern behavior in the gallery. The museum visit is considered to be organized by a normative order imposed by the physical and visual environment and enforced by museum wardens and all those visitors present in the gallery who monitor each other's conduct and create an environment of mutual observation and observability (Trondsen 1976; Bennett 1995). In art museums this ritualistic organization has been described by Hirschauer (2006) as "museum discipline," characterized as silent shuffling along the gallery walls. This relatively undisturbed viewing of art in a public place, however, is the product of an aesthetic organization of the actions of visitors who explore and experience exhibits in interaction with companions and other people who are in the galleries at the same time (Jafari, Taheri, and vom Lehn 2013).

Detailed video-based studies of interaction in art museums reveal that people accomplish their exploration of an exhibition moment by moment and in interaction with all those who are present. While the action and interaction in art museums are contingently organized, people's actions are not randomly produced but in a systematic manner, resulting in what Garfinkel (1967) described as a "familiar scene." Two visitors standing next to each other looking at a work of art move to the next exhibit by slowly and progressively transforming their bodily configuration, a side-by-side arrangement, into a configuration that allows them to jointly move on and take a standpoint at the next exhibit (vom Lehn 2013). Visitors manage to accomplish their concerted onward movement without, or with only little, talk by reacting to their aesthetic perception of the situation. They monitor, often from the corner of the eye, other visitors' "state of involvement" with the exhibit and notice changes, for example, in posture, which suggest they might be ready to move on. When, as in Figures 11.4a–c, a visitor turns to the right and moves away from the exhibit she is looking at with a friend, the latter may treat that bodily turn as an invitation to leave and align with that invitation by taking a step backward and turning his upper body to the right. In other cases, visitors feel encouraged to bring their engagement with the exhibit to a close when other people arrive in the locale. Following an aesthetic perspective, these cues are not only perceived visually, but are a corporeal reaction to the alterations of the atmosphere co-created

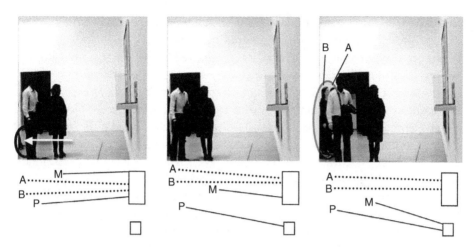

FIGURE 11.4a–c   Interactional organization of a museum visit (vom Lehn 2013). A, B, M, and P refer to the four visitors visible in the picture. A and B arrive from behind and become visible in (c). P is the man nearest to the reader, M the woman to his left.

between people present and in relationship to the material, corporeal, and visual environment around them.

These interactions, which arise between friends and strangers, can be described as forming a "pragmatic aesthetics" (Knoblauch 1998) in the museum, that is, an aesthetic organization produced for the pragmatic purposes of accomplishing the museum visit. The interaction that facilitates the concerted withdrawal and onward movement is embedded within a material and visual environment that the participants orient to bodily and visually while at the same time being aware of other people and their actions.

Despite all efforts to design and curate museums, visitors explore exhibitions in different ways. Baker emphasizes that:

> the meanings that the single individual might read into the objects encountered along the way – will only rarely coincide with the strategic thinking of museum planners. How a visitor interacts with artworks and their settings is determined by personal needs, associations, biases, and fantasies rather than by institutional recommendations. (Baker 1999, 18–19)

Moreover, the route visitors take through an exhibition – where they stop, what they look at and for how long, and how they see it emerges in and through social interaction and talk at and around exhibits (Heath and vom Lehn 2004). The aesthetic experience of people in museums cannot be understood independently from their action and interaction. The experience is not a cognitive process but a practical achievement produced in interaction with and around the works of art. In this sense, visitors too are creators of the aesthetic work that produces the atmosphere in museums, complementing and altering the product of the aesthetic work of museum managers, designers, and curators.

The atmosphere is also influenced by unexpected factors, for example, families visiting with noisy children, construction work, or a fire alarm that may disturb the museum experience. These events correspond with negative elements that marketing research commonly tries to avoid in retail atmospheres (Jones 1999). Other elements that can counter visitors' expectancies are the deployment of modern technology, such as hand-held computers or information kiosks in traditional art galleries. Curators and designers take particular care in the design and placement of such systems and devices and strive to have the technology accompany the original works without drawing undue attention to itself. Thus, they hope to avoid disturbing the aura of the original works of art and to maintain the museum atmosphere. However, when people encounter a traditional art exhibition where information systems stand next to paintings and sculptures, they often spend relatively more time with the technology and struggle to embed the technology within their interactional and collaborative examination of the exhibits. As Heath and vom Lehn found in their research of stationary and mobile systems in art museums, pairs and groups of visitors often separate and continue their visit individually, if only for the duration of their engagement with a piece of art or furniture, or they become frustrated with the systems and abandon them (vom Lehn and Heath 2005; Heath and vom Lehn 2008). An art museum atmosphere that differs from the expected or hoped-for encounter with works of art can also be observed in blockbuster exhibitions. For the practical purpose of gaining access to the works, visitors may deploy strategies such as waiting for a gap to open into which they then sprint, or using a stroller to get close to paintings. While "normally" they would deploy a pragmatic aesthetics, such a co-created atmosphere perceived perhaps as tense or unpleasant, impacts the visitor's behavior and aesthetic experience of the exhibition.

Conclusion

We have discussed some of the ways in which museums today construct atmospheres similar to those found in consumption contexts. These include art museums and the broad range of museal institutions that provide experiences of science and nature, of technology, culture, and history, and of corporate artifacts. Some corporate museums do not present artworks but actual products, many of which can be consumed, thus reducing the differences between marketing spaces and a "museum." This blurring of the boundaries can also be found in design museums and galleries associated with financial institutions and corporations, where products are put on display not for purchase, but for appreciation (Waidacher 1996).

As we have argued, the interplay of marketing and museums goes beyond advertising, the website, media coverage, and the museum shop, infusing the history of the museum and contemporary practice that shapes its atmospheric and aesthetic form. Marketing pervades the entire institution of the museum, both the front-of-house contact with the public and the backstage activities conducted to develop exhibitions. Marketing research can help understand how these front- and backstage activities contribute but are not limited to the creation of a museum atmosphere. Strategies of aesthetic work and techniques used in retail settings produce atmospheres, but we need to recognize people's role in co-creation of the experience, by theorizing the interplay between the visual and material resources that museums offer visitors and the concrete ways in which visitors make sense of exhibitions in and through their interaction with each other.

From our interdisciplinary critical marketing perspective, the question arises regarding the relationship between, on the one hand, the renewal of traditional museums as an attempt to address the increased consumerism in many Western countries and, on the other hand, the maintenance of the art museum as a space for art appreciation and aesthetic experiences. On the one hand, there is an increasing interest in communicating art and culture to the wider public whereby museum managers and marketers try to attract visitors to their institutions by hosting blockbuster exhibitions and deploying novel interactive technologies that are attractive to younger audiences. On the other hand, museums are criticized for blockbuster exhibitions and for deploying interactive technologies in traditional settings because they are seen as a technique to feed consumerism in the disguise of widening access.

The atmosphere in museums may fulfill a special social function, namely the mediation of an encounter set apart from action contexts that we typically find in "seductive" marketing atmospheres (Böhme 1993, 116). It may enable people to emotionally and imaginatively explore and experience moods and moments without being influenced to a specific purpose such as consumption. In the light of the similarities between museums and consumption spaces, museums have a broader range of opportunities to aesthetically communicate with consumers, providing spaces that do not necessarily lure and numb people (Murtola 2010), but may contribute to, for example, a critical and embodied understanding of history.

Our perspective emphasizes that these architectures are not only symbolic and representational, and may be used for place marketing or to make material and manifest a certain political aesthetics and ideological thought. These architectures are vehicles for aesthetic experience and constitute a real social power because they influence people via bodily and sensual perception. Museum studies already recognizes that architecture and exhibition design in museums is part and parcel of the educational dimension, relating to national identity construction, influencing the values and beliefs of the visiting public, and expressing political power and status (Hooper-Greenhill 1994; Kaplan 1994; Bennett 1995; Hein 2000). Atmospheres touch, invade, and permeate people's bodies, subtly influencing and manipulating their emotions and moods, their sensual and mental states (Böhme 2003). Via their subtle impact on people at bodily and emotional levels, they can "influence our perception of reality, to the point of subtly shaping beliefs, norms and cultural values" (Gagliardi 1996, 575). When consumption artifacts are presented in museums or when consumption settings are presented in a luxury museum style, we can see how museums produce not only a certain kind of citizen, as writers like Tony Bennett (1995) have shown, but also, by educating taste and participating in constructing marketing atmospheres, a consumer.

Notes

1   On scenography see also Chapter 16 by Beat Hächler and Chapter 15 by Bettina Habsburg-Lothringen in this volume.
2   See Chapter 14 by Peter Higgins in this volume.
3   On the BMW Building in Leipzig, Germany, see Chapter 23 by Mark W. Rectanus.

References

Baker, Malcolm. 1999. "Museums, Collections and Their Histories." In *A Grand Design: The Art of the Victoria and Albert Museum*, 17–21, edited by Malcom Baker and Brenda Richardson. New York: Abrams.

Banksy. 2010. *Exit through the Gift Shop*. Film, 87 min. Produced by Holly Cushing, Jaimie D'Cruz, and James Gay-Rees. Paranoid Pictures.

Bendt, Vera. 1992. "Das Integrationsmodell" [The integration model]. In *Daniel Libeskind: Erweiterung des Berlin Museums mit Abteilung Jüdisches Museum* [Daniel Libeskind: Extension of the Berlin Museum with the section Jewish Museum], edited by Kristin Feireiss, 25–30. Berlin: Ernst & Sohn.

Benjamin, Walter. 1968. "The Work of Art in the Age of Mechanical Reproduction." In *Illuminations: Essays and Reflections*, edited by Hannah Arendt. New York: Schocken.

Bennett, Tony. 1995. *The Birth of the Museum: History, Theory, Politics*. London: Routledge.

Biehl-Missal, Brigitte. 2011a. "Business Is Show Business: Management Presentations as Performance." *Journal of Management Studies* 48(3): 619–645.

Biehl-Missal, Brigitte. 2011b. *Wirtschaftsästhetik: Wie Unternehmen die Kunst als Inspiration und Werkzeug nutzen* [Atmosphere: Essays on a new aesthetics]. Wiesbaden: Gabler.

Biehl-Missal, Brigitte. 2013. "The Atmosphere of the Image: An Aesthetic Concept for Visual Analysis." *Consumption Markets & Culture* 16(4): 356–367.

Biehl-Missal, Brigitte, and Michael Saren. 2012. "Atmospheres of Seduction: A Critique of Aesthetic Marketing Practices." *Journal of Macromarketing* 32(2): 168–180.

Bitner, Mary Jo. 1992. Servicescapes: The Impact of Physical Surroundings on Customers and Employees." *Journal of Marketing* 56: 57–71.

Böhme, Gernot. 1993. "Atmosphere as the Fundamental Concept of a New Aesthetics." *Thesis Eleven* 36: 113–126.

Böhme, Gernot. 1995. *Atmosphäre: Essays zur neuen Ästhetik* [Atmosphere: Essays on the new aesthetics]. Frankfurt: Suhrkamp.

Böhme, Gernot. 2003. "Contribution to the Critique of the Aesthetic Economy." *Thesis Eleven* 73: 71–82.

Böhme, Gernot. 2006. *Architektur und Atmosphäre* [Architecture and atmosphere]. Munich: Wilhelm Fink.

Bryman, Alan E. 2004. *The Disneyization of Society*. London: Sage.

Chong, Derrick. 2013. "Institutions Trust Institutions Critiques by Artists of the BP/Tate Partnership." *Journal of Macromarketing* 33(2): 104–116.

de Certeau, Michel. 1984. *The Practice of Everyday Life*. Translated by S. Rendell. Berkeley: University of California Press.

Dennis, Charles, and Tamira King, eds. 2007. "Social and Experiential Retailing Part 1 and 2." Special issue, *International Journal of Retail & Distribution Management* 35(6–7): 421–611.

Dewey, John. 1934. "Art as Experience." In *The Later Works, 1925–1953*, edited by J. A. Boydston, 1–352. Carbondale: Southern Illinois University Press.

Duncan, Carol. 1995. *Civilizing Rituals: Inside Public Art Museums*. London: Routledge.

Duncan, Carol. 1999. "From Princely Gallery to the Public Art Museum: The Louvre Museum and the National Gallery, London." In *Representing the Nation: A Reader: Histories, Heritage and Museums*, edited by David Boswell and Jessica Evans, 304–331. New York: Routledge.

Featherstone, Mike. 1992. "Postmodernism and the Aestheticization of Everyday Life." In *Modernity and Identity*, edited by Scott Lash and Jonathan Friedman, 265–290. Oxford: Blackwell.

Fiore, Ann Marie, and Jihyun Kim. 2007. "An Integrative Framework Capturing Experiential and Utilitarian Shopping Experience." *International Journal of Retail & Distribution Management* 35(6): 421–442.

Gagliardi, P. 1996. "Exploring the Aesthetic Side of Organizational Life." In *Handbook of Organization Studies*, edited by Stewart R. Clegg, Cynthia Hardy, and Walter R. Nord, 565–580. London: Sage.

Garfinkel, Harold. 1967. *Studies in Ethnomethodology*. Cambridge: Polity.

Goffman, Erving. 1983. "The Interaction Order: American Sociological Association, 1982 Presidential Address." *American Sociological Review* 48(1): 1–17.

Gombrich, Ernst H. 1982. *The Image and the Eye*. Oxford: Phaidon.

Grove, Stephen, and Raymond Fisk. 1992. "The Service Experience as Theater." *Advances in Consumer Research* 19: 455–462.

Haug, Wolfgang Fritz. 1971. *Kritik der Warenästhetik* [Critique of commodity aesthetics]. Frankfurt: Suhrkamp.

Heath, Christian, and Dirk vom Lehn. 2004. "Configuring Reception: (Dis-)Regarding the 'Spectator' in Museums and Galleries." *Theory, Culture & Society* 21(6): 43–65.

Heath, Christian, and Dirk vom Lehn. 2008. "Configuring 'Interactivity': Enhancing Engagement in Science Centres and Museums." *Social Studies of Science* 38(1): 63–91.

Hein, Hilde 2000. *The Museum in Transition: A Philosophical Perspective*. Washington, DC: Smithsonian Institution.

Henning, Michelle. 2006. *Museums, Media and Cultural Theory*. Maidenhead, UK: Open University Press.

Hirschauer, Stefan. 2006. "Animated Corpses: Communicating with Post Mortals in an Anatomical Exhibition." *Body & Society* 12(4): 25–52.

Holbrook Morris B., and Elizabeth C. Hirschman. 1982. "The Experiential Aspects of Consumption: Consumer Fantasies, Feelings, and Fun." *Journal of Consumer Research* 9(2): 132–140.

Hooper-Greenhill, Eilean. 1994. *The Educational Role of the Museum*. London: Routledge.

Jafari, Aliakbar, Babak Taheri, and Dirk vom Lehn. 2013. "Cultural Consumption, Interactive Sociality, and the Museum." *Journal of Marketing Management* 29(15–16): 37–41.

Jones, M. A. 1999. "Entertaining Shopping Experiences: An Exploratory Investigation." *Journal of Retailing and Consumer Services* 6(3): 129–139.

Kaplan, Flora. 1994. *Museums and the Making of "Ourselves": The Role of Objects in the National Identity*. London: Leicester University Press.

Klages, Ludwig. 1972. *Vom kosmogonischen Eros* [On the cosmogenic Eros]. Bonn: Bouvier.

Klonk, Charlotte. 2009. *Spaces of Experience: Art Gallery Interiors from 1800 to 2000*. New Haven: Yale University Press.

Knoblauch, Hubert. 1998. "Pragmatische Ästhetik: Inszenierung, Performance und die Kunstfertigkeit alltäglichen kommunikativen Handelns" [Pragmatic aesthetics: Staging, performance and the skills of everyday communicative action]. In *Inszenierungsgesellschaft* [Society of staging], edited by Herbert Willems and Martin Jurga, 305–324. Wiesbaden: Westdeutscher.

Kotler, Philip. 1973. "Atmospherics as a Marketing Tool." *Journal of Retailing* 49(4): 48–64.

Kozinets, Robert V., John F. Sherry, Jr., Diana Storm, Adam Duhachek, Krittinee Nuttavuthisit, and Benét Deberry-Spence. 2004. "Ludic Agency and Retail Spectacle." *Journal of Consumer Research* 31(3): 658–672.

Lanza, Joseph. 2004. *Elevator Music: A Surreal History of Muzak, Easy-Listening, and Other Moodsong*. Ann Arbor: University of Michigan Press.

Lehmann, Hans-Thies. 2006. *Postdramatic Theatre*. London: Routledge.

Michon, Richard, Yu Hong, Donna Smith, and Jean-Charles Chebat. 2007. "The Shopping Experience of Female Fashion Leaders." *International Journal of Retail & Distribution Management* 35(7): 488–501.

Murtola, Anna-Maria. 2010. "Commodification of Utopia: The Lotus Eaters Revisited." *Culture and Organization* 16(1): 37–54.

Pallasmaa, Juhani. 2012. "On Atmosphere: Peripheral Perception and Existential Experience." In *Encounters*, vol. 2, *Architectural Essays*, edited by Peter MacKeith, 237–251. Helsinki: Rakennustieto.

Pine, Joseph, and James Gilmore. 1999. *The Experience Economy: Work Is Theater and Every Business a Stage*. Boston: Harvard Business School.

Rectanus, Mark W. 2002. *Culture Incorporated: Museums, Artists and Corporate Sponsorships*. Minneapolis: University of Minnesota Press.

Saren, Mike, Pauline Maclaran, Christina Goulding, Richard Elliott, Avi Shankar, and Miriam Catterall, eds. 2007. *Critical Marketing: Defining the Field*. Oxford: Butterworth-Heinemann.

Schmitz, Herrmann. 1964. *System der Philosophie* [System of philosophy]. Bonn: Bouvier.

Sherry, John F., Jr. 1998. "The Soul of the Company Store: Nike Town Chicago and the Emplaced Brandscape." In *Serviscapes: The Concept of Place in Contemporary Markets*, 109–146. Chicago: NTC Business Books.

Soto, Pablo. 2002. *Shop Window Design*. Barcelona: Loft.

Staniszewski, Mary A. 1998. *The Power of Display: A History of Exhibition Installations at the Museum of Modern Art*. Cambridge, MA: MIT Press.

Stiftung Jüdisches Museum Berlin. 2013. "The Libeskind Building." Accessed August 12, 2014. http://www.jmberlin.de/main/EN/04-About-The-Museum/01-Architecture/01-libeskind-Building.php.

Stoel, Leslie, Vanessa Wickliffe, and KyuHye Lee. 2004. "Attributes Beliefs and Spending as Antecedents to Shopping Value." *Journal of Business Research* 57(10): 1067–1073.

Thompson, Craig J., and Zeynep Arsel. 2004. "The Starbucks Brandscape and Consumers' (Anti-Corporate) Experiences of Glocalization." *Journal of Consumer Research* 31(3): 631–643.

Trondsen, Norman. 1976. "Social Control in the Art Museum." *Journal of Contemporary Ethnography* 5(1): 105–119.

Turley, Lou W., and Ronald E. Milliman. 2000. "Atmospheric Effects on Shopping Behavior: A Review of the Empirical Evidence." *Journal of Business Research* 49(2): 193–211.

Underhill, Paco. 1999. *Why We Buy: The Science of Shopping*. New York: Simon & Schuster.

Veblen, Thorstein. (1899) 1953. *Theory of the Leisure Class*. New York: New American Library.

Venkatraman, Meera, and Teresa Nelson. 2008. "From Servicescape to Consumptionscape: A Photo-Elicitation Study of Starbucks in the New China." *Journal of International Business Studies* 39(6): 1010–1026.

vom Lehn, Dirk. 2013. "Withdrawing from Exhibits: The Interactional Organisation of Museum Visits." In *Interaction and Mobility: Language and the Body in Motion*, edited by Pentti Haddington, Lorenza Mondada, and Maurice Nevile, 65–90. Berlin: De Gruyter.

vom Lehn, Dirk, and Christian Heath. 2005. "Accounting for New Technology in Museum Exhibitions." *International Journal of Arts Management* 7(6): 11–21.

Waidacher, Friedrich. 1996. *Handbuch der Allgemeinen Museologie* (Handbook of general museology]. Vienna: Böhlau.

Welsch, Wolfgang. 1997. *Undoing Aesthetics*. London: Sage.

Brigitte Biehl-Missal is a professor at BSP Business School Berlin Potsdam, Hochschule für Management, Germany, and a visiting researcher at Essex Business School, University of Essex, UK. Her research interests include the interplay of art, aesthetics, marketing, and organizations, and critical approaches. She holds a doctorate in theater, film, and media studies from the University of Frankfurt, Germany, and has been involved in a number of artistic projects concerned with contemporary economic developments. Her recent work has been published in the Journal of Management Studies, Consumption, Markets & Culture, and the Journal of Macromarketing.

Dirk vom Lehn is a member of the Work, Interaction and Technology Research Centre in the Department of Management at King's College London. His research is primarily concerned with video-based studies of interaction in museums and galleries, as well as with optometric practices and with street markets. His most recent publication is a book on Harold Garfinkel (Left Coast, 2014).

12 MUSEUMS, INTERACTIVITY, AND THE TASKS OF "EXHIBITION ANTHROPOLOGY"

Erkki Huhtamo

On a recent visit to Manchester's Museum of Science and Industry (MOSI), I came – once again – to think about the challenges museums are facing these days. I had decided to spend the rainy day in this excellent institution improving my under-standing of the origins of the industrial revolutions. In spite of the profuse offer-ings, I found myself driven to exasperation by hordes of hyperactive schoolchildren constantly running around. Having young people visit the museum (remarkably, there is no entrance fee) is basically a wonderful thing. The staff and the designers have done their best to offer multifaceted "object lessons." There are many won-derful historical objects in display cases with detailed captions; however, they seem to be outnumbered by exhibits that solicit active intervention. Interactive inter-faces abound. Besides, there were entertaining experiences hosted by human guides in period costumes. The overall scene was lively, with a lot of laughter and astonishment, and many spontaneous comments addressed to the presenters from the audience. The youngsters were having a good time within a kind of magic circle, far away from the relentless rain soaking the everyday reality just outside.

My exasperation was caused not so much by the noise and hassle as by my observations of the visitors' behavior. That the traditional exhibits – no matter how thoughtfully designed – received little more than fleeting glances did not surprise me; I knew it from other museums where they also have to compete with interactive exhibits. I was mainly concerned about the latter. *Any* exhibit with something to click, pull, or rotate drew hands like a magnet, but normally the experience both started and ended there. It was as if there had been nothing at all

The International Handbooks of Museum Studies: Museum Media, First Edition.
Edited by Michelle Henning.
© 2015 John Wiley & Sons Ltd. Published 2020 by John Wiley & Sons Ltd.

to be gained beyond the momentary acts of punching and tapping, pushing and pulling. The user interface had become The Thing, instead of serving as a gateway to more cerebral pleasures and discoveries (as I believe it is supposed to do). Beyond moments of rather physical fun, the interactive exhibits seemed to divulge little once their sensorimotor interest had become exhausted. It did not take long, as the visitors demonstrated by their restless feet. I found myself wondering what legacy the visit left in the young people's minds. Did they still remember MOSI the day after? Did they learn anything? Did they plan to come back one day?

I found a refuge in the basement of the Great Western Warehouse building, where the Collections Centre is located. In its silence I encountered another interactive experience of sorts – a long line of mechanically moved, thematically arranged archival cabinets with drawers that could be pulled open at will. Behind their protective glass panels one could observe many curious objects at close range. In a way, the cabinet offered an intermediate solution between passive and active displays, but it was not for the general public. For help and information one could turn to an archivist who seemed to have plenty of free time. I quickly secured a private tour of the reserves. In marked contrast to the commotion raging on the floors just above my head, everything was peaceful and quiet at the Collections Centre; only a handful of people came and went during my entire visit, obviously with a purpose. None of them were children or adolescents. Although linked thematically with the exhibition floors, and in some cases by identical objects, the Collections Centre was a world apart. In fact, there seemed to exist two separate worlds in the same building.

I have made similar observations at other institutions – particularly those dedicated to science and technology – around the world. As a trained cultural historian, I have opened many museum doors expecting to see "auratic" objects I know the museum has in its collection; over and over again I have been disappointed. The objects have either been taken into storage or are displayed in limited numbers. The most prominent places have been reserved for educational interactive exhibits. The situation bothers me in a rather complicated way because the prospects of interactive technology have been one of my main research topics over the past quarter century. I have followed the emergence of the "culture of interactivity" and written about its manifestations (Huhtamo 1999; 2005; 2006; 2011; 2012). Besides, I have closely observed utopian discourses extolling its revolutionary potential. Interactivity has been claimed to announce a transition into a world where the initiative belongs to individuals rather than to faceless corporations or bureaucracies. It has been associated with decentralization, customization, self-service, and reorganized time management. It is the user of interactive media who decides what to do and when; the enforced "flows" of working life and television-saturated leisure alike will be replaced by "negotiated" experiences.

Interactivity has seeped into the fabric of contemporary life. One only needs to think of smartphones, their countless "apps," and their omnipresence in social spaces from city streets to private bedrooms. As tokens of always-on lifestyles, they have become so ubiquitous that they are not necessarily designated as interactive any longer – if interactivity is everything, it may just as well go unmentioned (and perhaps unnoticed). The educational sector has not been unaffected by these developments. In fact, its affair with interactivity goes further back than the adoption of the word into common parlance. The nineteenth-century ideology of object lessons emphasized not just the replacement of the textual with the visual, but also the pedagogical benefits of actual objects (Bak 2012). Tactile experiences were recommended in a manner reminiscent of hands-on laboratory experiments. In the 1950s and 1960s (but anticipated earlier), "teaching machines" were developed by behaviorist psychologists and others for the purpose of personalizing the learning experience and making it fun (Skinner 1968; Benjamin 1988). Later developments, from personal computers to iPads in classrooms, stem from such experiments, although they are also part and parcel of the infiltration of interactivity into ever newer fields, including museum displays and contemporary art.

Whether or not the culture of interactivity has matured, it is certainly controversial. Cultural critics have begun dissecting the utopian rhetoric that promotes it as a panacea, questioning the claims made about its roles and benefits (Lanier 2010; Crary 2013). It is becoming clear that an interactive relationship between a human, an artifact, and (often but not always) other humans does not guarantee the quality of the experience. The pros and cons of interactive systems must be assessed against the social, ideological, and economic contexts within which they are utilized. Like any cultural products, they are put to divergent uses. Utopian promises may disguise agendas that counteract the stated goals. As a case in point, companies like Google and Facebook offer useful interactive services, but they also track users' actions in the interest of financial gain and behavioral regulation.

What roles does interactivity play within the museum context? How do the museum's own expectations match those of the visitors? There are no fit-all answers to such questions. Sociologists may well be able to provide some clarity by means of questionnaires, but that is not the purpose of this chapter. Rather than giving any conclusive answers, the goal is to identify meaningful questions, partly by theoretical speculation, partly by personal observations at museums and exhibitions. I will not focus solely on interactive exhibits, but also on the repercussions of interactive applications manifested by the behaviors of museum-goers. The underlying assumption is that, as a widely disseminated cultural technique, interactivity becomes internalized by its users to varying degrees. Through constant involvement, it becomes part of identity formation. It may even turn into an automatism we practice involuntarily. The "naturalization" and "automation" of interactivity may empower the subject, but they can also lead to confusions – for all social actions cannot be translated into interactive operations. There are areas where limited or prohibited interactivity still reigns. The museum institution is one of them.

I call my approach "exhibition anthropology." It is a deliberately constructed mindset with (de)constructive intentions, influenced by the proxemics of Edward

T. Hall ([1959] 1990), the "thick description" endorsed by the cultural anthropologist Clifford Geertz (1973), and the cultural semiotics of Roland Barthes ([1957] 1972), Umberto Eco (1986), and Dean MacCannell (1976). Exhibition anthropology pays attention to issues that may at first seem trivial and innocuous, ones that escape attention within the flux of everyday life. It argues that "spontaneous" or "improvised" acts by museum visitors may be only partly such. Objects, ideas, and attitudes are transported to the museum from the outside, in pockets as well as in minds.

Exhibition anthropology purports to figure out how the momentary relationships between visitors and the exhibits manifest shared – and sometimes discrepant – principles and habits. For this purpose the semiotic distinction between encoding and decoding suggested by the cultural studies scholar Stuart Hall (1980) is useful. It emphasizes the disparities between the intentions and interpretations by different cultural agents, both individual and institutional. Hall proposed a taxonomy of possible modes of encoding, but it has to be emphasized that different individuals can never interpret what they see, hear, and try out in absolutely identical ways, because the combinations of cultural codes they have internalized through their life processes are unique. Generalizations in terms of social groups are needed, but even in the case of closely knit subcultures whose members share many values and attitudes, one has to deal with approximations. I will therefore refrain from proposing sociological models superimposed on the practices of museum-going. I will merely engage in acts of observation, treating my findings symptomatically in order to disclose processes of (dis)signification taking place within contemporary media-saturated environments.

Freedom, control, and confusion in the art museum

A museum is a highly regulated environment.[1] The creation of an atmosphere that seems open and welcoming – a free zone for reflection and relaxation – is essential. When the Kiasma Museum of Contemporary Art opened in Helsinki in the late 1990s, it promoted itself as the citizens' "living room." An infrastructure that monitors the visitors, guiding them along desired routes and making sure they will not get hurt or engage themselves in unwanted acts, is equally important. The trick is to achieve a balance between these two aspects, giving the visitors a sense of freedom, but also reminding them of the limits of what is allowed. The museum is a panopticon of sorts, but overly emphasizing its nature as a surveillance machine would distress and alienate the visitors.

I thought about such issues in the summer of 2006 at Oslo's Astrup Fearnley Museum of Modern Art in its Tom Sachs exhibition. At the entrance I was greeted by a sign: "PLEASE HELP US TAKE CARE OF THE ARTWORKS. Several of the art works [sic] should not be touched. When in doubt, ask a museum-host. Parents are encouraged to look after their children." The choice of words caught my attention. By claiming that "several" of the artworks "should not be touched" the notice seemed to indicate that *some* of them were excluded from the rule. But which ones? This was far from obvious. Sachs often uses inexpensive material – found or even stolen junk – that does not look like it would suffer from a little bit of tapping. His works contain potentially tactile elements such as handles, switches, triggers, and knobs. Although these features imply everyday interactions with objects, the works themselves are not interactive. Even if the *Chanel Guillotine* (1998), the electric chair of *(What Would James Brown Do?)* (1999), and the cabinet-mounted handguns of *London Calling* (2003) look as if they might work (and, according to the artist, they do), they are not meant to be "fingered." *Nutsy's 1:1 McDonald's* (2002) is a functional hamburger stand that has been used to make junk food in performances, but in Oslo it was shown as a sculptural object, referring to its functionality only indexically.

Where were the touchable works? This could have referred to Sachs's life-size reconstructions of Le Corbusier furniture, but nobody dared to sit on them. Perhaps it simply meant the bench opposite a video monitor displaying Sachs's (meta-)architectural projects? I read the description first and understood the bench as part of the work, so I decided to stand next to it while watching the video, sheepishly missing an opportunity to test the message of the sign. I did not ask a "museum-host" either, although I was "in doubt." Most likely the touchable works were mere phantoms, brought to life by bad "Norwenglish." Still, the sign was symptomatic of issues affecting museum-going today. I don't mean acts by mad-men slashing Van Goghs or attention-hungry artists attacking Duchamps and Rothkos.[2] There is uncertainty about what one should or should not do. The confusions have been partly caused by cultural and institutional developments, such as interactivity, and partly by tendencies within the contemporary arts themselves.

Although the so-called serious art audience supposedly knows how to behave, for many the art museum seems to have become just another weekend amusement. Art museums compete with other family-oriented pastime activities, such as visits to science centers, theme parks, and entertainment centers, where interacting with the exhibits is not only tolerated, but often encouraged. Tactile activity is reinforced by the reflex-like habit of constantly fingering ATMs, laptops, game controllers, and, last but not least, smartphones. Touching things that don't belong to you was in earlier times an exception to a rule that generally forbade it, a sanctioned privilege only granted occasionally and case by case. As a result of the fingering habit, it may gradually be turning into a default behavioral mode, at least when it comes to the attitudes of the generations that have grown up under the spell of interactivity from their earliest childhood. The viral spreading of graffiti all over the world may be part of this phenomenon, testifying to a widespread disregard for the untouchability of private and public property, and to a disappearing sense of distinction between them. There is a real need for an approach that investigates how the impact of such habits affects behaviors in highly coded and regulated places like museums.

Although many museums and galleries still see themselves as touch-free zones, separating themselves from places where tactile approaches are tolerated and even encouraged, habits are seeping in from the outside, as was demonstrated by Game On, a video game exhibition shown at London's Barbican Gallery (Barbican Centre) and elsewhere in 2002–2003 (Lightfoot 2002). The majority of the exhibits consisted of functioning commercial games and game machines. There were a few game-inspired interactive artworks, such as Thomson & Craighead's *Triggerhappy* (1999) but, according to my observations, these were nearly ignored. Compared with the games, they may have seemed dull and alien for the overwhelmingly young audience. Perhaps they had been included to convince skeptics that games *do* inspire artists and therefore have a place in the gallery.

Exhibitions like *Game On* may be interpreted as efforts to "keep abreast of the times" – to make the museum "cool" for potential visitors who might otherwise ignore it. In an era of shrinking public support it would be naive to belittle the economic motives behind such programming decisions. One may assume that financial reasons have played a role in prompting prestigious institutions like the Franklin Institute in Philadelphia to keep much of their historical collections in storage, and to replace them with interactive hands-on exhibits. Family-oriented entertainment is offered in the guise of light enlightenment, as I witnessed some time ago. One may question the educational benefits of having screaming children jump rhythmically in front of a blue screen, seeing themselves transported into a fantasy landscape (not unlike those they know from games or animation films). Without guidance from parents, teachers, or museum staff, such experiences are likely to remain superfluous, blurring – rather than accentuating – the line between museums, game centers, playgrounds, and homes, where interactive "exercises" are offered. I consider this a disservice – a form of institutional prostitution. No matter how difficult it may be, the museums should find better ways of attracting visitors.

An interesting example of the challenges museums are facing as they try to refresh their profiles and attract new audiences was *Art in the Streets*, an extensive exhibition organized by the Museum of Contemporary Art (MOCA, Los Angeles) in its Geffen Contemporary annex in 2011. It was the first major effort by its new director Jeffrey Deitch, a commercial gallerist from New York, who was ostensibly brought in to stabilize the financially troubled institution.[3] Deitch had a reputation of supporting street arts, so his mega exhibition was no surprise. However, even before it opened it raised public controversy, not only because of its subject matter, but also because Deitch decided to have a mural he had commissioned from a well-known Italian street artist named Blu for the museum's back wall painted over. It depicted a field of coffins covered with huge one-dollar bills, which made it politically volatile in the less than permissive cultural climate of the contemporary United States.

Deitch tried to justify his decision by referring to the proximity of a veterans hospital and a memorial to Japanese American soldiers, but the true reasons must have been more complex (Mac Donald 2011). His turnaround highlighted a cluster of issues, from the risks of depending on private sponsors and their values (in 2008 MOCA was saved from bankruptcy by the billionaire board member Eli Broad) to pressures for political correctness, divisions concerning property rights, and the troubled relationships between public and private space, and high and popular culture. In the heated debate that erupted, the exhibition was accused of glorifying illegal activities by legitimizing graffiti writers and taggers as artists. It was also pointed out that a contradiction existed between the exhibition's topic and MOCA's own zero tolerance policy against graffiti in its own premises, both indoors and outdoors. An increase in illegal tagging in the museum's neighborhood was noted by the police, which put MOCA in an awkward position (Blankstein 2011). (Not everyone agreed there was an increase of such activities. The museum promised a clean-up.) Deitch's explanation, according to which the exhibition "put out an inspirational message: If you harness your talent you can be in a museum someday," did not convince everyone (Blankstein 2011). The essentially anarchic nature of untamed street art was emphasized by its more hard-core proponents.

What happened inside the exhibition was unexpectedly tame. During my four visits I saw long lines at the entrance and unusually broad demographics, reflecting Deitch's stated wish to attract inner city youth with little experience of museum-going. In spite of the topic and all the buzz it created, the curatorial policy and exhibition design were largely conventional, emphasizing an orderly historical presentation of the topic. Although large-scale installations made of urban junk, and some technology-based work (such as animatronic figures) were included, they did not radically deviate from what has been seen within contemporary art exhibitions. I saw no signs of transgressive behavior, but I did witness much picture-taking – it was allowed – of visitors posing in front of their favorite exhibits (predictably, Banksy was one of them) and no doubt posting the results online.

The exhibition attracted altogether 201,352 visitors, making it one of MOCA's three top successes of all time, according to the *Los Angeles Times* (August 10, 2011). I saw many satisfied and even enthusiastic – literally glowing – faces, but almost no expressions of disgust, hubris, or indifference, even from MOCA's customary middle-aged visitors. There was a surprising amount of concentration and silence in the exhibition halls, and many visitors seemed to stay for a long period. Particularly among the younger visitors, the exhibition seemed to strike a chord in a manner I have rarely witnessed in an art exhibition. I found myself wondering whether the orderly atmosphere was simply the result of an awareness of the museum's regulatory practices. More likely, a bridge between dire everyday realities and their museal "transfiguration" was created. It is possible that for some visitors, who may have been involved in graffiti writing themselves (it is nearly omnipresent in LA), saw its transformation into an accepted and even celebrated phenomenon as something solemn, even sublime. If so, Deitch may be said to have achieved his goal, although his populist stance proved untenable among the art elite of the city. In July 2013 he announced his resignation.[4]

To touch or not to touch?

Exhibitions of interactive art are rare, but interactive pieces are often shown together with "untouchable" works.[5] The situation provides opportunities for activating the visitor, but the result may be the opposite: alienation, confusion, and frustration. Visitors are in doubt about what they are allowed to do. The stressful situation is not resolved by the notices art museums now routinely display on their walls. These notices not only warn the visitors about potentially insulting or transgressive subject matter; they also provide detailed explanations about how to interpret or operate the works, and warnings against unwanted behavior. Tactile and interactive works could lead to more flexible, playful, and democratic experiences, but this does not happen automatically. The institutions are nervous, display pre-emptive rules and instructions, and enhance security with CCTV cameras, beeping signals, and omnipresent guards (a tendency that was scrutinized by perceptive artists like Julia Scher (2002) years ago). No longer does the museum world believe in the existence of codes and modes of behavior that would be automatically shared by the visitors.[6]

An exhibition called *Ecstasy: In and About Altered States*, shown at MOCA in 2005–2006, made me reflect on such issues (Mark 2005). I ended up visiting it four times, taking notes and snapshots, observing visitors, trying out limits, and talking to the guards. While the exhibition contained no examples of interactive media art, my observations provided evidence about the tensions between the desire to touch and the efforts to control or contain it. Issues like temptation, resistance, and capitulation were at the core of the exhibition itself, which had "altered states" (including drug-induced ones) as its theme. While they were deliberately dealt with by the artists and the curators, they were also inadvertently manifested by the exhibition design and MOCA's institutional policies. Even occasional messages, such as the following note taped next to a 16 mm EIKI film projector used to show Paul Sietsema's *Untitled (Beautiful Place)* (1998) could raise them: "This is not an Interactive Piece. Please do not play with the Projector." Because the film was shown only at certain times and there was no guard permanently standing in the room, the temptation to switch on the projector or just to play with its knobs ("exotic" remains from another technological era) may have been irresistible for some visitors – or could they really have expected the work to be interactive?

At the doorway leading to Olafur Eliasson's installation *Your Strange Certainty Still Kept* (1996) I noticed the following warning: "Viewers with light sensitivities please be advised: the artwork uses strobe lights." Entering the darkened space, I discovered a "curtain" of water dripping from the ceiling. It was illuminated by strobe lights, which made the water drops "dance" in changing formations.[7] The installation was close to the narrow entrance, and there was no barrier preventing the visitors from standing right next to it; it was even possible to walk around it to the other side. Therefore I found it quite natural to stretch out my hand and touch the water, as I saw others doing. Touching the water caused interesting changes in the light patterns. I assumed this to be intentional, and there was no signboard forbidding it. But when I started playing with the water drops, a guard immediately interfered, informing me that it was "forbidden to touch the water." When I asked him for an explanation, he bluntly stated that he had "received instructions." I began suspecting that this unexpected "tactiloclasm" had nothing to do with Eliasson's intentions, but much to do with poor exhibition design. The museum may have simply been concerned about the floor getting wet and somebody slipping on it. Indeed, in front of the *other* entrance to the installation room I discovered a yellow plastic "Cuidado piso mojado / Caution wet floor" sign, familiar from public restrooms; I later noticed there was one at the other entrance as well, leaning folded against the wall.

Pierre Huyghe's *L'expedition scintillante, Acte 2 (Light Show)* (2002) had no operating instructions either. It was a kind of *son et lumière* box in a darkened room, with pillows around it. Most visitors sat silently, watching smoke rise from the bottom part of the box, accompanied by music and illuminated by switching colored lights hanging from a frame above the construction. One teenage girl, however, was amusing herself by blowing at the smoke during her entire visit, delighted with her fun which no one else (including her girlfriends) was joining in. She sat very close, almost bent inside the box, constantly blowing at different intensities. The open sides of Huyghe's work permit this type of interaction, but whether it was something the artist had anticipated or just an accidental by-product inspired by design and a moment's fancy is difficult to judge. The behavior may have revealed the girl's nervousness and uneasiness with the codes of the situation, her obsession with interactivity, or her need for attention. The girl's intervention may have testified to her inability or refusal to immerse herself in the work's subtle combinations of smoke, light, and music. She certainly destroyed its (meta?)meditative quality. There were no guards in the room to enforce "correct" behavior.

Mounted on a wall just outside Huyghe's installation was Fred Tomacelli's *Echo, Wow and Flutter* (2000). At first it seems flat, but at a closer look one notices layers of cut-out images and small objects (including pills) immersed inside a thick layer of transparent resin. Although the surface is plain, the work creates an extraordinary impression of three dimensionality. There was a black line on the floor in front of the work, but it was generally ignored. Almost everyone I saw reached out their hand to touch the work. A guard stood next to it, interfering again and again. An elderly lady, who looked like a regular museum-goer, went to him to ask for permission to touch, which was expressly denied. The guard told me that he felt extremely exhausted, adding that he could not understand the constant urge to touch. Obviously he had not grasped the artist's cunning gesture. Apparently the work, which evoked drug addiction, is meant to create an irresistible temptation, which is denied, because it evokes a painting and paintings belong to the class of untouchable objects.

Works like *Echo, Wow and Flutter* are the guards' nightmares. But keeping the viewers behind a metal bar would not work – they would miss the opportunity to observe the work's delicate details, and indeed its *raison d'être*. Unintentionally, the situation brings to mind the spectators, whom I have seen trying to grasp virtual objects "sticking out" from the canvas while watching a 3D movie. There is a difference, however. In a specialty cinema or theme park such a behavioral gesture is encouraged as part of the thrill and also of the total experience. The visitors know the codes from previous experiences, stories, or pictures they have seen, and want to activate them because others have done so before them. How many of them do so as a form of ritualistic enactment, as an involuntary reflex, or because they believe it possible to actually touch something is difficult to judge. A 3D picture is a virtual image. It has no "surface," just an illusion produced by light and optics. "Touching" a stereoscopic image is like touching smoke, but the experience is – or at least should be – very different from playing with Pierre Huyghe's installation in an art museum.

The most intriguing case was Carsten Höller's *Upside-Down Mushroom Room* (2000). Its presentation evoked the ways theme park attractions are organized to regulate visitor traffic and to create expectations through delays and promises (kinds of rites of passage), while keeping the audience under surveillance. The visitors had to queue in line, while a guard stood by talking to a walkie-talkie. Just a few people were allowed to enter a long dark tunnel at a time, and only after reading a notice: "Please be advised: low hanging sculpture in motion. Please do not touch." They reached a brightly lit room full of huge red fly agaric mushrooms hanging from the ceiling, upside down and in slow rotation. It took an effort to navigate through the room without touching their deceptively real-looking surfaces: one was traversing a space of hallucinations and secret temptations.[8] Real life interfered in the form of another guard, who had been positioned inside the installation. This was the other end of the walkie-talkie line. The loud crackling communications between the guards echoed in the space, making concentration difficult. The museum became a super-panopticon that took over the visitors' fantasies about immersion in a dreamlike space.

Museums and the challenge of the smartphone

The uncertainties about touching or not touching exhibits arise from institutional and ideological transformations (Huhtamo 2006). The academic art of the nineteenth century was considered untouchable. The aesthetic experience was associated with distance. The taboo of physical contact was translated into theories about haptic gaze, a way of looking that was said to incorporate features from physical touch. As Constance Classen (2005) has explained, at early private collections and cabinets of curiosities touching artifacts was often not only allowed, but encouraged. Visitors took it as self-evident and were offended if the right to touch the objects was denied. Not just three-dimensional objects like statues, but even paintings, were touched as a complement to the act of looking. While access to early museums was restricted to privileged visitors who were assumed to know the proper codes of behavior, the situation changed with the emergence of the age of the masses and new democratic ideals in education. Artworks were enclosed in display cases or put behind protective sheets of glass and kept under the inspecting eyes of museum guards, because the new audiences could not be trusted to master the codes of behavior. Even the *potential* for touch was eliminated. The nineteenth-century museum, where nontactility reigned supreme, was therefore not a given, but a cultural and ideological construct.

Early twentieth-century avant-garde art began calling for the destruction of the barrier separating art from life. Classic avant-garde works, such as Duchamp's *Bicycle Wheel* (1913), Man Ray's *Object to Be Destroyed* (1923–1932), and Meret Oppenheim's *Breakfast in Fur/Fur Teacup* (1936), implied the act of touching, while true tactile art was called for by the Futurists and also anticipated by Dadaist and Surrealist actions, as well as by the experimental exhibition designs of Frederick Kiesler and others (Huhtamo 2006).[9] The happenings of the 1960s, actions like Valie Export's *Tapp und Tast Kino* (1968) and *Action Pants: Genital Panic* (1969), as well as the works of Marina Abramovic, Orlan, and others were signposts along the route toward tactile relationships between the visitor and the work, and in some cases also with artist performers. The most obvious example is interactive media art, where the visitor's active interventions are required to activate the work (Huhtamo 1995; 2004). Exhibition visitors are invited to push buttons, type at the keyboard, swipe screens, or swing their bodies in front of video cameras connected to responsive computer systems.

The museum institution emerged in the nineteenth century as a response to the challenge of educating the masses. It was also a disciplinary measure: the new urban masses had to be tamed so that they would not revolt and overturn the existing social order (Hooper-Greenhill 1989; Bennett 1995). In this sense the museum was not entirely different from such phenomena as spectator sports, the circus, or the cinema. Audiences were positioned as spectators rather than as "actors." They observed trained performers or spectacles, and paid for it. They may have shown their emotions, but were conceived as passive nonagents. The visitors had some freedom to negotiate the experience – to decide their routes, rhythms, and what to watch – albeit within premeditated controlled environments. Although the museum offered exhibits with cultural value and elevating potential, it was part of the great and invisible bourgeois panopticon put in place during the nineteenth century – a disciplinary institution.[10] The new museums did not tolerate tactility or deviant behavior. Paintings were displayed in massive frames that segregated them from surrounding reality and objects sealed behind protective glass. Lightly touching a statue, perhaps as an involuntary reminiscence of popular religious practices, was easier, but not encouraged either.

Today's museums encounter the challenge of the masses as well, but a different one. The crowds that spill out from tourist buses at museum entrances have been educated in the "open universities" of global tourism, mass immigration, and integrated media culture. Video games, laptop computers, iPads, and smart-phones have familiarized – and perhaps infected – millions with interactive media. The borderline between the public and the private has been blurred, and so have distinctions between behavioral modes. To make things more complicated, today's museum audiences are heterogeneous and multicultural. The world may superficially resemble Marshall McLuhan's global village, but behavioral differences, rooted in powerful and often incompatible cultural traditions, are not easily set aside (McLuhan [1962] 1990).[11] The ensuing tensions can be creative, but also raise anxieties.

It could be argued that museums simply cannot cope without all the instructions, warnings, and apologies any longer. Too much is at stake economically; being sued by an injured or insulted visitor is a museum's nightmare; small scandals and incidents, even pretended ones, are easily magnified by social media, damaging the institution's reputation. This is a reflection of a troubled and divided global society. Technological development has brought with it new contradictions, including ones related to smartphones. In less than a decade the smartphone has become a near global phenomenon that is often accused of having created manias, epidemics, and dependencies. This has to do with its versatility, its ease of use, and its always-on nature. It is very easy to switch from one function to another in an instant. The temptation to keep checking incoming text messages and sending one's own even while walking and driving seems difficult to resist for many. Built-in cameras have improved rapidly, and uploading digital picture files on Facebook or Tumblr can be done in a matter of seconds. It could be claimed that snapshot photography has never been practiced as intensively and extensively as today. Uploadable Instagram videos have followed and transformed the current snapshot craze.

Smartphones cause problems, but also provide opportunities. The ongoing smartphone craze is often claimed to have shortened attention spans, which had already been challenged by other devices in the thickening multimedia environment. Efforts have been made to counter this trend in a seemingly paradoxical way by encouraging smartphone use in the museum environment rather than forbidding it.[12] Museum audio guides have been used for years. They normally take the form of dedicated devices lent to the visitor for the duration of the visit. These are now often replaced by uploadable smartphone apps. Encouraging visitors to use their own device exploits their expertise and emotional attachment to it (it can also save costs for the museum). The museum experience can be enhanced by distributing "smart" QR (Quick Response) codes or radio frequency identification (RFID) triggers in the halls. When these are sensed by the smartphone or snapped with its camera, they offer information, including videos and virtual "augmented reality" objects that seem to float in the surrounding exhibition space.

In 2010 the Museum of London released an app called Streetmuseum, which broadened the museum experience into the public city space.[13] When visiting certain hotspots around the city, the user is able to superimpose photographs from the museum's collection on the actual site. Gamification is a recent design trend meant to harness the smartphone user's existing habits and preferences in the viewing of art.[14] An example is Tate Modern's Tate Trumps, an iPhone and iPad touch application based on the card game Top Trumps.[15] Users are encouraged to roam the galleries snapping pictures of artworks according to three criteria: the "battle mode," the "mood mode," and the "collector mode." In the first one, for example, the player is instructed to ask, "If this artwork came to life, how good would it be in a fight?"[16] After the gallery round, the visitor got together with friends who had accomplished the same tasks to play an endgame by comparing the choices and finding out the winner. The game may be entertaining and increase the recognition of artworks, but it is also a populist attempt to court people for whom the art museum has little significance. One suspects that the artworks are easily reduced to mere surfaces that are no different in kind from the billions of digital images pouring out from social media sites, or invoked by a Google image search.

The temptation to snap photographs in an environment that has traditionally limited or forbidden it is a difficult issue to resolve. It is notoriously hard to control what users actually do with their smartphones (as airlines know). The American artist Cory Arcangel commented on this in a work titled 777, which was positioned at the entrance to his one-man show at the Whitney Museum in New York (2011). It was a wall-mounted announcement that temporarily reversed the museum's strict photographic policy by allowing anyone to snap photos at will and encouraging them to post the results on the Internet. With the visitors' collaboration, the exhibition spread outside the museum's walls. Some museums seem to have loosened their policies, no doubt hoping that snapshots uploaded on social media sites will provide them with free publicity and "followers." Many museums are now posting stickers next to the artworks, indicating which ones may be photographed and which ones not. My observations indicate that such measures often have little effect, because many smartphone users have come to believe that they have the right to snap photos of anything and anywhere and to post them online. The problem is made more serious by the improving quality of smartphone cameras, which threatens copyright regulations. Photo snapping in the gallery also seems to encourage the tendency to look at and to frame artworks through the device instead of contemplating them directly with one's eyes.

The tasks of exhibition anthropology

In this chapter I have reflected on various observations I have made at museums and exhibitions over the past several years with a certain purpose in mind: namely, to make a plea for an approach I would like to call exhibition anthropology. In conclusion, I would like to offer preliminary remarks about what it could and perhaps should be, summarizing some of its tasks. It should have become clear by now that such an endeavor can never focus on any single issue pertaining to the museum experience, such as the nature and typology of exhibits, exhibition design, the constitution of the audience, or the museum's institutional organization; what is at stake is the complex and constantly changing interplay of all these (and other) aspects. Exhibition anthropology would investigate how such factors are organized in relation to each other, how they affect each other and give rise to actions, meanings, and interpretations in concrete circumstances.

The approach should not be conceived of as purely empirical, focused on case-by-case analyses. My basic idea is to treat the museum as a kind of experience apparatus – a combination of material features, social roles, and institutional practices and policies that provide a framework for visitors' experiences. Understood as an apparatus, the museum is a system of anticipations and regulations visitors are supposed to follow. One of its functions is to analyze potential deviations from its norms (including transgressive actions). The approach has been influenced by theories of the cinematic apparatus that were widely discussed in the 1970s and 1980s, as well as by Michel Foucault's "archaeology of knowledge," a theoretical stance that excavated the discursive constitution of disciplinary institutions such as the school and the prison. As other museum scholars have already suggested, the museum can be also analyzed as an institutionally and commercially determined and discursively maintained disciplinary system (Hooper-Greenhill 1989; Bennett 1995).

The cinematic apparatus is a kind of experience machine, partly technological, partly metapsychological (de Lauretis and Heath 1980). The standard example is the movie theater. It has many constitutive elements: the external facade and the entrance, with posters, lights, and other signs; the ticket booth; the lobby with its sales counters; and the auditorium where the main part of the experience takes place. The lights are dimmed, the curtains opened, and the beam of the projector shot to the screen through the darkness. The spectators are then persuaded – by means of "film language" – to identify with simulated worlds on the screen, made more mentally involving by a soundscape. The cinematic apparatus is an abstraction, a model to describe theoretically what happens in a movie theater. Theorists nowadays admit that it provides only the basis, not the full description, of the cinematic experience. The actual spectators negotiate their own experiences in ways that depend not only on the apparatus, but also on their personal life histories and ideological leanings (Cartwright and Sturken 2001). According to many apparatus theorists, spectators do not totally lose awareness of the reality around them. The presence of fellow spectators, the darkness, the size and shape of the screen, and even the temperature of the auditorium contribute to the total experience, which varies from spectator to spectator. The cinematic apparatus is a site where encoded meanings are actively decoded, as Stuart Hall (1980) famously explained.

The museum naturally differs radically from the movie theater when it comes to its elements, configurations, and goals (some museums, of course, contain auditoriums where films are shown). Still, it could be suggested that the museum experience can be analyzed in a related way by paying attention to the tension between the givens of the situation and the visitors' share in the constitution of the experience. Taking this into account, one goal of exhibition anthropology would be to match the constitutive elements of the museum apparatus with the ways in which it is activated – utilized, tested, and perhaps contested – by actual museum visitors. As I have tried to demonstrate with my examples, the encounters are ideologically loaded and involve sets of codes to different degrees in each museum-goer. As media culture infiltrates both museums themselves and visitors' habits and minds, the encounters become increasingly complex. There is an urgent need for analytic tools to help us come to terms with issues like smartphone use at museums, both as policies are implemented by institutions and as they are tested by the practices of actual mobile phone users.

One of the tasks of exhibition anthropology is to note down patterns of use, and also to reflect on their wider theoretical and cultural underpinnings. To achieve this, exhibition anthropology can learn much from work that has been done on areas like proxemics, which was established by Edward T. Hall ([1959] 1990; [1966] 1990; 1968) and others half a century ago. Proxemics is still a useful tool for making sense of social and cultural face-to-face (short-range) encounters taking place within physical spaces. However, because many encounters in today's media culture are mediated by devices like smartphones, classic proxemics has to be reassessed; we should ask, for example, what is at stake in a situation where somebody looks at a painting in a museum while listening to a guide, chatting with other visitors and perhaps sending text messages, snapping and uploading photos, and perhaps checking information about the painting from online databases. The phenomenological approach practiced by Sherry Turkle (2011) can be useful as a supplement, because it focuses on encounters between humans and new technology. Because the issues that involve museum visitors are often cross-cultural, cultural anthropology can help. I am thinking in particular about the "media anthropology" practiced by the late Eric Michaels (1994), who studied encounters between Australian Aboriginals and photography, television, and video cameras.

Michaels's work reminds us that, however standardized media technology may have become, its applications and interpretations vary depending on local traditions and behavioral patterns. To understand the subtleties involved in the reactions and communications between cultural agents like museum-goers, we need what another anthropologist, Clifford Geertz (1973), has called "thick description." Geertz famously demonstrated that what is often at stake in communications and exchanges between individuals is expressed by fleeting gestures, barely noticeable facial expressions, or highly oblique linguistic utterances. Hidden and implied rather than overt, they need to be dug out by an observer trained in reading signs with complex connotations. Here cultural semiotics, as practiced by pioneers like Roland Barthes, Umberto Eco, and Dean McCannell can still serve as an auxiliary. In his definition of culture, which I endorse, Geertz emphasized the value of semiotics:

Believing, with Max Weber, that man is an animal suspended in webs of significance he himself has spun, I take culture to be those webs, and the analysis of it to be therefore not an experimental science in search of law but an interpretive one in search of meaning. (Geertz 1973, 5)

Finally, a slightly subversive note: like any anthropologist, exhibition anthropologists should not be afraid of exposing themselves to embarrassment and ridicule. Sometimes it is not enough to observe, passively hidden in the crowd, and hastily scribble down notes in a corner – we have to have the guts to test the situation. I am not saying that we should break any rules, but it may be necessary to stretch them a little to make the museum's invisible regulations and boundaries appear for a moment. I am advocating an attitude I call "tactical transgression." The test can be explained as an "accident," as I have seen others do when they have been unable to resist the temptation to use a camera where it is forbidden. The exhibition anthropologist is also a museum-goer – with an attitude and a mission.

Notes

1   Parts of the following discussion have been previously published online at http://www.neme.org/1375/freedom-control-and-confusion (accessed August 18, 2014).
2   An attack on Marcel Duchamp's ready-made *Fountain* (1917) by the self-defined avant-garde artist Pierre Pinoncelli was explained by the attacker as "a wink at Dadaism," an effort to "pay homage to the Dada spirit." Pinoncelli had attacked the same piece years earlier. His attack represents the most "art history conscious" case of those that come to my mind. The court had no tolerance for Pinoncelli's act and gave him a three-month suspended sentence plus a fine of €214,000 ($262,700). *Fountain* itself was "slightly cracked." Reuters reported the abovementioned information on its website on January 24, 2006. Another example is the graffiti scribbled on a painting by Mark Rothko at London's Tate Modern by Vladimir Umanets in the name of an art movement called Yellowism in October 2012. For background, see Gamboni (2007).
3   It was curated by Deitch himself with street art afficionados Roger Gastman and Aaron Rose as associate curators. See Deitch, Gastman, and Rose (2011).
4   *Los Angeles Times*, July 24, 2013. In addition to objections to his leaning toward popular culture, it was obvious that Deitch had failed in his fundraising efforts. His turbulent stint at MOCA led to the resignations of the museum's respected long-term chief curator Paul Schimmel and of four high-profile artist members of its board. Deitch took with him his project for an exhibition on the influence of disco on art and culture.
5   This section contains elements from an essay first published in *Framework: The Finnish Art Review* 5 (July 2006): 110–113.
6   See also Chapter 16 by Beat Hächler in this volume for discussion of the roles of guards and signage.

7   Similar ideas were explored by Weng-Yin Tsai and other cybernetic artists already in the 1960s. It is not clear if Eliasson's work is a spontaneous rediscovery or deliberate comment on this tradition. Tsai's cybernetic sculptures were often responsive, reacting to sounds made by the users.

8   The experience may feel like entering an enchanted game world, a spatial version of Nintendo's Super Mario world where the visitor is one's own avatar and the goal is to avoid obstacles and get safely through. My thanks to Andrew Hieronymi for suggesting this.

9   There are conflicting stories about whether Man Ray himself destroyed versions of this piece as performative acts (he claimed so). In 1957 a group of protesting Italian students smashed one version. See Mileaf (2004).

10   The idea of the panopticon as an architectural "disciplinary machine" was proposed by Jeremy Bentham in the late eighteenth century. It was famously applied by Michel Foucault. For how it has been applied to exhibition contexts, see Levin, Froehne, and Weibel (2002).

11   McLuhan presented his famous idea in *The Gutenberg Galaxy*. He characterized it as a "simultaneous 'field'" recreated by "electro-magnetic discoveries," where the "human family" lives in a "single constricted space resonant with tribal drums" ([1962] 1990, 36).

12   See Chapters 22 by Nancy Proctor and 25 by Michelle Henning in this volume.

13   http://www.museumoflondon.org.uk/Resources/app/you-are-here-app/noflash/no-flash.html (accessed August 18, 2014).

14   I learned much about this topic from a talk by the journalist Bill Thompson (and from other contributions) at the Digital Creative Conference, organized by Mori Art Museum with the British Council, Tokyo, Japan, March 4, 2011.

15   http://www.tate.org.uk/context-comment/apps/tate-trumps (accessed August 18, 2014).

16   Tate Collectives, Twitter post, February 4, 2013, 5:48 a.m., https://twitter.com/TateCollectives/status/298427923893981185.

References

Bak, Meredith A. 2012. "Democracy and Discipline: Object Lessons and the Stereoscope in American Education 1870–1920." *Early Popular Visual Culture* 10: 147–167.

Barthes, Roland. (1957) 1972. *Mythologies*. New York: Hill & Wang.

Benjamin, Ludy T. 1988. "A History of Teaching Machines." *American Psychologist* 43: 703–712.

Bennett, Tony. 1995. *The Birth of the Museum: History, Theory, Politics*. London: Routledge.

Blankstein, Andrew. 2011. "Tagging Outside an L.A. Street Art Exhibit Fuels Debate." *Los Angeles Times*, April 20.

Cartwright, Lisa, and Marita Sturken. 2001. *Practices of Looking: An Introduction to Visual Culture*. Oxford: Oxford University Press.

Classen, Constance. 2005. "Touch in the Museum." In *The Book of Touch*, edited by Constance Classen, 275–286. Oxford: Berg.

Crary, Jonathan. 2013. *24/7: Late Capitalism and the Ends of Sleep*. London: Verso.

Deitch, Jeffrey, Roger Gastman, and Aaron Rose. 2011. *Art in the Streets*. New York: Skira Rizzoli, with MOCA.

de Lauretis, Teresa, and Stephen Heath, eds. 1980 *The Cinematic Apparatus*. London: Macmillan.

Eco, Umberto. 1986. *Travels in Hyperreality*. San Diego: Harcourt Brace Jovanovich.

Gamboni, Dario. 2007. *The Destruction of Art: Iconoclasm and Vandalism Since the French Revolution*. London: Reaktion.

Geertz, Clifford. 1973. *The Interpretation of Cultures*. New York: HarperCollins.

Hall, Edward T. (1959) 1990. *The Silent Language*. New York: Anchor.

Hall, Edward T. (1966) 1990. *The Hidden Dimension*. New York: Doubleday.

Hall, Edward T. 1968. "Proxemics." *Current Anthropology* 9: 83–108.

Hall, Stuart. 1980. "Encoding/Decoding." In *Culture, Media, Language*, edited by Stuart Hall, Dorothy Hobson, Andrew Lowe, and Paul Willis, 128–138. London: Hutchinson.

Hooper-Greenhill, Eilean. 1989. "The Museum in the Disciplinary Society." In *Museum Studies in Material Culture*, edited by S. M. Pearce, 61–72. Leicester: Leicester University Press.

Huhtamo, Erkki. 1995 "Seeking Deeper Contact: Interactive Art as Metacommentary." *Convergence* 1(2): 81–104.

Huhtamo, Erkki. 1999. "From Cybernation to Interaction: A Contribution to an Archaeology of Interactivity." In *The Digital Dialectic. New Essays on New Media*, edited by Peter Lunenfeld, 96–110. Cambridge, MA: MIT Press.

Huhtamo, Erkki. 2004 "Trouble at the Interface; or, The Identity Crisis of Interactive Art." *Framework: The Finnish Art Review* 2: 38–41.

Huhtamo, Erkki. 2005. "Slots of Fun, Slots of Trouble: Toward an Archaeology of Electronic Gaming." In *Handbook of Computer Games Studies*, edited by Joost Raessens and Jeffrey Goldstein, 1–21. Cambridge, MA: MIT Press.

Huhtamo Erkki. 2006. "Twin-Touch-Test-Redux: Media Archaeological Approach to Art, Interactivity, and Tactility." In *MediaArtHistories*, edited by Oliver Grau, 71–101. Cambridge, MA: MIT Press.

Huhtamo Erkki. 2011. "Pockets of Plenty: An Archaeology of Mobile Media." In *The Mobile Audience: Media Art and Mobile Technologies*, edited by Martin Rieser, 23–38. Amsterdam: Rodopi.

Huhtamo Erkki. 2012. "What's Victoria Got to Do with It? Toward an Archaeology of Domestic Video Gaming." In *Before the Crash: Early Video Game History*, edited by Mark J. P. Wolf, 30–52. Detroit: Wayne State University Press.

Lanier, Jaron. 2010. *You Are Not a Gadget: A Manifesto*. New York: Knopf.

Levin, Thomas Y., Ursula Froehne, and Peter Weibel, eds. 2002. *CTRL Space: Rhetorics of Surveillance from Bentham to Big Brother*. Cambridge, MA: MIT Press; Karlsruhe: ZKM.

Lightfoot, Jo, ed. 2002. *Game On: The History and Culture of Videogames*. London: Laurence King.

MacCannell, Dean. 1976. *The Tourist: A New Theory of the Leisure Class*. New York: Schocken.

Mac Donald, Heather. 2011. "Radical Graffiti Chic." *City Journal* 21(2). Accessed August 21, 2014. http://www.city-journal.org/2011/21_2_vandalism.html.

Mark, Lisa, ed. 2005. *Ecstasy: In and About Altered States,* organized by Paul Schimmel and Lisa Mark. Los Angeles: Museum of Contemporary Art.

McLuhan, Marshall. (1962) 1990. *The Gutenberg Galaxy: The Making of Typographic Man.* Toronto: University of Toronto Press.

Michaels, Eric.1994. *Bad Aboriginal Art: Tradition, Media and Technological Horizons.* Minneapolis: University of Minnesota Press.

Mileaf, Janine. 2004. "Between You and Me: Man Ray's Object to Be Destroyed." *Art Journal* 63(1): 5.

Scher, Julia. 2002. *Tell Me When You're Ready: Works from 1990–1995.* Boston: PMF.

Skinner, B. F. 1968. *The Technology of Teaching.* New York: Appleton-Century-Crofts.

Turkle, Sherry. 2011. *Alone Together: Why We Expect More from Technology and Less from Each Other.* New York: Basic Books.

Erkki Huhtamo is Professor of Media History and Theory at the University of California, Los Angeles, Departments of Design Media Arts and Film, Television, and Digital Media. He holds a PhD in cultural history and is internationally recognized as one of the founders of media archaeology. His most recent book is *Illusions in Motion: Media Archaeology of the Moving Panorama and Related Spectacles* (MIT Press, 2013).

13 KEEPING OBJECTS LIVE

Fiona Candlin

It is often assumed that museum exhibits are inert. Writing on the National Museum of American History website, the education specialist Jenny Wei (2011) comments that "most history museums face the challenge of bringing objects to life." Her strategy involved one of the institution's landmark exhibits being temporarily put back into service. Museum staff, dressed in period costume, fired up the John Bull locomotive and filmed it being driven along a track, subsequently using the video for an education program aimed at schoolchildren.

In this instance, the process of "bringing objects to life" involved hands-on interaction (driving the train and being able to touch it *in situ*) and educational material on the social history of the train's production and use. When the National Museum of Scotland "identified five subjects they wanted to bring to life," they also organized hands-on events and designed interactive digital materials that provided background information for each exhibit.[1] The British Museum took a slightly different tack in its Talking Objects program which has been rerun in other UK museums. Focusing on a Neolithic bone carving known as "swimming reindeer," young people from Westminster Kingsway College worked with curator Jill Cook "to take a closer look at this magical object. As part of this project the young people created a performance to bring the object to life."[2]

This chapter begins by considering why museum exhibits are commonly perceived to be in need of resuscitation. It then develops that analysis to show how the converse situation occurs in small museums in Devon and Cornwall, the southwesterly counties of England. In contrast to exhibits in most mainstream museums, those at the Museum of Witchcraft, the Valiant Soldier community museum, and the Dartmoor Prison Museum are already felt to be fully functioning and, to some extent, potent or dangerous. Notably, the three venues also share

The International Handbooks of Museum Studies: Museum Media, First Edition.
Edited by Michelle Henning.
© 2015 John Wiley & Sons Ltd. Published 2020 by John Wiley & Sons Ltd.

other characteristics insofar as they have few or no paid members of staff and limited opportunities for gaining state funding. Operating largely independently of the public sector, these organizations have no need to adopt official priorities and, in consequence, their modes of practice differ somewhat from those encountered in major institutions. Focusing on these museums therefore raises the possibility that the "death" of objects is not a necessary condition but that their demise depends on the specific character and circumstances of display.

"May God keep us safe"

The Museum of Witchcraft concentrates on the "wayside" or "hedgerow" magic that is associated with wise women and rural life. Within this tradition, which involves healing, protection, divination, curses, charms, and weather-working, objects are thought to possess power.[3] Some artifacts – usually glass bottles or balls filled with colorful materials – are made to capture spirits that may then offer protection. Other objects are considered to be inherently magical – for instance, the museum's Cock Rock fertility charm – or they can become so. A shoe that has been enchanted in order to manipulate its owner is an example of this latter category, as are oyster shells incised with love charms.

According to practitioners of witchcraft, these objects can continue to have power long after their spell has been cast.[4] They are not, as it were, defused once their influence has been wrought, and visiting witches regularly attest to their potency. In the collection of essays published to mark the museum's sixtieth anniversary, a contributor called Arizona remembers "feeling that everything behind the glass was alive" (Arizona 2011, 112) while Judith Noble recalls:

> a black glossy bag in a black glossy cup, a phallic stone, a box studded with pins, two bees in a bag, horn cups … All were made for magic … They had their own logic and what mattered most was that they exuded a strength; a power that flowed out of them through the dusty glass cases and into me. (Noble 2011, 31)

Given their worldview, it is expected that witches would feel that the collections were powerful. It is more surprising to discover that nonpractitioners often respond in similar terms. Over the years the proprietors have received several letters from visitors who neglected to leave donations and subsequently suffered misfortunes. Mrs. Holly Janek declared that, "While we are not normally superstitious, one of my sons feels that it may be prudent after all to make up for the omission and our belated contribution is enclosed" (Document 341, Museum of Witchcraft archives). Likewise, Mr. M. entreated the owner, "Please do me the favour of accepting these coins" (Document 289). More recently, a series of walking sticks have arrived by post. The museum provides them for visitors should they decide to venture onto the steep coastal paths which lead up from their doorstep, but asks that they be

FIGURE 13.1   Exterior of Museum of Witchcraft, Boscastle, UK. Note the walking sticks adjacent to the rear door.
Photo: Fiona Candlin/Museum of Witchcraft.

returned (Figure 13.1). Wives usually send them back on behalf of their husbands, with apologies and accounts of recent tribulations.

The museum comments box is also full of notes which employ the term "scary" or otherwise remark on the potency of the exhibits. Reeling between pleasure and shock, an anonymous tourist wrote: "It was very nice. I can't believe my eyes. It is an abnormal museum 10/10," while "Clare" wrote: "I believe in witches now." Chris from Essex commented, "Some weird and wonderful items and may God keep us safe," and another contributor found the museum frightening because "you never know what the voodoo dolls are doing at this very moment in time" (comments dated between January 2009 and April 2012).

The Museum of Witchcraft is not exceptional in exhibiting objects that are thought to be active and powerful. In her book *Making Representations*, Moira Simpson explains that Maori, Australian Aboriginal, and Native American communities believe that some objects have a life force and need to be cared for appropriately, whether they are located in museums or elsewhere (Simpson 1996; see also Kreps 2003). Crucially, however, only members of the correlative communities consider these museum artifacts to be animate beings or to be imbued with strong spiritual powers. As Simpson remarks, the vast majority of viewers think that they are inanimate objects: to the collector they may be curiosities or valuable works of art; to a curator or anthropologist they provide evidence of cultural traditions or religious beliefs; and, to "the visitor, they may well be of no more than passing interest" (1996, 195).

A similar dynamic occurs with regard to museum exhibits from a Christian tradition. As part of her PhD research on museum visitors' engagement with the divine, Steph Berns observed and interviewed visitors at the British Museum's 2011 exhibition *Treasures of Heaven* which focused on sacred masterpieces of medieval Europe. Berns noted that some Catholic and Eastern Orthodox visitors, and to a lesser extent those who held other religious or spiritual beliefs, meditated or prayed in front of exhibits and touched crosses or pictures to the glass display cases in order to produce "contact relics." For them, the objects on exhibition provided a means of making active connection with the saints and ultimately with God. Other attendees did not respond similarly; indeed, Berns found that the spiritual encounters of devotees were sometimes disrupted by overhearing the skeptical comments made by nonbelievers.[5]

As in the examples above, practitioners and believers perceive the Museum of Witchcraft's collections to be powerful but, importantly, their view is shared by visitors who are not affiliated to that community or belief system. This situation is analogous to a European museum visitor seeing a carved Ahayu:da on display and being struck by the presence of the Zuni war god that it embodies or a Hindu visiting the *Treasures of Heaven* exhibition and feeling that they must acknowledge the power of the Christian God. Given this anomaly, it might be tempting to ascribe the obeisant responses made by erstwhile nonbelievers to the objects' reputedly magical properties, but many public sector museums display similar objects without them having comparable effects. Although the British Museum holds the Elizabethan astrologer Dr. John Dee's black scrying mirror and the National Museum of Scotland has a collection of objects used for cursing, they do not prompt visitors from other faiths or with no religious affiliation to declare a newly discovered belief in witches. According to a curator at the latter museum, they elicit a "slight frisson or shiver" at most (Cheape 2008).

Why, then, do visitors who are "not normally superstitious" feel the artifacts at the Museum of Witchcraft to be potent? What qualities does the Museum of Witchcraft have or what does it do to achieve this end? In order to address these questions, it is important to first understand why museum exhibits are conventionally considered "dead."

Killing off exhibits

The idea that museums neutralize their collections dates back to Antoine-Chrysostome Quatremère de Quincy, who began writing on the subject in 1791, two years after the beginning of the French Revolution. During the immediately preceding years, revolutionaries had torn down religious monuments and those connected with the monarchy. Some carvings were destroyed but others were removed for safekeeping, and in 1795 the salvaged carvings were used to form the Museum of French Monuments (McClellan 1994). Sculptures looted by the French army as it conquered the Austrian Netherlands, Flanders, and the Italian peninsula also flooded back to Paris, and in 1796 Napoleon made the surrender of artworks a condition of armistice (McClellan 2008). Artworks by Rubens, Van Dyck, and Flemish masters were duly seized from the vanquished states and brought in triumph to the newly opened Louvre.

Quatremère was voluble in his criticisms and repeatedly argued against the removal of artworks and the foundation of public museums, perhaps most forcibly in *The Destination of Works of Art*. This was initially given as a lecture in 1807 and then published in 1815, the year Napoleon was defeated and some (but by no means all) of the appropriated artworks were returned. Focusing on classical sculpture, Quatremère argued that carvings were inextricably linked to their surroundings. Viewers may believe that they are enjoying the statuary but in actuality a "subtle transposition" takes place and "a thousand minor associations indirect and foreign to the object substitute themselves in the place of the principal ones, so that what we are looking at frequently has but little share in what we feel and admire" (Quatremère [1815] 1821, 103). To illustrate his point, Quatremère imagined a temple located in a sacred grove. The outside of the building was entwined with roses and myrtle, while inside it was resplendent in purple and gold. A mysterious veil hung at the center of the room and then, when sacred music played, it dropped to reveal a statue of a deity amid clouds of perfumed incense, or, as Quatremère puts it, "the goddess suddenly blazes on the sight" ([1815] 1821, 62).

In this instance, the effect of the carving relied on the setting and on the accompanying sensory experience of music and scent. It also involved the spiritual framework within which the sculpture was situated. The devotee's faith in the deity amplified their aesthetic response while, conversely, the allied sensory pleasure reinforced their belief. According to Quatremère, the principal function of these carvings was to produce and maintain religious commitment; prized away from this structure of worship and stripped of social utility, they lost their ability to "appeal to feelings," becoming "mere matter" ([1815] 1821, 64). "How many monuments owe the loss of their powerful effect to their being removed from their original situations!" lamented Quatremère. "How many works have lost their real value in losing their use!" (67).

One objection to Quatremère's rhetoric is that antique statuary had long since lost its ritual function. Even if it had remained in the place for which it was made, it would no longer be appreciated in the manner he described. Anticipating such an objection, Quatremère argued that the original location of works remained important because seeing something *in situ* allowed the viewer to make imaginative connections with the past. Quatremère wrote that, when strolling among ancient monuments, "my eyes see the identical objects which were seen by Pericles, by Plato and Caesar. Horace and Virgil have walked before the columns I am now admiring. Here is a point where we meet" ([1815] 1821, 85).

For him, museums had an entirely detrimental effect. Removing statues from their original setting, collecting fragments of monuments, methodically classing the remains, and composing them into a chronology, "killed" art in the name of historical investigation. "It is a living being attending its own funeral," he announced: "It is not writing its history, but its epitaph" (Quatremère [1815] 1821, 59).

When Quatremère described objects as "living beings," he did not mean that they are animate in the way that the exhibits at the Museum of Witchcraft are considered to be. Nor was he saying that museum collections are entirely without effect or interest, although the idea of killing something does suggest that. Rather, he contended that removing objects from context changes their status and the way they are perceived. Museums enable antiquarian interest or scholarly erudition, not emotional, spiritual, or imaginative engagement.

Quatremère's idea that art is "alive" and exhibits "dead" has been repeatedly reworked and developed (e.g., Malraux 1954; Valéry 1960), perhaps most notably by the Frankfurt School philosopher Theodor Adorno. Adorno opened his essay "Valery Proust Museum" by stating that the German word *museal* ("museumlike") has negative connotations since it describes "objects to which the observer no longer has a vital relationship and which are in the process of dying … Museum and mausoleum are connected by more than phonetic association. Museums are like the family sepulchres of works of art" (Adorno 1967, 175).

Adorno took a slightly different position to Quatremère. Although he agreed that objects are changed and diminished by their removal into a gallery, he also pointed out that, unless one was in possession of a private collection, museums provided the only means of becoming familiar with art and other treasures. "Museums will not be shut," he declared, "nor would it even be desirable to shut them" (1967, 185). Adorno also differed from Quatremère in linking aesthetic effect to the gallery and not to daily life. To explain his position, Adorno conjured someone who lives in an ancient town. Although they may know every corner and portal, when a visitor remarks on the beauty of the buildings, the resident replies with a peremptory "yes, yes." For them, seeing art was as "ordinary as breathing." The implication is that, in museums, everyone is like a tourist visiting a historic town. Visitors can only view the objects with a certain remove and this distance both creates the conditions for aesthetic appreciation and raises the question of the exhibits' "vitality." This later issue, as Adorno said, would probably never occur to anyone who was "at home with art and not a mere visitor" (1967, 179).

For Adorno, then, the quality of "life" derived from an object being embedded in an environment. The inhabitants of that environment might view an object with some indifference, barely noticing it on a day-to-day basis, yet they still know it in a profound and intimate way. Placing the object in a museum detaches it from the interests and habits of an evolving community, so the question of an object's "death" only arises when one is in the position of a visitor. (Quatremère and Adorno were principally concerned with art, but Daniel Sherman (1994) has suggested that their arguments could encompass almost any kind of exhibit. Philip Fisher (1991) gives the point further nuance when he argues that museums actually turn objects into art.)

Unless one adheres to a pagan or animist worldview, the idea of artifacts living or dying is a conceit, a shorthand device to indicate their transition from complex functional environments to exhibits. Museums also rely on and generate systems of belief (for instance, in the value of art) and their collections are still used, but emotional, embodied, and spiritual responses are actively suppressed in favor of aesthetic attention or historical analysis. Still, the terms "live" and "dead" are useful in that they abbreviate lengthy arguments and, more importantly, because they provide a way of conceptualizing and trying to account for otherwise elusive qualities of effect and response. If an exhibit is "dead," it means that the practices and responses associated with its former functions have been sidelined and that scholarly and aesthetic responses dominate. If, in contrast, an object is "live," it has the capacity to prompt reactions that are more appropriate to its former role in a nonmuseum world – in this instance, as a magical instrument or spell. The notion of "dead" and "live" objects also points to an object's putative ability to act. Due to its transposition into a gallery, the former type of object can no longer contribute to religious feeling or aid in spell casting, whereas the latter category of things retains that instrumental capacity.

Quatremère and Adorno both argued that objects lose their vitality partly because they are removed from a context of belief and use, but also as a result of the conditions established within museums. The literary scholar Philip Fisher has developed the second aspect of this position. He points out that museums arrange objects chronologically or geographically, provide technical or historical information, remove any extraneous decoration or sensory cues, and post signs instructing visitors not to touch. In doing so, they create "a script that makes certain acts possible and others unthinkable" (Fisher 1991, 18). "It would be "an act of madness,"" Fisher writes, "to enter a museum, and kneel down in front of a painting of the Virgin to pray for a soldier missing in battle, lighting a candle and leaving an offering on the floor near the picture before leaving" (1991, 13).

At the Museum of Witchcraft visitors do light candles, some leave offerings, and others meditate. Understanding why this venue produces the emotional, spiritual, and embodied engagement that characterizes "live" objects involves following the logic of Quatremère, Adorno, and Fisher's analyses and considering the qualities or connections that museums are presumed to lose. Accordingly, I investigate the museum's relationship to associated circuits of (nonmuseological) belief and practice, that is, to its immediate community and spiritual context. Then, in order to consider why visitors who are "not normally superstitious" feel that the exhibits are potent, I examine the museum's "script." What forms of presentation keep these objects vital and make these responses possible?

Location, use, and museum scripts

The Museum of Witchcraft was founded by Cecil Williamson in 1951, the year that the Witchcraft Act was repealed. It was originally located on the Isle of Man, which is situated in the Irish Sea, midway between the islands of Great Britain and Ireland, but the museum moved three times before opening at its current site in Boscastle on the north coast of Cornwall (Williamson 1976; 2012; King 2002; 2007).[6] The first relocation was prompted by disagreements between Williamson and his partner, Gerald Gardner, but subsequent removals were a response to local antagonism. Having reopened the Museum near Windsor Castle, one of the royal family's residences, Williamson was visited by "two grey-suited gentlemen" who apparently offered him a good financial incentive to move again and he did so, this time to Bourton-on-the-Water in the countryside of west central England. Here, the village priest preached on the evils of witchcraft and some residents staged protests outside the museum. The local press ran libelous articles, Williamson received death threats, and dead cats were hung from trees in the garden until, finally, an arson attack destroyed one wing of the building, and in 1961 Williamson shifted premises for the last time.

Williamson's early years in Cornwall were almost as fraught as his earlier ventures. The windows were daubed with paint and he claimed that a curse comprising a dog's heart pierced with thorns was left on his doorstep, but local dissension gradually passed. He continued to run the museum until 1996 when, at midnight on Halloween, it was sold to Graham King. Like Williamson, King also encountered antipathy from neighbors. Staff at the visitor center, which is located in the same building as the museum, refused to put his leaflets on display and a long correspondence with the neighborhood heritage officer ensued. Mention of the museum was omitted from tourist maps, the local authority declined to erect the usual brown signpost allotted to attractions and, in 1997, an application to open a small shop on the premises elicited numerous strong objections. In his letter to the planning office, a Mr. Hague opined that "the witchcraft museum has been the black spot of an otherwise beautiful place and to have its influence extended by a retail outlet would be a dreadful thing." His protests were echoed by Mr. MacLeod, elder of the Church of Nations in Camelford, who wrote of the "dangers occultism and such matters often carry with it," and by another local preacher who quoted the verse from Ephesians which reads "that in this life we fight not against flesh and blood but against Principalities and Powers of Darkness" (uncataloged correspondence, Museum of Witchcraft archives).

Eventually, though, the Museum of Witchcraft was given permission to sell souvenirs and today it stocks a very small range of books, postcards, candles, and T-shirts. The irony is that many of the local shops were already selling merchandise pertaining to magic and entirely outpaced the museum in the range of products they offer, as they do now. Crafty, which is situated on the main street, has a large window that is packed with clay models of wizards and hook-nosed witches wearing black pointy hats. Across the road is Rocky Road, which offers stone toads, a skull with Gothic decorations, crystals, and dream catchers, while the neighboring store called Things stocks a range of mugs that bear the legend "I'd rather be in Boscastle" and a range of witch balls for protecting one's home against evil spirits.

Contrary to the protestors' fears, this trade annuls rather than promotes witchcraft. Whereas objections to the museum selling supposedly magical merchandise credited witchcraft with having power, the current retail outlets offer commodities that align it with the caricatures of storybooks or with a benign interest in New Age topics. Witchcraft becomes a matter of gift-giving, interior decoration, self-reflection, or spiritual inquiry and not a magical force capable of animating objects or of bringing misfortune on ungenerous tourists.

Nonetheless, the outcry shows that witchcraft is a contentious subject and is not simply a matter for history books. In their letters of complaint, the protestors repeatedly pointed to the presence of witchcraft and "occult" practices in the area. They adduced no evidence, but this immediate region is an important locus of pilgrimage for witches, Goddess worshippers, neo-pagans, druids, and advocates of earth mysteries (which encompasses ley lines, power sites, dowsing, and astrology), all of whom share in a loose continuum of belief (Lowerson 1994; Hale 2002). The focus of their attention is Tintagel, a neighboring village to Boscastle, where, according to the twelfth-century chronicler Geoffrey of Monmouth, the legendary sixth-century hero King Arthur was conceived and born. Advocates of earth mysteries connect Arthurian legends to the zodiac and treat the area as a site of spiritual power, while other practitioners of neo-Celtic spirituality (a catchall term for the groups mentioned above) concentrate on Merlin's cave which is at the base of the Tintagel headland. Practitioners of neo-Celtic spirituality also make pilgrimages to the nearby village of Bossiney where two small carvings of labyrinths are etched into the walls of a valley and where the sixth-century St Nectan reputedly lived in an adjacent glen. This latter location is decorated with makeshift altars, clouties (fabric strips tied to trees), and offerings, making its status as a pilgrimage destination evident to other tourists and to residents in the area.

According to the cultural geographer Amy Hale and the anthropologist Helen Cornish, Tintagel and the two sites outside Bossiney are functionally interrelated with the Museum of Witchcraft (Hale 2004; Cornish 2005b). The Pagan Federation of Devon and Cornwall clearly see some concordance because they recently donated half the proceeding of their annual raffle to the museum, with the other half going to the Woodland Trust (Pagan Federation 2011). Likewise, the people who protested against the museum extending into retail drew a similar conclusion: that its collections are echoed by "occult" practices in the area.

Whether it is viewed positively or negatively, the Museum of Witchcraft operates in an environment which is broadly consonant with its interests. Although individual objects may have been geographically relocated, its collections are shown within a context that is congruent with their use. In this, the Museum of Witchcraft is akin to other faith-based or quasi-religious exhibitions such as the Museum of Wesleyan Methodism which is housed in the movement's foremost chapel, or the Museum of Freemasonry in London which is accessed through the institutional headquarters. Some police or army galleries that are situated in operating stations and barracks also show exhibits in close proximity to the activities undertaken in their immediate surroundings, as is the case at the Dartmoor Prison Museum, which I discuss below.

For Quatremère and later commentators, removing objects from a relevant working or functional environments was one of the factors that rendered them "dead" and, in this instance, the Museum of Witchcraft's location in an area that is a focus for Celtic spirituality helps account for why the exhibits are perceived to be "live." Yet, even if museums are based in surroundings appropriate to their subject, their architecture or presentational mode can still create a degree of dislocation. High walls, forecourts, flights of steps, ramps, or lobbies create buffer zones between the artifacts and adjacent spaces, while academic styles of interpretation can imply that the material belongs to another age or to a distinct subset of the population. Thus it is also important, as Fisher advises, to attend to the museum's script.

In this instance, the Museum of Witchcraft actively emphasizes its connections to the surrounding landscape. At the front of the whitewashed stone building is a box holding the wooden sticks that visitors may use if they decide to venture up the adjacent paths (see Figure 13.1). The museum's sign shows an old woman and two fishermen who have evidently taken this route, for the picture shows them standing on the hillside above the museum. Stepping inside the museum, visitors find themselves in a small stone-flagged lobby at one end of which is a grotto that has been built around a natural spring. Lit by candles, scented with incense, figures of the Great or Mother Goddess are perched on the ledges on the rock crag and a sign notes that it is a place for quiet contemplation. Unlike the exhibits that Quatremère describes, these collections have not been prized away from the habits and interests of the community. On the contrary, the museum is conceived in relation to its physical and spiritual context. Open to its surroundings, it is continuous with an environment that is closely associated with magical and spiritual practices.

Having paid the entrance fee, visitors are directed into the first gallery which presents a relatively conventional overview of images of witches, while the second room outlines the history of their persecution. The third room, however, has huge mirrors joined at right angles. In the space between them are three vertical stones interspersed with branches and the floor is strewn with flat rocks (Figure 13.2). The illusion is momentary but striking: walking in, visitors see themselves standing inside a large stone circle. As if subject to a fleeting enchantment, they appear to have been transported out onto the moors.

FIGURE 13.2   Stone circle in the Museum of Witchcraft. (For a color version of this figure, please see the color plate section.)
© John Hooper/Hoopix/Museum of Witchcraft.

The stone circle reiterates the museum's relationship to the locality and also marks a change in the conceptual framework of the museum. From here onward, the exhibition stops portraying witches as historical or literary figures and starts presenting witchcraft as a matter of fact. In the next display a series of objects are labeled: "Spell crafts by Kate McCarthy. Kate is making these protection dolls from horsehairs etc. She also makes herbal remedies, cat calling oils, horse enchanter oils." Similarly, a notice pinned outside the recreation of a wise woman's cottage reads: "The spells Joan speaks are traditional and collected locally. Many are still used by witches today. Please don't be frightened of witches. Most are like Joan and believe in helping, healing, and in harming no-one." The references to living witches and the use of the present tense, which continues throughout the museum, situate witchcraft in the contemporary world and assert that the exhibits are not simply historical artifacts but belong to continuing tradition. This perspective prepares visitors to conceive the objects as functional, possibly functioning and, indeed, subsequent displays are presented in these terms.

The exhibition of protective magic, for example, informs visitors that stones which are naturally pierced by holes – hagstones – can avert malevolent spirits, while lemons absorb curses: their power is destroyed as the fruit withers and blackens. Likewise, glass witches' balls are thought to capture troublesome spirits and mirrors can deflect negative energy. These modes of magical defense are the subject of exhibition and they are also actively used in the gallery. Mirrors line several cabinets, lemons suspended in woven strings are hung inside and above the case of curses, and a group of poppets have been laid on a large flat hagstone (Figures 13.3 and 13.4).

FIGURE 13.3 Cabinet of protective magic: note the mirrors to the rear, Museum of Witchcraft.

Photo: Fiona Candlin/Museum of Witchcraft.

FIGURE 13.4 Poppets arranged on a protective hagstone, Museum of Witchcraft.

Photo: Fiona Candlin/Museum of Witchcraft.

The cases containing curses have also been placed directly opposite those containing protective magic, and Graham King confirmed that the arrangement is intended to ensure both conceptual and magical balance.[7] One of the most alarming objects in the museum is an exquisitely rendered rag doll. She has minutely embroidered blue eyes and pursed pink lips, and a small dagger obtrudes from her red nurse's uniform with its white apron. It was made to induce a miscarriage. Another poppet – the name given to dolls made in the image of an individual – has the same function, but, countering them, a spell in the facing case was worked to maintain a pregnancy. Made by a local witch, this spell comprised a swift wrapped tightly in the bedclothes used when the woman lost a previous child. The bird has been offered in exchange for the child's life to come. Likewise, the case of curses contains a dog's heart that has been stuck through with thorns, and there are similar objects in the collection of protective magic. The artifacts are arranged not only to create instructive displays but to contain or neutralize threatening powers. Placing protective objects opposite the display of curses implies that both forms of magic are functional: that the curses need managing and that the protective spells do so. The curation suggests that both types of objects are operational, that they are in this sense "live."

In the company of witches

For Quatremère, Adorno, and Fisher the life of objects is intricately connected to their surroundings and to their use. The objects must contribute to religious or civic life or be generally sewn into the warp and weft of a society's life. At the Museum of Witchcraft the exhibits are connected to the elements and surroundings but, as the exhibition progresses, it gradually becomes clear that the members of staff are themselves practicing witches.

The cabinet containing the objects used for cursing and ill-wishing includes a number of poppets. One, which has a large pin through its mouth and is wrapped in thorns, was made to stop an ex-lover from gossiping after the end of an affair. It had originally belonged to the Museum of Pagan History in Glastonbury but because it was believed to emit such strongly negative energies, they decided that it was more appropriate to place it under the control of the Museum of Witchcraft. So many other individuals and organizations have done likewise that King is planning an exhibition of objects that their owners considered too dangerous to keep.[8]

The poppet shares space with a number of other items, including things that were removed from Williamson's house after he died. His family asked the museum for help in clearing away his magical tools, and in the center of an upstairs room the museum staff found a table with the manufacture of a spell in progress. It comprised a large tray filled with sand and fenced with a string of bones. At its center was a forked stick with an effigy of a face made with wax and human hair.

Believing it to be potent, the staff used magic to protect themselves and cleanse the room before removing the spell and bringing it to the museum. They do not, the text informs us, know at what or whom the curse was directed.

The tenor of the exhibition changes again in the penultimate room. As before, the texts reinforce the idea that magic is a matter of daily practice and that the staff are experts but, additionally, several of the labels suggest that the visitor could potentially require magical assistance and proffer advice on how to achieve it. A charm box made for a spirit to inhabit bears the text: "This spirit's name is said to be Fred and was once the protector of Dora from St Ives," while another label written by Cecil Williamson reads: "If you conjure up a spirit what do you do with it? Kate Honiton filled this lace-maker's globe magnifier with hundreds and thousands and invited the spirit to make itself at home." Williamson's question can be interpreted as rhetorical or as an actual query: What would you do if you conjured a spirit? He then offers a suggestion – you could make a house filled with shiny things to distract and amuse it. Other notices similarly instruct the reader:

> Candle magic is simple, effective and popular. Carefully choose the colour of a candle and inscribe a rune, name or magical sign in the wax or magically charge a pin or two and push them in. Light the candle at an appropriate time and watch it while meditating on the desired outcome. This forms the basis of many a powerful spell.

While several of the displays indicate that the objects are used by practitioners, these labels suggest that the visitors could similarly make or employ them. They implicitly invite the visitor into a community of practice.

That invitation is repeated more forcefully in the display on sea magic. The main panel announces that the church considered all tempests to be the work of the devil and his minions, the witches. They found their proof in the fact that the witches "frequented vantage points, set high up on the cliff tops when seas and storms were raging. There in unison and harmony with the storm, they swirled and turned, shrieking and howling into the face of the wind." The text continues:

> Yes witches did and still do dance with the wind in high places above the sea. You should try it some time. It is an experience never to be forgotten. I can guarantee that you will be carried away by the wind. You will experience greater emotional release and revelation than is obtainable through the most potent, and lethal, of drugs. For you have cast yourself into the arms of the universal creator.

Thus, the text invites visitors to join the witches, to act and to feel as they do. The tense then changes at the end of the passage: "you *have* cast yourself" into the wind. Williamson proposes that it has already happened, that the visitor has decided to take a leap into a magical world and has joined the group.

As they are about to leave, visitors might spot a small note pinned to a rabbit skin amulet. The text admits that the museum staff do not know the object's exact purpose, adding "if you are familiar with this type of charm please let us know." Of the 50,000 people who come to the museum every year approximately one-third are pagans, and it is likely that someone will be able to identify the charm, yet the text also includes people who are nonpractitioners. It credits them with magical knowledge.

The Museum of Witchcraft takes its visitors on a journey. It begins with a history and then shifts its conceptual framework. Having taken visitors through the looking glass, the museum intimates that the world might not be entirely amenable or subject to reason. It suggests that magic is in everyday use and presents spectators with objects that are understood to have powerful functions or effects. It gives visitors some strategies for coping with such forces and assumes that they may want to use them. It then addresses them as if they have already joined the ranks of the witches and can contribute to the museum.

To adapt Adorno's image, then, visitors to the Museum of Witchcraft are like tourists who come to visit an ancient town. They start by looking at the exhibits as though viewing carvings that have survived from ancient days. They are then welcomed into the buildings and are given the opportunity to see and experience these objects from the perspective of a resident. Instead of being distanced from the exhibits, the visitors start to view them as part of a functioning environment. Finally, they are tacitly invited to stay.

Clutter, unseen occupants, and life elsewhere

At the Museum of Witchcraft, the architecture connects the collections to a wider environment, while the curation and labeling locate the objects within an ongoing community of practice. In presenting the exhibits as functional and integral to the habits and interests of the witches, the museum implicitly grants permission for practitioners to treat it as a resource and as a site of pilgrimage. For many contemporary witches the museum does not displace objects from a context of use; it *is a* sphere for practice and their responses are more akin to ritual than they are to a conventional museum outing. Nonbelievers register this "script" and, recognizing that witchcraft is part of contemporary life within that area, judge the magical objects to be powerful.

The museum creates a situation in which the objects are live in the sense that Quatremère and Adorno meant. In this specific instance, the objects on display were used with magical intent and so, in creating the conditions for "life," the exhibits are felt to be powerful or animate. It would be a mistake to think that the objects are live because their provenance is magical. Rather, the perception of magical potency is predicated on the recognition of the objects' utility and agency.

If, then, the collections at the museum are felt to be live because of their continued use and their connection to a relevant group, the same conditions could apply

FIGURE 13.5   The public bar at The Valiant Soldier, Buckfastleigh, UK.
Photo: Fiona Candlin. Reproduced with permission of The Valiant Soldier see:
http://www.valiantsoldier.org.uk/photos/.

elsewhere. In order to develop that point I will briefly discuss two further museums that are not connected with magic or with spiritual belief. Again, I will consider the ways that their collections are perceived to be vital.

The Valiant Soldier is in the small village of Buckfastleigh, Devon, and it ran as
a public house from 1813 until 1965 when the brewery withdrew the license. On
the final evening, when the last customers left the premises, the landlord and land-
lady, Mr. and Mrs. Roberts, simply shut the door behind them and retreated to
their upstairs accommodation. Mr. Roberts died in 1969 but his wife, Alice, stayed
there until 1995 when the building was offered for sale. On gaining access to the
premises, local residents realized that the pub had remained untouched and that
the flat was relatively unchanged. Anxious to keep this time capsule intact, they
successfully campaigned to open The Valiant Soldier as a museum.

Visitors buy their tickets in the modern reception block next door to The Valiant
Soldier and are then left to enter the inn by themselves. They step onto the dark
red hard linoleum floor of a hallway which has one room to either side. A brown
door with stains around the handle leads to the public bar with long wood benches
fixed against two of the walls. Heavy plastic ashtrays, filled with the butts from
unfiltered cigarettes, rest on the tables. Two unwashed beer glasses, a packet of
cigarettes, and some matches stand on the bar, behind which are rows of optics,
still half-filled with spirits (Figure 13.5). On the other side of the hallway is the

"ladies' snug" which has a number of faded Lloyd loom basketry chairs and tables arranged in front of a 1930s tiled fireplace.

An audiotape plays quietly in the bar. It features men talking in Devon accents and snippets of news programs read in the plummy tones of 1950s broadcasters. A recording of people who remember drinking in the pub can be heard in the snug, but neither of these soundtracks conjures the presence of customers so much as the ingrained odor of tobacco smoke and the fainter aroma of bitter beer. The smell has not been artificially enhanced and, as the volunteers threw almost nothing away, the cigarette butts are those that were left behind on the night that the pub closed. Sandra Coleman, the volunteer museum manager, commented: "sometimes the smell is stronger than others, as if someone's been in here overnight." Laughing slightly nervously, she said she often wondered if anyone else had a key and had let themselves into the building, only to disappear out the back entrance when she arrived in the morning.[9]

Behind the bar is a steep uncarpeted flight of stairs which leads up to a narrow landing. A door opposite the head of the stairs stands open to reveal a small room with a queen-sized bed made up in white flannelette sheets and a blue satin counterpane. A cotton nightdress has been casually folded on the pillow while lacy and crocheted bed jackets hang over the headboard. Hatboxes and hats have been stored on top of a small wardrobe and a row of worn shoes is lined up beneath. An alarm clock, Bible, various pamphlets, a glass water bottle, saucers, and other odds and ends sit on the bedside table, while the dresser bears a similar array of clutter.

Throughout my visit I had a strong sense of intruding into someone's private space. Afterward, Sandra concurred and remarked that every morning she felt "like someone will stop and ask me what I'm doing here." This sense that the building is still occupied and at any minute the owner may return to question our presence is created by the conditions of visiting and other aspects of the museum "script." Although mainstream museums often arrange rooms in period style, their exhibits are framed by the infrastructure of reception desks, explanatory panels, directional signs, and conventional galleries. At The Valiant Soldier, visitors buy their ticket elsewhere and then step directly from the high street into the pub. On first arriving there is no indication that the venue is in fact a museum and, with the exception of a low and very discreet Perspex screen to prevent visitors from sitting on the basket chairs in the ladies' snug, the downstairs spaces have been left unprotected.

Visitors not only enter the pub by themselves, but are often left unaccompanied for the duration of their stay. The Valiant Soldier is run by volunteers so the building is sometimes left unstaffed and, with limited resources for publicity, the venue only attracts audiences of 2000–3000 people a year. If there were guards, other tourists, or actors playing roles (as they do in the recreated houses at Blists Hill Victorian Town in the Ironbridge Gorge), then their presence would legitimate that of the lone visitor. Even mannequins would be reassuring since they point to the simulated quality of the experience (Sandberg 2003, 18) but, as it is, wandering through the unpeopled building feels close to trespass.

FIGURE 13.6   Living room at The Valiant Soldier. (For a color version of this figure, please see the color plate section.)
Photo: Fiona Candlin. Reproduced with permission of The Valiant Soldier.

The feeling of intrusion is also connected to the venue's sensory cues and to the mass and disposition of the objects. There are shoes and cosmetics for different occasions and several bed jackets, providing Mrs. Roberts with a choice for warm or cold nights or allowing her to wash one while wearing another. Some of the objects are slightly misplaced: an old pipe has been left in the china cabinet, a tea towel is draped across the back of a dining room chair, and an ironing board stands next to the living room sideboard (Figure 13.6). It is as if the residents had been in the process of using something and had deposited it wherever convenient, as one might at home. These objects have also been worn. Nothing has been drastically restored, thoroughly cleaned, or replaced with new. The shoes are scuffed and molded to the shape of Mrs. Roberts's feet, the soap in the bathroom is half-used, and the doors are stained with the grease of repeated touch.

Although some outdoor folk museums have buildings that are left unstaffed, are free of mannequins, and may be relatively quiet, their rooms generally feature indicative objects rather than being recreations of inhabited space. Those that do simulate a domestic environment, such as the Skye Museum of Island Life, which Sharon Macdonald (2007) has discussed, tend to use mannequins. Historic houses have unstaffed, furnished rooms and rarely include dummy figures but everything remains in its correct and logical place and there is little personal litter or strong odor. Here the combination of minimal institutional infrastructure; unattended

FIGURE 13.7   Exterior of Dartmoor Prison Museum, UK.
Photo: Fiona Candlin. Reproduced with permission of Dartmoor Prison Museum.

rooms; the smell of tobacco, beer, and cold tar soap; the densely packed and mis-matched accoutrements of daily life; and the signs of wear create the sense that the owner has only just stepped out of the flat. These objects are perceived to belong to someone, to be embedded in an environment and part of an ongoing intimate life, and hence to be vital.

Twenty miles east of The Valiant Soldier, motorists pass a police notice which reads "No stopping on this road." The sign is there because, from this vantage point, there is a clear view across the moors to Dartmoor Prison. The road contin-ues on through Princetown, where most of the officers live, skirts the penitentiary walls, and passes a barricaded entrance before reaching the old prison dairy where the museum is located. Identical blue metal signs, each printed with a white crown and lettering which reads "HM Prison Service" and "Dartmoor Prison Museum," are positioned on either side of the heavy double doors (Figure 13.7).

Inside the museum the temperature drops, the granite walls resisting any warmth from the sun. Concrete garden ornaments in the shape of animals are arrayed around the reception area, along with a price list and a note which informs visitors that they have all been made by inmates. A man in uniform stands at the reception desk and, as I pay my admission fee, introduces himself as an ex-officer who worked at the prison "across the road" for 39 years. Unprompted, he tells me that the prison was never a high-security unit but a hard labor camp, that it was notorious for the severity of its regime, and that it had housed some of the most dangerous British criminals.

Continuing his introduction, the ex-officer explains that, when inmates have been "D-catted" (that is, those who can be trusted not to escape and are designated "Category D"), they are allowed to work under supervision at the current prison farm. If this assignment progresses smoothly, then the inmate can be employed outside of the prison grounds either at the guards' club or at the museum, where they clean, undertake maintenance work, build exhibitions, or write labels as required. Recounting this information leads the ex-officer to an anecdote about an elderly woman visitor who prodded one of the prisoners with her finger and asked him what he was in for. The prisoner replied "being stupid" and the ex-officer commented: "I know him, and what he did, and I wouldn't have poked him in the back." The implication is that men who were and may still be dangerous are working in the building.

The exhibition itself consists of a number of cases containing a mishmash of objects and images pertaining to the prison. One cabinet displays tiny carvings that French prisoners of war, who were incarcerated in the first decades of the nineteenth century, made from bones and fruit stones. There is a tunic button from 1879 and trophies from prison competitions, although it is unclear if these were won by the inmates or the officers. A collection of contemporary improvised weapons includes a plastic toothbrush that has been sharpened to a point, razors set into toothbrushes and sticks, and a shard of black plastic that has been bound at the blunt end to create a handle and which resembles a giant claw. This display also includes makeshift tattooing equipment constructed from Biros and batteries, while the neighboring exhibit is devoted to items of restraint and punishment that are no longer used. Escape tools smuggled in by recent visitors, tobacco tins with hidden sections for smuggling contraband, and equipment for smoking cannabis or crack cocaine are shown alongside photographs of a nineteenth-century flogging frame in a room full of shackles and an early twentieth-century restraint book that lists the names of prisoners who were kept in lockdown.

The combination of historic and contemporary objects conveys the impression that little has changed over the past 200 years. Whereas most mainstream museums present narratives of progress, these exhibits seem to blur past and present and thereby prevent the straitjackets, flogging frame, or peat railway being viewed as a moment in social history: instead they seem to be part of an ongoing situation. The lack of differentiation, in this case between the warder's punishment apparatus and the inmate's weaponry, also creates an image of continuing violence. The implication of the display is that all the men behave brutally and this undermines any notion that the guard's presence guarantees either the inmates or the prison visitors' safety.

At the end of the gallery is a fire exit covered in a thick plastic curtain and above it is a sign which reads "to the quarry." I could hear music and, assuming that prisoners working on a lower level were listening to the radio, felt nervous of going through the door by myself. After some hesitation, I did so, followed a passageway to metal stairs which dropped into a huge deserted milking parlor, and then walked through to a diorama of shackled men working with pickaxes. Barely pausing, I hurried through to the rest of the lower floor and looked through a window to check if anyone was in the yard outside. Relieved to find that it was empty, I paid only cursory attention to the mock-up cells and quickly returned upstairs by a second staircase. The final room was light and painted white, and a video about the progress made by prisoners on contemporary rehabilitation schemes was playing but, somewhat unnerved, I left.

The museum is a department of the prison and, although that information is not explicitly stated, it can nonetheless be deduced from the announcement that prisoners work there and from the painted concrete wares. The connection between the museum and the prison is further reinforced by the presence of ex-officers who, on retirement, move from the prison on one side of the road to the museum on the other, by jokes they make about visitors being admitted for a stay, and by the architecture of the building which adheres to a common perception that penitentiaries are dark and cold. Instead of being physically and organizationally removed from the prison, the museum functions as an extension of it.

Precisely because the museum operates as a precinct of the prison, the collections have not been removed from but repositioned within their original context. To visit the museum is to enter into the prison complex and, because the displays portray the penitentiary, inmates, and officers in the most adverse light, the museum feels unsafe – "live" in the most oppressive of ways.

Feeling for "life"

Quatremère, Adorno, and Fisher propose that objects lose their vitality once they are moved into museums. They may, according to Adorno and Fisher, gain a new role insofar as they become art or historical documents, but they are not used in any other capacity and they can no longer prompt the practices or emotions that were common to their earlier lives.

This model of museums relies on a conventional conception of the institution wherein there is a distinct separation between the inside and outside of the museum, where the objects are physically displaced from their previous sites of use, the decor attempts to establish neutral surrounds, and any noticeable smells are eradicated. Likewise, it presupposes that objects are organized according to rational classificatory systems, that they are uniformly lit, and that the accompanying texts are impersonally written by museum professionals.

Given the prevalence of these technical and epistemological forms, it is unsurprising that commentators presume that most exhibits are detached from their previous circuits of use, community, and belief. Yet, if one shifts the focus from national or the major independent institutions to consider smaller venues such as those I have described here, a very different picture emerges since these exhibits often retain close links with their originating environment and communities of practice. The objects at The Valiant Soldier have remained in their original location while those in the Dartmoor Prison Museum have been moved only slightly. The Dartmoor Prison Museum and the Museum of Witchcraft are both staffed by the same group of people as those who made and used the exhibits, and in the latter case some of the exhibits are still actively employed by a wider community of believers. In these two museums, the verbal and written interpretation of objects is also delivered from the perspective of a participant rather than that of a disengaged observer. Not all museums' objects are subject to the transformations that Quatremère, Adorno, and Fisher describe.

Quatremère, Adorno, and Fisher used the terms "live" and "dead" as a way of describing the emotional and spiritual losses and intellectual gains incurred when objects were put on display. As such, they presented that change as a fact, something that necessarily occurred, but if exhibits' connections to their prior contexts of use and belief are accepted to be variable then their levels of animation must be similarly inconstant. Instead of assuming that the vast majority of artifacts wither and die once they are incarcerated in museums, it may be more productive to consider the heterogeneity of museums and the varying degrees of vitality within their displays. Depending on the situation of and the conditions established within the museum, it is possible for things to live on; so, rather than just asserting that exhibits are alive or dead, those qualities must be felt for and noticed.

Notes

1 "Preloaded: The Royal Museum Project," http://preloaded.com/work/national-museums-scotland/ (accessed August 18, 2014).
2 "Talking Objects," http://www.britishmuseum.org/channel/object_stories/talking_objects/video_swimming_reindeer.aspx (accessed August 18, 2014).
3 There are numerous types of magic and of witchcraft, including Dianic, Gardnerian, ceremonial magic (also known as high or ceremonial magic), voodoo, and wicca. Contemporary wayside witches commonly assume a continuous tradition of folk magic but this claim has been contested by Ronald Hutton (2000). For a discussion of witches' conceptions of their past which mentions the Boscastle Museum see Helen Cornish (2005a).
4 Although one protection spell on display at the Museum of Witchcraft apparently needs to be renewed once a year.
5 Steph Berns, "Seeing the Sacred in the Museum: Exploring the Significance of Visitor Engagement with Sacred Objects," doctoral thesis (forthcoming), University of Kent, UK.
6 An account of the history of the Museum of Witchcraft which differs in some details is provided in Williamson (2012).
7 Conversation with Graham King, Museum of Witchcraft, Boscastle, September 24, 2010.
8 Conversation with Graham King, Museum of Witchcraft, Boscastle, April 23, 2012.
9 Conversation with Sandra Coleman, The Valiant Soldier, Buckfastleigh, September 27, 2010.

References

Adorno, Theodor W. 1967. "Valery Proust Museum." In *Prisms*. Cambridge, MA: Neville Spearman.

Arizona. 2011. "Living Proof." In *The Museum of Witchcraft: A Magical History*, ed. Kerriann Godwin, 112. Bodmin, UK: Occult Art Co., with Friends of Boscastle Museum of Witchcraft.

British Museum. 2010. "Talking Objects." Video, 07:24 min. Accessed August 18, 2014. http://www.britishmuseum.org/channel/object_stories/talking_objects/video_swimming_reindeer.aspx.

Cheape, H. 2008. "'Charms against Witchcraft': Magic and Mischief in Museum Collections." In *Witchcraft and Belief in Early Modern Scotland*, edited by Julian Goodare, Lauren Martin, and Joyce Miller, 227–248. Basingstoke, UK: Palgrave Macmillan.

Cornish, Helen. 2005a. "Cunning Histories: Privileging Narratives in the Present." *History and Anthropology* 16(3): 363–376.

Cornish, Helen. 2005b. "Recreating Historical Knowledge and Contemporary Witchcraft in Southern England." Doctoral thesis, Goldsmiths, University of London.

Fisher, Philip. 1991. *Making and Effacing Art: Modern American Art in a Culture of Museums*. New York: Oxford University Press.

Hale, Amy. 2002. "Whose Celtic Cornwall: The Ethnic Cornish Meet Celtic Spirituality." In *Celtic Geographies: Old Culture, New Times*, edited by David Harvey, 157–170. London: Routledge.

Hale, Amy. 2004. "The Land Near the Dark Cornish Sea: The Development of Tintagel as a Celtic Pilgrimage Site." *Journal for the Academic Study of Magic* 2: 206–225.

Hutton, Ronald. 2000. *The Triumph of the Moon: A History of Modern Pagan Witchcraft*. Oxford: Oxford University Press.

King, Graham. 2002. "The Museum of Witchcraft: 50 Years of Controversy." Boscastle, UK: Museum of Witchcraft.

King, Graham. 2007. *Museum Guide*. Boscastle, UK: Museum of Witchcraft.

Kreps, Christina F. 2003. *Liberating Culture: Cross-Cultural Perspectives on Museums, Curation, and Heritage Preservation*. London: Routledge.

Lowerson, John. 1994. "Celtic Tourism – Some Recent Magnets." *Cornish Studies* 2: 128–137.

Macdonald, Sharon. 2007. "On 'Old Things': The Fetishization of Past Everyday Life." Reprinted in *Cultural Heritage: Critical Concepts in Media and Cultural Studies*, edited by Laurajane Smith, 269–286. London: Routledge.

Malraux, André. 1954. *The Voices of Silence*. Translated by Stuart Gilbert. London: Secker & Warburg.

McClellan, Andrew. 1994. *Inventing the Louvre: Art, Politics, and the Origins of the Modern Museum in Eighteenth-Century Paris*. Cambridge: Cambridge University Press.

McClellan, Andrew. 2008. *The Art Museum from Boullée to Bilbao*. Berkeley: University of California Press.

Noble, Judith. 2011. "Dark Light." In *The Museum of Witchcraft: A Magical History*, edited by Kerriann Godwin, 31. Bodmin, UK: Occult Book Co., with Friends of the Boscastle Museum of Witchcraft.

Pagan Federation. 2011. *Conference Report*. Exeter: Pagan Federation of Devon, Cornwall and Isles.

Quatremère de Quincy, M. (1815) 1821. *The Destination of Works of Art and the Use to which They Are Applied, Considered with Regard to Their Influence on the Genius and Taste of Artists, and the Sentiment of Amateurs*. Translated by Henry Thomson. London.

Sandberg, Mark B. 2003. *Living Pictures, Missing Persons*. Princeton: Princeton University Press.

Sherman, Daniel J. 1994. "Quatremère/Benjamin/Marx: Art Museums, Aura and Commodity Fetishism." In *Museum Culture: Histories, Discourses, Spectacles*, edited by Daniel J. Sherman and Irit Rogoff, 123–143. London: Routledge.

Simpson, Moira. 1996. *Making Representations: Museums in the Post-Colonial Era*. London: Routledge.

Valéry, Paul. 1960. "The Problem of Museums." In *Degas, Manet, Morisot*, 202–206. New York: Pantheon.

Wei, Jenny. 2011. "Bringing a Museum Object to Life: The John Bull Locomotive." National Museum of American History. Accessed August 18, 2014. http://blog.americanhistory.si.edu/osaycanyousee/2011/03/bringing-a-museum-object-to-life-the-john-bull-locomotive.html.

Williamson, Cecil. 1976. "Witchcraft Museums – and What It Means to Own One." *Quest: A Quarterly Review of the Occult* 28: 25–28.

Williamson, Cecil. 2012. "How the Witchcraft Museum Came into Being." In *The Museum of Witchcraft: A Magical History*, edited by Kerriann Godwin, 12–19. Bodmin, UK: Occult Art Company with Friends of the Boscastle Museum of Witchcraft.

Fiona Candlin worked in the Education Department at Tate Liverpool and at the University of Liverpool before being appointed to a lectureship jointly held by the British Museum and the Faculty of Continuing Education, Birkbeck, University of London, in 2000. She subsequently joined the History of Art Department at Birkbeck where she is now Senior Lecturer in Museum Studies. Fiona is the author of *Art, Museums and Touch* (Manchester University Press, 2010) and coeditor of *The Object Reader* (Routledge, 2008). Her most recent research, for which she was awarded a Leverhulme Fellowship, asks how museology would change if small, independent single-subject museums were afforded serious scholarly attention. Her new book, *Micromuseology*, is due out in 2015.

PART III

Design and Curating in the Media Age

14 TOTAL MEDIA

Peter Higgins

This chapter reflects on a personal journey that has ultimately enabled my involvement in the process of museum-making with my company, Land Design Studio. This journey has combined a training in architecture; an involvement with TV, film, and theater; and more recently an interest in the potential of new technologies as refined and appropriate communication media. The chapter also investigates the role and function of the museum as a component of urban placemaking, especially in the context of what I believe to be profligate National Lottery funding, which often presents a grand gesture in the manner of the Victorians. In my view, the evolution of museums requires a process that considers the "power of the real": real objects, real people in real time, supported by coherent, nonesoteric curation of our material culture. Alongside this, we need to enthrall our audiences through the creation of immersive scenographic journeys that store, interpret, and distribute ideas by exploiting emerging technologies. This can happen only through a collaborative process that promotes mutual respect between museum professionals, designers, and funders, combined with an understanding of the diverse disciplines described above that may be collectively titled "total media."

Museums in the context of placemaking

Museums now need to survive in a very volatile marketplace where they compete with brand experiences, theme parks, high-end domestic digital technology, and a whole stream of other market-led competition. If a family chooses a day out they will consider primarily cost, quality of entertainment and hospitality, and only marginally the educational value for their children. Those demographic sectors

The International Handbooks of Museum Studies: Museum Media, First Edition.
Edited by Michelle Henning.
© 2015 John Wiley & Sons Ltd. Published 2020 by John Wiley & Sons Ltd.

that acknowledge the importance of their museum experience might now expect institutions to present their collections and interpretive messages in the most imaginative experiential way. This heightened expectation and increase in visitor numbers has had a particular impact on our national museums since the introduction of free access in 2001. The consequence of a diminished revenue stream has been a much more aggressive approach to branding, marketing, and the consideration of the museum as a destination. Internal teams and external consultants support strategies that provide a significantly improved product for consumers including high-quality food and beverage provisions, sophisticated retail experiences, profitable temporary exhibitions, and corporate out-of-hours events. At the Natural History Museum in London the prime external frontage hosts, among other things, London Fashion Week in the summer and a popular ice skating attraction at Christmas, neither of which has any synergy with the museum experience.

Temporary exhibitions have emerged as an important revenue driver. In 2012–2013 we witnessed the return of the blockbuster, with "sold out" signs for *Hollywood Costumes* and *David Bowie* at the Victoria and Albert Museum (V&A) and *Life and Death: Pompeii and Herculaneum* at the British Museum. The need for sponsor-friendly and easily accessible themes has raised criticism from ex-director of the V&A, Roy Strong, who challenges the desire to play safe and cites his controversial exhibitions, which raised awareness of the plight of country houses, churches, and gardens and ultimately had a lasting impact on government policy (Alberge 2013). I support his search for more inspiring concepts that may be less predictable, less market-driven, and more risky. Having worked on *Pompeii and Herculaneum*, I was aware of how valuable such a mainstream theme and critical acclaim were to the sponsor, Goldman Sachs, who may not have been so enthusiastic about a more obscure or esoteric exhibition.

As part of the urban condition, museums have always been given special status as portals of knowledge. At established cultural destinations such as Washington's Smithsonian, London's South Kensington, or the remodeled Museum Island (Museums Insel) in Berlin we are expected to assume a learning attitude as we pass through the doorway and may relax only as we leave (Hooper-Greenhill 1992; Conn 1998). We must search for a new way of incorporating our cultural centers into the city plan other than by replacing the portals of knowledge with slick stand-alone contemporary alternatives, such as the Museum of Liverpool or Glasgow's Riverside Museum, both of which stand defiantly isolated without any sensitive integration into the city grain. A more extreme example of public realm development may be found in the United Arab Emirates where, over the past decade, there has been increasing investment in international tourism through visitor attractions with complementary resort and retail development. In Abu Dhabi, under the direction of the Tourism Development & Investment Company, Sadiyat Island is to be transformed from a sandy moonscape into an extensive cultural quarter. This unprecedented piece of cultural master planning will host five iconic museums set within an evolving infrastructure hosting sublime permanent collections and blockbuster temporary exhibitions (TDIC et al. 2008).

To return to the more familiar economic constraints: there is no doubt in my view that our cities require the intelligent integration of museums or informal learning centers to help support sensitive placemaking. There would, of course, have to be a shift from the symbolic grand staircase and elevated classical portico that have graced many inner city public realms over the past 200 years (Duncan 1995; Giebelhausen 2003). Surely these architectural statements have for too long become increasingly isolated from the educational experience for the Google generation of schoolchildren, whose teachers now refer to a YouTube clip as an inspirational link rather than a stuffed mammal in a glass case.

In London an enlightened developer, Argent Group, is reclaiming and developing a vast leftover site adjacent to King's Cross station. This initiative, unlike that in Abu Dhabi, involves private investment, reflects on an extensive historic context and diversity of this inner city site, and has attracted significant public investment in the transport interchange. Argent has nurtured the visionary concept by locating the new Central Saint Martins College of Art and Design as the anchor attractor sited on the primary axial approach. There is, of course, a significant residential and commercial component but, at the same time, they have valued cultural assets such as the British Library, The Wellcome Collection, the Foundling Museum, and a new Aga Khan cultural center some of which are on the periphery of the site but have nevertheless been rationalized into the conceptual master plan. The developer has genuinely recognized the value of such activity as part of the marketing strategy that will ultimately attract investment (Sutton Young 2011).

When we interrogate the role and functions of twenty-first-century museums, it is possible to arrive at very different solutions that would never attract funding support from key stakeholders. Could our museums be deconstructed and distributed through towns or cities, perhaps sometimes located within vacant property, or would this be too modest, without political gravitas and the loaded view of how we should present our material culture? During the temporary closure of the Ars Electronica Center (Museum of the Future) in Linz, Austria, in 2007, director Gerfried Stocker decided that the annual festival should decamp throughout the city. One particular street accommodated a critical mass of installations in empty premises and open yards while others were distributed through the city. This implicitly meant that the experience of the festival also became an experience of the working city, thus democratizing the exposure and enjoyment of the media art. The Brucknerhaus concert hall provided the hub functions of information center, meeting place, and conference facility. This is an inspiring antidote to the UK lottery-funded grand gestures. Build a modest hub as a promotional center with auditorium facilities, shop, cafe, and a multipurpose temporary exhibition space and treasury of valuable objects, and distribute galleries throughout the city, along with education centers and accessible reserve collections, in what would be satellite locations. The Venice Biennale may also be cited as a demonstration of the distributed museum with Giardini pavilions and Arsenale buildings acting as the motherships, supported by cleverly curated installations threaded throughout the city. Already we find museums in airports; should they be in shopping malls? It would be futile to suggest that this distributed strategy be applied to major lottery-funded city museum investments when politicians, planners, lottery bodies, and the public have a predetermined desire for major architectural icons.

In 2005 we worked on a project in Swansea in south Wales, a city badly in need of regeneration with the familiar empty retail units that reflect economic decline. The National Waterfront Museum Swansea is a major £32 million waterside museum complex where we encountered the common situation that much of the reserve collection would stay locked away in remote warehouses even after completion. Our response to these apparently disconnected issues was an approach to the city council that we appropriate the empty shops as object vitrines with ready-made lighting and some security. Interpretation of the contained objects could even be extended to external sound installations, and themes could be curated and clustered in specific areas. Sadly, the council did not respond to this idea, though the initiative did anticipate the concept of the temporary "pop-up shop" that is now a familiar part of our retail high street landscape. A development of this concept of shopping and learning was proposed at the Westfield shopping center in west London, when we carried out a study commissioned by the developer to embed a BBC Experience in what would have become a media zone, along with multiplex cinemas, themed restaurants, and synergy retail such as software and electronics. Imagine if the BBC were to provide the "science behind" stories of telephony, computing, and Internet communication to help inform and educate the consumer. Here we had to demonstrate that the financial investment could work only if the developers acknowledged that this initiative would add value to the retail experience, enhancing footfall and rental values: shopping and learning.

Working from the inside out

Sadly, the biggest mistake of twentieth-century museum design continues as we hire superstar architects to create our cathedrals of culture. The exterior is the heroic wrapper while the all-important interior experience is a secondary process that has to be retro-fitted to suit the architect's seductive objects.

In the United Kingdom, National Lottery funding seems to have encouraged institutions to fall into familiar traps as demonstrated at the Liverpool Museum, the National Maritime Museum in London, and the Darwin Centre at the Natural History Museum in London. The functional brief is written and architects join the competition beauty parade. The winning shape is selected and often handed over to a secondary completing architect, project team, and designer to retro-fit coherent visitor experiences. The National Maritime Museum commissioned a new wing in 2012 to help reverse the main entrance to Greenwich Park, but the resulting solution fails to provide a coherent orientation function, and has an uncomfortable relationship with Neptune Court, which is the manifestation of previous lottery funding in 1999. The symbolic eight-story cocoon that forms the £78 million Darwin Centre has attracted many design superlatives in articles describing its external presence (Merrick 2009; Purnell 2009). But it is the internal legacy that passed on an impossible task to the exhibition designers who had to try and make sense of a dislocated movement system, dominant exposed services, and views of scientists who do not want to be exposed to passing voyeurs.

For 15 years my company, Land Design Studio, has benefited from our involvement in exhibition installations of over £35 million, supported by lottery-funded cultural initiatives. Unprecedented investment has exposed us to many diverse clients, procurement processes, and potentially unique creative opportunities. However, my view is that this profligate investment in cultural centers has happened too quickly and that we have not had time to review and learn from our mistakes.

The issue of architecture being fit for purpose is not an exclusively British phenomenon. Zaha Hadid's Phaeno Science Centre in Wolfsburg, Germany, has a beautifully refined concrete form while the interior hosts a random collection of science-based interactives probably sourced from the San Francisco Exploratorium, where they sit more comfortably in a darkened utilitarian space. In California, the originating research and development workshops (where the installations are devised and built) are visible and form part of the visitor experience; they do not need to have any relationship with the architectural aesthetic. I can only imagine that in Wolfsburg the client brief simply demanded an iconic architectural form within which they could install ready-made science interactives with no concern for synergy or an understanding of the holistic visitor experience. By contrast, in Berlin at the Neues Museum architect David Chipperfield has collaborated with Julian Harrap to help integrate the extensive remodeling of the building, along with the sensitive assembly of objects and narrative treatment. The palimpsest of the original building remains while contemporary interventions are justified and help make sense of the narrative stories embedded in the object collection. For the visitor the journey is controlled from exterior to interior, from new to old, using both the building and the objects within it to hold their attention and engage them with the fascinating stories.

The process of museum-making is one of most complex design typologies. Institutions have to bring together museum directors, curators, interpreters, educationalists, and marketing teams who have a really in-depth and sometimes esoteric understanding of their subject fields, associated narratives, and visitor needs. Architects, on the other hand, are forced to work through a professional work plan process which requires them to fulfill their conceptual stage very quickly, before they can move on to their comfort zone of space and mark making. The imperatives of both parties are often mismatched and require mediation. This opportunity to generate an integrated solution is often not understood by clients, which is not surprising as normally they will not have the experience that architects and project managers have in driving large-scale capital projects.

My view is that, in developing a new museum, the creative approach must involve the architect, an informed client team, and representation from exhibition designers at the stage of inception in order to create a truly holistic visitor experience. We have found at the early stages that our fundamental objective is to extend and articulate the primary information contained within the client content brief. The initial conceptual design response provides important technical proposals for the flow, dwell time, narrative sequence, activity adjacencies, communication and media protocols, lighting and acoustic strategies, power and data distribution, and important interfaces with both structural and mechanical engineers. There are also surprising creative and practical contributions that the designer may offer on operational and functional planning (back of house, shop, cafe), and even issues that impact on the funding business, branding, and marketing strategies. Our experience has demonstrated that this "inside out" approach enables solutions that are more coherent for the visitor and more efficient and cost effective for the client. In consequence, the architectural container respects the needs of the holistic visitor experience and is therefore more likely to be fit for purpose.

For example, as exhibition designers for the National Maritime Museum Cornwall (Figure 14.1), we were simultaneously appointed alongside the architects Long & Kentish and spent five valuable years crafting the "inside out solution" (Long 2003). Working with M. J. Long confirmed for us that both architect and interpretive designer must acknowledge each other's function and develop genuine mutual respect. A critical part of the brief was for us to display the small boats collection held by the National Maritime Museum in London. It became clear that we would not be able to contain this sizable collection within the modest

FIGURE 14.1   Exhibition design model of National Maritime Museum Cornwall, UK, 2002/2010. (For a color version of this figure, please see the color plate section.)
Photo: Nick Wood.

footprint of the building. Rather than treat this as a problem, we were able to transform it into a creative organizing principle. A central large volumetric space was created and equipped to enable a periodic rehang, along with a clever interpretation device. This starting point inspired the architects to create an elegant hull-like wall that would conveniently bisect the building, enabling us to create a dark, immersive introductory sequence, along with a ramped system that moves visitors effortlessly through the main body of the museum. The desire for a tower to punctuate the presence of the building on the waterside encouraged us to use the upper level to interpret the estuary and the lower level to investigate the tides and tidal movement that impacted the building. Also we worked together to internalize interpretation galleries and to exploit the seductive views of the water by introducing fenestration as part of the movement system or cafe. The iterative creative process was enjoyed by the whole team of clients, developers, architect, exhibition designers, project managers, marketing consultants, all under the scrutiny of the Heritage Lottery Fund and a regional development agency (for further discussion of this example, see Higgins 2005, 223).

Since the opening of the museum, a new director, with a background in tourism, has elected to deconstruct many components of the building. The architecture has been significantly changed, new galleries have been introduced, and there is a tangible shift from museum to visitor attraction, which may be valid but which challenges the original brief and positioning of the project. This situation probably raises familiar issues of retrospective change and modification, which seem inevitable once any experience is subjected to public use and scrutiny. Few, if any, funding bodies acknowledge or reflect on the need to provide significant funds to administer controlled and responsive changes. In Falmouth it is my view (and the architect's) that changes have been insensitive and random, undertaken without any consultation with the original team and without the iterative rigor that was central to the original process.

Designing for museums is a genre that has yet to be given the professional status that it richly deserves. Historically, it is difficult to track how creative disciplines emerge and establish a professional gravitas. The twentieth century has seen the growth of new creative disciplines such as graphic design, product design, automotive design, and now digital media. These disciplines have established themselves through a need in the marketplace and a desire on the part of willful practitioners to teach, write about, and promote them through events, awards, and professional bodies. Yes, of course, "exhibition designers" participate in all of these things but my view, which is shared by many of my contemporaries, is that the general perception of our discipline sees it as lightweight, as part of an end process, and in consequence it is undervalued.

It is worth considering the process of design consultancy selection, where through the conditions of public funding we are beholden to procurement bodies that believe they are qualified to select designers for their capital projects. It is often the case that they do not have the appropriate knowledge or experience to do this, especially when they are guided by project managers with generic selection criteria, leaving no room for visionary or conceptual approaches or, indeed, smaller, younger design practices. All too often the drivers of selection are lack of risk, lowest price, biggest office, turnover, and the rigorous demands of overcomplicated health and safety and environmental policies. Clients are frequently unaware that the impressive team of pitch-winning principals drawn from the large practices will often hand over the job to the junior designers to complete. The industry spends far too long completing prequalification material; then, if a company is fortunate enough to be shortlisted, it is expected to spend hundreds of unpaid hours competing with a "short" list that may consist of 10 companies. I believe that, in the public domain, project and procurement teams need to be more accountable. Museums should consider using external consultant designers to support them even at policy level to demonstrate an acknowledgment and respect of the extensive experience and skill sets that we have. As a personal example, since forming my company 20 years ago, I probably make a formal documented pitch about 10 times a year, covering a wide range of themes and genres. Yet I have never been invited by lottery bodies, government agencies, or even museum bodies to provide feedback or support in trying to streamline and improve the creative process. Imagine the accumulated knowledge held by established designers who have benefited from working across the platforms of both national and international institutions.

As a departure, I would even encourage a much more significant role for my contemporaries, extending to cultural placemaking which is now firmly on the city planning agenda. It would not be presumptuous to suggest that the exhibition designer's skills with space, narrative, and media may help generate a sense of place that impacts on the conceptual master plan and ultimately the architectural program. The diverse disciplines that I claim for the designer may be represented in a Venn diagram which integrates spatial design, narrative development, and the appropriate use of communication media (see Figure 14.2), all of which have to reflect and respond to the destination (visitor profile).

It is at this point that I confess that I struggle with the nomenclature of "exhibition designer" when really I am considering our value as the auteurs of the holistic creative process, the engineers of experience. My frustration with my inherited job description or title of "exhibition designer" was challenged when I was asked by Central Saint Martins, University of the Arts London, to help introduce a master's course in Exhibition Design. I actually redirected their energies to establish a much more complex program of validation for a course titled "Creative Practice for Narrative Environments" (now titled "MA Narrative Environments"). The course reflects the aspirations of the diagram, and is now establishing both academic and industry recognition. It may be that we need design courses to help explain the commissioning and procurement of talent rather than simply focusing on developing practitioners.

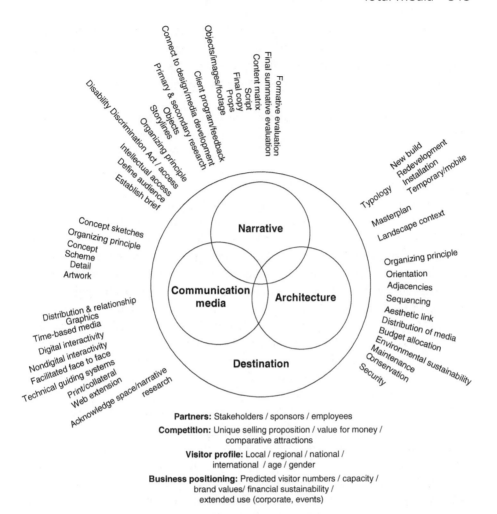

FIGURE 14.2   Land Venn diagram, showing the interrelationship of factors involved in the design process.

The emergence and context of the designer's craft and the influence of film and theater

The design craft associated with exhibitions may have been defined as a significant discipline only over the past 60 years. Before this, although there existed some exceptional and influential exhibition designers, this skill was often seen as technical support subservient to the curatorial display requirements and the fixed criteria of the architectural envelope.[1] For many there is a deep-rooted historic notion that the primary function of the designer is to provide technical support for case layouts in deterministic architectural spaces, and at best to produce the more prosaic outputs of plans, elevations, sections, and drawing packages. Curatorial demands would encourage very dense and often badly lit displays before the arrival of the modern movement, which at last challenged the opaque box and solidity, transforming it into more flexible open floor plans. There was an absence of mediation between the space and object to be exhibited through the neutral nature of the architectural vessel (Higgins 2005).

My own creative journey started with an architectural training at the Architectural Association. As an introduction to the modern movement, we were encouraged to consider Joseph Paxton's Great Exhibition of 1851, which inspired many aspects of structural engineering. This lightweight prefabricated industrial glazed shed was built in 19 weeks, and it was only later that, as an exhibition designer, I discovered how it encouraged participants to exhibit in a more fluid and imaginative way. The displays were a mixture of cultural and technological wonders drawn from around the world; it was, in fact, a trade show with little academic curation. The stained glass clipped to the glazed cladding may be described as an early form of mixed media by virtue of exploiting the source of natural light. This extraordinary event was a resounding success that captured the public's imagination through the simple display of objects that connected them with other worlds (Auerbach 1999; Purbrick 2001). It was also the origin of the World Expos that have continued the tradition of experimental communication wrapped around chosen themes and often set within spectacular architectures. The narrative journeys inspire a diverse range of designers, artists, and communicators to experiment and imagine.

My growing appreciation of the expo experience was enhanced when Land Design Studio was selected to design the UK pavilion at the 2005 Aichi Expo in Japan. Here we took the themes of "Nature's Wisdom" and demonstrated through smart but simple digital media how British innovators have learned from the natural world. With an acute understanding of the simple communication protocol, we were able to accommodate up to 35,000 people per day through a tiny immersive 500 square meter installation (Figure 14.3).[2]

The remodeling of existing galleries or designing for temporary or touring exhibitions involves a very different skill set from an expo pavilion or the creation of a new "green field" museum. Without the extreme demands of creating a new architectural envelope, the exhibition designer has a critical role in the creative process. There is normally a greater degree of comfort for the internal curatorial/interpretation team who would normally have generated a significant body of work to be handed over to the designer at the briefing stage.

With a defined architectural footprint and normally a clear understanding of visitor profile, the designer is in an exciting, liberated position to propose powerful organizing principles and visual stimuli. I would readily compare it to my work in the theater where you are provided with a stage plan and a script. Our design solution for *The Golden Age of Couture* at the V&A in 2007 was driven by the concise brief to describe and disseminate the making and production of couture in the 1950s. A visit to the original Dior headquarters in Paris inspired a design solution for the first

FIGURE 14.3 UK pavilion, Expo 2005, Aichi, Japan, designed by Land Design Studio. (For a color version of this figure, please see the color plate section.)
Photo: Lee Maudsley.

space that deconstructed the Dior and other famous buildings into a series of physical ateliers that also doubled as large vitrines. It was to be as if the separate studios had been extracted from the building and scattered across the floor of the gallery. The concept was conceived as a powerful architectural assembly, creating a sense of place; photo blow-ups were mounted on two sides of the vitrines which enabled interpreted object display on the other sides. As an idea, this then had to be tested with people flow (in this case free flow) and object distribution which impacted on the proposal for a large-format, dynamic projected backdrop at the end of the gallery. This conceptual leap is at the very heart of the design process: the origin and evolution of ideas is complex but ultimately they have to be holistically conceived and, most importantly, to respect the imperatives of the brief.[3]

I now know retrospectively how shifting from architecture to work in TV, film, and theater impacted my design philosophy. It has been fascinating to follow the emerging debate which involved such eminent designers as Stephen Greenberg, KOSSMANN.DEJONG, and Uwe Bruckner who refer to the film and theatrical scenographic process in their exhibition work. I would concur that there is a value in such comparisons but believe that there is a limited crossover.[4] For me, the most interesting link is the extraordinary creative process that needs to take place between the designer and director/curator. For the former, the mediating document is a script and for the other it is a brief. Our task rests in the quantum leap to express their written materials and their imagined situations, transforming them into spatial worlds and time-based experiences. For film designers there is the imperative to create tangible architectural worlds, though, increasingly, with the potential to extend the built form through the use of computer-generated imagery (CGI). The nature of the process normally demands that the finished scenographic product is handed over for others to complete, ultimately within the disconnected edit suite that provides the controlling filter for the auteur. In contrast, the theater designer may well be part of a wider collaborative creative process that engages directed performance, architecture, lighting, sound, and other media in an evolving way. The appreciation of the end product does, however, benefit from the "real time" collective experience.

Suzanne Mulder raises an interesting issue in the parallel world of Disney. It is the design rigor that underpins the Disney theme parks, involving the conventional architectural master plan with the "imagineers" working in the style of moviemakers, using detailed storyboards, close-up and long shots, whereby rides become the camera moves with the rhythm of the show totally controlled (Mulder 2010). As exhibition designers, we may reflect that such visceral experiences are about the thrill of movement and rarely have any extended intellectual value.

The exhibition designer does borrow from the scenographic impact of the film designer or the theatrical "power of the real" in its role to promote and transmit the exchange of ideas and information using a multitude of media. I would interrogate the role of the curator who usually has an extensive knowledge of tangible material and associated narrative but probably a limited understanding of the language and materiality of design in comparison to a film or theater director. It is through the need to display collections of material objects in sequenced narratives that I part company with my exhibition design colleagues. Greenberg suggests that, "because the exhibition is conceived as a 'film in space' rather than a film in two dimensions, each visitor can explore and edit at their own pace and in their own creative space" (2005, 230).

I would argue that there is a distinct difference between the deterministic narrative structure of a film (or theater piece) and the personalized sequence that our visitors undertake through our exhibitions. Yes, they may view the material in their own chosen order, at their own pace with possible unexplained omission or concentrations, but surely this weakens our role as auteur. By contrast, the film or theater director imposes a much more time-based order, allowing the introduction of powerful tools to enhance the story line such as the jump cut or flashback.

However, there are hybrid productions of theater and film that may offer some inspiration to the exhibition designer. For example, the site-sympathetic productions of theater group Punchdrunk, originated by Felix Barrett and Maxine Doyle, enable the audience to be immersed in a promenade experience in their own time, at their own pace, with no time-based sequence. It is entirely self-motivated, and the participating individual collects a series of powerful memories from apparently isolated narratives/performances which are always heavily supported by atmosphere, incredible props, sound, and light. For their finale in the production of *The Masque of the Red Death*, the cast move frenetically from their distributed settings to a gathering space, a ballroom where the Victorian performers come together to dance among the audience. As with a museum experience, these productions have a self-selected sequence and rely on incredible scene setting to enable the participant to engineer their own experience (Cavendish 2013). Film is much less fluid, but I will cite Coppola's *One from the Heart* which, in fact, borrows from theatrical conventions, allowing the audience to see glimpses of adjacent action through gauze reveals. It is intentionally ambiguous, proudly enabling the audience to celebrate the craft of filmmaking in the Zoetrope Studios. As exhibition designers, we may learn how to play with physical layered space from a medium that can only present it as an illusion.

Though I clearly acknowledge the relative control of narrative enjoyed by the genre of film and theater, I believe that the exhibition visitor leaves with a very different completion mindset. By virtue of their own personal edit process, suggested by Greenberg (see above), the exhibition visitor is much more participatory, selective, and personalized in their understanding of interpretive messages, and therefore prepared to extend their knowledge base in their own time.

This experiential designer (exhibition designer) puts the visitor at the center of a promenade that has to acknowledge architectural/spatial conditions, object, light, sound, the tactile, and the olfactory, as well as the more familiar aspects of time-based media (audiovisual), digital–analog interactivity, graphic information, and guided mediation. The design process becomes even more complex when we consider sequential movement and events, the power of real objects, and the impact of other visitors on the dynamics of engagement. Here French filmmaking nomenclature comes to my rescue as I would claim the need to create the *mise-en-scène*.

An ironic media moment arose following our design of the *Pompeii and Herculaneum* exhibition at the British Museum. The brief had driven the need to present the objects in the context of the people that used them by setting them within an architectural construct. I had to squeeze my version of a stylized Roman villa into the imposing round Reading Room, along with an introductory video and all-important end sequence that was to reveal the human casts. I enjoyed the possibility of returning to my days as a theater, film, and TV production designer. The rooms had physical relationships with one another (sometimes through gauzes, Mr. Coppola!) and were defined through scale and color. There was also the consideration of very different lighting levels which created changing moods and atmosphere as I introduced more scenographic techniques such as ceiling pieces and heavily textured paint finishes. (I had provided Rothko as a reference for my painter, and was thrilled to discover that Rothko had in fact been influenced by Pompeii's frescos.) It was only midway through the design process that I discovered the exhibition was to be transmitted live to cinemas across the world. The artifice of a movie set as exhibition was to become a real movie set. There was, of course, some serendipity in this situation, though the experience of real objects that were initially to be viewed in real time and space being transformed into a live filmic event is a fascinating one. Surprisingly, the cinema ticket was more expensive than the exhibition ticket.

Interactivity, digital media, objects, and audiences

My fortuitous crossover of disciplines has encouraged a fascination with the use of time-based media within the context of museum environments. With its roots in *son et lumière*, normally referred to as AV (audiovisual), the compelling and immersive opportunities created by the linear combination of "sound and image" may now be recovering ground against the more fashionable digital interactive scenarios. Recently we have experimented with such concepts as: 360 degree immersive "cave" environments; "table talk," whereby a projection table augments multiperson conversations as if at a virtual dinner party (Figure 14.4); a "frame shift" railway journey supporting the display of the Flying Scotsman; and an optically evolving backdrop providing a context for 30 ball gowns at the V&A. These

FIGURE 14.4   British Music Experience, Table Talk, The O2, London, 2009–2014.
Photo: Nick Wood.

experimental installations, of course, borrow from cinematic references inspired by production designers such as Dean Tavalouris (*One from the Heart*) or from CGI live action matting into digital settings, which is ubiquitous in many of the movies created for younger audiences. It is interesting to observe the influence that this medium has had in the development of scenographic theater design which now frequently incorporates large-scale or digitally projected backdrops, first seen in European experimental theater and the expos. For example, for the National Theatre production of *The Curious Incident of the Dog in the Night-Time*, Bunny Christie and Finn Ross contrived a dynamic digital grid that shifts the sense of time and place effortlessly through the play and reminds us of the visual sophistication of our audiences.

It is fascinating to track the growth of interactive digital media over the past 30 years which has been well documented by Ars Electronica in Linz, Austria. It is the experimental work of new media artists that has led to the contemporary mantra for interactivity in informal learning environments. Our response at Land has been to encourage the appropriate use of new media but not to use it gratuitously, which is especially important now that many of our visitors are familiar with sophisticated user-friendly digital media.

I believe that the growth of interactivity in the museum domain has the central objective of engaging the visitor through "discovery learning," which is most success-ful when we can encourage an emotional link with information delivery. With an understanding of input/output and the feedback loop, it is possible to promote cogni-tive exploration such that initiative and experiment are rewarded (Caulton 1998).

Another revelation has been our concept of "passive interactivity." If the protocol is clear and the delivery mechanism big enough, then one person, the avatar, is able to operate the system on behalf of much larger user groups who may be engaged with the learning process. Our solutions need to appeal to an extremely broad-based user profile and intergenerational users. We encourage systematic evaluation in respect of the intuitive use of the interface and the robustness of manufacture. While working on the British Music Experience at the O2 in Greenwich, the audio-visual hardware company Sysco set up a media lab facility where we could soak test and provide public evaluation and demonstrations for the client.[5]

It is the recently developed technologies that have enabled us to process this data or material in a rapid, responsive, and sensory way. Interfaces or reactive space may now be intuitive and unlike anything that visitors have seen before, and con-sequently we must be aware of sophisticated devices such as the Nintendo Wii and Microsoft Kinect, which are available to the public in the marketplace. A recent TED lecture by Mike Matas (2011) presented a complete media-rich journey through the story of climate change, all beautifully played out on an iPad. Eighteen months earlier, the Science Museum in London had to rely on 40 touchscreens set within a gallery to communicate the same narrative. This is a domestic technology that should stay in the home; visitors now demand smarter thinking when they venture into public institutions.

One of the most important features of the digital domain is the opportunity to build and capitalize on data management systems that provide storage and access, supporting visitor profiles and the growing need for self-selected and bespoke visits. There are presently investigations into developing how object displays can be identified and interpreted by using hand-held digital devices and, more recently, smartphones through GPS or proximity sensors. The augmented reality work of Art Com at the Natural History Museum in Berlin animates the static dinosaurs on foreground screens and is particularly relevant, though more sophisticated than most media available in galleries. In London, the King's College Work, Interaction and Technology Group run by Christian Heath has carried out extensive research of hand-held devices which has raised the issue of the screen detracting from the actual enjoyment of the object. Their study at Tate Modern demonstrated the worrying outcome that more time was consumed by the screen media than by the real object (Heath and vom Lehn 2010).

It is the need to impact on the narratives of source material that provides fascinating opportunities. Apart from data accessing, other typologies may be considered. It is possible to exploit visitors' fascination with physical mapping using large projected landscapes or maps that may be searched either personally or on a large multiuser scale. Reactive immersive environments can provide a collective experience not available on a large scale elsewhere, and semiotic interfaces can engage visitors through symbolic links to the narrative message.

The material culture that has preoccupied us for many centuries has encouraged us to curate, classify, and conserve, and in consequence present sterile objects in glass cases. The mantra of "less is more" often challenges institutions which are seduced into overdisplaying their collections, as is demonstrated at the Imperial War Museum's Duxford site, where its rich collections of aircraft are uncomfortably crammed into hangers that present them totally out of context. This unfortunate situation is, however, counterpointed by a compelling "operations room" which, as an authentic space, is delicately dressed with original material that augments the important story of World War II communications.

Within museums, we need to exploit technologies that can challenge the growth and popularity of the entertainment marketplace by valuing and celebrating "the power of the real" real time, real space, real people, and real objects, all of which may be carefully blended into the digital domain. As a response to the sterile cased/protected object, we have investigated the concept of giving users devices that provide a synthetic connectivity to protected or inaccessible objects by metaphorically unlocking the glass case. Our first embryonic study of this concept was for *Dinobirds*, a touring exhibition at the Natural History Museum in London in 2002, where we provided a joystick light that enabled the visitor to interrogate the surface of a precious fossilized archaeopteryx and be rewarded with in-depth screen interpretation linked to their navigation (Figure 14.5).

We have to also be mindful that only some of our visitors are familiar with smart digital media devices. For *The Book of the Dead* at the British Museum, we

FIGURE 14.5   Dinobirds, Natural History Museum, London.
Photo: Nick Wood.

were perplexed by how the visually rich papyri have to be presented at a scale and a level of conservation lighting that do not necessarily enable the visitor to enjoy them fully. Our proposal to provide adjacent projected image enhancement, which did not devalue or detract from the overall visitor experience, was at first resisted but ultimately proved to be a success.[6]

The process of developing contemporary museum installations may now shift to a more participatory public domain as visitors make significant contributions through personal objects that may be easily curated through Internet research, then passed on to curatorial teams for authentication. Long gone is the preoccupation with building exhibitions and telling stories based on convenient reserve collections. Our active response to our visitor demographics is often included in briefing documents prepared by established museums. It provides empirical data that usually underpins the imperative that the visitor experience be for everybody: families, adult experts, cultural tourists, young children, and so on. The inevitable outcome is for us to generate a communication strategy that would satisfy the median intellectual level of a 12-year-old visitor.

At the British Music Experience (BME), an exhibition dedicated to the history of British popular music at the O2 in London, designed for the American Anschutz Entertainment Group, we were conscious that there would be a wide range of expectations, from a 12-year-old who thinks that there are only four boy bands in the world to a 65-year-old who thinks that there is only one band in the world: Led Zeppelin! The serious challenge was to satisfy the differing needs of the audience and also to acknowledge the familiar need to attract repeat visits from local visitors and the inherent audience attracted to this incredibly successful O2 music venue. Three factors impacted on our creative solution: the plan/sequence that provided a group entry and exit experience with completely self-selected free flow for the main body of the exhibition; the layering of digitally stored media that enables self-selected curation possibly mediated by an elder/expert; and a serious interactive music studio that has universal appeal for young, old, expert, and novice. The BME has been acclaimed by the music press and received a special commendation from the European Museum of the Year Award, but probably the most rewarding review was in *Time Out* magazine, which carried a photograph of three generations expressing the value of their own individual day out (Arthur 2010).

We have recently developed the concept of tracking visitor activity with the objective of enhancing the overall quality of their experience in response to individual profiling. By encouraging visitors to provide semantic data, we could provide bespoke fields of interest including gender, language, and intellectual point of entry (useful for the various National Curricula in the United Kingdom), and also the opportunity to revisit them via the website or social media. Imagine if a soldier were able to feed in personal details of regiment, military action, and comrades which could be augmented through light, sound, or media as they passed through galleries at a war museum. There are emerging radio frequency identification (RFID) technologies that provide effective mechanisms to help detect and feedback data on a personal and consequentially engaging level. Recent developments in gaming interfaces are even predicting the passive measurement of alpha wave activity in the brain to provide apparently subconscious responses to physical stimuli.

Dynamic websites can extend the visitor experience way beyond the tangible architectural space, to school or home. It is my view that some of the "real time" journey may become part of the "extended web" which, as a complementary experience, should be built into the complete design strategy. We need to understand how to integrate all media into the total experience, and not to view the website as a separate bolt-on experience. I believe that the website is an extremely valuable preview and reprise of the visit and, in consequence, it should be handled in a complementary and sympathetic way, in response to the experience of the live visit, possibly through smartphones.

The past five years have been a revelation in respect of the growth of digital media and associated activity through the use of smartphones and social networking. We cannot deny that our visitor profile is changing fast. Social media have impacted on many dynamics, especially, at this moment, on the harder to reach 18- to 30-year-olds, but even this will change quickly. There has been significant activity within certain museum bodies to investigate their digital services. In 2012 the V&A produced a research document showing that 60 percent of its visitors use a smartphone to enhance their gallery or cultural visit. In particular, visitors took photographs, searched information, and were even positive about the idea of finding music relating to a period or place (V&A 2012). An extended Online Manager's Forum (including the V&A, Tate, the National Gallery, and the Imperial War Museum) went on to debate issues of potential distraction, tensions between visitor needs, and the requirements of new etiquettes.[7] A major observation was the need to design experiences from the perspective of user need and motivations rather than that of technology. Michael Dixon (2013), director of the Natural History Museum, reminded us of the smartphone-wielding public offering the potential for democratized crowd-sourced science. At the Science Museum in London, hundreds of people participate in Friday night science events, which have no formal marketing. In one of educationalist Ken Robinson's (2010) famous TED lectures he noted that young people don't use watches because they now carry devices that not only tell the time but a whole lot more. We know that their smartphones will easily capture images and experiences, distribute them to their friends, and store them for later use. Our young visitors are now our marketeers, or detractors. Advertising agencies hire young graduates just to track and respond to their social media profile. As Lucy von Weber (2011) said at a recent TiLE conference, "if there is a conversation going on out there about you, you had better be a part of it."

In this short review of museum making I have attempted to embrace and disseminate some of my personal experiences gathered through a privileged rollercoaster career. As an introduction I used the expression "total media" which I adopted absurdly from the better-known tactical theory of football pioneered by the Dutch in the 1970s, described as "total football" (Dutch, *totaalvoetbal*). This theory focuses on a team dynamic of adaptability, spatial awareness, fluidity, and collaboration. At the same time, I am not advocating a complete democratization of process because, as with football management, we still need visionaries to identify, build, and manage the team. It is critical in our profession that we search out the most accomplished thinkers who understand the huge complexities of the issues that I have raised and lead their teams to reinvent and perpetuate the value and function of museums in our everyday lives.

Notes

1   See also Chapter 18 by Sue Perks in this volume.
2   "UK Expo '05 – Visitor Experience," http://vimeo.com/10231653 (accessed August 19, 2014).
3   See "V&A – The Golden Age of Couture," http://vimeo.com/9351370 (accessed August 19, 2014).
4   For more on the combination of film and exhibition design, see Chapters 3 by Nils Lindahl Elliot, 5 by Jenny Chamarette, and 15 by Bettina Habsburg-Lothringen in this volume.

5 "British Music Experience," http://vimeo.com/9379070 (accessed August 19, 2014).
6 "British Museum – Ancient Egyptian Book of the Dead," http://vimeo.com/17325834 (accessed August 19, 2014).
7 "Making Visitor Information Easier for Mobile Phone Users," http://www.vam.ac.uk/blog/digital-media/making-mobile-users-experience-better (accessed August 19, 2014).

References

Alberge, Dalya. 2013. "Galleries Are Playing It Safe with Bowie and Endless Renoir." *Observer*, January 20.

Arthur, Tim. 2010. "Get into Dad Rock." *Time Out*, June 17.

Auerbach, Jeffrey A. 1999. *The Great Exhibition of 1851: A Nation on Display*. New Haven: Yale University Press.

Caulton, Tim. 1998. *Hands-On Exhibitions*. London: Routledge.

Cavendish, Dominic. 2013. "Punchdrunk: Plunge into the World of Extraordinary Theatre." *Telegraph*, August 12.

Conn, Steven. 1998. *Museums and American Intellectual Life*. Chicago: University of Chicago Press.

Dixon, Michael. 2013. "Technology Can Bring the Magic of Museums to All." *Evening Standard*, July 13.

Duncan, Carol. 1995. *Civilising Rituals: Inside Public Art Museums*. London: Routledge.

Giebelhausen, Michaela, ed. 2003. *The Architecture of the Museum: Symbolic Structures, Urban Contexts*. Manchester: Manchester University Press.

Greenberg, Stephen. 2005. "The Vital Museum." In *Reshaping Museum Space*, edited by Suzanne MacLeod, 226–237. London: Routledge.

Heath, Christian, and Dirk vom Lehn. 2010. "Interactivity and Collaboration: New Forms of Participation in Museums, Galleries and Science Centres." In *Museums in a Digital Age*, edited by Ross Parry, 266–280. Milton Park, UK: Routledge.

Higgins, Peter. 2005. "From Cathedral of Culture to Anchor Attractor." In *Reshaping Museum Space*, edited by Suzanne MacLeod, 215–225. London: Routledge.

Hooper-Greenhill, Eilean. 1992. *Museums and the Shaping of Knowledge*. London: Routledge.

Long, M. J. 2003. *National Maritime Museum Cornwall: The Architect's Story*. London: Long & Kentish.

Matas, Mike. 2011. "A Next-Generation Digital Book." Video. Accessed August 18, 2014. http://www.ted.com/talks/mike_matas#t-754 .

Merrick, Jay. 2009. "What a Creation! Darwin Centre's New Wing Is Both a Mystery and a Triumph of Design." *Independent*, September 9. Accessed August 18, 2014. http://www.independent.co.uk/arts-entertainment/architecture/what-a-creation-darwin-centres-new-wing-is-both-a-mystery-and-a-triumph-of-design-1783870.html.

Mulder, Suzanne. 2010. "Context." In *Engaging Places: Exhibition Design Explored*, edited by Herman Kossmann and Mark De Jong, 11–41. Amsterdam: Frame.

Purbrick, Louise, ed. 2001. *The Great Exhibition of 1851: New Interdisciplinary Essays*. Manchester: Manchester University Press.

Purnell, Sonia. 2009. "Natural History Museum's Darwin Centre Can Rival the Dinosaurs." *Evening Standard*, September 8. Accessed August 19, 2014. http://www.standard.co.uk/arts/natural-history-museums-darwin-centre-can-rival-the-dinosaurs-7416437.html.

Robinson, Ken. 2010. "Bring On the Learning Revolution." Video. Accessed August 18, 2014. http://www.ted.com/talks/sir_ken_robinson_bring_on_the_revolution.

Sutton Young, ed. 2011. *Stories King's Cross*. London: King's Cross Central Ltd Partnership.

TDIC (Tourist Development & Investment Company) et al. 2008. *Introduction to Saadiyat Island Cultural District*. Abu Dhabi: Motivate.

V&A. 2012. "Understanding the Mobile V&A Visitor." Accessed September 8, 2014. http://www.vam.ac.uk/__data/assets/pdf_file/0009/236439/Visitor_Use_Mobile_Devices.pdf.

von Weber, Lucy. 2011. "Digital Tourism: Tomorrow's Guest Has Checked In Early." Paper presented at the TiLEforum 2011, Florence, Italy, October 17.

Peter Higgins trained at the Architectural Association and has worked as a designer for the BBC and in London's West End theaters. In 1992 he formed Land Design Studio, which has built a reputation in integrating architecture, narrative design, and communication media for museums, science centers, visitor attractions, and commercial environments. Clients include the Foreign and Commonwealth Office, Anschutz Entertainment Group, Miraikan Tokyo, National Parks Singapore, the V&A, the Natural History Museum, and the British Museum, where in 2013 they designed *Pompeii and Herculaneum*. He has worked with the museum studies department at Leicester University and at Central Saint Martins where he helped develop their MA in Narrative Environments. In 2009 he was awarded an RDI (Royal Designer for Industry).

15 FROM OBJECT TO ENVIRONMENT
The Recent History of Exhibitions in Germany and Austria

Bettina Habsburg-Lothringen
[Translated by Mark Miscovich]

More and more, museums and exhibitions are drawing on the immersive strategies refined and professionalized by theme parks and shopping centers over the
past decades – visualization and materialization, the creation of three-dimensional
environments, the blurring of lines between reality and fiction, the leveling of
time and landscapes, personalization and personification, and the atmospheric use
of light, tone, color, smells, and architectural features – as ways of attracting a
larger audience. There are two reasons for this. First, museums and exhibitions
have begun to address new, more abstract themes and areas of the sciences, the
present and future which are not represented by classical museum objects. Second,
the aesthetic and medium of the museum exhibition has been redefined and
inspired by artists, filmmakers, cartoonists, designers, and choreographers using
new media, and by the incorporation of related professions into the field of exhibition design. Drawing on examples from the German-speaking world, this chapter
will investigate what these developments mean for the traditional museum
medium (objects, texts, architecture) and how they can be assessed in a museum
historical context.

The International Handbooks of Museum Studies: Museum Media, First Edition.
Edited by Michelle Henning.
© 2015 John Wiley & Sons Ltd. Published 2020 by John Wiley & Sons Ltd.

Museum exhibitions: Classification and chronology

Cabinets of curiosities were the forerunners of what we now call museums, and are still considered to be one reference point for designing exhibitions up to the present today. There were no limits to the content of Renaissance cabinets of curiosities. Although there were changing fashions and interests, it can be said that they contained the entire diversity of the known world. Not only was no attention paid to the spatial separation of art, technology, and nature – a separation that was felt to be absolutely essential in later museum presentations – but they also seemed to care very little about the opposition between reality and fiction, which was later to become insurmountable in the centuries that followed. The fantastic was treated as equally valid in these collections, and everything wonderful and curious worked to break down the hierarchy of norms and conventions.

Cabinets of curiosities focused on objects, which were stored and presented in one place. Since they differed greatly in size and appearance, depending on their origin, there was no standard form for presenting the exhibition pieces: pictorial works leaned against or decorated walls from floor to ceiling. Objects were positioned in the middle of the room or set on tables. Preserved specimens hung from the ceiling, preferably next to cabinets, chests, shelves, and sideboards on the same theme, which were found along the walls or in the middle of the room and were used to house the pieces of the collection. Written commentary such as labels on the exhibition objects and the connections between them were found only occasionally, which was also true of inventories and catalogs.[1]

The true significance of the individual pieces of the collection in a cabinet of curiosities only became apparent in relation to the other objects. Every piece was part of an entire composition, which included the storage furnishings and the exhibition room. As a kind of walk-in exhibit object, the cabinets aimed to produce an overall artistic and monumental effect. There was no standard classification system for arranging the objects, no generally valid principles, but there was a notion of the ideal cabinet. For instance, the objects could be classified according to art objects, natural and ethnological objects, instruments and weapons, and so on. Or the objects could be arranged according to material, which meant that objects made of gold, silver, wood, porcelain, glass, or ivory would be grouped together, regardless of their origin, form, and function. The objects were also ordered according to ideas of resemblances and affinities, of sympathies and antipathies between objects, of associations and correspondences, which, as Michel Foucault described, had to be deciphered first from the secret signs ([1966] 1994, 31–32).

At the end of the seventeenth century, it seems that cabinets of curiosities started to lose their attractiveness. Horst Bredekamp (1995, 86) points to the fate of the cabinet of curiosities (*Kunstkammer*) in Dresden, Germany. Its closure, which began in 1720, was typical and anticipated the fate of all the important cabinets during the course of the eighteenth century. The cabinets of curiosities were closed because their collections of objects were incomplete, their compositions were uninspired, and they were not organized into recognizable disciplines. It is clear today that the "chaos" of the cabinets was, in Bredekamp's words, "deliberate" and that they were mirrors of a world as people up to the seventeenth century imagined it to be (Bredekamp 1995, 113). Nevertheless, in the eighteenth century, at the beginning of the modern history of museums, they were denounced as cluttered junk rooms without any comprehensible system.

In this new context, the presentation of collections and exhibitions of the museum set out to reveal a new conception of the world, a transformed way of thinking, according to which resemblances were no longer credible and their signs could no longer be granted the power of classification. The ideas and concepts associated with modernity challenged the worldview of the past by emphasizing a world of superficial visibility and a reality that could be compared and described systematically on the basis of this visibility. In accordance with this, classification and chronology became the guiding concepts of the new museums.

As Jana Scholze has observed, exemplary, largely interchangeable, objects are used as representatives of scientific systems in the context of classifying exhibitions (2004, 86, 122). As early nature exhibitions clearly show, individual pieces are reduced to their formal and functional properties, and the accompanying information is limited to name or title, provenance, and date. Individual histories and social, regional, and cultural backgrounds are left unexamined. Objects in classifying exhibitions are presented in rank and file. Despite their variety and diversity, the order of the exhibitions creates the impression of harmony, homogeneity, and conformity. Since they are equally present and current, regardless of their age, the objects seem to be timeless. This is also reinforced by using as few means of presentation as possible and through standard plain display cases.

In terms of reception, classification implies a comparative view of things. And it can be assumed that there is a direct connection between the opportunity to learn something and one's previous knowledge: the less previous knowledge the viewer has, the more likely it is that they will let the aesthetic of the object alone have an effect on them. In traditional arrangements of minerals, for example, non-specialists have no other choice but to compare them according to color, material substance, and place of origin.

Chronologically ordered exhibitions also, clearly, differ from the spatial creations of cabinets of curiosities: in the case of linear chronological orders, the remains of objects and events are defined as sequences. Chronologies help to represent time sequences, periods, and so-called turning points in history; they are, however, constructs and are neither objective nor definitive. They respond to the wish to make the past tangible and to picture people and things in it. In exhibitions, chronologies are mainly created by written texts, and then suggested through the arrangement of the objects, as well as the sequence of rooms. The individual object in the chronological stories, however, often seems subordinate; this leads to a reduction in its range of meaning.

Chronological orders have played a key role in museums of art and cultural history since the eighteenth century. The development of art museums led to less emphasis being placed on aesthetic criteria and overall visually attractive scenarios, and more importance being given to selecting representative works based on their historical development with the goal of providing an encyclopedic overview. Scholars were from now on interested in composition, color, and lighting as an expression of artistic quality. Exhibition pieces now had to be grouped in rooms according to periods, schools, and geographical origins. In the nineteenth century, these rooms were still often staged in a conspicuous way, furnished with murals and frescoes or decorated with flower arrangements and matching furniture. Only later was it thought that a homogeneous setting made it easier to compare objects (Joachimides 2001).

In historical museums, scholars endeavored to restructure the historical remains according to the modern idea of a metanarrative. With the aid of written sources and evidence in the form of objects, a coherent picture of historical world events would be drawn, and a universal as well as purposeful plan revealed on closer consideration of episodes connected by cause and effect. In this way, well into the twentieth century, historical exhibitions could still create the impression that the past not only could be reconstructed and objectively described in texts, but that it could also be represented factually using labeled objects in serial presentations and accompanying texts (Beier 2000).

Chronologies, narrative structures, and narrative schemes make the reception of objects easier for the audience. They provide a clear way to read the exhibition and are familiar to the audience from fairy tales, media, and everyday storytelling. Classification and chronology were also used as ordering principles to communicate ethnological themes in the museum. These also included methods of presentation designed to create environments. The term "environment" here refers to sometimes expansive combinations of objects and design elements in the exhibition space, arranged in such a way as to give the most authentic impression of a period or the life of people in that period. Information on the dates, materials, or functions of the individual objects does not play an important role in this form of presentation, and language-based commentary is used sparingly.

The pioneering events for these reconstructive visualization and staging concepts of the nineteenth and twentieth centuries were the world's fairs (Kretschmer 1999). The enormous number of objects on display and the cultures represented forced the organizers of the world's fairs and the participating countries to continuously develop new, unconventional forms of presentation. To beat the competition, they always sought to incorporate the most spectacular architecture and the most sensational decorations, parades, and festivities, and to integrate new technology and media.

In this way, recreated street scenes, villages, and urban neighborhoods, for instance, were supposed to act as excursions to faraway worlds or past times. The buildings and landscapes, reconstructed out of wood and papier-mâché, were decorated with mannequins and traditional accessories. Reconstructed scenes of everyday life and celebrations, paintings and panoramas, were supposed to provide atmosphere. However, these were soon found to be too lifeless and the desired density and dynamic of thoroughly idealized pictures was achieved only by the introduction of live animals, poets, musicians, and actors in magnificent costumes.

At the start of the twentieth century, the presentation of scientific and technological innovations at world expositions required completely different concepts. Visitors' interest in these was aroused by transforming abstract content into comprehensible pictures. The goal of driving simulators, "transparent humans," walk-in periodic tables, and other interactive attractions that appeal to the senses was to use visual means to make difficult scientific or technical knowledge more understandable and accessible. Later presentations of technology and the sciences, for example, in science centers, have drawn on the experiences gained from the world expositions.[2]

Thus, presentation methods designed to create a classification, a chronology, and an environment were the main forms used by early museums to create a picture of the world. Their development has been linked to the development of modern science since the beginning of the modern period. However, their development is also an indication of the understanding and identity of the institution of the museum as a scientific establishment. Ultimately, the methods of presentation could be considered as a mirror of the visual culture and perceptual habits of the time.

All three methods of presentation mentioned above can still be found in museums. Classifying arrangements are used, for instance, in the currently popular accessible depot. Such "open storage displays" can be seen, for example, in the ethnographical Übersee-Museum Bremen in Germany, the Historisches Museum Luzern in Switzerland, and the new regional museum of Vorarlberg, in Bregenz, Austria. Chronological order is still the most commonly used form for conveying history, for example, in the German Historical Museum [Deutsches Historisches Museum] in Berlin. And reconstructive methods of presentation, which were designed to create an environment, can still be found relatively unchanged in ethnographic and open air museums, like in the Swiss Open-Air Museum in Ballenberg. However, in other places, these methods have been critically examined and widely reinterpreted over the course of the twentieth century.

Stagings of the 1980s: The exhibition as montage and essay

Starting in the 1970s, the German-speaking world experienced an increase in the number of museums and a differentiation of their contents. The medium of the exhibition also underwent a momentous change, becoming more didactic. Under the battle cry of "Lernort kontra Musentempel" [Places of education versus museum temples] (Spickernagel and Walbe 1979), the elitism of the museum institution was the subject of passionate debate, and there was a call for a clear commitment to its communicative and educational mission, including the use of didactic media and techniques. Whereas, up to the beginning of the 1970s, exhibitions had traditionally been characterized by objects and accompanying texts, the graphic arts now found their way into the museum. The medium of the text grew in importance and use as the fundamental bearer of meaning.

This process of making the exhibition more didactic had already provoked a countermovement in the 1980s. During this decade large-scale exhibitions, dedicated to historical periods or important historical figures, established themselves in the German-speaking world. The German ethnologist Gottfried Korff curated several of these exhibitions and thus founded and promoted a new type of staged exhibition. Examples include *Preußen – Versuch einer Bilanz* [Prussia – Attempting an assessment] in 1981 and *Berlin, Berlin: Die Ausstellung zur Geschichte der Stadt* [Berlin, Berlin: The exhibition on the history of the city] in 1987, both staged by the Berliner Festspiele GmbH at the Martin-Gropius-Bau, Berlin (see Eckhardt 1982; Korff and Rürup 1988). This new type of exhibition, with its emphasis on objects and accompanying texts, broke with the distanced, Enlightenment-inspired purism of traditional museum exhibitions. Likewise Korff adopted a position contrary to the didactic presentations of the 1970s, which, in his view, pushed the object into the background and gave too much room to texts and graphics. Ultimately, he opposed the exhibition practice of many cultural, scientific, and folklore museums, which in the 1980s were still attempting to reconstruct as detailed and authentic a picture of the past as possible.

In this new type of cultural history exhibition, the exhibits were now supplemented by audiovisual media and art and design features, and were arranged in self-explanatory environments.[3] These environments allowed the ever increasing number of exhibits to be structured more clearly for the audience and the objects to be contextualized according to an overriding theme. The focus of the exhibition was always on the object, which, as the "historical informant" and "core and quintessence of the museum," was supposed to be emphasized by the form of its presentation and to become the undisputed center of the exhibition once again. Korff was convinced of the nature of the object as historical witness and of the aura of the original. Walter Benjamin had once characterized this as the stimulating dialectic of an emotional and intellectual, and thus unapproachable, distance of the original and its simultaneous spatial, sensuous, and material proximity and presence (Benjamin [1939] 2003, 255).

Thus, for Gottfried Korff, an exhibition was not only a "thing archive" and a "place to collect and display material culture"; it was also an "agency of sensuous knowledge" and should be used to further communicate the perspectives and positions on cultural theory of a specific time period (1982, 16; 1988, 14; Korff and Roth 1990, 15–16). In the 1980s, these included the questionable nature of (the theory of) progress and of grand historical narratives; insight into the inaccessibility of the past and, thus, the constructed nature of any representation of history;

and the undoing of oppositions such as dream and reality, reason and madness, and high and popular culture.

The first display technique to fall victim to the assumption that the past cannot be represented was the reconstructive staging. A variety of museums today still rely on replicas of historical spaces and events, which involves the danger of reinforcing clichés and showing the past as a pleasant idyll. The new historical exhibitions of the 1980s refused any naturalistic images that purported to transport the viewer to distant places and different time periods. They ultimately rejected any impression of illusionary authenticity and the pretense of any possibility of documenting history from A to Z. To describe this, Gottfried Korff appropriated the term "ironic museography" from the British art historian Stephen Bann (1988, 63): The artificial character of any world created by the museum should be made apparent through specific alienating effects and distortions. This should enable a critical and plural approach to history, which reveals history in its splendid diversity of "penetrating, conflicting and complementary constructs and force fields," in its "coexistence and opposition," and with its "connections and breaks, and changing images and models" (Korff and Rürup 1988, 16).

The inclusion of different perspectives and alternative narratives strongly supported a transdisciplinary approach to themes, and the attempt to arrive at a productive integration of documents and discourses from political and cultural history; the technical, social, and natural sciences; and religion. Art was granted a special, higher, role. For a long time, the purpose of art in historical exhibitions was to portray rulers or to provide a picture to make it easier to envisage events. The idea now began to gain acceptance that artistic objects as historical remains are, in some way, perhaps more suited to capturing the complexity of events and of facing the impossibility of representing the past in a sublime and witty way (Ernst 1991, 27). In addition to this combination of disciplines and objects as historical witnesses, there was also the combination of high and popular culture: objects of everyday culture were now given equal space in historical exhibitions, and the design of the exhibition was also guided and inspired by everyday cultural forms and genres. Ultimately, copies and reproductions were awarded a new role. Traditionally, they were frowned on in exhibitions and were opposed to the original, but now they were used specifically to call the visitor's attention to the fact that any approach to the past, even through an original object, is possible only to a very limited extent (see, for example, the exhibitions at the Martin-Gropius-Bau mentioned above).

The pathos and solemnity of some traditional historical presentations were relativized by revealing the history of their reception and research. The idea was to show that the state of scientific knowledge, and the mindsets and worldviews that went along with it, were constantly changing, that images of history were subject to formative processes, that there were always responsible and interested parties behind interpretations and representations of history, and that other, alternative, contradictory interpretations and theories could always be found.

Therefore, these exhibitions had to make clear to a wide audience that any judgments presented were based on current understanding of the theme, and that an exhibition was only a contemporary attempt to interpret the past, a mirror of current research results, scientific discourses, and particular tastes.

The high degree of reflection ultimately also included the conditions and possibilities of the exhibition as a medium. It was important to communicate that exhibitions can be understood only in the context of social codes, of knowledge and understanding, and as a repository of changing historical constructs and the expression of changing power relations, and that exhibitions are always necessarily bound to the value systems and worldviews of their curators and designers.

But how could these main conceptual ideas be expressed, and how did they influence the appearance of exhibitions? These new principles could never have been implemented without a re-evaluation of the importance and role of design. Exhibition designers were still responsible for taking appropriate measures to frame and protect exhibits, for arranging and structuring them, as well as for defining the specific path through the exhibition and rhythmic sequences. However, the shift to staging as the main design principle increased the importance and share of design in the overall outcome of the exhibition and, at the same time, gave proof of a new awareness of the museum as an aesthetic medium. As in the theater, exhibitions now had to make a story available to all the senses by placing it within the proper setting, by realizing an interpretation of the content, and by offering a visual interpretation. Attitudes toward the philosophy of culture and the theory of history, such as the idea of the basic impossibility of representing history, found expression in design, in distortions and illusions, which (de)composed the happy appearance of complete presentability. The desire to emphasize the relativity of any scientific knowledge now made it possible to include poetic and artificial images, and metaphorical and playful translations, in historical presentations. The audience's expectations were consistently disappointed through unexpected collisions of objects and compositional counterpoints. The unbridgeable gap between present and past was demonstrated by exposing the exhibits in a structure that was clearly recognizable as contemporary, for instance, through the confrontation with new media and aesthetics. Interpretations and meanings were supposed to be provoked and guided by atmospheres and moods, which could be produced only through the introduction of new media and technology capable of conveying meaning through staging. This led to an increased use of atmospheric media such as architecture and colors, sounds and light, in addition to objects, which were deliberately put into a meaningful relationship with one another, and the traditional means of display case and pedestal. Two examples for this are the exhibitions *Traum und Wirklichkeit: Wien 1870–1930* [Dream and reality: Vienna 1870–1930] in Vienna (1985) and *AEIOU* in Stein, Lower Austria (also 1985).

As a whole, these disorienting conceptual and design features pursued the goal of triggering a "productive shock" in the viewer. Walter Benjamin, who coined this phrase, defined it as *the* modern form of perception that focuses the attention, as the disturbing element and didactic means that leads to knowledge in a "lightning flash" ([1927–1940] 1999, 457).

Immersion and reflection: Developments from the spirit of the 1980s

The fractured stagings of history in the 1980s set a new standard. Today these sometimes seem like only a timid beginning in the light of sensational exhibition concepts and design solutions, but it should be noted that they laid the foundation for these and gave a foretaste of the later and current appearance of many exhibitions through the radical upholding of principles and demands made 30 years ago. In addition, it also seems essential that the influence of this practice of staging was not limited to cultural history exhibitions, but can also be found in historico-scientific and natural scientific exhibitions.

So, what developments can be identified over the past two decades in the German-speaking world? First, the number of exhibitions has continued to increase. There has been a shift to more and more spectacular locations outside the museum, and new themes and contents have led to new methods of conveying meaning and new curatorial and design professions. On the level of concepts and design, there is not just one clearly identifiable trend but, rather, many at the same time. Since the 1990s there has been a revival of interest in cabinets of curiosities as a benchmark for a wide variety of exhibition projects. A purism of presentation, which had been considered, in the meantime, to be obsolete, and a focus on the inquiry of the individual object, have experienced a renaissance in a variety of categories and for different reasons (a countermovement directed specifically against the practice of staging of recent years, a return to the collection as the centerpiece of the museum, financial reasons, etc.). Historical exhibitions tend either to belong to the critical tradition of the 1980s, or to be shaped by historians who persistently ignore any theoretical treatment of the question of exhibiting. Science exhibitions have been booming and run the gambit from reduced object–text combinations to opulent inventions of images and space. This also applies to technology exhibitions, which have faced new competition in the form of highly successful and decidedly interactive science centers. A holistic understanding of themes has spread throughout natural history museums. Traditional systematic presentations and environments still exist and, on the level of design, aside from the increased use of media, the influence of developments in cultural scientific fields can be observed. Folklore and ethnology have shown a tendency either to critically examine their traditional idyllic constructions and make the history of their collections clear, or to ignore any critical reassessment of their own tradition, an approach often evidenced by singling out and aestheticizing the pieces of their collections and presenting them as pieces of art.

The following discussion will focus on a recent trend. A number of exhibitions have been staged in a new way in the German-speaking world since around the year 2000. What is distinctive about them is the way they resist reducing their themes to individual disciplines while, at the same time, considering perspectives from the history of culture, nature, and science. They follow in the footsteps of the 1980s idea of the exhibition, in which the exhibition was considered to be a sensuous-aesthetic, pictorial medium; and they continue to develop the staged exhibition by drawing on means and strategies from various recreational institutions and culture-related media. Following from this, I would like to suggest a second form of exhibiting as an alternative, one that also continues to pursue previously discussed aspects of 1980s exhibitions. This encompasses exhibitions from a wide range of categories which make certain theoretical positions or museological thought a fundamental component of the overall concept, relatively independent of the specific theme but equally significant. These theoretical positions are concerned with the institution of the museum and the medium of the exhibition; questions of representation, reception, and perception; the role and social responsibility of curators and designers.

Since the turn of the millennium, there have been several large exhibitions in the German-speaking world, located somewhere on the border between the cultural and natural sciences, which were thoroughly designed as visual and spatial media.[4] In contrast to the familiar large exhibitions devoted to persons and periods, these presentations have in common the fact that they tackle complex themes, which are difficult to define objectively – such as health, brain research, belief, age, or "the future of nature." These themes do not suggest any single meaningful narrative, they are not associated with just one specific scientific discipline, and they are not necessarily connected to any particular collection or object. While traditional portrayals of individuals or representations of periods involved a particular body of source material and a clear number of objects, in the case of these new themes, the choice of narrative (among other possible ones) and a particular manner of communication appropriate to the theme has been increasingly left to curators and designers.

Another characteristic feature of these exhibitions is that they do not necessarily concentrate on original objects or tell one single coherent story. The focus is on terms and messages ("Health is more than conventional medicine" or "Nature is something people can manipulate and construct," for example), which are secondary to the various exhibition techniques used for conveying meaning. Furthermore, the documentation of historical circumstances now also includes questions and perspectives with respect to the present and future.

A wide range of professionals with spatial and visual skills have started to work as exhibitions designers. Whereas in the 1990s most of the exhibition designers in the German-speaking world were stage designers and architects, now they are representatives from the fields of art, film, comics, costume design, music, and dance. With the background of their respective media and professional experience, they have a strong understanding of exhibitions as spatial media and holistic spaces of experience. They combine objects with images, sounds, interactive options, and living protagonists to produce a balanced representation. Their commitment to the institution of the museum and the traditions of the various disciplines only goes so far and, contrary to the traditional Enlightenment-inspired educational imperative of the museum, they only want to provoke people to examine the theme critically. And, most of the time, this provocation is brought about by staging (*Inszenierung*).[5]

The new terminology seeks to convince us of the qualitative difference between this staging and those of the 1980s. The term "scenography" was not used in connection with exhibitions in the German-speaking world until the year 2000. It eventually became familiar to a wider public via its use in discussions of reactions to the theme park at the world's fair in Hanover. In the context of the world's fair, scenography refers to the artistic interpretation and scenic implementation of content, which should make the effect and the intended message of the exhibition clearer and more significant through the use of creative means (Roth 2000). This corresponds to an understanding of the term in relation to the 1980s stagings. While the stagings were primarily characterized by architectural and stage design features, scenography breaks down boundaries through the integration and combination of elements of various origins, such as dance, film, music, choreography, and art, and also utilizes the possibilities presented by technical advances. Scenography could be understood to be the process of making familiar stagings more intense and dynamic: no more cautious suggestions in abstract translations but, rather, completely integrated spatial environments; no compositions of objects merely accentuated by light in rooms clearly recognizable as exhibition rooms but, rather, the blending together of design arrangements, interior, and architecture into an all-encompassing counter-reality; and no static images but, rather, flexible, atmospherically dense, and interactive illusory spaces, in which the viewer is immersed temporarily.

The immersive power emanating from these kinds of exhibition scenarios are reminiscent of the captivating character and manipulative strategies of commercial theme parks. As H. Jürgen Kagelmann (1998) has explained, these parks translate their content into easy-to-understand three-dimensional pictures. These are then combined together to form stories with a beginning, a middle, and an end, which merge together smoothly and consistently. The audience moves through the three-dimensional picture stories as if through a reconstructed film, which takes place within familiar narrative structures, now enriched by surprising colors, forms, and materials and enlivened by personalized objects and interactive options, while at the same time creating a world that differs spatially and aesthetically from the familiar world. This break with the familiar world is further reinforced by hermetically sealing off the outside world. There are no windows to the outside, and the interiors are covered with colors, materials, sounds, and light, or blanketed or neutralized by projections. The fact that there are no empty spaces or gaps allows visitors to temporarily forget about the outside world and makes it possible to create a new tangible and seemingly "authentic" world. In addition to architectural techniques, light, and sound installations, smells and fluctuating temperatures are used and visitors' sense of balance may be deliberately unsettled. Thus, there could be a sensational transition from day to night every five minutes, a forest might arise from the atmospheric choir of its inhabitants, and a trip to ocean floor could be simulated through the manipulation of air pressure. Theme parks are temporary immersions in fantasy worlds and counter-realities. The rules of traditional museum exhibitions are not part of their vocabulary. This can be seen, for instance, in how reality and fiction are arbitrarily combined, or the limits of time and space are simply ignored, in theme parks.

Scenographic exhibitions are now approaching this level. For instance, there is a need to visualize and materialize, which manifests itself in visualizations and materializations of scientific knowledge or cultural processes: it is no longer enough to hint at traces in exhibitions, but rather it has become necessary to invent visually impressive and objectively tangible signs for the small, the complex, and the intangible. Thus, the process of cell division is no longer described, but is performed as a dramatic trip in a three-dimensional virtual space. Whatever can be recognized on the level of two- and three-dimensional objects is also important at the level of the whole presentation, which is defined by metaphorical and allegorical pictorial spaces and visually dynamic and acoustically enhanced illusory spaces.

Moreover, on the basis of a very theme-oriented overall concept, wrapping the content into stories seems very promising. The exhibition piece is needed at most as a signal of a story, whose episodes the audience can explore and wander through as with a film set. Optical textures take the place of connecting verbal explanations: from beginning to end, a semantically loaded architecture interweaves the various methods of conveying meaning into forward moving, linear sequences of events with causes and effects, and climaxes and happy endings. At the same time, the dramatic composition seeks to purposefully control the formation of hypotheses and associations, as well as rhythms of excitement and relaxation. The fact that this is mainly the same as the traditional narrative scheme helps promote understanding. However, playful ways of dealing with dramaturgical patterns and systematically provoked breaks with convention do not necessarily conflict with the audience's ability to notice and remember if the content at issue is at least known in part, and thus individual signs or pictures are sufficient to evoke associations and stories in the viewer's mind.

Another characteristic feature of exhibition staging is a very creative way of dealing with conventional concepts of time and space. Although the museum has always been a place of alternative spatial arrangements and condensed geographies, what is new is the selection and combination of specific objects according to attraction and sensation and the goal of enabling rapid reception on a quick walkthrough. In terms of the approach to time and duration, it should be noted that traditional concepts are becoming less important, giving way to an apparent simultaneity of depicted events as technically elaborate "individual times" are being created. Complete isolation from the outside world is achieved through architectural and design methods. Without the means to locate their position and orient themselves, visitors then experience, for example, the annual cycle of seasons every hour. Examples of this could be seen in the "Planet of Visions" and "The 21st Century" exhibits at the Themenpark Expo 2000 in Hanover, Germany.

In addition to the dissolution of time and space, there is the blurring of reality and fiction. This means that, not only is fiction allowed to enter, but the hierarchy between imagination and reality is broken down, so that there is no longer any difference between the fantastic and that which can be scientifically proven. Therefore, it is perfectly natural to include digitally generated organisms in exhibitions – as seen, for example, at the exhibition *7 Bilder und Zeichen des 21: Jahrhunderts* [7 hills: Images and signs of the 21st century] in Berlin in 2000, in the *Dschungel* [jungle] section – or to organize visually stunning journeys from the Big Bang all the way to the end of the universe.

Other promising strategies for immersion are personalization, personification, and participation. In historical and ethnographic exhibitions, the personal fates of both real and fictional persons are used to address the audience on an emotional level. In nature and scientific exhibitions, animals and objects are personified, as they were, for example, in the knowledge and communication pavilions at the Themenpark Expo 2000. Participation turns visitors and viewers into active contributors, who are able to take sides in historical conflicts, or be responsible for positive and negative environmental developments in virtual worlds, as in the exhibition *Die Zukunft der Natur* [The future of nature] in South Tyrol, in 2005.

Finally, moods and atmospheres are essential for captivating the audience. The recipes of "emotional design" for constructing "scenarios of feeling" are as simple as they are well known: modifying colors and lights are placed over the architecture (size, shape, and sequence of rooms), and acoustic stimuli are added as mood elements. Materials, smells, and temperatures contribute to further condensing the atmosphere, which strives to represent a stimulus-intensive alternative to filmic acceleration. The goal of all these measures is to create self-contained worlds, in which the audience can focus on the content presented, without distractions from the outside world.

However, if scenographic exhibitions use the same strategies as commercial theme parks, how can we still tell them apart? One clear difference can be found in whether scenographic spatial creations – in the tradition of the cultural history stagings of the 1980s described above – make reference to and are based on cultural theory. This finds its expression in the appearance and character of the images and environments that are created, which are not merely superficial reconstructions or trivial transpositions of content into the exhibition space, but instead independent design or artistic translations of a theme full of wit, spirit, or irony. Exemplary in this respect are the temporary exhibition *Kosmos im Kopf: Gehirn und Denken* [The cosmos in your head: The brain and thought], at Deutsches Hygiene-Museum

Dresden [German Hygiene Museum] in 2000 and the permanent exhibition *Helden & Hofer* [Heroes and Hofer] in the MuseumPasseier in South Tyrol (since 2009).[6]

It is obvious that communicating content in the manner described above has tremendous implications for the importance and role of the methods used to create and convey meaning and exhibition media. In a situation where content cannot be represented in conventional ways, because it is abstract, processual, or invisible, and where the current present, with its wealth of objects, and the objectively incomprehensible future are integrated into a presentation with the finished past, there must be consequences for the traditional museum media of object, text, and architecture.

But what do these "abstract" themes mean for the role of the traditional object? There is no doubt that the new themes of recent years have entailed very far-reaching changes for the object: the object tends to play a secondary role in scenographic exhibitions. It is disempowered in favor of overall atmospheric impressions, and it loses its special status as an original relic, work of art, and so on when it becomes an equal part of the design or artistic environment. When this practice is taken to the next level, the exhibition object is not only neglected, but is completely omitted as an apparently negligible element. One simply dispenses with the central bearer of meaning in the museum and finds a replacement in design installations, artistic works, and symbolic signs. One reason for this development is that conventional exhibits, in terms of the content of exhibitions, are becoming harder to find or must actually be invented first, whereas the new technical and medial capabilities now provide very promising additional bearers of meaning, suitable for staging and full of aesthetic potential (examples of these can be found in all of the exhibitions listed in n. 4).

The medium of writing is still used to explain objects, to create connections, and to basically provide context. However, scenographic exhibitions try to do without texts as far as possible in order to facilitate international reception as well as in recognition of a presumably changed perception. Texts, whether in their quantitative scope or in their visual appearance, do not play a defining role. Ideally, they should not disturb the overall visual impression.

The importance of museum and exhibition architecture, as well as the outer representative building and interior design, has been unchallenged since the beginning of the museum age, but their function has changed completely. The task of interior design has always been to divide areas and rooms, to organize correspondences and relationships, to provide insights and vistas, and to give collections a dignified setting. However, now, in the case of scenographic exhibitions, interior design is increasingly used to support conceptual considerations and content messages. It serves the purposes of message and information, of moods and atmospheres. It should not only be attractive and decorative, but also tell part of the story, using aberrations and disruptions to confuse, or sloping walls, slanting floors, perspectival distortions, or labyrinthine passages to provoke anxiety. There was no lack of this in the staged exhibitions of the 1980s, but a new quality results from using immaterial media to enhance the architecture. Light and sounds, smells and temperatures, intensify, contrast, or make the messages of the architecture more concrete and turn rooms into atmospheric spaces. In an opposite scenario – and this also did not exist in this form in the 1980s – the architecture is deliberately neutralized and the constructed space is reduced to acting as a flexible projection surface for images and information (again, examples of these can be found in the exhibitions listed in n. 4).

This is mainly communicated using audiovisual media. Audiovisual features have become a permanent part of exhibitions in recent years and have established themselves as information systems for conveying knowledge and information specific to target groups: texts, images, films, and sounds make it possible to offer additional content on the themes, which gives visitors an interactive and individual option of defining for themselves how much detail they prefer. In scenographic exhibitions, media are now particularly used to create spaces and atmospheres. Designers create flexible worlds of play, perception, and illusion, using images and sounds as well as visual, musical, and acoustic effects. In addition, media technologies make it possible to add virtual contexts to objects, to arrange settings and interactive tours, or to integrate objects into the presentations using external realities. The difference between new illusion technology solutions and historical extensions of real space is that the spaces created by modern media are dynamic and can always be replaced and supplemented, as needed, by new virtual spaces.

As the new protagonists of exhibitions, dancers and actors also set the created spaces in motion and contribute to a hybridization of the medium of the exhibition, which can also be seen where aquariums and libraries or entire planetariums, zoos, and cinemas become an integral part of exhibitions. Art plays a special role in scenographic exhibiting. As previously mentioned, art was integrated into historical exhibitions on account of its content up to the 1970s, but the artistic quality of its implementation was not particularly important. Starting in the 1980s, awareness developed in the value of artistic visualizations, particularly for themes and aspects of themes that evade objective documentation through the traditional medium of the object and can only be described in long texts. Today, art can be found in every museum category as a semantically concise and sublime means of expression. In scenographic exhibitions, which have freed themselves from the idea of a definitive story or the ability to present a true picture of the past, artists and designers create exhibition pieces and produce colorful visualizations of findings, processes, and developments, for which there is no pictorial equivalent in reality. What is surprising and new is that art is only partially recognizable as art and, in many cases, works of art are not identified as such. However, art is found not only in the form of individual objects or installations, but also at the level of design, when artists are active as exhibition designers.

Other kinds of presentations, which one could describe as discursive exhibitions, pursue completely different strategies of communication and other goals than the scenographic exhibitions described above. As in the case of the image-based, scenographic thematic exhibitions, these exhibitions address current scientific, political, or social problems and issues, which, on account of their complexity and intricacy, cannot be approached through one particular story as the only meaningful one or through specific objects. The curators and designers responsible for the exhibition can develop narratives and formulate messages as they think best, using objects and texts as well as artistic and design installations to help them do this. In contrast to scenographic exhibitions, these discursive exhibitions are not content with communicating simple individual messages, but instead attempt to give objective and spatial expression to various attempts at explanation and interpretive approaches using the exhibition as a medium. As in the 1980s, this is realized by the density and arrangement of objects and the use of design features and artistic interventions. The difference between them can be found in the tendency to focus not on sound scientific knowledge on the theme or issue of the exhibition, but rather on the history and the current state of the scientific and/or artistic treatment of the theme or issue. As in the 2012 exhibitions *Objekt Atlas: Feldforschung im Museum* [Object atlas: Fieldwork in the museum] and *Trading Style: Weltmode im Dialog* [Trading style: World fashion in dialogue], at the Weltkulturen Museum [Museum of World Cultures] in Frankfurt, Germany, the object no longer stands for itself or for a discovery, knowledge, or event, but rather it becomes a piece of evidence in the museum's process of interpretation and scientific research.

Another characteristic of these discursive exhibitions is a strong sensitivity to the conditions of exhibiting and the apparent desire to make the audience aware of the power of the institution of the museum to give meaning, of the traditions and particular characteristics of the medium of the exhibition, or of the role and responsibility of designers and curators. In attempting to shake the foundations of apparently incontrovertible laws and cherished traditions, the audience takes part in the happening of the exhibition in the form of event- and process-based works, performances, and experiments. Freed from their role as passive consumers, visitors suddenly finds themselves obliged to contribute actively to the development and success of an exhibition. A very interesting institution in this context is the Stapferhaus in Lenzburg, Switzerland.[7]

Although discursive exhibitions seem to be more cumbersome and less accessible than the opulent scenographic exhibitions, they have found their way into contemporary art and into museums of ethnology, culture, and the natural sciences. Both discourse exhibitions and scenographic exhibitions are part of the museum's tradition of interpreting and communicating the world. They carry within them ideas and inspirations from cabinets of curiosities, traditional museums of modernity, and the history of museums and exhibitions in the twentieth century in different forms and to varying degrees, and they are more or less based on their key media: object and text. However, they have also been influenced by the forms of presentation and communication of art, world's fairs, and commercial theme parks and the high street.

Scenographic exhibitions, in particular, have received a great deal of attention from museum practitioners and journalists in the German-speaking world, who have criticized them time and again.[8] The main target of criticism has often been how they deal with the object as the traditional and central subject of museum exhibition, its reduction to one source of information among others, its casual integration and degradation in multimedia spatial creations, and the resulting impression of a depreciation of content in favor of elaborate and self-conscious exhibition design. This criticism is based on legitimate concern about the aestheticization, media overload, and technical upgrading of exhibitions which, in terms of presentation, are not necessary but are often included for good measure rather than for any communicative function. But it is also based on a power struggle over the question of what an exhibition should be, how it should be made, and where the limits of museum exhibition should be drawn. Curators tend to favor linking the concept of museum exhibition to the actual object. They feel a duty to the collections they manage, whose cost-intensive maintenance they, it seems, increasingly have to justify. Furthermore, curators in charge of collections mainly think of themselves as scholars and consider museums to be object archives and places to display material culture, places for object-based research and object-based knowledge transfer. Media, architecture, and design experts, however, see themselves less as advocates of museum collections, and consider it their duty to convey the message of the content by any means possible, taking into account the audience's interests and habits of perception.

In conclusion, it is difficult and, at this point, too early to make a general statement on scenographic exhibitions. Scenographic exhibitions have contributed, like discourse exhibitions, to making exhibitions in the German-speaking world more diverse and colorful. They will not replace the traditional object-based exhibitions, but they have further potential, and thus their continued existence is justified. Their relation to the present and to society allows them to treat themes in museums and exhibitions that are important today but difficult to capture in collections. And they contribute to reinforcing the museum's role as a place for representing current issues and as a forum.

Notes

1   On cabinets of curiosity, see, e.g., Pomian (1990); Grote (1994); Bredekamp (1995); Schramm, Schwarte, and Lazardzig (2008); Mauriès (2011).
2   Sources on world's fairs and expos include Greenhalgh (1988); Rydell and Gwinn (1994); Mattie (1998); Kretschmer (1999); Roth (2000); Wörner (2000); Wyss (2010).
3   See, e.g., the exhibitions of Gottfried Korff (Korff 1981; Korff and Rürup 1987); see also Eckhardt (1982); Mai (1986); Korff (1988; 1995); Korff and Rürup (1988); Rüsen, Ernst, and Grütter (1988); Korff and Roth (1990); Schober (1994); Biermann (1996).

4   For example, Themenpark Expo 2000 in Hanover, Germany with its pavilions "Planet of Visions," "The 21st Century," "Mobility," "Knowledge," "Communication," "The Future of Work," "Basic Needs," "Health Futures," "Humankind," "Nutrition, Energy and Environment"; *7 Hügel: Bilder und Zeichen des 21. Jahrhunderts* [7 hills: Images and signs of the 21st century] at the Martin-Gropius-Bau in Berlin in 2000; *Kosmos im Kopf: Gehirn und Denken* [The cosmos in your head: The brain and thought] at the Deutsches Hygiene-Museum Dresden [German Hygiene Museum] in Dresden in 2000; *Die Zukunft der Natur, Landesausstellung Tirol* [The future of nature: State Exhibition, Tyrol] in Tyrol–South Tyrol–Trentino in 2005; *C'est la vie*, in the Naturhistorisches Museum [Museum of Natural History] of the Burgergemeinde of Berne, a permanent exhibition since 2008; *Helden & Hofer* [Heroes and Hofer] in the MuseumPasseier in South Tyrol, permanent exhibition since 2009; the exhibitions *nonstop* (2010), *Glaubenssache* [Matter of faith] in 2006–2007, and *Entscheiden* [Decision-making] in 2013–2014 in the Stapferhaus Lenzburg, Switzerland; the exhibitions *Glück* [Luck] in 2008, *Arbeit* [Work] in 2009–2010, and *Leidenschaften* [Passions] in 2012 at the Deutsches Hygiene-Museum Dresden, Germany; and, finally, the DDR Museum in Berlin, with its permanent exhibition, which was renewed in 2012.

5   For the German term *Inszenierung*, see Scholze (2004).

6   Andreas Hofer was a Tyrolian "freedom fighter" in the eighteenth century who fought against Bavaria and France/Napoleon

7   See Chapter 16 by Beat Hächler in this volume, which focuses specifically on the exhibition strategies of the Stapferhaus.

8   See, e.g., Assheuer (2000); Becker (2000); Eggebrecht (2000); Jessen (2000); Kemp (2000); Kamann (2000); Seibt (2000); Urban (2000).

References

Assheuer, Thomas. 2000. "Die Evolution frißt ihre Kinder" [Evolution devours its children]. *Die Zeit*, October 26.

Bann, Stephen. 1988. "Das ironische Museum" [The ironic museum]. In *Geschichte sehen: Beiträge zur Ästhetik historischer Museen* [Visualizing history: Contributions on the aesthetics of museums of history], edited by Jörn Rüsen, Wolfgang Ernst, and Heinrich Theodor Grütter, 63–68. Pfaffenweiler, Germany: Centaurus.

Becker, Peter von. 2000. "Wer der Göttin Kali in die Augen schaut: Berlins Jahrhundert-Schau, '7 Hügel' und Hannovers Expo mit ihrem 'Themenpark' gehen zu Ende: Letzte Fragen vor Torschluss" [Those who look the goddess Kali in the Eye: Berlin's century-show "7 Hills" and Hanover Expo with its "Theme Park" come to an end: Last questions before gate closure.] *Der Tagesspiegel*, October 27.

Beier, Rosmarie, ed. 2000. *Geschichtskultur in der zweiten Moderne* [Historical culture in second modernity]. Frankfurt: Campus.

Benjamin, Walter. (1927–1940) 1999. *The Arcades Project*. Translated by Howard Eiland and Kevin McLaughlin. Cambridge, MA: Harvard University Press. Based on Walter Benjamin's *Das Passagen-Werk*, edited by Rolf Tiedemann (Frankfurt: Suhrkamp, 1983).

Benjamin, Walter. (1939) 2003. *The Work of Art in the Age of Its Technological Reproducibility* (3rd version). In *Selected Writings, vol. 4, 1938–1940*, edited by Howard Eiland and Michael W. Jennings. Cambridge, MA: Harvard University Press. Originally published as *Das Kunstwerk im Zeitalter seiner technischen Reproduzierbarkeit* (Frankfurt: Suhrkamp, 1963).

Biermann, Alfons W., ed. 1996. *Vom Elfenbeinturm zur Fußgängerzone: drei Jahrzehnte deutsche Museumsentwicklung: Versuch einer Bilanz und Standortbestimmung* [From the ivory tower to the pedestrian zone: Three decades of German museum development: An Attempt at Balance and Positioning]. Opladen, Germany: Westdeutscher.

Bredekamp, Horst. 1995. *The Lure of Antiquity and the Cult of the Machine: The Kunstkammer and the Evolution of Nature, Art and Technology*. Princeton: Markus Wiener.

Eckhardt, Ulrich, ed. 1982. *Preußen – Versuch einer Bilanz: Bilder und Texte einer Ausstellung* [Prussia – An Attempt at Balance: Pictures and texts of an exhibition]. Berlin: Berliner Festspiele.

Eggebrecht, Harald. 2000. "Odyssee durch den Weltmüll: Die Berliner Millenniumsschau, Sieben Hügel" lenkt den Blick auf eine beunruhigende Zukunft" [An odyssey through global waste: The Berlin millennium show "Seven Hills" draws attention to a worrying future]. *Süddeutsche Zeitung*, June 3.

Ernst, Wolfgang. 1991. "Das historische Museum" [The historical museum]. *Österreichische Zeitschrift für Geschichtswissenschaft* 4: 25–43.

Foucault, Michel. (1966) 1994. *The Order of Things: An Archaeology of the Human Sciences*. New York: Vintage.

Greenhalgh, Paul. 1988. *Ephemeral Vistas: The Expositions Universelles, Great Exhibitions and World's Fairs, 1851–1939*. Manchester: Manchester University Press.

Grote, Andreas, ed. 1994. *Macrocosmos in Microcosmo: Die Welt in der Stube: Zur Geschichte des Sammelns 1450 bis 1800* [Macrocosm in microcosm: *The world in a room:* On the history of collecting 1450–1800]. Opladen, Germany: Leske & Budrich

Jessen, Jens. 2000. "Der achte Hügel: Die Expo wird das Zwischenlager für den geistigen Restmüll des 20. Jahrhunderts" [The eighth hill: The Expo is the interim storage for the mental waste of the 20th century]. Die Zeit, May 18. Accessed August 22, 2014. http://www.zeit.de/2000/21/200021.sprechmuell_expo.xml.

Joachimides, Alexis. 2001. *Die Museumsreformbewegung in Deutschland und die Entstehung des modernen Museums 1880–1940* [The museum reform movement in Germany and the emergence of the modern museum 1880–1940]. Dresden: Verlag der Kunst.

Kagelmann, H. Jürgen. 1998. "Erlebniswelten" [Worlds of experience]. In *Erlebniswelten: Zur Kommerzialisierung der Emotionen in touristischen Räumen und Landschaften* [Worlds of experience: Commercialization of emotions in tourist areas and landscapes], edited by Max Rieder, Reinhard Bachleitner, and H. Jürgen Kagelmann, 58–94. Munich: Profil.

Kamann, Matthias. 2000. "Die Kathedrale des Wissens" [The cathedral of knowledge]. *Die Welt*, May 13.

Kemp, Wolfgang. 2000. "Geiler als Playstation Two oder zurück zu den Fingerfarben? Erste Impressionen eines leicht beeindruckbaren Expo-Gängers aus Hannover" [Hotter than Playstation Two or back to the finger paints? First impressions of an impressionable Expo-goer from Hanover]. *Die Zeit*, May 31. Accessed August 22, 2014. http://www.zeit.de/2000/23/200023.expo-flaneur_.xml.

Korff, Gottfried. 1981. *Preußen – Versuch einer Bilanz* [Prussia – An attempt at balance]. Reinbek, Germany: Rowohlt.

Korff, Gottfried. 1982. "Zur Einführung" [Introduction]. In *Preußen – Versuch einer Bilanz: Bilder und Texte einer Ausstellung* [Prussia – An attempt at balance: Pictures and text of an exhibition], edited by Ulrich Eckhardt, 14–17. Berlin: Festspiele.

Korff, Gottfried. 1988. "Die Popularisierung des Musealen" [The popularization of the museal]. In *Museum als soziales Gedächtnis? Kritische Beiträge zu Museumswissenschaft und Museumspädagogik* [The museum as social memory? Critical contributions to museum science and pedagogy], edited by Gottfried Fliedl, 9–23. Klagenfurt, Germany: Kärntner Druck- und Verlagsgesellschaft.

Korff, Gottfried. 1995. "Läßt sich Geschichte musealisieren?" [Can history be a musealized?]. *Museumskunde* 60: 18–22.

Korff, Gottfried, and Martin Roth, eds. 1990. *Das historische Museum: Labor, Schaubühne, Identitätsfabrik* [The historical museum: Laboratory, stage, identity factory]. Frankfurt: Campus.

Korff, Gottfried, and Reinhard Rürup, eds. 1987. *Berlin, Berlin: Die Ausstellung zur Geschichte der Stadt* [Berlin, Berlin: The exhibition of the city's history]. Berlin: Nicolai.

Korff, Gottfried, and Reinhard Rürup, eds. 1988. *Berlin, Berlin: Bilder einer Ausstellung: Eine Dokumentation* [Berlin, Berlin: The exhibition of the city's history]. Berlin: Festspiele.

Kretschmer, Winfried. 1999. *Geschichte der Weltausstellungen* [A history of world expositions]. Frankfurt: Campus.

Mai, Ekkehard. 1986. *Expositionen: Geschichte und Kritik des Ausstellungswesens* [Exposures: History and criticism of exhibitions]. Munich: Deutscher Kunstverlag.

Mattie, Eric. 1998. *Weltausstellungen* [World's fairs]. Stuttgart: Belser.

Mauriès, Patrick. 2011. *Cabinets of Curiosities*. London: Thames & Hudson.

Pomian, Krzysztof. 1990. *Collectors and Curiosities: Paris and Venice, 1500–1800*. Translated by Elizabeth Wiles-Portier. Cambridge: Polity.

Roth, Martin, ed. 2000. *Der Themenpark der EXPO 2000: Die Entdeckung einer neuen Welt* [The EXPO 2000 theme park: The discovery of a new world]. Vienna: Springer.

Rüsen, Jörn, Wolfgang Ernst, and Heinrich Theodor Grütter, eds. 1988. *Geschichte sehen: Beiträge zur Ästhetik historischer Museen* [Visualizing history: Contributions on the aesthetics of historical museums]. Pfaffenweiler, Germany: Centaurus.

Rydell, Robert W., and Nancy Gwinn, eds. 1994. *Fair Representations: World's Fairs and the Modern World*. Amsterdam: VU University Press.

Schober, Anna. 1994. *Montierte Geschichten: Programmatisch inszenierte historische Ausstellungen* [Assembled stories: Programmatically staged historical exhibitions]. Vienna: J&V.

Scholze, Jana. 2004. *Medium Ausstellung: Lektüren musealer Gestaltung in Oxford, Leipzig, Amsterdam und Berlin* [The exhibition medium: Readings of museum design in Oxford, Leipzig, Amsterdam and Berlin]. Bielefeld, Germany: Transcript.

Schramm, Helmar, Ludger Schwarte, and Jan Lazardzig, eds. 2008. *Kunstkammer – Laboratorium – Bühne: Schauplätze des Wissens im 17. Jahrhundert* [Kunstkammer – laboratory – stage: Scenes of knowledge in the 17th century]. Berlin: De Gruyter.

Seibt, Gustav. 2000. "Data Morgana: In der Berliner Ausstellung 'Sieben Hügel' zeigt sich das vormoderne Weltbild der neuen Wissensgesellschaft" [Data Morgana:

The premodern worldview of the new knowledge society at the Berlin exhibition "Seven Hills"]. *Die Zeit* 21.

Spickernagel, Ellen, and Brigitte Walbe, eds. 1979. *Das Museum, Lernort kontra Musentempel* [The museum, a place of learning versus a temple of the Muses]. Giessen, Germany: Anabas.

Urban, Martin. 2000. "'Alles echt!' – 'Alles Blödsinn!' Die große Berliner Ausstellung Sieben Hügel präsentiert 'suggesto-fiktive' Absurditäten als Relikte einer unbekannten Kultur" ["It's all real!" – "It's all nonsense!" The great Berlin exhibition Seven Hills presents "suggesto-fictive" absurdities as relics of an unknown culture]. *Süddeutsche Zeitung*, July 4.

Wörner, Martin. 2000. *Die Welt an einem Ort: Illustrierte Geschichte der Weltausstellungen* [The world in one place: An illustrated history of world expositions]. Berlin: Riemer.

Wyss, Beat. 2010. *Die Pariser Weltausstellung 1889: Bilder von der Globalisierung* [The Paris World Fair of 1889: Pictures of globalization]. Frankfurt: Insel.

Bettina Habsburg-Lothringen is a historian and, since 2010, has been head of the Museumsakademie Joanneum at the Universalmuseum Joanneum in Graz, Austria. Since 2014 she has also been head of the Cultural History Department of the Joanneum which includes the Museum im Palais and the Styrian Armoury. She is the editor of *Dauerausstellungen: Schlaglichter auf ein Format* [Permanent exhibitions: Spotlight on a format] (Transcript, 2012); *Die Praxis der Ausstellung: Über museale Konzepte auf Zeit und auf Dauer* [The practice of exhibition: On museological concepts of time and duration] (Transcript, 2012); and *Das Schaudepot: Zwischen offenem Magazin und Inszenierung* [Visible storage: Between open storerooms and staged presentation] (Transcript, 2010). Her research interests include the history of display in museums, permanent exhibitions, the representation of history in museums, and the social role of the institution.

16 MUSEUMS AS SPACES OF THE PRESENT
The Case for Social Scenography

Beat Hächler
[Translated by Niall Hoskin]

"Social scenography" is a working concept. It has evolved in recent years as a result of reflection on my own practice with regard to exhibitions, and stands for an attempt to explicitly address the performative aspect of exhibitions and the actions and effects they trigger, rather than being limited to the design of what is visible in concrete terms. In this sense, social scenography represents a change of emphasis, an attempt to fathom the social aspect of the scenographic more profoundly, and thereby to extend the focus onto all actors within the scenographic space, but especially visitors. How can scenographic means be used to enhance the social, interactive, communicative dimension? What makes an exhibition into a social performative space? What is the role of the visitor in the production of the exhibition as social space? This chapter takes an empirical approach. It sets out to use a case study of the Stapferhaus Lenzburg, and my own experiences of exhibitions from the period 1994–2010, to derive methodological insights which could be grouped under the term "social scenography." The Stapferhaus Lenzburg, an exhibition provider active in Switzerland and abroad which also goes by the name of Haus der Gegenwart, a "museum of the present," is unique in that it is organized along interdisciplinary lines (Hächler 2009, 131). To this day it is consistently dedicated to staging contemporary topics from the real world, without being able to fall back on either a collection of its own or permanent exhibition spaces.

The International Handbooks of Museum Studies: Museum Media, First Edition.
Edited by Michelle Henning.
© 2015 John Wiley & Sons Ltd. Published 2020 by John Wiley & Sons Ltd.

Please touch

The following incident occurred in Vienna's renowned Albertina, in the *Andy Warhol Cars* exhibition (*AK für Sie* 2010; Odendahl 2010, 44). The exhibition showed, among other things, an installation by the Genevan artist Sylvie Fleury. Fleury's work consisted of a group of images with nine large-format aluminum panels, placed directly on the floor and simply leaning against the wall: the panels showed oversized covers of old American car magazines. On this particular morning, a senior attendant was making his customary tour of inspection through the exhibition rooms when a junior attendant pointed out to him that one of the nine panels in Fleury's piece had slipped slightly. At that time there was as yet no barrier in front of the installation. It is possible that a visitor or the cleaning lady had knocked the panel the previous day and no one had noticed. The senior attendant did not hesitate and carefully moved the artwork back to its original position. He did not move the panel by more than a centimeter, he later explained. For the senior attendant, that was the end of the matter – not so for the Albertina's museum management, which heard of the incident. The museum employee was called to account for acting without authority and summarily dismissed from service in the museum. The reason given for this step by the deputy director of the museum was the resultant "loss of trust." She asserted that a senior attendant should not touch any art "be it by Rembrandt, Dürer or Fleury." He should have informed restorers, curators, and exhibition management, and not have laid hands on it himself. The 45-year-old defendant appeared before an employment tribunal. He acknowledged that he had acted on impulse and expressed regret. The court was lenient and simply issued a warning: the employee was allowed to stay in post as a senior attendant.

A thousand kilometers west, in the small Swiss town of Lenzburg in Greater Zurich, a quite different story took place. Lenzburg is the home of the Stapferhaus Lenzburg, which has been active since 1994 as an exhibition provider. The Stapferhaus is not a museum in the strict sense: it has no collection and no exhibition spaces of its own; instead, it presents themes of the present through spatial arrangements in specifically chosen venues. Thus, in 2006, *Glaubenssache: Eine Ausstellung für Gläubige und Ungläubige* [A Matter of Belief: An Exhibition for Believers and Nonbelievers] was presented for 12 months in a warehouse on a former military site, although the exhibition was also later shown in the Luxembourg City History Museum. The creators of *A Matter of Belief* set out to examine belief and religion in everyday modern life.

What many found surprising was that the exhibition did not begin indoors, as museum visitors expect, but outside the door (Figure 16.1). Instead of the expected entrance, the public was greeted by an installation with two labeled entrances: on the one side, the entrance for believers, on the other that for nonbelievers. There was no third door, not even for deliveries or staff. The doors were expensively fitted out, but each to the same standard. Brilliant white with gold lettering, encased in a frame clad in brass panels. Visitors wanting to approach one of the doors did so on a 5 centimeter high tarmac walkway which extended into the hall. Thus the choice

FIGURE 16.1   Self-enactment: the scene at the entrance to the exhibition *A Matter of Belief*, Lenzburg, Switzerland. (For a color version of this figure, please see the color plate section.)
Photo: Donovan Wyrsch. © Stapferhaus Lenzburg.

of door began five meters outside with the first step onto the walkway. Those wanting to step into the exhibition had to identify themselves as "believers" or "nonbelievers." By means of this self-exposure – proceeding along the walkway, reaching for the handle, opening the door – the actual exhibit, the action, was produced.

Why am I recounting this? Because the two exhibition scenes show in abbreviated form two fundamentally different conceptions which must exercise us as we think about the museum as a space of the present. Naturally the term "space of the present" itself implies certain characteristics, which might be discussed as aims: being a social space, being meant to stimulate an examination of material from the here and now, or being a space for reflection and self-reflection. Here I should like to touch on just five elements which are inherent in the two conceptions, and then to consider the outline of a social scenography.

Social scenography: Approaches to the concept

Touch versus don't touch

Sylvie Fleury's piece, with its nine aluminum panels, doubtless makes a visual statement on the subject of "cars." However, the work consists primarily of a spatial ensemble of picture panels, whose arrangement within the white cube is determined and fixed by the artist in a series of overlaps, specific spacings, and angles of inclination. The piece stands for itself and becomes accessible through its physical presence and materiality. The visitor's role is to look at the piece, to read it, and, if possible, to understand it.

If one were to apply this process precisely to the initial phase of *A Matter of Belief*, the experienced visitor to the Albertina would have to pause a while in front of the entrance to *A Matter of Belief*, inspect the brass panels, read the lettering on the door, ponder on the meaning of the installation, and carry on past regardless. In the case of *A Matter of Belief*, the simple gesture of looking does not lead to access. Instead, it is necessary for visitors to perform an action. In this case, doors are not objects to be looked at but instructions for action. They are there in order to be opened. In the Albertina – as we already know – the arrangement of space was quite the reverse. The pictures leaning against the wall are not sending out the signal "Who hangs us on the wall?" or "Who clears us away?" but rather "Here stands an untouchable work of art." Action (in the sense of handling) was not only not intended, but it broke certain elementary rules in the game of art museum activity, and was punished as a "loss of trust." The museum as institution relies here on employees carrying out only certain authorized actions, and on visitors conducting themselves as mere observers of what the curator and artist have devised for the public, and who must accept unquestioningly this division of roles into active and nonactive. From this arises a second fundamental element which has already been touched on.

Static work versus performative, ephemeral work

Inherent in the contrast between the two approaches of action and nonaction is the differing materiality of the two types of exhibition. Fleury's picture piece is material and static; the performative work of choosing a door is immaterial and ephemeral. The performative work is, at most, visible to other chance observers outside and, in any event, visible to the active participants themselves. By acting within the wholly artificial context of the Zeughaus Lenzburg, participants pose the classic question "Do I believe?" themselves. The spatial disposition makes the visitor who is interested in questions of belief into a visitor-actor. The physical distance required in the Albertina, and, after the incident, explicitly emphasized in Fleury's installation by means of a barrier tape, is exactly what is not needed in the performative context. The design of walkway and door had to be conceived so that approaching and touching the installation could take place without inhibition or doubt. This could, however, be achieved only by a scenographic fait accompli, designing the required action in a very specific spatial context. This leads to a dynamic concept of space.

Space versus place

In his book *The Practice of Everyday Life* (1984), the French philosopher and historian Michel de Certeau makes a clear distinction between place (*lieu*) and space (*espace*):

A place (*lieu*) is the order (of whatever kind) in accord with which elements are distributed in relationships of coexistence. It thus excludes the possibility of two things
being in the same location (*place*) ... A place is thus an instantaneous configuration
of positions. (de Certeau 1984, 117)

Conversely, space for Certeau is "composed of intersections of mobile elements.
It is in a sense actuated by the ensemble of movements deployed within it ... In
short, *space is a practiced place*" (Certeau 1984, 117; emphasis original). The dividing
line between the two case studies is similar to the distinction between place and
space. In Sylvie Fleury's installation, precise positioning and microscopically accurate juxtaposition are crucial. The important thing is localization, the instantaneous
configuration of positions, as de Certeau calls it: panel next to panel, but also visitors there and artwork here. This is not the case with the arrangement of visitors,
walkway, and door in *A Matter of Belief*. The entrance installation positioned outside
the Zeughaus is only a precondition for the space, which is yet to be created. The
space arises only from the actions of the visitor-actors. This space is as immaterial
as the actors themselves, but, above all, the space becomes emancipated from the
"indivisible place." It is quite possible for different spaces to occur in the same place
depending on who is here carrying out what actions. This raises the question of
visitor-observer versus visitor-actor.

Visitor-observer versus visitor-actor

The museum is always a sphere in which there are actors with different roles
allocated to them. In the two case studies, however, the actors' spaces are differently arranged. On the one hand, there is the art museum with a precise hierarchy of museum management, curator, artist, attendants, senior and junior, and
visitors. Their different fields of activity are arranged in a vertical ranking. The
further down an actor is, the smaller his radius of action. On the other hand,
we have the theme-based exhibition provider with a temporary project team
composed of culture experts, scenographers, architects, media technologists,
mediators, and so on, presenting the public with a participative and performative
spatial arrangement – where they are themselves players and, to a certain extent,
on an equal footing.

Of course, there are hierarchies and spheres of influence here as well; scenography imposes non-negotiable guidelines and projects visitors willy-nilly into a predetermined situation. But the level of activity imposed on visitor-actors comes
about only once they are within the situation. It arises of itself and is a necessary
component in creating the space. The space arises from the intersection of content-
based conception, spatial arrangement, *and* social praxis/activity on the part of
the visitors.

The final element we need to help us think about the museum as a space of the
present is the white cube versus the laboratory.

White cube versus laboratory

This question is as old as museums themselves. The first cabinets of curiosities were probably more like the laboratories of the present than many of today's museums. The question arises: to what extent are museums shaped, bound, limited in terms of their ability to create space simply by their institutional architecture and operating culture? What difference does it make if one shows Sylvie Fleury's picture installation in the Albertina's white cube, the arsenal hall of the Stapferhaus Lenzburg, or on a stand at the Geneva Motor Show? If we juxtapose these venues, we can intuitively deduce the existence of wholly different spaces. Or, conversely, we could formulate it as follows: If, for the sake of argument, we were to expect identical effects from the two institutions, the interventions in the two places would turn out quite differently, as the elements constituting the spaces are so differently configured. How then must museums look if they are to be of some use as spaces of the present? How far does such a space of the present belong in a museum at all, and not in a supermarket or a community center? How far can a performative, participative approach be reconciled with the received perception of the museum as a sacred realm of the untouchable?

Museums as zones of stability in representing the present

The question of the museum as a space of the present goes far beyond matters of participative methods and interactive tools. In essence, it is a question of the ability of the museum as institution to create new social spaces in the present: spaces (i.e., not simply places) which make the present recognizable, negotiable, and accessible to reflection; far from ruling out historical material, this definitely includes it. As I see it, a museum as a space of the present acts as a resonating chamber for one's own behavior. For in such a setting, what museum visitors are confronted with above all is themselves. A mirroring of one's own presence is the first step toward reflection.

But what does "present" mean in this context? The sociologist Hartmut Rosa describes the present as "a space of stability for which current experiences and expectations, supported by institutional practices, have validity" (Rosa 2009). Of course this is expressed as an ideal, as stability is always a product in decay: the present has no fixed existence. Hence Rosa defines the present in relative terms. The present is the period of time in which institutional rules and social practices remain valid with little alteration, giving the majority a means of orientation.

Rosa asserts at the same time that the periods of stability of each present moment are becoming ever shorter. He takes up the notion already popularized by Hermann Lübbe of an accelerated "shrinking of the present" (*Gegenwarts-schrumpfung*) (Lübbe 1992, 18–19). The "rates of decay of activity-oriented experiences and expectations" are, according to Rosa (2005, 133), increasing progressively, rendering the construction of a collective present increasingly difficult. Rosa suggests that perception of the present is distinguished by the fact that we have more and more experiences per unit of time, but that these experiences remain episodic and are no longer linked to each other and to their own identity: "A society characterized by the ultra-short-term pattern … could thus turn out to be a society rich in experiences [*Erlebnisse*: the immediate and lived experience of moments] but poor in experience [*Erfahrung*: accumulated and reflected experience which forms knowledge]" (Rosa 2005, 470).

Against this backdrop, the museum as an institutional "space of the present" would play its part as a temporary zone of stability in which the present is represented, that is, constructed. In other words, in the museum the present becomes tangible because visitors' experiences are given space and become themselves museum objects. One can think of such a zone of stability in terms of a "freezing" in a public space, in which total strangers freeze their movements for a minute, thus making this movement visible.

The Swiss sociologist Kurt Imhof uses a fine German word for the zone of stability: *Vergegenwärtigung* (re-present-ation). Museums, he claims, are "institutions for re-presenting the present for the purpose of taking control of the future" (Imhof 2008, 49). This is necessary because conscious perception of the present does not manifest itself automatically from contemporaneity and the reproduction of experiences, but needs re-presentation, the social construction of reality (Berger and Luckmann 1966). Experience (*Erfahrung*) has to be filtered out of experiences (*Erlebnisse*): the potential value added is a gain in sense of direction, an increase in competence, an ability to act. Re-presentation derives from perception and reflection on the part of the actors in the present: these can only be achieved by having a minimal viewing distance from their own behavior.

Scenography as the creation of performative spaces

The discipline which has guided exhibition praxis in some countries for years is that of scenography. The concept derives from the realm of theater in the ancient world: for a good 10 years now the definition of the term has been constantly expanding. Scenography now encompasses the

> cultural praxis and theory of the creation of performative spaces in the realms of, and at the interface of, architecture, theater, exhibition and media. In its emphasis on process, event and construct, it combines the previously separate genres of design, through architecture, theater, exhibition, trade fair and museum to create scenic gestures of spatiality. (Brejzek, Mueller von der Haegen, and Wallen 2009, 371)

Thus social and performative aspects are always present within the notion of the scenographic. However, in the actual scenographic practices of such diverse institutions as art and art history museums, science centers, commercial brand environments, and exhibition providers such as the Stapferhaus Lenzburg, this is not the case. As I perceive it, scenography is still widely understood as being synonymous with exhibition architecture, 3D design, and hi-tech media presentations. Scenography tends to be used to refer to the spatial product of its creators, but does not generally refer to performative content initiated in visitors by the architecture of an exhibition.

Therefore, to describe exhibitions such as *A Matter of Belief* I shall use the amplified term "social scenography," which is to be understood as a meta-design of content, form, and activity, with an emphasis on actions. In her book, *Raumsoziologie* [Sociology of space], Martina Löw drew up a relational concept of space which contains essential elements of an action-oriented scenography. She understands space purely as a social phenomenon: "Space is a relational arrangement of living beings and social goods in places" (Löw 2001, 271). This concept is to be distinguished particularly from an absolute concept of space as a container. Löw states that "The expectation of a basic sociological concept of space must therefore be that it covers the process of its own creation and does not assume its result, e.g., that of being a receptacle" (2001, 270–271).

The emphasis on process is certainly a key element in understanding exhibitions as performative spaces. However, Markus Schroer is right to object that it is not just a matter of recognizing that space is created socially, but of taking into account what this space itself determines. By this Schroer means the inclusion of "spatial arrangements" which are "not without their effect on our behavior" (2006, 178). In this way, he brings the "classical" arrangement of form (space as receptacle) back into his consideration of space. From the practical perspective, this is also very plausible. I experience "social scenography" myself very similarly, as the creation of performative stages by means of engineered environments. The spaces thus created elicit in the visitor-actors by means of actions a better perception of their own cultural praxis or, at any rate, of their cultural praxis at a given moment.

The practical realm: Stapferhaus Lenzburg

What does this mean then in terms of practice in the realm of museums? As a relatively young exhibition provider, the Stapferhaus has been working toward social scenography in an experimental way since the mid-1990s. Initially, it did this by using historical materials that it sought to link to the present, then increasingly and eventually exclusively, by employing present-day themes from everyday life. The historical aspects gradually dwindled and yielded to a documentary approach to the present which was partly socioanthropologically, partly sociologically, and partly psychologically oriented. In abandoned buildings, principally factories and warehouses over 1000 square meters, the Stapferhaus created large-scale exhibitions on broad everyday themes. These were not tied to specific events, items from collections, or particular people, but rather they arose in a journalistic way, from our own research, in a certain sense *ex nihilo*. Two crucial questions always underscored the exhibition concept: "Why? What is our thesis? What do we want?" And "For whom? Who are we aiming at? Who is our public?" The answers were not as simple as the questions. But, as a rule, they led very soon and very directly to the actors in these topics and, through them, necessarily to the present. We soon realized that the public is not just a willing recipient but a resource, a source of knowledge, and a participative player; and this recognition was crucial in informing our various approaches to social scenography.

This is also clear from the chronology of the projects. The activity in the Stapferhaus began in 1994 with *Anne Frank und wir* [Anne Frank and us], an exhibition about the Holocaust, Swiss refugee policy in World War II, and links with Swiss migration policy in the 1990s. Even at that time, the exhibition was based largely on eyewitness accounts and powerful source material. In 1997 there followed *A Walk on the Wild Side*, a large-scale show on youth cultures in twentieth-century Switzerland. This exhibition turned out to be a popular intergenerational project: grandparents and grandchildren, social workers and teenagers, parents and children, together discovered in the exhibition each other's youth as recurrent rites of passage.

In 1999 *Last Minute* came into being: this was an exhibition about the discrete professional worlds relating to dying and death in the present. The exhibition appealed primarily to the caring professions, to social workers, and to those in funeral services, professionals who normally have to deal on their own with their experiences at work. They used the exhibition for group visits, discussions, and intensive workshop sessions. In 2002 the Stapferhaus turned to a quite different emotional topic and one which had some difficulty in reaching its audience; it did, however, begin to experiment with participative elements within the exhibition. *Autolust*, an exhibition about the irrational, emotional aspects of car driving, mobilized 50 schoolchildren in one village to photograph their parents, neighbors, and friends together with their cars. This formed a whole section of the exhibition and a publication.

From 2004 onward there followed ever bigger large-scale productions which used a whole variety of methods of participation, interaction, and self-reflection. In 2004 the exhibition *Strafen* [Punish] set out to examine concepts and experiences of punishment in the public and private spheres; in 2006 *A Matter of Belief*, discussed above, examined the multiplicity and variety of beliefs in the broad realm of religion and culture; in 2009 *Nonstop*, addressed questions about time management and increasing shortage of time; and in 2010 the exhibition *Home* was devoted to the digitalization of everyday life.

From this body of concrete experiences and developments, five rough categories of methods of social scenography may be derived and described: personalization, self-questioning, participation, dialogic interaction, and exposure. In their outlines they show the interplay of content, form, and design of activity, but they are anything but clear-cut.

Method 1: Personalization

Personalization is primarily a journalistic principle, according to which a phenomenon is individualized and reduced to a few faces. The theme gains an identity and this creates closeness. The zoom effect creates closeness but at the risk of becoming specific. Applied to exhibitions, it involves the decision of the exhibition creators as to who may speak: a choice between man and woman, between old and young, between an engaging and a distancing style. The sample of people involved should be, to some extent, representative of the society which is supposed to be portrayed or of the target groups which the exhibition is intended to reach.

These performative attributes determine a greater or lesser readiness to identify on the part of visitors. Therefore, it is equally important to establish suitable background parameters by which to select appropriate individuals from the world of the theme being examined. In recent years the Stapferhaus has increasingly worked with personal typologies which have been developed in different scientific disciplines, and which set out solely to represent complex social realities via the fewest possible individuals and thus to facilitate intelligent identification. In the case of *A Matter of Belief*, faith profiles from the sociology of religion led to the identification of nine target individuals who would contribute in the exhibition through the audio and film format and with texts and loan items. For the selection of this sample, a casting process in several steps was necessary. The individuals not only had to meet the parameters that had been established, such as age, gender, religious affiliation, faith, or specific geographic origin, but they also had to be able to express themselves in front of a camera or a microphone. Besides that, friendliness and charisma were necessary, so that profiles that differed in terms of content nevertheless had more or less the same chances in competing for attention within the context of the exhibition.

At the start of *A Matter of Belief*, videos of individuals were presented life size and face to face with the visitors. They had been asked how they imagined God to be, and the nine selected individuals who replied were: an intellectual man who was an atheist; a traditional Catholic believer (a woman); the teenage son of liberal Jewish parents; a well-educated Muslim mother; an evangelical young man with a sense of mission; a secular Hindu man who only goes to the temple on account of his wife and for the food; a nondenominational woman who sends her children to Protestant religious classes; a Zen Buddhist manager who was once a Catholic; and an esoterically inspired syncretist who designs her own rituals. The opportunities for identification offered to the public were broad but not shallow. These people were not representatives but individuals, standing for themselves. So, as opportunities for identification, they were multilayered and approachable.

A Matter of Belief used personalization as a narrative leitmotif. The nine characters representing belief who were presented at the start subsequently had their say on several occasions. They remained reference points for visitors throughout their stay in the exhibition. Form and content served to make visible a secularized, individualized, and patchwork landscape of faith. At the level of the active involvement of visitors, identification served primarily to activate self-reflection and in this way to deliver the central message: *A Matter of Belief* is not mediating a topic for an audience, but the audience itself becomes the topic.

Another exhibition which used personalization was *Last Minute: On Dying and Death* [Last minute: Über Sterben und Tod; 1999], which was comparable in its intention but organized quite differently in terms of the media chosen. The basic tenet of the exhibition was that dying and death have been outsourced to a professional world where practices are heavily characterized by a division of labor. Instead of talking about the creation of taboos, the exhibition examined techniques of delegation, distancing, and alienation. The angle taken here followed the research methods of the sociologist Ursula Streckeisen. In her research project *The Ordinary Death* (1995) she was concerned with an intensive examination of "professional strategies relating to the end of life" in the working environment of a hospice. As a sympathetic observer she looked over many participants' shoulders as they worked. Visitors to the exhibition were intended to experience what Streckeisen had described and analyzed verbally. Of course there existed filmic visualizations such as that of the Berne-based filmmaker Damaris Lüthi with her crematorium film *1000 Degrees Celsius*. However, in the end we decided to use not film but sound. A documentary would have taken more time to tell one person's story. On the other hand, an audio narration in the form of a monologue made it possible to zoom in on the professional life of our subjects in a direct and vivid, yet abstract, way. In this particular case, it was important that the references made to professionalism and division of labor should not be perceived as negative per se, and that visitors to the exhibition should not start to long for "the good old days" of the *Ars moriendi* (art of dying) as Philipp Ariès does in *The Hour of Our Death* (1981). Instead, we wanted them to be able to perceive the current culture of dying as the sum of individual, highly differentiated professional cultures around dying and death.

The spatial layout used freestanding separate cubes (booths representing each profession), arranged in the same room. The world of work, with its division of labor, was represented and personalized by 10 selected figures: the intensive care specialist, the pathologist, the hospice counselor, the priest, the undertaker, the organ transplant coordinator, the news editor of the evening news broadcast, the mortality rate statistician, the leader of a seminar on grieving, and the crematorium technician. Visitors could press a button and hear ambient sound in the form of a narrated monologue. Specific working practices were dealt with, such as how the care expert places swabs on the closed eyes of dead patients. Objects, in this case the swab, mentioned on the soundtrack, were extravagantly displayed as isolated museum objects in a showcase at the entrance to the cube. In the 10 cases were displayed very everyday, unspectacular objects, such as the priest's reading glasses, the undertaker's scented oil, the laboratory samples of the pathologist, the transplant coordinator's mobile phone. All these objects were displayed without explanatory labeling. Similarly the name and profession of the individual speaking was only disclosed inside. There was no way of zapping from one to the other; the different professional worlds had to be discovered. The detailed description which these players gave of microscopic parts of their own sphere opened up wide themes which were dealt with in greater depth as the exhibition continued.

The world of work that was personalized in this way was made concrete by the construction of 10 3-meter walk-in cubes. Outwardly these boxes were indistinguishable; only their interior life made them distinctive: different floor coverings which visitors could see from outside and – as mentioned above – the various objects in the illuminated glass cabinets by the entrances to the listening booths. The floor coverings implied the professional worlds and spheres of activity: solid timber planks in the undertaker's cube, a needle-pile carpet in the statistician's realm, white tiles (and not tile-effect laminate) in the pathologist's domain. The sound in the room, the object displayed, and the floor material formed a unity of associations.

Method 2: Self-questioning

Self-reflection is an implicit form of self-questioning. But self-questioning can also take place explicitly, as actual questioning of the public. In recent years the Stapferhaus has worked on several occasions with questioning tools, generally in the form of a test which presented visitors with a personalized result. *Last Minute* playfully presented visitors with a "death notice generator." Visitors were able to use pre-existing text elements to compose a death notice, perhaps even their own. In this way they were indirectly made to question their ideas of an individualized culture of death. For *Autolust* a car test was developed in collaboration with the DemoSCOPE research institute: this determined which car suited each user. The test was based on an actual research tool working with the "social profiles" of makes of car.

The configuration of all the tests in the Stapferhaus exhibitions used existing scientific typologies, but these had to be put into a scenographic context. This meant, at every stage, simplifying and abbreviating them, as well as making them playful and thinking of them within the exhibition context as an exhibit, that is, arranging the test site so as to make each individual result visible to all as part of the exhibition. This can be illustrated in depth using *A Matter of Belief* as an example.

In *A Matter of Belief*, self-questioning was employed as a leitmotif, parallel to the personalization already mentioned. The exhibition involved visitors in a test on belief which identified types of belief across the denominations, thus going beyond religious affiliations. Right at the start, "believers" and "nonbelievers" were issued with a USB memory stick as their admission ticket to the exhibition: on this they

FIGURE 16.2   "Believer" or "Nonbeliever" USB sticks to be worn by visitors to the exhibition *A Matter of Belief.*
Photo: Theres Bütler © Stapferhaus Lenzburg.

were to save their responses. It was designed as an amulet to be worn around the neck (Figure 16.2). Of course there were a few visitors who refused to wear it in this way, and simply put the stick and its lanyard in their trouser pockets. At three points around the exhibition there were questioning checkpoints, which all visitors were meant to go to (Figure 16.3). These checkpoints were reminiscent of ATMs. Golden touch screen locations with discrete control panels, where "believers" as well as "nonbelievers" could log on and answer questions on their own attitude to belief. There were 40 questions to work through. This test on belief types was based in methodological terms on the "religiosity structure test" of the Munich psychologist of religion Stefan Huber (2003). It measures religiosity independently of affiliation to any specific religion. It assesses the intensity of faith on the one hand and, on the other, the orientation of its content. This includes, particularly, the religious experience and behavior of people, be it in prayer, worship, or other spiritual practices. The essential distinction is between a theistic concept of faith (God as a tangible counterpart) and a pantheistic one (the divine as an all-pervading principle). For *A Matter of Belief* the test was slightly expanded and adapted to the examples in the exhibition. The aim of the exercise was to enable a differentiated consideration of religiosity and belief which spanned religions, and not to assess religions wholesale. For a visitor to receive a result, he/she had to answer all the questions. At the final checkpoint, the saved responses produced a personal faith

FIGURE 16.3   Checkpoint surveying individuals' belief profiles in *A Matter of Belief*.
Photo: Theres Bütler © Stapferhaus Lenzburg.

profile, closely matching one of the five predefined templates. These profiles were: traditionally religious, culturally religious, patchwork religious, alternatively religious, and without religion.

More than 95 percent of the over 40,000 visitors took part in the self-questioning. The final screen announced the resultant faith profile to the participants in the test, and directed them to a large round table where they could find out more about their result (Figure 16.4). The table had the five belief profiles arranged around the circle, so that the visitors assembled in a ring at the table. Some individuals who until then had been in different religious affiliations (e.g., pupils in school classes) could, after the test, be grouped together in the same belief profile. This opened up surprising spaces for discussion. The result confirmed some in what they already knew, irritated some, and led others to contradict it. The important thing is that the process of self-questioning brought the theme of the exhibition closer to the individual, but also made valid statements about the faith landscape of modern-day Switzerland.

Method 3: Participation

The involvement of visitors in the conception, realization, and operation of an exhibition is an increasingly important and popular type of social scenography; museums are just starting to discover participation for themselves (see Simon

FIGURE 16.4   Round table finale: the exhibition *A Matter of Belief* assigns visitors to new faith profiles extending beyond their religious affiliations.
Photo: Donovan Wyrsch © Stapferhaus Lenzburg.

2010; Gesser et al. 2012). The Stapferhaus has been using participation since 1994, notably where the content of exhibitions was to be generated by the public, because no one else could generate this content. But that also means that design and scenography define the frame within which participation is to take place. Here again *A Matter of Belief* is a good example.

A Matter of Belief presented exhibition visitors with statistical statements on the size of individual religious communities in Switzerland: 42 percent Catholic, 33 percent Protestant, 11 percent nondenominational, 4 percent Muslim, and so on. These government statistics were able to identify membership of institutions but not to indicate anything about the individual attitudes to faith of the members of these religions. Anyone wanting to know more about this will not find any official figures, since individual belief goes beyond the traditional affiliations to religion that surveys usually measure. There are only investigations in the field of the sociology of religion, which make qualitative statements about the patchwork faith landscape of the present.

This was an important reason to develop a participative project such as this. The idea was that a sample of 100 people in the same distribution as the figures from the Federal Office of Statistics – that is, 42 Catholics, 33 Protestants, and so on – would lend the exhibition an object which would stand for their personal attitude

FIGURE 16.5 What does Switzerland believe? These representative objects gathered from the population in the exhibition *A Matter of Belief* show how attitudes to belief have been individualized. (For a color version of this figure, please see the color plate section.) Photo: Theres Bütler © Stapferhaus Lenzburg.

to faith. There were no limiting guidelines as to the object: sacred or profane, they could be chosen freely. In addition, a commentary was to be supplied in the form of a short text explaining why the object had been chosen and what it meant to the lender. The Stapferhaus set in motion a complex communication system, via print media, the Internet, and appeals in old people's homes and schools, as well as through a wide network of personal contacts, in order to produce a meaningful selection of objects and stories linked to them. The objects, which varied in weight and size, were presented in clear plastic bags like confiscated pieces of police evidence (Figure 16.5). The bags were hung on fine wires up to a height of 5 meters and over a 30 meter length. The bright colors of the wall made them reminiscent of the votive offerings in rural Italian churches. As was expected, the choice of objects did not only encompass sacred things, as might be assumed from the statistics on religion, but a crazy multicultural mix of sacred and profane objects from different religious sources: a Protestant might show a Buddha, an agnostic or atheist present a Madonna complete with halo, or a pious creationist might choose a simple piece of wood because it evokes God's nature. The complicated, thoroughly contradictory faith landscape derived from this participative project portrayed the real topography of faith in Switzerland far more precisely than the Federal Office of Statistics ever could.

Method 4: Dialogic interaction

Social scenography always depends on interaction. Dialogic interaction, that is face-to-face encounters, goes one stage further. If it is true that, in exhibitions on present-day topics, the visitors are the experts on their own everyday lives, then it also makes sense to make use of this expertise by scenographic means and to make it speak. *Nonstop: An Exhibition about the Speed of Life* (2009) took up a topic which was difficult to visualize. How can one show shortness of time, speed, the acceleration of our culture of time? During our discussion of the principles underlying the concept, the idea of the Life Time Bar came about. The Life Time Bar is a real bar with stools, a counter, and bar staff; however, there is nothing to drink, but instead much more to hear and to say. Instead of drinks, there were stories, life stories, served up on vinyl discs and slowly revolving record players. In scenographic terms, the content of the Life Time Bar was in three layers. The curated content, in the classic sense, took the form of the prepared audio stories of people of different ages. The selected individuals mused on their relationship to time (of life) and speed in their daily life. They observed themselves from the perspective of the narrator of their own lives. For example, the former bank director of the Swiss Banking Association, Roland Rasi, reflected by speaking about how his own culture of time had changed since leaving the bank. The stories were carefully chosen personalizations, as described in Method 1 above. Part of the staging of the story was an appropriate choice of media: slow vinyl discs instead of nippy MP3 players. There was no way of hopping quickly from one statement to another. One had to listen to one and then order another, disc by disc.

At the same time, a social situation was set up by the spatial arrangement of the guests in this bar. It is well known that customers in a bar are never alone. It is more or less certain that, at a bar just a few meters long, there will be interactions between customers who happen to be there, especially if they are members of a group with a leader. Up to 24 people could sit at the Life Time Bar at any time, in front of 12 record players, two people sharing each listening post. Thus, the guests were aware of each other, noted the stories that were ordered, observed thoughtful or happy reactions to the content, and to some extent also shared this information.

Finally, there was another central character: the barmaid, who actively facilitated the choice of stories, moderating and answering queries. From the bar menu, guests learned that the barmaid was not a permanently employed project worker but a volunteer. She was thus devoting some of the time in her life to the "nonstop" project and its guests. She too had a life story and a motive, related to the theme, for spending her time here in this role, just as the man at the bar had his reasons for giving time to the statement by the ex-banker. This multilayered arrangement based on having time and using time led – depending on the combination of visitors – to conversations which were just as completely centered on the meaning of working time and living time, time and money, career and the common good, as the contents of the vinyl discs on the turntable. In scenographic terms, the crucial thing is this: the layer of content structured in the space cannot be pre-formulated, limited, or controlled. Its development is purely emergent: it arises out of the social situation. The only thing that can be planned is what the term "social scenography" means at heart: that is, the structuring of the content and form of a spatial situation, so that it can occur in a performative, participative, and thematically focused way, and thus itself becomes part of the portrayal of the theme.

Method 5: Exposure

However, social scenography can go one step further and make visitors themselves into an exhibit. At this point we reach a gray area of social scenography where the boundaries blur between enactment being a powerful tool and it being an unacceptable encroachment. It is an ethical question: How far may visitors be made, unasked, into objects of exhibition without the option of withdrawing from this allotted role? The entrance to A Matter of Belief, with its two doors, is an example of this. The two doors compelled those entering to make a statement about the wholly stereotypical terms "believer" and "nonbeliever," before they had made up their minds what the terms mean. There was no third neutral door, nor a discreet way of dealing with the imposed assignment. Beyond the door visitors had to continue on the gangway to the ticket office, which made them identifiable to the ticket office staff as believers or nonbelievers. For the ticket also bore the legend "believer" or "nonbeliever" and, as the ticket office staff indicated, was to be worn as a pendant around the neck – which, of course, some individuals refused to do. Within a short time the twin entrances to A Matter of Belief became the true symbol of the exhibition. They summed up essential fundamental statements which could be physically experienced in a simple image. Faith, once a publicly practiced and required norm, has largely become a private affair in the secular Western social context. The twin entrances made this change almost grotesquely visible, by vehemently refusing visitors any privacy or confidentiality (Figure 16.1). The walk to the door on the catwalk-like gangway was like a compulsory public performance. At the same time this trick with the doors forced visitors to their first personal statement of position, which was then variously differentiated through the exhibition. The truly decisive element, however, was that the trigger for the anticipated debate was not set in motion by a museum exhibit, nor by some media installation, but solely by the scenographically planned actions of the visitors. These actions needed visitors to be active and emotionally involved, and other visitors to bear witness, in order to produce the exhibition content in such depth.

The deliberate exposure of visitors has a specific character in terms of content, when it is concerned with changing the role of visitor-observer into that of visitor-participant. The idea is therefore to turn the theme from a general subject to a personal subject for the approaching visitors. The Stapferhaus practiced this technique on several occasions, and in a particularly emphatic way in the introductory phases of the *Autolust* and *Punish* exhibitions, in *A Matter of Belief* as already described, and again in *Nonstop* and *Home*. That is, in every case, in the spatial settings preceding the exhibitions themselves: on the piazza outside the Zeughaus area, just outside the entrance to the lobby, or inside the building but before the reception desk.

In *Autolust*, the whole Zeughaus area was transformed into a car park roundabout, bounded by a sea of flowers formed by 3000 plastic daffodils planted in the asphalt. Thus, visitors arriving by car involuntarily became part of a staged car spectacle reminiscent of the motoring innocence of the 1950s, when the Touring Club was still organizing Sunday drives. Visitors to *Punish* were welcomed by a lawned area of some 8 by 12 meters and a "Keep off the grass" sign. The lawful paved path was laid out so as to invite unlawful access in a straight line across the grass. What happened on the grass was transmitted by a video camera to a monitor at the ticket office.

The exhibition *Nonstop: On the Speed of Life* had visitors approach along a 100 meter long ramp, in a dead straight line, which was the quickest way across the square into the exhibition. Inside there were two ways down: the slow way down the stairs or the quick way down the fireman's pole. In the next room, the "Rush Hour" audio space, busy visitors got to sit on perch rails as if waiting in a subway station or in a tram or lift. The active sources on this sonic stage were not sounds but the visitors themselves, on display and listening. The exhibition *Home* received its visitors in a digital home. With their tickets, visitors, irrespective of age, sex, or clothing, were handed a pair of "home socks" to be worn throughout the exhibition.

What can social scenography achieve?

For many years, social scenography has restricted itself to the creation of new physical spaces. Scenographers have devised exhibition environments, moods, furniture, lighting concepts, and interactive computer displays. Social scenography is involved with the creation of social spaces via the design of actions *as well as* the devising of physical spaces. Social scenography creates arrangements of artifacts and people in order to bring about something performative – let us call it "content." This content appears in an emergent way, but not at all by chance. The door-related events in *A Matter of Belief* were planned in their effect but it had to remain open as to who would have this experience and with what outcome for the individual. Social scenography proposes that exhibitions and museums can be arranged as spaces of the present and thus fulfill the role of self-reflective platforms for questions about contemporary society. The practice of the Stapferhaus illustrates this interpretation.

References

AK für Sie. 2010. "Museumsaufseher zurück im Job" [Museum attendant back on the job]. September, 16.

Berger, Peter L., and Thomas Luckmann. 1966. *The Social Construction of Reality: A Treatise in the Sociology of Knowledge*. Garden City, NY: Doubleday.

Brejzek, Thea, Gesa Mueller von der Haegen, and Lawrence Wallen. 2009. "Szenografie" [Scenography]. In *Raumwissenschaften* [Sciences of space], edited by Stephan Günzel, 370–385. Frankfurt: Suhrkamp.

de Certeau, Michel. 1984. *The Practice of Everyday Life*. Berkeley: University of California Press.

Gesser, Susanne, Martin Handschin, Angela Jannelli, and Sibylle Lichtensteiger, eds. 2012. *Das partizipative Museum: Zwischen Teilhabe und User Generated Content* [The Participatory Museum: Between Engagement and User-Generated Content]. Bielefeld, Germany: Transcript.

Hächler, Beat. 2009. "Gegenwart vergegenwärtigen: Wie das Stapferhaus Lenzburg seinen Vermittlungsauftrag versteht" [Representing the present: How Stapferhaus Lenzburg sees its task as an agency]. In *Kultur macht Schule: Kulturvermittlung in der Praxis* [Culture sets a precedent: Imparting culture in practice], edited by Gunhild Hamer, 130–134. Baden, Germany: Hier & Jetzt.

Huber, Stefan. 2003. *Zentralität und Inhalt: Ein neues multidimensionales Messmodell der Religiosität* [Centrality and content: A new multidimensional model for measuring religiosity]. Opladen, Germany: Leske & Budrich.

Imhof, Kurt. 2008. "Europäische Museen der Zukünfte" [European museums of the futures]. In *Europa als Museumsobjekt* [Europe as a museum exhibit], edited by Georg Kreis, 48–61. Basel: Europa Institut.

Löw, Martina. 2001. *Raumsoziologie* [Sociology of space]. Frankfurt: Suhrkamp.

Lübbe, Hermann. 1992. *Im Zug der Zeit: Verkürzter Aufenthalt in der Gegenwart* [In the course of time: Shortened stay in the present]. Berlin: Springer.

Odendahl, Bernhard. 2010. "Verrückte Kunst" [Topsy-turvy art]. *Der Bund*, April 17, 44.

Rosa, Hartmut. 2005. *Beschleunigung: Die Veränderung der Zeitstrukturen in der Moderne* [Acceleration: The alteration of time structures in the modern world]. Frankfurt: Suhrkamp.

Rosa, Hartmut. 2009. "Schrumpfende Gegenwart und Zeitoase? Die Rolle von Museen im Beschleunigungszeitalter" [A shrinking present and an oasis in time? The role of museums in an accelerating age]. Paper presented at conference on "Gegenwart ausstellen" [Exhibiting the present], Stapferhaus Lenzburg, May 1–2, 2009.

Schroer, Markus. 2006. *Räume, Orte, Grenzen: Auf dem Weg zu einer Soziologie des Raums* [Spaces, places, borders: Toward a sociology of space]. Frankfurt: Suhrkamp.

Simon, Nina. 2010. *The Participatory Museum*. Santa Cruz, CA: Museum 2.0.

Streckeisen, Ursula. 1995. *Der ganz gewöhnliche Tod: Professionelle Strategien rund um das Lebensende* [The ordinary death: Professional strategies relating to the end of life]. With contributions from Lilo Roost Vischer and Corina Salis Gross. Final Report to the Swiss National Science Foundation. Berne: Institut für Soziologie.

Beat Hächler is the Director of the Swiss Alpine Museum in Berne. Under his leadership, the museum was redesigned in 2011, and reopened in 2012 as a contemporary exhibition space. Until 2010 Hächler was joint director in charge of the Stapferhaus Lenzburg, which specialized at that time in exhibitions on subjects relating to everyday life and the present. Hächler studied history, German literature, and media sciences in Berne and Madrid. In 2012 he obtained a postgraduate qualification in scenography at the Zurich University of the Arts.

17 (DIS)PLAYING THE MUSEUM
Artifacts, Visitors, Embodiment, and Mediality

Karin Harrasser

This chapter sets out to develop an approach to (dis)playing the museum. It develops ideas about learning and knowledge appropriation – and about modes of studying these – by giving particular attention to the interrelations of museum media and the way they are used by visitors, in this case by children. It is based a research project conducted in three children's museums and science centers in Austria and Germany over 30 months in 2007–2009. The research team of social scientists and humanities scholars concentrated on interactives and hands-on objects which have become frequently used in exhibitions for both children and adults.[1] The extensive use of interactive media and the paradigm of playful learning mark a break in how museums conceive themselves. By studying them in detail, we wanted to address the question of what kind of agencies museums will be in the future and what kind of agency they will be able to trigger within their visitors. What modes of subjectivization and learning are connected with such objects and what kind of knowledge is at stake in playful learning?

The approach of (dis)playing the museum involves a number of aspects that we regard as central to an understanding of learning and knowledge appropriation in museums. First, it encompasses a certain idea of how exhibitions are structured (as narrative or in terms of dramaturgy) and how they address visitors. Second, it contains a theorization of the way visitors appropriate exhibitions. Third, the relation between displays and the actual and embodied micro-practices of visitors can be seen as one dynamic process. And, fourth, it allows for a reflection on our own research practice, on our own involvement in research as a specific "audience" for the children's practices of showing (they "perform" the exhibition for themselves, for others, and also for us). The approach thus offers answers and methodological tools to a number of questions raised in various fields of museology. Current research literature (e.g., Macdonald 2006) shows that, apart from the history and

The International Handbooks of Museum Studies: Museum Media, First Edition.
Edited by Michelle Henning.
© 2015 John Wiley & Sons Ltd. Published 2020 by John Wiley & Sons Ltd.

practical operation of museums, museology is divided into two major areas: studies about museum architecture, spaces, and media, that is displays (see Schade and Richter 2007), and those about visitors, learning, and interaction. Our research positions itself between these two areas and is thus forced to consider the relations between exhibits and visitors more systematically. Following the discussion of central concepts and two case studies, the chapter will broaden the perspective to more general questions about how interactive media transform museums and how and to what extent museums can be conceived as media.

The research aimed at a better understanding of a specific type of museum displays (interactives, hands-on). We chose predominantly to observe children aged 6–12 years, at whom such displays are often – though not exclusively – targeted. Such displays, though claiming the status of museum objects, cross the boundary to educational media and performative modes of showing and learning. Often they are conceptualized both as objects that are able to address "all the senses" and as media to transport factual knowledge. In our reading they are media in the strict sense of a means of transportation of meaning that transforms the subject who interacts. We were interested in learning more about the integration and functioning of such objects within the setting of the museum which traditionally relies on auratic objects and distancing gestures as well as on the magic of the material object itself. How do hands-on objects transform the idea of the museum? What ideas and concepts of learning enter the museum with interactives? And, most importantly, how do children interact with such objects? Do they follow the built-in scripts or to what extent do they invent alternative meanings? On the basis of numerous observations (in total 128 protocols[2]) the team focused on interactions between artifacts and museum visitors. We interpreted interactions as performances of self-conceptions and identity as well as of the children's relation to (gendered and class- and race-biased) knowledge. For this we used the methodological tools of ethnographic data collection and grounded theory (Strauss and Corbin 1990). The findings are based on micro-observations and thick descriptions (Geertz 1973) of interactional situations.

How did we arrive at the formula "(dis)playing the museum"? The English word "display" encompasses a wide array of meanings. Its semantics range from the act of showing off (e.g., in bird dances) and cross the realm of exhibiting to its current use as a term for visualizing technologies. Display, in the sense of an exhibit, one could also argue, marks the very coincidence of techniques of attraction and techniques of knowledge. The current predominant meaning of display as a device to visualize computer data is, of course, the most recent, and includes certain types of interactive museum displays. Our reason for mentioning the definitions here is in order to highlight one of the older meanings of the word. From around 1900 zoologists and ethologists used the word "display" to refer to the expressive behavior of animals and humans. Although we by no means follow a behavioristic idea of agency, the basic idea became quite important for our research: What can children show us – what do *they* display while interacting with displays? How is their playing "playing for somebody"? Is it a performance of some kind?

This led to the initial extension of the commonly used museological notion of display to include the active dimension of display*ing*. Schade and Richter define display in keeping with recent discussions in media studies as an interface between humans and machines (2007). Accordingly, both the individual interactive display, and the museum or the exhibition itself, are considered to be "machines" of visualization. This modifies the concept of "display" in the direction of the idea of the museum as a *dispositif* in the Foucauldian sense (see, e.g., Teckert 2007). The French historian of science Michel Foucault conceptualized the *dispositif* as a historically contingent infrastructure that permits certain statements and precludes others. It is a set of rules and/or architectural or technical features that facilitates or limits what can be articulated. In an interview from 1977, Foucault defined *dispositif* as follows:

> a thoroughly heterogeneous ensemble consisting of discourses, institutions, architectural forms, regulatory decisions, laws, administrative measures, scientific statements, philosophical, moral and philanthropic propositions in short, the said as much as the unsaid ... The apparatus [*dispositif*] itself is the system of relations that can be established between these elements. (Foucault 1980, 194–195)

However heterogeneous the elements of the *dispositif* may actually be, it is not heterogeneity that results. The given assembly of elements is, rather, the very condition and (technical) infrastructure of what can possibly be perceived, articulated, and known. Exhibiting as a "practice of showing" (see Bal 1992) thus tends at first toward a rather technical notion of the interface and, only in the second place, toward a concept of the active involvement of the visitor. But, by interacting with the display, the visitor constitutes himself or herself *as* visitor and by that – and this is the crucial point – shows that something is being shown. Display*ing* therefore means – and here is our first conceptual shift – that, as part of the reception and perusal of an exhibition, while something is perceived, something is always being shown. The one who perceives or uses a display, more or less unwittingly displays something that has not been included into the display, something that escapes the curatorial process.

"Museum-as-text" approaches, developed most systematically by the art historian Mieke Bal (1992; 2006) and by Muttenthaler and Wonisch (2006) are based on the assumption that every display has an intentional meaning and an (unconscious) subtext that usually eludes the exhibition makers, but that lurks in the narrative context, in the sequence of objects, as well as in the nooks and crannies of exhibitions. This additional stratum of meaning can be elucidated by semiotic analysis. The subtexts, it is claimed, contain implicit statements that produce inclusions and exclusions, for example, statements about the superiority of a cultural group or about who or what constitutes the object and the subject in art. Thus, it is through the expository arrangement and media aesthetics – more than through content in the strict sense – through the underlying narrative, associations, and judgments made on the formal level, that agency and affiliation are ascribed and produced. And so it is not the case that museum-as-text approaches do not take visitors into consideration; on the contrary, Rhiannon Mason (2006) points out that approaches based on a poststructuralist-influenced concept of textuality do not consider the exhibition makers to be the sole producers of meaning, but stress visitors' readings as central to the production of meaning. Mieke Bal (1992) coined the term "expository agent" to describe this prompting aspect of actual exhibition arrangements. However, in studies of this kind visitors usually appear only as secondary effects of the museum-as-text. They are called on by the displays and are not being explicitly studied. The exhibitions and spaces analyzed are generally void of people and reception is basically conceived as an effect of the display.

Our approach involved combining semiotic analysis with a close observation of visitors' interactions. However, we need to be careful: meaning-making as a sensual and cognitive process is empirically accessible only through an indirect approach: all that we can observe are acts, operations, gestures, and communications. We can establish which exhibits, images, and interactives attract which children, how much time they spend with them, and which displays trigger communication (with peers, with parents, with teachers). As we wanted to go beyond the superficial construction of an abstract visitor that decodes subtexts, we had to find means to explore *how* and *what* children see or experience, and, even more crucially, how they *interpret*, how they make sense of what they encounter. Such information is, of course, accessible only to a limited degree, as these processes are invisible and can only be estimated via language. However, by cooperating closely with two schools, we were at least able to ask children about their experiences and interpretations. We conducted interviews but also acquired information with the help of games. In our observations, special attention was given to situations in which children communicated about what they had seen and experienced with their peers or with the educators in the exhibition. Facial and gestural expressions were noted in detail and interpreted systematically. But it still needs to be stated: The kind of displaying we were interested in is hard to study, even with the support of ethnographic methods. It lies between expression and behavior, between reaction and semiosis and is notoriously resistant to observation and analysis.

In the past few years the kind of interactions we were interested have been studied as *performances*. In the wake of social constructivist approaches, the formation of agency and the production of knowledge are considered by many researchers in the cultural and social sciences as performative acts (West and Zimmerman 1987; Hirschauer 1989; Butler 1997; for an overview, see Wirth 2007). It is through performances that identities and relations to others are ritually stabilized or destabilized. And the museum is a specific place for the performance of subjectivity and identity: remote from everyday family and classroom contexts, though in a sense still attached by an umbilical cord, exhibitions and science centers designed to involve the body and the senses offer beautiful and effective "stages" for both the training and transgression of culturally coded identities.

What we found in our research was a complex children's knowledge culture that oscillates between mimicry and imagination, between the learning of a canon of knowledge and individual and playful "theorizing" of what is encountered. We found the museum to be (still) a heterotopic place, a place in which the rules of the everyday world both do and do not apply, in which the scope of validity of social norms can be tested and assessed in ever new ways. Accordingly, our concern was to make the "play" in *displaying* apparent. As the media theorist Roger Silverstone pointed out, in the museum not only children but all visitors "can play in a safe world, an extension of childhood involvement with other objects" (1992, 40). This game involves not only subjects and objects but, in the first place, interactions.

"(Dis)playing the museum" is, therefore, to be understood basically as a model, an approach, a system of navigation that allowed us to relate the semiotically inspired "readings" of museum objects to empirically observed micro-sequences of interaction. This permitted a more detailed view of learning practices than is possible in studies of visitors, which are often restricted to quantifiable data. However, in order not to get stuck on anecdotal moments at the microlevel that could readily be interpreted as "subversive" or "adversary" – since the children's playful interaction with museum displays is full of "abuses" of all kinds – we also regularly adopted approaches that permitted us to situate our observations in broader social contexts. Although the sociologist Pierre Bourdieu's work is at the opposite extreme to Bruno Latour on the social theoretical level, we found ourselves referring again and again to his analysis of cultural processes of distinction and class, ethnic- and gender-conditioned habits, as we tried not to ignore the conditionality of the observed forms of the children's acts and expressions. We came to also see them as struggles for agency and sovereignty.

As early as the 1970s, Bourdieu had observed that the paradigm of "open learning" is in itself class- and gender-based, despite its universalistic claims (see Bourdieu and Passeron 1990). This paradigm, which is present in many museums and not just children's museums, holds that children are "natural explorers," that their "natural curiosity" has to be strengthened, and that therefore "free choice" learning is the magic bullet for successful learning. Bourdieu argued that this is a model of learning that is not at all universal, but that supports and is supported by a specific "habitus" which is cultivated in well-educated bourgeois families, with their high esteem of education and culture. Such a habitus can quickly appear hostile to children from other milieus. They quite often find it hard to interact "freely" with what the museum offers as they are unfamiliar with the whole environment and don't feel entitled to appropriate the hands-on displays. Hands-on and "free choice" seem to appeal best to children who are already sovereign learners.

This interpretive framework allowed for the exemplification of structures of meaning embodied in exhibits and played out by the young visitors. We conceptualized not only the museum object as a medium but also the bodies of the visitors as media which display and expose the meaning of exhibitionary arrangement. The approach combines cultural studies concepts of active consumers with approaches from media studies and science studies that emphasize the agency of objects. We therefore enriched our empirical research with interpretive models drawn from actor network theory (ANT). ANT researchers such as Bruno Latour, Madeleine Akrich, and others are inspired by ethnographic research and study media technological practices such as the use of laboratory technology, the way simple technology (such as keys) restructures the social, or how large-scale technological infrastructures (such as railway systems) generate an urban public.[3] This mode of interpretation appeared to be useful for the analysis of the relations between museum media and visitors, but only if it does not forget the fact that displays are made for learning. Their "function" is quite a tricky one, at least more complex then the function of a key.

Back and forth: Encoding, decoding, recoding

The tracking of the back-and-forth movement between exhibition analysis and the observation of young visitors, between museum-as-text and (dis)playing as a gesture performed by visitors became a central research strategy within the project. It was also important as a switch of attention between accumulation of data and interpretation through theoretical lenses. The back-and-forth movement, for example, helped in an analysis of an incident within an exhibition on ecology in a children's museum. The object of analysis and observation was the "Kilometer Kitchen," an exhibit intended to transmit the idea that buying local and regional products is better for the environment than consuming products that have to be transported over long distances. A supermarket checkout counter was modified in such a way that, instead of scanning the price of the wooden toy food that was presented in baskets on the shelves, it showed the number of kilometers that it had been transported. The children would receive a receipt with the result printed out. The exhibit was thus more of a store than a kitchen. This arrangement was completed by a menu resting on the floor, a map of the world with symbolic figures of people and animals, photographs of people shopping, and a poster with comic-book figures hung above the whole arrangement. Under the heading "It matters what you eat!" ["Es ist nicht Wurst, was du isst!"] it displayed scenes of "cannibalism": a pig about to eat a sausage, a carrot with a baby carrot on a plate, a fish with a small fish, a hen with an egg. In contrast to the manifest text of the poster heading, the subtext of the pictures was not that it *matters* what you eat, but that you literally *are* what you eat.

Within this arrangement we observed the following scene. A little girl went up to the checkout counter with her basket and was praised by the educator for the "good" purchase of a regional product, an apple. Surprisingly, the little girl responded by giving information about her own background: "I come from Turkey" (BP_KS_070530, 114–117).[4] The educator in charge did not react to her association and we can only speculate what effect this had on the girl's self-perception. What seems at first to be a misinterpretation on the little girl's part is, in fact, a rather literal interpretation of what was presented in the display: the short circuit between identity (you are …) and product (… what you eat) has moral implications, and the girl immediately applied this moral (it matters where you come from) to her person. Here, the second shift away from an understanding of the display as an unproblematic interface comes into play: the girl refers not just to what is represented but also twists the meaning – in this case, back on herself. It is hard to determine whether the whole moral of the display (faraway = bad) is incorporated in her answer, but something must have struck her as touching on her identity. Her reaction is a (dis)play, a distortion of what was intended to be taught.

In a way, our approach here comes close to the reception model of cultural studies that Stuart Hall elaborated on the basis of semiotic theories in his article "Encoding/Decoding" ([1973] 1980), which has often been used in research on audiences and youth cultures. Hall suggests that "linear" receptions – what he calls "hegemonic readings" – occur only rarely. "Negotiated" or "oppositional" readings, as he puts it, are more frequent, and these appear when the conditions of knowledge, the control over the communicative infrastructure, or the overall production relations between "author" and "recipient" do not coincide. Thus, negotiated and oppositional readings are to be expected, and all the more so in cases where social stratifications such as class, ethnicity, gender, and age are not explicitly addressed. But whereas Hall emphasizes the empowering effect of oppositional readings, we would like to argue that the need to negotiate a nonharmful reading is not only subversive but often means stress for children who already have difficulties "fitting in." One of our findings is that the additional interpretive work of those who are not addressed by a display in terms of both content and the habitus called for is highly original but at the same time has to be considered as real effort, not easily performed in any situation. Ambivalence can be a good starting point for learning, but it can also become quite demanding.

It is not only the visitors who express ambivalence; often it is also the objects exhibited, the nonhuman agents in the museum that, by their presence, "speak in tongues" (Haraway 1991, 181). If exhibition displays are not analyzed as mere means of transmission of content that need to be optimized, they are often studied in Foucault's sense as *dispositifs*, as mentioned above. We applied Foucault's understanding of the preconditions of knowledge production to our reconstruction of the institutional conditions of exhibitions: questions about the sociocultural location of certain exhibition spaces within the topography of the city interested us as *dispositifs* as much as the self-imposed educational programs of individual museums. In this way, the paradigm of "open," self-acquired learning of science centers and children's museums as such can likewise be understood as *dispositif* in the sense of an educational paradigm. "Open learning" is generally understood as opposed to the (older) paradigm of the disciplinary regulation of bodies, minds, and things in traditional museums of technology or the sciences.[5]

The drawback of the Foucauldian mode of critique is that, for one thing, the analysis is theoretically tailored in such a way that it tends to take large social entities into account (the disciplinary society, neoliberalism as a whole) and so forces the gaze away from concrete practices. For another, in our opinion, the disciplinary or governance factor of displays is conceptualized in a reductionist way. If we speak about *dispositifs*, power relations tend to appear to be frozen within objects and media that regulate what can be known: the infrastructure more or less determines interaction and experience. This is why we worked with selected concepts from actor network theory, which allow us to look at human–thing constellations in quite a different way.

The two positions (Foucault and ANT) are not entirely dissimilar at first glance. Bruno Latour (2005), sociologist of science and cofounder of ANT, talks about "scripts" that are incorporated into things and apparatuses by way of "delegation" of meanings, which are then translated back into and forced onto human action. His famous examples are the "sleeping policeman" (Latour 1999, ch. 6), and the "Berlin key" – in which, according to Latour (2000), an entire sociotechnical paradigm of inclusion and exclusion, complete with a temporal order (the door has to be locked at night), is inscribed or encoded. The "Berlin key" is a key and lock system that forces the user to lock the door from the inside, whenever he or she wants to close it: The key is stuck in on one side of the door and can only be released from the inside, if the door is thoroughly locked. The "sleeping policemen" performs a similar material force: the speed bump does not need to be interpreted semantically like a road sign, but "punishes" reckless drivers immediately by damaging their suspension; the object changes human interaction and behavior.

The major appeal of ANT for museum studies lies in its ability to analyze the process of delegation of meanings into things and back, not as a determined and determining process but as a "chain of translations" that generates new and unforeseen effects, new entities, and new partnerships within each delegation and connection. Thus, it supports our conviction that it is not the case that some "ideological" program of action is "embedded" in museum objects and their spatial arrangement; an ideology that is subsequently to be affirmed by the visitor. Museum things and visitors instead constantly create ever new collectives or assemblages with new possibilities of knowing and new ways of doing, which often imply a possibility of *de-scription* (Akrich 1992), that is, a destabilization of inscribed programs and social orders.

This happens when an object is given a new purpose by a way of using it. An example of this could – again – be the supermarket checkout counter already introduced, which obviously dominated the scenario of the shop / kitchen and at the same time sabotaged the intention of the assemblage. As mentioned already, the intended learning content was the idea that a lower number of kilometers in the transport of goods is good for the environment. But some children, of course, got a kick out of racking up the most kilometers on their receipts, so as to be "rich in terms of kilometers." One could say that the capitalist script of accumulation, as dominator of the

FIGURE 17.1   The *Mirakulosum*. (For a color version of this figure, please see the color plate section.)
Photo: Doris Harrasser, 2007.

scene, overruled the ecological script. The assemblage cashier/educator/child does not automatically lead to environmentally aware behavior, but to a scenario in which ecological and capitalist codes of behavior are brought into opposition such that some children are logically provoked to act in an antiecological manner.

In this line of analysis we were, for example, able to observe significant differences between girls and boys when it came to the interaction with machine-like displays. The display at stake was part of a laboratory arrangement called the *Mirakulosum* (Figure 17.1) in an exhibition about colors, which was held in an Austrian children's museum in the winter of 2007 (see Wöhrer and Harrasser 2011). The whole setting suggested an experimental situation and included a second hands-on station which taught different methods to isolate pigments from plants and ticks. The machine is a color-mixer containing a big transparent box placed on a wooden table (Figure 17.2). Inside this box are two bowls of water covered with a metal grid. On a clipboard little bottles with colored pigments are waiting to be used. Standing next to each other, two children can use this arrangement at the same time. They have to slide a hand into rubber gear that is used in sterile environments to reach into the box to start the game. Additionally, two handles, which function like gear-shifters, can be used to renew the water supply.

At first sight, the machine looked enigmatic. Children were often insecure about what to do with it. This is a typical scene from numerous observations:

Lena is the first at the object. She asks the educator: "How does this work?" He explains that she has to pour the powder into the water and that the water takes on color. But before that, she has to drain the water that was already colored. He shows

FIGURE 17.2   The color-mixer.
Photo: Doris Harrasser, 2007.

> her the hand gear, which she has to pull. After that, the educator turns to the other
> children at the table. Lena starts to color the water. Shortly after this Claus and
> Stephan enter the room, turn to Lena and ask: "What can be done here?" Lena
> explains how the coloring of water works. All three children start to color the two
> water basins. (BP_DH_071221, 187–195)

Many children started their interaction by asking for an explanation of how to
use this object before they even touched it: they called for an expert. Differences in
expertise are quickly established between newly arriving children and those who
have knowledge, even if it was only acquired a couple of minutes earlier. Not a
single child was observed to use the object without being given information. The
observation that the children cannot easily read the script for the handling of the
technical object corresponds with Harry Collins's (1990) findings that technology
in general needs explanation when used in everyday life. Real "experimenting" is
not easily possible with this strange object, but experimentation can be performed
as a reward for quite exhausting bodily effort: fitted with the rubber gear, the children grasp the bottles, shake them above the water, and color it with yellow, red,
blue, and black pigments. Many children are short of breath, their cheeks turn red,
some start to sweat or complain that this is "painful" or that their arm hurts (BP_
DH_080123, 309–310). In these exclamations the children express the physical
effort that is needed to carry out the experiment. They display the causal relation
of exhaustion and success that is inscribed in the object. If they are successful in
performing the task, they can watch their output immediately: colorful filaments
draw lines through the water before they dissolve. When children watch this phenomenon, they are amazed, cry out "oh" or "ah," "wow" or "Look, Mum!" and
show their work to peers or adults (e.g., BP_DH_080213, 353–360).

This is striking because usually the young "users" of the machine already know the factual result before the performance of "the experiment." They have often practiced color mixing before, but now they experience the process in a new way within a quasi-experimental setting. One could even say that, because the material technology and the social setting strongly restricts their bodily movements and actions, this otherwise banal fact is being highlighted as an insight. We can see that it is the very disciplining of the body and the strangeness of the machine that generate a specific form of isolated attention that has been identified as the core of a scientific habitus (Daston 2004). The historian of science Lorraine Daston characterizes curiosity, amazement, and the involvement of the body as basic elements of scientific knowledge production of the early sciences. But what distinguishes scientific practice from other forms of involvement and passion is the type of media of observation and the scientific genres of description that tend to a "purification" of scientific knowledge. One could thus say that by exhibiting the techniques of observation, by pointing to the laboriousness of knowledge acquisition, and by exhibiting the aesthetics of the new, the display did a good job in demonstrating how scientific knowledge is fabricated.

So far we have discussed how children in general (dis)played the machine. We then observed variations along the lines of gender. Both boys and girls were curious to learn the script of the object, both experienced exertion when following the instructions, and both expressed astonishment over the results. However, other practices differed depending on the child's gender. Many girls had a quite skeptical attitude to the object. They adjusted to the given setting and explanations more carefully than boys, that is, they waited more patiently before they used it, they carried out their "experiments" strictly according to the instructions, they let boys intervene in their game and let them explain how the object was to be handled, and so on. Some of the girls were enthusiastic about the colors, but they seemed to be more interested in the results of their experiment than in playing around with the device as such. They also made suggestions for the improvement of the object. Their criticism of the disproportion between the complicated machinery and the demonstration of a well-known, actually banal, fact, moved beyond the inscribed functionality of the machine. They reflected, questioned, criticized, and developed further ("recoded") the given setting.

The girls' reflections about the overall intentions of the machine resemble other studies' results of girls being better at "strategy knowledge" than boys of the same age who "scored higher" than girls in tests of science content (O'Reilly and McNamara 2007, 184). Most boys showed less ambivalence toward the given setting. They were enthusiastic about the object itself and started playing and experimenting right after they had been introduced to its handling. Boys often started explaining and intervening in other children's play. They evidently derived pleasure from handling the object in various ways: they developed games, explanations, and interpretations on their own, in which, for example, the act of pouring became more important than the mixing of colors. Boys also developed games and theories around the object: they pretended to create drinks to be sold in the museum or poison to pollute the river Danube. We only rarely observed boys explicitly questioning the arrangement. Only one boy within our sample suggested optimizing the instrument to make the handling easier (BP_DH_080205: 242–270).

The children (girls as well as boys) overperform, and decode the instrument and display the fact that it is possible to use the instrument not only in one way (to mix colors) but in more varied ways. Their activities were the result of creative processes within an experimental, though polysemic, setting. Our observations showed a wide spectrum of practices, which ranged from testing the already known results of mixing different colors to the discovery of new questions and/or new answers and even to reflecting and questioning the whole arrangement and its purpose. Of course, the gendered differences we observed are tendencies. We want neither to generalize nor to disregard other social factors shaping children's practices in museums and we have to take into account that the children had already experienced a process of gender-related socialization. Research has shown that children's education is shaped by gender and gender differences in many respects; and the same is true for science and technology museums. Borun and Chambers (2000) observed that boys are more likely to be taken to a science museum by their parents than girls, while Crowley et al. (2001) came to the conclusion that parents were three times more likely to explain science to boys than to girls while using interactive science exhibits in a museum. We suggest that the girls' careful comprehension of the given instructions and simultaneous maintenance of a skeptical distance to the arrangement can be interpreted not simply as an affirmation of gender roles but also as a means of self-empowerment, as a strategy to gain competence with unfamiliar technical objects they would otherwise not deal with habitually. The de-scription and (dis)play takes place on the level of physical interaction and theoretical reasoning in this case rather than of identity and meaning-making as it does in the first case study.

What kind of museum is at stake? What kind of knowledge? What kind of learning?

Are these findings of relevance only in the field of educational media in museums? Given the fact that hands-on and "free choice" learning have made their way into traditional museums for quite some time now, we may as well ask: What kind of museum is at stake if we consider "hands-on" and "free choice" as persistent paradigms for museum media? What kind of knowledge and what kind of learning are we dealing with in contemporary museums? If the traditional museum with its object-oriented displays and great narratives (historical, geographical, biological), which are played out in spatial arrangements, is entangled with the civilizing and educational projects of the nineteenth century (see Bennett 1995), what can we learn from contemporary display design? We can take the question further: If the traditional museum paradigm is a showcase of imperialism and of the superiority of scientific knowledge over other forms of knowing, what do flat and interactive technologies in exhibiting tell us about contemporary society? Who is the playful explorer envisioned by designers of all these interactive displays that have now proliferated in almost every museum?

The slogan "Hands on!" refers to a concept of learning and understanding by way of bodily, emotional, and intellectual experiences. The pioneers of children's museums in the United States, who coined the term, based their exhibition prac- tices on progressive educational and psychological theories, such as John Dewey's "learning by doing," Maria Montessori's findings that children need freedom to move and a stimulating environment for individual development, as well as Jean Piaget's work, which is based on the belief that children acquire knowledge through play and imitation (König 2002). The concept combines these approaches, which became part of a didactic framework for children's museums but also for the modernization and audience orientation of traditional museum displays.

This need for modernization is an impulse that is intermingled both with iden- tity politics and with the paradoxes of postenlightenment education. The need to rework museum displays has an important root in political demands to dismantle existing hierarchies of knowledge. It is connected to demands to involve those who had formerly been displayed (e.g., women, ethnic groups). "Involvement" and "participation" are important keywords in discussions about the democratiza- tion of museums. But involvement and participation, the constant engagement in processes of knowledge production, have meanwhile become ambivalent educa- tional goals. As an effect of the (normative) self-description of modern societies as "knowledge societies," we perceive a constant tension between the empowering effects of learning and knowing and the compulsory, even repressive, nature of the imperative of "lifelong learning." The imperative fuels the need for ever better and more effective educational tools which should address all senses and the whole personality of the learning individual. It is our impression that "the child as explorer" has become the prototype of the much desired informed citizen, who is willing to learn constantly.

What we observed with children has a lot to do with this tension, as they were asking (themselves, their peers, the educators) what kind of knowledge, what kind of competences, were valued as necessary or at least interesting. We could observe how they made explicit with their play not only hidden agendas of educational objec- tives but also the normative character of learning as such. We could see clearly that undoing hierarchies of knowledge with hands-on and participatory methods does not produce equality, certainly not automatically. It does produce interesting and new forms of expertise, though: narrative competence, "freestyle theory-making" and improvisational skills could be observed in many variations. But we could also see stress and excessive demands for those not familiar with "open" formats of learn- ing or with technologies. What we were able to learn from the children is that the spatial organization and the interplay of artifacts and narrations are both part and counterpart of the process of being subjectified *as* museum visitor that performs his or her civil right and duty to learn. We were able to observe both the seductive character of spatial organization and of interactives and a certain obstinacy of objects. And it remains open as to what the effects of the addressing of visitors as "users" of displays does to the experience of a museum visit.

Conclusions: What kind of medium is the museum?

As mentioned at the beginning, our research on learning focused on specific educational media. We were interested in interactives and hands-on objects which are materializations of a certain idea of learning, namely the idea of self-organized and playful learning. Given the fact that interactive media and the paradigm of playful learning are strong tendencies within contemporary museum planning and exhibition design, we can situate them within the larger question as to the extent and in what respects the contemporary museum can be conceived as a medium. Media are frequently defined as (technical) means or (cultural) methods to process, store, and transmit data. I would like to add that media are more and less than that. They are more than "means" as they play an active role in processing, storing, and transmitting; it makes a difference whether "data" ("content") is transmitted via images, letters, diagrams, or objects. And they are less than this, for media as such do not exist. As German philosopher and literary scholar Joseph Vogl states: "There are no media – no media, that is, in a substantial and historically stable sense" (2012, 73). Media do – of course – somehow exist but they cannot be reduced to their actual representations (film, theater, display) or to their technical features, which are themselves historically contingent. They are notoriously hard to study, as "media make things readable, audible, visible, and perceptible, but they do all this with a tendency to extinguish themselves in these operations – to make themselves imperceptible" (Vogl 2012, 73). However, they do make an appearance in certain situations: in breakdowns, in dysfunctional usage, whenever they are reworked and recoded, or when they become obsolescent. It is when media go out of fashion or don't function properly that we perceive them. It was our project to study such situations in order to learn more general things about the museum as a medium that stabilizes and destabilizes epistemological values and cultural codes and thus transforms both what we conceive as "knowledge" and as a "museum."

I would like to return to the initial question: What are the possible consequences of the prevailing "interactive mode" in exhibition design and of the paradigm of playful learning? Given the fact that they reconfigure museums and their audiences, what kind of agencies will museums be in the future? What kind of agency will they be able to trigger within their visitors? For sure they are no longer temples of Culture with a big C, be it art or scientific culture. They are no longer a medium of national interest to teach bourgeois citizens how they became what they are, as

Tony Bennett (1995) has argued for the national museums of the nineteenth century. Bennett described these museums as sites for the self-assurance of a privileged group of people who saw their own culture reflected in them as the most advanced, the most civilized, culture. At the same time these museums aimed to transform the working classes into self-motivated, self-civilizing sovereign learners. With interactive media we can observe an extension but also a modification of this tradition. In the course of their democratization museums have been transformed into hybrid places that oscillate between educational tasks and entertainment programs. This is evident in the mix of museum objects that can be found in different concentrations in different museums: precious (and not so precious) originals with and without showcases cohabit with "functional" media such as mock-ups, hands-on objects, and interactive digital media. We see an intermingling of the Urania principle of education – the social democratic idea of education for everybody – with genuine entertainment formats. We see marriages of politically highly desired participatory approaches with pure consumer opportunism. We consider participatory approaches important because inequality in cultural capital is still at stake. We can see this in multiple surveys about the bias in educational chances depending on class and ethnicity (see Jacob and Klein 2013). The findings we arrived at when studying the children's (dis)plays were both promising and irritating: more than ever it seems impossible to finally stabilize any meaning within the museum. Objects are constantly unsettled, recoded, (dis)played. Spontaneous theories are being invented, desires are being triggered, and new uses are being performed, no matter how well thought out the objects and displays are.

On the other hand, it could be the case that the museum loses its heterotopic potential if it nestles up all too easily with current media aesthetics of interaction that tend to render their mediality imperceptible. The museum as a space that allows for a questioning and skeptical gaze on what is considered normal and real traditionally relied on media that gave the objects an aura. Paradoxically, these media manufactured presence by distancing the objects visually and haptically. In the space between the eye and the object, the imagination was able to flourish, but so too were ideologies of various kinds. Interactives promised to shorten the distance between the eye and the object, suggesting direct insight or learning. But do directness and insight go together that well? Is it not the crystal of the showcase that reflects the gaze, the moment when the medium creeps into perception that triggers complex learning processes? Such a process includes the content or the object, the way it is presented (the curatorial narrative), and the visitor's awareness of his or her own position with regard to the arrangement? The more we get used to "intuitive," "sensual," "interactive" media the less such devices will probably be able to trigger the sense of wonder so necessary for any substantial learning (see Greenblatt 1991). Museum objects will line up with the visitor's media reality, with worlds of information they are continuously dealing with already. A thought experiment as a conclusion: It could be the recurrent use of "old media" that guarantees the heterotopic character of the museum in the future because it is old media that trip up perception. Obsolescent media, for example, often have an alienating effect. A song played from an old record full of scratches, a Super 8 film with its strange colors, but also a huge collection of minerals in showcases (such as in the Museum of Natural History in Vienna): such items are disturbing. They foreground the fact that somebody has made this, has fabricated it to be seen or to be heard. We cannot overlook this fact, as the medium is persistently present within the aesthetic experience; we cannot delete it from our perception. In the best case, a gap for interpretation and imagination opens up and is not immediately reframed by institutional effects. Could the museum please vanish for a moment?

Notes

1   The research project, titled "Science with all Senses: Gender and Science in the Making," was supported by the Vienna Science and Technology Fund (WWTF) and was carried out by Science Communications Research, Vienna. Research was conducted in three children's museums and science centers in Austria and Germany over 30 months between 2007 and 2009 with a team consisting of both social scientists and humanities scholars. The researchers were Veronika Wöhrer, Doris Harrasser, Stephanie Kiessling, Karin Schneider, Sabine Sölkner, and the author.

2   Eighty-nine observations were carried out in ZOOM Children's Museum in Vienna, 21 at the Museum of Technology, 16 at the Spectrum, the science center at the German Museum Museum of Technology in Berlin, and two additional observations in the main museum.

3   For an introduction to topics and methods of actor network theory, see Latour (2005).

4   The abbreviation BP refers to internal field notes and protocols. All names of children have been changed.

5   For critical readings of the paradigm of open learning as governmental mode of education, see Ricken and Rieger-Ladich (2004) and Dzierzbicka (2006).

References

Akrich, Madeleine. 1992. "The De-Scription of Technical Objects." In *Shaping Technology/Building Society: Studies in Sociotechnical Change*, edited by Wiebe E. Bijker and John Law, 205–224. Cambridge, MA: MIT Press.

Bal, Mieke. 1992. "Telling, Showing, Showing Off." *Critical Inquiry* 18(3): 556–594.

Bal, Mieke. 2006. "Exposing the Public." In *Companion to Museum Studies*, edited by Sharon Macdonald, 525–542. Oxford: Blackwell.

Bennett, Tony. 1995. *The Birth of the Museum: History, Theory, Politics*. London: Routledge.

Borun, Minda, and Margaret Chambers. 2000. "Gender Roles in Science Museum Learning." *Visitor Studies Today!* 3(3): 11–14.

Bourdieu, Pierre, and Jean-Claude Passeron. 1990. *Reproduction in Education, Society and Culture*, 2nd ed. London: Sage.

Butler, Judith. 1997. "Performative Acts and Gender Constitution: An Essay in Phenomenology and Feminist Theory." In *Writing on the Body: Female Embodiment and Feminist Theory*, edited by Katie Conboy, Nadia Medina, and Sarah Stanbury, 401–417. New York: Columbia University Press.

Collins, Harry M. 1990. *Artificial Experts: Social Knowledge and Intelligent Machines*. Cambridge, MA: MIT Press.

Crowley, Kevin, Maureen Callanan, Harriet Tenenbaum, and Elizabeth Allen. 2001. "Parents Explain More Often to Boys than to Girls During Shared Scientific Thinking." *Psychological Science* 12(3): 258–261.

Daston, Lorraine. 2004. "Attention and the Values of Nature in the Enlightenment." In *The Moral Authority of Nature*, edited by Lorraine Daston and Fernando Vidal, 100–126. Chicago: University of Chicago Press.

Dzierzbicka, Agnieszka. 2006. *Vereinbaren statt anordnen: Neoliberale Gouvernementalität macht Schule* [Agree rather than give orders: Neoliberal governance in schools]. Vienna: Löcker.

Foucault, Michel. 1980. "The Confession of the Flesh." In *Power/Knowledge: Selected Interviews and Other Writings 1972–1977*, edited by Colin Gordon, 194–228. New York: Pantheon.

Geertz, Clifford. 1973. "Thick Description: Toward an Interpretive Theory of Culture". In *The Interpretation of Cultures: Selected Essays*, 3–30. New York: Basic Books.

Greenblatt, Stephen. 1991. "Resonance and Wonder." In *Exhibiting Cultures*, edited by Ivan Karp and Steven D. Lavine, 42–56. Washington, DC: Smithsonian Institution.

Hall, Stuart. (1973) 1980. "Encoding/Decoding." In *Culture, Media, Language: Working Papers in Cultural Studies 1972–79*, edited by the Centre for Contemporary Cultural Studies, 128–138. London: Hutchinson.

Haraway, Donna. 1991. "A Cyborg Manifesto: Science, Technology, and Socialist-Feminism in the Late Twentieth Century." In *Simians, Cyborgs and Women: The Reinvention of Nature*, 149–181. New York: Routledge.

Hirschauer, Stefan. 1989. "Die interaktive Konstruktion von Geschlechtszugehörigkeit" [The interactive construction of gender affiliation]. *Zeitschrift für Soziologie* 8: 100–118.

Jacob, Marita, and Markus Klein. 2013. "Der Einfluss der Bildungsherkunft auf den Berufseinstieg und die ersten Erwerbsjahre von Universitätsabsolventen" [The impact of educational background on the career and the first few years of employment of university graduates]. *Beiträge zur Hochschulforschung* 35(1): 8–37.

König, Gabriele. 2002. *Kinder- und Jugendmuseen: Genese und Entwicklung einer Museumsgattung: Impulse für besucherorientierte Museumskonzepte* [Children's and youth museums: Genesis and development of a museum type: The impetus behind visitor-oriented approaches to museums]. Opladen, Germany: Leske & Budrich.

Latour, Bruno. 1999. *Pandora's Hope: Essays on the Reality of Science Studies*. Cambridge, MA: Harvard University Press.

Latour, Bruno. 2000. "The Berlin Key; or, How To Do Words with Things." In *Matter, Materiality and Modern Culture*, edited by Paul Graves-Brown, 10–21. London: Routledge.

Latour, Bruno. 2005. *Reassembling the Social: An Introduction to Actor-Network-Theory*. New York: Oxford University Press.

Macdonald, Sharon, ed. 2006. *Companion to Museum Studies*. Oxford: Blackwell.

Mason, Rhiannon. 2006. "Cultural Theory and Museum Studies." In *A Companion to Museum Studies*, edited by Sharon Macdonald, 17–32. Oxford: Blackwell.

Muttenthaler, Roswitha, and Regina Wonisch. 2006. *Gesten des Zeigens: Zur Repräsentation von Gender und Race in Ausstellungen* [Pointing the finger: On the representation of gender and race in exhibitions]. Bielefeld, Germany: Transcript.

O'Reilly, Tenaha, and Danielle S. McNamara. 2007. "The Impact of Science Knowledge, Reading Skill, and Reading Strategy Knowledge on More Traditional 'High-Stakes' Measures of High School Students' Science Achievement." *American Educational Research Journal* 44(1): 161–196.

Ricken, Norbert, and Markus Rieger-Ladich, eds. 2004. *Michel Foucault: Pädagogische Lektüren* [Pedagogical readings]. Wiesbaden: Verlag für Sozialwissenschaften.

Schade, Sigrid, and Dorothee Richter. 2007. "Ausstellungsdisplays: Reflexionen zu einem Zürcher Forschungsprojekt" [Exhibition displays: Reflections on a Zurich-based research project]. *Kunstforum International* 186: 55–64.

Silverstone, Roger. 1992. "The Medium is the Museum: On Objects and Logics in Times and Spaces." In *Museums and the Public Understanding of Science*, edited by John Durant, 34–41. London: Science Museum.

Strauss, Anselm L., and Juliet Corbin. 1990. *Basics of Qualitative Research: Grounded Theory Procedures and Techniques*. Thousand Oaks, CA: Sage.

Teckert, Christian. 2007. "Display als Dispositiv: Die Ideologie der Ausstellung als Thema zeitgenössischer Architektur" [Display as device: The ideology of the exhibition as a subject of contemporary architecture]. *Kunstforum International* 186: 180–187.

Vogl, Joseph. 2012. "Taming Time: Media of Financialization." *Grey Room* 46: 72–83.

West, Candace, and Don H. Zimmerman. 1987. "Doing Gender." *Gender & Society* 1: 125–151.

Wirth, Uwe. 2007. *Performanz: Zwischen Sprachphilosophie und Kulturwissenschaft* [Performance: Between the philosophy of language and cultural studies]. Frankfurt: Suhrkamp.

Wöhrer, Veronika, and Doris Harrasser. 2011. "Playful Experiments: Gendered Performances in a Children's Museum." In *Science as Culture* 20(4): 471–490. doi:10.1080/09505431.2011.605925.

Karin Harrasser is Professor for Cultural Studies (Kulturwissenschaft) at the University of Art and Design Linz. She studied German literature and history at the University of Vienna and completed her dissertation on the narratives of digital cultures there. After a postdoctoral position at Humboldt University of Berlin, she followed her research in the cultural history of prosthetics at the Academy of Media Arts Cologne. She conducted a research project on the production of gender and knowledge in museums and has realized numerous projects at the intersection of arts and science communication. Her most recent books is *Körper 2.0: Über die technische Erweiterbarkeit des Menschen* [Body 2.0: On the technical extendibility of the Human] (Transcript, 2013).

FIGURE 2.2 Melik Ohanian, *Invisible Film*, 2005, video projection, 90 minutes.
Courtesy of the artist and Galerie Chantal Crousel, Paris.

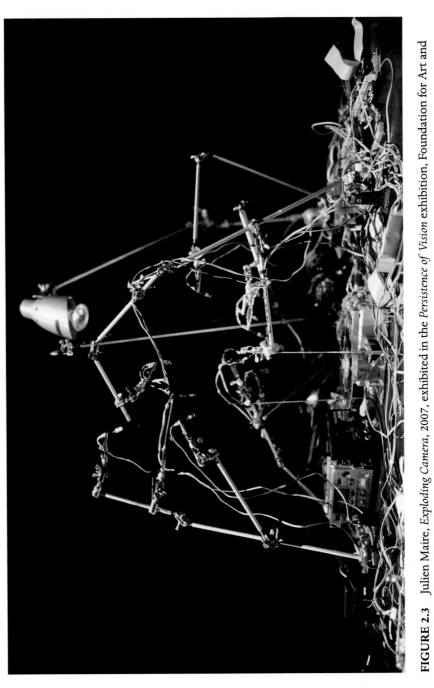

FIGURE 2.3 Julien Maire, *Exploding Camera*, 2007, exhibited in the *Persistence of Vision* exhibition, Foundation for Art and Creative Technology (FACT), Liverpool.

Photo: Brian Slater.

FIGURE 4.1 Pavel Boyko and Arkadi Lebedev, *The Battle of Kursk: A History Lesson.*
© Royal Museum of the Army and of Military History, Brussels.

FIGURE 6.2 Installation view of *Remote Control*, Institute of Contemporary Arts, London, 2012.
Photo: Mark Blower.

FIGURE 6.3 LuckyPDF's James Early and Chloe Sims at *Remote Control*, Institute of Contemporary Arts, London, 2012.
Photo: Victoria Erdelevskaya. Courtesy of LuckyPDF and Institute of Contemporary Arts.

FIGURE 10.2 Rupert Cox and Angus Carlyle, *Air Pressure*, 2012. View of installation at Whitworth Art Gallery, Manchester, UK.

FIGURE 10.3 Rupert Cox and Angus Carlyle, *Air Pressure*, 2012. Another view of installation at Whitworth Art Gallery, Manchester, UK.

FIGURE 11.3   Menashe Kadishman, *Shalechet*, Libeskind Building, Jewish Museum, Berlin. Donation Dieter and Si Rosenkranz.
Photo: Jens Ziehe.

FIGURE 13.2   Stone circle in the Museum of Witchcraft.
© John Hooper/Hoopix/Museum of Witchcraft.

FIGURE 13.6   Living room at The Valiant Soldier.
Photo: Fiona Candlin. Reproduced with permission of The Valiant Soldier.

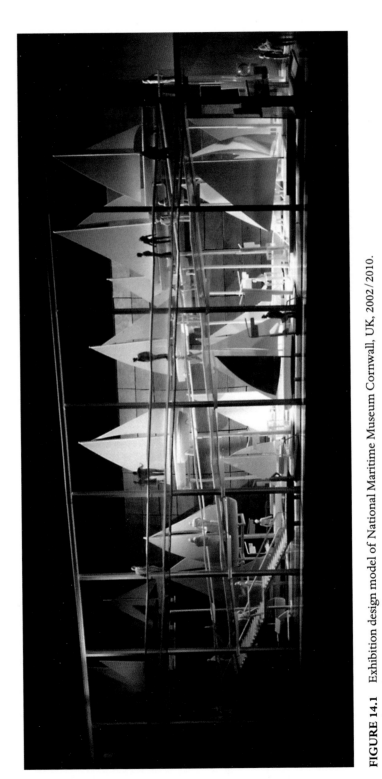

FIGURE 14.1 Exhibition design model of National Maritime Museum Cornwall, UK, 2002/2010.
Photo: Nick Wood.

FIGURE 14.3 UK pavilion, Expo 2005, Aichi, Japan, designed by Land Design Studio.
Photo: Lee Maudsley.

FIGURE 16.1   Self-enactment: the scene at the entrance to the exhibition *A Matter of Belief*, Lenzburg, Switzerland.

Photo: Donovan Wyrsch. © Stapferhaus Lenzburg.

FIGURE 16.5   What does Switzerland believe? These representative objects gathered from the population in the exhibition *A Matter of Belief* show how attitudes to belief have been individualized.

Photo: Theres Bütler © Stapferhaus Lenzburg.

FIGURE 17.1   The *Mirakulosum*.
Photo: Doris Harrasser, 2007.

FIGURE 18.6 The Hall of Human Biology, ca. 1977, Natural History Museum, London.

© The Trustees of the Natural History Museum, London.

FIGURE 19.2 The Interactive Desk, with a tangible token visible inside the basket, Bunratty Folk Park.

Photo: Don Moloney – Press 22.

FIGURE 20.3 Rafael Lozano-Hemmer, *Pulse Room*, 2010, Manchester Art Gallery, Manchester, UK.

Photo: Peter Mallet. Reproduced by permission of Rafael Lozano-Hemmer.

FIGURE 21.3   Physical marker indicating the presence of an artwork in John Bell's *The Variable Museum.*

FIGURE 23.1   BMW Welt, Munich.
Reproduced by permission of BMW AG.

FIGURE 23.3 "Going to the Schirn is not art," Frankfurt.
Photo: Mark W. Rectanus.

FIGURE 24.3 Mark Dion, Cabinet of Curiosities, Musée Océanographique, Monaco.
© Musée Océanographique. Photo: M. Dagnino, 2011. Reproduced with permission.

FIGURE 25.1 Hans Holbein the Younger, *The Ambassadors*, 1533. Note the famous distorted skull in the foreground of the picture.

By permission of the National Gallery, London.

18 TRANSFORMING THE NATURAL HISTORY MUSEUM IN LONDON
Isotype and the New Exhibition Scheme

Sue Perks

*The transformer is someone who is working on behalf of the audience and interme-
diary, someone who mediates between the experts and the lay audience you're trying
to communicate with. It seems strange, you would think haven't museums always
been doing that? And I think manifestly not when you look at the work that had been
done. Often, exhibitions, mounted by subject specialists … were for a specialist to
show other specialists that they were fully up-to-date with their subject. No thought
was given to the audience at all.*

Miles 2008

In 1975 the Natural History Museum in London took a leap of faith when it
adopted the 50-year-old concept of the transformer in the development of its
"New Exhibition Scheme." This way of working has had a fundamental influence
on the design of educational exhibits ever since. The original role of the transformer stems from Isotype (the International System Of TYpographic Picture
Education) originated by Dr. Otto Neurath in 1925 for use at the Gesellschafts-
und Wirtschaftsmuseum [Social and Economic Museum] in Vienna. The transformer mediated between academics and designers to create accessible charts and
exhibits. Neurath's charts were designed to educate and inform the citizens of
"Red Vienna" about important social and political matters, under the auspices of
the Social Democratic regime (1919–1934).

The International Handbooks of Museum Studies: Museum Media, First Edition.
Edited by Michelle Henning.
© 2015 John Wiley & Sons Ltd. Published 2020 by John Wiley & Sons Ltd.

Half a century later, Roger Miles and his team at the Natural History Museum (hereafter NHM) used the role of the transformer to devise the New Exhibition Scheme in response to their need to fulfill the 1753 mandate that stated that exhibitions existed "for the general use and benefit of the public." According to Miles, it was fair to say that, before the New Exhibition Scheme, the needs of the audience were not being considered by either museum curators or designers, who were guilty of "packaging" displays rather than providing the audience with accessible exhibits. Miles referred to the frustration of the educator within museums as they tried to make academic exhibits accessible when in reality they were only of interest to other curators and the educated public (Miles 2008).

Roger Miles and Mick Alt cited the Isotype transformer as one of the three main contributing factors that went into the formulation of the New Exhibition Scheme (Miles and Alt 1979, 158–162). Transformation was adopted to attempt to communicate effectively with a largely undefined general audience and to enhance a visitor-friendly approach in the design of new exhibitions. Miles considered that the Isotype transformer was the "inspiration" behind the scheme; and the NHM's adoption of the role during the 1970s has been much documented (Kinross 1979; 1981; Kraeutler 2003; 2008; M. Neurath and Kinross 2009). But why was this historic role considered relevant for the design of audience-friendly exhibitions? And how was the role of the transformer applied and adapted to work on a much larger scale for a 1970s audience? Common themes that bridge the 50 year gap are a sound emphasis on education, integrity in conveying information, and the need to communicate effectively with the audience. Evidence to show how the museum implemented these themes and adopted transformation can be found in official documents, journals, papers, and publications in the Natural History Museum Library and Archives in South Kensington.

The New Exhibition Scheme ran from 1975 to 1991, beginning as a radical experiment to shake up the way that the NHM related to its audience. Despite media controversy and internal struggle, what began as an experiment culminated in the controversial almost object-free exhibition *Human Biology: An Exhibition of Ourselves*, which opened to great acclaim in 1977, swiftly followed by *Introducing Ecology* in 1978. Experience gained from designing and producing these early phases of the New Exhibition Scheme formed the basis of "museum technology," a pragmatic body of evidence-based knowledge that Miles developed to design educational exhibitions for further phases of the scheme, ultimately solving the museum's problem of remaining progressive and fulfilling their educative mandate (Miles and Tout 1979).

This chapter will examine how and why the NHM adopted this 50-year-old methodology – conceived in Vienna for a social and economic museum under very different political circumstances. It will also discuss how the museum redefined the role of the Isotype transformer for a 1970s audience in the context of a

FIGURE 18.1   (a) Otto Neurath, 1944. (b) Marie Neurath.
Courtesy of the Otto and Marie Neurath Isotype Collection, Department of Typography & Graphic Communication, University of Reading.

British national museum, concentrating on the collaborative relationship between scientist and designer – the transformation partnerships and the extended teams that supported them.

The origins and definition of the transformer

Dr. Otto Neurath (Figure 18.1a) became the first director of the Gesellschafts- und Wirtschaftsmuseum in 1925 (hereafter GWM) and primarily formulated the principles of Isotype (then known as the Vienna Method) to explain sociological and economic issues to working-class Viennese citizens using a system of visual statistics. The GWM formed part of the Social Democrat experiment to blend culture and politics in Red Vienna from 1919 to 1934. Neurath's particular aims were to establish a museum to educate and inform citizens of their rights and to provide unbiased information on important social issues (Gruber 1991, 84).

It has been argued that Neurath gained his initial ideas on social museums from examples set by the ambitious world expositions of the nineteenth century, the outdoor hygiene and science exhibitions of the early twentieth century, and the Musée Social, which presented ideas on the welfare state in turn-of-the-century France (Vossoughian 2008, 49). But Neurath began to develop more focused ideas on visual communication in a social context in his role as director of the Museum of War Economy in Leipzig in 1916. There he began to incorporate visual statistics into his museum displays. Neurath's work on the visual dissemination of social facts continued in 1921 when he became general secretary of the Austrian Housing and Allotment Association.

The success of the GWM and the Vienna Method – developed as a simple picture language for use in the museum, attracted many home and overseas visitors,

FIGURE 18.2   The Gesellschafts- und Wirtschaftsmuseum, Vienna ca. 1927.
Courtesy of the Otto and Marie Neurath Isotype Collection, Department of Typography &
Graphic Communication, University of Reading.

all eager to find new ways to present visual information. Rudolf Modley, the popularizer of the pictogram in America during the 1930s, interned at the GWM in the late 1920s, commented on the large number of Americans who visited the museum between 1927 and 1934. He described it as a "classroom in social science for thousands of residents and visitors" (Modley and Lowenstein 1952, 6). American visitors included representatives from the newly founded Chicago Museum of Science and Industry (one of the first of America's many science museums), keen to use Neurath's Vienna Method in their own museum.

The many thousands of local visitors to the GWM enjoyed a convivial atmosphere and late evening and weekend opening hours where they could see informative, entertaining charts and simple interactive self-testing devices to reinforce the concepts put forward. Charts were arranged in bays to allow small groups to informally discuss content with friends and family and to form opinions based on the visual arguments presented. Apart from the main museum in the New Town Hall, the GWM (Figure 18.2) had sub-branches in accessible places so that it was easy for all working people to visit in their leisure time.[1]

The GWM formed a constantly changing platform showcasing the work of the Vienna District Municipality, where the audience was treated as an equal partner, rather than as an uneducated underclass, by providing accessible, visitor-friendly displays. Neurath used the medium of the museum to communicate his ideas on housing, hygiene, health, and social and economic developments. He was against the amassing of collections, only ever exhibiting three-dimensional objects to support statements made in the charts on display, never as stand-alone *objets d'art*.

Audience opinion was monitored and charts were adapted in response to visitor feedback. Neurath and his team were among the first museologists to monitor feedback in this way (M. Neurath and Kinross 2009, 25–26). The museum was at the height of its popularity during the late 1920s and early 1930s, employing 25 staff in a prime central Vienna location, with 500 square meters of exhibition space. The Social Democrats, as sponsors of the museum, promoted measures to improve the education system and encouraged the collaboration of schools and museums. School tours were welcome, and Marie Neurath's (née Reidemeister) training as a teacher proved useful in facilitating the association.

Marie Neurath (Figure 18.1b) was the first employee of the museum in 1925 and, along with Otto Neurath, became one of the first transformers. In a 1974 article entitled "Isotype" she outlined the role of the transformer (M. Neurath 1974). This was reprinted in the NHM's in-house training manual for transformers *The Transformation Reader* (1979):

> It is the responsibility of the "transformer" to understand the data, to get all necessary information from the expert, to decide what is worth transmitting to the public, how to make it understandable, how to link it with general knowledge or with information already given in other charts. He has to remember the rules and keep to them, adding new variations where advisable, at the same time avoiding unnecessary deviations which would only confuse. (M. Neurath 1974, 13)

Otto Neurath's transformer or "trustee of the public" was responsible for acquiring and extracting facts from information supplied by the subject expert and for having enough general knowledge, integrity, and graphic skills to turn the information into a chart, using repeated Isotype symbols to represent magnitude. The transformer translated academic or statistical information into rough visuals of charts and made decisions on all major details such as the graphic form of the argument, the quantity represented by each pictogram, the use of guide images (*Führungsbilder*) to reinforce the message, color coding, titling, captions, and annotation. This design would then be handed on to the graphic artist who assembled and pasted up the final artwork, which consisted of linocut printed symbols and printed letterpress type set in Futura font.

In the context of the New Exhibition Scheme at the NHM, the transformer's role was to bring complex scientific facts and ideas to life in an entertaining and educative way for a wide lay audience – in simple terms, to turn the form of information chosen by the expert into a form that most suited the learner, through the combined skills of designer and subject expert, curator, or scientist. Miles's thoughts on transformation had their roots in Neurath's definition of the transformer, but the outcome was not governed by a formal visual system and was produced by a team equipped with far greater technological resources. It must be remembered that Miles could not have considered such a radical departure from traditional methods for designing exhibitions without the funding, infrastructure, and staffing that only a national museum could offer. In addition, while the GWM comprised only 500 square meters of exhibition space, the NHM during the mid-1970s comprised 14,000 square meters of exhibition space.

For the transformers at the NHM during the 1970s and 1980s, the process began with an equal partnership of scientist and three-dimensional designer. Initially, the scientist transformer's job was to make the designer understand the facts so they could use their communication skills to make the information accessible. The designer transformer's job was to understand the content provided by the scientist and translate it into educative, visually attractive graphic solutions suitable for a lay audience. The museum employed three-dimensional designers as designer transformers (even though the work would have been better suited to graphic designers, as "skilled professional communicators"[2]). The resulting rough visuals were then passed to graphic designers, illustrators, and model makers to produce artwork for the production of exhibits. The museum graphic design teams during the 1970s and 1980s were based in west London, 15 miles from the designer–scientist transformation partnerships at the museum in central London. Miles (2008) admits that early on they were a little hazy about where the weight of responsibility lay for graphic interpretation. For this reason, exhibits in the New Exhibition Scheme, particularly early on, were highly ambitious in their use of three-dimensional design, but less so in two-dimensional terms.

A need for change

A good illustration of the reasons why the NHM needed to change its ideas on how a national museum should communicate with its audience can be found by looking back at issues of *Museums Journal* from the late 1950s to the early 1980s; they paint a lively picture of museums struggling to come to terms with the problem of making displays more accessible to the visiting public. During the 1950s, very few museums in the United Kingdom employed full-time designers. Numbers had not significantly changed at the end of the 1960s, but they swelled during the mid-1970s as museums recognized the need for designers – used not as display technicians but as equal team members in a challenging, expanding role. By the end of the 1970s *Museums Journal* was discussing the employment of "communicators" as the way forward for museum design. During the Museums Association Annual Conference in 1970, discussion took place not so much on *whether* or not to employ a designer, but on *how* to use designers in museums (Belcher 1970, 63–66).

The traditional 1950s method for delivering museum exhibits was for the curator (or scientist) to supply facts, select relevant exhibits, write text and titles, and then hand everything over to the graphic designer. It was the function of the graphic designer to make everything look attractive and neat; specify the typography for the labels, main introductory text, and headings; produce or commission illustrations; and fit it all into the case – a role described as "window dressing" by museum commentators of the time. As more museums gradually began to employ in-house designers, two divided camps emerged; the designer was employed to service the graphic needs of the curator and was not seen as a valued part of the process of formulating exhibits. It was apparent that the museum curator and the museum designer had little in common, and approached their work from very different perspectives.

Two Museums Association Annual Conferences held in 1970 and 1972 (Bristol City Museum and Art Gallery and Guildhall Museum, London), chaired by Michael Belcher (then head of the Exhibition Section at the NHM), reported on the role of the designer in museums from varying viewpoints (Belcher 1970, 63–66; 1972, 58–62). Delegates summarized situations that could impede communication and lead to poorly functioning educational exhibits:

- dominance of designer *or* curator;
- curators who employed designers as extensions of themselves;
- scholarship seen as a barrier to communication;
- failed dialogue between curator and designer.

The need for a mediator between curator and designer was discussed, envisioned in the role of scriptwriter, content editor, interpreter, or communicator which was to be incorporated into the museum design process. Delegates discussed how to structure information by dividing it into easily accessible sections along with who should be responsible for ultimately communicating with the audience. The eminent Viennese art historian and museum scholar Alma Wittlin had referred to this need to structure information in *Museums: In Search of a Usable Future* (1970), highlighting the fact that curators did not necessarily possess pedagogical skills and that a wider team was needed to effectively engage with the audience – in particular a communicator. She suggested that subject matter specialists should take a fresh look at how they conveyed facts to a lay audience and embrace the communication process, rather than hiding from it. She called for "public authenticated information" to be delivered by teams of scholars, communicators, and designers. Wittlin also berated the fact that, "At present, communicators have not yet entered the realm of museums, and a condition of imbalance exists due to the dominance of either curator or designer" (1970, 210). She referred back to Neurath's museum, stating that: "'Relationships,' in the form of comparison or of evolution, were the keynotes in the presentation of information in the Museum of Social Science (Gesellschafts- und Wirtschaftsmuseum), Vienna" (Wittlin 1970, 159).[3]

At *Museums Journal*'s second design conference in 1972, museum designer Robin Wade suggested that designer and curator should take equal responsibility for the display of the exhibit. He pointed out that neither designer nor curator was wholly qualified to communicate effectively with the visiting public and highlighted the need for a professional interpreter, possibly in the guise of an editor with a journalistic background. Wade went on to describe the special nature of museum design and how museum professionals should embrace the discipline of communication rather than adhere strictly to more traditional roles:

> The designer must overthrow the tendency to design for beautifully composed glossy magazines, and must not neglect the intellectual content of display. The curator, for his part, seems often to be obsessed with scholarship. But neither curator nor designer is necessarily the best person to interpret the collections to the public – maybe an editor with a journalistic background is required. (Wade 1972, 62)

In summary, what was needed was a role to "bridge the gap" between display and academic staff. At the same conference, Margaret Hall from the British Museum described how this position could work:

> Someone else is perhaps needed to interpret the information, to process and edit it, and present it to the public. He would be a useful addition to the design team and also most useful in an educational role; perhaps academic curators should be the source of information and should not present it directly to the public. (1972, 62)

In 1975 Sir John Wyndham Pope-Hennessy (then director of the British Museum) also referred to the problem of curators with a far too intimate knowledge of their collection being unable to take an overview: "And if he is a hidden pedant, then practically anything is liable to occur. No one should underrate how obstinate substantial scholars are" (Pope-Hennessy 1975). David Gosling, exhibition designer and latterly head of design at the NHM from 1975 to 1984, suggested that the activities of a NHM designer before 1975 amounted to no more than "sugaring the academic pill" and exhibitions were "organised along the lines of textbooks suitable for graduate students" (1980, 66). He considered that the designer's brief was rarely formulated and exhibits were often developed in an ad hoc way, with texts and specimens presented to the designer by the specialist for arrangement in cases. The following quotation from Miles sums up the balance of professional input that he considered was required to take ideas for a visitor-centered approach to museum design forward. It is essentially a description of the transformation partnerships that Miles introduced to the NHM in 1975:

> If the specialist is concerned to *communicate* his knowledge and expertise, and if the designer is concerned with *design for communication*, then they share substantial common ground. This is also the ground of the educationalist; so all three are engaged in the same pursuit. The problem now becomes getting all three together, so no one is over shadowed. (Miles 1981, 116; emphasis original)

Ideas emanating from discussions found in publications such as *Museums Journal* and conferences went toward the realization that things had to change at the NHM. The British Museum Act of 1963 had officially divided the collections of the

British Museum from those of the British Museum (Natural History). After the split, the renamed NHM became much more acutely aware that it was failing to live up to the 1753 Act that had originally brought about its existence, which stated that its purpose was to entertain and benefit the general public (Clarke and Miles 1980).

Until 1968 the heads of botany, geology, mineralogy, palaeontology, and zoology had enjoyed independent control over their own areas of the museum, which appeared to have lost any coherence as a unified body. The museum trustees recognized that the galleries and public areas of the museum were perceived as dull, overly technical, and badly in need of updating, and requested that the director, Frank Claringbull, make recommendations for their redevelopment.[4]

A number of different factors now needed to be considered alongside the display of specimens in museum design – television, universal education, and the development of mass media were changing the world and the public had more leisure time to make use of it all – but museum workers were slow to recognize the developing social importance of museums as places of entertainment and learning. Concurrently, there was a huge growth in the dissemination of scientific knowledge and more experimental approaches were emerging in the presentation of biology, which challenged the NHM to explore interconnections and relationships between exhibits, rather than simply placing them in cases with taxonomic details.

According to Wittlin, museums in the United States during the 1960s were "progressing in great strides" in the founding of new museums and increasing visitor attendance (1970, 174–175). Several main trends were emerging: an increasing interest in ecology and biology in museums of natural history, the fostering of links between museums and schools, a new emphasis on research, the shift from presenting a static to a dynamic view of the natural world, and a desire to make museum environments reflect the content of the exhibits. It is unlikely that a national museum of the calibre of the NHM would have been unaware of these international trends in their desire to bring displays up to date in a more dynamic environment.

By the early 1970s it was acknowledged that the NHM's exhibitions were failing because they were conceptually static, overly subject-focused, and inconsiderate of the needs of the lay visitor. It was also recognized by the museum and scholarly community that the intrinsic role of the museum was changing from being simply a storehouse of objects to a more questioning study of the world. The NHM needed to adapt its scholarly voice to reach out to a nonspecialist audience in an entertaining manner. The visiting public could see TV programs on natural history, so museums had to work much harder to attract audiences. E. V. Gatacre's paper "The Limits of Professional Design," read at the Museums Association Annual Conference on July 8, 1976, summed up the changing museum audience when he discussed how Pope-Hennessy, director of the British Museum, had described his public as having "responses determined by the television screen, unaccustomed to looking intently at static images" (Gatacre 1976, 96).

The development of the New Exhibition Scheme

In December 1968 Claringbull, on behalf of the museum trustees, took the radical first step to update the galleries. He started by removing control from the heads of the five science departments, and took sole responsibility for the galleries. This was the first initiative toward the formation of the New Exhibition Scheme.[5] Work began in earnest to develop the scheme, initially through an exhibition panel chaired by Claringbull, which included 12 members of the scientific staff and the education officer. In February 1972 the museum trustees approved a paper entitled "British Museum (Natural History): A Proposal for a New Approach to the Visiting Public," and a unified policy for exhibition development was formally activated. The failings of the current exhibition policy were clearly described in this 1972 proposal:

> The present exhibition fails because it is primarily concerned with the diversity of nature, and omits three-quarters of its rightful subject matter. It is piecemeal and conceptually static, neglectful of natural processes and interactions, and reflects to its loss the division of the Museum into five separate departments. (Miles 1975, E)

Claringbull set up small working parties to investigate four different themes (man, ecology, life processes and behavior, evolution, and diversity) and the decision was made to mount a pilot project. The New Exhibition Scheme was officially launched with an exhibition based on the life history of man, with the working title "Being and Becoming." To ascertain the right level to pitch the content for the pilot project, visitor surveys were staged, which identified the audience as the "interested layman" – not the academic. This was a revelation, as previously the museum had been largely unaware of whom their audience consisted. Focusing on the needs of the audience was a significant change; as Miles said, they moved from "concentrating purely on the subject matter, to realising it was more about communication than it was about biology. The key was shifting from being subject matter oriented to visitor-oriented."[6]

Miles has cited the three main factors which went into the design and final realization of the New Exhibition Scheme: Otto Neurath and Isotype, educational technology (developed by the Open University), and Karl Popper's trial-and-error approach to problem solving. Originally, the NHM learned about Isotype and the transformer from the Open University (which was established during the late 1960s to bring degree-level learning to those unable to attend traditional campus universities). In the early 1970s Claringbull contacted the Open University in relation to developing ideas on distance learning. The Open University had been using educational technology to design literature and course units to develop "active learning," a technique evolved from learning techniques used in World War II to train troops of mixed abilities.

Michael Macdonald-Ross from the Insitute of Educational Technology at the Open University played a key role in introducing transformation to both the Open

University and later the NHM. During the early 1970s Macdonald-Ross and his small team of consultants were researching methods of communication to enhance distance learning techniques for the design of new course literature. As part of his initial research, Macdonald-Ross approached Prof. Michael Twyman in the Department of Typography and Graphic Communication at the University of Reading, where Marie Neurath had recently deposited the Isotype Institute archive. Macdonald-Ross was impressed with what he saw, and took his ideas on Isotype and transformation back to the Open University. With Rob Waller, he wrote the paper "The Transformer" (Macdonald-Ross and Waller 1976), an examination of the role – which they considered had lain dormant for nearly half a century – and a call to arms for graphic designers to collaborate with other disciplines.[7]

At the NHM, educational technology was used to design the production system needed to develop and implement the New Exhibition Scheme and to structure scientific information by breaking it down into smaller, manageable sections, to avoid oversaturation of material and to encourage the active participation of the visitor. Miles stated that programmed learning (the ability to deliver self-paced infomation in small bites, which gives the audience immediate feedback) had alerted the museum of the need to establish a clearly defined purpose, aims, objectives, structure, story line, and a starting point which matched the visitor's existing knowledge, but educational technology was used as the tool to provide a more "systematic, problem-solving approach to education" (Miles and Alt 1978, 160). He considered it particularly useful when dealing with mixed ability teaching and the self-paced learning required by museums with an undefined audience (Miles and Alt 1978).

The NHM was initially interested in how the Open University was approaching the problem of distance learning. An Open University biologist, Beryl Crooks, was seconded to the museum for six months in March 1974 to facilitate the rewriting of a new outline for "Being and Becoming." Behavioral objectives were applied to each individual planned exhibit (a technique used in educational technology to identify exactly what the audience should have learned before moving on to the next exhibit). Preliminary work on the content and treatment of the first brief identified far too many overall and specific behavioral objectives for the average museum visitor to digest in one visit, which highlighted the problem of using this method as a theoretical basis for designing educational exhibits (Miles 1986, 228). Overcomplexity made the scheme unworkable, overly subject-focused, and not at all visitor-focused. Otto Neurath had been well aware of this dilemma, as he stated:

> Of course, as in everything educational, success in this field is secured by giving up something else; in order to create pictures that can easily be remembered one has to omit many details. But that only proves the maxim that he who knows best what to omit is the best teacher, and one who can omit nothing from his demonstrations should not be a teacher at all. (1973, 220)

It was clear that a more condensed overview of biology and a simplification of the content were needed to make the museum audience engage with the science. Crooks's input had not served to clarify the situation. The NHM was still struggling to identify a valid visitor-centere approach for the design of its galleries. It was at this point that Macdonald-Ross suggested to Miles that Isotype might be a worthwhile area to investigate to progress the New Exhibition Scheme.

On Macdonald-Ross's recommendation, Alan Tout, an educational technologist, began work with the museum in November 1974 and set out a new schedule for exhibit development and a new team structure. On January 1, 1975, Miles was appointed head of the newly formed Department of Public Services (DPS), created through the merging of the existing Exhibition Section with newly employed science, editorial, and design staff. Miles was responsible for the management of all the museum's biological galleries with the main task of bringing the New Exhibition Scheme to fruition.

Miles was clearly inspired by Isotype. On June 24, 1975, as a consequence of a growing interest in Neurath's museum work, he arranged for 28 members of the newly formed DPS team to visit University of Reading Library to see the exhibition *Graphic Communication through ISOTYPE*, followed by a seminar given by Prof. Michael Twyman.

New recruits to the Department of Public Services contracted ca. 1975–1980 attended an intensive two-week training session where they were introduced to the principles of Isotype through the *Transformation Reader*. This was a 28 page A4 document produced in-house at the museum, compiled by Roger Miles, assisted by Rodney Eastwood (British Museum 1979). Its aim was to provide a framework from which to create communicative exhibits. It featured a collection of writing by prominent authors on many aspects of exhibition design, learning theory, educational technology, planning, and communication including Otto and Marie Neurath, Michael Tywman, Michael Macdonald-Ross, Rob Waller, Alma S. Wittlin, and other communication experts. In the introduction Miles defines transformation as "that process by which relevant knowledge, usually of a specialist nature and known only to a minority, is made available to a wider audience by using forms capable of being comprehended by non-specialists" (British Museum 1979, 2). It forms a key piece of evidence to show the extent to which the principles of Isotype were adopted by the NHM. The *Transformation Reader* introduced Isotype through extracts from Otto Neurath's *International Picture Language* (1936) and extracts from Marie Neurath's *Instructional Science* (1974). It also contains a passage from Alma Wittlin, "Hazards of Communication by Exhibits," in which she lists factors leading to the failure of communication in exhibits: intellectual overload and deficit, sensory monotony, and sensory overstimulation (British Museum 1979, 4–9). Transformers from the 1970s and 1980s still quote "The Enchanted Loser" (Figure 18.3) as a warning to avoid designing exhibits that are so visually overpowering that the underlying educational concept is lost. The *Transformation Reader* also included a large number of extracts derived from the Open University, which suggests how closely Miles was considering their ideas on distance learning and educational technology.

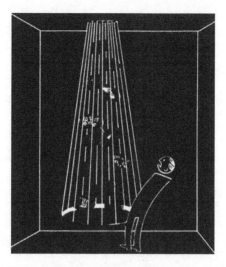

FIGURE 18.3   Alma Wittlin's "The Enchanted Loser" from the *Transformation Reader*. The original caption reads: "Enchanted by the rich design, the viewer turns into all enchanted loser – he never discovers that the pretty mobiles represent cells in the human body." Courtesy of the Trustees of the Natural History Museum, London.

The *Transformation Reader* also discussed how to achieve the style of graphic language found in Isotype. Interviews with NHM transformers from the 1970s and 1980s reinforce the fact that Neurath's original graphic language (depicted in the background of Figure 18.1a) was at least considered and followed, if the material was thought to be appropriate (although they clearly found it difficult to relate to themes of a nonstatistical nature). Richard Meakin, a designer transformer recalls that only certain types of comparative information proved suitable for the strict application of the original principles of Isotype's graphic language, but that the clarity, simplicity, and elimination of unnecessary detail inherent within the Isotype system were certainly adhered to. Examples of the graphic language found in the *Transformation Reader* provided clear guidelines for how to produce archetypical simplified, comparative diagrams with horizontal arrangements of same-sized units, and the text also discussed adaptations to the principles.

Isotype not only provided the inspiration for the New Exhibition Scheme, but also gave the NHM a set of rules to design exhibits that clearly communicated with their audience. Miles reprinted an extract from Marie Neurath's *Instructional Science* in which she stated:

> The rules … are the concern of that step in the total process of production, which we called "transformation." From the data which are given in words and figures a way has to be found to extract the essential facts and put them into picture form. It is the responsibility of the "transformer" to understand the data, to get all necessary information from the expert, to decide what is worth transmitting to the public. (M. Neurath 1974, 136)

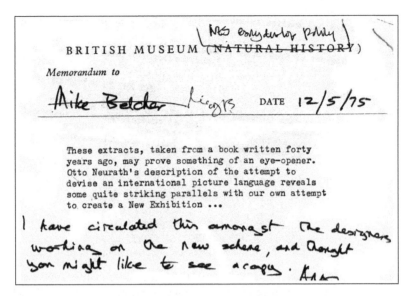

FIGURE 18.4   Memo from NHM Archives (originally attached to copies of pages from Neurath's *International Picture Language*) which evidences how Isotype was an informing factor in the formulation of the New Exhibition Scheme.
© The Trustees of the Natural History Museum, London.

Marie Neurath also emphasized the adaptability of the principles of Isotype, which is particularly relevant to museum designers struggling to come to terms with what appeared to be a very rigid set of rules, designed for a very different time and place (British Museum 1979, 10).

The influence of the principles of Isotype manifested themselves in many layers of the museum's working practices. A memo from Anne Bedser (editor) to Mike Belcher (exhibitions) of March 7, 1975, illustrates the fact that Isotype was being incorporated into the working methods of the museum (Figure 18.4). There is also documented evidence that Isotype shaped the team structure in the Department of Public Services (centering on the process of mediation between subject specialist and designer). In a 1993 paper, "Too Many Cooks Boil the Wroth – Exhibits, Teams, Evaluation," Miles presented the diagrams shown in Figures 18.5a–c.

Figure 18.5a shows the traditional curator/designer model used at the museum before the New Exhibition Scheme was introduced in 1975. The "expert," or curator, is ultimately responsible for the exhibit. Miles's definitions of the roles of the curator ("selects objects and writes labels"), the designer ("makes things look good"), and the teacher ("makes the best of things after the opening") could be thought of as rather tongue in cheek, but are very much in line with common museum practice of the time. The introduction of Neurath's 1925 team model (Figure 18.5b) seems all the more radical when compared with this traditional approach to designing museum exhibits. Miles's 1975 team model (Figure 18.5c) links the exhibit researchers and exhibit designers to parallel the role of the

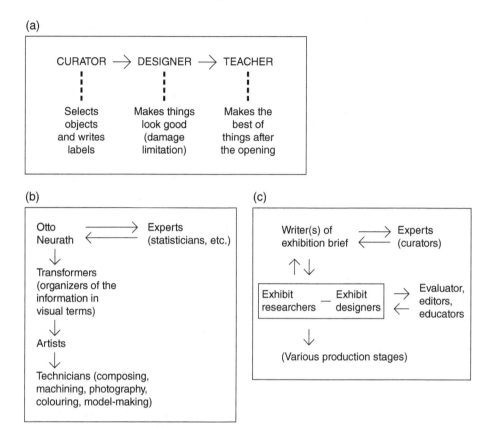

FIGURE 18.5   (a) Traditional curator/designer model used at the NHM before the New Exhibition Scheme was introduced in 1975; (b) Neurath's team model from the Gesellschafts- und Wirtschaftsmuseum, 1925–1934; (c) Miles's post-1975 NES team model. Diagrams from Miles (1993).
Reprinted by permission of Taylor & Francis.

transformers – the "who were responsible for organising the information in visual terms" (Twyman 1975, 11). He refers to the exhibit researchers and exhibit design-ers as transformers within the text of this paper, but not in the diagram. Both team models have "experts" at the top of the table and both make use of transformers – Macdonald-Ross and Waller's "skilled professional communicators" (2000, 178) – to bridge the gap between subject expert and the general public, working in a 1:1 partnership. The subject expert is not solely responsible for the exhibit. There are differences in the structure of both Miles's and Neurath's team models, mostly due to the fact that there are far more processes involved in Miles's model (evaluators, editors, and educators) but it is obvious that they both rely heavily on the meeting of academic and designer minds in the transformation process.

Miles and Tout were the key decision-makers and architects of the New Exhibition Scheme, along with Brian Lewis, professor of educational science at the

Open University, who was brought in to help with the practical implementation of the New Exhibition Scheme. Lewis argued:

> The teaching points must be fully explained. Misleading statements and irrelevant scholastic displays must be eliminated. There must be no mistakes, non-sequiters [*sic*], gaps or other defects in the argument. All written materials need in fact to be well structured and self-explanatory and pitched at the right level of difficulty. Even this may not be enough. Unfortunately, it is all too easy to be clear and accurate with respect to subjects that most visitors regard as being irrelevant and unimportant. Some effort must therefore be made to arouse in the visitor a sense of excitement and purpose. In the very act of imparting knowledge, the instructional materials must explain why the knowledge is worth having and how it fits into the broader scheme of things. (1980, 154)

Some of Lewis's ideas on educational technology concurred with the principles of Isotype and Neurath's thinking on museums, in particular, the problem of oversaturation of information ("less is more"). Lewis stated that, "If museums took their educational remit more seriously, they would exercise a self-denying ordinance on the selection of exhibits" (1980, 154). He also believed that analogy underpinned all other methods of communication, referring the visitor to a known idea to enable them to understand a more alien concept. Miles and Alt also associate transformation with analogy and problem solving:

> In developing the Exhibition Scheme we are attempting to apply the concept of transformation in wider fields than Isotype charts and diagrams, including three-dimensional design, but still with its basic meaning. We particularly associate it with the construction of analogies or conceptual bridges, whether in the form of graphics models or interactive devices. (Miles and Alt 1978, 161)

Miles and Alt cite a particular exhibit on the cerebral cortex as being a good example of the NHM's adapted use of transformation. The composition of the brain is illustrated using a crumpled sheet of newspaper – an analogy, a method used in educational technology. Using analogous concepts to succinctly tell a story is a far more economical aid to understanding than applying unwieldy amounts of behavioral objectives. Miles considered that the visitor would learn more from fewer well-designed exhibits than from filling the space with mediocre ones. This concurs with Neurath's ideas on a good teacher's ability to edit information, and leave out the rest (O. Neurath 1936, 27).

Ideas taken from Karl Popper, the Viennese philosopher of science, underpinned the theoretical trial-and-error approach to the New Exhibition Scheme, taking small steps at a time and emphasizing the importance of evaluation. Popper advocated refinement through continual evaluative testing, but in practical museum terms this was uneconomic and impracticable (Miles and Tout 1979, 210). The trial-and-error approach was not new to American museums. Miles visited several science centers and museums in North America[8] and Australia during 1976, and was impressed with what he found.

The Exploratorium in San Francisco had opened its doors in 1969, and evaluated exhibits by placing roughly finished interactive prototypes in the exhibition spaces accompanied by museum staff called "Explainers" who were able to observe the public's responses to the exhibits. Through constant evaluation, exhibits were adapted and improved. The Lawrence Hall of Science (Berkeley) used graphic-based mock-ups and more formal evaluation procedures housed in a special evaluation space; final exhibits would be built in response to the evaluation. Miles favored the Lawrence Hall of Science model – as the pilot project was an experimental exhibition and had to be completed within a set time frame.

As well as the effective use of evaluation, Miles was inspired by the North American use of interactive exhibits, the participatory attitude toward the visiting public, and the emphasis placed on contemporary physical and biological science, technology, and industry rather than on objects from the past, all of which he incorporated into the New Exhibition Scheme.[9] The former London Geological Museum (now part of the NHM) had mounted a much acclaimed permanent exhibition in 1972, *The Story of the Earth*, which had broken the mold in the United Kingdom for creating spectacular immersive scientific exhibitions. However, according to Miles, it was the Exploratorium, which based itself on the philosophy that science should be fun and accessible for people of all ages, that formed one of the three main influences behind the formulation of the New Exhibition Scheme.

Because it was unlikely that everything would be right at the first attempt at using such an experimental approach to the design of educational exhibits, and there was so little time for formative evaluation (except in the case of a few mock-ups), final exhibits were put on display and amended if necessary through summative evaluation. The museum installed closed-circuit television to allow visitors to be observed as they viewed the exhibition (Miles 1986, 234). An annual visitor survey was established to monitor the makeup of visitors and their responses to the new exhibitions, and the results were published in *Museums Journal* every four years (Alt 1980). Miles believed that this approach to evaluation was unique among British museums during the mid-1970s; it led to the museum becoming known as a pioneer in this field – although there is evidence that evaluation was used at the GWM 50 years earlier from the late 1920s to 1934 (M. Neurath and Kinross 2009, 25).

The Hall of Human Biology

On May 24, 1977, the pilot project *Human Biology: An Exhibition of Ourselves* (Figure 18.6) was opened by the secretary of state for education, Shirley Williams. The director pronounced it "Stunning, a foretaste of a revolution" (Miles 1986, 231). The exhibition was introduced as an experiment to test out museum technology – Miles's new approach to the design of educational exhibits. *Human Biology* was widely acclaimed by the public, who flocked to see it, leaving other galleries virtually empty. Visitor levels continued to rise, reaching over three million in 1977, and visitor surveys indicated that it was the most popular permanent exhibition

FIGURE 18.6   The Hall of Human Biology, ca. 1977, Natural History Museum, London. (For a color version of this figure, please see the color plate section.)
© The Trustees of the Natural History Museum, London.

that the Natural History Museum had ever produced. The museum felt that it had justifiably begun to realize its aims and objectives for the New Exhibition Scheme in the creation of an enjoyable, visitor-centered approach.

Professional acclaim centered on the fact that *Human Biology* was considered to be a new, adventurous departure from the traditional method of designing exhibitions which, as an exercise in museum design, made fascinating viewing for curators. It covered new ground in dealing with human biology on such a large scale, using biological ideas and processes rather than collections of objects. The lack of real specimens gave *Human Biology* one of its most distinguishing traits – which, as Miles pointed out, stemmed from the nature of the subject matter rather than any desire to do away with traditional museum realia. It was constructed as a new stand-alone modern interactive environment within the museum, hiding all references to the gothic interior. The content had a strong narrative basis, broken down into "mind-sized chapters" of tightly structured groups of largely interactive exhibits, forming separate but interconnected episodes. Visitor surveys indicated that the content was memorable and succeeded in both educating and enthralling visitors. The visitor was no longer a passive onlooker, but a participant in a journey based on intelligible language and analogous concepts. The structure of the learning hierarchy was based around a rational arrangement of ideas, to help the visitor explore and be motivated to find out more. Content was pitched at two levels, the majority suitable for a 15-year-old, with a secondary level accessed through raised island exhibits known as "Enrichment Assemblies" (which were subsequently scrapped as they failed to indicate that they presented more advanced knowledge, were inaccessible to disabled users, and posed a safety hazard).

But there was also widespread criticism of *Human Biology* from museum professionals, much of it centering around the huge budget spent on an experimental concept, coupled with an element of envy that Miles had been given such freedom to produce this radical new approach to exhibition design. This was perhaps also tinged with the fear that curators might be forced to produce exhibitions in this new style, restructure their own galleries, and lose their power bases. Miles's ideas were also viewed by some as paying homage to fashionable 1970s liberalism, which offended conservatives. The "Letters to the Editor" pages of *Museums Journal* from 1977 to 1979 outline much of the praise (some of it veiled) along with the outright criticism leveled at *Human Biology*. Museum critic Tony Duggan identified technical imperfections and ambiguous concepts in *Human Biology* and felt that its staging in such an important architectural setting was money badly spent. But, although he had reservations, he did view *Human Biology* as the physical realization of what museologists had been talking about for the previous 10 years:

> From the professional point of view, the Hall is mandatory viewing for all curators. The role of the educationalist in museums has been one of the great debating points over the last ten years. This Hall, with so many unusual exhibits presented with the philosophy, which differs radically from that of traditional curatorship, reveals something of what the educationalists have been trying to tell us (and sell us) for a long time. (Duggan 1978, 5–6)

Alison Whyman of the Hunterian Museum praised Miles for his visitor-centered approach, stating that *Human Biology*

> represented the first time that a museum in Britain had designed an exhibition in a scientific manner, attempting to define the essential characteristics of its audience and aiming to fulfill a specific purpose, i.e. the communication of various biological ideas. (1979, 36–37)

In general, Miles was praised for his application of current research in psychology and education, the designer–scientist transformer partnerships, visitor participation, and museum technology, which he had developed through a combination of theoretical, inspirational, and practical influences. Some museum commentators, initially critical of *Human Biology*, had a change of heart after seeing the exhibition for themselves:

> I have followed the growth of the new exhibition policy at the British Museum (Natural history) with much interest, knowing it would have implications for our

own programme of exhibit renewal. Initially, on reading the policy for the new exhibition scheme I was instinctively opposed to the whole policy, since the display was too concept, and not specimen based. After spending over one whole day in the Hall of Human Biology, however, and observing the way in which the public is fascinated by this new approach, I suffered conversion, and came away convinced that the new methodology of the scheme was of profound importance for all museums wishing to educate as well as entertain. (Rolfe 1978, 194)

But opinion was heavily divided and some extremely harsh criticism emerged. *Human Biology* was likened to a "cheap disco" and a "hideous portent of modernization yet to come" (Miles 1986), and seen as lacking actual exhibits in a traditionally exhibit-rich institution. Miles's response to this was that *Human Biology* was an experimental exhibition. Further exhibitions in the New Exhibition Scheme (e.g., *Introducing Ecology*) did make extensive use of the collections within the museum.

Philip Doughty (general secretary of the Geological Curators Group) famously described the exhibition as "a kind of lewd offal-shop nightmare [that] escaped curatorial control and fell into the hands of pure, tasteless communicators" (1978, 56). Richard Fifield (1977), museum critic for *New Scientist*, considered *Human Biology* to be "tainted" and to hamper visitor comprehension by its inconsistent terminology, likening the new display conduits to a fairground "tunnel of love." *Human Biology* and *Introducing Ecology* (which swiftly followed) were also criticized by science historian Frank Greenaway, who was concerned about a national museum giving "elementary instruction" – dumbing down content. He stated:

We should all give some degree of assent to this until faced with a museum gallery which resembles a modern popular science text, all graphics and VDUs with museum objects incorporated, not as items in a traditional collection but just as illustrations to the product of a "script-writer." (Greenaway 1983, 8)

But some of the most scathing comments came from curator and museum critic Patrick Boylan in 1979. He criticized the display policy, the fact that Miles had not made early working papers more accessible, the philosophical approach, the misuse of public funding, and the misguided attitude to academic research. Boylan objected to the fact that the NHM, as one of the foremost international institutes for research was allowing its scientists to be taken away from their academic activities to partner designers in constructing exhibitions outside their traditional areas of expertise. He did not consider Miles's visitor-centered approach to be new, or the claim that the museum was one of the first to be designed in a scientific manner, or that the look was in any way original. He considered *Human Biology* to be self-consciously "modern tasteful" in style – "pure Middle Class 'Habitat'" – and that Miles was overly concerned with educational psychology and learning theories, remarking that the museum was reinforcing "fashionable, mildly liberal, educational and social theory and practice" (Boylan 1979).

Boylan articulated the position of the museum scientists aptly in this 1979 critique of the New Exhibition Scheme, stating that previously the museum's public galleries had been "regarded as a closely integrated adjunct of the curatorial and research programme of the Museum … funded out of the annual Research Council's parliamentary vote" (Boylan 1979). Miles, in defense, makes the point that the new way of constructing exhibitions was based on scientists fitting into the framework of exhibition design, no longer taking overall responsibility for it (1987, 183). The once powerful position of the scientist-curator had been severely downgraded from team leader to equal team member. Trained scientists were not all happy to relinquish their research activities for a more general educational role within a content development team even if it was a fixed secondment. This reinforced Miles's case for the introduction of open-minded "skilled professional communicators."

Boylan was critical of scientists being taken away from core research to take part in communicating science to the public – the transformation partnerships, and the

FIGURE 18.7   "Survival of the Fittest in SW7," *Sunday Times Weekly Review*, May 24, 1981. Photo: Duncan Baxter; drawings: Michael Heath. Reproduced by permission of the Sunday Times/ Newssyndication.com. This cartoon illustrates a NHM centenary report by Bryan Silcock which highlights the "seething disputes" occurring in a "museum whose real business is science." It shows the different parties involved in the argument: (*left to right*) traditional curators, NES exhibit designers, a veiled attack on Miles (a fossil fish expert), an attack on schemes which did not respect Waterhouse's architectural interior, and finally a poke at anti-Darwinian theories.

diminishing of power of the scientist in the museum environment. He expressed the fears of many museum curators at that time – that they too would be forced to adopt similar expensive and radical approaches in their own institutions.

In July 1978 Miles gave a lecture about *Human Biology* at the Museums Association's Annual Conference in Edinburgh and "very strong views" were expressed in response to his visitor-centered approach (Densley 1978). Miles was criticized for being wasteful of massive budgets in a time of stringent financial constraints. Delegates considered the experimentation healthy, but agreed that a smaller pilot exhibition would have sufficed to introduce this new style of working. Miles's answer to the criticism was that *Human Biology* could only be regarded as an experiment to show the way forward. It was not perfect. The project continued to cause controversy well into the 1980s, as can be seen in the 1981 cartoon from the *Sunday Times Weekly Review* (Figure 18.7).

The influence and legacy of Isotype at the Natural History Museum

The majority of the designers in Miles's designer–scientist transformer partnerships came from three-dimensional design backgrounds (although Richard Meakin was originally a medical illustrator and designer of statistical diagrams). Dierdre Janson-Smith (recruited in 1979 as part of the second wave of transformer partnerships) answered an advertisement for a "content developer with a science background." The title "transformer" did not appear within job advertisements of the time, but appeared frequently within documents found in the museum archives. Janson-Smith recollects that Miles had considered bringing in existing museum curators who were more interested in communication than research, but was forced to look outside the museum for the right staff, with "no museum agenda and open, malleable minds."[10]

From the evidence of the *Transformation Reader* and interviews with transformers, it is apparent that the transformation partnerships were broadly encouraged to use some of the principles of Isotype as a starting point: primarily the hierarchical ordering of information and use of comparison. Neurath's charts attempted to present unbiased factual information so that the audience could then draw their own conclusions. Exhibits found in early phases of the New Exhibition Scheme also tried to set out unbiased factual information, but their primary function was to educate and entertain. Miles's extended use of comparison included analogy and metaphor, techniques borrowed from educational technology, instead of adhering to the Isotype principle that objects should be clearly expressed in immediate terms. The "Cortex" exhibit (cited as an effective example of this kind of analogous exhibit) is still present in *Human Biology* after over 30 years. Museum audiences in the 1970s were visually sophisticated through media exposure to the metaphor (a staple technique used in advertising), so Miles had to try much harder to capture and retain his media-conversant audience and to compete with television and the other national museums on his doorstep.

Miles's style of presenting graphic material is very different from Neurath's; and, while there is tacit evidence of the use of Isotype graphic language present in a few exhibits, in general NHM transformers considered this approach rigid and unsuitable for anything but statistical information.

As one ex-NHM scientist transformer stated:

I found it very exciting, to be asked to think hard how to "transform" information into something that a non-scientist could understand. The approach was, I can now see, extremely didactic – what we were taught was grounded firmly in learning theory, and the aim was very much to get across what you needed to get across ... With a lot of feedback from our in-house educational technology/visitor survey team, we were taught that we needed to develop exhibits that attracted and held visitors for long enough for them to absorb what we wanted them to learn. Transformation was about hooking and holding them, starting where they were. Our concept of engaging with the visitor was a lot less sophisticated – we were in a way being taught long-distance learning techniques ... We were introduced to "the enchanted loser" – one of the images in the book [*Transformation Reader*] that I remember very well – the basic message being that less is more, that crowded displays with loads of objects and labels actively hindered communication. I am sure this must be a key influence of Isotype.[11]

Conclusion

One of the most significant principles that Miles borrowed from Isotype was to view the subject matter from an audience's perspective, rather than from the subject expert's perspective. Fidelity to material and viewer was respected above all, as it was with the GWM team – it could also be said that both museums, in theory, share the NHM's founding 1753 mandate of being "for the general use and benefit of the public." The New Exhibition Scheme, like the GWM, was designed to be socially inclusive, and both museums were noncommercial and had an educational basis. They also shared the primary purpose of disseminating social knowledge in an enjoyable and convivial setting. The New Exhibition Scheme was designed as a set of visual arguments clearly set out in words, moving and static imagery, and interactive exhibits, building in complexity as the viewer moved through the gallery. Empirical experiences formed through participating in interactive tasks, considering questions posed and facts presented, led the audience to a more informed position. Visitor testing revealed that *Human Biology* audiences retained far more facts than audiences of other more traditional object-based exhibitions at the museum (Alt 1980, 10–19). It is not difficult to see why the museum became known as a pioneer of evaluation during the 1970s and 1980s.

Diedre Janson-Smith considers that, through the process of transformation, the designer was able to take an equal part in the communication process rather than being an accessory to it, and that the most important legacy of Isotype was to give the designer a critical role in the design of educational exhibits. As a scientist transformer, she had to first explain the scientific content to her designer partner so they could understand it, and find a way to coherently explain it to the audience. Alan Ward, a designer transformer, considered that Isotype brought an "information-based" approach to the design of educational exhibits, addressing the interpretation of subject matter, and turning it into a form that was accessible to the museum visitor. He also stated that the introduction of the transformer partnerships brought designers and scientists into a close working relationship, and required them to view the information from a layperson's perspective rather than from the perspective of the expert (or taxonomist).[12] The adoption of transformation helped take ultimate control away from the curator, through the equal status of the designer–scientist partnerships. Knowledge became visitor-oriented and not subject-oriented. The museum lost its "window dressers" and gained professional communicators.

In his article in *Museums Journal* on the design of New Exhibition Scheme Phase 6, *Man's Place in Evolution*, David Gosling (1980) illustrated the practical effect of the principles of Isotype on the NHM. He thought that the integration of biologists and designers (the transformer partnerships) into a full-time exhibition development team was the first step in rectifying gaps in visitors' knowledge. The combination of the two disciplines of design and science engendered a mutual respect between the partners, and they in turn provided a change in emphasis from the needs of the teacher to those of the learner.

Isotype scholar Robin Kinross (1981) described transformation as a "fruitful influence" on designers and all those concerned with graphic presentation of information. He considered that the NHM had a real understanding of the historic principles behind Isotype and was able to produce a new body of work, applying the principles of Isotype in new surroundings, under very different circumstances.

Miles gave many papers and spoke widely on museum technology from the mid-1970s to the late 1990s. *The Design of Educational Exhibits* (1982), written in collaboration with Alt, Gosling, Lewis, and Tout, was one of the first publications to discuss the design and implementation of a system for the delivery of didactic exhibitions in a national museum context. It offered practical guidelines on how to design educational exhibits based on the pragmatic ideas developed during the formulation of the early phases of the New Exhibition Scheme. Since then many books have been written on aspects of museology, and formative and summative evaluation has become an integral part of the development of new exhibitions. Evaluation forms one of the key legacies of the visitor-centered approach developed at the museum, which Miles considers shifted to the nearby Science Museum in the mid-1990s.[13]

Miles remained as head of the Department of Public Services from 1975 to 1991, during which time 10 permanent exhibitions (or phases) were produced. The New Exhibition Scheme became the "Exhibition Scheme" and the visual appearance of the exhibitions became more traditional, as artifacts and specimens were integrated into the original experimental specimen-light concepts. The designer–scientist transformation partnerships continued to form the backbone of the Department of Public Services, and Miles's notion of museum technology became more firmly established within the NHM and was widely discussed in papers, conferences, and journals.

However, by the late 1980s the once enthusiastic transformer partnerships appeared to have run out of steam. Fueled by media controversy, stringent budgetary constraints, and internal power struggles, they were no longer producing the innovative exhibitions characterized by the early phases of the New Exhibition Scheme. The scientists and designers who worked on exhibitions for any length of time gradually lost their inspiration and enthusiasm against a background of declining resources and less creative freedom. The Department of Public Services needed revitalization, but in a Civil Service work environment it was difficult economically to inject fresh talent. Since the inception of the New Exhibition Scheme, the museum scientists had been wary of their loss of power and, although initially some were enthusiastic, many never fully appreciated being taken away from their research. Experience also showed that only a few scientists were actually suitable for the role of scientist transformer and the museum's pool of talent was too small to sustain such a mode of operation. So the museum moved toward employing new scientists. This move was made with the blessing of the five keepers, who in any case did not like losing their best scientists for up to two years at a time. Miles was forced to admit that the relative security found in a government post was not conducive to sustaining creativity over long periods of time (Miles 1996; 2007).

In 1989 the new Conservative government under Margaret Thatcher brought in museum admission charges. The NHM had to concentrate on marketing itself to find sponsorship from major corporations rather than relying on public funding. Funds were diverted away from exhibitions and staff restructuring took place, with a raft of redundancies, including the majority of the transformation partnerships that had previously formed the backbone to the New Exhibition Scheme. Internal disputes and political battles forced the Department of Public Services to disband in 1991.

Transformation has been shown to be a significant factor in new ways of designing educational exhibits at the NHM; but its effects are more far-reaching, and ideas that were thought of as radical during the 1970s (as they were in the 1920s) now appear logical and commonplace to today's museum designers. For transformation to take place effectively, an understanding between the partners was essential, which was sometimes haphazard owing to the personalities involved. Not all transformer partnerships enjoyed fruitful relationships, and the resulting transformation was not always as erudite as it could have been.

Macdonald-Ross stated that all systems of communication, from Isotype to operational research and educational technology stem from basic communication strategies, which he defines as "the human organisation of learning which has been in existence for centuries."[14] Both Neurath and Miles assembled their own versions of this notion. In much the same way that Neurath had taken elements from philosophy, sociology, pedagogy, "education by the eye," and a whole host of other disciplines to construct Isotype, Miles took aspects of Isotype and combined them with educational technology, operational research, evaluative studies, philosophy, education, and cybernetics to construct museum technology.

It could be said that through the application of museum technology – Miles's experimental new museum philosophy based around sound pedagogical issues and a visitor-centered approach – the NHM succeeded in reinterpreting its original mandate as a social institution to educate the public. It could also be said that transformation formed a key role in making this happen. Transformation also helped to raise the profile of designers within museums from "window dressers" in the 1960s, to transformers of complex information during the 1970s and 1980s, and has given the inquiring designer a far more important role in the development and design of educational exhibits.

The legacy of transformation in a contemporary museum context lies in the methodology used by museum professionals, but today it is more likely to be known as "interpretation" and to involve teams of academics, scriptwriters, editors, audience advocates (a nondesign role which ensures that exhibitions remain visitor-centered), designers (used in a more traditional role), technicians, and support staff. Interpretation is most effective when editors are able to visually conceptualize academic information and vividly relay ideas to designers who can, in turn, enhance and refine the graphic outcome.

Ex-transformers (designers and scientists) now function as independent design consultants and interpreters working with large museums and visitor attractions in the United Kingdom and further afield. They admit to taking the visitor-centered, Isotype-inspired approach they gained from the New Exhibition Scheme with them. The NHM currently employs staff engaged in the planning and formulation of exhibitions, but currently no NHM employee bears the job title "transformer" and designers employed by the museum currently take on a more traditional graphic design role.

The legacy of transformation in the NHM (and originally derived from Neurath's Isotype at the GWM) is far-reaching. Ideas that appeared radical to the museum community during the 1970s now appear commonplace; it is unthinkable today that an exhibit would be designed without the close collaboration of designer and subject expert, as Miles reinforced in a recent interview. Museum transformers also clearly illustrate how important transformation was to museum professionals. Transformation as a method was disseminated when the Department of Public Services closed and ex-NHM transformers populated the wider museum community, taking their New Exhibition Scheme experience forward into new museological environments. The museum has outsourced all major exhibitions since 1991, many to organizations employing ex-NHM transformers:

> The work at the Natural History Museum was the basis of all I have done since, really, and I have long been grateful for it. However, while it may have been the truth it wasn't the whole truth, neither was it new. And, given that the idea spawned a whole industry, I'm constantly amazed by how often one sees "The Rules" ignored, or as I suspect, not known.[15]

Acknowledgment

I would like to extend very special thanks to Dr. Roger Miles for his profound scholarly advice on this essay and his patience and enthusiasm.

Notes

1   Otto Neurath describes in detail how the GWM was configured (1973, 214–233).
2   An expression used by Macdonald-Ross and Waller (1976).
3   Wittlin also cited Neurath's 1936 book *International Picture Language* in the footnotes (1970, 278). Her essay "Hazards of Communication by Exhibits" featured in the *Transformation Reader*, the Natural History Museum in-house training manual for transformers (British Museum 1979).
4   Dr. Roger S. Miles, interview with author, September 1, 2008.
5   Dr. Roger S. Miles, interview with author, September 1, 2008.
6   Dr. Roger S. Miles, interview with author, September 1, 2008.
7   They revised this paper in 2000 (Macdonald-Ross and Waller 2000). It shows how Neurath's ideas have been updated and why they were still appropriate many years on.
8   On the North American stage of this study trip Miles was first introduced to the evaluative work of Harris Shettel and his strategies for determining exhibit effectiveness.
9   See "Preliminary Report on a Visit to 18 Museums in North America and Australia, January and February 1976," generalized observations by Roger Miles, February 25, 1976, NES PP 1976. Miles visited museums in Washington, New York, Cleveland, Chicago, Milwaukee, San Francisco and Oakland, Toronto, and Perth (*Annual Report 1976–77* (1976), DF 935/28, Natural History Museum Archive).
10 Dierdre Janson-Smith, email message to author, 2008.
11 Dierdre Janson-Smith, email message to author, 2008.
12 Alan Ward, email message to author, 2008.
13 Dr. Roger S. Miles, interview with author September 1, 2008.
14 Michael Macdonald-Ross, interview with author June 25, 2008.
15 Susan Jones, scientist transformer, email message to author, 2008.

References

Alt, Mick B. 1980. "Four Years of Visitor Surveys at the British Museum (Natural History) 1976–79." *Museums Journal* 80(1): 10–19.

Belcher, Michael G., convener. 1970. "The Role of the Designer in the Museum." *Museums Journal* 70(2): 63–66.

Belcher, Michael, G. comp. 1972. "Second Design Conference." *Museums Journal* 7(2): 58–62.

Boylan, Patrick J. 1979. "The New Exhibition Policy and Programme at the British Museum (Natural History): A Contribution to a Debate St Andrews, September 1979." Natural History Museum Archive, NES Correspondence and History 1968–1984.

British Museum (Natural History) Department of Public Services. 1979. *Transformation Reader*, 2nd ed. In-house publication.

Clarke, Giles, and Roger Miles. 1980. "The Natural History Museum and the Public." *Biologist* 27(2): 81–85.

Densley, Michael. 1978. "Specialist Session: Report of the Group of Designers / Interpreters in Museums." *Museums Journal* 78(3): 131.

Doughty, Philip S. 1978. "Britain Before Man – A Review." *Museums Journal* 78(2): 54–56.

Duggan, Tony. 1978. "The Shapes of Things to Come? Reflections on a Visit to the Hall of Human Biology, South Kensington." *Museums Journal* 78(1): 5–6.

Fifield, Richard. 1977. "Heritage Displaymanship." *New Scientist*, February 3, 293.

Gatacre, E. V. 1976. "The Limits of Professional Design." *Museums Journal* 76(3): 93–99.

Gosling, David. 1980. "Man's Place in Evolution: A New Exhibition at the British Museum (Natural History)." *Museums Journal* 80(2): 66–69.

Greenaway, Frank. 1983. "National Museums." *Museums Journal* 83(2): 7–12.

Gruber, Helmut. 1991. *Red Vienna Experiment in Working-Class Culture 1919–1934*. New York: Oxford University Press.

Hall, Margaret. 1972. "Second Design Conference." *Museums Journal* 72(2): 62.

Kinross, Robin. 1979. "Otto Neurath's Contribution to Visual Communication 1925–1945: The History, Graphic Language and Theory of Isotype." Master's thesis, University of Reading.

Kinross, Robin. 1981. "On the Influence of Isotype." *Information Design Journal* 2(2): 122–130.

Kraeutler, Hadwig. 2003. "Otto Neurath – Museum and Exhibition Work: Spaces (Designed) for Communication." Doctoral thesis, University of Leicester.

Kraeutler, Hadwig. 2008. *Otto Neurath: Museum and Exhibition Work Spaces (Designed) for Communication*. Frankfurt: Peter Lang.

Lewis, Brian N. 1980. "The Museum as an Educational Facility." *Museums Journal* 80(3): 151–155.

Macdonald-Ross, Michael, and Rob H. Waller. 1976. "The Transformer." *Penrose Annual* 69: 141–152.

Macdonald-Ross, Michael, and Rob H. Waller. 2000. "The Transformer Revisited." *Information Design Journal* 9(2–3): 177–193.

Miles, Roger. 1975. "British Museum (Natural History): A Policy Guide for the New Exhibition Scheme." Internal document, February 25, NHM Archive DPS 42.

Miles, Roger S. 1981. "Information as an Experience: Exploitation of a Museum's Resources." *Library Association*: 112–118.

Miles, Roger S., with Michael B. Alt, David C. Gosling, Brian N. Lewis, and Alan F. Tout. 1982. *The Design of Educational Exhibits*. London: Allen & Unwin.

Miles, Roger S. 1986. "Lessons in Human Biology: Testing a Theory of Exhibition Design." *International Journal of Museum Management and Curatorship* 5: 227–240.

Miles, Roger S. 1987. "Museums and Public Culture: A Context for Communicating Science." *Chicago Academy of Sciences* 157–169.

Miles, Roger S. 1993. "Too Many Cooks Boil the Wroth – Exhibits, Teams, Evaluation." *Visitor Studies* 5: 58–70.

Miles, Roger S. 1996. "Otto Neurath and the Modern Public Museum: The Case of the Natural History Museum (London)." *Museums Journal* 79(1): 23–26.

Miles, Roger S. 2007. "A Natural History Museum in Transition: Reflections on Visitor Studies in Practice." *Visitor Studies* 10(2): 129–135.

Miles, Roger S. 2008. "Origins of the New Exhibition Scheme and its Pilot Exhibition ('Human Biology')." Unpublished paper.

Miles, Roger S., and Michael B. Alt. 1978. "British Museum (Natural History): A New Approach to the Visiting Public." *Museums Journal* 78(4): 158–162.

Miles, Roger S., and Alan F. Tout. 1979. "Outline of a Technology for Effective Science Exhibits." *Special Papers in Palaeontology* 22: 209–224.

Modley, Rudolf, and Dyno Lowenstein. 1952. *Pictographs and Graphs: How to Make and Use Them*. New York: Harper.

Neurath, Marie. 1974. "Isotype." *Instructional Science* 3: 127–150.

Neurath, Marie, and Robin Kinross. 2009 *The Transformer: Principles of Making Isotype Charts*. London: Hyphen.

Neurath, Otto. 1933. "Museums of the Future." *Survey Graphic* 22: 458–463.

Neurath, Otto. 1936. *International Picture Language: The First Rules of ISOTYPE*. London: Kegan Paul.

Neurath, Otto. 1973. *Empiricism and Sociology*. Edited by Marie Neurath and Robert S. Cohen. Dordrecht: Reidel.

Pope-Hennessy, John. 1975. "Design in Museums." *Journal of the Royal Society of Arts* 123: 717–727.

Rolfe, Ian W. D. 1978. "Letters to the Editor." *Museums Journal* 78(4): 194.

Twyman, Michael. 1975. "The Significance of Isotype." *Graphic Communication through ISOTYPE* (University of Reading) 6–17. Reprinted in *Icographic* 10 (1976): 2–12.

Vossoughian, Nader. 2008. *Otto Neurath: The Language of the Global Polis*. Rotterdam: Nai.

Wade, Robin. 1972. "Second Design Conference." *Museums Journal* 72(2): 62.

Whyman, Alison. 1979. "Letters to the Editor." *Museums Journal* 79(1): 36–37.

Wittlin, Alma S. 1970. *Museums in Search of a Usable Future*. Cambridge, MA: MIT Press.

Further Reading

Henning, Michelle. 2006. *Museums, Media and Cultural Theory*. Maidenhead, UK: Open University Press.

Perks, Sue. 2013. "The Legacy of the Principles of Isotype." Doctoral thesis, University of Reading.

Sue Perks is an information designer and educator. Her doctoral research was on the legacy of the principles of Isotype. She has been a partner in Perks Willis Design since 1989 and her expertise is in the design of educational exhibits within museums and the organization and management of information. Recent projects include the graphic interpretation of Tudor House Museum in Southampton, permanent and temporary exhibitions in the Natural History Museum, corporate rebranding and publication design for the British Academy, and design commissions for the BBC, Carluccio's, English Heritage, the Royal Air Force, British Airways, Boots, London Borough of Merton, and the British Red Cross. She is currently also subject leader for MA Graphic Design at the University for the Creative Arts, Epsom.

19 EMBODIMENT AND PLACE EXPERIENCE IN HERITAGE TECHNOLOGY DESIGN

Luigina Ciolfi

Interactive technology has been an important part of cultural heritage practices for decades and for a variety of purposes: from visitor attraction, engagement, and education, to support for guides, curators, and other heritage professionals. From early examples of interactive information displays and portable guides available at museums, to more recent installations involving technological platforms such as augmented reality and social media, interactive technology design in heritage contexts has been the subject of extensive practice and research, within both human-centered computing and heritage and museum studies (Hindmarsh et al. 2005; Kalay, Kwan, and Affleck 2008; Hornecker 2010; Ciolfi 2013).

The fields of human-centered computing and of cultural heritage have independently evolved through the years, developing ways of thinking and hands-on practices within their own remits. However, there are interesting parallels to be made between the two fields concerning ideas of visitors' active experience and agency in heritage. For example, within heritage studies, conceptualizations of the very nature of heritage have evolved to consider intangible, digital, and personal heritage as worthy of preservation and exhibition; moreover, the relationship that visitors can have with heritage has shifted from a rather didactic to a more active and dialogic one. This is connected also to a rethinking of the role of professionals and of how heritage can be communicated, exhibited, and often reconfigured through social practices. The role of visitors has evolved from mere recipients of packaged content to active participants in heritage (e.g., from simply choosing content that they prefer, to being encouraged to express their reactions, to even contributing to exhibits in

The International Handbooks of Museum Studies: Museum Media, First Edition.
Edited by Michelle Henning.
© 2015 John Wiley & Sons Ltd. Published 2020 by John Wiley & Sons Ltd.

some situations), and the role of heritage professionals has seen a shift from authoritative figures to mediators and facilitators of a more active visitor experience.

> The process of introducing community groups to museums is not about high levels of educational achievement. Rather it is concerned with negotiating, confidence-building and provoking opportunities. ... A fundamental change is taking place in the relationship between the public and museums; a change towards a collaboration of joint interest, joint views, feelings and sensitivities. (Dodd 1994, 132–133)

Simon (2010) observes how participation has increasingly become a concern of museums, and how even low-technology strategies for engagement can be successful in making visitors active contributors to heritage sites. As well as new practices and expectations surrounding heritage visitors and professionals, there has also been an increasing attention to how to mediate issues of materiality and tangibility in heritage displays, which are often far removed from visitor experience owing to conservation issues, and how the human sensory, emotional, and aesthetic experience of objects can be supported and enhanced in museums to establish richer relationships with heritage holdings (Dudley 2009).

Human-centered computing has explored similar issues: technology is seen more and more as a tool mediating human agency within an environment. Subsequently, the conceptualization of humans has changed from that of merely reactive "users" to active agents in the process of interaction. It is no surprise that the process of interaction in itself has also evolved to move beyond point-and-click modalities to include a consideration for the body and the senses, the physical environment, and the social world.

A second similarity between these two fields is the increasing attention toward material, bodily, and felt aspects of human experience and how technology can mediate them and/or support them. Important work in human-centered computing has proposed an embodied and situated view of interaction (Suchman 1987; Dourish 2001; Hornecker 2012). The embodied nature of human experiences is something that technology design must take into account, overcoming the overly cognitivistic views of earlier human–computer interaction scholarship. The experience of technology is a physical and embodied one, no matter what form interaction takes. Moreover, people are situated in a rich physical environment, where structural accommodation to activities, environmental characteristics, and the presence of others shape practices and sense-making. Phenomenological theories of embodiment and experience have been influential in shaping new frameworks and concepts to guide technology design (Dourish 2001; Robertson 2002; McCarthy and Wright 2004) and in revisiting methodological approaches to study human experience in the world (Cahour and Salembier 2012; Giaccardi 2012).

As part of this trend, an attention to *place* has also emerged: looking at interaction as something that features humans in the physical environment, we must also focus on the physical world, and not just as a background structure but rather as it is lived and experienced – something that is constantly reconfigured and remade by experience (Harrison and Dourish 1996; Ciolfi and Bannon 2005; Dourish 2006).

Adopting an experiential perspective to the study of the physical world is useful, for it takes the perspective of actors, rather than that of structure (Tuan 1977). Where space normally refers to geometrical extension and location, *place* describes our experience of being in the world and investing a physical location or setting with meaning, memories, and feelings. Space and place must be understood with respect to the human body, as "the human being, by his mere presence, imposes a schema on space" (Tuan 1977, 36). Space is organized by people so that it conforms with and caters to their biological needs and social relationships thus becoming lived place. Places are entities that "incarnate the experience and aspirations of people" (Tuan 1971, 281). The presence of technology, either on our person or in the environments we occupy, is a component of place experience – in other words, of our lived experience of the world. Therefore, place becomes a key concept for designing engaging interactions with technology and it can guide a process of technology study, ideation, and development (Fitzpatrick 2003; Ciolfi and Bannon 2007; Rossitto and Severinson Eklundh 2007).

As well as refining its conceptual framework, human-centered computing has researched novel forms of interaction, such as tangible and embedded interaction modalities that see humans and interactive systems connected by interfaces involving bodily movements and sensory capabilities well beyond "traditional" graphical user interfaces. Interactive environments have also been explored, whereby elements of the physical world have been endowed with digital interactive capabilities with the idea of providing opportunities for interaction "beyond the desktop" (Weiser 1991).

Combining a more holistic and rich view of people and of practices with the consideration of body and place is key for developing innovative technologies and interactions in heritage contexts. It is essential to have such a rich view of human interaction and experience if we are to meaningfully support activities in the evolving context of heritage.

Specifically, a focus on embodied and emplaced interaction is essential for the design of engaging heritage technologies, which require a sensitivity to the physical environment, to the role of visitors, and to the important active and dialogical relationship between heritage artifacts and sites and human beings. Moreover, interactive technologies should support the novel possibilities for agency identified in the heritage domain: the focus on a more "active" human user of technology, considered as part of the complex physical and embodied experience of the world, is something that links to an evolving view of heritage experience by visitors and stakeholders.

In the following section, I will discuss some relevant examples of heritage technology research informed by a concern for embodiment and place. This overview will outline some of the existing contributions and recurrent challenges within human-centered computing in the context of museums and heritage sites.

Designing for embodied and emplaced heritage experiences

Designing technology to support embodied and emplaced experiences of heritage presents unique challenges. The physical environment is designed in a particular way for exhibition purposes, and the artifacts are displayed in specific sequences to support an underlying narrative and curatorial intent. Often, these curated aspects cannot be modified, and technology needs to be introduced in these settings with sensitivity and respect.

In some cases, the physical place of the exhibition has been "augmented" via a virtual space overlaid onto the physical one where interactions can occur, as in the Charles Rennie Mackintosh exhibition at the Lighthouse, Scotland's national center for design and architecture in Glasgow (Galani and Chalmers 2002; Brown et al. 2005). In other cases, digital technology has been brought to environments where interesting heritage activities take place, to facilitate people's engagement and access. One example is the "experimental zones" described by Stuedahl and Smørdal (2012) in their study of the interactive installations at the Norwegian Maritime Museum in Oslo.

Yet another approach has been to create additional exhibition rooms with embedded interactivity that provide an extension to the museum space. In the SHAPE project (Fraser et al. 2003; Bannon et al. 2005), different kinds of heritage sites were thus augmented through technology. In the "Re-tracing the Past" exhibition created by the SHAPE project for the Hunt Museum in Ireland, replica museum objects were also used as tangible props to support people's activities in the interactive space (Ferris et al. 2004). Finding ways in which heritage objects can be involved in tangible interaction is an important issue, as experimenting with novel interaction modalities can clash with conservation and preservation issues in museums and other heritage contexts.

Other examples of work leave the physical structure of an exhibition space untouched, but a stand-alone tangible interaction component introduced within it adds an element of bodily involvement and engagement. This approach has been followed, for example, at Vancouver Aquarium with the introduction of multi-touch interactive tables (Hinrichs and Carpendale 2011), and at the Museum of Natural History in Berlin through the "Jurascopes" – viewing stations where visitors can see augmented reality content overlaid onto a physical exhibition (Hornecker 2010).

Beyond museums, the relationship between heritage and the multitude of media platforms that can facilitate contextualization and place-making has been discussed by Giaccardi and Palen (2008) as an essentially social process, where designing to facilitate a person's sense of place ownership and of social synergies with others is key to ensuring that feelings, values, and experiences are invested in the interaction with heritage and with technology.

These examples reinforce my argument that technology design should be concerned with the compound of human embodied activities and the lived physical environment, particularly in museums and heritage sites where the physical display is at the core of the visitor experience. Only by understanding how visitor interactions occur, and in turn shape the physical context of an exhibition or display, can we design to augment these activities and to encourage greater access, engagement, and participation. Moreover, technology design can be a way of maintaining rootedness to a place and embodying specific characterizations of interactions that occur there by coupling digital content with artifacts related to a place, or by making the heritage value of a place more visible and accessible: for example, at Museon, the museum for science and culture in The Hague, a digital wayfinder designed for the exhibition on the Inuit of Greenland took the form of a magnifying glass, thus representing the spirit of investigation and discovery that the museum encourages.[1]

In the following sections I will present two recent examples of my own work intended to provide a rich embodied and situated experience at two outdoor heritage sites. Although outdoor heritage has not been much studied in human-centered computing, it has the potential to inspire innovative design interventions supporting embodied interactions. Sense of place is a very important component of the visit to outdoor heritage sites, as the environment is an essential part of the exhibition and often in itself a heritage artifact. I will give an introductory description of outdoor cultural heritage and discuss two projects conducted at two different outdoor heritage sites – an open air living history museum and an historic cemetery – detailing how the sites were studied in order to gain an understanding of their physical qualities and of the visitor experience, and outlining how design ideas were developed and realized.

Outdoor heritage sites: Offering possibilities for novel interactions

Research has been conducted within human-centered computing that examines the challenges of designing interactions for living history museums and other outdoor historic sites: two examples are the mobile social photography app developed for the Valle Crucis Abbey open air museum in Wales (Baber et al. 2008), and the installation at the Viena Carelia historic village in Finland, where the projection of digital content on the walls of one of the historic houses is triggered by the light of a candle (Ilmonen 2007). Another type of technology widely developed for open air heritage sites and now commonly used is location-sensitive mobile guides, which can detect the location of the visitor and deliver appropriate content. Technology such as this has been deployed and studied by human-centered computing researchers at the Culloden Battlefield Park in Scotland (Pfeifer, Savage, and Robinson 2009) and at the Rock Art open air exhibition in Northumberland, England (Mazel et al. 2012). Through these studies of actual technological intervention, a finer understanding of mobile activities – not just as guided tours but also as deeper and more active explorations of a site – has been gleaned (Ilmonen 2007).

Augmented reality and mixed reality have also been explored as suitable technologies to support visitor experience at outdoor sites owing to their ability to unobtrusively overlay digital content on the actual environment. A pioneering project examining the potential of this technology was the "Augurscope": a mobile telescope-like device that visitors to Nottingham Castle could use to view a reconstruction of the original medieval castle superimposed on the current landscape and buildings (Schnädelbach, Galani, and Flintham 2009; Schnädelbach et al. 2002). Augmentation technology offers an added layer, providing visitors with the opportunity to see a reconstruction of the past environment, showing things that are no longer there, or populating it with additional content such as textual descriptions, and visual additions.[2]

In public and urban computing, mobile outdoor experiences, including city trails and games on various themes, also provide useful insights (see, e.g., the mobile shared visitor experiences at London Zoo described by O'Hara et al. 2007). Geotagging – the adding of geographical information to media, for example, the location where a photo was taken, has also been used to allow for rich annotation of large public spaces by participants, thus augmenting actual locations with added layers of content (Lane 2003). Geotagging is nowadays encouraged by many museums: visitors are often invited to take photos of exhibits or of particular artifacts, or to leave a geotagged comment on them via platforms such as Facebook, Twitter, or bespoke museum smartphone apps.

Aspects of collaboration and sharing that have been identified as key to positive museum visiting experiences (Falk and Dierking 2012) are also important to keep in mind for outdoor heritage, as the interpersonal interactions that characterize the visit to outdoor heritage sites are shaped by the qualities and features of the environment and of the particular exhibits.

Outdoor heritage sites are settings where an approach to design that focuses on place and embodiment could benefit visitors and other stakeholders for a number of reasons: the multisensory nature of the visit, the importance of the physical environment, and the centrality of place as part of the visitor experience (e.g., appreciating "being there") are qualities that can be addressed by a mindful approach to design. Interactive technology for outdoor heritage has the potential to support truly innovative forms and narratives of interaction, providing inspiration and insights for design at other heritage institutions. For these reasons, outdoor heritage is a setting that I have focused on in recent collaborative research, and explored from the point of view of the interactions and experiences people have there, as well as the added value technological interventions could provide.

Outdoor heritage sites differ greatly in terms of the nature of what is on display, management and curatorial approach, and what is offered to visitors: from living history museums that house reconstructions of buildings, to archaeological sites, to historic landmarks and landscapes in different stages of preservation that are open to visitors. In this chapter, I focus on research conducted at two types of outdoor heritage sites: an open air living history museum – Bunratty Folk Park in Ireland – and a historical cemetery – Sheffield General Cemetery in England.

These two collaborative projects aimed at understanding and designing outdoor heritage sites with particular focus on experiences of place, embodiment, and materiality – concerns that have not been addressed in great depth by other work to date. In both projects, the potential of technological interventions focused on emplaced and embodied interaction was explored, based on a thorough understanding of the space, the visitors, and the activities taking place in each context.

Living history museums are challenging environments to augment through interactive technology: they present complex heritage displays that usually include entire buildings, historical artifacts, and often live performances, all within an outdoor site that is often also part of the display, whether or not it is landscaped/designed to be so. At living history museums, a key curatorial goal is to provide visitors with reconstructions of everyday life in times past, not only by showcasing material for viewing but also by engaging visitors through the recreation of costumes and crafts.

Living history museums are organized in ways that are to some extent similar to "traditional" object-centered museums but in other ways profoundly different. A major similarity is that an explicit curatorial approach underpins what is on display: which buildings are selected for the museum, how they are restored and fitted, what objects are displayed within them, and what kind of human activities are enacted, usually by professional animators and actors. Another similarity is that living history museums are constituted by a sequence of exhibits: there is a narrative to the physical exploration of the site that can be organized, for example, around the temporal progression of the buildings (e.g., from older to newer), or by the choice of different themes to cluster them such as urban life, rural life, geographical location. At the same time, living history museums have a unique character: they are more informal than most museums, allowing behaviors and activities such as consuming food and discussing loudly, for example. They are also physically different by virtue of being outdoor sites where the exhibits can be walked into: this offers a more multisensory and immersive experience which is not often possible in enclosed museums, and which includes smell and taste as important ways of exploring what is on display, for example, where demonstrations of traditional cooking are held. Because of their physical and organizational nature, living history museums usually lack traditional forms of information support such as poster boards, labels, and so on: the character of the site seldom can be maintained with the presence of such artifacts and, although living history museums certainly grant visitors the possibility to get close to the display, they often do not provide a lot of information about them. Geographical distribution is also a crucial feature, and so are environmental conditions, such as the weather, in affecting how the visit will take place and how long it will last.

Some similar characteristics apply to open access historical sites that present some degree of interpretation, such as the historical cemetery I will describe further on in this chapter. With historical sites, there is less scope for designing an exhibition as such, as the site cannot be altered in its structure, and its remaining true to its original layout and atmosphere strongly characterizes the visitor experience. The goal is to immerse visitors in the historical atmosphere of the site, helping them interpret what they see and reflect on the experience of being there. Curatorial interventions usually relate to proposing visiting paths (e.g., the sequence in which a site is to be explored), and providing information and/or guidance in a sensitive and nonintrusive way. As with living history museums, geographical distribution and environmental conditions are key features that significantly shape the visitor experience. Both types of sites allow for "immersive" visits, where being physically enveloped by a stimulating and atmospheric environment is memorable and engaging for visitors.

In the following sections I will present two projects in outdoor heritage sites that I have been involved in. The first space (Bunratty Folk Park) is a curated outdoor museum, the second (Sheffield General Cemetery) is a historical site with minimal interpretation. The former is a designated exhibition site, managed by the government agency that owns it; the latter is a historic space that has become a heritage destination after its original purpose ended and a volunteer community group was created to facilitate visitor access. In describing the two projects, I will outline some challenges faced in designing for embodiment and place experience at open air heritage sites.

"Reminisce" at Bunratty Folk Park

Bunratty Folk Park is an open air museum located in County Clare, Ireland, and one of the country's most successful tourist attractions. Opened to the public in the early 1960s, it displays 32 historic dwellings within a 26 acre parkland site. Most of the dwellings were moved to Bunratty from their original location and reconstructed on site (Figure 19.1). These include, among others, craftsmen cottages, a village street, a schoolhouse, working mills, and a church. The landscape is also an important component of what is on display, featuring, for example, walled gardens, farmyards, and animal enclosures. The goal of Bunratty Folk Park is to provide visitors with insights into life in Ireland in from the 1890s to the 1950s, particularly rural lifestyles and traditional activities. Each building is also fitted with original furniture and decorations so as to recreate the atmosphere of this period.

A team of professional animators is active on site to impersonate characters such as the *Bean an Tí* (Irish for "woman of the house"; plural *Mná Tí*), the schoolteacher, and the constable. The animators socialize with visitors, showcase and describe places and activities, and also help with the maintenance of the site (for

FIGURE 19.1   Cottage on display at Bunratty Folk Park, Co. Clare, Ireland.
Photo: Luigina Ciolfi.

example, by minding the open fires in some of the buildings and baking goods for the park's tearooms). During the high season (from May to September) the team of animators grows to a total of eight members, whereas only three or four are on site during the rest of the year. Their number is relatively small considering the size of the folk park and the number of buildings that visitors can access. This means that visitors encounter them at only few of the buildings and that the animators are extremely busy during opening hours.

Our project was funded by the Irish tourism agency Fáilte Ireland with the goal of assessing the potential of interactive technology to enhance visitor attractions. We first conducted a series of field activities in order to gain a thorough understanding of the site, its inhabitants, and their activities. These were followed by a set of creative workshops aimed at developing design scenarios, and finally by the development of a prototype which was tested on site.

We conducted several sessions of naturalistic observations at Bunratty Folk Park to gather information on how the park is structured and organized, and to understand what paths visitors follow, which buildings engage them the most, and how they discuss what they see. Therefore, in our observations we took note of the different groups of people (age, nationality) visiting, recorded which trajectories around the park were followed, which sites were visited, and where prolonged discussions and conversations took place. We were particularly concerned with documenting the visitors' relationships to the place and how they experienced it in terms of physical accommodation, cultural understandings, social interaction, and personal and emotional connections.

The methods used to collect qualitative data during the visits included notetaking, video observations, and "shadowing" – following selected visitors as they moved through the space and documenting their actions via field notes (Czarniawska 2007). We also conducted informal interviews with animators, clarifying their role and goals in communicating and presenting the exhibits to visitors, and their perception of what engages and motivates visitors to explore more of the site.

People enjoy the atmosphere above all, and many return to Bunratty for further visits – a good indicator of the appreciation of the site. Its open and informal nature encourages social interaction between visitors, particularly when facilitated by staff such as the Mná Tí. Discussions among visitors regarding the buildings and objects on display are commonplace, showing the engaging nature of the place. The site presents a number of other important features: its size means that visitors spend a considerable amount of time there (sometimes an entire day). Indeed spatial distribution is an issue that emerged strongly from the data: a full journey around the park is long and may be exhausting, especially for elderly people or children. So a lot of visitors' attention is taken up with managing other family members, making sure they keep up and are not left behind. The further reaches of the park are also less frequented.

The observations also revealed that the information available to visitors through the simple map they receive on arrival is quite disconnected from the actual landmarks they see. It is also not easy for them to understand what particular sites represent, and sometimes visitors misunderstand the purpose and nature of certain buildings. This is because of the difficulties of placing more detailed information on site without interfering with its atmosphere and rural setting. There is a tension between providing visitors with enough information for them to appreciate the place in terms of its full cultural and historical significance and engaging them through an atmosphere of "authenticity."

Visitors to the folk park represent a wide demographic in terms of age and nationality. This is important, for it impacts on how the place is recognized and interpreted by various people. For example, older visitors may be able to recognize the different artifacts and places, buildings and situations, that are presented in the park: their personal memories of visiting houses such as those on display at the park, or of using farm tools, brought the exhibition to life for them in a way that cannot be replicated for younger visitors (particularly non-Irish ones).

For all visitors, the experience is enlivened by interacting with the animators: from engaging them in conversations, to seeing them occupying the spaces and creating interesting displays, such as the *Bean An Tí* slicing freshly baked bread, and the school teacher engaging visitors in singing a song in the Irish language. The work of the characters is crucial in bringing the environments and artifacts to life for the visitors, and in facilitating a richer embodied interaction with the site.

The overall immersiveness of the folk park is talked about by the visitors in their conversations on site and by the animators discussing their role in the context of the museum. The very concept of Bunratty Folk Park is to recreate scenes from Irish history through the reconstruction of buildings and sites, therefore, the developers of the park have gone to great lengths (in most cases relocating entire buildings and refurbishing them with authentic artifacts) to recreate each scene to be faithful to the original historical context. The role of human animation at certain sites is to further convey the character of the building and of its original setting. This sense of authenticity and full immersion is an essential part of how visitors experience their visit to the museum, and it is strongly related to issues of embodiment and place as it concerns both physical immersion and multisensory engagement.

Developing design scenarios

Our field studies suggest that designing technological interventions at Bunratty Folk Park will have to be mindful of several critical issues relating to embodied and emplaced visitor experience. The issue here is not simply the provision of information in the form of interactive guides or information points, but the sensitive creation of a manifold set of digital artifacts that seamlessly integrate with the physical environment and with the ongoing activities of people as they peruse the objects and move through the buildings.

To discuss these issues, a series of design workshops were held, and people who had visited the folk park at least once in the past were recruited by the project team to participate. The discussions referred to many aspects of the visit to Bunratty: the general look and feel of the place, but also the availability of information and the general layout of the site. A strong theme that emerged was that of developing narrative around broad activities, rather than simply providing snippets of content describing individual objects or buildings, for example, baking, tools for grinding flour, the kitchen, and cooking.

The participants suggested that technology could provide some further information about how artifacts and buildings were used and how they fitted into their surroundings, and also highlight connections between them. They discussed how older visitors found it easier to appreciate the site because of their own personal recollections and experiences of rural life. It is sometimes difficult to convey to the majority of visitors the personal importance that certain artifacts or buildings can carry.

Finally, a major issue discussed was the heterogeneity of the park's attractions and the large variety of buildings and artifacts available, and how technology should support visitors' explorations of the entire site but also of individual components: design should allow for fragments of content and/or interaction to work independently as well as together. The project team embarked on a number of scenario-building activities. The main concepts that were generated were:

- *personal narratives*: the importance of delivering information that is not just descriptive of a building or artifact, but informative of its context of use by people;
- *paths and trails*: allowing visitors to explore a meaningful set of places/objects, which would be connected to a theme, rather than simply collecting snippets of disconnected content;
- *augmentation*: presenting visitors with additional information that is not simply what they can see in front of them. It is crucial, at the same time, to allow visitors to fully appreciate what is physically present, and to discuss it in a social and collaborative manner.

Several scenarios were storyboarded, and one was chosen by the project team as it addressed some of the most important themes that had emerged from both the work in the field and the discussion with participants.

The "Reminisce" prototype

The team designed and developed a prototype interactive installation for Bunratty Folk Park called "Reminisce" (Ciolfi and McLoughlin 2011; 2012). Our final design concept played heavily on the physical, tangible qualities of the experience at Bunratty Folk Park: smelling the turf fires and the freshly made butter, tasting the freshly baked bread, touching the buildings, and petting the animals are activities that people enjoy, talk about, and seek actively during their visit and that we wanted to build on and support through our design. To achieve this, we included in the sequence of interaction physical objects related to some of the farmhouses at Bunratty Folk Park as essential components of the interactive experience of "Reminisce."

The theme of "Reminisce" was that of memories and recollections inspired by the buildings in the folk park, and the goal was to bring a layer of personal content that would add to the site in terms of lived experience and personalization. Fictional characters were created for visitors to follow around the site and from whom they would hear reminiscences about their past lives at particular houses in the form of sound snippets. This theme is a common one in designing visitor trails for museums.

Memories were marked by QR codes placed at different locations around the folk park; visitors could access them by scanning the codes with a mobile phone.[3] The choice of QR codes, printed on small (20 × 10 cm) simple placards was decided on with the agreement of the folk park management group as an acceptable solution to provide some visual cue to the visitors that additional content was available at a particular location, being much smaller and simpler than an information panel. The codes would trigger an audio recording of a chosen character's memory at that site, to be played on the handset. Participants were also able to record their own thoughts in real time at these locations, adding a layer of personal information to that collected during the trail.

A similar project has been deployed at the Frilandsmuseet, an open air museum near Copenhagen in Denmark, where a visitor trail operating through QR codes and a mobile app also utilized fictional characters as a way to engage visitors with additional digital content. Another example of utilizing fictional characters as a way to personalize digital content is *Ghosts in the Garden* at the Sydney Gardens in Bath, where visitors "hunt" for particular locations where auditory narratives from historical characters can be played on a portable device.[4] "Reminisce," however, presented some novel characteristics: the use of tangible "tokens" for controlling parts of the installation, and the capability of the system to take visitors' contributions in real time in the form of audio recordings (Ciolfi and McLoughlin 2011).

The tangible tokens took the form of small packs of keepsakes, each containing a physical souvenir that participants could take home with them and that was associated with each site: for example, the turf could be found in the Shannon Farmhouse where turf fires were always burning, and different recipes at houses where baking demonstrations would normally take place. The keepsakes included traditional recipes, pieces of turf, small hanks of wool, and so on. The tangible tokens provided clues about where the participants could find other memories in the trail, but also provided the key to access yet another interactive component of "Reminisce," the interactive desk in the folk park's schoolhouse, the last site of the trail: the clues were printed on cards with RFID (radio-frequency identification) tags embedded in them.[5] When they reached the schoolhouse, the last site on the "Reminisce" trail, participants could use the tangible tokens as input devices (Figure 19.2).

In the schoolhouse, the interactive desk allowed people to listen to recordings that other visitors had left at the sites in the trail. Placed on the desk were books with embedded RFID tags, each of them relating to one of the characters from whom visitors could collect memories. A book holder and a basket with embedded RFID readers were also placed on the desk. When one of the books was placed on the holder and one of the tangible tokens placed inside the basket, the recordings left by other visitors were played back (Figure 19.2). These recordings were of the site where the tangible token was collected.

Through these tokens, participants gathered mementoes of their visit, simple keepsakes that were, however, connected with the complex experience of the site, reminding them of what they had encountered in the folk park, both digital and physical. The tokens were also mementoes of "Reminisce" itself and provided the experience with an element of tangible simplicity and straightforwardness that technology can sometime lack. They also guided participants to other memories available to them: having clues in the form of a physical object was a way of not letting the technology take over the entire story line of "Reminisce"

FIGURE 19.2   The Interactive Desk, with a tangible token visible inside the basket, Bunratty Folk Park. (For a color version of this figure, please see the color plate section.)
Photo: Don Moloney – Press 22.

and grab the visitors' whole attention. The participants had to use a mobile phone for the collection and recording of memories; therefore, we wanted to avoid too strong a focus on a digital artifact and we introduced a low-tech way of finding clues and connecting the houses to each other, encouraging visitors to consider their surroundings – and not only the technology – when progressing in their exploration.

Finally, the tangible tokens allowed participants to access the memories that other people left at the site: they contained a hidden high-tech element, the RFID tags, that was the key to interacting with the installation in the schoolhouse. The interactive desk looked very low-tech, in keeping with the surroundings: on top of the desk were a wooden book holder, the two books, a wicker basket, and a small blackboard with the words "Place Your Souvenir in the Basket" written in chalk. No screens, keyboards, or other computer technology were visible in the installation (Figure 19.2). The desk, however, provided a way to access the "cloud" of digital content created in real time by the participants.

The evaluation data collected during "Reminisce" shows that participants in the installation appreciated the presence of the tangible tokens both as ways to navigate through the folk park and to connect with the content available at each site, and as simple, lightweight keepsakes that were interesting and evocative in themselves (Ciolfi and McLoughlin 2012). "Reminisce" played on the atmosphere of the park and on the characteristics of the houses, providing added value without taking away from the existing tangible qualities that visitors enjoy so much in their time at Bunratty. The tokens embodied themes of the visit (farming, cooking, turf-cutting, etc.) and linked strongly to the features of the place. The presence of tangible elements enriched the interaction with the installation as well as fitting into the atmosphere of Bunratty Folk Park.

Exploring tangibles at Sheffield General Cemetery

The Sheffield General Cemetery is a historic parkland cemetery located in the city of Sheffield in England. Opened in 1836 and closed for burials in 1978, it is now a free and open access historical, architectural, and natural conservation area owned by Sheffield City Council but managed by a community group, the Sheffield General Cemetery Trust.[6] The trust offers regular guided tours on several themes, from history to wildlife, as well as providing assistance to people interested in locating a particular grave or memorial. The trust volunteers also engage in conservation and maintenance activities aimed at keeping the cemetery accessible and safe for visitors.

Eighty-seven thousand people were buried in the cemetery and, although part of the site was cleared of gravestones during the 1980s for safety reasons, it still features a large number of memorials and gravestones, as well as two chapels and a row of semi-interred catacombs (Figure 19.3). Moreover, the site (originally a quarry) was landscaped to include trees and plants of symbolic value (such as "weeping" trees and shrubs associated with mourning), and to provide visitors to the cemetery with a peaceful and reflective experience. For example, the cemetery's gatehouse was built over the river Porter to represent the idea of "crossing the river" to the afterlife, common in many ancient myths related to death and rebirth. Therefore, the historical landscape of the cemetery is also particularly important.

The cemetery was purpose-built and not consecrated to a particular religious confession, thus it is the final resting place of a wide variety of people of different social extraction and of various political and religious beliefs. Many well-known and historically important citizens in Sheffield's history are buried or commemorated there as well as ordinary people, including people from the lower social classes, thus representing interesting insights into the social reality of nineteenth-century England.

The cemetery has also gained the status of "area of natural history interest" and "local nature reserve" as it hosts a variety of significant plants, trees, and fungi as well as several species of birds and insects. The natural history aspect of the cemetery is showcased through themed tours that the volunteers offer and host: there are regular birdwatching tours throughout the year as well as special events on plants, fungi, and bats.

FIGURE 19.3   A view of the Sheffield General Cemetery, UK: gravestones and memorials and the Nonconformist chapel.
Photo: Luigina Ciolfi.

The cemetery is open access and free of charge around the clock; it has no artificial street lighting and some of the less frequented paths can be treacherous in hours of darkness. The guided tours are also free, although participants are encouraged to make a small donation to the Sheffield General Cemetery Trust. The tour guides offer their services on a voluntary basis and also base the tours on their own knowledge and interests around the cemetery. The area where the cemetery is located was, at the time of construction, in the rural outskirts of Sheffield. However, the city has expanded significantly and the cemetery is now a large green space between busy roads, residential areas, and commercial streets. It is used as a local amenity, with many nearby residents and workers using it for dog walking, jogging, and generally as an urban park.

Our study of the site has been conducted as part of the European Union Project "meSch – material encounters with digital cultural heritage" (Petrelli et al. 2013), which seeks to explore ways in which digital technology can bridge the divide between material aspects of cultural heritage holdings and digital information about them. The project has therefore a strong focus on how the tangible and embodied qualities of appreciating heritage should be supported and not disrupted by the use of interactive technologies for visitor access.

Field studies and workshop

In an initial phase of fieldwork, we conducted observations of the site in order to understand its structure and layout, and to gain insights on the visitors that access the site. We also observed a historical guided tour, taking note of the strategies that the guide employed to show the participants around the site, the themes that characterized the narration, and the reactions of and commentary by the participants. The observations were documented through field notes, photography, and video recordings. In a second phase of empirical work, we conducted semistructured interviews with Sheffield General Cemetery Trust volunteers on site, following the ideas of walking ethnography and walk-throughs (Lee and Ingold 2006; Ciolfi 2007). At the end of the walk-through, participants were shown sketches of design concepts that our team had proposed following the first phase of fieldwork, with the idea to generate some design concepts that could inspire the cemetery volunteers to join in codesign activities and propose novel interaction concepts of their own.

The fieldwork showed that there are many different motivations for visiting Sheffield General Cemetery, and that the historical and architectural importance of the site is only one of them. The many regular visitors go to the cemetery for its peacefulness, to exercise in beautiful surroundings, for relaxation and for informal exploration of the space while walking their dog, or to break up the working day with a walk. As the site is open access, there are also many passers-by who use the main path crossing the cemetery as a shortcut between two busy roads. One-off visitors are usually more interested in the historical aspects of the site, and visit the cemetery for this purpose. Many visitors to the Sheffield General Cemetery are historic cemeteries enthusiasts; others come to visit the grave of a relation or a person of interest.

These individual experiences are quite different from guided tours. Individual visitors do not seem to follow a particular pattern of movement, and dedicate varying amounts of time to different parts of the landscape (which is also linked to the scant presence of information around the cemetery), while guided tours follow a more defined path which highlights locations of particular historical or architectural significance.

For all visitors, the physical experience of the cemetery is structured along the main pathways crossing the site, since only a few paths are accessible owing to the risks of treading on unstable ground in some places: some areas are fenced off, and others made very difficult to enter, for example by keeping them overgrown. Plants and trees are an important feature of the visit, as are birds and their calls, which provide a constant auditory backdrop to any visit. Seasonal changes are a very important aspect in shaping the visitor experience of the cemetery. The landscape changes significantly throughout the year, and seasonal changes also affect the perception and identification of monuments and structures: for example, thick vegetation in the summer makes it more difficult for people to see gravestones and other monuments at a distance. Furthermore, the lack of artificial lights in the cemetery means that visiting hours are more limited during the winter months. There is also a distinctly different atmosphere between the part of the cemetery that was cleared of gravestones and the one that retains all the original structures; moreover, people entering the cemetery from the former might not know that the site is indeed a cemetery, and that there are historic monuments a short distance away.

The interviews with volunteers showed a wide variety of different interests motivating their commitment to the cemetery: all commented on the community value stemming from being a member of the team and on the pride they feel in caring for an important heritage site. They enjoy spending time in the cemetery not only because they are surrounded by fascinating history, but also because of the peacefulness and beauty of the area, and because of the satisfaction they draw from their involvement: personal well-being and health, the value of community work, and the contemplative atmosphere were themes that emerged in many of the interviews.

When asked to point out their favorite locations around the cemetery, many volunteers included important historical landmarks and aspects of the landscape in their selection, but they also treasured those areas of the cemetery where they and the local community conducted conservation work, which included making a gravestone more accessible or visible by clearing shrubbery and consolidating paths, planting a new tree, and replacing a dead hedge. Their efforts have become part of the heritage value associated with the site: something to be preserved and noted. Other favorite locations are certain secluded paths that give some of the volunteers a sense of peace and reflection.

The analysis of data collected during both phases of fieldwork inspired a set of design themes:

- *making things visible*: making the presence of things more visible to visitors, whether structures that are no longer present (e.g., the cleared-out section of the cemetery), or things that are hidden for whatever reason (e.g., by vegetation, structures built underground);
- *enhanced interpretation*: helping visitors "read" the landscape in richer ways by providing them with additional tools for interpretation (from information provision, to wayfinding, etc.) on a variety of themes;
- *peace, reflection, and nature*: sensitively building on the felt atmosphere and on the immersive physical nature of the place, providing means for deeper reflection, relaxation, and so on.

The themes were taken by the project team as inspiration for the creation of a first set of design concepts. They were also used as discussion points during a creative workshop featuring a small group of Sheffield General Cemetery volunteers. This was organized and attended by four trust volunteers and four researchers from our team. The goals were to engage the volunteers in the design, encouraging them to express opinions on our design ideas, and to suggest their own. The design themes outlined above were heavily discussed, with the volunteers making suggestions on how, for example, novel types of interactive signage could support "enhanced interpretation," and what types of information could help in "making things visible." Other design constraints were discussed at length, for example, how to design technology that would work as effectively in different environmental conditions; how to overcome power issues, bad weather, wear and tear, and possible antisocial behavior.

Prototypes

An initial set of concepts and prototypes has been developed to address the three design themes. From an interactional point of view, the design ideas revolved around three degrees of engagement: grabbing attention, inviting closer exploration, and in-depth engagement. The first type of design intervention is meant to grab the attention of the visitor, without demanding too much full interaction and simply hinting that there is more to be discovered. An example of this type of intervention is the "Bird Box": a stand-alone, solar-powered box that projects an animation of birds in flight to attract the visitor's attention toward certain paths in the cemetery (Figure 19.4). The initial prototype was realized by using the components of a rotating lamp, with the light shining through a revolving carton cut out with bird outlines. The follow-up prototype uses a miniature projector connected to a circuit board, although this version of the prototype cannot yet be powered wirelessly. The animation can be regularly updated to reflect the seasons and the birds currently present at the cemetery.

The second type invites closer exploration, providing relatively simple occasions for interaction. An example of this is the "Binoculars," a rugged set of binoculars (which can either be handheld or fixed on the ground) that provides an orientation-based augmented reality visual overlay to particular areas of the cemetery to aid interpretation (Figure 19.5).

The third type is focused on those visitors who wish to engage more deeply with the site and are willing to explore more information and to undertake more prolonged interaction during their visit. The example of this is "The Companion Novel," an interactive book that visitors carry with them during the visit. By selecting a particular page of the book through a specially designed bookmark, the visitor selects a different narrative theme around the cemetery, and appropriate auditory information on that theme is provided to them by wireless speakers located at specific hotspots (Figure 19.6) (Ciolfi et al. 2013). By virtue of the distributed audio, the locations themselves invite the visitors to approach them, thus adding a new sensory layer to the site and avoiding the problem of social isolation that has been found with certain audio guides (Simon 2010).

The three prototypes are a first attempt at addressing the design themes relevant to the cemetery, with a concern for embodied and emplaced interaction: the form for all of them is intended to support intuitive handling and to fit in with the

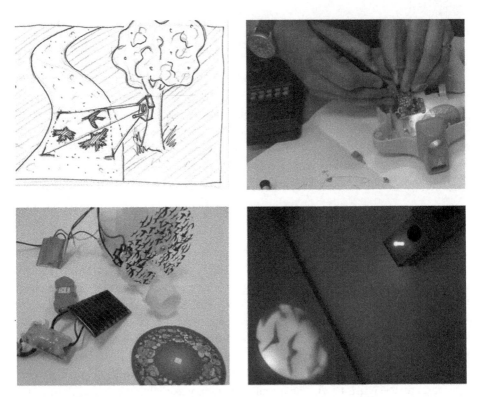

FIGURE 19.4   The Bird Box prototype from sketch to realization.
Photos: Nick Dulake, Daniela Petrelli.

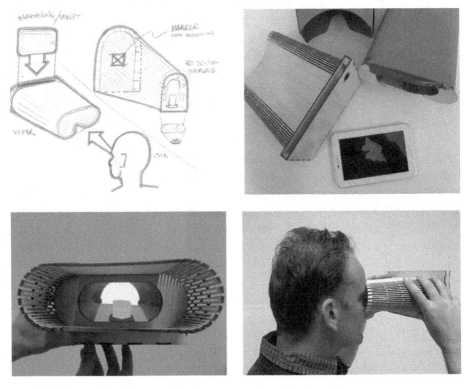

FIGURE 19.5   The Binoculars prototype from sketch to realization.
Photos: Nick Dulake, Daniela Petrelli.

FIGURE 19.6   The Companion Novel prototype from sketch to realization.
Photos: Nick Dulake, Daniela Petrelli.

environment in an unobtrusive way. The interaction that the three prototypes support is also inspired by the lived qualities of the place, from wildlife to social and landscape history. While certain technical components of the prototypes can be compared to other existing pioneering projects (such as the environmental projections and mobile augmented reality used in the "Future Cemetery" installation at Arnos Vale Cemetery in Bristol, UK), the way in which the prototypes address the design themes is unique to the narrative of Sheffield General Cemetery. However, the three types of interactive engagement addressed (i.e., attracting attention, inviting closer exploration, and engaging deeply) can be transferred overall to other sites where different levels of visitor engagement may need to be targeted.

Discussion and Conclusions

The projects described in this chapter are examples of the challenges posed by two outdoor heritage sites that present different characteristics, both of which offer rich embodied experiences for their visitors. From understanding the space and their inhabitants to exploring design possibilities and finally realizing prototype installations, it is necessary to be mindful of a complex set of issues surrounding the places, the people, and the material and tangible qualities that characterize them and that characterize visitors' practices.

Place as compound of personal, social, cultural, and physical experiential qualities, and embodiment as a fundamental quality of human practices from movement to sensory immersion, are essential frames for approaching the design of technology for this type of heritage site. Therefore technology at the two sites was strongly focused on embodied and emplaced aspects of visitor interaction on site. The physical environment is relevant not only in terms of what is on display, but in terms of the overall surroundings, an overall visitor experience which is immersive and sensorially rich.

Cultural heritage professionals and practitioners worldwide have pioneered projects with the goal of engaging visitors in ways that are emplaced, tangible, and embodied. Some examples have been mentioned earlier, most of which are situated in open air sites. Another installation addressing issues of embodiment at an open air site is the "Sculpture Garden Experience" designed for the gardens of Rufford Abbey (England), whereby the content of a more traditional audio guide has been adapted to include invitations to visitors to perform certain physical actions around each sculpture: from viewing them from unusual viewpoints to touching them and approaching them performing particular gestures (Fosh et al. 2013). The idea of the guide was to focus the visitor experience not only on finding out information about the sculptures, but also on their embodied experience of the exhibition.

But open air sites are not the only heritage setting where interactive installations have addressed issues of embodiment and place. Indoor galleries have been, and are being, designed to accommodate technology in ways that make the physical space assume new meanings and relevance. In other words, the environment does not simply house interactive digital technology, but is designed to convey that tangibility and embodiment are part of the "exhibition rules" for visitors – an approach pioneered by the SHAPE research project mentioned earlier.

From the two practical cases, and from other examples of heritage technology I have mentioned in the chapter, we can gain a set of valuable insights which can also be useful for other types of museums and heritage sites. A first consideration is that a concern for place and embodiment should be kept in mind from the initial phases of the design process, for example, when conducting preparatory studies of a site; therefore, grounding methodology on a site as much as possible and choosing techniques that enable the capture of practices in a situated view are key in shaping the subsequent steps toward design.

A second important insight is that studies of visitors on site should not focus only on the tasks and actions that they perform, but also pay attention to less structured activities and practices: not everybody has a specific goal when visiting a museum or heritage site, and not everybody wants to engage deeply with it from the point of view of structured content presentation. For some visitors, a positive experience is about taking in their surroundings in their own time, without being loaded with complex information. At both Bunratty Folk Park and Sheffield General Cemetery the interaction can be lighter or deeper, and this entire spectrum should be supported. In "Reminisce" visitors could access the content for as few or as many buildings as they wished; they could choose whether or not to contribute with a comment, or to ignore the digital information completely and focus on the tangible tokens. At the cemetery, each prototype works independently and visitors can decide to engage in more or less demanding interactions.

Embodiment is also about emotion and sensory immersion, and too much digital information when it is not wanted can disrupt this. A memorable experience of a place can be linked to interactions that are very simple and not content-related: for example, at Bunratty, smelling the fresh turf contained in one of the tangible tokens; at the Cemetery, listening to the sound of birds and rustling trees while wandering about. Overloading visitors with digital content and diverting their attention from the artifacts on display is a risk in all museums. At outdoor sites this can disrupt a key part of the visitor experience – the appreciation of the material qualities of a space and the experience of being fully immersed in a fascinating physical environment – even more. Another strategy might be to use interactive technology simply as a way to "nudge" visitor attention to the physical space, such as is described in the concept of the Bird Box at Sheffield General Cemetery.

Furthermore, if and when full-on interaction with technology is wanted, it is important to incorporate embodied elements, whether in the physical form factor of the technology – for example, the tangible artifacts at the cemetery – or in the nature of the interactions – such as with the tangible tokens in "Reminisce," which needed simply to be put inside a basket in the schoolhouse in order to trigger the archive of comments left by visitors. This is important so that the visitors would not perceive a gap between the physical, material experience of the exhibition and the digital interaction available: providing elements as a bridge between an exhibit and the multimedia content sustains the visitor's embodied and emplaced engagement.

Overall, linking to the place's structural, cultural, social, and emotional qualities is key: the design of technology should be mindful of, provide anchors for, and be connected to place. The materials and form factors in which technology is embedded can help in this respect: they can provide contrasts or similarities to the material aspects of a place, and inspire different reactions from visitors by creating an "ecology" of analogue and digital artifacts to populate the physical environment. A consideration for place and embodiment in technology design directly addresses current trends in heritage practices on fostering new forms of material engagement for visitors. Lessons learned by human-centered design research can be instrumental in this respect.

Acknowledgments

"Reminisce" at Bunratty Folk Park was funded by Fáilte Ireland and by the University of Limerick Seed Funding initiative. The work at Sheffield General Cemetery is funded by the EU FP7 Project meSch (Grant Agreement 600851). Thanks to Marc McLoughlin and to Daniela Petrelli and the other members of the meSch team for their key contributions to the projects described in this chapter, and to the staff and volunteers at Bunratty Folk Park and at Sheffield General Cemetery.

Notes

1   "Seal Hunting in the Museum, Testing a Mesch Prototype," http://mesch-project.eu/seal-hunting-in-the-museum-testing-a-mesch-prototype/ (accessed August 25, 2014).
2   See Chapter 21 by Bell and Ippolito in this volume for more on augmented reality in an art context.
3   Quick Response (QR) codes are unique visual codes, similar to bar codes, that can be machine-read (for example, by using a webcam or a smartphone camera) and which, when scanned, link to the delivery of unique content. An extraordinary number of museums around the world, from large institutions such as the Museum of Modern Art (MoMA) in New York and the Victoria and Albert Museum in London, to smaller museums such as the National Museum of Scotland and the Museum of Art in Stuttgart (Germany), have introduced this form of informal guidance within their exhibitions, usually as part of bespoke mobile apps.
4   http://www.react-hub.org.uk/heritagesandbox/projects/2012/ghosts-in-the-garden/ (accessed August 28, 2014).
5   Radio-frequency identification (RFID) tags are labels for the storing and wireless transmission of information, thanks to a circuit and an antenna embedded therein. RFID tags can be read by an RFID reader and do not need to be powered or to be in the line of vision of the reader for the information to be delivered. Therefore, they can be easily embedded into portable objects.
6   See www.gencem.org/ (accessed August 25, 2014).

References

Baber, C., J. Cross, T. Khaleel, and R. Beale. 2008. "Location-Based Photography as Sense-Making." In *BCS-HCI '08: Proceedings of the 22nd British HCI Group Annual Conference on People and Computers: Culture, Creativity, Interaction*, 133–140. Swinton, UK: British Computer Society.

Bannon, L., S. Benford, J. M. Bowers, and C. Heath. 2005. "Hybrid Design Creates Innovative Museum Experiences." *Communications of the ACM* 48(3): 62–65.

Brown, B., M. Chalmers, M. Bell, M. Hall, I. MacColl, and P. Rudman. 2005. "Sharing the Square: Collaborative Leisure in the City Streets." In *ECSCW 2005: Proceedings of the*

Ninth European Conference on Computer-Supported Cooperative Work, 18–22 September 2005, 427–447. London: Springer.

Cahour, B., and P. Salembier. 2012. "The User Phenomenological Experience: Evoking the Lived Activity with Re-Situating Interviews." In *CHI '12: Theories behind UX Research and How They Are Used in Practice*. New York: ACM.

Ciolfi, L. 2007. "Taking a Walk: Investigating Personal Paths in the Museum Space." In *CREATE 07: Proceedings of the Conference on Creative Inventions, Innovations and Everyday Designs in HCI*, edited by D. Golightly, T. Rose, B. L. W. Wong, and A. Light, 29–34. London: British Computer Society.

Ciolfi, L. 2013. "The Collaborative Work of Heritage: Open Challenges for CSCW." In *ECSCW 2013: Proceedings*, edited by O. W. Bertelsen, L. Ciolfi, M. A. Grasso, and G. A. Papadopoulos, 83–101. London: Springer. doi:10.1007/978-1-4471-5346-7_5.

Ciolfi, L., and L. Bannon. 2005. "Space, Place and the Design of Technologically Enhanced Physical Environments." In *Space, Spatiality and Technology*, edited by P. Turner and E. Davenport, 217–232. London: Springer.

Ciolfi, L., and L. J. Bannon. 2007. "Designing Hybrid Places: Merging Interaction Design, Ubiquitous Technologies and Geographies of the Museum Space." *Co-Design* 3(3): 159–180.

Ciolfi, L., and M. McLoughlin. 2011. "Physical Keys to Digital Memories: Reflecting on the Role of Tangible Artifacts in 'Reminisce.'" In *Museums and the Web 2011: Proceedings*, edited by D. Bearman and J. Trant, 197–208. Toronto: Archives & Museums Informatics.

Ciolfi, L., and M. McLoughlin. 2012. "Designing for Meaningful Visitor Engagement at a Living History Museum." In *NordiCHI '12: Proceedings of the 7th Nordic Conference on Human–Computer Interaction: Making Sense through Design*, 69–78. New York: ACM.

Ciolfi, L., D. Petrelli, F. Caparrelli, N. Dulake, R. Goldberg, M. T. Marshall, and M. Willox. 2013. "Exploring Historical, Social and Natural Heritage: Challenges for Tangible Interaction Design at Sheffield General Cemetery." In *Proceedings of NODEM 2013: Nordic Digital Excellence in Museums, Stockholm, December 2013*. Stockholm: NODEM.

Czarniawska, B. 2007. *Shadowing: And Other Techniques for Doing Fieldwork in Modern Societies*. Copenhagen: Copenhagen Business School Press.

Dodd, J. 1994. "Whose Museum Is It Anyway? Museum Education and the Community." In *The Educational Role of the Museum*, edited by E. Hooper-Greenhill, 31–33. London: Routledge.

Dourish, P. 2001. *Where the Action Is: The Foundations of Embodied Interaction*. Cambridge, MA: MIT Press.

Dourish, P. 2006. "Re-Space-ing Place: Place and Space Ten Years On." In *CSCW 2006: Proceedings of the ACM Conference on Computer-Supported Cooperative Work*, 299–308. New York: ACM.

Dudley, S. 2009. *Museum Materialities: Objects, Engagements, Interpretations*. London: Routledge.

Falk, J., and L. Dierking. 2012. *The Museum Experience Revisited*. Walnut Creek, CA: Left Coast.

Ferris, K., L. Bannon, L. Ciolfi, P. Gallagher, T. Hall, and M. Lennon. 2004. "Shaping Experiences in the Hunt Museum: A Design Case Study." In *Proceedings of DIS 04: International Conference on the Design of Interactive Systems*. New York: ACM.

Fitzpatrick, G. 2003. *The Locales Framework Understanding and Designing for Wicked Problems*. Dordrecht: Kluwer.

Fosh, L., S. Benford, S. Reeves, B. Koleva, and P. Brundell. 2013. "See Me, Feel Me, Touch Me, Hear Me: Trajectories and Interpretation in a Sculpture Garden." In *Proceedings of CHI 2013: International Conference on Human Factors in Computing Systems*, 149–158. New York: ACM.

Fraser, M., D. Stanton, K. H. Ng, S. Benford, C. O'Malley, J. Bowers, G. Taxén, K. Ferris, and J. Hindmarsh. 2003. "Assembling History: Achieving Coherent Experiences with Diverse Technologies." In *ECSCW 2003: Proceedings of the Eighth European Conference on Computer Supported Cooperative Work*. London: Springer.

Galani, A., and M. Chalmers. 2002. "Can You See Me? Exploring Co-Visiting between Physical and Virtual Visitors." In *Proceedings of ICHIM 2002: The International Cultural Heritage Informatics Meeting*, 31–40. Toronto: Archives & Museum Informatics.

Giaccardi, E. 2012. "Embodied Narratives: A Performative Co-Design Technique." *Proceedings of DIS 2012: Designing Interactive Systems*. New York: ACM.

Giaccardi, E., and L. Palen. 2008. "The Social Production of Heritage through Cross-Media Interaction: Making Place for Place-Making." *International Journal of Heritage Studies* 14(3): 289–298.

Harrison, S., and P. Dourish. 1996. "Re-Place-ing Space: The Roles of Place and Space in Collaborative Systems." *Proceedings of the ACM Conference on Computer-Supported Cooperative Work CSCW '96*, 67–76. New York: ACM.

Hindmarsh, J., C. Heath, D. vom Lehn, and J. Cleverly. 2005. "Creating Assemblies in Public Environments: Social Interaction, Interactive Exhibits and CSCW." *CSCW Journal* 14(1): 1–41.

Hinrichs, U., and S. Carpendale. 2011. "Gestures in the Wild: Studying Multi-Touch Gesture Sequences on Interactive Tabletop Exhibits." In *Proceedings of CHI 2011: International Conference on Human Factors in Computing Systems*, 3023–3032. New York: ACM.

Hornecker, E. 2010. "Interactions around a Contextually Embedded System." *Proceedings of TEI 2010: International Conference on Tangible, Embedded and Embodied Interaction*, 169–176. New York: ACM.

Hornecker, E. 2012. "Beyond Affordance: Tangibles' Hybrid Nature." *Proceedings of TEI 2012*, 17–182. New York: ACM.

Ilmonen, T. 2007. "Tranquil Interaction: Exploring Archaic Culture in the Kylä Installation." In *Proceedings of Designing Pleasurable Products and Interfaces*, edited by I. Koskinen and T. Keinonen, 92–106. New York: ACM.

Kalay, Y., T. Kwan, and J. Affleck, eds. 2008. *New Media and Cultural Heritage*. London: Routledge.

Lane, G. 2003. "Urban Tapestries: Wireless Networking, Public Authoring and Social Knowledge." *Personal and Ubiquitous Computing* 7(3–4): 169–175.

Lee, J., and T. Ingold. 2006. "Fieldwork on Foot: Perceiving, Routing, Socialising." In *Locating the Field: Space, Place and Context in Anthropology*, edited by S. Coleman and P. Collins. Oxford: Berg.

Mazel, A., A. Galani, D. Maxwell, and K. Sharpe. 2012. "'I Want To Be Provoked': Public Involvement in the Development of the Northumberland Rock Art on Mobile Phones Project." *World Archaeology* 44(4): 592–611.

McCarthy, J., and P. Wright. 2004. *Technology as Experience*. Cambridge, MA: MIT Press.

O'Hara, K., T. Kindberg, M. Glancy, L. Baptista, B. Sukumaran, G. Kahana, and J. Rowbotham. 2007. "Collecting and Sharing Location-Based Content on Mobile Phones in a Zoo Visitor Experience." *Computer-Supported Cooperative Work* 16(1–2): 11–44.

Petrelli, D., L. Ciolfi, D. van Dijk, E. Hornecker, E. Not, and A. Schmidt. 2013. "Integrating Material and Digital: A New Way for Cultural Heritage." *ACM Interactions*, July–August, 58–63.

Pfeifer, T., P. Savage, and B. Robinson. 2009. "Managing the Culloden Battlefield Invisible Mobile Guidance Experience." In *MUCS '09: Proceedings of the 6th International Workshop on Managing Ubiquitous Communications and Services*, edited by T. Pfeifer, D. O'Sullivan, and S. Das, 51–58. New York: ACM.

Robertson, T. 2002. "The Public Availability of Actions and Artefacts." *Computer Supported Cooperative Work* 11(2–3): 299–316.

Rossitto, C., and K. Severinson Eklundh. 2007. "Managing Work at Several Places: A Case of Project Work in a Nomadic Group of Students." In *Proceedings of ECCE 2007: 14th European Conference on Cognitive Ergonomics*, 45–51. New York: ACM.

Schnädelbach, H., A. Galani, and M. Flintham. 2009. "Embedded Mixed Reality Environments." In *Engineering of Mixed Reality Systems*, edited by E. Dubois, P. D. Gray, and L. Nigay, 57–78. London: Springer.

Schnädelbach, H., B. Koleva, M. Flintham, M. Fraser, S. Izadi, P. Chandler, M. Foster, S. Benford, C. Greenhalgh, and T. Rodden. 2002. "The Augurscope: A Mixed Reality Interface for Outdoors." In *Proceedings of CHI 2002: International Conference on Human Factors in Computing Systems*, 9–16. New York: ACM.

Simon, N. 2010. *The Participatory Museum*. Museums 2.0. Accessed August 28, 2014. http://www.participatorymuseum.org/read/.

Stuedahl, D., and O. Smørdal. 2012. "Experimental Zones – Spaces for New Forms of Participation in Museum Exhibition Development." In *Proceedings of the DREAM Conference "The Transformative Museum"*, May 23–25, 2012, Roskilde University, Denmark, edited by Erik Kristiansen, 375–387. Accessed August 28, 2014. http://www.dreamconference.dk/wp-content/uploads/2012/06/TheTransformativeMuseumProceedingsScreen.pdf.

Suchman, L. 1987. *Plans and Situated Actions: The Problem of Human–Machine Communication*. Cambridge: Cambridge University Press.

Tuan, Y. F. 1971. "Geography, Phenomenology and the Study of Human Nature". *Canadian Geographer* 15: 181–192.

Tuan, Y. F. 1977. *Space and Place: The Perspective of Experience*. Minneapolis: University of Minnesota Press.

Weiser, M. 1991. "The Computer for the 21st Century." In "Communications, Computers, and Networks," special issue, *Scientific American*, September.

Luigina Ciolfi is Reader in Communication at Sheffield Hallam University, UK. She holds a *Laurea* (University of Siena, Italy) and a PhD (University of Limerick, Ireland) in human–computer interaction, and for many years has researched the design and evaluation of interactive technologies for human use and enjoyment. She has worked on several international projects on cultural heritage technologies in collaboration with academic and museum partners. She has initiated the "Re-thinking Technology in Museums" conference series and has published extensively in international conferences and journals. Details on her work can be found at www.luiginaciolfi.com.

PART IV

Extending the Museum

20 OPEN AND CLOSED SYSTEMS
New Media Art in Museums and Galleries

Beryl Graham

Augmented reality has changed the scope of "public space." … Even physically walled private spaces are now open areas for anyone to use or re-shape. … the former "helper" criterium of whether something was placed within museum walls or not, is no longer valid. Virtual artworks by "non artists" could mix with officially curated art within an official museum. The museum offers the white cube and walls, the visitor decides what to see, and curators are bypassed.

Veenhof 2010

Museums might be familiar with the idea of their audiences using new media technology as part of an officially authored marketing device, gallery guide, or collections interface, but when the technology is used for art rather than interpretation, then boundaries can be pushed in interesting and productive ways. Augmented reality (AR), for example, is a set of technologies where global positioning system (GPS) data combines with lens-based imaging – you can look at the scene in front of you through your smartphone camera, and see digital images superimposed in certain positions in that scene. The technology is usually used for military or educational purposes, for example, looking at a building and being able to also see images of proposed architectural extensions on that site. What artists Sander Veenhof and Mark Skwarek did in 2010 with the technology was to add digital objects and images into the Museum of Modern Art (MoMA) in New York: new virtual sculptures by Veenhof and others who responded to an "open submission" call, "augmented" existing sculptures like halos or filled vacant spaces. The artists also decided to take images from MoMA's online documentation of its collection, so that the public could see all of the works in the collection at the same time in the gallery spaces, not just the ones that the curators had selected. Those who saw

The International Handbooks of Museum Studies: Museum Media, First Edition.
Edited by Michelle Henning.
© 2015 John Wiley & Sons Ltd. Published 2020 by John Wiley & Sons Ltd.

the advance publicity could go along with their smartphones for a day event as part of the Conflux Psychogeography Festival. The artists' website shows a helpful gallery map indicating the location of certain AR artworks, and generously adds an extra floor to the museum building, especially for AR art. The fact that MoMA did not know in advance about this additional exhibition on their program was part of the concept of the piece: "featuring augmented reality art in its proper context: a contemporary art museum." This mischievous bypassing of curatorial gatekeeping is gentle on the other artworks, however; no artworks were damaged, and the other artworks were enabled to virtually "mix" with the unofficially curated artworks, and to be viewed at the visitors' choice. It is this rethinking of the role of the visitor, the artist, and the curator which is perhaps the most signifi-cant recent development associated with media in the museum, and new media in particular, leading to a consideration of whether museum systems are "open" or "closed." If openness exists beyond merely fashionable rhetoric, then there are critical delineations to be drawn between openness to artists and to visitors, and also between differing levels of interaction, participation, or perhaps even control of decision making.

There are also, of course, examples where such works are done with permis-sion, as part of the official curatorial program. Margriet Schavemaker is head of collections and research at the Stedelijk Museum in Amsterdam and, unusually, has been involved in using new media in the museum as marketing media, as inter-pretation media, and as new media art in its own right. Schavemaker has made new exhibitions from the documentation in the museum archives of iconic 1960s exhibitions, and so is no stranger to the curatorial complexities of differentiating between media used as document and media used as art. In 2010 she commis-sioned an augmented reality work by artist Jan Rothuizen, where drawings and texts appeared on the blank white walls of interstitial spaces in the galleries, each of which was specific to the meaning of a museum location, including the text "This is not a church" (Schavemaker et al. 2011). Curators who take "educational technology" seriously as art media are admittedly unusual, but not without his-tory. The exhibition *Les immatériaux*, for example, curated by Jean-François Lyotard for the Centre Pompidou, Paris, in 1985, has left a legacy of exhibition installation shots including enigmatic computer screens and keyboards (Dernie 2006, 72–73). While these might have been assumed to be interpretation devices in many exhibi-tions, research reveals them to be showing the project "Writing Tests" commis-sioned by Lyotard from a collection of philosophical writers and experts, using an online bulletin board system in advance of the exhibition, and illustrating an early example of new media appearing as art where it might more usually be under-stood as education (Gere 2006, 18–22; Graham and Cook 2010, 19–29).

"New media" covers a wide range of newish technologies including the web, software code, GPS devices, and interactive fridges. "New media art" (or, as Sarah Cook and Steve Dietz would have it, "The Art Formerly Known as New Media") has to deal with a particular conundrum: the same new media are used for Internet porn, cheesy advertising, war, medicine ... and art. In a museum, the same media are used for publicity, interpretation, collections management, building security ... and art, which makes the confusion between new media educational technology and new media art a particularly productive issue in this chapter. To add to this confusion, "the computer" can be both a means of art production and a means of distribution or storage. Understandably, the media are often identified in terms of the first or most frequent encounter and, like imprinted ducklings, it can be difficult for people to shake off this first impression. As Cook (2011) states, substantial physical and conceptual negotiation is often required to imprint the idea of new media art: "As is the case with other museums and galleries around the world, it was often necessary to negotiate with the administration of the The Banff Centre to show that new media was art, not just technological innovation" (2011, 426).

Even if the idea of new media art is accepted, then much of the rhetoric characterizes the field either as ugly duckling or impossibly utopian swan: demonized as populist, shallow spectacle, flash in the pan, distanced, or overlauded as democratic, engaging, future building, connecting communities. Commenting on museums and art centers in general, Nick Prior firmly connects new technologies with a faintly *déclassé* flamboyance which may taint a hyped-up hypermodern future:

> They still, on the whole, celebrate values worked up by nineteenth-century aesthetics, including ideas of genius, expression, and cultural transcendence, but to these they have added new approaches, technologies, and flamboyant modes of exhibition more suitable to a hypermodern era. (Prior 2003, 67)

Artists, however, can usually be trusted to cut through the hyperbole around technology with a critical eye, especially if they work with those technologies every day as media. If curators are led by the new art, then they too need to be critical of how the art appears in museums and galleries, even down to the fundamental considerations of art exhibitions, those of time and space, before moving on to consider visitor behaviors in relation to behaviors of the artwork itself.

Time and space

Photography as storyboard, exhibition as film.

Bal 2007, 71

It is in the installation design of the first half of the twentieth century that the sources of such practices as viewer interactivity and site specificity, as well as multimedia, electronic and installation-based work, are to be found.

Staniszewski 1998, xxiii

As Mieke Bal succinctly indicates, for the audience, exhibitions are time-based, even if the objects are not. Exhibitions are a dynamic thing for any kind of art or media, whether that be photography or ceramics, with a variable cast of characters including the audience. As Mary Anne Staniszewski points out, if the "sources" of certain practices lie in exhibition installation, then the very nature of how time and space is dealt with in exhibitions becomes particularly important to these practices. Note that Staniszewski identifies the practices most affected here, first, through the characteristics of how they work (viewer interactivity and site specificity) rather than through specific media. This approach has also proved useful when applied to curating new media art. To briefly summarize, in 1999 Steve Dietz identified three characteristics of net art: connectivity, computability, and interactivity. As discussed in the book *Rethinking Curating*, each "behavior" presents different challenges to curators, and can be related to different histories of curating (Graham and Cook 2010). Connectivity, for example, might be familiar to curators of live art or 1960s conceptual art including mail art. In relation to "computability," the generative and algorithmic nature of computer software offers evolution over time. The third behavior of "interaction," such as Veenhof's augmented reality work already mentioned, has been much discussed in recent years, and is covered later in this chapter. These three behaviors might be present singly or in combination in new media art; they form a useful way of understanding not each new medium (which might change rapidly), but the ways in which the behaviors might demand a rethink of the processes involved in exhibiting these works.

These three behaviors all affect considerations of time and space for curating new media art in museums, but these can be informed by, and yet differentiated from, other art forms. Some forms of new media art might be time-based (like video) or live (like live broadcast), but neither of those encompasses the concept of computer "real time," or the difference between online "chat" and a telephone conversation. In terms of space, some new media art might be "immaterial," like some conceptual art, but how are the instruction sets of Fluxus works different from the instructions of computer code, with the algorithmic ability to generate and evolve? (Graham and Cook 2010, 51–110). There are still regrettable examples where curators more used to objects struggle with the time-based nature of video, and hence leave their audiences also struggling – with tired legs and vague expectations of duration. The "immateriality" of some forms of new media art has also encouraged curators to rethink the ways in which they exhibit in response to how the artworks behave. Given that new media art is not just one medium or behavior, it is particularly encouraging to see how various museums and art venues have evolved their own tactics for their own interests, different departments of the museum, and social context, both online and offline.

San Francisco Museum of Modern Art is an example, with a history of collecting and showing media art, then new media art, across various departments. The Media Arts Department collected notable video installation works from the 1980s, including Nam Jun Paik's *Egg Grows* (1984–1989). In the 1990s the Architecture and

Design Department showed and archived websites on the museum website and in galleries, which might have been regarded as either design or art. The Media Arts Department then exhibited works which were more formally "art" including net art. The online material was formally presented on the museum website as an "online gallery" e.space for only one year (2001–2002) and showed new media art including Thomson and Craighead's *e-poltergeist* in 2001. e.space is now not visible on the museum website's main page, and is categorized as a past "exhibition" rather than an ongoing space for exhibiting. The works are still available to view online, but they do not appear in the online database of the museum collection. In the physical galleries of the building, exhibitions have included a regular space for showing media work from the collection, and larger temporary exhibitions which included both new media works and painting or photography, for example, the exhibition *010101: Art in Technological Times* in 2001, which was instigated by then director David Ross in a very deliberate effort to show new media alongside other contemporary art. This demanded a highly inclusive approach whereby departments of the museum were included in developing the exhibition of new media art, including the curator of education and the Conservation Department, and helped to ensure that the acquisition of new media works into the collection was made possible. More recently, exhibitions such as *The Art of Participation* in 2008 have been able to show both new media and non-new media participatory works from the collection (Frieling 2014).

In the United Kingdom, the Victoria and Albert Museum (V&A) has a rather different history of collecting in relation to exhibition. The museum has been collecting "computer art" in the Print Department since the 1960s, with recent acquisitions and further archives acquired since 2000, led by Douglas Dodds from the Word and Image Department. Because the collected works are predominantly prints, the means of exhibiting the work is in some ways little different from showing other prints. As the Computer Art Collection web page is careful to point out:

> Although the term "computer art" is used by some to refer to computer-based art practices in general, the term should be understood as being separate from that of digital art, which implies a much freer or more open use of technologies. Aspects such as connectivity or interactivity often play a key part in contemporary digital or new media art, but were less a part of the vocabulary of the early technology. (V&A 2010)

The exhibition strategies on the website and for the *Digital Pioneers* temporary display in the V&A in 2009 were therefore to include some material which might differentiate how the *processes* of production were different from other kinds of printmaking: The collection website, for example, links to a page named "Drawing Techniques: Digital Technology" – in the same way as the processes of bronze casting might be explained to an audience who would not be able to read the processes behind a finished sculpture. However, histories of technology more recent than bronze casting are perhaps less well documented than other art histories, and the museum has benefited from a substantial Arts and Humanities Research Council (AHRC) grant to the V&A and Birkbeck, University of London, to help fill the gaps. It is interesting to note that the collection web page also includes an installation photograph from *Event One* in 1969 at the Royal College of Art, perhaps due to a curatorial awareness that both technological histories and exhibition installation histories are not usual inclusions in museum archives, or collections. Documentation of most of the V&A collection is available on the museum website, and is well interpreted, but *Digital Pioneers* is perhaps key here because it was deliberately arranged to coincide with a larger V&A exhibition, *Decode: Digital Design Sensations*, an exhibition of contemporary work curated by Louise Shannon from Contemporary Programmes. *Decode* was situated in the V&A's contemporary Porter Gallery, with interventions situated throughout the museum. It was the first exhibition of contemporary digital work at the V&A, and included international loans of contemporary digital art and design, alongside new commissions. As a substantial number of the exhibits involved interaction, and the exhibition was extremely popular, with long queues to buy tickets, the approach to display demanded the rethinking of museum strategies concerning time and space: this involved not only timed ticketing, but also the curator collaborating on the education programs and, when the opportunity arose, liaising with artists and designers on developing their work from prototypes to exhibition-standard pieces. The supporting material used for the exhibition included an "open source" marketing campaign, new methods employed by the Conservation Department, as well as new approaches taken by the Exhibitions Department during the tour of *Decode* to China, Russia, and Israel (Shannon 2014). Importantly for the museum and the future of new media art, the experience of the show led to a piece of contemporary work being acquired after the show: rAndom International's *Study for a Mirror*. This kind of fundamental reconsideration of media in the museum both as art in itself and how the media are used for exhibition, production, education, collection database, marketing, and networking in general is somewhat typical of the ways in which curators of new media art need to work with many areas of the museum in considering how work is exhibited, whether offline or online.

For all the rhetoric concerning "virtual galleries," there are rather few examples of art museum websites which take a serious long-term view of the Internet as a venue for exhibiting net art. The Whitney Museum's Artport, founded in 2002, is one of the few: listed under "exhibitions," it both functions as an online gallery space for commissions of net art and new media art, and also links to documentation of net art and new media art exhibitions at the Whitney, and new media art in the museum's collection. There have been occasional exhibitions in the gallery spaces of the Whitney relating to new media art, but Artport forms the coherent thread over a longer duration – reflecting, perhaps, associate curator Christiane Paul's expert input over a long period but with relatively modest institutional resourcing.

A rather smaller-scale example with an interestingly experimental approach is Arnolfini in Bristol – a contemporary arts center which covers live art/dance, sound/music, and film as well as events, and hence might be expected to be able to integrate non-object-based art into its program. Listed as "online projects" rather than as an exhibition, project.arnolfini was renamed in 2011, and is described, significantly, not as art but as "an online experimental production and research platform linked to the curatorial programme of Arnolfini."[1] Works commissioned since 2007 are included, with recent works such as *120days of *buntu* by Gordan Savicic and Danja Vasiliev in 2011. Geoff Cox, associate producer of the project, has also worked offline with Arnolfini on events and exhibitions, and is keen to "respond through artistic critique of social media as a reinvigoration of what was once called net.art."[2] An example where the method of the curating particularly reflects the behaviors of new media is *antisocial notworking*, from 2008, a "repository of projects that explore the pseudo-agency of online social platforms"[3] including work by Cory Arcangel, Les Liens Invisibles, and sumoto.iki. These works are primarily selected by the associate producer working in a traditional curatorial role, but the project is ongoing through time, and also seeks open submissions, critically reflecting that new media can facilitate "user-generated content." The *project.arnolfini* website also links to concerns for archives in general and issues for archiving live art in particular, not just new media art. The *Performing the Archive* wiki by Paul Clarke, by being open to editing by more than one authorial voice, aimed to explore "interrelationship and interactivity between the archives and communities of practitioners, scholars and audiences."[4] Like the V&A, it can therefore be seen that the behaviors of new media affect how curators and other museum workers work in time and space, online and offline. That *antisocial notworking* is both curated and open submission for artworks, like Veenhof's augmented reality project, reflects the potential for crowdsourcing the content of exhibitions: a new media behavior which sometimes causes confusion for other institutions, however large they might be.

In New York, the Guggenheim Museum's *YouTube Play: A Biennial of Creative Video* was a project started in 2010. From an open submission of 23,000 videos, a team of Guggenheim curators narrowed it down to a shortlist of 125. The *YouTube Play* jury of 11 people, including designers, artists, musicians, animators, and video (but not new media) curators, chose the top 25 videos from the shortlist. The selection was shown at the New York Guggenheim for two days only and include: an evening event featuring large, frenetically edited projections covering the inside and outside of the building; music and dance performances; and acknowledgment of the selected 25 artists. In the video documenting the evening event, the artists look somewhat stunned, perhaps by the contrast between the cloistered life of production and distribution production online, and this all-singing and dancing version. The physical gallery display of the selected videos is rather reminiscent of a Royal Academy Summer Exhibition, with individual videos stacked up and across the walls, so that viewers need to physically move from one to another, wearing headphones. The selected videos look, for the most part, like video art, animation, or documentation of live art, although they are generally shorter in duration than nononline equivalents. Although the URL for the project is http://www.guggenheim.org/new-york/

interact/participate/youtube-play, there is very little opportunity for participation by the viewer: "The Take" is a blog for the project, and features commissioned posts from people including new media curators, but commenting on these posts is difficult and unsurprisingly sparse. On the ongoing YouTube site where you can watch all the shortlisted videos, in order to comment you must exit the special YouTube Play site and watch on the general YouTube site. An interesting concession to new media behaviors, however, is the framing provided by some interpretive material in the form of frequently asked questions (FAQs). One reads: "Doesn't video art already exist? How is this different?" In the context of this project, this is a very good question. The mode of exhibition does attempt to reflect the sublime mass of video material on the Internet, but it also reveals a common institutional anxiety (although one not shared by Jean-François Lyotard), that new media is too immaterial, too fast, too slow, too much, or too little to be shown in a physical gallery without considerably "flamboyant" modes of display.

Precisely to help institutions who may be familiar with video but not with new media art, Robert Sakrowski has suggested some solutions (albeit rather tongue in cheek) to fitting the time and the space to the behaviors of the media used. Sakrowski is an art historian, artist, and curator based in Berlin who headed the project netart-datenbank.org at TU Berlin and has curated several exhibitions in the field of net art. His blog (http://curatingyoutube.net/) discusses and showcases examples of how people are curating YouTube, by selecting and arranging works around ideas of, for example, particular characteristics of soundtracks, moving between online and offline behaviors of the videos and database format, whether for viewing or for producing user-generated content. His own proposal is for *Curating Youtube BOX* (CYB), an easily transported physical box installation, a room within a room, which can

> easily be installed in the context of a museum, a gallery, a studio or an art fair. CYB enables curators and scientists to present net videos in a format that is adequate to the art business ... The net videos presented in the various exhibitions will be presented in their original size, using apt players and thereby creating a feeling of "authenticity." (Sakrowski and Bäucker 2010)

A tablet computer as part of the system would enable both a curator to supply interpretive material around the videos, and a viewer to use the database features by creating personal playlists and add comments and links. This gleefully universal panacea for struggling curators concerning new media space, time, aesthetics, interpretation, interaction, and audience wittily highlights the sheer range of factors which new media curators need to consider in order to achieve "authenticity" in reflecting new media behaviors, which involve an "original size" of a domestic screen rather than a large spectacle.

Arts workers, therefore, although they might have experience of curating immaterial conceptual art or of using media as a means of distribution, might find themselves still dealing with new questions of space and time. The *Broadcast Yourself* exhibition in 2008, curated by Sarah Cook and Kathy Rae Huffman, included both old and new media in exploring the differences in access to broadcasting systems for artists. They varied enormously in concepts of space and time, from the deliberately low-tech *Joanie 4 Jackie* from 1996, a video chain letter instigated by Miranda July, where women video-makers used postal services to mail videotapes in a widening network, to *TV Swansong* in 2002, curated by Nina Pope and Karen Guthrie, which was a one-day webcast of artists' work, broadcast live from significant locations including a ballroom. Viewers of the *Broadcast Yourself* exhibition could be streamed live from the exhibition, interviewed by a computer program in a commissioned work by Active Ingredient, and also watch documentation of Shaina Anand's CCTV projects in India, which demonstrated how artists continue to create their own systems to contest the fact that they have limited access to the technologies needed for conventional television broadcast.

New media, of course, flow not only through the museum but around it, into public and social spaces, and through the airwaves. Considerations of time and space therefore extend more widely than strictly "museum media" for those working with new media. Yukiko Shikata has curated for the InterCommunication Center (ICC) in Tokyo as well as continuing to work as an independent curator, and has a particular delicate and far-reaching experience of curating space and time. In 2005 she was producer of *MobLab: Japanese–German Media Camp 2005*, which involved a group of artists working on a bus to make and show work for three weeks as the bus toured Japan. The accompanying website both documented the process and formed a means of exhibition. Shikata explains that,

> In Japan and most of the Asian countries, there is no strong desire for the "construction" or "overview," like in the West. I think the European notions of "construction" and "overview" are established on the premise of the Cartesian notion (and notation) of space, and "chronos," the notion of time, and in Asian countries time and space were not articulated in this Western way. (Shikata 2009)

Her project *Mission G: Sensing the Earth* exhibition ran for around nine months at the ICC (2009–2010). The long duration reflected the nature of the exhibition, where data gathered from international locations via the Internet fed live into installations in the gallery, slowly tracking and illuminating shifts and patterns, including those relating to climate change, in real time. The work was not interactive with the viewer, but was reacting to data in its code, and evolving algorithmically and slowly. Considering that those marketing new media art often appear to feel obliged to stress the frenetic speed and hands-on fun aspects of new media, this example of minimalist contemplation is a reminder that new media take many forms.

Considerations of time and space for new media art in museums are therefore not purely formal concerns, but relate strongly to the intent of each work, and the kinds of characteristics or behaviors that might occur in the work singly or in combination. To return to Steve Dietz's three behaviors of connectivity, computability, and interactivity, it is perhaps the last that presents the most fundamental challenge to museums, in particular in rethinking the structure of institutions in relation to audiences.

Interaction, and the participatory turn

[A]t Information it was not the institution of the Museum of Modern Art that was staging a dialogue with its viewers: that role was now commandeered by the artist.
                                                                    Staniszewski 1998, 270

Ask three times …
Can't hear the hecklers 'til they sit down …
Cultivate conflict …
Encourage the quieter people …[5]

Although there is a current fascination with dialogues, viewers, audiences, the relational, participation, and interaction in art, there tends to be a dangerously vague feeling on the part of funders and others that these are the kinds of nice things that art museums *should* be doing, rather than a firm critical grasp of different varieties of participation or of research which might help the extreme rigors of doing this kind of practice well. It is very questionable how much of these facets of exhibition are documented and valued in museum work, although, again, there is a blur between knowledge in education departments and curatorial departments concerning participation.

Staniszewski in the quote above refers to the *Information* exhibition of 1970 at MoMA in New York, curated by Kynaston McShine. The exhibition was notable not only for the way in which McShine responded to conceptual art with new curatorial tools and methods, but also for the integration of ideas of interaction and participation. Hans Haacke's work in the show, *MoMA Poll*, for example, was founded on active participation, where the audience voted on a political question and their votes were visible to other members of the audience in clear plastic posting boxes. As Staniszewski points out, these considerations of interaction and installation were more traditionally the responsibilities of different departments of a museum, but were now brought together via artists' practice. New media art practices do not, of course, have the monopoly on participatory systems, but because so many new media systems are by their nature interactive in behavior, practitioners who have been wrestling with the different systems of interaction, connectivity, social networking, or even open source coproduction, are likely to have a highly critical appreciation of what they mean by participation.

FIGURE 20.1   *Talkaoke* at the Barbican Centre, London, 2012.
Photo: Hektor P. Kowalski. Reproduced by permission of The People Speak.

The People Speak, quoted in the second epigraph above, is a group which provides "Tools for the world to take over itself. The People Speak makes it easy for people to talk to each other …"[6] Its projects include *Talkaoke*, a mobile doughnut-shaped desk with lights and microphone where a host encourages people to talk about whatever is important to them, and to have a conversation with each other (Figure 20.1). The tips above about "cultivating conflict" are part of their website, where knowledge is shared so that the skills of hosting conversations can be passed on. Another of their projects, *Who Wants To Be* …, uses a more formal method of voting with different colored cards, recognized and counted by video camera, in order to reach important decisions – often on local planning issues or how to spend collective pots of event ticket money on art projects. The group have developed the systems over time, such as a "heckling" system which works both with technology like mobile phones and face to face, and hence uses hybrid sets of technological and social skills. The case studies on the web have worked in the contexts of art festivals, creative industries conferences, and the Safer Croydon planning campaign. The cofounders Saul Albert and Mikey Weinkove cite their experience as including participatory art and chat show hosting, but should this project be described as education or art? It is interesting to note that, like Hans Haacke and his *MoMA Poll*, The People Speak are using participatory systems from politics, entertainment, or education rather than art itself.

In museums, the extensive audience knowledge of those who work in education can greatly inform curatorial practice. Nina Simon (2010), for example, uses four categories of different levels of participation, where the museum has a decreasing level of control over the visitors: contributing to institutions; collaborating with visitors; co-creating with visitors; and hosting participants. This acknowledgment of loss of control, however, is precisely what disturbs some curators, critics, and institutions, for participation challenges some deeply held value judgments around the participating body and audience behaviors. The Robert Morris retrospective *Bodyspacemotionthings*, installed in 1971 and 2009 at the Tate, has been widely discussed in relation to participation, and for good reason. The hands-on participatory sculpture exhibition closed after five days, after reports of audience injuries and press reviews which opined that the shallow "assault course" meant that the trouble with participation was that it made people behave like "wild beasts" (Dietz 2004; Graham and Cook 2010, 127). Interestingly, the reinstallation of the exhibition in original participatory form was instigated by live art and intermedia art curators as part of *The Long Weekend* (2009), perhaps because these areas have an existing interest in and respect for audience participative behaviors as an inherent characteristic of the art forms.

The long debate about Nicolas Bourriaud's "relational aesthetics" can be very briefly summarized as exploring the tension that participatory systems cannot be serious as art unless there is space for conflict in the system. However, the artists cited by Claire Bishop (2006) as offering space for conflict, such as Thomas Hirschhorn, tend to have an oppositional political stance such as offering audiences in working-class areas of cities the chance to destroy or change his installations if they choose to (although, arguably, all audiences might have the choice to do this to any art). Because the examples in the debate between Bourriaud and Bishop are artists who are at the center of traditional fine art star systems, this leaves little room for discussing other systems of authorship, contribution, or coproduction. Graham and Cook's book *Rethinking Curating*, however, carefully distinguishes between interaction, participation, and collaboration, which like Nina Simon's categories, acknowledge very different levels of control and "openness" (Bishop 2006; Graham and Cook 2010, 116–118). Even "simple" kinds of interaction can radically affect the reading of the artwork and, although simple, can escape the caricature of assault courses and wild beasts. It has perhaps been artists who have been most skeptical of the tendency of relational and educational turns to "misleadingly conjure a level playing field in the room" (Zolghadr 2010, 163), and have seen the potential for close audience engagement to deal with conflict and "difficult knowledge" (Frenkel and Zemans 2007, 123). Artists who have worked with the inherently interactive behaviors of new media can offer particular understandings of both interaction between audience and artwork, and interaction between people that might be hosted by the artwork.

In their artwork from 2006, *Seen – Fruits of Our Labor*, Osman and Omar Khan work with hidden experiences, and how the ways in which artworks behave fundamentally affects interactions between people. The work was presented in a public square in San Jose, and appeared as a shiny black slab taller than a person. There were instructions on a plaque nearby, but the more common interface was watching people behaving strangely around the slab: peering at it through cameras or

FIGURE 20.2   Osman Khan and Omar Khan, *SEEN – Fruits of Our Labor*, 2006, installed in the public plaza in front of San Jose Museum of Art, California.
Reproduced by permission of Osman Khan and Omar Khan.

mobile phone cams (Figure 20.2). The infrared text scrolling down the slab was only visible through a digital camera, and the text concerned three communities of San Jose's labor: the tech-savvy workers of Silicon Valley; the undocumented workers (migrant workers from Mexico, Vietnam, etc.) engaged in menial tasks in San Jose; and the virtual community of outsourced tech workers in India. The texts are responses from these three groups of people being asked "What is the fruit of your labor?" Viewers of the work often took photographs of the work, with their own image reflected in the shiny surface along with the text.

> The resulting picture/video, a personal artwork, shows the participant, the means of production (camera) and the responses in a revealing relationship. What was hidden from your view, the other's thoughts and motivations, is revealed through the technical device. You become witness in the most personal way to this exchange. (Khan and Khan 2006)

FIGURE 20.3   Rafael Lozano-Hemmer, *Pulse Room*, 2010, Manchester Art Gallery, Manchester, UK. (For a color version of this figure, please see the color plate section.)
Photo: Peter Mallet. Reproduced by permission of Rafael Lozano-Hemmer.

What was also remarkable about the work was the interactions between viewers in the center of a bleak American city plaza. People took it on themselves to explain what they were looking at to others and even went so far as to loan that most intimate and covetable of devices, the mobile phone, to strangers without a camera, in order to pass on the experience.

This kind of sensitivity not only to interactions between artwork and audience, but between audience members, is also evident in many of the works of the artist Rafael Lozano-Hemmer. *Pulse Room* from 2006 is a work where the viewers slowly realize that the pleasure of seeing their own heartbeats pulse in the form of a delicately fluttering lightbulb is balanced by the responsibility for pushing someone else's recorded heartbeat out of the spectacle of the artwork and into darkness (Figure 20.3). His *Body Movies, Relational Architecture No. 6* (2001–) is a huge installation in outdoor plazas and public squares, and offers users the opportunity to make giant shadows with their bodies. The work actually enables at least two kinds of reaction or interaction. First, there are projected photographic images of people, which the audience can see properly only when they cover the photographs with their own shadow – they may find themselves copying the body shape of someone of a different gender or race. If individuals in the audience collaborate to cover all of the photographs at the same time, then the computer program reacts by projecting a new crop of photographs. Audience readings of the artwork may therefore be complex, but here the computer program is simply reacting to their movements. Second, the audience can freely improvise with the huge shadows to interact with each other. Lozano-Hemmer vouches that "Successful pieces that feature 'interactivity for groups' are usually out-of-control" (Lozano-Hemmer 2001).

From these subtle understandings of interactions, those working with new media art are therefore able to offer critical tools for mapping what interacts with whom, beyond the limited scope of traditional fine art relationships. One mapping which has proved useful for thinking about participatory systems has been Paul Baran's diagrams of three kinds of network: *centralized* networks (one to many), *decentralized* networks (several to many), and the rhizome-like *distributed* networks (many to many). Broadcast media can be seen as a centralized network, whereas the distributed network of the Internet works in a way that is fundamentally different in terms of understandings of distribution, and of audience participation. New media vocabularies have to be very specific about the control of what connects with what – the points where the lines of communication in a network meet are called "nodes," and nodes where many lines converge become "hubs," so that actually some nodes can be more important than others, even in a rhizomatic network. Vocabularies of "behavior" are thus emerging which are proving more useful than attempting to describe artworks by specific medium. If the nodes are understood as people, then the power relationships between artists, curators, and the "audience" can be understood in a more accurate way (Graham 2010, 288).

Audience contributions to documentation

[W]hat was wonderful to see was that we were learning through what people were posting online. We would see all kinds of documents come up either on Flickr or on YouTube and then say, "Wait a minute, what actually happened in the galleries?"
Frieling 2009

Before discussing the more complex area of considering audiences as coproducers of art, it should be briefly acknowledged that audiences have been contributing to the documentation and archives concerning art for some time, in ways which might be more familiar to museum education staff than to curators. *The Art of Participation* exhibition curated by Rudolf Frieling for San Francisco Museum of Modern Art in 2008 proved to be a learning experience for the whole institution. After some earlier institutional anxiety about images appearing online, outside institutional control, the museum changed some fundamental administrative systems: existing default restrictions on photography were lifted, and the informal online documentation of this exhibition was considered to be not only a useful supplement to formal documentation, but a way of further publicizing and encouraging participation after the museum visit.

While unlikely to replace institutional archives, this kind of documentation will by its nature tend to include people in installation shots of participative work because, for the informal photographer, the people are the most important thing. As recognized by Jon Ippolito (2008), the debate around the conservation and preservation of new media art has been crucial for the development of such art, not because everyone needs to be a preservation expert, but because the artwork, in order to be collected, also needs to be documented, classified, and exhibited, and its most essential characteristics need to be discussed. This is particularly important for participatory art, because there are few "histories of exhibitions" rather than histories of art, and the nature of audience behaviors in participatory exhibitions is particularly badly documented for future display. Where audience studies are present in archives, they tend to be of a demographic kind most useful for the berating of arts organizations by funders and governments, and so institutions may be reluctant to reveal them. My own research concerning interactive artworks in gallery settings identified patterns of interaction between audience members as well as interaction between artwork and audience (Graham 1997; 2008). More recently, researcher and curator Lizzie Muller has pushed audience studies of interactive art way beyond the conventional demographic approach of museums, into documentation that looks in detail at complex audience experiences of interaction. She worked with Caitlin Jones at the Daniel Langlois Foundation Centre for Research and Documentation to develop documentation of David Rokeby's artworks in ways intended to inform future artists and curators, and perhaps form an "oral history" of new media art (Jones and Muller 2008). As Rokeby's work is in many international art collections, this resource adds a larger and deeper independent body of documentation that may be beyond the means of individual institutions. Again, the potential for the audiences to "crowdsource" their own audience studies online could complement formal research: the more audience members comment, tweet, and add their own oral histories, the more of a picture of audience complexity might be available to future researchers (Graham and Cook 2010, 268–273).

Audience contributions to art

In the case of Learning to Love You More, we are not using some kind of stealth software to learn about the lives of people and then publish what we find. The participants are willingly contributing, so it has never come up in that way. There have been a few cases where people have contacted us and asked us to take things out of their submissions but later changed their mind. It might be that circumstances had changed in some way or they just found it too revealing and then we would just remove it.

Fletcher 2007, 88

Artists such as Harrell Fletcher and Miranda July, who worked on the long-running *Learning to Love You More* project (2002–2009), can draw on a detailed working knowledge of the ethics of participatory new media art systems. In the project, the artists drew up "assignments" for people to complete and submit to the website. The artists did have editorial control over the submissions, but exercised this only rarely. While this is basically a centralized system, where people are contributing to the artists' project, each person is credited with their own work: this addresses the issue of artistic authorship which arises in certain relational aesthetic artworks. When the work was shown in the Whitney Biennial in New York in 2004, the museum was concerned with issues of artistic quality of the open submissions, and perhaps sought to allay these concerns by also commissioning Fletcher to make a site-specific artwork for the elevator in the museum, which edited together some audio submissions from *Learning to Love You More*. In this case, the artwork was credited to Fletcher, but the individual audio works were also credited by name as material used. These systems of fair participation are perhaps more familiar to those editing books or producing films than to the systems of fine art, and demand different understandings or participation. When dealing with the delicate balance between the public and the private involved in online social networking sites, both artists and curators can benefit from experience and expertise.

When considering participatory systems which involve the distributed coproduction of artwork rather than contributing to a centralized artwork, the issues of credits and copyright become even more key to the system. Again, new media has particularly useful ways of understanding this. Digital media can obviously be cut and pasted very easily, and the web is a public distributive space, but, rather than trying to impose traditional notions of copyright and control at all points, new media offers systems of "copyleft" where credit is still assigned but copying and use are less restricted. If considering art projects which are distributed coproductions, where all nodes are equally important, then open source systems are useful. "Open source" is a term from software production, where many people contribute to developing software: the source code is available to all, and is written in such a way that the structure (the recipe, if you like) is open to other programmers/users to copy, improve, or adapt. Open source software is often available at no monetary cost to the user, and hence is an alternative system opposed to proprietary software where the code is hidden and closed for copyright and financial benefit. Here the distinctions between programmers and users of the software become blurred, in a similar way to how the boundaries between artists and audiences become blurred in participatory projects.

"Open source" is a term often applied rather loosely to participatory art projects to mean an essentially nonhierarchical structure, but this is not necessarily the case. As artist and curator Simon Pope testifies, there is "a subtle difference between technical freedom and social freedom" (2011, 815). There may well be hierarchies of skill and time involved in open source production systems, and as artist and curator Dominic Smith identified in his research, a key characteristic of the systems centered on crediting work, and the ability to share the recipe in a way which makes it more likely that people will want to adapt that recipe in their own way, even if that recipe then "forks" into a very different kind of software (Smith 2011). He also identified that if a particular person instigates a project, then the tendency is for the project to remain centralized on that person rather than being distributed, simply because some people find it more alluring to start their own thing and expect people to contribute, than to always contribute to or develop a larger whole. He therefore made a conscious decision to develop a project instigated by someone else. *The Shredder* was originally devised as part of the *Geekosystem* project by Julian Priest, David Merritt, and Adam Hyde, and involved shredding old proprietary software manuals, mixing them with coffee grounds, and hence using "upgrade culture" as a growing medium for spinach seedlings. This project was adapted by Smith to grow edible fungi, which were exhibited in bell jars in Tyneside Cinema in Newcastle as part of AV Festival, and the recipe shared via cocktail hour talks. The instigators were credited on the work, as well as those who codeveloped the project, including a mycology consultant on fungus growth conditions.

New media can therefore draw on participatory methods far wider than the traditional fine art centralized star system, and understandings of authorship far wider than single copyright, to help with the substantial challenges of participatory art and also to rethink the role of curating itself.

Audience as curators?

… a collective of young people who would come up with projects and lobby all of the museums in the city, and start their own museum if necessary.
Graham and Yasin 2007, 170

The idea that "the audience" might be interested in participating or collaborating, not only in making art but also in curating their own museum, will come as no surprise to those involved in education, "community art," or new media. As Friedrich Kittler states, data-based new media can easily facilitate the desire that "Visitors too – they especially – should be given access not just to lovingly presorted information but to all available information" (1996, 73). There are therefore many good examples already on museum websites, including the Walker Art Center, where users can select artworks from documentation of museum collections, to add to their very own "collection" which can be saved for later additions and development. Not only can people select works, but they can input keywords and tags. In the case of the runme.org repository of software art this contributes to a "folksonomy" – forming those very taxonomies and categories of kinds of art that curators fight so hard over (www.runme.org). In the case of software art, these categories are not yet firmly formed, and so a folksonomy shaped by artists and viewers can be seen to be a useful thing. For older fields of art, art historians, curators, and educators might be less willing to relinquish control over their lovingly presorted information. In reality, of course, as Kittler recognizes, this expert information can exist alongside the more chaotic crowdsourced information and can be used in accordance with context and taste.

The idea of collaborative curating of exhibitions is again not a new idea, but new media can make this more feasible, with more people, over a greater distance. The arts group Furtherfield in London, for example, were able to collaboratively curate the project *Do It with Others (DIWO)* in 2007 with other people online and in the physical gallery space. Anyone who subscribed to their discussion list could join in: artworks were viewed using a webcam, and reviewed and selected by live text "chat." The artworks were moved around the physical gallery space by collective decision, again observed by webcam. This experimental and hybrid approach was in line with the organization's experience of collaborative projects, and what they learned from the process was shared online via discussion lists and blogs, in a way open sourcing the participative system and the recipe. This kind of "self-institutionalization" is feasible whatever medium you are working with, but new media can simply make this easier to achieve over distances and with more people, and to develop over time. Furtherfield were also highly active in the network NODE.London, which coordinated a media art season in 2006 with no lead curator but a series of linked nodes.

As with Robert Sakrowski's curatingyoutube.net project in the introduction to this chapter, new media can be inherently participatory, and that includes curating as well as making art. Whether people are good curators or not, as with the non-new media world, depends on the skills of the individuals.

Conclusions: Systems of museum media

For me, it is not "the media" that enter the gallery (the media are positioned, received or generated there) but it is the audience that enters the gallery. What I find exciting about dealing with new media is the extraordinarily complicated relationship between audience and artwork.

Ride 2011, 81

In acknowledging that the role of the audience is intimately linked to considerations of how new media appear in museums and galleries, there is fundamental questioning of the roles of the viewer, user, or participant – not only in producing art, but also in creating exhibitions. This reconsideration of audience highlights just how many areas and people involved in museums and galleries might be involved in rethinking media in museums, from marketers, gallery attendants, and education staff to curators, archivists, and conservators. This network of linked issues might demand new systems or, as curator and artist Vince Dziekan would have it, "new programme architectures" (2012, 190).

There are an encouraging number of examples of institutions that are willing to take on these changes and to draw in the wider potential of crowdsourced documentation or audience curating. In particular, those making a link between commissioning, collection, and exhibition seem to understand the wide range of issues. *Current: An Experiment in Collecting Digital Art*, for example, is a partnership by the Harris Museum and Art Gallery and folly in the United Kingdom, which included an exhibition, acquisition, documented public debate, and audience considerations, presented as a practical case study in a wider research project (Taylor 2014).

If audiences are truly important in considering museum media not simply as marketing tools, then there is a strong argument for building on the "productive confusion" between educational and art new media to share knowledge in order to address the considerable challenges – triangulating from as many sources as possible would seem to be valuable. At a time when funders of both research and art are particularly keen on new media understood primarily as a flamboyant means of distribution, marketing, and participation, it is, however, still important to differentiate one from the other (CRUMB 2012). Too often the research about audiences and behaviors is simply asking the wrong questions: "rather than succumbing to the market researcher's command to 'answer this!' we continue to ask, as Judith Mastai always did: 'So – what do you want to do'" (Graham and Yasin 2007, 171).

If the idea of fully coproduced distributed art or exhibitions is taken seriously by museums, then the systems chime with new media ideologies of open source work processes. As Alexa Färber identifies, there is a growing demand for, and some response to, an idea of openness which rather works against a tendency for curators to keep exhibition processes behind a velvet curtain until opening night:

> By applying ethnographic procedures of experience-based reflection and to some extent revealing themselves publicly, curators meet an apparent public demand to know how an exhibition and how the curators "tick." This kind of transparency also meets a public pressure to lay bare everything for which tax and other spending was spent. (Färber 2007, 235)

While institutions might not be ready to provide all available information just yet, there is some evidence that consideration of participation is growing in curatorial literature, even if it appears in some unusual forms. If the documentation of exhibitions and behaviors lies not only outside the museum but on the sublime mass of the Internet, and quite possibly in the hands of the viewers themselves, then this information – not only on art or exhibitions, but also on audience behaviors in relation to those exhibitions – promises a more critical grasp of the practicalities of working with new media time and space, or participatory art practices.

As explored in this chapter, certain "behaviors" of new media art, such as participation or interaction, might be placed with a firm hand in museum "education" departments, rather than in collections, archives, or libraries from whence the distant gleam of the historical canon might be glimpsed. If these areas of knowledge can be connected together and can inform each other, then both critical art histories and working knowledge of how open or how closed systems of museum media can be, then new media in the museum could fully reach their potential.

Notes

1   http://www.project.arnolfini.org.uk (accessed August 25, 2014).
2   http://www.arnolfini.org.uk/about/cookies/learning/projects/online-projects (accessed September 8, 2014).
3   http://project.arnolfini.org.uk/antisocial-notworking (accessed September 8, 2014).
4   http://oldproject.arnolfini.org.uk/cgi-bin/wiki/read.cgi?section=PerformingTheArc hive&page=Home (accessed August 25, 2014).
5   "Tricks of the Trade," http://thepeoplespeak.org.uk/blog/2013/01/07/tricks-of-the-trade/ (accessed August 26, 2014).
6   http://thepeoplespeak.org.uk/about/ (accessed September 8, 2014).

References

Bal, Mieke. 2007. "Exhibition as Film." In *Exhibition Experiments*, edited by Sharon Macdonald and Paul Basu, 71–93. Oxford: Wiley-Blackwell.

Bishop, Claire, ed. 2006. *Participation*. Cambridge, MA: MIT Press.

Cook, Sarah. 2011. "Showing New Media Art at Banff." In *Euphoria and Dystopia: The Banff New Media Institute Dialogues*, edited by Sarah Cook and Sara Diamond, 426–444. Banff, Canada: Banff Centre Press.

CRUMB. 2012. "Distribution and Dissemination After New Media." Professional development workshop, March 5. Accessed August 25, 2014. http://www.crumbweb.org/getSeminarDetail.php?id=17.

Dernie, David. 2006. *Exhibition Design*. London: Laurence King.

Dietz, Steve. 2004. "Is It All Robert Morris's Fault?" *Yproductions*. Accessed August 25, 2014. http://www.yproductions.com/WebWalkAbout/archives/is_it_all_robert_mor riss_fault.html.

Dziekan, Vince. 2012. *Virtuality and the Art of Exhibition: Curatorial Design for the Multimedia Museum*. Bristol: Intellect.

Färber, Alexa. 2007. "Exposing Expo: Exhibition Entrepreneurship and Experimental Reflexivity in Late Modernity." In *Exhibition Experiments*, edited by Sharon Macdonald and Paul Basu, 219–239. Oxford: Wiley-Blackwell.

Fletcher, Harrell. 2007. "Tell Me Your Story: An Interview with Artist Harrell Fletcher." By Marisa Sanchez. In *Searching for Art's New Publics*, edited by Jeni Walwin, 79–90. Bristol: Intellect.

Frenkel, Vera, and Joyce Zemans. 2007. "A Place for Uncertainty: Towards a New Kind of Museum." In *Museums After Modernism: Strategies of Engagement*, edited by Griselda Pollock and Joyce Zemans, 119–130. Oxford: Blackwell.

Frieling, Rudolf. 2009. "An Interview with Rudolf Frieling." By Beryl Graham. CRUMB. Accessed August 25, 2014. http://www.crumbweb.org/getInterviewDetail.php?id=34.

Frieling, Rudolf. 2014. "The Museum as Producer: Processing Art and Performing a Collection." In *New Collecting: Exhibiting and Audiences After New Media Art*, edited by Beryl Graham, 135–158. Farnham, UK: Ashgate.

Gere, Charlie. 2006. *Art, Time and Technology*. Oxford: Berg.

Graham, Beryl. 1997. "A Study of Audience Relationships with Interactive Computer-Based Visual Artworks in Gallery Settings, through Observation, Art Practice, and Curation." Doctoral thesis, University of Sunderland. Accessed August 25, 2014. http://www.berylgraham.com/cv/sub/thesisi.htm.

Graham, Beryl. 2008. "Serious Games – Case Study." In *New Media in the White Cube and Beyond: Curatorial Models for Digital Art*, edited by Christiane Paul, 191–206. Berkeley: University of California Press.

Graham, Beryl. 2010. "What Kind of Participative System? Critical Vocabularies from New Media Art." In *The "Do-It-Yourself" Artwork: Participation from Fluxus to New Media*, edited by Anna Dezeuze, 281–305. Manchester: Manchester University Press.

Graham, Beryl, and Sarah Cook. 2010. *Rethinking Curating: Art after New Media*. Cambridge, MA: MIT Press.

Graham, Janna, and Shadya Yasin. 2007. "Reframing Participation in the Museum: A Syncopated Discussion." In *Museums After Modernism: Strategies of Engagement*, edited by Griselda Pollock and Joyce Zemans, 157–172. Oxford: Blackwell.

Ippolito, Jon. 2008. "Death by Wall Label." In *New Media in the White Cube and Beyond: Curatorial Models for Digital Art*, edited by Christiane Paul. Berkeley: University of California Press. Accessed August 25, 2014. http://thoughtmesh.net/publish/11.php.

Jones, Caitlin, and Lizzie Muller. 2008. "David Rokeby, *The Giver of Names* (1991–): Documentary Collection." Daniel Langlois Foundation, Centre for Research and Documentation. Accessed August 25, 2014. http://www.fondation-langlois.org/html/e/page.php?Repere=200812&NumPage=2121.

Khan, Osman, and Omar Khan. 2006. "SEEN Screens Exposing Employed Narratives." Accessed August 25, 2014. http://www.osmankhan.com/works.asp?name=Unviewed.

Kittler, Friedrich. 1996. "Museums on the Digital Frontier." In *The End(s) of the Museum*, edited by John Hanhardt, 67–80. Barcelona: Fondacio Antoni Tapies.

Lozano-Hemmer, Rafael. 2001. "Too Interactive (Belated)." To New-Media-Curating discussion list (New-Media-Curating@jiscmail.acuk), December 6. Accessed August 25, 2014. https://www.jiscmail.ac.uk/cgi-bin/webadmin?A2=ind01&L=new-media-curating&F=&S=&P=317411.

Pope, Simon. 2011. "Bridges II." In *Euphoria and Dystopia: The Banff New Media Institute Dialogues*, edited by Sarah Cook and Sara Diamond, 814–819. Banff, Canada: Banff Centre Press.

Prior, Nick. 2003. "Having One's Tate and Eating It: Transformations of the Museum in a Hypermodern Era." In *Art and Its Publics: Museum Studies at the Millennium*, edited by Andrew McClellan, 51–74. Oxford: Blackwell.

Ride, Peter. 2011. "Enter the Gallery." *Public: Art Culture Ideas* 44: 81–89.

Sakrowski, Robert, and Sven Bäucker. 2010. "Curating Youtube BOX [CYB]." Accessed August 25, 2014. http://www.curatingyoutube.net/cyt-box/.

Schavemaker, Margriet, Hein Wils, Paul Stork, and Ebelien Pondaag. 2011. "Augmented Reality and the Museum Experience." In *Museums and the Web 2011: Proceedings*, edited by J. Trant and D. Bearman. Toronto: Archives & Museum Informatics. Accessed August 25, 2014. http://www.museumsandtheweb.com/mw2011/papers/augmented_reality_and_the_museum_experience.

Shannon, Louise. 2014. "Historic Collection, Contemporary Audience: Victoria and Albert Museum." In *New Collecting: Exhibiting and Audiences After New Media Art*, edited by Beryl Graham, 171–182. Farnham, UK: Ashgate.

Shikata, Yukiko. 2009. "An Interview with Yukiko Shikata." By Verina Gfader. CRUMB. Accessed August 25, 2014. http://www.crumbweb.org/getInterviewDetail.php?op=3&sublink=1&id=37.

Simon, Nina. 2010. *The Participatory Museum*. Museum 2.0. Accessed August 25, 2014. http://www.participatorymuseum.org/ (accessed September 24, 2013).

Smith, Dominic. 2011. "Models of Open Source Production Compared to Participative Systems in New Media Art." Doctoral thesis, University of Sunderland.

Staniszewski, Mary Anne. 1998. *The Power of Display: A History of Exhibition Installations at the Museum of Modern Art*. Cambridge, MA: MIT Press.

Taylor, Lindsay. 2014. "From Exhibition to Collection: Harris Museum and Art Gallery." In *New Collecting: Exhibiting and Audiences After New Media Art*, edited by Beryl Graham, 111–134. Farnham, UK: Ashgate.

V&A. 2010. "The V&A's Computer Art Collections." Accessed August 25, 2014. http://www.vam.ac.uk/content/articles/t/v-and-a-computer-art-collections/.

Veenhof, Sander. 2010. "DIY Day MoMA Oct 9th 2010: Augmented Reality Art Invasion!" Accessed August 25, 2014. http://www.sndrv.nl/moma/?page=press.

Zolghadr, Tirdad. 2010. "The Angry Middle Aged: Romance and the Possibilities of Adult Education in the Art World." In *Curating and the Educational Turn*, edited by Paul O'Neill and Mick Wilson, 157–164. London: Open Editions; Amsterdam: de Appel.

Beryl Graham is Professor of New Media Art at the School of Arts, Design and Media, University of Sunderland, United Kingdom, and is cofounder and coeditor of CRUMB. She curated the international exhibition *Serious Games* for the Laing and Barbican art galleries, and has also worked with SF Camerawork. Her book *Digital Media Art* was published by Heinemann in 2003, and she coauthored with Sarah Cook the book *Rethinking Curating: Art after New Media* for MIT Press in 2010, and edited *New Collecting: Exhibiting and Audiences* for Ashgate in 2014. She has presented papers at conferences including *Navigating Intelligence* (Banff), *Museums and the Web* (Vancouver), and *Decoding the Digital* (Victoria and Albert Museum).

21 DIFFUSED MUSEUMS
Networked, Augmented, and Self-Organized Collections

John Bell and Jon Ippolito

Not Here

> The Samek Art Gallery at Bucknell University is very pleased to announce that we
> will *not* be presenting the Augmented Reality artwork of the art collective, Manifest.AR
> from June 4 through November 27, 2011. (Samek Art Museum 2011)

So began the press release for the exhibition *Not Here*. Curiously, the artists of
Manifest.AR weren't featured in the 2011 Venice Biennale either. Even more of a
coincidence: the same works not featured in the Biennale were not featured in the
Samek show in Pennsylvania and not featured at the Kasa Gallery in Istanbul, all
during the same period. This exhibition/nonexhibition, reminiscent of Robert
Smithson's Site/Non-Site works, was made possible by augmented reality (AR).
Originally conceived to overlay useful data over a live video feed, AR software also
allows enterprising artists to position virtual versions of their works in real spaces,
at least on smartphones with cameras and AR apps. Point your phone at a street sign
or bush in a garden, and through its camera you might see a seemingly three-dimensional toad, or a wall text, or some other apparition floating in that physical location.
For the *Not Here* show, museum director Richard Rinehart, formerly of the Berkeley
Art Museum, tapped the same irreverent crew that hijacked the lobby of the
Museum of Modern Art in 2010 for the exhibition *We AR in MOMA*. This guerrilla
exhibition planted virtual artworks in MoMA's foyer, leaving guards and unaware
gallery-goers scratching their heads when they saw clued-in visitors pointing mobile
phones at blank walls and chattering about their favorite works (Sterling 2010).[1]

The International Handbooks of Museum Studies: Museum Media, First Edition.
Edited by Michelle Henning.
© 2015 John Wiley & Sons Ltd. Published 2020 by John Wiley & Sons Ltd.

Augmented reality lets artists and curators have their cake and eat it too, empowering them to exhibit multiple, conflicting installations in the same venue – and the same installation simultaneously in multiple venues. What's not (here) to like? Plenty, if you're a curator accustomed to deciding which art gets into your museum and which stays out. One of the Manifest.AR artists reports that the director of the otherwise avant-gardist Transmediale festival branded augmented reality art "offensive" (Tamiko Thiel, email to author, February 2, 2012). It's hard to believe such vehement reactions are based on AR's crude three-dimensional aesthetics rather than its boundary-crossing politics. Ironically, some of the same curators who seem blind to the promise of AR often espouse the ideals of openness exemplified by the technology. Manifest.AR's "AR Intervention" manifesto plays on this contradiction by bending quotes by 2011 Venice Biennale curator Bice Curiger to its own purpose:

As "one of the world's most important forums for the dissemination and illumination about the current developments in international art" the 54th Biennial of Venice could not justify its reputation without an uninvited Manifest.AR Augmented Reality infiltration. In order to "challenge the conventions through which contemporary art is viewed" we have constructed virtual AR pavilions directly amongst the 30-odd buildings of the lucky few within the Giardini. In accordance with the "ILLUMInations" theme and Bice Curiger's 5 questions our uninvited participation will not be bound by nation-state borders, by physical boundaries or by conventional art world structures. (Manifest.AR 2011)

The Venice Biennale has not invited Manifest.AR to exhibit these artworks. The Samek Art Gallery has invited the artists to not exhibit the works. Manifest.AR's Venice Biennale 2011 AR Intervention descends from the artistic lineage of Salons des Refusés and Institutional Critique. This project imbues healthy critique with a sense of play and offers a new lens through which to view questions of absence and presence, of center and periphery. Artists from Marcel Duchamp to Michael Asher to Andrea Fraser have shown that when an artist gestures beyond the limits of the current art world, they do not leave that world behind; instead they expand its borders. Manifest.AR is expanding the art world in a discursive sense as well as technologically and spatially. (Samek Art Museum 2011)

Of course, augmented reality doesn't do away with spatial coordinates, like net art often does (Ippolito 2006). Rather, it maps new information and imagery onto existing coordinates – in this case, latitudes and longitudes in the city of Venice and the environs of Bucknell University. So you have to be standing at one of those coordinates, as registered by the mobile phone in your hand, to see one of the works. As the Samek press release notes snarkily, "These artworks can be viewed from only two places on Earth: Venice, Italy and Lewisburg, PA. They can be not viewed from anywhere" (Samek Art Museum 2011). Some of the artworks on "display" echo the theme of who's not there, such as German artist Tamiko Thiel's *Shades of Absence*:

FIGURE 21.1   *Not Here* exhibition, as viewed by mobile phone, showing John Cleater's *Sky Pavilions*, Samek Art Museum, Bucknell University, Pennsylvania, August 29, 2011. Courtesy of Samek Art Museum.

> In these pavilions of absence images of contemporary artists whose works have been censored in this century are reduced to gold silhouettes and placed in the midst of terms of transgression. Each erased silhouette stands for countless unknown or lesser known artists who face censorship or persecution with no public support. Touching the artist silhouettes brings the viewer a website with information on censored artists, and instructions on how viewers can add new names and information via the web or Facebook.[2]

Manifest.AR chose to "exhibit" their works in some of the art world's most exclusive venues. Unlike creators of conventional public sculpture, augmented reality artists don't need permission to overlay data or imagery on a neighborhood, building, or even museum wall. Realizing the paradoxical relationship between real and virtual at the heart of augmented reality, Manifest.AR decided to replicate their Venice show at the Samek Art Gallery in Pennsylvania and the Kasa Gallery in Istanbul. The same works are "present" in all three locations, just identified with a different set of latitude and longitude coordinates (Figure 21.1).

Augmented reality is only one of the latest in a long chain of technologies initially resisted by museums despite their almost immediate embrace by artists. Some of those apparatuses, from holograms to Minitel, have died on the vine; others, like AR's elder brother virtual reality (VR), cling to life but have yet to bear fruit.[3] Others have transformed from an artistic plaything to a curatorial necessity. In 1995 artists produced 8 percent of all websites (Atkins 1998); almost two decades later, it is rare in the developed world for a museum to have no footprint at all on the web.

This chapter looks at two opportunities that have arisen for museums: the World Wide Web at the turn of the millennium, and hybridized digital–physical spaces in its second decade. We examine how museums responded to these challenges, including provocations initiated by the authors themselves, and how the altered versions of collection, exclusivity, and curation made possible by these new modes of operation question the definition of "museum." We conclude by comparing the struggles for control played out in curatorial circles with a model drawn from a very different community organized around creativity and culture: the producers and players of the strategy game *Civilization*.

The .museum ("Dot's not a museum!")

Augmented reality is only the latest virtual upstart to have muddled the definition of the museum. In 2000 the Internet Committee for Assigned Names and Numbers (ICANN), the nonprofit organization that oversees the use of Internet domains, approved the "dot-museum" global top-level domain (TLD). Up to that time, ICANN and its predecessors had only approved a handful of such global top-level domains, including .com, .org, and .net. These domain suffixes serve as an organizing scheme for web names at the highest level, so it was a surprise to many netizens when ICANN authorized the idiosyncratic .museum generic TLD (gTLD) to give a special place to museums on the web. Some observers noted the unprecedented specificity of .museum, wondering whether it would open the door to comparable domain suffixes like .travelservice and .florist. Yet for years afterward ICANN never used its authority to unilaterally designate any other industry-specific gTLD, with the exception of .aero.[4] Despite the initial resistance, especially among art museums, to embrace the web for their own purposes, ICANN had just handed brick-and-mortar curators an august pedestal on which to display their collections in cyberspace.

But some cried foul. On December 4, 2000 one of the authors of this essay, then Guggenheim curator and artist, Jon Ippolito, published an open letter to Cary Karp, then president of the Museum Domain Management Association and director of the Department of Information Technology at the Swedish Museum of National History.[5] Ippolito wrote that "in a time of accelerated change, small decisions can have far-reaching effects," noting that "even as innocent a choice as how to name websites can gently steer us toward a more open or closed society." Pointing to the identity crisis facing museums at the dawn of the digital age, Ippolito wrote:

> In a world where artists, musicians, and other producers can tap into the Internet to reach a far-flung audience instantaneously, it's understandable that brick-and-mortar institutions would be anxious to redefine themselves beyond their previous roles as centralized repositories of culture ... Of course, you can't redefine a plot of real estate – geographic or virtual – without redefining your neighbors' estates. Yet one question that I have not seen discussed in the public debate is how the addition of a .museum suffix might affect online creativity that takes place *outside* a museum setting.

The letter goes on to explain why .org offered museums a foothold on the web that stimulated rather than restricted innovation:

> Before .museum, all someone needed to try out a new curatorial paradigm was twenty-five dollars for a domain name, a healthy dose of sweat equity, and some

interesting content. Armed with .orgs and .nets, creative people found new ways to share culture outside of the constraints of the offline status quo. For artists, this meant exhibiting on the Web's boundless frontier instead of trying to get a foot in the door of a SoHo gallery. For critics, it meant posting to unmoderated listserves instead of pining to be published in *Art in America*. For viewers with a modem, it meant looking at art anytime, anywhere – without paying MoMA's admission price. Art thrived in this environment ... And because there was no special naming convention to segregate artworks from the rest of culture, many people stumbled upon art sites who might never have stepped foot inside a museum.

Enter .museum. In contrast to generic suffixes like .org and .edu, .museum represents a much more restricted criterion. For the first time, permission to register a top-level domain was determined by membership in a private association, the International Council of Museums (ICOM), the vast majority of whose members – we must be honest here – had hitherto treated the Internet primarily as an electronic billboard to advertise their offline programs. (By comparison, academic institutions have a reasonable claim to .edu given that they helped get the fledgling Internet on its feet; indeed a handful of prominent universities, including Carnegie Mellon University and the University of California, Berkeley, had already registered .edu domains by 1985.)

For its part, ICOM had already stated that a major goal of the new domain suffix was to bridge the digital divide:

> Many museums already have a presence on the Internet, while others, due partly to financial and technical limitations, are moving into cyberspace more slowly. Developing a clear cyberspace identity for the museum community as a whole is expected to help bridge this digital divide. Proponents believe that .museum, along with value-added services that can be provided to its members, will give museums that have not yet participated actively in the development of the Internet the support to do so. (ICOM 2000a)

This goal seemed in line with ICANN's task of expanding the web's namespace without undermining its open architecture. And, although they had rejected suffixes like .union and .health as insufficiently democratic, ICANN's governors seemed convinced that the availability of .museum domains would encourage more small museums to take the leap into cyberspace.

Ippolito and like-minded critics were unconvinced. What of the countless offline alternative spaces and exhibition halls that do not maintain a permanent collection of objects? Many have played critical roles in nurturing contemporary artists and movements. Artists Space nurtured Cindy Sherman's career, while a show at the Cincinnati Contemporary Art Center guaranteed Robert Mapplethorpe's notoriety. Yet, once museums have claimed the best of the virtual real estate, what chance do these numerous alternative spaces have of competing for hits from web surfers who've never heard of them? In an attention economy like the web, small advantages can make big differences. Suppose an art history student looks up the artist Bill Viola in a search engine and gets links for five .orgs and one .museum. Which link is she going to follow?

The gap between .museum haves and have-nots looks even wider once we take into account the countless virtual studios and exhibition spaces where artists create and exhibit their work. There are a host of fascinating and valuable museum-like resources online that would not qualify for ICOM's definition of a museum – which in 2000 still required institutions to collect *material*.[6] This definition excludes all online cultural archives, whether they collect Internet art projects, digital videos of political conventions, or audio testimonies to the Holocaust.[7] Some in the online community at the time viewed ICOM's support for .museum as a smokescreen to cover the embarrassing fact that artist collectives and online art sites, from äda'web to Nicholas Pioch's WebLouvre, had established important online presences well before their brick-and-mortar equivalents. If the shoe were on the other foot, wouldn't brick-and-mortar institutions balk at a rule that forbade them from using the word "museum" in their signage if they didn't have a website?

If .museum doesn't exactly bridge the digital divide, then perhaps its true benefit lies merely in convenience. Certainly .museum would make it easier for people specifically in search of brick-and-mortar museums, though studies indicate that surprisingly few people actually look for things online by guessing the URL – they use search engines instead.[8] Another convenience ascribed to .museum was the reduction in time-consuming cybersquatting litigation. Yet registering "museumofmodernart.museum" by itself will do nothing to stop others from registering such homonyms as "themuseumofmodernart.org" or "museum-of-modern-art.org" (memo to MoMA: you missed these).

To a curator at a prestigious museum like MoMA, watching hundreds of visitors stream through the main entrance, the fuss over .museum probably seemed like a tempest in a teapot. The year 2000 was a dozen years before the Google Art Project offered digital paintings at higher resolutions than the artists themselves saw them and the San Francisco Museum of Asian Art let visitors scan their artifacts in 3D using handheld cameras and phones (Ippolito 2012). In the 1990s the typical virtual museum had been little more than a handful of postage stamp sized GIFs of artifacts, dithered in 216 web-safe colors, set against one of Web 1.0's frightful tiled background textures. It doesn't make sense that curators would kick up a fuss about the URL that showed in a browser's location bar at a time when websites were just crappy versions of print brochures, and online visitors represented such a tiny sliver of visitors.

The curators who created innovative websites cared, because they knew something the brick-and-mortar curators didn't – something they saw in their server logs. Online visitors were already rivalling offline ones. In 2003 the Metropolitan Museum of Art, New York, perhaps the best-known brick-and-mortar museum, contained two million artworks and had five million visitors per year, for a total of 2.5 visits per artwork. That same year, the online art portal Rhizome.org, one of the best-known virtual "museums," showed only 600 artworks but had four million visitors per year, for a total of 7,000 visits per artwork.

To their credit, forward-thinking brick-and-mortar curators like Cary Karp anticipated this flood of online visitors back in the 1990s, which is why they lobbied ICANN hard to approve .museum. Yet critics saw .museum not as paving the way for virtual museums as but paving *over* museum-like virtual collections that had already established a foothold in cyberspace. These ranged from Nicholas Pioch's WebLouvre, which was far more comprehensive and better researched and illustrated than the Louvre's official website, to the Last Real Net Art Museum, which exhaustively documented a single work's social context, to UbuWeb, whose extensive online archive made avant-garde audio and video more accessible than any videotape distributor of its time (Goldsmith 2011; Lialina 2011). Pioch's WebLouvre, created when he was only a student, was later rechristened WebMuseum to avoid litigation, and mirror sites prevented it from being shut down.

To counteract the shadow that .museum might cast on the broader cultural landscape, Ippolito asked whether ICOM should drop the requirement that registrants of .museum fit its definition of a museum, and suggested provocatively that ICANN could require registrants to supply new definitions to be uploaded to www.icom.org to stimulate debate on the subject. His letter concluded:

> Our mandate as museums is not to compete with the cultural production going on outside our walls, but to reflect and preserve it. How unfortunate it would be for established museums to unwittingly erase the heritage they are meant to preserve by gerrymandering the name space … It would be especially misguided for institutions whose mandate is to preserve history to condone a protocol that would encourage its erasure.[9]

In the end it was .museum that was effectively erased. By July of 2001 the director of the Whitney Museum of American Art, Maxwell Anderson, was lamenting the suffix's elitism in the *New York Times* (Mirapaul 2001). Today, although it is an official gTLD, only about 10 percent of brick-and-mortar museums have registered a .museum domain and the vast majority of web surfers don't even know it exists.[10]

What did this dot-fizzle mean for the definition of a museum? It meant that brick-and-mortar museums had to prove their mettle on the Internet by creating robust and innovative sites rather than resting on their gTLD laurels. And it made room for models like UbuWeb and the Last Real Net Art Museum to extend the definition to exploit the interactivity and reach of the Internet. As if in sympathy, the very ICOM definition of museum changed in 2001 to include "tangible and intangible" collections (ICOM 2001).

The vernacular museum

What has been the result of this extended definition of the curatorial instinct? A decade later, now that the typical Internet user swims in a sea of social media, brick-and-mortar museums represent less than 1 percent of curating. If curating means making sense of cultural creations via selection, organization, and presentation, then there are now scores, if not hundreds, of digital platforms devoted to this: Tumblr, Delicious, Instagram, Flickr, and on and on. To be sure, some activities that are today called "curating" are a far stretch from the term's original scope. Do you really "curate" a food stand, or your Facebook time line? Choire Sicha of *The Awl* dismisses this everyday curating altogether:

> As a former actual curator, of like, actual art and whatnot, I think I'm fairly well positioned to say that you folks with your blog and your Tumblr and your whatever are not actually engaged in a practice of curation. Call it what you like: aggregating? Blogging? Choosing? Copyright infringing sometimes? But it's not actually curation, or anything like it. (Sicha 2012)

It's easy for curators of prestigious museums to pooh-pooh this form of vernacular curation. After all, in many museums the role of the curator is defined not just by the activities performed but by the power vested in the office. Curators often receive ranks based on the academic model, from adjunct to assistant to associate to full curator. In the United States, traditional museum departments are even more hierarchical than university departments, in that full curators are often the bosses of curators under them, and in general curators decide exhibitions and policies much more than registrars, conservators, or visitor service staff.

Vernacular curating breaks the hierarchy of curating, especially the stereotype of curator as alpha male. In the early 2010s one in five women online in the United States use Pinterest, a social network that enables users to "re-pin" images and other snippets from websites. Some observers chalk up Pinterest's rapid take-up among women to a preponderance of gender-stereotypical content, from cupcake recipes to gardening tips to wedding invitations. Others, including Carina Chocano writing in the *New York Times,* see advertising as an influence:

> Your average Pinterest board or inspiration Tumblr basically functions as a longing machine … Pinterest's sudden and spectacular rise has been met with some skepticism, and it's often talked about in that particular dismissive way reserved for things that have the temerity to seem both frivolous and feminine. Not surprisingly, some of this loathing is internalized. Someone on Pinterest once posted a slide that read: "Pinterest: Where women go to plan imaginary weddings, dress children that don't exist and decorate homes we can't afford." But to focus on the "aspirational" aspect is to miss the point. People don't post stuff because they wish they owned it, but because they think they are it, and they long to be understood, which is different. (Chocano 2012)

Surprisingly, another reason for Pinterest's popularity among women may be that it offers one of the most curatorial of social media interfaces. A typical pinboard tiles images across the entire screen in two dimensions, in contrast to the inappropriately named "wall" of Facebook, which as of 2013 is actually a linear time line in which images play a supporting role to textual updates. By contrast, Pinterest's crowded pinboards call to mind nineteenth-century salon-style hangings, in which the walls were covered with a mosaic of individual paintings. While the Paris Salon hung paintings chockablock from just below eye level all the way up to the ceiling, Pinterest turns this wall upside down, so that the images begin at eye level and the user must scroll down to follow their (seemingly) endless progression back in time.

So it may be more than high heels and hairdos that attract women to Pinterest. Writer Rahel Aima claims Pinterest and similar microblogging platforms remind us of the feminine roots of the curatorial instinct:

> Rather than simply creating as an artisan might, the microblogger-as-curator brings objects together, contextualizing and co-producing the space at hand – be it in a physical gallery or online – with the help of various network technologies. Curation is a word long associated with the performance of traditionally feminized labor: A putting together, an assembling, a nurturing, a taking care of things and people. Curing hams and charcuterie and "putting up" produce for the winter. Chicken soup for the common cold; restoratives, remedies, and healing. It's unpaid labor that structures and enables paid, productive labor. (Aima 2012)

Today, some brick-and-mortar museums are determined not to be left behind the curve again – whether technological or gendered – and are beginning to supplement their gallery curating with this vernacular curation. Steve.museum is a multi-institution effort which enables visitors to add descriptive tags to works in an online collection. Visitors from the Internet helped to select the works on view in New York's Museum of Modern Art for the exhibition *The Residents: Re-viewed* (2006), the Brooklyn Museum's *Click! A Crowd-Curated Exhibition* (2008), and the Guggenheim's *YouTube Play* (2010) (Lavallee 2006). Some programs for curators-in-training, including the University of Maine's Digital Curation program founded by the authors of this essay, teach both professional and vernacular curating.[11]

The Variable Museum

As of this writing, in the 2010s, augmented reality projects – whether authorized by a museum or not – carry on the Internet's decentering of the authoritative curatorial voice in a mobile context. Like the ill-fated .museum suffix, handheld apps developed or commissioned by museums offer an "official," trusted guide to the collection and exhibitions. But that hasn't stopped unofficial augmented reality

FIGURE 21.2 John Bell, *The Variable Museum.*

from wrapping the museum in its own mantle, as we saw in the case of Manifest. AR mentioned in this chapter's introduction.[12]

Museums can no longer make authoritative statements because works are multivalent and visitors need to negotiate their meanings among themselves. In John Bell's AR artwork *The Variable Museum* each museum-goer in a group has her own viewer which, when pointed at the same physical location, shows a different digital artifact added to the space (Figure 21.2). As a trivial example, one might see a playing card, such as an ace of hearts, floating in a corner; this might not mean much by itself, but when combined with cards viewed by other visitors may convey the concept of a royal flush. In *The Variable Museum*, augmented reality doles out a different vision to each visitor, forcing them to share descriptions with each other to understand the collective experience.

In a recent article, Bell argues that *The Variable Museum*'s implementation of augmented reality requires a slightly different set of definitions than the standard museum experience:

> *The Variable Museum* makes third party contextualization an integral part of the work. However, doing so requires tweaking the vocabulary of art and coming up with some new definitions.
> - Artifact – an individual work, what would usually be called an artwork (e.g., a painting, a sculpture, an installation).
> - Set – A collection of multiple artifacts that form a paradigmatic group. For the purposes of *The Variable Museum*, the individual artifacts are fungible.

FIGURE 21.3 Physical marker indicating the presence of an artwork in John Bell's *The Variable Museum*. (For a color version of this figure, please see the color plate section.)

- Artwork (or piece) – in *The Variable Museum*, an artwork can be understood to be a physical location in the gallery where a set is placed. The artwork is represented to individual visitors as a single artifact. Construction of the final piece is only possible when multiple visitors combine their experiences of the artifacts they perceive in that location. (Bell 2013, 18)

The Variable Museum's use of augmented reality leaves little room for authoritative curatorial statements. The people who see each of the individual artifacts are charged with defining them to others, so a description from museum staff would subvert their participation in the artwork. Explaining the paradigm that unites a set would also give the game away. The most a museum could do would be to point out where in the room visitors should point their smartphones or AR goggles; but even that is a function made unnecessary by *The Variable Museum*'s use of physical markers to indicate where an artwork exists (Figure 21.3).

Which is not to say that there is no curatorial role at all involved in an exhibition of *The Variable Museum*. Bell's model is based on artist-curators who select the artifacts seen and determine the sets linking them at each instantiation of the museum. While he insists on some basic ground rules designed to facilitate communication, such as visitors only being allowed to enter in groups and that the AR viewers used should not be easily shareable whenever possible, *The Variable Museum*'s thesis boils down to an interpretation of how individualized augmented reality experiences differ from both shared physical or virtual experiences. As he has explained:

This set of rules clearly leaves a great deal open to interpretation. Specific means of displaying artifacts, the paradigms and artwork under consideration, and the installation of *The Variable Museum* itself are all left to the artists in charge of each iteration of the piece. Instead, the core of *The Variable Museum* is an idea: when several people in the same space are given partial experiences of an artwork, communication between them will develop a shared connotative meaning that is different than if they were all given the complete experience. (Bell 2013, 19)

The Variable Museum hands a great deal of the responsibility for curation over to the people who walk through it by encouraging them to provide context to others about the works they see. The artist-curator nominally in charge may select the artifacts and define the sets that go into it, but the individuals put the pieces together and ultimately decide what they mean. The woman who sees a paper crane and describes it as a table decoration is curating into existence a different artwork than the man who recalls it as part of a Senbazuru at his wedding, prompting different responses and associations from the other visitors they are talking to.

Augmented reality provides a mechanism for further pushing the museum out into the world, but it also allows the world to push into the museum. The argument that a .museum gTLD would only serve to dismiss museum-like behavior if it is not officially sanctioned is now being brought to the physical world. Augmented reality works like *The Variable Museum* allow curators to be defined by their actions rather than their museum job titles. Just as a museum's website gains little prestige from its web suffix – which forces it to innovate online – in the augmented reality world an exhibit will gain little from being held in a museum if it is not also innovative, engaging, and open. Augmented museums should be willing to compete for meritocratic clout rather than assume autocratic authority, or else understand that they will be sharing that authority with the visitors themselves.

The self-organized museum

While vernacular and variable museums may share the idea that curation is not the sole right of museum-appointed staff, they still maintain that it is an individual that is responsible for curating. Pinterest boards are individual collections created when a user plucks images from the larger stream of content flowing through the system. *The Variable Museum's* artifacts and sets are chosen by whoever is staging an iteration of the piece. The strength of both models is that the end user is given the ultimate responsibility to remix inputs and customize his experience, but in neither system is that experience shared with more than a few virtual or physical friends.

Other networked museums are built around community curation, where not only do the members of the community have input on what work is featured, but the work itself dictates its own curation. This is often the case when the work has a functional aspect as well as an experiential side, as in the case of video game archives. While large brick-and-mortar museums like MoMA and Stanford have begun to collect games in the 2010s, game communities have been curating a variety of game experiences on the web since its inception. Unlike institutional curators or even artist-curators, these game communities have been truly group-based mechanisms for determining significance and quality for much of their existence.

The *Sid Meier's Civilization* line of games is widely acknowledged as one of the most significant game franchises ever made and has a correspondingly large community of fans (Adams, Butts, and Onyett 2007). In 2014 the largest fan site is the Civilization Fanatics Center with over 60,000 active contributors discussing the franchise. In addition to discussing the games, though, this community has been creating game mods – add-ons that alter the game experience – since *Sid Meier's Civilization II* was released in 1996. Civilization Fanatics Center lists almost 19,000 mods, utilities, and content packs spanning the seven games it follows, with well over 12 million downloads of those files.

Archiving 19,000 files on any given subject is not a particularly unique accomplishment for a website. These mods are not only archived, though; they have been created and curated continuously through years of changing game platforms and player expectations. This Darwinian mode of curation rewards mods that provide the most unique, fun, or satisfying gameplay experience as judged by the community itself. Individual creators are responsible for many of the files, but the most visible mods are maintained by stewards more than coders. One mod, titled *Fall from Heaven*, has almost 300,000 posts discussing what should be in, what should be out, and even collections of secondary mods that alter its alterations to the original game. The community has demonstrated that it is more than a mechanistic debugging tool by supporting unique gameplay experiences whether they are fully functional or not, working to get them to the level of playability, and then polish. The result is a diverse set of curated experiences that the entire community can download and share.

Under this model, the community of curators grants relevance to its host institution – in this case, Civilization Fanatics Center. Should the community decide that Civilization Fanatics Center is no longer suitable, they will simply move themselves and their content to another host and declare it the new institution. The *Civilization* game community has done this several times already, with previously leading sites turned into virtual ghost towns in a matter of months. A curator at MoMA may find that freedom difficult to copy. The prestige that MoMA holds is based on its history and collection; it is shared with its curators as they come and go far more than the other way around.

The self-organized museum can only thrive in certain kinds of environments, some of which are becoming increasingly threatened by encroaching commercial interests. Supporting communities are both the creators and consumers of a self-organized museum, but as networked communities have faced greater algorithmic moderation they have fractured and been distanced from collective creation. Facebook, Google, and other intermediary sites impose structures that older host software like bulletin boards or Usenet did not (Pariser 2011). The success of the

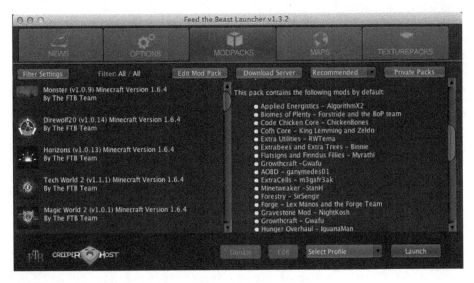

FIGURE 21.4   "Feed the Beast" launcher showing mod pack.
© Feed-the-beast.com.

self-organized game museum has prompted game developers to create their own specialized community software which enforces rules empowering the company over the community.[13] From Apple's App Store to Valve's Steam environment, attempts to monetize the community have instead separated it from its roots. It is instructive to see how these systems have damaged the communities they ostensibly support by enforcing assumptions that are either expedient to the development of their software or supportive of monetization over creative freedoms. Inherent in social networking era game communities is the idea that curated objects are atomic and that individuals create them. Unlike *Fall from Heaven*'s 300,000 posts of give-and-take discussion, community feedback about a mod on Steam is limited to a thumbs up or thumbs down and a brief comment (Valve Software 2012). As a result, Steam-based mods are algorithmically ranked and displayed to users based on data so simple that they are not curated in any meaningful sense of the term. When the community lacks the tools to communicate, it cannot create or curate.

In more open environments self-organized collections are growing in new directions. An even more mod-friendly game launched in 2009 is Mojang's *Minecraft*. *Minecraft*'s community is vast, decentralized across many different forums and wikis, and – because of the nature of *Minecraft* as a game – composed of individuals who are very interested in working together to build. An exact count of *Minecraft*'s mods is difficult to obtain, but one index site lists 569 as of this writing.[14] Beyond the group development and feedback model of *Civilization*'s community curation, *Minecraft*'s community has built complex loaders that package multiple mods together to provide radically different gameplay and aesthetic experiences. The "Feed the Beast" loader allows subgroups within the community to collect a series of interoperable mods and publish them to other players as their ideal variant of the game (Figure 21.4). Some "Feed the Beast" packs are relatively simple, while others can contain more than 60 discrete mods and create a game that would make the head of a player used to vanilla *Minecraft* spin.

The idea that curation results in diverging sets of possibilities is antithetical to the traditional role of narrowing exhibition possibilities down to a single display, but it is the result of self-organization. Community-based curation will rarely end in total agreement but the flexibility of the network ensures that, no matter which perspective on a work wins the day, the runners-up will not be shunted to the side and neglected. Even the brick-and-mortar museum has to accept that they are no longer singular authoritative voices on the artifacts they exhibit and that the voices of outside experts are at the fingertips of anyone with a smartphone should they decide to use it. The only question is whether future curators will embrace their community co-curators or attempt to reject them and fail.

The disappearing museum

Bell's *Variable Museum* challenges the expectation that all visitors see the same thing when they look at a museum wall. This chapter will conclude with a look at how augmented reality can do away with museum walls altogether.

In 1947 writer Andre Malraux argued that the reproductions of artworks circulating throughout society in the form of photographs, engravings, and the like form a *musée imaginaire*, which English commentators translated as a "museum without walls."[15] In the 1960s and 1970s Malraux's notion seemed reborn in art conceived and performed in the open, such as Daniel Buren's striped sandwich boards carried through the streets of Paris. By the 1990s advocates of museums on the web were applying the term to online collections, and in the 2000s the advent of mobile devices that could access place-based multimedia content encouraged innovators to extend the concept to the urban histories.

Many of today's device-guided "exhibitions" still follow the model of the Acoustiguide gallery tour popular in late twentieth-century museums, whereby museum-goers could press a button on their earphones corresponding to an artifact on view to hear a celebrity or museum director interpret it for them.[16] Some, such as Philadelphia's public art program, have begun to broaden the range of perspectives voiced in mobile devices and to deploy them outside the museum proper:

> Museum Without Walls™: AUDIO is a new kind of interpretive program for Philadelphia's public art. Each audio program is told by a variety of people from all walks of life who are connected to the sculpture by knowledge, experience or affiliation. Nearly 100 "voices" at 35 stops explore 51 sculptures along the Benjamin Franklin Parkway and Kelly Drive.[17]

In a 2012 Humanities, Arts, Science, and Technology Alliance and Collaboratory (HASTAC) discussion on "The Future of Museums," a number of participants raised cautions about the distancing nature of digital technology. Susana Bautista of the University of Southern California observed that, more than predigested interpretation, audiences now want to experience culture directly. Amy Atticks of Brown University Library struck a familiar note:

> The sense of the "sublime" and some amount of "aura" might be lost in translation between the physical and the digital, and there is definitely invested social and cultural value in places, presence, and the senses (smell, touch, and otherwise), that screens and current digital technologies can't quite replicate. (HASTAC 2012)

Vivian Shaw of the University of Texas at Austin pointed to emotions associated with particular places that might only be tapped by physical proximity, such as the Hiroshima Peace Memorial Museum:

> I am thinking about how museums' ability to craft and produce experiences is particularly important in the contexts of "trauma site museums" … places of historical violence (prisons, death camps) that have been converted into museums. An argument can also be made to add to this definition museums that have been built post-facto in places that have suffered catastrophic trauma, violence, and disaster … the museum authority and expertise, then, connects intimately with their physical and geographic proximity to this trauma. (HASTAC 2012)

Shaw extended her implicit critique of virtual museums to suggest that their disconnection from a geographic site could contribute to consolidating one authoritative interpretation of the site.

> In looking at the changing experience of the digitized museum, perhaps we can meditate on how, in addition to centralizing information, "authority" stakes a claim over the ethical and sensory meanings associated with physical spaces. As museum websites display narratives that are arguably more limited and less experiential is some consolidation of authority at work? Do tourists become less motivated to visit "far-flung" museum sites if they can already "see what's inside" on a website? (HASTAC 2012)

Shaw's concerns are entirely legitimate for the vast majority of digital museums – because the vast majority of digital museums consist merely of websites offering authoritative, predigested interpretations. Yet, for a site of historical importance, augmented reality can be *less* virtual than a physical museum.

Imagine letting visitors wander the grounds of a site such as Ellis Island or Dachau in its original uncurated state, accompanied by an augmented reality app that lets them share their personal histories with, and reactions to, specific artifacts (via image recognition) or locations (via GPS). Such a "museum" would require only a smartphone – no wall panels, no labels, no gift shop, maybe a few "experts" hired to add their perspectives. It could be deployed anywhere there is mobile coverage – on the train to the site, in the surrounding woods – truly a museum without walls.

An urban trauma zone that has already inspired augmented reality apps is Ground Zero, the former site of the World Trade Center in New York City destroyed during the 9/11 blowback attacks. Working with the National September 11 Memorial & Museum, Jake Barton helped create the iPhone app *Explore 9/11*, which overlays photographs taken on the day the towers came down, geo-located to the phone's current position, to what is currently seen in the camera. For example, a tourist exiting the Fulton Street subway might see images of smoke, debris, and scrambling firefighters superimposed on the routine bustle of lower Broadway (Segall 2011). Another AR app, meanwhile, recreates a floating outline of the Twin Towers when the phone is aimed at the place they once stood. This app by Brian August lets a user post a photo of the skyline including these ghostly towers with a note to a shared map that shows all the images posted by users from different angles and locations, from the East River Ferry to the Brooklyn–Queens Expressway (Kessler 2011).

Clearly such AR apps offer new techniques for presenting and generating historical information related to a landmark – not to mention entirely new social expectations for what it means to "visit a museum."[18] Barton thinks so: "It's really important to basically meet people where they are in their daily life. You don't think about history as just ending up on books or in encyclopedias" (Segall 2011).

Yet we might still ask whether this strategy ultimately distances the viewer from the physical matter at hand, whether footprints where T. rex once walked or holes where towers used to be. Isn't AR used this way yet another digital doppelgänger, a distracting virtual add-on to the museum's traditional interpretive arsenal of wall texts and catalogs?

No: AR cuts sideways across the apparent spectrum between the physical and the virtual. We think of digital overlays or representations as mediation of real experience, and rightly so. But what about wall labels, pedestals, mannikins, special lighting? These are compulsory intrusions into the physical neighborhood of an artifact – and more often than not replacements for the artifact's native neighborhood.

When we look through the glass screen of a smartphone pointed at a physical object, is that so different from looking at the object through a vitrine silk-screened with didactic text? Sure, we're used to associating vitrines with the respectable distance accorded *La Gioconda* in the Louvre or *La Pietà* in St. Peter's Basilica, and mobile phones with the disrespectful intrusiveness of paparazzi chasing celebrities on the streets of Paris and Rome. But is "distance" the correct touchstone for appreciation or respect? When a proud mother snaps a photo of her baby to text to grandma, is that a sign she doesn't appreciate her child? Many historical sites, especially those in cities, are alive with a shifting population of inhabitants and a changing built environment; it makes no more sense to put them behind a vitrine than to put a human baby behind one.

With augmented reality, we might view museological data overlaid on a Māori dugout moored in New Zealand, or a cannonball embedded in a house facade in Stockholm. Would this experience be more mediated than viewing these objects in a glass case in New York? And wouldn't the option *not* to add a museological layer to the experience – to turn off the screen and view the object in its uncurated state – make AR more respectful of the physical ambience that gives these objects meaning?[19] In *Re-collection: Art, New Media, and Social Memory*, Richard Rinehart and Jon Ippolito (2014) look at examples of museums that have chosen to strip away conventional layers of mediation, whether virtual or vitreous. In place of a gallery with didactic panels, archaeologists chose to plant a 12 acre grove on the original site of ancient Greek garden of Kolymbetra. Naturalists like Vanessa Vobis at the Los Angeles Museum of Natural History are foregoing dioramas of taxidermied animals for real critters living in an urban wildlife habitat (Shahbazi 2012). Do visitors need a museum cafe if they can pick oranges grown in ancient groves and bring them home? Do visitors need a lecture on indigenous culture, if they can step into a dugout canoe and paddle out with the Māori?

To some, this radical regrounding in the world may smack of what Barbara Kirshenblatt-Gimblett (1998) calls "destination culture," a theatrical process by which contemporary museums emulate theme parks to privilege the destination over the source. For example, Ellis Island's Immigration Museum supposedly documents the experience of the millions of would-be Americans who wound their way through its processing facility. Yet, Kirshenblatt-Gimblett argues, the ongoing exhibition glosses over the messy details of these immigrants' varied ethnic and geographic points of origin to focus on their story of becoming US citizens. Even sites of primarily scientific interest can suffer from "destination culture"; when dinosaur animatronics trump dinosaur bones, the resulting spectacle may become more entertainment than edification.

Is the solution to "destination culture" for museums to retreat from the world, cloistering their collections safely inside vitrines girded by authoritative wall texts? Perhaps even to forbid the use of personal devices in their galleries, to prevent highbrow culture from being contaminated by spectacle?

Certainly not. If museums are to shift the way they engage visitors, the goal should be not to make the world more like a museum, but to make museums more like the world. Augmented reality and other nonexclusive forms of information juxtaposition offer the possibility of overlaying new perspectives onto dusty artifacts and orthodox interpretations – of diversifying rather than homogenizing culture. The river paddled by the Māori may be a destination, but it is also the source – and no one knows its history and significance better than the Māori. When anthropologists at the Museum of Archaeology and Anthropology at Cambridge discovered that 70 percent of their Zuni artifacts were wrongly cataloged, they partnered with Zuni representative Jim Enote to invite Zuni tribespeople to describe the artifacts themselves, and added a new field to their database to accommodate these alternative descriptions (Budka 2008).[20] Prompted by concern that a Passamaquoddy dictionary under development at the University of Maine omitted the cultural context of this native tongue, Ian Larson distributed iBooks to Passamaquoddy children and asked them to videotape the stories of their grandparents. The children then uploaded these videos to a website that made it easy to tag and define vocabulary words used in one or more of the stories.[21] Thanks to distributed means of documenting and curating culture, "indigenous peoples are thus regaining authorship and ownership of their objects" (Budka 2008).

Writing in "The Future of Museums" forum, Bautista observed that museums need to be smarter mediators to adapt to a changing society (HASTAC 2012). What is often forgotten is that conventional museums remain stuck like amber in a form of mediation that derives from papal collections of the fifteenth century: untouchable relics ensconced in vitrines and on pedestals, described in wall texts written from an omniscient perspective.[22]

Technology by itself is no panacea for this anachronistic autocracy. Five-figure climate control systems, video surveillance, infrared detectors that buzz when a visitor steps too close – these all reinforce a work's aura at the expense of genuine human connection. Even efforts to squeeze collections onto websites or into interactive kiosks usually end up reproducing the one-to-many broadcast paradigm of a museum's physical galleries.

Curation always implies mediation. Yet, as this chapter has argued, recent curatorial paradigms have expanded both the range of mediators – from professional to amateur – and the sites of mediation – from geographic to virtual. Museums need to learn these new paradigms, and in order to do this they need curators trained with social media skills as well as an open mind. (Who are the experts in the Passamaquoddy language if not the native speakers themselves?) In recent years, several digital curation programs have emerged in universities across the United States. How many will teach that privileging wall texts over augmented reality may unintentionally dissociate viewers further from first-hand experience?

Curators in training aren't going to leap to that sort of curb-jumping conclusion from studying how museums have done things in the past. Museum studies and curation programs need to ensure their curricula are designed to help curators see the deeper effects of their choices of mediation, hopefully informed by more than knee-jerk reactions to new forms of presentation and preservation.

Conclusion

As popular media industries have learned (with much distress), the large-scale deployment of new network, storage, and output technologies since the early 1990s has led to a sea change in the way people consume media. Museums have been partially insulated from these changes by their emphasis on unique artifacts as well as conventions and demographics that favor slower technological adoption. When museums have explored new technologies, by and large they have deployed hierarchic systems that further their traditional forms of control over audience experience and interpretation. This has put them at odds with the global trend since the early 2000s toward technologies of participation, including the Web 2.0 dynamic that now drives most vernacular curation, from reputation economies like Amazon and Netflix to social media such as Tumblr and Facebook. Likewise, art museum cataloging systems don't allow multiple viewpoints, or even admit that an artifact may change over time. Their paradigm for preservation looks to experts in labs, whereas the most energized preservation strategies are emerging from amateurs distributed across the Internet in a manner similar to *Civilization*'s modders (Rinehart and Ippolito 2014).

The strapline of ICOM's 2000 press release touting the new .museum domain declared, "General public to benefit from unified museum presence on Internet," while Kenneth Hamma, director of MuseDoma and assistant director of the J. Paul Getty Museum, stated: "this shared domain will help museums coalesce their efforts on the World Wide Web. It will be of special benefit to museums that have yet to establish themselves online. A shared domain identity is precisely what is needed" (ICOM 2000b). While indirectly signaling that museums had been behind the technological curve, these quotes made the claim that a remedy would be found in a unified identify for all museums that "coalesces" their online presence.

Perhaps the creators of .museum really didn't mean to apply domain names exclusively, but in fact to diversify the Internet's native namespace. If that's truly so, then they are about to get their wish in spades. In February 2014 ICANN opened up over 1000 newly approved global top-level domains, with names as arbitrary as .ninja, .pink, and even .wtf (Shankland 2013). On the one hand, the riot of new domains is bad news for Goliaths like Pepsi and KFC, which are now obliged to police their trademark across a plethora of domains like Pepsi.buy or KFC.food (Bachman 2014). On the other hand, an organization has to fork over $185,000 to ICANN to become the official registrar of one of these new domains, a cost that puts controlling a new domain out of reach of the Davids – including most if not all museums (Shankland 2014). In its atypical specificity compared to the more generic .com and .org, .museum inadvertently paved the way for new domains such as .show, .gallery, .photography, and the like.[23] Unfortunately for curators bent on shoring up their institutional clout, the potential chaos of hundreds of proliferating domains seems to have furnished museums with more competition than visibility.

In the end, it doesn't help for museums to embrace widgets and gizmos if they deploy them to constrain access to culture. The best way for curators to surmount obstacles to networked, augmented, and self-organized collections isn't to hire more IT staff or increase their budgets; it's to recognize and enlist co-curators outside their walls who can help shoulder the daunting responsibility of sustaining cultural memory. In this way, by enabling alternative voices and models, museums can learn to augment their patrons' view of reality instead of policing it.

Notes

1 See also Chapter 20 by Beryl Graham in this volume.

2 http://www.manifestar.info/venicebiennial2011/descr-shades.php (accessed September 10, 2014).

3 As of this writing (2014), many VR advocates hope the inexpensive Occulus Rift headset will lower the bar to virtual reality gaming.

4 Like .museum, .aero struck many Internet observers as overly specific in 2000, yet it appears to be actually used in the industry (http://en.wikipedia.org/wiki/.aero, accessed August 25, 2014). As we'll see, ICANN eventually approved a wide swath of gTLD designations to be managed by any organization that could raise the $185,000 fee.

5 The letter was also addressed to Valerie Jullien, communications officer of the International Council of Museums, and Kenneth Hamma, assistant director of the J. Paul Getty Museum, and was published in several locations online, including http://www.nettime.org/Lists-Archives/nettime-l-0012/msg00070.html (accessed August 25, 2014). Ippolito was not writing on behalf of the Guggenheim Museum, his employer at the time.

6 The ICOM definition operative in 2000 was the one ratified in 1995, which began: "A museum is a non-profit making permanent institution in the service of society and of its development, and open to the public which acquires, conserves, researches, communicates and exhibits, for purposes of study, education and enjoyment, material evidence of people and their environment" (ICOM 2001).

7 Of course, there were many quirky collections already on the web in 2000; the website of the Museum of Jurassic Technology, whose exhibitions include supernatural remedies and micro-mosaics made from butterfly wings, dates back to 1996 (Internet Archive Wayback Machine search for "www.mjt.org," http://web.archive.org/web/19961001000000*/http://www.mjt.org/, accessed February 6, 2014). Then again, many websites of "mainstream" museums from the period seemed to be just as quirky as their nonaccredited counterparts; at the time when the controversy over .museum came to a head, in December 2000, the main feature of the website of the Swedish Museum of Natural History, where Cary Karp worked, was an exhibition on "dung mosses" (Internet Archive Wayback Machine, "Swedish Museum of Natural History," snapshot from December 3, 2000, http://web.archive.org/web/20001203064700/http://www.nrm.se/, accessed February 6, 2014).

8 Remarkably, even in 2010 an astounding number of Internet users still found Facebook via Google rather than directly visiting Facebook.com (Barry Schwartz, "Facebook Top Search Query at Google, Bing & Yahoo," Search Engine Land, April 28, 2010, http://searchengineland.com/facebook-top-search-query-at-google-bing-yahoo-40923, accessed August 25, 2014). In 2000 online directories of art and culture were still common, such as the Musee d'Art Contemporain de Montreal's *Médiathèque* at http://www.macm.org/mediatheque/.

9 http://www.nettime.org/Lists-Archives/nettime-l-0012/msg00070.html (accessed August 25, 2014).

10 http://www.dmoz.org/Reference/Museums/ (accessed September 10, 2014).

11   "Digital Curation at the University of Maine," http://digitalcuration.umaine.edu/ (accessed August 25, 2014).

12   Historically artists haven't always needed digital means to mess with museums. Banksy claimed to have installed his own artworks surreptitiously at the Brooklyn Museum, Metropolitan Museum of Art, MoMA, and Museum of Natural History all at once in 2005. Krzysztof Wodiczko projected images onto the city hall and a statue of Abraham Lincoln under cover of night.

13   Even the term "mod," used by the gaming community since the 1980s, has been replaced with the legally sterilized "user-generated content" in several of these systems.

14   http://modlist.mcf.li/version/1.4.7 (accessed August 26, 2014).

15   See Chapter 25 by Michelle Henning in this volume.

16   See Chapters 22 by Nancy Proctor and 26 by Haidee Wasson, both in this volume.

17   Note the trademark: apparently a museum without walls can still maintain ownership (Museum Without Walls Audio, http://museumwithoutwallsaudio.org/, accessed August 26, 2014).

18   Michelle Henning reports that one of her students visited Ground Zero but was reluctant to use the AR app owing to concerns among visitors about the inappropriateness of holding up their phones as if taking holiday snapshots (private correspondence with Jon Ippolito, September 9, 2013).

19   HASTAC (2012) participant Susan Hazan wrote: "My only problem with all of this digital festivity is that – at the end of the day – if someone turns off the electricity – it all simply vanishes into thin air!" Try running the Metropolitan after turning the electricity off. Ironically, your smartphone will keep working.

20   See Chapter 13, "'Get to Know Your World': An Interview with Jim Enote, Director of the A:shiwi A:wan Museum and Heritage Center in Zuni, New Mexico," by Gwyneira Isaac, in *Museum Transformations*.

21   "The Passamaquoddy Living Language System," http://www.universalpantograph. com/passamaquoddy5 (accessed August 27, 2014). Larson worked with developer Sam Hunting and University of Maine faculty Mike Scott and Joline Blais. For an overview, see http://nmdprojects.net/student_work/capstone_2009/larson_ian_passamaquoddy/ media/larson_ian_passamaquoddy_demo.mp4 (accessed August 27, 2014).

22   The problem remains even when the stuff of culture is born digital. The contemporary equivalent of those Vatican reliquaries that stored saints' knuckles for 1000 years are the boxes in which we now entomb inert assemblages of metal and plastic, as curators put video decks and computers into crates and are surprised to find they're unusable when they pull them out 20 years later.

23   These are all actual approved gTLDs. The interested reader can browse or search among the approved domains at https://gtldresult.icann.org (accessed August 27, 2014).

References

Adams, Dan, Steve Butts, and Charles Onyett. 2007. "Top 25 PC Games of All Time." IGN Entertainment, March 16. Accessed August 25, 2014. http://www.ign.com/ articles/2007/03/16/top-25-pc-games-of-all-time?page=3.

Aima, Rahel. 2012. "Desiring Machines." *New Inquiry*, May 29. Accessed August 25, 2014. http://thenewinquiry.com/essays/desiring-machines.

Atkins, Richard. 1998. "What is äda'web?" Accessed August 25, 2014. http://www.walker-art.org/archive/4/B5737118FB210DAF6169.htm.

Bachman, Katy. 2014. "Icann: Brands Are at Risk of Domain Abuse with New Top Level Domains." *Adweek*, February 7. Accessed August 25, 2014. http://www.adweek.com/news/technology/icann-brands-are-risk-domain-abuse-new-top-level-domains-155584.

Bell, John. 2013. "The Variable Museum: Off-Topic Art" *Leonardo Electronic Almanac* 19(1): 12–19. Accessed August 25, 2014. http://www.leoalmanac.org/wp-content/uploads/2013/01/LEAVol19No1-Bell.pdf.

Budka, Philipp. 2008. "Subversion, Conversion, Development." Centre for Research in the Arts, Social Sciences, and Humanities at the University of Cambridge Mesh. Accessed August 25, 2014. http://thoughtmesh.net/publish/87.php.

Chocano, Carina. 2012. "Pinterest, Tumblr and the Trouble with 'Curation.'" *New York Times*, July 20. Accessed August 25, 2014. http://www.nytimes.com/2012/07/22/magazine/pinterest-tumblr-and-the-trouble-with-curation.html.

Goldsmith, Kenneth. 2011. "UbuWeb." Accessed September 10, 2014. http://www.ubu.com/resources/.

HASTAC (Humanities, Arts, Science, and Technology Alliance and Collaboratory). 2012. "The Future of Museums." Participatory forum launched May 16, 2012. Accessed August 27, 2014. http://hastac.org/forums/future-museums.

ICOM (International Council of Museums). 2000a. "ICOM Seeks New Internet Domain for Museums." Press release, October 4. Accessed September 10, 2014. http://home.ease.lsoft.com/scripts/wa-HOME.exe?A2=ind0010&L=icom-l&T=0&P=1375.

ICOM (International Council of Museums). 2000b. "Dot-Museum (.museum) Named as One of Seven Winners in Expansion of Internet Domain Names." Press release, November 20. Accessed August 25, 2014. http://archives.icom.museum/release.museum2.html.

ICOM (International Council of Museums). 2001. "Development of the Museum Definition according to ICOM Statutes (1946–2001)." Accessed August 25, 2014. http://archives.icom.museum/hist_def_eng.html.

Ippolito, Jon. 2006. "Internet Art, Net Art, and Networked Art in Relation: Interview with Jon Ippolito." Interview by Karen Verschooren. Accessed August 25, 2014. http://three.org/ippolito/writing/ippolito_verschooren_interview.html.

Ippolito, Jon. 2012. "Re-collection: Trusting Amateurs with Our Future." Accessed August 25, 2014. http://three.org/ippolito/writing/trusting_amateurs/index_2012.html#learningfrom1.

Kessler, Sarah. 2011. "Augmented Reality App Puts Twin Towers Back in the New York Skyline." Mashable, August 4. Accessed August 25, 2014. http://mashable.com/2011/08/04/twin-towers-augmented-reality.

Kirshenblatt-Gimblett, Barbara. 1998. *Destination Culture: Tourism, Museums, and Heritage*. Berkeley: University of California Press.

Lavallee, Andrew. 2006. "Museums Try YouTube, Flickr To Find New Works for the Walls." *Wall Street Journal* (New York), October 13. Accessed August 25, 2014. http://online.wsj.com/article/SB116040543414086891.html.

Lialina, Olia. 2011. "Last Real Net Art Museum." Accessed August 25, 2014. http://myboy-friendcamebackfromth.ewar.ru/.

Manifest.AR. 2011. "Manifest.AR Venice Biennial 2011 AR Intervention." Accessed August 25, 2014. http://manifestarblog.wordpress.com/venice2011.

Mirapaul, Matthew. 2001. "So Is It or Isn't It a Museum? Only the Web Suffix Knows." *New York Times*, July 9, E2.

Pariser, Eli. 2011. *The Filter Bubble: What the Internet Is Hiding from You*. New York: Penguin.

Rinehart, Richard, and Jon Ippolito. 2014. *Re-collection: Art, New Media, and Social Memory*. Cambridge, MA: MIT Press.

Samek Art Museum. 2011. "Current Exhibition/Not Here." Accessed September 10, 2014. http://galleries.blogs.bucknell.edu/2011/07/08/current-exhibitionnot-here/.

Segall, Laurie. 2011. "Explore 9/11 through the Eyes of Your iPhone." CNN Money, September 7. Accessed August 25, 2014. http://money.cnn.com/2011/09/07/technology/911_apps/.

Shahbazi, Rudabeh. 2012. "Natural History Museum to Open the North Campus Nature Exhibit." Los Angeles News, April 19. Accessed September 10, 2014. http://abclocal.go.com//story?section=news/local/los_angeles&id=8628888.

Shankland, Stephen. 2013. "Here Come the Arabic, Russian, and Chinese Net Addresses." CNET, July 15. Accessed August 25, 2014. http://www.cnet.com/news/here-come-the-arabic-russian-and-chinese-net-addresses/.

Shankland, Stephen. 2014. "ICANN CEO Sets Off Explosion of New Internet Names (Q&A)." CNET, January 28. Accessed August 25, 2014. http://www.cnet.com/news/icann-ceo-sets-off-explosion-of-new-internet-names-q-a/.

Sicha, Choire. 2012. "You Are Not a Curator, You Are Actually Just a Filthy Blogger." The Awl, June 1. Accessed September 11, 2014. http://www.theawl.com/2012/06/you-are-not-a-curator-you-are-actually-just-a-blogger.

Sterling, Bruce. 2010. "Augmented Reality: Invading the Museum of Modern Art." Wired, October 11. Accessed August 25, 2014. http://www.wired.com/beyond_the_beyond/2010/10/augmented-reality-invading-the-museum-of-modern-art/.

Valve Software. 2012. "Steam Workshop." Valve Developer Community, Valve Software, May 24. Accessed August 25, 2014. https://developer.valvesoftware.com/wiki/Steam_Workshop#Rating.

John Bell is a senior research fellow for Still Water and Adjunct Professor of New Media and Assistant Professor of Digital Curation at the University of Maine. He has contributed to the development of numerous digital humanities projects including The Pool, a system for fostering and documenting distributed creativity in digital arts, the Variable Media Questionnaire, a database that provides insight into the preservation of ephemeral artworks, and is the architect for the Media Ecology Project, a system designed to increase scholarly access to rights-encumbered media stored in siloed archives. With nine coauthors, he wrote *10 PRINT CHR$(205.5+RND(1)); : GOTO 10*, a single-voice book exploring the social and technological environment around the eponymous BASIC program and the Commodore 64 it ran on. More information can be found at http://johnpbell.info/.

Jon Ippolito is an artist, writer, and curator born in Berkeley, California, who turned to making art after failing as an astrophysicist. After applying for what he thought was a position as a museum guard, Jon was hired in the curatorial department of the Guggenheim, New York, where in 1993 he curated *Virtual Reality: An Emerging Medium* and subsequent exhibitions that explore the intersection of contemporary art and new media. In 2002 he joined the faculty of the University of Maine's New Media Department, where with Joline Blais he cofounded Still Water, a lab devoted to studying and building creative networks. His writing on the cultural and aesthetic implications of new media has appeared in the *Washington Post* and *Art Journal* as well as in his 2014 book with Richard Rinehart, *Re-collection: Art, New Media, and Social Memory*. More information can be found at http://three.org/ippolito/.

22 MOBILE IN MUSEUMS
From Interpretation to Conversation

Nancy Proctor

Museums are often portrayed as conservative in their use of technology, and even as resistant to innovation. But, in terms of mobiles, museums have been early adopters of personal handheld devices since at least the 1950s, when the Stedelijk Museum in Amsterdam pioneered a multilingual audio tour of its exhibition *Vermeer: Real or Fake*.[1] Significantly, the new radio technology used for this early tour system was originally deployed in cinemas to enable access for people with hearing impairments, and the aim of the museum tour was to provide multilingual translation for The Netherlands' many foreign visitors. This symbiotic relationship between mobile technology and accessibility in all its forms has continued to inspire some of the most innovative uses of mobile platforms to this day, as well as leading examples of universal design.[2]

Audio tours are still the most common form of "self-guided" mobile experience at cultural sites. Arguably, they are also the oldest source of "augmented reality" (AR), enabling us to "overlay" the observed environment with interpretation and other content we hear. The Stedelijk Museum was one of the first cultural organizations to adopt AR for its new mobile applications. This and other examples of mobile innovation in decades- and centuries-old institutions suggest that the foundational experiences and expertise required to deploy even the most cutting edge of twenty-first-century mobile technologies effectively lie at museums' fingertips – and well within their traditional purview. By building on this long history of innovation with mobile technologies, museums and cultural organizations can and should lead the field in terms of mobile content and user experience design.

Since the invention of the audio tour, the number and kind of mobile devices used by museums have proliferated. In addition to audio and multimedia tours on

The International Handbooks of Museum Studies: Museum Media, First Edition.
Edited by Michelle Henning.
© 2015 John Wiley & Sons Ltd. Published 2020 by John Wiley & Sons Ltd.

made-for-museum devices that are loaned to museum visitors, museums now produce a wide range of downloadable media, ranging from audio and video podcasts to PDFs and e-books and now apps, for use on their audiences' personal mobile phones, media players, and tablet computers. Even with smartphones and tablet computers soon to become our primary means of accessing the Internet, a significant part of the world's mobile phone use is still limited to voice and text messaging. Mobile-phone-based audio tours, using the simple voice connections that are available to all mobile phones, emerged at the same time as the first podcast museum tours; both were hailed as low-cost alternatives to distributing tours on museum-owned devices. Mobile phone tours and downloadable tours made for personal media players like the iPod started museums thinking about how they could encourage and even expect people to BYOD ("bring your own mobile device") to access mobile tour content – in order to avoid the expense of both the hardware and the staffing to hand it out.

What these forms of mobile media – the traditional audio tour, the mobile phone tour, the podcast, and similar downloadable content – have in common is that they are typically deployed in a broadcast model, that is, the one-way delivery of content from museum to consumer with no built-in feedback loop or dialectic functionality. But with today's new networked mobile devices – smartphones, tablet computers, and wi-fi-enabled media players and gaming devices – two- and multiway communications are easier and more available. Not just "narrowcast" audio tours, but interactive mobile multimedia, including games, crowdsourcing activities, and social media, can be delivered via apps to the visitor's own Internet-enabled phones and media players instead of or to supplement devices provided on site by the museum.

The term "mobile" has therefore come to encompass an ever expanding field of platforms, players, and modes of audience engagement. Mobile in museums today means:

- both pocketable devices (phones, personal media players, gaming devices) and larger portable devices (tablets, e-readers);
- both smartphones which run apps and access the Internet and simpler mobile or feature phones which do little more than make voice calls and send text messages;
- both podcasts of audio and video content and other downloadable content, including PDFs and e-books;
- both mobile websites, which are optimized for or automatically scale to the small screen ("responsive" websites) for audiences on the go and "immobile" websites, which are designed for the larger screens of laptop and desktop computers but which are increasingly visited by mobile devices;
- both BYOD mobile experiences, designed for visitors' personal devices and traditional on-site device distribution for visitors who do not have or do not wish to use their own phone or media player.

Mobile's disruptive power comes from its unique ability to offer the individual intimate, immediate, and ubiquitous access combined with an unprecedented potential to connect people with communities and conversations in global social networks: mobile can be both private and public, personal and political. Today's Web 2.0 zeitgeist challenges us to think beyond the audio tour and to broadcast formats for mobile content and experiences. With audiences expecting to be able to access content and networked services on demand – whenever, wherever, and however they want – museums are also being inspired to conceive content and experiences that operate across platforms and contexts, both inside the museum and beyond. In this expanded field of the museum as a "distributed network" of platforms, content and people, mobile plays a unique role as connector, bridge, and glue, uniting communities and experiences across time, space, and interfaces.

At the same time as the rise of mobile reshapes the museum's thinking about its digital interfaces, it broadens access to the museum exponentially. Not only are more people able to connect with the museum through their mobile devices, but there is also the potential for them to personalize their museum experience and integrate collections, exhibitions, and other museum offerings into a much broader range of use case scenarios than we have ever imagined. The museum can not only enter people's homes and classrooms, but also accompany them during their daily commutes, their international travel, and their work and leisure activities as never before. Museums are beginning to open up access to their content for reuse in creative and educational ways that may go far beyond their original purpose. Mobile plays a key role in enabling museums to understand and cater to this huge range of contexts and demands for cultural content and experiences.

It is increasingly difficult to talk about "mobile" as distinct from the web or the in-gallery experience or practically any other media we encounter in a cultural context. Mobile in all its forms has become the "web" that connects nonmobile platforms and experiences and, increasingly, all of the museum's audiences. As mobile Internet overtakes desktop use of the Internet, mobile is redefining the very term "World Wide Web."[3] As a result, we have reached a certain tipping point for mobile in the cultural sector: after generations of playing a relatively marginal role (if any) as the traditional audio tour in most museums' interpretation programs and budgets, mobile has reached maturity as a technology discourse and platform, extending its reach to audiences far beyond the museum's walls. Mobile is no longer a "nice to have": we hear museum professionals echoing the sense that the pervasiveness of mobile make it an essential part of the museum experience, both on-site and beyond (Fusion Research & Analytics, AAM, and Museums Association 2012).

With smartphones becoming nearly ubiquitous among museum visitors, mobile technology is increasingly taken for granted and even "invisible," freeing up content specialists and experience designers to focus on what is truly transformative and memorable for museums' constituents. Perhaps ironically in this age of technological revolutions, mobile in museums is less about the technology today than it has ever been. Instead, the main challenges facing museums and their digital teams today are the development of cross-platform content strategies and linking contexts of use to create immersive experiences that go beyond the informational library and archive paradigms of museums on the Web 1.0 and even Web 2.0.

The museum as distributed network

Museums' potential online audiences greatly exceed the number of visitors who will ever have the opportunity to visit their physical sites. Online interactions with the museum now include social media sites – for example, Facebook pages, Flickr groups, YouTube channels, blogs, and Twitter streams – as well as digital content about its collections, exhibitions, and programs that is not authored, sanctioned by, or even known to the museum. The museum experience can now be said to extend well beyond the platforms that museums control – their brick-and-mortar buildings as well as their own websites and social media presences – to the spaces where online audiences and others publish their own images, videos, texts, and more about museum collections, topics, and events without any editorial recourse to museum staff at all.

This expanding landscape for museum audience engagement lends a new urgency to the questions: What is the museum's responsibility to those who may never be able to visit the physical museum in person? And how can museums engage online audiences on all the platforms they now use with the same degree of impact, if not the same kind of experience, as the "real world" museum encounter? These are questions not just of audience engagement today, but that touch on the very quality, relevance, and sustainability of the museum experience in the future as well. Museums need strategies for content and experience design that address audiences effectively and efficiently across these many digital destinations, both those controlled by the museum and those that are created by visitors and other third parties. These new methods take us beyond a simple multiplatform museum to a more radical distributed network model – proving, perhaps, that humble grass roots structures are better than even the trusty spoke and wheel in carrying the museum's messages to its many audiences.

The multiplatform museum model

At first glance, "multiplatform museum" is a perfectly serviceable term for the multifaceted nature of museums' interactions with audiences today: it makes us think beyond the physical site and suggests the museum's presence in multiple digital contexts. It is also true to say that "multiplatform" accurately describes common current approaches to social media and online publishing. But this is not to say that the "multiplatform" museum makes the best use of and the greatest impact with digital media. Another metaphor, the distributed network, offers a more effective approach to cross-platform engagement in the twenty-first-century museum – one which yields "network effects," meaning that the system is both more sustainable and improves in quality and impact as the distributed network grows in breadth and number of participants. In what we might call museums on the Web 3.0, a networked approach to the museum's platforms is also better able to create immersive environments and transformative encounters with collections and museum content in the digital as well as "analogue" world.

Technically speaking, "multiplatform" implies publishing to many outlets or "platforms" from a single content source. In other words, the aim is to create an accurate copy of the same original (content, message) on each platform, or at least to control the content and experience from a central publishing source. But, like any wholesale export of culture without sensitivity to the "native" context and its communities, multiplatform publishing results at best in forcing square pegs into round holes, at worst in a sort of colonizing effort; either way, it ultimately fails to be faithful either to the message or the target audience's needs. Content designed for one use, context, or platform rarely ports directly and easily to another. Brochures do not make good websites. Texts written for catalogs and wall labels sound stilted and dry as audio guide scripts. And, just as physical artifacts have to be photographed or scanned in order to create a digital representation for online use, at a minimum videos and photographs are reformatted and retagged to meet the requirements of the different digital platforms. As long as museums remain bound by Web 1.0 thinking, which seeks to create – at best – a digital version of the "real world," the digital museum encounter will remain a hollow echo, its mobile experiences a soulless transcription of the living museum's voices.

Moreover, because of its spoke-and-wheel structure, the multiplatform model does not easily incorporate feedback loops or ways for user-authored content and experiences to be combined with museum content and redistributed without passing through centralized channels, where editors and censors monitor and shape the conversation. When museums adopt even "networked" social media platforms using a multiplatform approach, we typically see not conversation but a rebroadcast of the museum's messages: Facebook, Twitter and other social network sites become simply digital mouthpieces for the museum's analogue marketing campaigns. The reach of these messages may be extended through retweets, links, or repostings, but there is little if any two-way interaction or exchange between the museum and online audience members. Success is measured in "hits" and audience size rather than impact on the individual and the museum encounter.

This is not to say that there is no value in broadcast, retweets, or other quick and relatively superficial forms of audience engagement; on the contrary, they are part of the comprehensive set of tools and approaches the museum needs for communicating the rich variety of its offerings to an even more diverse audience and ever broadening contexts. But if museums aim at more than one-way communications, and at developing new and compelling ways of reaching online visitors who may never have the opportunity to experience the wonder of museum offerings in person, then strategies are required for creating content and messages with a more discursive dynamic and greater sensitivity to the specificity of the many platforms, audiences, and contexts now within their compass. Instead of a multiplatform model, museums are increasingly adopting more flexible modular structures and methodologies, akin to what technologists might call a "distributed network" or rhizomic model, in the philosophical concept elaborated by Gilles Deleuze and Félix Guattari.

The distributed network model

There is no center to a distributed network: no panopticon tower from where the entire system is visible, no Hegelian master or slave. The constituent platforms work together to create a whole that is greater than the sum of its parts. In terms of content, we speak less of the "original" and more of Baudrillard's (1988) elaboration of the "simulacrum" – the copy without an original. Notions of authority and hierarchy are not very helpful in describing relationships and processes that work together more like digital "mash-ups" than pronouncements. Knowledge, rather than being disseminated outward from a center point, is discovered in its intersections and interstices, through the (sometimes surprising) juxtapositions that can happen when experiences are assembled collaboratively along the many-branched paths of a rhizome. In the museum as distributed network, content and experience creation resembles atoms coming together and reforming to create new molecules, or "choose-your-own-ending" adventure stories.

The Internet is one of the few present-day examples of a true distributed network. By design, it is structured in such a way that it is impossible to destroy the entire network through an "attack" or service outage at any single center. In the loosest sense, every time you perform an Internet search, you have tapped into a distributed network. The original content that forms the results page – itself a mash-up – exists on a number of different computers, physical and virtual, each potentially in its own network or grid. It is delivered to you in an entirely new and personalized context on the basis of your search interests and terms *at that precise moment*; yet the original digital assets are completely untouched in their original form, and you can easily trace the results content back to discover its full context and original publication environment. The value and authority of the "original" is not diminished but, rather, increased by being placed in new contexts alongside content from other sources. Quality is determined by the content's relevance, depth, longevity, and quantity of what could be called "peer reviews" and recommendations, that is to say, links.

Other than the Internet itself, distributed networks don't really exist yet in the technical sense, because most computer systems are built on the master–slave model. But we do see the products of master–slave systems being distributed, for example, in peer-to-peer gaming, social media environments, and some wikis. As museums begin to design interpretation and information systems for the age of social media, the distributed network can serve as an inspirational metaphor and a practical model to suggest new ways of authoring and supporting museum experiences that are conversational rather than unidirectional, engaging, and relevant for audiences rather than simply didactic, and generative of content and open-ended questions rather than finite and closed answers. Content and experiences in such systems become more sustainable across platforms, communities, and time, and "smarter" – that is to say, more effective and useful – the more they are used: rather like Pandora or the Amazon recommendations system. Distributed approaches to museum experience design increase the quality of both the visitor experience and the online museum itself, and mobile can be a key driver of this transformation.

Like the Internet, the museum as distributed network is enhanced, not diluted, by multiple voices and authors. But it requires powerful tools for making the ever increasing data and metadata of assets, interpretations, and interpreters findable and relevant, and for connecting communities of interest in meaningful ways across oceans of content and contributors. The mobile technologies that underpin this network require correspondingly radical approaches to content and experience design in order to deliver on the potential of the distributed model.

"From we do the talking, to we help you do the talking"

"Traditional" museum tour development on the broadcast model usually begins with the question "What are the most important messages we want visitors to take away from the encounter with this collection, exhibition, or object?" – and content is developed to support those goals, overlaying the physical reality of the museum with interpretive content and information. As the audio tour platform evolved from analogue tapes to digital media players, the kinds of media that could form this content and the devices that could deliver it proliferated to include text, images, video, animations, and interactive content as well as virtual reality and location awareness.

A multiplatform approach might repurpose and publish the museum's existing audio tour content to the new generation of mobile devices: mobile phones, personal media players like iPods, and web-enabled phones – as podcasts, mobile phone tours, mobile websites, and native applications. Especially with some planning ahead for cross-platform content design and minor versioning of assets for the different delivery platforms, this is not a bad strategy: museums should seek to "meet our audiences where they are" by publishing their content in as many places as possible.

As Koven Smith (2009) has asked, however, will delivering what is fundamentally the same, narrowcast tour experience to shiny new gadgets really "take museums' audiences some place new"? Will adding images or video or a sexy new smartphone platform really improve the take-up or penetration rates of mobile technology use by museum visitors – in other words, better help the museum engage audiences and deliver on its educational mission? Although visitors self-report higher usage of mobile interpretation in museums (Petrie and Tallon 2010), in reality the audio tour reaches a sobering minority of the museum's audience. One also has to ask how well podcasts, mobile phone tours, and iPhone apps serving up the same basic content, usually designed with the on-site visit in mind, fulfill the needs of those audiences who'll never be able to come to the museum in person. And if people are increasingly using their mobile devices to connect to social media experiences, will they really leave those expectations at the door of the museum?

Applied to mobile platforms, the distributed network model can include but also go beyond the narrowcast audio tour and basic informational services for museum mobile websites and apps. Whether audio tour, "un-tour," "de-tour," or "para-tour" (Schavemaker 2011, 52), the connected mobile platforms available to museums today invite the development of networked visitor experiences. Mobile can be understood in this light as social media and an integral part of a web of platforms that connect communities of interest and facilitate conversations among audiences as well as with the museum itself. As an indispensable part of the 2.0 museum, mobile supports the key indices of the museum's success vis-à-vis its core mission and responsibility to the public good: accessibility, relevance, quality, accountability, and sustainability. At its most effective, mobile introduces network effects into museum systems, so that accessibility and relevance lead to greater quality, accountability, and sustainability of the museum's mission.

Accessibility, relevance, and accountability

From its origins in audio systems for people with hearing impairment in the 1950s, and even from the invention of the telephone (which was conceived initially by Alexander Graham Bell as a listening aid for people who were hard of hearing), mobile development has been inspired and motivated by a need to increase accessibility to content and conversations. And just as ramps and large, clear signage have been proven to offer universal advantages by making museums more user-friendly for all patrons, regardless of their mobility and vision, accessible design increases the quality and impact of the mobile experience for everyone. The Smithsonian has set "accessibility" as its number one mobile product development principle. As a tool for broadening access, mobile increases the museum's ability to meet people wherever they are – physically, culturally, linguistically, and in terms of educational and other abilities – and take them some place new or on new paths through familiar collections and contexts.

Mobile can also make museums more relevant and help deliver on the museum's responsibility to make its collections, content, and activities meaningful and accessible to the broadest possible audiences. Relevance is a two-sided coin, however, requiring an in-depth understanding both of the museum's target audience(s) and of the museum's own mission and aims.

The museum's mission, goals, resources, and objectives for the mobile program serve as a framework and touchstone for developing the content and services that respond to visitors' interests and needs. These should be clearly articulated at the outset of the mobile project and understood by all involved in the project, both internal staff and external contractors. In 2007 the Education Department at the San Francisco Museum of Modern Art (SFMOMA) adapted an Interpretive Goals questionnaire originally developed by the Getty to foreground the key information that structures and informs interpretive project development at the museum. The eight questions asked by the cross-functional teams at the beginning of each initiative include:

- Please list one to three main ideas visitors will take away from viewing the exhibition. What objects or didactic components of the exhibition will help them learn this?
- Describe the rationale and originality of the project. Is the exhibition bringing new scholarship to the field, exposing an under-recognized subject, etc.? Why is this exhibition important now at SFMOMA?
- Please note other interpretive, multi-media components that should be considered (audio tour, in-gallery videos, interactive feature, blogs, etc.). Are you aware of existing media created by other organizations on this topic? (Samis and Pau 2009)

If the museum's and audience's goals are not aligned, mobile initiatives are likely to fall on deaf ears and add to the long list of one-hit mobile wonders: perhaps innovative and newsworthy in the moment but ultimately unsustainable and unsupportive of the museum's and the audience's core aims.

In order to sustain relevance to its audiences and accountability to its stakeholders, the mobile program can capture data (metrics) and feedback from these visitors on where they go, what they do, and what questions they ask of the museum's content and collections, events, and so on. Traditional audience research can be central to understanding our mobile visitors' interests and needs but, as Lynda Kelly (2010) has argued, so can data-mining social media content. User-generated content and data gleaned from commenting, collecting, and sharing functions on both the mobile and related social media platforms the museum uses provide important insight into how audiences' interests and needs are and can be engaged by the museum's collections, activities, and resources. By the same token, it is critical that audience research and uses of the data gleaned from social media by the museum do not violate the public trust, but continue to uphold the museum's reputation and brand values.

Location-based services (LBS) can bring the museum to the visitor both on site and beyond, making content and collections more relevant to the visitor's current context. LBS also offer the ability to place museum content and interpretation in surprising places, enabling serendipitous encounters and giving the visitor a powerful emotive experience linked to the museum despite the absence of the actual artifact. Various technology solutions for LBS are discussed at greater length below, but meeting audiences where they are takes much more than advanced technology: it requires mobile experiences that deliver on the museum's mission, and the mobile metrics of success begin with asking what audiences want to know about our collections, exhibitions, research, and scholarship, both on site and beyond the museum's walls, and *not* with what we want to tell them.

By responding first to our visitors' actual interests and needs, we create content and experiences that make the museum more relevant to their interests and lives. Starting with understanding our audiences also means we can increase the quality of the networked museum through both better focused museum-authored content, and linking to related content from audiences both expert and amateur. The quality and relevance of the museum's discourse are the preconditions for its sustainability, and enable network effects that grow audiences and foster self-perpetuating conversations about the museum's collections, activities, and messages. Mobile products and services do not yield these benefits on their own, but rather as an integral part of the ecosystem of platforms that now make up the museum as distributed network (Proctor 2011b).

Quality

As Chris Anderson (2009) has noted, "Quality is in the eye of the beholder[s], and … what is most important to them … is relevance." On the basis of better understanding of both audiences and institutional goals, the museum can create content that is calibrated to engage with audiences and that connects their interests to the museum's mission and goals, thereby increasing the quality of both the museum experience and its digital assets. Mobile content is likely to outlive the technologies for which it has initially been developed, so adopting industry standards and investing in the highest-quality productions possible (high definition, 3D, etc.) will enable the museum to get a longer-term return on their content investment. But for short-term and small budget programs, relevance may be a more important factor in mobile success than production values.

Beyond responding to audiences' immediate questions and interests, mobile can increase the quality of the museum's experience by drawing on its traditional strengths: its collections, exhibitions, events, and interpretations of the invaluable artifacts and key stories, ideas, and concepts that it preserves. Far from diluting the value of the curatorial voice, mobile offers museums the opportunity to take conversations somewhere new – to content, experiences, and ideas that participants may never have thought to inquire about. The museum's subject experts are uniquely placed to identify and leverage audience members' interests to take them to new levels of understanding, and to introduce new concepts and content of which they may otherwise have remained unaware, without necessarily falling into lecture mode. The museum expert who joins a conversation with an audience is at the same time just one voice and a privileged node in the peer-to-peer network of the conversation. Museums are bastions of niche expertise that has enormous interest and value to the communities already engaged with related content. These communities offer an opportunity for museum experts to curate not just collection displays and exhibitions, but conversations that extend well beyond the museum's walls and exhibition lifespan. Once engaged, the community and its conversations can grow and change with the museum's audiences as well as new scholarship and acquisitions.

Part of a quality visitor experience is being able to find the content that is relevant to the visitor's interests and context in a given moment. This means that great interface designs and mobile-optimized search facilities for collections and exhibition content, as well as interactive maps, are both critical and expected tools for helping visitors find the content that responds to their questions and interests. But a good search relies on good metadata – with quality here once again having a lot to do with relevance to the user. In addition to museum-authored metadata and geo-data, social tagging can enhance the discoverability of museum content for those who are not familiar with specialist terminology and ontologies often used to describe collections. For example, the Brooklyn Museum's mobile application uses social tagging, along with "liking," as an additional tool for audience engagement: by tagging and liking objects in the collection, visitors make them more findable and interesting to others.[4]

Location-based social media platforms incorporate gaming elements and can be adapted by the museum to create cultural tours and routes of discovery, with "badges" and other rewards, both virtual and real, for fulfilling tasks. Meaningful and sustainable engagement can also be found in crowdsourcing and citizen scientist or citizen curator initiatives in which audiences truly contribute to the work of the museum and therefore to what they will experience there. Scapes, Halsey Burgund's audio installation at the deCordova Sculpture Park and Museum provides a platform for visitors to record their comments on the artworks as they move around the Park (Burgund 2010). An algorithm blends these voices with each other and an original location-based score by Burgund, and plays them back via visitors' iPhones at the locations at which they were recorded. Instead of a cacophony of banal visitor comments, the effect is profound: given the impactful task of leaving a vision and questions for those who come after, the visitors have collaborated asynchronously to create a guide to the sculptures that opens eyes and sensibilities even more than carefully curated expert interpretation. Again, this project finds that the line is blurred between "quality" and "relevance" when the content is proximate to the visitor's interests and context.

Sustainability

As social media, mobile doesn't just engage audiences more powerfully in its 2.0 forms, but it also creates a more sustainable museum discourse by distributing its content, messages, and digital collections through a self-perpetuating network of connected audiences. Objects from the collections, events, and individual content assets (images, videos, audio recordings, texts) can all serve as ambassadors that reach out to people on whatever platform they may be using, and offer multiple paths to discovering more on other platforms, including but not limited to the museum's brick-and-mortar presence. Functions that allow visitors to save, annotate, and redistribute content along with their experience and insights to others help build the network around museum collections and activities. The museum can also help communities of interest form around objects and exhibits by facilitating the conversation both directly with individuals and between audience members. For example, The Australian Museum, among others, has created Facebook pages for specific objects from its collection, which take on personalities and their own voices, engaging people online in passionate and lively dialogues (Kelly 2010). The wider the network, the more self-sustaining the conversation is around the museum, its collections, and activities. And, just as appreciation of the museum has been shown to increase the more platforms for interpretation the visitor uses (Samis 2007), the value and "intelligence" of the conversational network increases with use.

The potential for reuse of museum assets in a variety of contexts and conversations also encourages us to think in a modular and rhizomic way about content development: In how many different ways, on how many different platforms, can a given asset be used? How will the conversations and communities take on different aspects in different contexts? In the museum as distributed network, every platform is a community, not just an outlet for content publication and distribution. By combining established social media platforms like Flickr, YouTube, Facebook, and Twitter with mobile social media and analogue content and publications built by or for the museum, museums can create a whole that is greater than the sum of its parts – they can think holistically about the museum as a network *through its content* rather than through the technology.

The main challenge remains content and asset management across the ever expanding array of platforms the museum uses. As the platforms that museums use and are represented on expand and change, the adoption of mobile content standards becomes perhaps the most critical cross-platform content management strategy. Museums can ensure the longest possible future use of assets by employing platform- and technology-independent standards where they exist, and creating them where they don't. For example, the Indianapolis Museum of Art has led the development of TourML, a mobile content mark-up schema built for use in museum guides and interpretive mobile experiences.[5] Strategies and best practices for increasing the efficiency of cross-platform content deployment continue to evolve and will likely remain in constant development as both technology and cultural use of it change (see, for example, Bicknell 2010).

Location, location, location

Outdoors, GPS is the leading means of triggering location-based mobile content and experiences, and many visitors wonder why they can't enjoy the same services inside a museum. Simple network connectivity, through wi-fi or mobile access in the galleries, alone can offer important means for people to record and share their on-site museum experiences with wider networks, and also to access interpretive content and educational activities, created by both the museum and others. Indeed, without publicly accessible and free networks (usually wi-fi), the range of content and experiences that museums can create for mobile users is confined to traditional broadcast modes with no social media or other network effects.

But wayfinding and other location-based mobile services have represented a sort of holy grail for museums since the 1990s (Proctor 2005). Millions of dollars have been spent trying to get interpretive content to play automatically and seamlessly on mobile devices based on visitors' locations in the gallery. The GettyGuide and the Smithsonian's SIGuide, both dating from 2005, are examples of ambitious mobile projects that were designed around – and ultimately sunk by – reliance on a level of accuracy and responsiveness in indoor positioning that proved impossible to achieve with the technology then available (Honeysett 2008).

Many such attempts have relied on signals from wi-fi, mobile, and other networks to triangulate mobile users' locations indoors where GPS has limited, if any, reach. The American Museum of Natural History, working with Cisco, Spotlight Mobile (now Meridian), and Bloomberg funding, installed over 300 access points in the museum to enable location detection via wi-fi triangulation in their 2010 Explorer app. Although there have been some mixed reviews of the app's performance – caused mainly by the varying quality of users' mobile devices, operating systems, and wi-fi connections and signal strength – it was the first truly robust and successful implementation of this technology in a museum. The Museum of Old and New Art (MONA) in Tasmania added radio frequency identification (RFID) to their wi-fi-based positioning system – and an ingenious interface that turns any fluctuations in the location-based response into an opportunity for serendipitous discovery of nearby artworks – to offer a nearly bullet-proof solution in their O guide. Both museums invested heavily in their buildings' infrastructure to install the necessary networks that drive the apps.

Other solutions include lacunae and other anomalies in buildings' radio maps, noting that an absence of radio signals can mark a spot as well (Rowe 2012). Magnetic fields and low-frequency 3D signal technology that penetrate where GPS and network signals can't reach can also be measured by mobile devices (Aron 2012; Piesing 2012). On mobile platforms, location-based services go hand in hand with personalization: solutions that customize content and experiences to people's interests and activities (Bickersteth and Ainsley 2011; Chan 2011). Major online map providers have ventured into interior cultural spaces to provide museum floor plans, offering possibilities for location-based and personalized information delivery to mobile users through the platforms and interfaces they are most familiar with.

As these solutions evolve and new ones emerge, important questions will remain: Will the quality of the positioning vary from building to building, in much the same way that the reliability of GPS varies out of doors? How easy will it be for museums to incorporate mapping services offered by leading platform and service providers into their own apps and mobile websites to create a complete offering of location-based content and experiences? Who will ultimately "own" the map and user data generated by museums, and how much effort will it take to maintain?

Museums will continue to interrogate whether the new mobile technologies provide a real return on investment and a sustainable solution for visitors' needs in any given project and context, asking if a location-based app is the answer if more and better signage will provide greater accessibility, for example. Would museum visitors be just as well served by solutions that require less or no technology infrastructure (such as computer vision solutions), that use the mobile camera's lens to "see" where the user is compared to a visual model of the environment, or the humble numbered label and a keypad? Undoubtedly, in many cases, all of these will be required, and more. The good news is that, thanks to commercial interest in these technologies, powerful mobile tools are ever more readily available both inside and beyond the museum sector.

Are we there yet? Finding the participant in the mobile experience

Just as important as the technology are the content and experiences that location-based technologies can enable. There are two emerging technologies of particular interest for museums that work both indoors and outdoors to bring new kinds of services and content to museum experiences. Computer vision, such as that provided by Google Goggles, do not just deliver mobile content related to specific objects in a collection, but also tell us something about where the visitor is in the museum, opening the door to a new way to trigger other location-based services, including wayfinding. The mobile camera effectively recognizes where it is by comparing the images seen through its lens with a visual model that has been constructed of the environment and can be referenced through a wi-fi or other network.

Although it has been argued that audio tours were the first form of augmented reality, today the term more commonly refers to overlays of text, images, or video onto the "real" world as seen through a mobile device's camera. AR can convey not just information but emotions and immersive experiences by creating rich audio and visual environments, for example, overlaying a contemporary landscape with historic photos taken at the same location. One example is the Museum of London's Street Museum app, which overlays the streets of London with images of those same locations from the eighteenth century and beyond at their correct geospatial coordinates, so that visitors can stumble on the Great Fire of 1861 at London Bridge, suffragettes on Downing Street 40 years later, Holborn Circus during the Blitz, or hippies in Hyde Park in 1970. Just as people all over the world can now create content about museums, their collections, and events for social media platforms, museum visitors and activists have begun placing augmented reality content in museums. The Layar augmented reality platform was used for exhibitions presented by the Stedelijk Museum on Museumplein in Amsterdam in 2010, and an augmented reality exhibition of digital art curated by Sander Veenhof and Mark Skwarek was exhibited "within" the New York Museum of Modern Art's (MoMA) galleries – this digital intervention was unauthorized by the museum, but also unopposed by it.[6] Will museums see these as new opportunities for audience engagement with the collections and concepts of digital curation, or violations of a new form of intellectual property right?

Even without sophisticated location-aware technologies, the museum can seek out and cultivate communities of interest around topics related to museum collections and events by providing timely mobile content and other contributions to the conversation through cross-platform social media outlets such as Twitter and Facebook. Although location-based technologies are rich with potential, low-tech solutions like good signage and manually driven interfaces (keypads, menus, etc.) can also be efficient and perfectly adequate to help users access location-based services. Regardless of what location-based solution is used, without good content and user-experience design, the mobile product will fail to engage its audiences. As always, content and experience design should be the primary focus of LBS projects in the museum, and will likely command the greatest investment in terms of budget and planning.

"Recruiting the world"

When it comes to content and user-experience design, listening is as important a skill as speaking for museums. As artist Halsey Burgund has said, "People say interesting things, and they say things in interesting ways" (Proctor 2010b). This "wisdom of the crowd" (Surowiecki 2004; Howes 2008) is a great and largely untapped resource in the museum economy of the twenty-first century.

At the same time, the great power of Mobile 2.0, in contrast to the first generation of broadcast audio tour and media players, is its ability to connect people, whenever, wherever, and however they may want to engage. This gives mobile platforms an unparalleled ability to leverage the power of crowdsourcing, which has led the Smithsonian to summarize its mobile strategy as "recruiting the world" (Proctor 2011c). Employing the principle that the best way to learn is to teach, mobile design based on the connective power of mobile platforms and a distributed network model turns visitors into curators and creators, docents and ambassadors, for museums by giving them the tools to contribute meaningfully to the development of the museum experience. The museum's passive audiences become active collaborators and key to the success and sustainability of the museum's mission. Supported by the networked capabilities of the latest generation of mobile devices, museum experiences today can move from headphones to microphones, "from *we* do the talking to we help *you* do the talking" (Anderson 2009) without, critically, abandoning the still relevant tools and approaches for mobile engagement that have been developed in "museum mobile 1.0" over the past 60 years.

In the beginning: Early soundtracks and soundbites

Whether given by live guides or prerecorded on tape, the first museum tours were linear. From starting point A to end point N, the exhibits interpreted on the tour were strung along the tour's linear route like pearls of wisdom on a necklace. The value of the tour was measured in "stops": points at which the visitor physically stopped to look, listen, and learn.

The messiness, but also the magic, happened in the spaces between the exhibit commentary or stops on the tour, where directions and contextual information could be provided as people moved from stop to stop. People got lost easily in the interstitial spaces, uncertain of where to find the next stop, or they lost track of where they were in the audio tour tape. When they got bored or distracted or tired of following the herd, they simply decided to get off the tour at the latest stop, so missing the culmination of the tour narrative.

But, in the best linear tours, the spaces in between were where it all happened: that was where visitors got the background information and context that brought the exhibits to life. The connective tissue of the tour could immerse its listeners in music and storytelling that carried them along effortlessly from one stop to another, transporting the museum visitor to a different, magical, world. In some courageous tours, the liminal spaces were an opportunity for audience participation. The tour could issue challenges to the visitors to play games, complete tasks, or simply give time to share impressions with a companion. The more marketing-minded tours gestured toward galleries and exhibits along the way as opportunities to return and find out more in another tour. The interstitial spaces were also opportunities to "add value" to the linear tour experience.

Fear and impatience with the messiness prevailed, however, and the second generation of audio tour technology – Mobile 1.1–1.9, we might call it – introduced "random access" tours. With the new digital platforms of the 1990s, visitors could choose which exhibits they saw, and hence which stops they listened to, absolutely at random. Random access to museum commentary via a telephone-style keypad was the first "personalization" in museum mobile tours, and was promoted in modernist terms as a liberation from the herd. Thanks to the new technology, visitors could finally do their own thing in the museum.

But as, Laura Mann, a veteran of the audio tour industry, put it: "We lost something when we moved away from the linear tour" (conversation with the author,

2007). By "upgrading" to the new mobile platforms and tailoring our content for random access, we lost the ability to tell stories in the museum through mobile tours. Without knowing what order visitors would listen to the commentaries in, it was impossible to build on information and provide context and background to interpretation about any given object. Without a regressive "hack" of the new digital tour devices, the ability to immerse visitors in a mobile audio experience was gone.

"People say interesting things, and they say them in interesting ways"

With the introduction of screen-based mobile devices, it is now possible to recover the magic of the linear tour without losing the flexibility and personalization of the visit that is possible only through random access technology. Both kinds of content – soundtracks and stops – are accessible through visual interfaces that permit viewers to watch a linear video from beginning to end if they like, but also to jump out of the video at specific points to go deeper and learn more about specific points of interest. The online art video platform, ArtBabble.org offered an example of this navigation in its first iteration, and today YouTube interfaces with annotations in the time line of the linear content give some idea of this kind of design.

But there are other ways than a visual interface to achieve a similar merging of the stop and the soundtrack in museum mobile tours. The mobile, sound-based installation and app Scapes by artist Halsey Burgund (Figure 22.1) took the traditional museum mobile content modalities – the stop and the soundtrack – and transformed them radically, using the visitor's body as the interface to the content. Scapes demonstrated how collaborating with visitors can have what we might call a radical and sustainable – rather than a temporary, "revolutionary" – effect on not just the mobile experience but the way museums do their work.

Scapes was installed at the deCordova Sculpture Park in Massachusetts from July 13 to December 31, 2010. In concept, it was a crowdsourced audio experience of the sculpture park. Burgund wrote a location-based score for the park that played through the Scapes app, which visitors could download from the iTunes store or use on iPhones loaned out by the park. As they moved around the park, the music they heard changed according to their location. This soundtrack was blended with the voices of visitors whose comments on their visit to the park were triggered via GPS to play back at the location where they were recorded. The app offered a short number of simple questions to prompt visitors' contributions:

1. Scapes is an excuse to talk to yourself about anything at all. Go for it.
2. Look straight up and describe what you see.
3. Tell us about someone you wish was here with you right now. Talk to her/him.
4. Tell a story inspired by something you see or feel here.
5. Ask a question of those who come after you.

FIGURE 22.1   The home screen of Halsey Burgund's app, Scapes.

Visitors' contributions went live in the app as soon as they were recorded, with no prior moderation by Burgund or the park. This instant gratification turned out to be a critical reward and motivation for visitors to contribute to the artwork. Over the six-month period of the installation, Burgund and the park reported no inappropriate contributions to the app. It seems that Burgund's score and the context of the visit literally set a tone, which visitors respected. The result was a deeply moving and engaging mobile "tour" of the park that was entirely choreographed by and unique to each visitor. The app, artist, and park "listened" and empowered visitors to do the talking. In the process, the traditional elements of the mobile tour were transformed:

1. Stops became soundtracks: wherever the visitor stopped to hear more, they received a continuous stream of music blended with the visitor commentaries that had been previously recorded at that location. Rather than being limited to a 1–2 minute commentary, they could listen for as long or as little time as they wished before moving on.

2. The "soundtrack" of the visit was alinear, in that visitors chose their own route and could wander randomly among sculptures and features of the park without any preconceived route.

3. The conversation among visitors, who could respond to each other's commentaries as well as to the park, was asynchronous and built up in layers over time as more participants added their voices.
4. And the participant's body was the interface to the mobile content. By triggering the app's location-based content to play, the visitor's movements wrote the mobile experience, in real time, kinetically.

Clearly there is a huge advantage to working with artists on new platforms, as it is in the nature of their work to push the boundaries of the technologies, content, and approaches we may think we know so well. But Scapes is not a unique example of how the connected nature of the new mobile technologies opens up possibilities to create new kinds of content and experiences for museum visitors that take us far beyond the traditional audio tour model, radically transforming both the format and the museum visit in the process. At the same time, the very structures of power that define the museum itself are "rewired" when the public becomes the voice of the museum. Important new ways of achieving the museum's mission emerge from collaborations with "the crowd."

"There is no such thing as a visitor"

In her 1997 critique of capitalist models and metrics in understanding the value of museums to their audiences – and vice versa – feminist museum practitioner Judith Mastai interrogated the very concept of museum "visitor," arguing against a "visitor services" model which is tied to a capitalist service economy. In this model, the visitor as customer is presumed to know what she or he wants; the museum's role in the transaction is simply to supply it. Instead, Mastai argues, the museum visitor should be seen as a learner who comes to the museum precisely because she or he doesn't know. In this economy, the museum's role is not only to answer the questions visitors ask, but also propose new questions and connections that may never have occurred to the visitor without the structure and guidance of a learning environment (Mastai 2007). In his 2006 essay "The People Formerly Known as the Audience," and its 2010 expansion, Jay Rosen echoes this skepticism of simplistic consumer models for understanding audiences in the age of social media. Building on Raymond Williams's 1958 observation "There are no masses, there are only ways of seeing people as masses" Rosen's work underscores the importance of audience research and new understandings of audiences based not on traditional marketing demographics but on the dynamics of the new discursive models that have emerged with online culture (Rosen 2006).

Museums are magnets for specialists and enthusiasts of all sorts, and often *amateurs* know more about specific objects than the institutional curators and experts responsible for them.[7] As Chris Anderson (2009) predicted, many museums have found that publishing their collections records online has attracted these "citizen curators" in larger numbers than ever before, and has contributed valuable information to the understanding and interpretation of their collections. At the same time, their contributions radically redefine the identity and role of the "curator" as well as the relationships between museum staff and communities.

Clay Shirky identifies a specific radical potential in participatory systems when they reach a certain scale: quoting Philip Anderson, he argues that "'More is different.' When you aggregate a lot of something, it behaves in new ways" (Shirky 2010, 28). Social media and networked communications aggregate not just museums' audiences but also their time, knowledge, and creativity as a global resource for "designing new kinds of participation" for the museum in the twenty-first century (Chan 2009). In so doing, those collectives thereby restructure the museum as not just a *communal* but a *civic* space, to use Shirky's terms – that is, to the benefit of society at large, rather than just a self-selected museum community. In an economy of what Shirky calls "cognitive surplus," the means of production and its ends become indistinguishable and self-sustaining: "We, collectively, aren't just the source of the surplus; we are also the people designing its use, by our participation and by the things we expect of one another as we wrestle together with our new connectedness" (Shirky 2010, 29).

We have seen an increasing number of experiments using connected systems for crowdsourcing in the cultural sphere. In some of the most highly developed examples, "enthusiastic amateurs" from around the world don't just contribute to but lead important work involving collections and research, from transcribing old documents (the "Old Weather Project" at the United Kingdom's National Maritime Museum), to identifying astronomical entities in photographs of outer space (Galaxy Zoo), to collecting data on species and their global distribution (Project Noah and the Encyclopedia of Life), to selecting representative collection photographs (Victoria and Albert Museum online crowdsourcing initiative), to adding metadata to make digital records more findable (Steve.museum), to creating oral history archives (Stories from Main Street) and crowdsourcing verbal descriptions of collection objects to assist visually impaired and other visitors in "seeing" the Smithsonian collections (Access American Stories).[8]

Museum mission and the mobile economy

The contemporary proliferation of participatory projects and practices in museums does not mean, however, that old interests and systems of power have disappeared in the revolution. As Jay Rosen wrote in response to criticism of his 2006 essay:

> The post I wrote does not say "the people" have the power now, and the media lost theirs. It says there's been a *shift* in power. (And there has, but only a partial one.) It also speaks of a new "balance of power," which is another way of talking about a limited change.

I'm not claiming that the power shift is total, or even decisive. Only that it's significant, and changes the equation.

Exclusive influence, monopoly position, the right to dictate terms, dynastic continuity, priestly authority, guild conditions for limiting competition – these have been
lost, not the entrenched media's social and market power, which as you say remain
considerable.[9]

The interrogation and investigation of entrenched interests and systems of power
in the museum as institution and discourse is relevant also to the development of
mobile experiences of the museum. Whose agenda is at work will condition the
nature of the experience, its voices, and its impact on further shifting the balance
of power.

Trevor Owens has argued that the real value of crowdsourcing is getting people
to think and operate in alignment with the museum's mission:

> Getting transcriptions, or for that matter getting any kind of data or work is a
> by-product of something that is actually far more amazing than being able to better
> search through a collection. The process of crowdsourcing projects fulfills the mis-
> sion of digital collections better than the resulting searches. That is, when someone
> sits down to transcribe a document they are actually better fulfilling the mission of
> the cultural heritage organization than anyone who simply stops by to flip through
> the pages. (Owens 2012)

In other words, if museums focus too exclusively on the idea of work product,
they can overlook the greatest value of crowdsourcing projects, which is the process itself. A strategy of using mobile to "recruit the world" potentially transforms
participants in the mission of the museum into stakeholders in a shared future and
success. But those new participants also have the potential to transform the
museum, the way it works, its structures of power, and even its mission.

Mobile is changing the way museums do business – whether they are aware of
it or not. As "the people formerly known as the audience" increasingly expect
information and experiences on demand, wherever and whenever they are, the
market is growing for mobile products and services for and about museums. At
the same time, museums are beginning to think of audiences in a more granular
way, recognizing more variation in needs and interests among their visitors, partners, and collaborators, both online and on site. As a result, museums aspire to
create mobile products and service that better suit specific audience groups and
contexts. In response, a wide range of new players has entered the mobile scene,
loosening the grip of the handful of audio tour companies who dominated the
field for over 50 years. Start-up app companies and smartphone manufacturers,
mobile network providers and social media gurus, students, freelance content
developers, open data protagonists, "citizen curators," new alliances among cultural organizations to co-create content – it seems that nearly every day new forces

are emerging to dramatically reconfigure both the museum mobile landscape and its business models (Samis 2011).

A review of the business strategies developed over the 60 year history of the audio tour shows that some persist in this Mobile 2.0 economy; others are the result of new functions possible on handheld computing platforms and the new business interests that are bringing them to market. What hasn't changed is that, whether "free" or "paid for" by the end-user, there is always a cost to the museum to develop a mobile program. (Some of the business models common for mobile in museums are discussed in Proctor 2011b.)

The value is in the network

In the summer of 2010 Fast Company blogger Aaron Shapiro (2010) warned that developers are unlikely to "get rich quick" on mobile apps. This is particularly true of museums, whose primary mission is not profit but education and outreach. Scant financial returns on mobile products are really nothing new to the museum field: with a few exceptions among the most visited cultural attractions, revenues have not been the most significant benefits to the museum from its audio tours and their progeny. Nonetheless, museums have been early adopters and innovators in the mobile space for some 60 years. The investment required for mobile programs has commonly been justified because of mobile's unique ability to meet other needs of the museum's mission: offering greater possibilities for extending outreach, improving the quality and accessibility of interpretation and education, and supporting other revenue initiatives and connecting platforms to create a whole greater than the sum of its parts.

The metrics of success for mobile, like its goals, are therefore not just the number of downloads and dollars received, but also the extent to which the mobile program is able to engage audiences and support other museum programs, activities, and revenue streams. These outcomes are clearly much more difficult to quantify, but devising metrics, measuring tools, and a management culture that evaluates and values them should be a focus of effort by the museum community as we experiment with new mobile business models. But, as the networked model helps museums find greater relevance to and dialogue with their constituents, its network effects also deliver greater sustainability for the museum against metrics of long-term cultural value – not the terms of capitalist and consumerist systems of exchange.

Becoming a sustainable, radical mobile museum

"As government support for museums has been reduced," noted Judith Mastai, "the financial strategies for maintaining the financial health of these institutions have shifted to serving the customer (or, in the jargon of Museum Studies, the visitor)" (Mastai 2007, 173). What is problematic here is not the idea of serving the people who walk into the museum (in person or, figuratively speaking, online) – responding to their needs and questions. Rather, Mastai noted the influence of market economics in positioning the visitor as the other side of a commercial transaction whose desires can be simply and fully satisfied with the "right" answer, an experience tailored to the individual's conscious wants and needs. Visitors are not merely "sources of information based in perceived needs and desires so that the museum can appear to be publicly accountable by meeting them," argues Mastai, informed by Lacan's critique of "the subject supposed to know." "The mandate of the museum is not to pander to 'felt' needs, but to use them as a starting point from which to build bridges between what is known and what must be known" (Mastai 2007, 175).

Building bridges and weaving more voices and participants into the museum as distributed network accomplishes many ends, ranging from those that support the museum's mission and existing structures of power, to those that can transform not only the way the museum does business, but the very nature and meaning of the institution itself. Crowdsourcing may open up new resources and ways of accomplishing the work of the museum, and produce innovative new products and experiences using mobile platforms among others. Perhaps more importantly, it can engage people in the mission of the museum, and make them stakeholders in the museum's success as an institution. But, on the radical end of the spectrum, letting the people have a say will change the very definition of what museums are.

At the heart of the challenge of radically restructuring museums and their discourses lies this question of democracy: Can museums survive the transformation into truly *civic* organizations that go beyond participation, collaboration, and community to welcome critical transformations of the institution itself? Or will the long, slow shift from Acropolis to Agora be experienced primarily, or even only, as a crisis in museum identity and a fragmenting of museum authority and ownership of the discourse?

Elsewhere I have argued that the project to move from "we do the talking" to "we help you do the talking," as Chris Anderson (2009) put it, is a feminist one. The museum as distributed network is a persistently radical, rather than temporarily revolutionary, model not only because it gives voice to the silenced but also because it decenters traditional structures of power, enabling relations both hierarchical and rhizomic between its nodes (people, communities, conversations) and their connectors. I would add that, even as it enables the bridges and the connections between nodes in the network, mobile can feed the fantasy, with all of its pervasiveness and power, that the museum as distributed network is a consistent and continuous fabric – that the new voices will sing in harmony with existing structures of power. Perhaps the next challenge, as we move from Mobile 2.0 to the next 3.0 generation, is how mobile can play a critical role in enabling the museum instead to map the gaps in its network, to define the edges of the occlusions, the losses and the silences that remain – to bring into question the very homogeneity and singularity of the institution itself.

Notes

1   This chapter summarizes and develops my research which has been published in earlier versions in Proctor 2010a; 2011a; 2011b. Loïc Tallon (2009) found what may be the earliest audio tour in a museum, the 1952 multilingual audio tour of the exhibition *Vermeer: Real or Fake* at the Stedelijk Museum in Amsterdam and blogged about this discovery. The original film can be found at "Draadloze rondleiding in het Amsterdamse Stedelijke Museum" (Wireless tour of the Amsterdam City Museum) in the archives of Polygoon Hollands Nieuws, July 28, 1952, http://www.geschiedenis24.nl/speler. program.7072658.html (accessed August 27, 2014).

2   Universal design aims to produce products and services that are accessible to everyone, irrespective of ability. For example, "Voice over" in the Apple iOS which enables vision-free access to the full range of smartphone access for blind users, drivers, and other multitaskers alike. Similarly, the *Word Lens* app from Quest Visual (http://questvisual. com/us/) uses the smartphone camera to recognize and translate signs between English, Spanish, French, and Italian. The Smithsonian is experimenting with "computer vision" via the smartphone's camera to assist visually impaired visitors with wayfinding and location-based content delivery, and has established accessibility as the number one mobile product development principle in its Mobile Strategic Plan (Proctor 2011c).

3   The famous prediction that mobile web users are expected to exceed desktop Internet users by 2014 was probably inspired by a 2011 Microsoft Tag study (http://www.digital buzzblog.com/2011-mobile-statistics-stats-facts-marketing-infographic/, accessed August 27, 2014). Mary Meeker of Morgan Stanley made a similar forecast in 2010 (http://gigaom. com/2010/04/12/mary-meeker-mobile-internet-will-soon-overtake-fixed-internet/, accessed August 27, 2014), while Dan Rowinski recorded in February 2012 that "Since 2009, mobile internet usage has doubled every year" (http://readwrite.com/2012/02/05/ since_2009_mobile_internet_usage_has_doubled_every, accessed August 27, 2014).

4   http://www.brooklynmuseum.org/community/blogosphere/2010/07/27/brooklyn-museum-mobile-web-on-iphone-and-droid/ (accessed September 15, 2014).

5   http://wiki.museummobile.info/standards (accessed August 27, 2014).

6   See Chapters 20 by Beryl Graham and 21 by John Bell and Jon Ippolito in this volume.

7   Bernard Stiegler has developed this concept of the "amateur" in the context of the museum visit in the "Politics and Technologies of the Amateur" seminar series at the Centre Pompidou's Institute for Research and Innovation (IRI) and "Figures de l'amateur" blog posts of June 22, 2010. See http://www.iri.centrepompidou.fr/category/ seminaire/figures-de-lamateur/?lang=en_us.

8   These examples can be located online as follows: the "Old Weather Project" at www. oldweather.org; Galaxy Zoo at www.galaxyzoo.org, Project Noah at www.project noah.org; the Encyclopedia of Life at www.eol.org; Victoria and Albert Museum online crowdsourcing at http://collections.vam.ac.uk/crowdsourcing/; Steve.museum at http://Steve.museum; Stories from Main Streets from the US Apple iTunes store; and Access American Stories at http://www.si.edu/apps/accessamericanstories.

9   Also at http://archive.pressthink.org/2006/06/27/ppl_frmr.html (accessed September 15, 2014).

References

Anderson, C. 2009. "The Smithsonian's Long Tail." Keynote lecture at "Smithsonian 2.0: A Gathering to Re-imagine the Smithsonian in the Digital Age" conference, January 24.

Aron, J. 2012. "App Uses Earth's Magnetic Field to Guide You Indoors." *New Scientist*, July 9. Accessed August 27, 2014. http://www.newscientist.com/blogs/onepercent/2012/07/earths-magnetic-field-guides-y.html.

Baudrillard, J. 1988. "Simulacra and Simulations." In *Selected Writings*, edited by M. Poster, 166–184. Stanford: Stanford University Press.

Bickersteth, J., and C. Ainsley. 2011. "Mobile Phones and Visitor Tracking." In *Museums and the Web 2011: Proceedings*, edited by J. Trant and D. Bearman. Toronto: Archives & Museum Informatics. Accessed August 27, 2014. http://www.museumsandtheweb.com/mw2011/papers/mobile_phones_and_visitor_tracking.html

Bicknell, T. 2010. "Digital Asset Management Strategies for Multi-platform Mobile Content Delivery." In *Museos, redes sociales y tecnología 2.0* [Museums, social media and 2.0 Technology], edited by Alex Ibañez Etxeberria, 89–101. Zarautz, Spain: Servicio Editorial de al Universidad del País Vasco. Accessed September 15, 2014. http://www.ehu.es/argitalpenak/images/stories/libros_gratuitos_en_pdf/Humanidades/Museos,%20redes%20sociales%20y%20tecnologia%202.0%20-%20Museums,%20social%20media%20&%202.0%20technology.pdf.

Burgund, H. 2010. "Scapes at deCordova Scupture Park and Museum." Accessed August 27, 2014. http://www.decordova.org/art/exhibition/platform-3-halsey-burgund-scapes.

Chan, S. 2009. "Another OPAC discovery – the Gambey Dip Circle (or the Value of Minimal Tombstone Data)." April 27. Accessed August 27, 2014. http://www.powerhousemuseum.com/dmsblog/index.php/2009/04/27/another-opac-discovery-the-gambey-dip-circle-and-the-value-of-minimal-tombstone-data/.

Chan, S. 2011. "Prototyping moveME – a Location-Aware Indoor Mobile App with Tracking." June 6. Accessed August 27, 2014. http://www.freshandnew.org/2011/06/prototyping-moveme-a-location-aware-indoor-mobile-app-with-tracking/.

Fusion Research & Analytics, AAM, and Museums Association. 2012. *Mobile in Museums Study – 2012: A Survey of American Alliance of Museums (US) and Museums Association (UK) Members*. Accessed September 15, 2014. https://aam-us.org/docs/research/mobilemuseums2012-(aam).pdf.

Honeysett, N. 2008. "GettyGuide Handheld (A Cautionary Tale)." Keynote presentation at the Tate Handheld Conference 2008. Accessed August 27, 2014. http://tatehandheld-conference.pbworks.com/w/page/19520884/Keynote%20Presentation%3A%20Nik%20Honeysett.

Howes, J. 2008. *Crowdsourcing*. New York: Crown.

Kelly, L. 2010. "The 21st Century Museum: The Museum without Walls." Paper presented at ICOM-CECA, Shanghai, November.

Mastai, J. 2007. "There Is No Such Thing as a Visitor." In *Museums after Modernism: Strategies of Engagement*, edited by G. Pollock and J. Zemans, 173–177. Oxford: Blackwell.

Owens, T. 2012. "Crowdsourcing Cultural Heritage: The Objectives Are Upside Down." Accessed September 15, 2014. http://www.trevorowens.org/2012/03/crowdsourcing-cultural-heritage-the-objectives-are-upside-down/.

Petrie, M., and L. Tallon. 2010. "The Iphone Effect? Comparing Visitors' and Museum Professionals' Evolving Expectations of Mobile Interpretation Tools." In *Museums and the Web 2011: Proceedings*, edited by J. Trant and D. Bearman. Toronto: Archives & Museum Informatics. Accessed August 27, 2014. http://www.archimuse.com/mw2010/papers/petrie/petrie.html.

Piesing, M. 2012. "Low-Frequency 3D Location Technology Flourishes Where GPS Fails." June 6. Accessed August 27, 2014. http://www.wired.co.uk/news/archive/2012-06/06/low-frequency-location-tracking.

Proctor, N. 2005. "Off Base or On Target? Pros and Cons of Wireless and Location-Aware Applications in the Museum." Paper presented at the ICHIM Conference, Paris, September 21–23. Accessed August 27, 2014. http://www.archimuse.com/publishing/ichim05/Proctor.pdf.

Proctor, N. 2010a. "Digital: Museum as Platform, Curator as Champion, in the Age of Social Media," *Curator: The Museum Journal* 53(1): 35-43.

Proctor, N. 2010b. "Mobile Social Media: Halsey Burgund's 'Scapes.'" MuseumMobile Wiki, October 21. Accessed August 27, 2014. http://wiki.museummobile.info/archives/16082.

Proctor, N. 2011a. *Mobile Apps for Museums: The AAM Guide to Planning and Strategy*, edited by Nancy Proctor, Washington, DC: AAM.

Proctor, N. 2011b. "The Museum as Distributed Network." In *Interactive Museums: Digital Technology, Handheld Interpretation and Online Experiences*, edited by Gregory Chamberlain, 1–20. London: Museum-iD. Accessed September 15, 2014. http://www.museum-id.com/idea-detail.asp?id=337.

Proctor, N. 2011c. "Recruiting the World: Mobile Strategy at the Smithsonian." Accessed August 27, 2014. http://my.si.edu/Media/Default/PDF/SIMobilestrategyDec2011.pdf.

Rosen, J. 2006. "The People Formerly Known as the Audience." Accessed August 28, 2014. http://archive.pressthink.org/2006/06/27/ppl_frmr.html.

Rowe, G. 2012. "Top 5 Indoor Geolocation Technologies." April 16. Accessed August 27, 2014. http://www.thoughtden.co.uk/blog/2012/04/top-5-indoor-geolocation-technologies/.

Samis, P. 2007. "Gaining Traction in the Vaseline: Visitor Response to a Multi-track Interpretation Design for *Matthew Barney: Drawing Restraint*." In *Museums and the Web 2011: Proceedings*, edited by J. Trant and D. Bearman. Toronto: Archives & Museum Informatics. Accessed August 27, 2014. http://www.archimuse.com/mw2007/papers/samis/samis.html.

Samis, P. 2011. "Models and Misnomers for Mobile Production." In *Mobile Apps for Museums: The AAM Guide to Planning and Strategy*, edited by Nancy Proctor. Washington, DC: AAM. Accessed September 15, 2014. http://mobileappsformuseums.wordpress.com/2011/08/05/models-and-misnomers-for-mobile-production/.

Samis, P., and S. Pau. 2009. "After the Heroism, Collaboration: Organizational Learning and the Mobile Space." In *Museums and the Web 2011: Proceedings*, edited by J. Trant and D. Bearman. Toronto: Archives & Museum Informatics. Accessed August 27, 2014. http://www.archimuse.com/mw2009/papers/samis/samis.html.

Schavemaker, M. 2011. "Is Augmented Reality the Ultimate Museum App? Some Strategic Considerations." In *Mobile Apps for Museums: The AAM Guide to Planning and*

Strategy, edited by Nancy Proctor, 46–55. Washington, DC: AAM. Accessed September 15, 2014. http://mobileappsformuseums.wordpress.com/2011/08/05/is-augmented-reality-the-ultimate-museum-app-some-strategic-considerations/.

Shapiro, A. 2010. "The Great App Bubble." Fast Company, August 20. Accessed August 27, 2014. http://www.fastcompany.com/1684020/great-app-bubble.

Shirky, C. 2010. *Cognitive Surplus*. New York: Penguin.

Smith, K. J. 2009. "The Future of Mobile Interpretation." In *Museums and the Web 2011: Proceedings*, edited by J. Trant and D. Bearman. Toronto: Archives & Museum Informatics. Accessed August 27, 2014. http://www.archimuse.com/mw2009/papers/smith/smith.html.

Surowiecki, J. 2004. *The Wisdom of Crowds*. New York: Doubleday.

Tallon, L. 2009. "About That 1952 Stedelijk Museum Audio guide, and a certain Willem Sandburg." Musematic, May 19. Accessed August 27, 2014. http://musematic.net/2009/05/19/about-that-1952-sedelijk-museum-audio-guide-and-a-certain-willem-sandburg/.

Further Reading

Anderson, M. 2007. "Prescriptions for Art Museums in the Decade Ahead." *Curator: The Museum Journal* 50(1): 9–18.

DaPonte, J. 2010. "Mobile Trends for Museums." Presentation at the Tate Handheld Conference 2010, "Museums in the Age of Social Media." Accessed September 15, 2014. http://entertheswarm.com/?p=49.

Proctor, N., ed. 2011. *Mobile Apps for Museums: The AAM Guide to Planning and Strategy*. Washington, DC: AAM.

Smith, A. 2010. "Mobile Access 2010." Pew Research Internet Research Project, July 7. Accessed August 27, 2014. http://www.pewinternet.org/Reports/2010/Mobile-Access-2010.aspx.

Trant, J., and D. Bearman, eds. 2011. *Museums and the Web 2011: Proceedings*. Toronto: Archives & Museum Informatics.

Nancy Proctor is Deputy Director for Digital Experience and Communications at the Baltimore Museum of Art, and co-chair of Museums and the Web. From 2010 to 2014 she was Head of Mobile Strategy and New Media Initiatives for the Smithsonian. With a PhD in American art history, she began publishing online exhibitions in 1995 with Titus Bicknell at TheGalleryChannel.com. TheGalleryChannel was acquired by Antenna Audio, where Nancy led new product development from 2000 to 2008. From 2008 to 2010 she was head of new media initiatives at the Smithsonian American Art Museum. She served as program chair for the Museums Computer Network (MCN) Conference 2010–2011, co-organized the Tate Handheld conferences 2008–2010, manages the MuseumMobile wiki, edited *Mobile Apps for Museums: The AAM Guide to Planning and Strategy* (AAM, 2010) and is digital editor of *Curator: The Museum Journal*.

23 MOVING OUT
Museums, Mobility, and Urban Spaces

Mark W. Rectanus

A collaborative project between the San Francisco Exploratorium and Harrell Fletcher titled *The Best Things in Museums Are the Windows* asked "Where does the museum end and the outside world begin?" The Exploratorium's Center for Art and Inquiry, which co-organized the four-day project with Fletcher in 2013, explained that:

> *The Windows* seeks to create a dynamic framework for discovery by drawing in members of the public as it moves across water, city, suburb, and country, building on the multidimensional perspectives of the participants. The path of *The Windows* will be seeded with demonstrations, screenings, talks, and workshops. (Exploratorium 2013)

Discussing the conceptual development of *The Windows*, Fletcher references the historical relations between the objects on display in museums and acts of viewing, that create the contexts of the museum experience. In doing so, he underscores the potential for an expanded context for engagement:

> The title of the piece is a quote from the painter Pierre Bonnard. You go to a museum and look at the paintings – which is great – but then you look out the windows and see how you can apply what you've learned in the museum to the world outside. You can see things anew because of that framework that's been established in your mind. (Exploratorium 2013)

Notions of a "museum without walls" (Malraux 1967), tearing down walls (Relyea 2013, 171–181), and opening gallery spaces within museums (Krauss 2005) have gained momentum as exhibition spaces, technologies, and audiences increasingly

The International Handbooks of Museum Studies: Museum Media, First Edition.
Edited by Michelle Henning.
© 2015 John Wiley & Sons Ltd. Published 2020 by John Wiley & Sons Ltd.

contextualize experience in terms of mobility. *The Windows*, as a metaphor for capturing experience and relating it to the outside world, also calls our attention to the museum's engagement in increasingly complex constellations of media use. As a view to the outside world of distant places, or a portal for "tele-vision(s)," the windows metaphor has also been used to capture the experiential impact of multidimensional, networked, media – most notably in Microsoft's use of the Windows™ brand (albeit in different contexts). *The Windows* project at the Exploratorium is indicative of a wide range of contemporary museum practices, curatorial initiatives, and collaborative projects (with artists and audiences) that are moving out of the museum's historically circumscribed spaces of archiving, exhibiting, and viewing culture.

The notion of "moving out" does not mean that there is a privileged position "outside" from which the "inside" can be viewed, nor does the museum possess a perspective from within which can be transferred to the "outside." Rather it refers to a process of change in which the fixity of space and boundaries – and how they are defined or conceptualized – is shifting, destabilized, and interrogated. This is happening in part through the strategies of museums themselves, but also in response to the forces of globalization or its contestation in diverse forms of "glocalization" (Virilio 2008, 144; Saybasili 2011, 412–413). As Andreas Huyssen observes, global–local binaries cannot fully address "the specificities of the global–local mix in any concrete urban imaginary" (2008, 5). In this regard, Terry Smith underscores the significance of "locality around the world, the specific histories of which should be acknowledged, valued, and carefully tracked alongside recognition of their interaction with other local and regional tendencies and with dominant art producing centers" (2012, 33–34).

An increasing engagement with contested notions of the global – for example, "world art," "global art," or "worldly art" – and how they intersect with museum discourses, is reflected in the projects and practices of curators and museum directors (Belting 2007; Harris 2011; Smith 2012; Weibel 2013). *Documenta 11* (2002), directed by Okwui Enwezor, received critical recognition as a pivotal moment in advancing and reconceptualizing notions of "global art" by more fully engaging the work of non-Western artists that stimulated new ways to think about locality (Belting 2013a, 73). In the introduction to dOCUMENTA (13) – sited in Alexandria, Banff, and Kabul as well as in the documenta's historical center of Kassel – Carolyn Christov-Bakargiev underscored the potential for destabilizing spatiotemporal relations (Smith 2012, 242–246):

> These places ... are phenomenal spatialities that embody the conditions in which artists and thinkers find themselves acting in the present – of being "on stage" / "under siege" / "in a state of hope" / "on retreat" – unfreezing the associations that are typically made with those places and stressing their continual shifting. (Christov-Bakargiev 2012, 7)

Lane Relyea (2013) points to the socioeconomic and political implications of an increasingly networked art world of freelance labor (artists, curators, designers) that has been shaped by the forces of globalization and neoliberalism, but he also observes apertures for alternative practices. Transborder collaborative projects between arts centers and artist collectives such as the Raqs Media Collective (India) and the Chronus Art Center (Shanghai), which seek to "untangle and compare the different paths of modernity taken by India and China," may represent lateral forms of engagement that create alternatives to Western exhibition cultures and museum models (Chronus Art Center 2013).

The emergence of global megacities in the non-Western world has also opened new spaces for diverse cultural practices and "imaginative geographies" (Huyssen 2008, 14). Within the context of "the postcolonial constellation," Enwezor notes that discourses on, and forms of, contemporary art "cannot be defined by simple, singular models" (2008b, 223), underscoring the diverse venues that shape contemporary curatorial practices and forms of display, including:

> the proliferation of exhibition forms – such as blockbusters, large-scale group or thematic exhibitions, cultural festivals, biennales, and so on – and their constant mutation. All of these have significantly enlarged the knowledge base of contemporary thinking about art and its commonplaces in museums and culture at large. This enlargement is crucial, because it has created new networks between hitherto separated spheres of contemporary artistic production, in both the everyday engagement with the world and its images, texts, and narratives. (2008b, 223–224; see also 2008a 156–178)

These developments have had a profound impact on contemporary curating (Smith 2012) but also on the museum's administration, organization, programming, exhibiting, and curating. In this regard Relyea observes that:

> Platforms and projects dominate the new organizational forms of the art world, replacing more closed, nonhorizontal forms. This has put tremendous pressure on museums (traditionally very opposite sort of structures, hierarchical and exclusive) and most are racing to adjust. (2013, 21)

In referring to emerging networks and processes of deterritorialization as part of the postcolonial constellation, Enwezor observes, "not so much the newness of these territories … but their systematic integration into mobile sites of discourse, which only become more visible because of the advances in information technology" (2008b, 228).

Although museums have also been physically moving out – most visibly with respect to their expansion into new wings, global satellites, and iconic architecture – a singular focus on interior museum spaces and architecture would overlook the increasing permeability of museum borders and projects that problematize notions of inside/outside by working across cultures and geographies (Papastergiadis 2008, 378–379). With regard to what might constitute a more "global museum," Hans Belting observes that:

> The issue is not whether these museums qualify as models for "a global museum" anywhere in the world. The question is rather whether in the global age the art museum will survive at all as an institution with a single purpose and a common appearance.
>
> The quest for new art worlds will provide museums with a new and critical role. The mapping drive which aims to develop interacting art worlds in geographic (but not in national) terms, calls for places on the map that symbolize an art world in the making. But such places do not require the same type of institution. (2013b, 251; see also Bharucha 2004, 130–133)

Referring to the "mobile sites of discourse" in which cultural production, mediation, and reception occur, Enwezor also directs our attention to the intersections of the museum and mobile media within and outside the museum, as well as the role that digital media play in the deterritorialization of museum contents and programming (Kelly 2013, 60–62; Weibel 2013, 25–26). The "mobile sites of discourse" – whether they are collaborative projects that move across diverse sites or are interconnected through mobile media – create the potential for dialogic interactions with audiences, including acts of reflection, performance, and consumption. That is, audiences interact with cultural sites by drawing on their past experience with other sites of memory-making and by communicating these experiences with other viewers in real or virtual communities. For example, the Jewish Museum Munich developed multiple pathways for experiencing the museum through exhibition spaces, on blogs (that included dialogues with the museum's director), and though installations, such as *Speaking Germany*. Sharone Lifschitz created this multidimensional communicative project through texts on the museum's windows and at (mobile) sites throughout the city (Fleckenstein and Purin 2007). Excerpts from Lifschitz's conversations with Germans – placed on billboards, inside subway trains, and on bridges – provided new, and sometimes unexpected, contexts for thinking about identity and life in contemporary Germany. For example, one statement and response on an advertising pillar read, "I cannot always be upset with who I am. / No, of course not, of course ..."[1] These dialogues exposed questions of German and Jewish identity by bringing the conversations out into the spaces of everyday life both in the pedestrian zone surrounding the Jewish Museum Munich and throughout the city (Bilski 2007, 71).[2]

The construction of metanarratives and discursive spaces outside the museum may also be considered in the context of historical shifts in the museum from private to public spaces, and in terms of "civic seeing," as Tony Bennett (2006) has shown. Bennett underscores the historical relations and "tension between the museum as civic educator and the negative pull of distracted vision" through the "incorporation of television, video, touch-screen computer displays, and Imax theaters into museums [which] has undermined the distinction between museums and other forms of audiovisual culture" (2006, 275–276).

"Civic seeing" may also inform our understanding of curatorial interventions that have emerged on the boundary zones of museums. In particular, this chapter will examine the construction of transdiscursive spaces for art and culture, sites for creating cultural meaning and experience, and audience engagement through a mobile *mise-en-scène*. The term "mobile *mise-en-scène*," as I am employing it here, assumes audiences who are mobile not only in terms of their physical movement across urban cultural zones but also with respect to their mobility across media (film, television, video, Internet), sites of cultural performance (museums, theater, symphony, cinema), and the sites for the consumption of culture (in virtual and real spaces). The shifting contexts of exhibitions or other forms of cultural display (e.g., art installations in public spaces) are mediated through the mobile *mise-en-scène*, that is, the formal and physical modalities of constructing the *mise-en-scène* (subject, lighting, setting, framing, performance), the conceptual development of a project (by artists and/or curators), the reception of the installation within diverse contexts ("static" or "mobile"), and the environments that may alter the work and its reception. The concept of *mise-en-scène*, taken from theater and cinema, literally refers to "placing on stage." The process of composing the subject, lighting, and setting, as *mise-en-scène*, creates a "frame" that structures how the performance of the persons (or objects) is "staged" and subsequently experienced by audiences. As Mieke Bal points out, *mise-en-scène* provides "a metaphor for the experience of an exhibition" by foregrounding the affective experience of spectatorship which is, in part, based on how exhibition spaces are created (2007, 74–75). The use of a *mobile mise-en-scène* may be found at diverse sites for exhibitions and installations – ranging from art, science, technology, and cultural heritage museums to biennials and art festivals. While some characteristics of a mobile *mise-en-scène* (e.g., in filmmaking or traveling exhibitions) have been discussed in other contexts (Bacher 1978; Bal 2007, 74–76), I am suggesting its use as an analytical tool that may inform our understanding of the transdiscursive dimensions of museums within contemporary urban culture(s) as well as projects that destabilize the borders of urban space.

The implications of "moving out" are visible in the reconceptualization of museum and exhibition practices within urban topographies. They are wide-ranging and include the development of urban cultural zones (e.g., clusters of museum buildings that are collectively branded for cultural tourism), strategies for engaging audiences in the museum's boundary zones throughout the city, local cultural politics that privilege mixed use entertainment complexes, collaborative projects with artists and curators that involve social activism, the museum's expanded role as a think tank, lab, or conceptual space, or projects that seek to engage audiences in everyday life and culture (e.g., in public transportation, streets, and shopping venues). The blurring boundaries between the museum, urban cultural space, and mobile media (which audiences may use to navigate and interact with these sites) underscore the multidimensional modes in which museum visitors are engaged as *spectators and participants* as they bring their memories and knowledge to the process of experiencing culture.

Transdiscursive spaces and the mobile *mise-en-scène*: *The Recovery of Discovery*

In March 2011 the Kunst-Werke Institute for Contemporary Art in Berlin launched Cyprien Gaillard's participatory installation *The Recovery of Discovery*. The installation, which became known as the "beer pyramid," was composed of 3000 imported cartons of Turkish Efes beer which formed the material for the pyramid (Pfeffer 2012). Over 3000 visitors at the opening climbed the pyramid, tore open cartons of beer, opened the bottles using their own devices, drank, talked, smoked, and stayed late into the night. As the installation progressed over three months, the pyramid became increasingly unstable as bottles were lined up along the wall, smashed, or broken. The visitors' incremental deconstruction and destruction of the pyramid became an integral dimension of the project.

Gaillard's installation formally and metaphorically references the Pergamon Altar located at the nearby Pergamon Museum, Berlin – underscoring the construction of transdiscursive spaces and cultural zones for staging art and culture within urban topographies (Gaillard and Pfeffer 2012, 33, 46; Pfeffer 2012, 10–11; von Osten 2012, 81). The installation not only calls our attention to urban cultural zones created by multiple museum complexes (such as Berlin's Museum Island or Munich's Pinakotheken) as sites of cultural tourism, events, and consumption, but also to visitor mobility in traversing these zones and participating in urban culture. As Marion von Osten observes, cities themselves are on display as exhibitions and "in contemporary art we find historiographic references have become a central focal point, the material of artistic interventions" (2012, 70).

The conceptual development of the installation is informed by notions of tourism, consumption, "creative destruction," and urban archaeology. Gaillard refers to tearing down hierarchies in ruins, that is, between the image of the Pergamon Altar as "high culture" and the beer pyramid as a signifier of the ruins of urban popular culture, arguing that "somehow all ruins should be equal" (von Osten 2012, 46). In terms of their respective functions as sites of touristic consumption and event culture, both the Pergamon Altar and Gaillard's beer pyramid allude to John Urry's notion of *Consuming Places* (1995). Gaillard's installation, however, attempts to engage visitors in an exploration of their multiple roles as consumers and participants in creating culture through a performative process of consuming (beer) and the destruction of the monument itself.

The Recovery of Discovery employs cinematic staging strategies that create a mobile *mise-en-scène* by inviting audiences to engage in a form of cinematic spectacle. Gaillard, like many other contemporary artists who work across multiple media platforms, used his experience in filmmaking (Gaillard and Pfeffer 2012, 46) to stage installations as a (cinematic) event – one in which the exhibition visitors function in the dual role of audience and performers. The construction of the beer pyramid became the literal and metaphorical stage on which the performance would take place. Gaillard created a cinematic frame defined by the aesthetics of the pyramid's size, shape, color, lighting, and placement and the use of the Efes beer cartons which staged references to Turkey, antiquity, and the iconography of pyramids as cultural artifacts. However, rather than following a script or storyboard which would determine each shot or scene in a performance, the narrative unfolded through the unscripted performance of the visitors as they consumed and deconstructed the stage (i.e., pyramid) while drinking, talking, smoking, and interacting in small groups, much like reality television. Exhibition curator Susanne Pfeffer and Cyprien Gaillard observed that the visitors became "a force that was difficult to control" as they refused to leave the installation at closing time (Pfeffer 2012, 13). As the visitors' images and stories of the beer pyramid spread via YouTube and blogs, social media created a discursive and sensory space that reflected the mobility of the visitor-performers as they moved in and out of the exhibition and across virtual spaces.[3]

Gaillard's project required that visitors "recover the discovery" of political links to the cultural contexts of monuments and their histories through a process of participation and reflection. Here, Grant Kester refers to the "multivalent and contradictory" dimensions of socially engaged art that emerge through collective action (2011, 210). The installation invited visitors to transform the exhibition space into a site for touristic consumption and destruction – simultaneously undermining the representational authority of the "white cube" and problematizing how audience interaction is situated (Pfeffer 2012, 15). While Gaillard's aesthetics of participatory art and performative *practice* engage the affective dimensions of experience in order to recover critical modes of discovery, that is, "the recovery of discovery," they also carry an uncertain outcome with regard to how visitors experience and reflect on their individual and collective participation. Gaillard's performative project does succeed in problematizing the intersections of exhibition space and the variegated spaces of everyday life (including architecture, urban nightlife, and consumption) by creating a boundary zone – between exhibition and urban landscapes – that engages the conflicts and contradictions of these spaces. In doing so, Gaillard destabilizes the participants' modes of experiencing and seeing by foregrounding their own "complicity" as "vandals" within urban landscapes of creation and destruction – in part through references to the Pergamon Altar. However, a performative process of "discovery" which would more fully challenge visitors to reflect on the appropriation of the past, including the discursive links to Germany, Turkey, and the Pergamon Altar (Foster 2012) and how they are inscribed in the cultural memory of the present, remains only partially excavated as a fragmentary dimension of Gaillard's project.

The Recovery of Discovery provides a paradigmatic example of the manner in which museums and galleries create transdiscursive spaces that mediate and interrogate contemporary cultural practices. Gaillard's project reveals discourses on the histories of cultural artifacts, urban tourism, and the performative role of visitors. These are issues of central importance for contemporary museums as they become multidimensionally mobile. The installation also reflects the dialogic and discursive aspects of visitor mobility as they interact with other visitors in the physical spaces of museums or galleries, but also on a transdiscursive level as they move across urban spaces (e.g., from one venue to another) and communicate their experiences via mobile media.

Thus, museums increasingly position audiences in multiple roles as viewers, spectators, performers, and consumers. These positions are informed by the aesthetics of museum media and the mediation of images and content on websites, in archives, or at multiple sites of display (e.g., traveling exhibitions), functioning as a mobile *mise-en-scène*. Smith comments that:

> Given this dispersal of information across so many mediums, the sense of loss, sometimes exclusion, felt by those who for good reason could not actually visit an exhibition – who obtained some sense of it through reading about it in the press or in magazines or by consulting the catalogue – is lessening. (2012, 237)

The proliferation and diversification of media use and aesthetics (e.g., from videography and filmmaking to YouTube) across platforms sited outside the museum may be creating more textured and complex engagements with museums, but they also challenge museums to rethink how visitors can be engaged in culture's multiple valences of entertainment *and* critical reflection. While audiences may be increasingly adept at navigating media platforms, they may also find it challenging to map out their own space for reflection and critical engagement of culture within the context of everyday life.

Corporate museums and cultural zones: BMW Welt and Leeum Samsung Museum of Art

In 2007 BMW Welt (BMW World) opened as the central hub of BMW's global corporate representation and as a platform for heightening its cultural profile in Munich. Designed by Coop Himmelb(l)au, BMW Welt provides a stage for visual and material consumption, event culture, performance, and exhibition. At BMW Welt, visitors view and sit in new BMW automobiles and on motorcycles, observe other customers as they descend the spiral ramp in their new cars, eat in the many restaurants, shop for BMW merchandise, and watch performances by

FIGURE 23.1   BMW Welt, Munich. (For a color version of this figure, please see the color plate section.)
Reproduced by permission of BMW AG.

motorcyclists, or other events, in the open spaces of the structure. Visitors are engaged in acts of performative consumption through their interaction in and around the automobiles – becoming actors on a metaphorical stage who observe, and are observed by, their fellow actors and spectators. In doing this, the visitors are not only coperformers on multiple stages in BMW Welt, they are also coconstructing the mobile *mise-en-scène* of each exhibition, that is, as each vehicle is dually signified as an interactive exhibit and as an imagined object for purchase that can be driven away – becoming a mobile exhibition in its own right (Figure 23.1).

Notions of mobility, consumption, and performance at the BMW complex are conceptually and structurally mediated through three buildings (BMW Welt, the BMW Museum, and the BMW factory), the BMW website, and a pedestrian bridge linking BMW Welt with the BMW Museum. BMW Welt, as the architectural centerpiece of the complex, shifts the focus from the representation of present pasts (Huyssen 2003) in the BMW Museum to present futures in BMW Welt. The exhibitions in both buildings engage visitors in processes of memory-making by linking pasts (and futures) to the present. The convergence of past and present may, as Huyssen observes, represent "the desire to anchor ourselves in a world characterized by an increasing instability of time and the fracturing of lived space" (2003, 18). At the same time, visitor interaction with vehicles as "exhibits for sale" in BMW Welt enables visitors to create memories for the *future* that can be retrieved in order to recreate or anticipate the BMW experience. While the BMW Museum remains a site for representing BMW's automotive history it also introduces futuristic discourses that elide the museum's institutional links to the past, for example, when it asserts that "contemporary museums have nothing in common with their predecessors of the 19th century" (BMW 2011).

BMW Welt and the BMW Museum operate in multiple dimensions of the mobile *mise-en-scène* by utilizing cinematic strategies of audience engagement

FIGURE 23.2   BMW Museum, Munich.
Photo: Mark W. Rectanus. Reproduced by permission of BMW AG.

through architecture, staging, and events that create contexts for the visitors'
shared experience of the BMW brand (i.e., shopping, viewing, and sitting in new
automobiles). These sites within the complex also construct new contexts for
imagining present pasts and present futures by evoking notions of mobility, innovation, experience, and exclusivity through the signage used in both exhibition
spaces (Figure 23.2). Examples range from "High Performance: The Epitome of
Power and Exclusiveness" to alternating English/German words on the walls of
the BMW Museum's upward walkway such as "Umwelt"/"Environment,"
"Fortschritt"/"Progress," or "Euphorie"/"Euphoria." Mobility is inscribed in the
branding of BMW vehicles through the open, cinematic stage within BMW
Welt – as customers drive down the ramp and exit the building onto the nearby
autobahn – but also in the representation of the automobiles that invite potential
buyers to imagine their own experience of being on stage and driving away. Thus,
the BMW complex, as part of a cultural zone linking the Olympic Village, Olympic
Park, and nearby Allianz Arena stadium (with its own museum for Bayern Munich
Football Club), offers interconnected modes of entertainment (sports, shopping,
driving) and spectatorship (concerts, exhibitions open air films, and music festivals) that reinforce BMW's globalized representation of individuality, mobility,
strength, and performance with a local inflection.

Another example of how corporate museums are shaping urban culture is provided by the Leeum Samsung Museum of Art in Seoul, South Korea. The Leeum has attempted to establish a new model for the contemporary Asian art museum by creating three museums under one institutional umbrella, but with each museum maintaining an individual visual brand or identity. Museum 1, designed by Mario Botta, exhibits traditional Korean art; Museum 2, designed by Jean Nouvel, presents works by contemporary Korean and international artists; and the Samsung Child Education & Culture Center, designed by Rem Koolhaas, "contributes to the education of future leaders" (Leeum Samsung Museum of Art 2013). As Birgit Mersmann observes, "With this act of mega-merging, it builds in itself a new museum corporation, thereby also structurally reflecting its core definition and mission as a Samsung corporate museum" (2013, 284). Unlike the BMW complex, the Leeum museums are primarily dedicated to the mediation of art and education rather than the explicit self-representation of product culture. In this sense, the founding concept for the Leeum museums, based on the collections of Korean art held by Samsung's founder and subsequent chairman, is similar to patronage models that establish named museums for the patron's collections or museum wings endowed by corporate sponsors (Leeum 2013). On the museum website, the Leeum positions itself as a cosmopolitan institution with a global outlook:

> Welcoming the emerging global age, Leeum seeks to be a center of Asian art. It is a museum of new ideas, and bridges the East and the West, with its eye on the future. Please enjoy a new world of art and culture in Leeum, where the past and present coexist, and where art, culture, and people share an urban architectural space in harmony with nature. (Leeum 2013)

As Mersmann observes, the Leeum's Western-style branding and image is "subordinated in order to build a new Korean corporate identity as a powerful part of a representation of the New Asia. In this way, it is the West that stands in the image of the New Asia" (2013, 287). Rather than creating sites for the exploration of what the "New Asia" might mean, or how these multiple museum concepts might contribute to diverse discourses on "East and West," the Leeum posits its status as a cultural center for the "New Asia" while Samsung's corporate role as a shaping force of globalized mobile culture is conspicuously absent. As Rustom Bharucha notes, attempts by any museum to lay claim to or represent "Asian art" within a region with so many diverse and competing identities and cultures is inherently problematic (2004, 130–131). Bharucha suggests an alternative path that would investigate contested notions of the "New Asian Museum" through an exploration of cultural, social, and geopolitical differences and conflicts rather than their erasure (2004, 131).

By merging "cultural tradition" with geopolitics, the Leeum aspires to become the definitive museum for Asian art: "Leeum desires to be, as an artistic and cultural root, the center of Asian art, and desires to be a leader for the future" (Leeum 2013). These objectives may represent attempts to simultaneously preserve cultural identity in response to the (homogenizing) forces of global media culture (which Samsung facilitates through its (mobile) product culture) while responding to the contestation of regional identities and competition for cultural tourism and strategic interests in Asia (ranging from the Korean peninsula to Singapore, China, and Japan). In this context, "moving out" may involve the Leeum's attempts to stake out a territory as *the* new center and leader for Asian art both in terms of a globalized corporate cultural politics and in response to regional competition.

Boundary zones

The development of cultural zones as a focus of urban planning or "cultural engineering" (Huyssen 2008, 9) and localized responses by museums, which stake out their own claims to urban space, reflect the contested status of urban cultural politics. Museums increasingly make use of their exterior structures for promotion and self-representation, and as a site for installations – ranging from banners for new exhibitions to signs and posters that are installed as art in public space. Light-projection technologies are utilized to project words and images on the surfaces of museum structures or on plazas surrounding the museum – attracting visitors to evening events, highlighting the visual profile of the museum and its artwork, in order to compete with other urban events. The use of images and words and their signification as hypertexts in public spaces are, as Simon Morley has observed, indicative of how the artist "becomes a cartographer of all media" (2003, 208). These hypertexts may also reference local cultural politics and urban planning. For example, Lars Ramberg mounted a sign with the word "ZWEIFEL" (doubt) on the top of the German Democratic Republic's Palace of the Republic in Berlin before it was demolished – drawing attention to debates over the future of the building (which housed the German Democratic Republic parliament and a cultural center) and its cultural legacy in post-unification Germany (Ramberg 2005).

While self-representation and promotion on museum facades have become commonplace, the Schirn Kunsthalle in Frankfurt am Main developed a project with the Frankfurt transit authority (VGF) which utilized the public spaces of the adjacent Römer subway station (Figure 23.3). A series of signs located in the subway leading to the Schirn included: "U-BAHN FAHREN IST KEINE KUNST" [Riding the subway is not art], "WERBUNG MACHEN / IST KEINE KUNST" [Advertising is not art], "KARTENKAUFEN / IST KEINE KUNST" [Buying [subway] tickets is not art]. Visitors ascending or descending the escalator leading to the Schirn could read: "HOCHSCHAUEN / IST KEINE KUNST" [Looking up is not art], "WÄNDEGUCKEN / IST KEINE KUNST" [Looking at the walls is not art]; and at the top of the stairs the final sign located directly before pedestrians turn to the

FIGURE 23.3   "Going to the Schirn is not art," Frankfurt. (For a color version of this figure, please see the color plate section.)
Photo: Mark W. Rectanus.

museum states "IN DIE SCHRIN / GEHEN IST / KEINE KUNST" [Going to the Schirn is not art]. Each sign is situated in a different location along the pedestrian's path, leading to or from the museum, and within a context which foregrounds the *performativity* of everyday actions, for example, "buying tickets" or "riding the subway."

The sequencing of the signs juxtaposes the concreteness of the everyday with the abstractness of "art." This emerges most clearly in the sign at the top of the steps which addresses and – depending on the reading – problematizes the action of going to an exhibition ("Going to the Schirn is not art"). The movement from outside to inside, of going into the Schirn's exhibition space, suggests that visiting an art museum or exhibition is not in and of itself related to art by negating the associative linkage to the word "KUNST" (art), but it also anticipates and destabilizes the link between the viewer and the artwork itself which the visit to an exhibition promises. Thus, the signs question the value and meaning of everyday activities *outside* the museum that have been elevated to forms of aesthetic connoisseurship in urban space, in short the aestheticization of everyday life. These include consumer culture as art ("WERBUNG MACHEN" (advertising)) or acts of visual consumption ("RÖMER FOTOGRAFIEREN" (photographing the Römer plaza)). The placement of the signs creates a mobile *mise-en-scène* through their sequencing, as pedestrians walk past each sign and view them as individual images but also as a moving sequence (similar to a slow motion video) – referencing the pedestrian's own mobility as a postmodern *flâneur* ("stroller") who traverses the urban landscape, by riding the subway, walking, photographing, looking, and visiting the museum.

The signs also ask viewers to question their subject positions with regard to everyday life and culture from an ironic, self-reflexive, and humorous perspective. Both modalities – that is, engagement with notions of art and postmodern irony – reflect the genesis of the project, not as art in public spaces, but rather as a joint venture between the Schirn, the VGF, and the global advertising firm Saatchi & Saatchi. Viewed from this perspective, the subway station was transformed into a themed environment and provocation which would stimulate reflection on notions of mobility (e.g., riding the subway) and urban experience – one which also encouraged viewers to create their own narratives and performative scenarios by acting out or reading the signs aloud to others as they move through the space.

Although the Schirn's promotional partnership with the transit authority would seem to reinforce an "image transfer," that is, between mass transit (as a vehicle of access to cultural institutions) and the museum, the signs also suggest the erasure of art and culture from everyday experience by telling the viewer what it is not. Understood as populism from the right, the signs reinstate the possibility of high art that cannot be experienced within or defined by everyday life, that is, creating a separate sphere for art that cannot be realized by simply *visiting* the museum. Read as populism from the left, the signs critique notions of urban tourism or "consuming places" (Urry 1995), including visits to the exhibition, which redefine engagement with art in terms of commodification rather than exploring the critical social contexts of art in the everyday.

In 2013 the Schirn expanded its conceptual move outside the museum through the project "Street-Art Brazil," which invited 11 leading artists and artists groups to create their works on bank towers, bridges, the Hauptwache pedestrian zone, the police presidium, a subway train, and the exterior of the Schirn. These murals, signs, and symbols became interventions that could "alter the everyday image of the city" (Schirn 2013). In order to enable pedestrians to locate and identify the individual works, the Schirn developed a mobile app that also included background information and artists' videos, thus linking the curatorial content of the project to its display in diverse urban spaces. Your Picture At The Schirn encouraged pedestrians to take a photo of one of the works from their own vantage point, tag the image(s) on Instagram, and activate the GPS. The images were posted on a constantly changing collage that arranged them (based on an algorithm that referenced size, color, and time of submission) and projected them in the Schirn's foyer. Visitors participated in the mobile *mise-en-scène* created by the Brazilian street artists by capturing images from their own perspectives and acting out the Schirn's suggestion: "So show us how you see art!" (Schirn 2013). "Street-Art Brazil" provided a more differentiated response to clichés of global graffiti by revealing a diversity of styles and techniques – that amplified the political and social references in the works – while creating new perspectives for reception and reflection as the works were inserted into sites of everyday life in a German city. The Schirn became a portal for experiencing the project by curating multiple platforms that created diverse perspectives on locality and simultaneously engaged visitors in participatory dimensions – linking the decentered sites of display and performance with visitors viewing the collage in the central foyer of the Schirn. "Street-Art Brazil" illustrates how artist residencies at museums are also moving out to mobile sites and in doing so are shifting the temporal and spatial modes of exhibition practice (Smith 2012).

Social activism and collaboration

The museum's increasing engagement in the urban landscapes of everyday life also signals forms of social activism that may be linked to artist residencies at museums and art centers, curatorial collaborations with individual artists, participatory installations, or interventions by artist collectives. Rather than considering these developments as separate spheres of activity, museums increasingly seek to identify intersections and forms of collaboration that map onto social, economic, political, and cultural networks – reflecting a conceptual shift that repositions museum space vis-à-vis public space in terms of permeability and openness. In this regard Nikos Papastergiadis observes:

> As contemporary art practice reimagines notions of place and exile, as artists trace connections that transcend the old geospatial boundaries, we not only witness new narratives of mobility and difference, but new patterns of social engagement and aesthetic production. The next challenge is to find a discourse that can articulate the complex interlocal connections that now operate in a global network. (2008, 380).

The *Populism* exhibition (2005), which traveled to the Contemporary Art Centre (Vilnius), the National Museum of Architecture and Design (Oslo), the Stedelijk Museum (Amsterdam), and the Frankfurter Kunstverein (Frankfurt am Main), problematized notions of inside/outside and signaled forms of "activist curating" (Smith 2012, 232–236). In this exhibition, organized by the Nordic Institute for Contemporary Art (NIFCA), the curators asked how "forms of populism – whether left wing or right wing, progressive or reactionary – promote themselves and their quest for mass appeal through a stylistic and aesthetic consciousness" (Stedelijk Museum 2005, 51). *Populism* did not aim to exhibit representative expressions of populist art but rather individual and collective works that registered and mediated the ideologies, aesthetics, and diverse expressions of populism. The project interrogated how "The political imagination of visual art can get involved in these economies of signs and desires, and address current cultural discussions through proposals of other directions for democracy" (Stedelijk 2005, 51). In addition to a *Populism* reader which provided theoretical essays and artists' statements, the project also appropriated populist media by publishing free copies of *The Populist* in a large, tabloid-like format. The exhibition reflects the impact of populism and meta-discourses on the nexus of museums, politics, media, and the civic, for example, by asking how museums "plan their programming and marketing in an attempt to reach wider audiences" or "What conception of the audience (and by extension, of citizenship) is inherent in … cultural populism?" (Stedelijk 2005, 51).

As issues of mobility and migration have become a focus of populist politics, artistic interventions have attempted to expose and destabilize mobility's links to ideology, for example, globalized notions of "freedom of movement" (which are manifest in the themed environment of BMW Welt). Exhibitions such as the Generali Foundation's *Geography and the Politics of Mobility* reflected a critical consciousness of the intersections of mobility, technology, and globalization by examining how artists and audiences interact and participate in projects that operate within multiple geographies. Here Ursula Biermann observed that:

> the participating artists and writers, are perfectly aware that they are personally involved in writing a geography that contributes to the building of the very space they describe. The exhibition space may be looked at as one such transient location whose meaning is generated through the passage of people and the appearance of temporary projects, which may inscribe themselves, over time, in the form of a program, into the space. … Each of the projects gives insight into a system, which is as much a system of navigation as a system of representation. (2003, 22–23)

Brian Holmes draws our attention to how we map the work of artist communities and collectives that operate outside exhibitions and museum spaces, in virtual space, or through interventions in public spaces – in part, creating "parallel and alternative circuits of experimentation, production, distribution, use, and interpretation" (2003, 169). Networked artist collectives have played an increasingly important role in shaping contemporary artistic practice and have provided further impetus for museums to "think outside the box" or more aptly "outside the white cube." Collectives such as Ala Plástica (Buenos Aires), Park Fiction (Hamburg), Wochenklausur (Vienna), and Huit Facettes (Dakar) create interventions at local levels, while others such as Shack/Slumdwellers International and Global Studio "bring a range of skills from a variety of distant sources to bear on specific, extreme problems of housing" (Smith 2009, 230–231). In this regard, Kester underscores the tensions between "the abbreviated, nomadic, nature of many of these projects" and the fact that the "artist is never able to enter fully into the complexities of a given situation" (2011, 135). For Kester, this dimension also references the relations between artists and museums, that is, a "tension that differentiates the museum or gallery space as an essentially accommodating receptacle for the artist's vision from the vicissitudes of the Tanzanian countryside" (2011, 135).

Art museums may also seek collaborators who contribute their knowledge and professional experience in order to design local interventions that address the impact of a globally networked economy on everyday life and culture. While exhibitions on architecture and design have become institutionalized within the collections and exhibition culture of many contemporary museums, New York's Museum of Modern Art (MoMA) intervened more directly in the politics of housing through the project *Foreclosed: Rehousing the American Dream* by creating "five teams of architects, planners, ecologists, engineers, landscape designers ... to develop proposals for housing that would open new routes through the mortgage-foreclosure crisis that continues to afflict the United States."[4]

Rather than focusing on the spatial politics of urban city centers, the MoMA project addressed the sometimes "invisible" impact of the financial crisis on suburbia in five regions of the United States, while calling attention to the connections between zoning policies, urban infrastructure, economic policies, and the flows of global corporate capital, all of which contributed to the collapse of financial markets in 2008. Within this context, "moving out" assumes a more physical and literal inflection in terms of both the families who left their homes as a result of mortgage foreclosures and unemployment and the museum's awareness of the impact of the recession on local communities. "Foreclosed" also signals broader discussions regarding the musealization and "repurposing" of former industrial sites into themed environments, "shrinking cities," and the museum's response to these developments (Barndt 2010).

Conceptual spaces

Museums are increasingly examining how they can reposition their practices with respect to their relations to the "outside." While education and outreach initiatives play a significant role in the museum's mission to engage diverse publics, many museums are developing new conceptual platforms that will facilitate experimental projects inside and outside museum spaces. The Hirschhorn Museum's "Bubble" project indicates the "asymmetrical thinking" that characterizes attempts to reconceptualize engagement with audiences. "The Bubble," developed by the Hirschhorn's director, Richard Koshalek, and architects Diller Scofidio + Renfro, resembled a large blue balloon inserted in the "doughnut hole" center (i.e., an open air space) of the Hirschhorn Museum, with a second small balloon protruding from the side of the round museum structure. Joseph Giovannini (2013) commented that "The design was described as a 'seasonal inflatable structure' that would house pop-up think tanks about the arts around the world, transforming the nation's contemporary art museum into a cultural Davos on the Mall."

"The Bubble" represented a continuation of new initiatives launched by Koshalek that would make the Hirschhorn more visible and attractive to museum visitors on the Washington, DC, Mall. Koshalek "turned the institution inside out," for example, by commissioning a 360 degree film (*Song 1*) by Doug Aitkin that was projected on the museum's exterior wall, creating an atmosphere similar to a drive-in movie on the Mall (Giovannini 2013). The asymmetrical form of "The Bubble" references both its experimental design, which required extensive consultations between the architects and engineers, and its "counter-intuitive" approach to repositioning the Hirschhorn's identity and programming within the competitive cultural space of other museums located on the Mall. "The Bubble" was also designed as an alternative cultural space whose architecture would signal a more radical response to, and departure from, the traditional museum architecture represented by other Smithsonian museums. Plans for programming "The Bubble" ranged from presentations in think tank forums to performing arts events that would complement but also expand the conceptual scope of the Hirschhorn (Giovannini 2013).

"The Bubble" as a seasonal, fluid, and dynamic space designed to attract visitors and artists also reflects its use as a mobile *mise-en-scène* by moving out of the museum's existing boundaries in order to create new spaces for visitor engagement. "The Bubble" becomes a medium whose form communicates the aim of its function(s) as flexible, movable, and mutable while incorporating components of spectacle and pop art that would attract audiences (Giovaninni 2013). Because funding for the project was not secured by the deadline and the museum's board could not reach consensus on its future, it was cancelled in 2013 and Koshalek subsequently resigned as director (Giovaninni 2013). While the brief history of "The Bubble" reflects the fragility of many museum experiments (with respect to their funding, implementation, and sustainability), it is also indicative of attempts by museums to increase their visibility and visitor engagement within highly competitive cultural zones.

The Museum of Contemporary Art (MCA), Chicago, has pursued the reconceptualization of the museum by focusing on increased interactions between artists and audiences. MCA director Madeleine Grynsztejn comments: "We want to be an artist-activated, audience-engaged platform for producing art, ideas and conversation around the creative process" (2011, 45). Grynsztejn's efforts to redefine the museum's engagement by focusing on exhibitions and think tanks intersects with the MCA's organizational realignment into a "convergence team" that merges formerly independent departments (performance, education, marketing, and visitor services) in order to create a more holistic operational framework. The MCA's efforts to create synergies between the museum concept and exhibition practice were reflected in the words "MUSEUMS ARE NOW," which were painted on the museum's exterior steps (and designed by Scott Reinhard) during Olafur Eliasson's exhibition *Take Your Time* (2009). The urgency of the message not only directs visitors' attention to the contemporaneity of the museum and curatorial practice (Smith 2012), but also illustrates how notions of the contemporary museum that are communicated on the boundary zones between "inside" and "outside" reference a rethinking of the museum's mission.

Like the Hirschhorn, the MCA is aware of the challenges of communicating and projecting a visual identity within the competitive landscape of urban event culture. In order to more effectively engage and communicate with audiences and artists, Grynsztejn merged media relations, marketing, and visitor services into a combined department of communications and community engagement – noting that the impetus for the restructuring emerged from the experience that "social networks are now more pervasive and impact which exhibitions audiences attend and how they respond" (2011, 47). This move not only illustrates the impact of social media on the museum's administrative structure but also the MCA's expansion into sociopolitical programming as a response to audience feedback, or what might be considered "crowdsourcing" on a smaller scale. Projects such as Jeremy Deller's "It Is What It Is: Conversations about Iraq" or the reconfiguration of the MCA's Mayer Education Center into an "Idea Lounge" seek to engage museum visitors in discussions of social issues (Grynsztejn 2011, 46). These initiatives also signal an institutional engagement with, and response to, global issues – exploring how they are locally instantiated through collaborations with artists and audiences. Grynsztejn is aware of the pivotal role of curators and museum directors in rethinking the roles of the museum when she concludes that:

> My passions migrated from working on a particular artist's work to applying that thought process to the museum itself, toward how to create, how to evolve a museum. I'm convinced that working with artists has led me to that. I'm "curating" an institution now. (2011, 48)

Mapping the mobile museum

The range of initiatives launched by museums, curators, and artists during the late twentieth century and early twenty-first century demonstrates an increased engagement in diverse forms of locality including platforms that address an expanded field of exhibition, museum, and curating practices. Most notably, this includes the pivotal role of biennials, cultural centers, and programs that have "created new networks between hitherto separated spheres of contemporary artistic production" and "mobile sites of discourse" (Enwezor 2008b). Commercial events such as Art Basel (and its expansion to Miami Beach and Hong Kong) are also "wired in" to networks that interconnect museums with global art markets (Horowitz 2011, 16–17). Relyea underscores the "interfunctionality" of these platforms, ranging from documenta to Art Basel, as they "maintain a minimal continuity of identity and … accommodate a maximum of product turnover, thus remaining as responsive as possible to shifts in outside tastes, trends, and conditions" (2013, 24). These developments have had an impact on how museums attempt to reposition themselves strategically or map their own locations within the cartographies of contemporary culture. As Smith observes, museums, art centers, and artists may increasingly utilize forms of regional collaboration and networking that do "not follow Western infrastructure models, notably the exhibitionary complex" (2012, 235).

The museum's engagement in competing and conflicting notions of the civic may range from forms of social activism to educational outreach, think tanks, or labs. The BMW Guggenheim Lab project created "a mobile laboratory about urban life" with a thematic focus for each city as it traveled from New York ("confronting comfort") to Berlin (civic participation), and Mumbai (privacy and public space) (BMW Guggenheim Lab 2013). An MCA Chicago think tank that questioned "how to be a civic agent" explicitly references the museum's own role in the public sphere (Grynsztejn 2011, 46). Movements such as Occupy Museums (a direct outgrowth of Occupy Wall Street) also signal a focus on museum economics and ethics as they relate to notions of the public sphere and the civic (Smith 2012, 233). Many contemporary museum projects are facilitated and supported through social networking and mobile technologies – indicating how local interventions become inextricably linked to globalized forms of support and activism that can mobilize constituencies. Occupy Museums also reveals how local movements (Occupy Wall Street) become globalized and create new localized interventions. In this regard Papastergiadis has observed:

> "Small gestures in specific places" – this could be the coda for the time when the place for art is on the move. Today the form of art bends to the circumstance, and the boundary with the everyday blurs. The placement of small gestures in specific places can at first glance be continuous with our daily stride, sight, breath, touch and reach. And yet it might also suggest that all these actions are more complex. (2008, 373–374)

Interventions by artists such as The Yes Men, who created fake editions of newspapers distributed on the streets in Beijing, Brussels, and New York (Thompson 2012, 254–255), provide one example of how artists are intervening in global (media) discourses through strategic local actions.

Bharucha reminds us that notions of mobility are also closely linked to diaspora and migration – forces that inform local projects and contribute to new forms of display and engagement that are not driven by the logics of maintaining "assets," "brands," or the value of the museum structure and location (2004, 131). Regional and transborder collaborations such as the Dutch Art Institute Istanbul (2013), which supports artist residencies and exhibitions in the Netherlands and Turkey, aim "to create fleeting collectivities that operate as 'interfaces' between art, education and the world." Projects such as the Schirn's "Street-Art Brazil" create short-term local interventions that signal increasingly mobile artist residencies that move across cultures.

As visitors move between the physically bounded and virtual spaces that mediate the museum (and its reconceptualization as a (virtually) unbounded territory), they are also reshaping the relations between the museum's inside/outside as part of the civic. For example, the organization cultureNOW seized on an expanded notion of a civic museum after 9/11 in order to launch a "Museum without Walls." "Over 75 public art collections ... are collaborating to create a digital National Gallery of art and architecture in the public realm" including "11,000 sites and 21,000 images supplemented by over 1,050 podcasts by artists, architects, historians and curators" (cultureNOW 2013).The project is also mapping cultural sites outside the United States and using GPS technology to develop an iPhone app and guide.

Increasingly, physical and mobile museum experiences supplement and inform one another. As audiences personalize their experiences inside the museum, by capturing and archiving them on mobile devices, their experiences outside the museum may become more museum-like as they are integrated into the larger constellations of individual and collective memory and experience. Relyea argues that, as the manner in which audiences experience and access exhibitions, archives, and collections becomes more "radically open-ended," museums become like databases that "are simply collections of individual items, each with potentially the same significance as every other item in its field" (2013, 181). While this fragmentation and relativization of the museum experience seems to relegate it to particularization or individualized connoisseurship, museums continue to play a significant role in creating pathways for visitor interaction that provide apertures for more critical forms of education, engagement, and imagination. In this regard, Wolfgang Ernst observes that "Museographical dramaturgy is about the art of displaying missing links and about creating a sense of distance; only when space is left can the imagination of the viewer step in, and objects communicate with one another" (2000, 33).

Certainly, the museum's multiple roles as site(s) of entertainment and critical engagement, and the aforementioned "tension between the museum as civic educator and the negative pull of distracted vision" (Bennett 2006, 276), will remain contested. With respect to the nexus of museums, social media, and audiences, Lynda Kelly concludes that:

> They will be mobile, accessing information wherever they are and at whatever time of their choosing, active participants, rather than passive receivers of content and information. Given the opportunities provided across the physical, online and mobile spaces, the connected museum must be flexible, mobile, vibrant and changing and "houses full of ideas." The question [that] still remains, however, is whether museums are really ready to meet these challenges and become truly transformative in a world that is increasingly connected. (2013, 69)

While forces on the "outside" such as social media, mobile technologies, and the mobility of audiences across virtual and urban spaces may be having a greater impact on transforming museums than interventions from "within," efforts to simultaneously turn the museum "inside out" and "outside in" may provide an opportunity for creating new discourses and forms of engagement that will alter how museums are "navigated" in everyday life. Andrew Dewdney, David Dibosa, and Victoria Walsh observe that: "Turning the museum 'inside out,' would create a more porous museum and enable it to embrace and map new groupings and collectivities, those which are busily reshaping the public commons" (2013, 245).

The forces of a decentered, deterritorialized museum landscape – characterized by movement across cultural zones – have gained further impetus through the emerging practices of virtual mobile communication that problematize notions of center–periphery. The tensions between mobility and locality (and defining a sense of place) create challenges for contemporary museums as they attempt to simultaneously identify new positions and collaborations – within rapidly changing platforms, practices, and media – that will be economically viable, flexible, and sustainable. The question raised by *The Windows* – "Where does the museum end and the outside world begin?" – has therefore become a pivotal one for contemporary museums. In his personal account of the four-day walk which composed *The Windows* experience, Jason Groves (2013) writes:

> Fletcher's project pushed the ecological thought beyond construction materials and into the thinking and performance of interconnectedness: the demonstration and enactment of the museum's entanglement in systems and scales that extend far beyond the physical location. The peripatetic defiance of any boundary between inside and outside was instrumental in uniting social, spatial, and ecological practices … In doing so we were moved beyond the self-satisfaction of a green environmentalism and into the domain of a "dark ecology" (Timothy Morton) that celebrates the messiness of a planet pervaded by non-human agencies, open-ended systems, deep time, and the derangement of scales characteristic of recent ecological thought.

Museums have recognized that there will be no singular model or path to follow as they experiment with multiple platforms and collaborations (Enwezor 2008b, 223). By investigating the process of "moving out" it may be possible to understand how museums are remapping their conceptual and physical boundaries as portals for experience that complicate notions of global mobility and locality and how mobile media (including the media of exhibitions and installations) increasingly problematize the fixity of those borders as the museum collaborates with curators, artists, and audiences in exploring these new cartographies.

Notes

1 Photo of poster at Münchener Freiheit on March 29, 2007, http://www.sharonelifschitz. com/files/gimgs/83_speakinggermanylifschitz14_v2.jpg (accessed September 2, 2014).
2 For additional information on the Jewish Museum Munich, BMW Welt, and the mobile *mise-en-scène*, see my forthcoming article (Rectanus, Forthcoming).

3 See videos filmed by Jimi Biondi, April 7, 2011, http://www.youtube.com/watch?v=TBpcky4cEOc (accessed August 29, 2015).

4 "Foreclosed: Rehousing the American Dream," http://www.moma.org/interactives/exhibitions/2012/foreclosed/ (accessed September 2, 2014).

References

Bacher, Lutz. 1978. *The Mobile Mise en Scène: A Critical Analysis of the Theory and Practice of Long-Take Camera Movement in the Narrative Film*. New York: Arno.

Bal, Mieke. 2007. "Exhibition as Film." In *Exhibition Experiments*, edited by Sharon Macdonald and Paul Basu, 71–93. Oxford: Blackwell.

Barndt, Kerstin. 2010. "Layers of Time: Industrial Ruins and Exhibitionary Temporalities." *PMLA* 125(1): 134–141. Accessed August 28, 2014. http://www.lsa.umich.edu/UMICH/german/Home/People/BarndtPMLA.pdf.

Belting, Hans. 2007. "Contemporary Art and the Museum in the Global Age." In *Contemporary Art and the Museum: A Global Perspective*, edited by Peter Weibel and Andrea Buddensieg, 16–38. Ostfildern, Germany: Hatje Cantz.

Belting, Hans. 2013a. "Documenta 11, Kassel, 2002." In *The Global Contemporary and the Rise of New Art Worlds*, edited by Hans Belting, Andrea Buddensieg, and Peter Weibel, 73. Karlsruhe, Germany: ZKM; Cambridge, MA: MIT Press.

Belting, Hans. 2013b. "The Plurality of Art Worlds and the New Museum." In *The Global Contemporary and the Rise of New Art Worlds*, edited by Hans Belting, Andrea Buddensieg, and Peter Weibel, 246–254. Karlsruhe, Germany: ZKM; Cambridge, MA: MIT Press.

Bennett, Tony. 2006. "Civic Seeing: Museums and the Organization of Vision." In *A Companion to Museum Studies*, edited by Sharon Macdonald, 263–271. Oxford: Blackwell.

Bharucha, Rustom. 2004. "Beyond the Box: Problematizing the 'New Asian Museum.'" In *Over Here: International Perspectives on Art and Culture*, edited by Gerardo Mosquera and Jean Fischer, 123–136. Cambridge, MA: MIT Press.

Biermann, Ursula, ed. 2003. *Geografie und die Politik der Mobilität/Geography and the Politics of Mobility*. Vienna: Generali Foundation.

Bilski, Emily D. 2007. "How Can Germans and Jews Speak to Each Other about Germany? How Can We *Not* Speak about Germany?" In *Jüdisches Museum München* [Jewish Museum Munich], edited by Jutta Fleckenstein and Bernhard Purin, 70–71. Munich: Prestel.

BMW. 2011. "Museen im 21. Jahrhundert: Die zweite Wechselausstellung:" [Museums in the 21st century: The second special exhibition]. Accessed August 28, 2014. http://www.bmw-welt.com/de/exhibitions/museum/temporary/museums_21st_century.html.

BMW Guggenheim Lab. 2013. "Where Is the Lab?" Accessed August 28, 2014. http://www.bmwguggenheimlab.org/where-is-the-lab

Christov-Bakargiev, Carolyn. 2012. *dOCUMENTA 13: The Guidebook*. Ostfildern, Germany: Hatje Cantz.

Chronus Art Center. 2013. "Raqs Media Collective at Chronus Art Center: Extra Time." Accessed August 28, 2014. http://www.e-flux.com/announcements/raqs-media-collective-3/.

cultureNOW. 2013. "Museum without Walls." Accessed August 28, 2014. http://culture now.org/mission.

Dewdney, Andrew, David Dibosa, and Victoria Walsh. 2013. *Post-Critical Museology: Theory and Practice in the Art Museum*. London: Routledge.

Dutch Art Institute Istanbul. 2013. "Dutch Art Institute Istanbul." Accessed August 28, 2014. http://dutchartinstitute.eu/page/4391/dutch-art-institute-istanbul-new-works-by-fifteen-dai-2013-graduates-exhi.

Enwezor, Okwui. 2008a. "Mega-Exhibitions: The Antinomies of a Transnational Global Form." In *Other Cities, Other Worlds: Urban Imaginaries in a Globalizing Age*, edited by Andreas Huyssen, 148–178. Durham, NC: Duke University Press.

Enwezor, Okwui. 2008b. "The Postcolonial Constellation: Contemporary Art in a State of Permanent Transition." In *Antinomies of Art and Culture: Modernity, Postmodernity, Contemporaneity*, edited by Terry Smith, Okwui Enwezor, and Nancy Condee, 207–234. Durham, NC: Duke University Press.

Ernst, Wolfgang. 2000. "Archi(ve)tectures of Museology." In *Museums and Memory*, edited by Susan Crane, 17–34. Stanford: Stanford University Press.

Exploratorium. 2013. "The Best Things in Museums Are the Windows: A Participatory Project Co-organized by Harrell Fletcher and the Exploratorium." Accessed August 28, 2014. http://www.exploratorium.edu/arts/the-windows.

Fleckenstein, Jutta, and Bernhard Purin, eds. 2007. *Jüdisches Museum München* [Jewish Museum Munich]. Munich: Prestel.

Foster, Hal. 2012. "Vandal Aesthetics." In *Cyprien Gaillard: The Recovery of Discovery*, edited by Susanne Pfeffer, 51–52. Berlin: Walther König. Originally published as "'Cyprien Gaillard: The Recovery of Discovery' – KW Institute for Contemporary Art," *Artforum* 50(4).

Gaillard, Cyprien, and Susanne Pfeffer. 2012. "In Conversation: Cyprien Gaillard and Susanne Pfeffer." In *Cyprien Gaillard: The Recovery of Discovery*, edited by Susanne Pfeffer, 33–49. Berlin: Walther König.

Giovannini, Joseph. 2013. "The Real Deal with the Hirschhorn Bubble." Smithsonian. Accessed August 28, 2014. http://www.smithsonianmag.com/arts-culture/The-Real-Deal-With-the-Hirshhorn-Bubble-204127181.html.

Groves, Jason. 2013. "Feedback: The Best Things in Museums Are the Windows." Accessed August 28, 2014. http://openhumanitiespress.org/feedback/newecologies/the-best-things-in-museums-are-the-windows/.

Grynsztejn, Madeleine. 2011. "MCA Chicago Today: Madeleine Grynsztejn Interviewed by Susan Snodgrass." *Art in America*, January, 43–48.

Harris, Jonathan, ed. 2011. *Globalization and Contemporary Art*. Oxford: Wiley-Blackwell.

Holmes, Brian. 2003. "Maps for the Outside: Bureau d'études; or, The Revenge of the Concept." In *Geografie und die Politik der Mobilität/Geography and the Politics of Mobility*, edited by Ursula Biermann, 164–169. Köln: Walther König.

Horowitz, Noah. 2011. *Art of the Deal: Contemporary Art in a Global Financial Market*. Princeton: Princeton University Press.

Huyssen, Andreas. 2003. *Present Pasts: Urban Palimpsests and the Politics of Memory*. Stanford: Stanford University Press.

Huyssen, Andreas, ed. 2008. *Other Cities, Other Worlds: Urban Imaginaries in a Globalizing Age*. Durham, NC: Duke University Press.

Kelly, Lynda. 2013. "The Connected Museum in the World of Social Media." In *Museum Communication and Social Media: The Connected Museum*, edited by Kirsten Drotner and Kim Christian Schrøder, 54–71. New York: Routledge.

Kester, Grant. 2011. *The One and the Many: Contemporary Collaborative Art in a Global Context*. Durham, NC: Duke University Press.

Krauss, Rosalind. 2005. "Postmodernism's Museum without Walls." In *Thinking about Exhibitions*, edited by Reesa Greenberg, Bruce W. Ferguson, and Sandy Nairne, 241–245. New York: Routledge.

Leeum Samsung Museum of Art. 2013. "Welcome." Accessed August 28, 2014. http://leeum.samsungfoundation.org/html_eng/introduction/welcome.asp.

Malraux, André. 1967. *Museum without Walls*. London: Secker & Warburg.

Mersmann, Birgit. 2013. "Asia Exhibited in Korea: Image Conflicts in the Making of Contemporary Art." In *The Global Contemporary and the Rise of New Art Worlds*, edited by Hans Belting, Andrea Buddensieg, and Peter Weibel, 282–290. Karlsruhe, Germany: ZKM; Cambridge, MA: MIT Press.

Morley, Simon. 2003. *Writing on the Wall: Word and Image in Modern Art*. Berkeley: University of California Press.

Papastergiadis, Nikos. 2008. "Spatial Aesthetics: Rethinking the Contemporary." In *Antinomies of Art and Culture: Modernity, Postmodernity, Contemporaneity*, edited by Terry Smith, Okwui Enwezor, and Nancy Condee, 363–381. Durham, NC: Duke University Press.

Pfeffer, Susanne. 2012. "Life in the Museum Is Like Making Love in a Cemetery." In *Cyprien Gaillard: The Recovery of Discovery*, edited by Susanne Pfeffer, 7–16. Berlin: Walther König.

Ramberg, Lars Ø. 2005. "Palast des Zweifels" [The palace of doubt]. Accessed August 28, 2014. http://www.larsramberg.de/1/viewentry/3890.

Rectanus, Mark. Forthcoming. "Refracted Memory: Museums, Film, and Visual Culture in Urban Space." In *Exhibiting the German Past: Museums, Film and Musealization*, edited by Peter McIsaac and Gabriele Mueller. Toronto: University of Toronto Press.

Relyea, Lane. 2013. *Your Everyday Art World*. Cambridge, MA: MIT Press.

Saybasili, Nermin. 2011. "Gesturing No(w)here." In *Globalization and Contemporary Art*, edited by Jonathan Harris, 407–421. Oxford: Wiley-Blackwell.

Schirn Kunsthalle. 2013. "Street-Art Brazil." Accessed August 28, 2014. http://schirn.de/STREET-ART_BRAZIL_3.html.

Smith, Terry. 2009. *What Is Contemporary Art?* Chicago: University of Chicago Press.

Smith, Terry. 2012. *Thinking Contemporary Curating*. New York: Independent Curators International.

Stedelijk Museum. 2005. "Populism." *Stedelijk Museum Bulletin* 18(2): 51–54.

Thompson, Nato, ed. 2012. *Living as Form: Socially Engaged Art from 1991–2011*. New York: Creative Time; Cambridge, MA: MIT Press.

Urry, John. 1995. *Consuming Places*. London: Routledge.

Virilio, Paul. 2008. *Open Sky*. London: Verso.

von Osten, Marion. 2012. "City in Ruins." In *Cyprien Gaillard: The Recovery of Discovery*, edited by Susanne Pfeffer, 69–81. Berlin: Walther König.

Weibel, Peter. 2013. "Globalization and Contemporary Art." In *The Global Contemporary and the Rise of New Art Worlds*, edited by Hans Belting, Andrea Buddensieg, and Peter Weibel, 20–27. Karlsruhe, Germany: ZKM; Cambridge, MA: MIT Press.

Further Reading

Pfeffer, Susanne, ed. 2012. *Cyprien Gaillard: The Recovery of Discovery*. Berlin: Walther König.

Rectanus, Mark. 2002. *Culture Incorporated: Museums, Artists, and Corporate Sponsorships*. Minneapolis: University of Minnesota Press.

Rectanus, Mark. 2006. "Globalization: Incorporating the Museum." In *A Companion to Museum Studies*, edited by Sharon Macdonald, 381–397. Oxford: Blackwell.

Smith, Terry, Okwui Enwezor, and Nancy Condee, eds. 2008. *Antinomies of Art and Culture: Modernity, Postmodernity, Contemporaneity*. Durham, NC: Duke University Press.

Mark W. Rectanus is Professor of German Studies in the Department of World Languages and Cultures at Iowa State University. His research interests include print culture and publishing, media, museum studies, cultural politics, performance studies, and conceptual art. He is the author of *Culture Incorporated: Museums, Artists, and Corporate Sponsorships* (University of Minnesota Press, 2002); "Globalization: Incorporating the Museum," in *A Companion to Museum Studies*, edited by Sharon Macdonald (2006); "Performing Knowledge: Cultural Discourses, Knowledge Communities, and Youth Culture," in *TELOS* (2010); and the editor of *Über Gegenwartsliteratur: Interpretationen und Interventionen* [About Contemporary Literature: Interpretations and Interventions] (Aisthesis, 2008).

24 BEYOND THE GLASS CASE
Museums as Playgrounds for Replication

Petra Tjitske Kalshoven

Skirting the museum: A skirmish and a scrimshander

In August 2008, on the sloping lawn behind the American Museum in Bath, England, a skirmish was performed, set in 1758 Ticonderoga (now in New York State). Redcoats, Rangers, and Black Watch were taking on French Bluecoats and militia, supported by a handful of Iroquois scouts, in an episode during the French and Indian Wars. Shots were fired and prisoners taken in front of an interested and at times excited crowd. The French won, an English officer was killed in cold blood – *Vive le roi!* Some booing occurred.

I attended this event, organized by living history association New France and Old England, as the guest of Alex[1] from Derbyshire, an active member of several living history and re-enactment groups focusing on the eighteenth century. Living history is a form of historical presentation where practitioners (either amateurs or professionals in the heritage industry), dressed in period costume, draw visitors into a virtual world of the past, offering a glimpse of daily life, in particular the domestic production of arts and crafts. Re-enactment refers to the staging of historic battles, where the emphasis is on spectacular (but historically plausible) actions (see Kalshoven 2012, ch. 1). At the event in Bath, visitors were treated to a mix of both practices. Particularly interested in Creek and Cherokee Woodland cultures, Alex performed an Iroquois scout in the skirmish, fighting on the French side, armed with a balled war club he had crafted out of maple wood. I had contacted him because of my interest in re-enactments of Native American role models, having previously studied replica-making and performance practices among so-called Indian hobbyists (non-Native amateurs fascinated by Native American lifeworlds from the past) on the European continent (Kalshoven 2012).

The International Handbooks of Museum Studies: Museum Media, First Edition.
Edited by Michelle Henning.
© 2015 John Wiley & Sons Ltd. Published 2020 by John Wiley & Sons Ltd.

After the performance on the lawn, visitors strolled among a number of stalls dedicated to crafts associated with the period that New France and Old England sought to bring alive. Alex's friend John, in his role as a trader in the English camp, attracted an intrigued audience by demonstrating a decorative technique developed by whalers. Scrimshawing, he explained, consisted in engraving horns or bone and then rubbing in soot or ink to make the engravings stand out: "Scrimshaw is a peculiar word of obscure and much disputed origins which has come to be used for the decorative craftwork which was developed by men engaged in the whaling industry" (West 1991, 39). Scrimshanders usually engraved whale products, "particularly the large ivory teeth of the Sperm whale," but (walrus) tusks, wood, or horn were used as well (West 1991, 39). John had mastered the technique, proceeding by trial and error, initially producing some awful results, as he put it – he acquired the skill through sheer perseverance. Examples of his making were positioned on a table in front of him for visitors to handle (Figure 24.1). All decorative elements and patterns he used on his horns, John explained, had been attested on originals – but obviously, the shape of the horns, which he had acquired through a friend who worked in a slaughter house, would always be unique. He did not apply artificial patina, which he said was used by people who sought to make replicas pass for originals. The objects he emulated, he pointed out, had started out new and acquired patina over the years, just as his own objects would through his use of them in living history events.

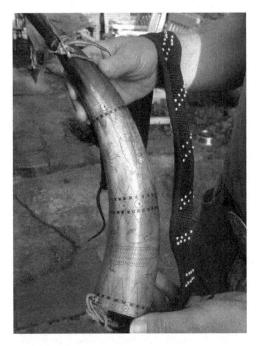

FIGURE 24.1   John displays one of his scrimshawed powder horns, August 2008.
Photo: Petra Tjitske Kalshoven.

While visitors were able to handle John's craftwork on the lawn, inside, in the American Museum, original scrimshawed powder horns and a sperm whale tooth engraved by nineteenth-century Nantucket whaler and artist Frederick Myrick were on display in a glass case. Myrick engraved several dozens of sperm whale teeth, known as Susan's teeth, during an 1826–1829 voyage on the whaling ship *Susan* (see Frank 2000). As I admired his work, a pair of re-enactors in costume were making the rounds of the museum, looking very appropriate in the period rooms. The American Museum, housed in the impressive Claverton Manor just outside Bath, focuses on decorative arts, furniture, china, and textiles. Scrimshaw is part of its folk art collection. By producing replicas of originals such as those kept in the museum, and engaging his replicas in demonstrations and actions, John effectively made material culture fit for situations of serious play outside: he had taken the artifacts out of their case and out of the museum in the guise of copies, turning people's engagement with them into a tactile, dialogic process centered on what had become a rather different kind of artifact.

Such amateur representation takes place through "life-size" replication and mimesis, but also through plays with scale, in particular miniaturization. As I expressed an interest in war gaming, which is a form of re-enactment on a miniature scale (Kalshoven 2013), Alex promptly introduced me to Brian, who performed an officer in the French artillery. Brian was organizing a game that night in the log cabin on the grounds of Claverton Manor. He showed me a small box containing a board game played with cards substituting for World War I planes and zeppelins; you can also play it with model planes, he explained, showing me one tiny example.

My encounters with Alex and his friends in the living history scene provided valuable insights into heuristic and ontological values invested in museum originals, replicas, hard-to-categorize in-between artifacts, and miniatures. Living history and re-enactment practices open up possibilities of thinking through specific "things" (Henare, Holbraad, and Wastell 2007) that are intimately related to museum culture; mimicking, mediating, and perhaps challenging it. What can a replica scrimshawed powder horn tell us about contemporary museums and about human curiosity? How does a tin figurine of a Redcoat mediate relations between individuals and worlds of practice and imagination? What is lost or gained in replica-making or miniaturization? What does imitation in re-enactment *do*? Such questions animate the present discussion which, taking its cue from fieldwork encounters with re-enactors and living historians, explores how museums and their collections have become models for emulation by amateurs keen to make artifacts perform outside their glass cases in an attempt to re-experience material cultures associated with geographical or temporal otherness. Fascinated by the historicity and tangibility of the "real thing" but frustrated by its inaccessibility in the museum environment, living historians and re-enactors create replicas and make them come alive through performances that, as I argue, both defy and celebrate the sanctity of the museum space.

This chapter is thus concerned with the tension between, on the one hand, the pleasure associated with the "real thing" displayed in museums and, on the other, mimetic practices modeled on museal representation. Rather than being plundered and copied, however, museums are active participants in practices of living history and re-enactment. Combining Johan Huizinga's ([1950] 1967) conceptualization of play as a generative societal force and Stephen Bann's (2003 and 2007) discussion of a "return to curiosity" in museum contexts, I conceive museums as playgrounds that invite play within the museal space, but that also allow for the generation of other forms of play in spaces outside the museum "proper" through re-enactment, that is, through practices of imitation and miniaturization.

Museums as playgrounds

My conception of museums as playgrounds is inspired by Johan Huizinga's influential study of humans at play, *Homo Ludens* ([1950] 1967). Reluctant to formulate any strict definition of play, Huizinga characterized it by describing actual practices of playing. He suggested that players create "temporary worlds within the ordinary world, dedicated to the performance of an act apart" ([1950] 1967, 10). Play, he wrote, was limited both in time and in space. Even though play was disinterested and pleasurable, he considered it an inherently serious activity, as there would be important things at stake for players, such as money or prestige. According to Huizinga, societal institutions should be seen as functioning in the realm of play whenever they could be classified under the headings of performance or contest, turning play into a genuine force in society.

Huizinga did not mention museums as potential playgrounds – indeed, he might have associated them with nonplay as temples of science. Science did not belong to the world of play, Huizinga maintained, for two reasons: it did not provide relaxation from everyday life and it was bound to strict demands of accuracy and veracity ([1950] 1967, 203–204). He suggested that eighteenth-century "enlightened man" was further removed from an understanding of play, which he associated primarily with "the world of the savage, the child and the poet," than "modern man," whose sense of aesthetics, in particular a new interest in masks, helped him reconnect with the "primitive" (26). I would like to make a case for the museum's inclusion in the play sphere in the light of recent developments in museum culture, and in conceptions of museum culture, that highlight connections between scientific practices and performance. Huizinga has been invoked by museum scholars before. Susan Pearce associated his ideas on play with the practice of collecting in particular, describing it as something that is

> set aside from daily life, like all the fenced-off enclosures in which games are played [affording it] a sacred character of apartness from the profane world, enshrined in its

display shelves and cabinets. Collecting ... has the character of ritual activity which is carried out for its own sake with all the social and emotional quality which this implies. (Pearce 1992, 50)

Pearce considered the inherently limited nature of collections integral to their play character and to their allure: "Games have endings, precincts have boundaries and collections must have limits, and this closure contributes hugely to the sense of rightness and so to our aesthetic pleasure" (1992, 53). She drew an analogy with games and game rules in her approach to exhibitions as well: "each exhibition is a production, like a theatrical production, and like a play, it is a specific work of culture with game rules of its own" (136–137).

To make my case for the museum as a playground, I will elaborate on the spatial and imaginative character of play rather than on its rules, taking my cue from Huizinga's insistence on play as taking part in a world apart and on its relationship with performance. The separate realm stipulated for play in *Homo Ludens* articulates well with phenomenologist Alfred Schutz's ideas on "finite provinces of meaning" (Schutz [1945] 1962, 230). Huizinga's cultural historical approach to play finds a cognitive complement in Schutz's theory of human experience, which begins from the premise that the origin of all reality is subjective. Whatever excites and stimulates our interest is real, and therefore it is the meaning of our experiences rather than the ontological structure of the objects that constitutes reality. The world, Schutz suggested, can be divided into sub-universes that he named finite provinces of meaning, each of which can be experienced as real from a specific cognitive perspective. A "certain set of our experiences" may be considered a finite province of meaning if all of these experiences "show a specific cognitive style and are – *with respect to this style* – not only consistent in themselves but also compatible with one another" (Schutz [1945] 1962, 228; emphasis original). Shifting from one province of meaning to another, he suggested, is accompanied by a shock experience that is routinely negotiated by the person involved in shifting. The examples of finite provinces of meaning that Schutz offers include the world of dreams, the world of imageries (especially art), the world of religious experience, the play world of the child, and the world of the insane (229). For each cognitive style, Schutz posited a specific tension of consciousness, form of self-experience, form of sociality, and a specific time perspective. Museums have been described as spaces that require a specific way of behaving (Classen and Howes 2006) or a special way of looking (Alpers 1991, on the "museum effect") and that instill a sense of awe (Gell [1992] 1995) or wonder in which time is suspended (Greenblatt 1991), qualities that dovetail with Schutz's characterization of cognitive styles. Huizinga's playground, informed by Schutz's conception of provinces of meaning, allows us to conceive of the museum space as a temporary world delimited in space enabling visitors to let themselves be engaged and adopt an appropriate attitude in the "performance of an act apart." What is more, Schutz's theory of cognitive shifts involved in moving from a straightforward reality to an experience of play and imagination is also useful for thinking about re-enactment. Re-enactors negotiate different temporalities that are not necessarily delimited in space (as the museum is) but that do lead participants to adopt a different form of sociality and a particular tension of consciousness. The museum world and the world of re-enactment, I suggest, invite modes of play that overlap considerably.

Re-enactment as experimental play

Before we left on a road trip from Derby to Bath for the French and Indian Wars event, Alex took me on a tour of his favorite museums. In Derby Museum, he introduced me to the curator, who took us to the stores to show us Native American artifacts including a tomahawk, moccasins, and pipe bowls. Alex had contributed to exhibitions at Derby Museum, one of which had been on the French and Indian Wars. He had lent out replicas for visitors to handle and had given talks. On excellent terms with the curator, Alex engaged him in a lively conversation on the objects, their provenance, and their possibilities for display, confidently and yet cautiously attributing these to particular peoples and places. The amateur and the professional shared their enthusiasm for their favorite artifacts, both taking pleasure in material conduits of former times.

Stores make for special spaces indeed – spaces that are significantly less democratized than the museum's exhibition halls and exude an inner circle appeal where objects allure those in the know, competing for informed attention. And yet, how can a museum and its stores not pale in terms of playfulness compared to the quite physical jousting and thrusting that goes on outside when re-enactors act out past otherness? Both museum practice and re-enactment revolve around acquiring and disseminating knowledge. One important heuristic difference is that re-enactors use their bodies as exploratory tools. They do so in actions that need not be fully scripted, allowing for scenarios to play out differently than in the model they seek to emulate (see Blackson 2007, 30). At times, they will fill in gaps in the historical or material record as the action unfolds both physically and imaginatively. Such action may concern military strategy, as in the skirmish performed at Claverton Manor. It may also concern material culture experimented through skilled craftsmanship. One example from my fieldwork with Indian hobbyists would be experimentation with obscure techniques such as the use of bird quills in decorative embroidery with a view to finding out how to achieve results evident in museum pieces.

Underlying each action, however, is the awareness that this is all about experimentation and trying out – what Erving Goffman called "rehearsals" (1974, 48) – rather than about ordinary living. Underlying each action is the message "this is play": even if participants achieve fleeting moments of how things could have been done in the past, they remain aware that "these actions in which we now engage do not denote what those actions *for which they stand* would denote," which is anthropologist Gregory Bateson's definition of play (1972, 180; emphasis original). Play, I suggest, is what occurs in the gap between straightforward experience of a primary reality and complete suspension of disbelief – in order to be play, play needs a cognitive shift (see Schutz, discussed above) that includes an awareness of its status. Re-enactors know that they will not die in that day's battle, but as they go through the motions they will feel a rush of adrenaline, and they will grudgingly play at dying if they fail to outdo their opponent. A living historian will go through expert motions of demonstrating scrimshawing and be satisfied with the day's work, knowing s/he has produced a convincing replica and has learned something about the original in the process. Neither activity is necessary or useful in a day-to-day sense, and this discrepancy with primary reality is precisely what makes it playfully serious. Whether re-enactment has indeed any heuristic potential is a matter of debate (see Handler and Gable 1997; Peers 2007; McCalman and Pickering 2010). According to performance studies scholar Rebecca Schneider, the sheer feel of fighting may be epistemically rich. Exploring re-enactment as a performance of "remains" in the present, she has distanced herself from scholarly critiques of historical re-enactment as privileging the "affective" rather than the "analytical," which, she suggests, betray an alliance to a Cartesian mind/body dichotomy (2011, 33–39).

Historical re-enactment as practiced by amateurs and re-enactment as a dedicated art practice share the awareness of discrepancy on which I insist. Tracing the roots of artistic re-enactment to action painting and performance art, Sven Lütticken suggests that postmodern society requires individuals to "perform themselves *as* commodities" (2005, 17). Recreating historical events as an artistic practice then becomes a way of using re-enactment against itself as a political comment on postmodern commodification (2005, 19). It can also be used to give voice to those that were not heard in the "original" event, as is the case with artist Jeremy Deller's *The Battle of Orgreave*, a 2001 re-enactment of the clash between police and striking miners in Yorkshire in 1984–1985 (Lütticken 2005, 51; Blackson 2007, 32). Some of these actions are difficult to distinguish from those performed by amateur re-enactors; others focus in particular on re-enactments of previous artistic performances (for examples of the latter, see Pil and Galia Kollectiv 2007). Lütticken calls for artistic re-enactment to appropriate historical re-enactment and experiment with "forms of repetition that break open history," implying that amateur re-enactors tend to be trapped in literalness, in "relaxing play" which amounts to a conservative diversion and fails to bring something new in the present (2005, 60). Blackson, on the other hand, considers re-enactment as a creative act in both artistic and amateur contexts, suggesting that historical re-enactment is able to free itself from an original source (2007, 40). In my fieldwork among Indianist re-enactors, this was indeed evident, although I found that creativity is crucial even when practitioners seek to emulate a style as faithfully as possible (Kalshoven 2012, ch. 4).

Unlike most artistic re-enactment, historical re-enactment and living history crucially depend on successful replication of artifacts. This is not a matter of straightforward imitation, but rather involves a process of learning to recognize styles. In my conversations with Indian hobbyists, I found that they consistently use the term "authentic" to characterize their own replicas: a well-made replica that may pass for an original in terms of materials, craftsmanship, and style, but is not an identical copy of an existing "original" piece, is called an "authentic" or "museum-quality" replica (Kalshoven 2012, ch. 5). Such a replica becomes an embodiment of the knowledge that practitioners acquire in museum spaces. This expert emulation takes place not only on the level of the artifact, but also on the level of performance. In other words, replicas must resemble originals both in the way they look or feel and in the way they are made and handled in action.

Authentic replicas constitute practitioners' capital in processes of exchange. Scrimshander John showed me a quilled knife sheath given to him by a German re-enactor who had previously participated in the annual French and Indian Wars event at the American Museum as an Indian scout working for the French. John had given the German scout a scrimshawed powder horn in return. Alex had made John a bag decorated with quill work to trade for a powder horn. These trading skills were an indispensable part of living history, Alex and John explained: engaging in gift-giving and barter was not only a way of benefiting from different skills available in their hobby, but it also reflected practices that would have occurred in the period of emulation, enhancing the quality of the overall performance. Trading skills contribute to the authenticity of the living historical present while encouraging practitioners to compete, that is, to play, at the pinnacle of their creative powers.

Mimetic pursuits: Copying as a competitive force

I have used the term "replication" above, but re-enactment and replica-making involve complex forms of imitation that call for some fine-tuning. Unpacking the mimetic effort involved in re-enactment, and in replica-making in particular, will clarify the relationship between the museum as a playground and practices of copying that generate additional layers of play. In literary criticism, the terms "replication," "simulation," and "formalization" are used in analyses of literary realism – despite the rather different context, such refining of the terminology is useful for my purposes here. Leona Toker defines these concepts as follows:

> Replication is an attempt to model the structure of the original by identifying its constituents; simulation consists in tracing the way things work, that is, the function of specific constituents; and formalization involves a competition with the original for philosophical or aesthetic coherence. (2000, 137–138)

Living history and re-enactment include all three of these mimetic pursuits, with replication and simulation involved in both replica-making and stagings; on the level of the object as it is made from the right materials and used in historically correct ways, and on the level of the performance (such as a skirmish) as participants learn about social and political structures, acting in accordance with the roles they embrace – while being acutely aware of the many compromises that must be made in historical simulation. Formalization occurs in the craftwork and stagings of the most dedicated practitioners, who tend to strive for replicas that are never straight-forward copies of an original but are unique artifacts faithful to a specific historical style, expressing an aesthetic coherence that would have fitted the time and place of emulation, but is also striking in the eyes of rival replica-makers, and of profes-sionals (including curators), in the here and now. The element of competition that Toker highlights in formalization recalls Huizinga's claim that contest is inherently playful. Formalization applies on the level of performances whose ideal aim is to succeed in bringing out the essence and the "feel" of an event or time period or otherness, both aesthetically and philosophically – perhaps something of the zeit-geist, at least in the experience of the performers and their audience.

Hybrid entanglements between objects, their makers, and their miniature forms appeared to be at work behind the performances I witnessed during my visit to the event at the American Museum. Not only were re-enactors engaging with objects simulating aspects of material cultures from a past, transforming the present into a new version of it; I found that they also played out versions of the past in which they themselves were turned into artifacts, downsized to plastic, tin, or cardboard figurines. While, during the day, the audience enjoyed a skirmish performed by re-enactors playing out the past on a one-on-one scale, at night the re-enactors camping on the grounds got out their board games and competitively enjoyed some warlike encounter on a miniature scale. In my discussions with living histo-rians and re-enactors in Bath and other places, and during visits to museums with various collections of miniature figures, it dawned on me that practically every re-enactment troupe has its equivalent in miniature – and miniatures are yet another way of making material culture fit for situations of play, either inside or outside museums.

Toker's threefold model of imitation can also be applied to the miniatures that are part of re-enactors' worlds when they are off duty. Miniatures used in re-enactors' play may stand for the historical figures that they portray life-size during their events. They can be bought ready-made or be hand-painted by players so as to look the appropriate part in the war game. Replication on a reduced scale requires respect for the right proportions and a knowledgeable selection of the appro-priate colors and attributes. Simulation is especially important in the interplay of figurines with the landscape of the board game. Individual soldiers, entire regi-ments, or a single figurine standing for an entire regiment play roles that are plau-sible within a battle scenario, but that must remain in line with the rules of the specific game as well. Rolling the dice determines battle movements. Representation of a historical reality thus goes hand in hand with abstraction from reality.

Formalization is of special interest since the aesthetic qualities of the miniature are a function of its smallness, which calls for expert stylization. I suggest that it

FIGURE 24.2   Iroquois scouts present themselves to the audience preceding a re-enactment of a skirmish during the French and Indian Wars; on the right is an English grenadier. American Museum in Britain, Bath, August 2008.
Photo: Petra Tjitske Kalshoven.

is stylization that allows the miniature to compete successfully with the original. In interviews with gamers and miniature enthusiasts (Kalshoven 2013) I was informed that it was particularly important to pay attention to specific details that needed to be added or "brought out" in painting in order to make the miniature effective. Bringing out details makes the figure recognizable and pleasing to the connoisseur – a "proper" figure. When I visited the event in Bath, I had photographs stored on my digital camera of a spectacularly complete collection of eighteenth-century tin figurines, the Molhuysen collection, recently acquired by the Tin Figurines Museum in Ommen in the Netherlands. On the lawn, I spotted an English grenadier wearing a distinctive miter that reminded me of the outfits in the Molhuysen collection (Figure 24.2). I approached him excitedly and showed him a picture on my camera. He corrected me at once: "Those are Prussians – just look at that piece of metal attached to the front of their miters." It was a detail brought out expertly by an eighteenth-century draughtsman or tin engraver that allowed the English re-enactor-grenadier to connect it confidently with its historical model.

Through the lens of formalization in particular, it becomes clear that re-enactment as a mimetic, sensual practice goes beyond a straightforward attempt at copying of museum culture in ways that invite more subtle consideration than the observation that re-enactment (or living history) allows objects to perform outside their glass cases. Miniatures, too, can be more than just reduced-scale copies, as they require very specific skills to make them look and perform in ways that are convincing in the playground of the board game, where other times and places are meant to come alive. Philosopher Hans-Georg Gadamer, who conceived of "play" as the ontological basis for the notion of aesthetics ([1960] 2004, 102–157), suggested that imitations may be better than the real thing in that "imitation and representation are not merely a second version, a copy, but a recognition of the essence. … They contain the essential relation to everyone for whom the representation exists" ([1960] 2004, 114). In Toker's terms, they compete with the original through formalization. Re-enactors acknowledge that they will never know what things were "really like," but they do strive for glimpses of insight, fleetingly acquired in particular during moments of intense movement such as dancing or charging – in the proper clothes, featuring the proper accoutrements. Such moments of emulation create something telling and new. That copies can be embodiments of creativity has also been brought to the fore in recent discussions of digital reproduction (Latour and Lowe 2012). Worlds of re-enactment in miniature provide a parallel to such virtual realms in that they offer simulations in a format that is just as convenient for handling, but that abstracts through formalized stylization. The formalization that occurs in re-enactment, which is a form of competition with the original (see Toker's definition), brings out the element of creative play in these mimetic pursuits.

Objections to the playful museum

Physical and visceral action, as demonstrated by re-enactors and living historians, is not what comes to mind when considering museum practice. Museum visitors are expected to display another type of attention that, at first sight, seems to lack a playful angle. If play connotes action and a performance or a contest, as Huizinga stipulated, it seems counterintuitive that museum artifacts, inviting private contemplation and musings on symbolism, enable the visitor to play at all. Two objections thus arise to the museum as a playground, one of a sensorial nature (museums cater to a cerebral, distanced gaze only), the other of a functional nature (museums are formal institutions that celebrate scientific knowledge as part of an educational enterprise), and the two are intimately entangled.

Since their emergence as educational and scientific institutions in the nineteenth century, museums have become repositories of artifacts, home to a material world that has been "carefully bottled and boxed" (Knell 2007, 3). Ethnology museums in particular have been reproached for subjecting artifacts to alien forms of classification, privileging the visually attractive by relegating aesthetically less striking objects to the storerooms, thus neglecting sensory aspects that may have had special significance in the non-ocularcentric cultural contexts in which the objects were originally embedded (Classen and Howes 2006).[2] While Huizinga did not mention the modern scientific museum as either playful or nonplayful, he dwelt on the eighteenth-century craze for natural history collections and curiosities as representative for the spirit of play in this particular period of history, when "natural history collections and curios [were] all the rage," and implied that play subsequently declined as a generative force in society ([1950] 1967, 187). As Romanticism was replaced by "Realism, Naturalism, Impressionism and the rest of that dull catalogue of literary and pictorial coteries," and democratization leveled the playing field, "culture ceased to be 'played'" (192–193). Most museum scholars consider cabinets of curiosities to be forerunners of the modern museum. Classen and Howes (2006) contrast the tactile affordances of the *Wunderkammer* with the asensual didactic space of the scientific institutions that swallowed and reorganized the private collections that had come before. The playful *Wunderkammer*, predicated on juxtaposition, aesthetics, synecdoche, and allusion, gave way to a drive for scientific completeness, classification in orders, genera, and species, and orderly contextualization of objects: in other words, to the modern, not-so-playful museum (Poliquin 2012, 124–132). As the marvelous became associated with frowned-on religious enthusiasm and superstition, wonder and wonders waned in European intellectuals' esteem in the first half of the eighteenth century: "Central to the new, secular meaning of enlightenment as a state of mind and a way of life was the rejection of the marvelous" (Daston and Park 1998, 331; see also Huizinga's critique of enlightened man, discussed above).

Things happening: Museum artifacts provoking play and emulation

Recent studies of museum display, however, point to a return to tactility and to wonder in the museum space, signaling a renewed appeal of the curious and playful (see Henning 2006, 143, on re-enchantment in a museal context). A volume with the telling title *Touch in Museums* (Chatterjee 2008) presents case studies in Britain in which museum artifacts are either made accessible to (more democratized) handling by interested parties going beyond connoisseurs or replicated through tactile artworks (Onol 2008) and digital simulation (Were 2008). In the same volume, Bernadette Lynch (2008) draws on phenomenological insights about human–thing relations to argue that picking up and touching things is fundamental to human experience of material culture. Whereas Graeme Were observes playfulness in the freedom to juxtapose artifacts in virtual space, Lynch situates play in tactile "doing," insisting on its centrality to learning. In both Were's and Lynch's examples, play and playfulness seem to be related to curiosity, and ways of satisfying curiosity that involve making active connections. Such developments are associated with a new role for the museum as a site for the return to curiosity (Bann 2003; Henning 2006, 145) – and, as I would like to argue, for the return to play.

It is not only visitors that do the playing in museums, however. In the humanities and social sciences, a recent surge in interest in studies of material culture has highlighted the active role that "things" and the materials they are made of play in identity construction and social relations (e.g., Brown 2001; 2003; Tilley 2004; Miller 2005; Tilley et al. 2006; Edwards, Gosden, and Phillips 2006; Henare, Holbraad, and Wastell 2007; Bennett 2010). In a fresh take on material worlds that owes part of its audacity to a rethinking of anthropological explorations of animism, things are considered curious in themselves; they are understood to have the potential to make things happen, to do more than "affording" alone (Gibson 1979). Applied to the museum context, this means that, while visitors may be performing, experiencing, and expressing a certain style of attention, museum objects have been made complicit in the performance and are, in fact, an integral part of it. In recent literature on museum worlds, it has been suggested that museum objects, as very particular "things," perform as a result of curatorial intervention and juxtaposition. Artifacts are now considered actors that turn the museum into a space for performance. One of the founders of thing theory, cultural historian Bill Brown, has argued that institutions such as ethnology museums have, in their contextualization of objects, "each in their own way fostered and depended on a kind of animism" (2003, 117). He implies that museum curators have made it seem, through the ways in which they arrange objects, as if such objects were endowed with life. Thing theory, according to Brown, involves an exploration of how it is that "inanimate objects" have a potential to "constitute human subjects" (2001, 7). One specific arrangement of objects that Brown discusses is the diorama or life-group exhibition that became popular in anthropology in the late nineteenth century, the kind of exhibit that "wrested anthropology away from natural history and insisted that the meaning of things is disclosed by their function within a specific environment" (Brown 2003, 92). The result of this kind of diorama is what he calls "synecdochal magic," through which an object comes to stand for a cultural thing. (On the appeal of dioramas, see also Kalshoven 2008.) Objects achieve a form of agency as a result of the way in which they are socially, culturally, or museologically embedded – but, rather than visitors or curators, it is the objects that subsequently *perform* the magic (see Bouquet and Porto 2005, on museum magic). In a similar vein, it has been argued that "Exhibitions are fundamentally theatrical, for they are how museums perform the knowledge they create" (Kirshenblatt-Gimblett 1998, 3).

This conception of acting objects is grounded in their potential as signifiers rather than in their sensual or material qualities. Alfred Gell's (1998) important investigations into social relations between artworks and people and into object agency similarly emphasize objects' semiotic qualities.[3] As part of his project to develop an anthropology of art, Gell situated the enchantment that art objects can provoke in the distance that such objects are able to maintain. Elaborating on

Georg Simmel's claim that the desire for objects experienced by subjects lies in their resistance to our desire and thus in our heightened wish to obtain them, Gell suggested that we may desire objects while knowing full well that we cannot possess them, as with a painting by an old master. He argued that it is not the objects as such in which the power of art resides – rather, this power lies in "the *symbolic* processes they provoke in the beholder" (Gell [1992] 1995, 48; emphasis original).

Objects performing and enchanting in museum or gallery spaces can do so, then, from the protective enclosure of their glass cases and under the watchful eye of security guards as they sit silently, enigmatically, as objects of desire. The contrast with Alex wielding his war club during the skirmish performed outside the American Museum and John demonstrating his scrimshawing skills could hardly be more pronounced – re-enactors and living historians are in the business of making the past come alive in the present through active use of (replicated) material culture, constituting a sensual engagement with past or unfamiliar worlds. And yet, such sensual engagement is directly related to the enigmatic beckoning that museum artifacts do. The magic that museum objects work on re-enactors and living historians provokes a desire of emulation – the distance maintained by the objects is partly overcome in that it inspires practitioners to possess them through a ruse, in the guise of the expert replica. Museum artifacts inspire living historians and re-enactors to replicate them. Semiotic play on the part of the object becomes embodied play on the part of the re-enactor, armed with replicas as crucial props. In its focus on lived, embodied immediacy and its emphasis on experiental learning, re-enactment is phenomenology in practice, nourished by research that must include museum visits. The playgrounds in which replicas demand and shape attention and the social relations in which they are embedded differ from those in which "original" museum objects feature and perform, and yet connections between living history practice and museum culture are not limited to neat schemata separating replicas from real things or semiotics from sensual practice. Part of the pleasure of playing at the past by doing living history resides in being knowledgeable about museum culture and moving in between museums and museum-inspired playgrounds. The most dedicated re-enactors and living historians are avid but critical museum-goers (and visitors of virtual museums online) who are sometimes invited to collaborate with professional historians and curators, as Alex regularly is in Derby Museum.

The return to curiosity, scrimshawing, and play: Huizinga revisited

As an example of the waning of play in contemporary culture, Huizinga referred to a past age of curiosity. As we have seen, however, play has made a comeback in museum contexts as artifacts are accorded performative magic, recalling the age of curiosity. As art historian Stephen Bann (2003; 2007) has argued, it is through interventions by contemporary artists that curiosity has of late re-entered gallery and museum spaces. During a visit to the Musée Océanographique in Monaco in January 2013, I was stopped in my tracks as I spotted a scrimshawed object – an engraved sperm whale tooth, another one of Frederick Myrick's famous Susan's teeth. Its museal context was rather different, however, from the scrimshaw pieces that I had seen in the American Museum in Bath. In the Musée Océanographique, the engraved sperm whale tooth was one of many curiosities brought together in the "world's largest marine curiosity cabinet" (according to a display panel) by American artist Mark Dion, who had been invited to rummage the museum's stores and collections in 2011 for the exhibition *Oceanomania* (Dion 2011). The "Cabinet of Curiosities," taking up an entire wall in the monumental building on Monaco's Rock, displayed "natural" objects on one side, including large taxidermied fish, a polar bear, and a walrus trophy, and "cultural" objects on the other, including ancient diver suits, ship models, and the scrimshawed tooth (Figure 24.3). Through Dion's intervention, the tooth had become a curiosity, a different thing from the otherwise very similar museum object in the display case in Bath. Although it was an original, unlike John's replica scrimshaw, it was quite similar to the replica in that it was no longer a straightforward museum object. As a result of its contextualization, Dion had turned it into a reference to a museum object – a play at it.

FIGURE 24.3 Mark Dion, "Cabinet of Curiosities," Musée Océanographique, Monaco. (For a color version of this figure, please see the color plate section.)
© Musée Océanographique. Photo: M. Dagnino, 2011. Reproduced with permission.

Not only did this tooth constitute a reference to other, similar, whale's teeth, changing something in the process of replication – Dion himself is very much a re-enactor. Through his art projects, Mark Dion *plays at* being an archaeologist, a naturalist, or a curator, using his body and persona in going through the gestures expected of such professionals. He subsequently invites the public to play along.

Dion's replication of a "Cabinet of Curiosities" is now a permanent exhibition at the Musée Océanographique. At the 2011 *Oceanomania* exhibition, a collaboration between the Nouveau Musée National de Monaco and the Musée Océanographique, Dion also displayed a series of smaller cabinets of curiosities he had created before, one of which ("The Phantom Museum," 2010) was a recreation in papier-mâché of illustrations of curiosities in an early eighteenth-century treatise on *Wunderkammern*, again, a play at similar objects in other contexts.[4] In her foreword to Dion's *Oceanomania* catalog, HRH the Princess of Hanover invites visitors of the exhibition to a "simultaneously fun and serious scenario" (Dion 2011, 5), a turn of phrase that resonates with Huizinga's conception of play as an inherently serious activity. And there is indeed a lot at stake here: toward the end of the catalog, Dion juxtaposes activities listed under the headings "oceanophilia" and "oceanocide," highlighting an environmental message (2011, 174–175).

While living historians re-enact the stories and histories that museums strive to tell by putting things on display, Dion mimics museum history, science, and practice, choosing a rather different object of seriously ludic emulation. While eighteenth-century cabinets of curiosities presented microcosms of exotic worlds, Dion's cabinets mimic these older display techniques in order to stage and rethink practices of curiosity and collecting, inviting a political angle. Imitation and special things (including originals and replicas) are at the core of both re-enactors' and Dion's practices.

In *Ways around Modernism* (2007), Stephen Bann associates the interplay between art and science with an ethos of curiosity. Elaborating on his earlier piece entitled "The Return to Curiosity" (2003), he heralds "curiosity" as a harbinger of postmodernity because of the way in which it has been embraced by contemporary artists. "Curiosity," a term that was used for practices of collecting and connoisseurship in the Renaissance and early modern period, was not without controversy, often associated with the less serious – a troublesome reputation it shares with play, according to theorists of play such as Huizinga (Kalshoven 2012, ch. 5). Drawing on Krzysztof Pomian, who situates curiosity in between religion and science, Bann suggests that curiosity can play a role in challenging existing paradigms of knowledge and classification. The return to curiosity in contemporary art practice, he argues, constitutes a reclaiming by the artist of "realms of knowledge previously relinquished to the scientist" (Bann 2007, 120). Curiosity, which combines an emphasis on the object's materiality with a story grounded in personal association, disturbs a normalized order and positions the displayed object as existing in "a nexus of interrelated meanings" (Bann 2003, 120). Bann notes that museums are in the process of recovering their performative potential; not only have some of the great surviving cabinets of curiosities become an object of fascination (2007, 130), but the cabinet is also making a comeback as a mode of display, as it does in Mark Dion's work. Bann associates it with a cognitive mode of "close attention and almost philosophical reverie" (2003, 118–119). His discussion of curiosity shows parallels with Huizinga's conception of play as situated in between the ritual and the profane. Huizinga referred to the eighteenth century when he wrote wistfully, "Natural history collections and curios are all the rage" ([1950] 1967, 187); nevertheless, this phrase would sound perfectly appropriate in discussing museum culture today – the return to curiosity can be glossed as a return to play in Huizinga's sense.

Bann's emphasis is on objects as carriers of meaning, or of multiple meanings, rather than on their sensoriality. In a passage on collecting inspired by curiosity, he suggests that objects tend to "acquire a status of semiotic hybridity, combining several strands of signification" (Bann 2007, 145). If we return to my ethnographic example and the artifact that caught visitors' attention on the lawn in Bath, the scrimshawed powder horn or whale's tooth may be shown to be an intriguing artifact from this point of view. According to Janet West of the Scott Polar Institute, scrimshawing involved a "choice of materials and decorative motifs" that was "often bizarre" (1991, 39). It was sometimes hard to distinguish from Native (such as Inuit) carvings in areas where whalers were active, which leads West to wonder where to draw the line in her definition of scrimshawing, implying some uneasiness with the hybridity involved.

The hybrid nature of some of the artifacts crafted by the living historians that I met at the event in Bath proved, on the contrary, to be a particular attraction, as was brought out by one participant's example of weaving a sash. Hilary, an art historian friend of Alex's who worked for a municipal museum, represented a French woman who took care of the laundry for the army. Her clothing, she explained to me, was usually more colorful than that of the women in the English camp, and the petticoats scandalously shorter – better adapted, she suggested, to the terrain in Canada. Hilary was busy finger weaving when I visited her in the French camp later that day, working in Osage style, experimenting with wool dyed with natural products – she was quite aware of and intrigued by the dye plants in the Claverton gardens. Finger woven sashes, she explained, were made both by Native people in North America and by Europeans. It was this hybridity that fascinated her, she said; Europeans appropriated techniques and artifacts from Indians, and Indians borrowed from the Europeans in turn. Her preference for exploring intercultural connections through semiotically rich things echoed Alex's enthusiasm for a splendid beaded Creek Seminole bandolier bag lined with Chinese silk that we could admire in the stores of Derby Museum. He pointed out to me that it was entirely composed of trade goods. When I asked Alex about his preference for materials, which some re-enactors insist should be sourced in the place of origin of an emulated model, he told me it would be contrived to do everything in purely American materials. He chuckled with amusement as he mentioned an example of the use of mink in one of his artifacts. Originally from North America, this particular mink had been trapped along the river close to his house in

Derbyshire. So he used local mink that originated in the original artifact's country of origin. When Alex presented his practice as a living historian in one of the anthropology modules I teach in Manchester, he brought an original tea cozy he had acquired, entirely Iroquois-made, but after a European design – another example of a fascination with interconnectedness and hybridity. He also brought an artifact that he had recently crafted himself: a mermaid. In Mark Dion's *Oceanomania* cabinet, an "original" version of this typical curiosity cabinet item featured in the cabinet's "cultural" half.

Bann's "semiotic hybridity" was an evident factor in the pleasure Alex and his friends derived from the artifacts they discussed with me. Because of the nature of their practice of replica-making, however, other aspects entered into their engagement with artifacts that borrowed from the sensorial rather than the semiotic realm. A replica scrimshawed powder horn acquires a social and tactile dimension as it is allowed to circulate in ways denied to the original, which can only enigmatically signal from its case – whether it is a standard glass case or a cabinet installed by Mark Dion. But already in the very act of reproducing scrimshaw, in the making of the sash, hybridity is scratched onto the horn or woven into the fabric as it is turned into a successful replica, both semiotically and sensuously pointing to its historical model kept in the museum but also emerging quite physically in the context of living history as its own thing in a new set of relations and connections. In a contemporary setting, scrimshawing and finger weaving are all the more curious and hybrid types of craftwork as they play at practices that came before, "playing culture" in a way that Huizinga thought had been lost. It has not been lost – whether it is contemporary artists or living historians engaging in actions that "do not denote what those actions *for which they stand* would denote" (Bateson 1972, 180), culture is played as re-enactment thrives.

Museums as permeable playgrounds

In re-enactment and living history practices, it is not so much the museum playground that is imitated, but the worlds to which objects in museums point by virtue of what Bill Brown called "synecdochal magic." Simon Knell has argued that objects in museums are able to tell stories only because these objects are "authentic" and are made to come alive through curatorial expertise conveyed on labels: "the object's active role ... is dependent upon it being real and authentic ... It is expertise ... which breathes life into the corpse-like object" (2007, 26). He cautions against heritage parks, as "authenticity is a fugitive quality easily lost" (17). While writers such as Latour and Lowe (2012) seek to undermine a notion of authenticity predicated on any sharp distinction between original "real thing" and facsimile, it is undeniable that the "real" exerts enormous attraction, also among living historians and re-enactors, in spite of the pleasure and instruction they derive from expert mimesis. Indeed, it is the fascination with the real that animates their mimetic practices. It is not enough for the original artifact to beckon and signal in an aloof kind of enigmatic materiality. Instead, the real must be retrieved through a live, functioning "thing"; in its expertly crafted form, the replica is able to breathe life into the performance, lending it its own authenticity as the replica turns performing bodies into tools of exploration.

In contrast to the bounded space of Huizinga's playground, the museum, then, is characterized by permeability, as processes of re-enactment make its contents spill over into other worlds of play. The amateurs responsible for such "appropriation" are deeply interested in tangible realities; and yet it is through the artifice of replication that they attempt to get in touch with the real thing, going so far as to mimic patination. Discussing fakes, reproductions, and modern scrimshaw, Janet West explains that "to a lay person, darkening is a sign of age, so a lot of modern scrimshaw is done on teeth dyed to a golden or brown colour to simulate age" (West 1991, 54). When simulated on replicas, patina lends a modern object time-depth. Patination in processes of imitation tends to be associated with dissimulation rather than creativity. What I argue here, is that re-enactment as a mode of performance can be considered a practice of patination that reveals rather than covers up.

Such revealing takes place on a range of different levels. The dynamics at work, I suggest, are reminiscent of the Mouse Trap board game in which a series of object actions – a plastic boot kicking a miniature bucket releasing a marble that will collide with a trap mechanism – leads to a cage being lowered onto a player's toy mouse. The game of re-enactment is set in motion by enigmatic artifacts triggering an urge to pick them up and run with them. The urge must be resisted in the museal playground, but finds an outlet in a simulation of how it could have been – sensuous inquiry is triggered by semiotically piqued desires. Rather than trapping the mouse within the confines of the board, however, the playground opens up into another playground where science meets with imagination. Replica-making is one action in the Mouse Trap game. Performing actions reliant on replicas, using the body as a tool of animation and inquiry, is another. So is making figurines of soldiers. Acting out with figurines calls into being yet another such playground bouncing off from other playgrounds. Where the action originates becomes increasingly unclear. Replicas may be modeled on pictures of real things found online or on examples in "how-to" hobby books rather than on "originals" displayed in a museum space. In the case of miniatures, replication is often mediated by representations of the original, such as photographs, which become the models of emulation, rather than by the original itself. Here, the thread between a specific miniature and its model becomes especially difficult to disentangle. But also on the level of life-size performance, as one re-enactment follows another, and practitioners study their own performance captured on film, the relationship between enactment and re-enactment becomes increasingly complex, as there is a "feedback system at work between representation and the real; each reflects, inspires, and copies the other" (Phelan 2005, 157).

Because of the wealth of images, copies, and facsimiles available and the increasing ease of access to these, mimetic creations of "other" worlds become increasingly possible and sophisticated. In relation to the artifact displayed in a museum, I mentioned how Bann notes a subversive element in the return to curiosity in that it disturbs a normalized order and positions the object as existing in "a nexus of interrelated meanings" (2003, 120). This is evident in the vivid practices of re-enactors and living historians, who combine science with imagination in wielding objects that are semiotically and sensorially highly charged; positioning their very bodies in playgrounds where meanings, things, and people interrelate. The return to curiosity noted by Bann, I suggest, goes hand in hand with "playing culture" in a spirit that Huizinga valued so highly but thought was lost. The sense of wonder and excitement associated with re-enactment practices does not so much reside in a fascination with otherness as in the connections between self and other, in the recognition of a hybridity that attention to "things" can bring to the fore. Looking at a piece of scrimshaw, an Iroquois war club, or an intriguingly ambiguous sash in a museum, I will think of the worlds in which these artifacts have performed, and I will think of John, Alex, and Hilary making and performing look-alikes. Living historians study museum originals thinking of how to turn them into functioning replicas, thus adding to the material life of the original. In a very real way, living historians and miniature enthusiasts affect and constitute, through their practices of imitation and play and through their own bodies, curious material worlds, as well as their afterlives in museums.

Acknowledgments

Life was breathed into this chapter thanks to the generosity of my discussion partners, who enthusiastically shared their time, knowledge, and skills with me as re-enactors and living historians – I thank David Spencer and Steve Thompson in particular. I also wish to express my gratitude to Patrick Piguet, curator at the Musée Océanographique, Monaco, for taking me on a tour of Mark Dion's "Cabinet of Curiosities," and to the Social Sciences and Humanities Research Council of Canada for financial support during my postdoctoral research at the University of Aberdeen (2007–2009). Finally, I am grateful to the editors for their helpful and insightful comments.

Notes

1 Names have been changed to protect discussion partners' anonymity.
2 For nuanced discussions of alleged ocularcentrism in the "West," see Marks (2000, 132–133); Edwards, Gosden, and Phillips (2006, introduction); and Grasseni (2007).
3 See in particular Gell (1998) on art's potential agency cast in terms of "distributed personhood."
4 For another intervention by Mark Dion resulting in a curiosity cabinet at the University of Minnesota, see Sheehy (2006).

References

Alpers, Svetlana. 1991. "The Museum as a Way of Seeing." In *Exhibiting Cultures: The Poetics and Politics of Museum Display*, edited by Ivan Karp and Steven D. Lavine, 25–32. Washington, DC: Smithsonian Institution Press.

Bann, Stephen. 2003. "The Return to Curiosity: Shifting Paradigms in Contemporary Museum Display." In *Art and Its Publics: Museum Studies at the Millennium*, edited by Andrew McClellan, 17–30. Oxford: Blackwell.

Bann, Stephen. 2007. "Curiouser and Curiouser." In *Ways around Modernism*, 103–172. New York: Routledge.

Bateson, Gregory. 1972. "A Theory of Play and Fantasy." In *Steps to an Ecology of Mind*, 177–193. New York: Ballantine.

Bennett, Jane. 2010. *Vibrant Matter: A Political Ecology of Things*. Durham, NC: Duke University Press.

Blackson, Robert. 2007. "Once More … with Feeling: Reenactment in Contemporary Art and Culture." *Art Journal* 66(1): 28–40.

Bouquet, Mary, and Nuno Porto, eds. 2005. *Science, Magic and Religion: The Ritual Processes of Museum Magic*. Oxford: Berghahn.

Brown, Bill. 2001. "Thing Theory." *Critical Inquiry* 28(1): 1–16.

Brown, Bill. 2003. "Regional Artifacts." In *A Sense of Things*, 81–135. Chicago: University of Chicago Press.

Chatterjee, Helen J. 2008. *Touch in Museums: Policy and Practice in Object Handling*. Oxford: Berg.

Classen, Constance, and David Howes. 2006. "The Museum as Sensescape: Western Sensibilities and Indigenous Artifacts." In *Sensible Objects: Colonialism, Museums and Material Culture*, edited by Elizabeth Edwards, Chris Gosden, and Ruth B. Phillips, 199–222. Oxford: Berg.

Daston, Lorraine, and Katharine Park. 1998. *Wonder and the Order of Nature, 1150–1750*. New York: Zone.

Dion, Mark. 2011. *Oceanomania: Souvenirs of Mysterious Seas – From the Expedition to the Aquarium*. London: MACK.

Edwards, Elizabeth, Chris Gosden, and Ruth B. Phillips, eds. 2006. *Sensible Objects: Colonialism, Museums and Material Culture*. Oxford: Berg.

Frank, Stuart M., ed. 2000. *Frederick Myrick of Nantucket Scrimshaw Catalogue Raisonné*, compiled by Donald E. Ridley, with contributions by Paul Madden, Paul Vardeman, and Janet West. Sharon, MA: Kendall Whaling Museum.

Gadamer, Hans-Georg. (1960) 2004. *Truth and Method*. Translated by Garrett Barden and John Cumming. London: Continuum.

Gell, Alfred. (1992) 1995. "The Technology of Enchantment and the Enchantment of Technology." In *Anthropology, Art and Aesthetics*, edited by Jeremy Coote and Anthony Shelton, 40–63. Oxford: Clarendon.

Gell, Alfred. 1998. *Art and Agency: An Anthropological Theory*. Oxford: Clarendon.

Gibson, J. J. 1979. *The Ecological Approach to Visual Perception*. Boston: Houghton Mifflin.

Goffman, Erving. 1974. *Frame Analysis: An Essay on the Organization of Experience*. Cambridge, MA: Harvard University Press.

Grasseni, Cristina. 2007. "Communities of Practice and Forms of Life: Towards a Rehabilitation of Vision?" In *Ways of Knowing: New Approaches in the Anthropology of Experience and Learning*, edited by Mark Harris, 203–221. Oxford: Berghahn.

Greenblatt, Stephen. 1991. "Resonance and Wonder." In *Exhibiting Cultures: The Poetics and Politics of Museum Display*, edited by Ivan Karp and Steven D. Lavine, 42–56. Washington, DC: Smithsonian Institution.

Handler, Richard, and Eric Gable. 1997. *The New History in an Old Museum: Creating the Past at Colonial Williamsburg*. Durham, NC: Duke University Press.

Henare, Amiria, Martin Holbraad, and Sari Wastell, eds. 2007. *Thinking through Things: Theorising Artefacts Ethnographically*. London: Routledge.

Henning, Michelle. 2006. "Archive." In *Museums, Media and Cultural Theory*, 129–155. Maidenhead, UK: Open University Press.

Huizinga, Johan. (1950) 1967. *Homo Ludens: A Study of the Play Element in Culture*. Boston: Beacon.

Kalshoven, Petra Tjitske. 2008. "Magic of the Mannequin: A Guided Look through the Dioramas in the Mashantucket Pequot Museum." *Acta Americana* 16(2): 5–25.

Kalshoven, Petra Tjitske. 2012. *Crafting "the Indian": Knowledge, Desire, and Play in Indianist Reenactment*. New York: Berghahn.

Kalshoven, Petra Tjitske. 2013. "The World Unwraps from Tiny Bags: Measuring Landscapes in Miniature." *Ethnos* 78(3): 352–379.

Kirshenblatt-Gimblett, Barbara. 1998. *Destination Culture: Tourism, Museums, and Heritage*. Berkeley: University of California Press.

Knell, Simon J. 2007. "Museums, Reality and the Material World." In *Museums in the Material World*, edited by Simon J. Knell, 1–28. London: Routledge.

Latour, Bruno, and Adam Lowe. 2012. "The Migration of the Aura, or How to Explore the Original Through Its Facsimiles." In *Switching Codes: Thinking Through Digital Technology in the Humanities and the Arts*, edited by Thomas Bartscherer and Roderick Coover, 275–298. Chicago: University of Chicago Press.

Lütticken, Sven. 2005. "An Arena in Which to Reenact." In *Life, Once More: Forms of Reenactment in Contemporary Art*, edited by Sven Lütticken, 17–60. Rotterdam: Witte de With Center for Contemporary Art.

Lynch, Bernadette. 2008. "The Amenable Object: Working with Diaspora Communities through a Psychoanalysis of Touch." In *Touch in Museums: Policy and Practice in Object Handling*, edited by Helen J. Chatterjee, 261–272. Oxford: Berg.

Marks, Laura U. 2000. "The Memory of Touch." In *The Skin of the Film: Intercultural Cinema, Embodiment, and the Senses*, 127–193. Durham, NC: Duke University Press.

McCalman, Iain, and Paul A. Pickering, eds. 2010. *Historical Reenactment: From Realism to the Affective Turn*. Basingstoke, UK: Palgrave Macmillan.

Miller, Daniel, ed. 2005. *Materiality*. Durham, NC: Duke University Press.

Onol, Isil. 2008. "Tactual Explorations: A Tactile Interpretation of a Museum Exhibit through Tactile Art Works and Augmented Reality." In *Touch in Museums: Policy and Practice in Object Handling*, edited by Helen J. Chatterjee, 92–106. Oxford: Berg.

Pearce, Susan M. 1992. *Museums, Objects and Collections: A Cultural Study*. London: Leicester University Press.

Peers, Laura. 2007. *Playing Ourselves: Interpreting Native Histories at Historic Reconstructions*. Lanham, MD: AltaMira.

Phelan, Peggy. 2005. "Hinckley and Ronald Reagan: Reenactment and the Ethics of the Real." In *Life, Once More: Forms of Reenactment in Contemporary Art*, edited by Sven Lütticken, 147–168. Rotterdam: Witte de With Center for Contemporary Art.

Pil and Galia Kollectiv. 2007. "RETRO/NECRO: From Beyond the Grave of the Politics of Re-enactment." *Art Papers* 20. Accessed August 29, 2014. http://www.kollectiv.co.uk/Art%20Papers%20feature/reenactment/retro-necro.htm.

Poliquin, Rachel. 2012. *The Breathless Zoo: Taxidermy and the Cultures of Longing*. University Park: Pennsylvania State University Press.

Schneider, Rebecca, 2011. "Reenactment and Relative Pain." In *Performing Remains: Art and War in Times of Theatrical Reenactment*, 32–60. New York: Routledge.

Schutz, A. (1945) 1962. "Multiple Realities." In *Rules and Meanings*, edited by M. Douglas, 227–231. Harmondsworth, UK: Penguin.

Sheehy, Colleen J., ed. 2006. *Cabinet of Curiosities: Mark Dion and the University as Installation*. Minneapolis: University of Minnesota Press.

Tilley, Christopher. 2004. *The Materiality of Stone: Explorations in Landscape Phenomenology*. Oxford: Berg.

Tilley, Christopher, Webb Keane, Susanne Küchler, Mike Rowlands, and Patricia Spyer, eds. 2006. *Handbook of Material Culture*. London: Sage.

Toker, Leona. 2000. *Return from the Archipelago: Narratives of Gulag Survivors*. Bloomington: Indiana University Press.

Were, Graeme. 2008. "Out of Touch? Digital Technologies, Ethnographic Objects and Sensory Orders." In *Touch in Museums: Policy and Practice in Object Handling*, edited by Helen J. Chatterjee, 121–134. Oxford: Berg.

West, Janet. 1991. "Scrimshaw and the Identification of Sea Mammal Products." *Journal of Museum Ethnography* 2: 39–79.

Petra Tjitske Kalshoven is Lecturer in Social Anthropology at the University of Manchester. Her research focuses on skilled manifestations of human curiosity, and her work on replicas and imitation ties into a more general interest in the relations between people, their "things," and the landscapes with which they engage, identify, or take issue. Kalshoven is the author of *Crafting "the Indian": Knowledge, Desire, and Play in Indianist Reenactment* (Berghahn, 2012), an ethnographic study of the social and performative dynamics of a contemporary amateur practice in Europe predicated on emulation of Native American lifeworlds from the past. Her current research agenda centers on the imitation of nature that underpins the skilled practice of taxidermy, with a view to shedding light on evolving human–animal relations.

25 WITH AND WITHOUT WALLS
Photographic Reproduction and the Art Museum

Michelle Henning

According to Peter Walsh, we are in the era of the "post-photographic" museum, something we take so much for granted that we have to work to historically reconstruct the pre-photographic museum (2007, 23). Photography thoroughly mediates visitors' experience of museums: from the publicity or educational material they encounter before their visit, on paper or online; to behind-the-scenes practices which employ photography for purposes of preservation, conservation, and documentation; to the snapshots that visitors take themselves and then circulate. Photographs are ubiquitous in contemporary exhibition contexts, to contextualize exhibits, and as artifacts in their own right. In this chapter, I do not plan to attempt to reconstruct the pre-photographic museum, but to show how photography has helped to shape the values that are commonly associated with modernism, such as artistic style, handling or facture, and originality. These aesthetic categories were naturalized by the post-photographic museum, even if it initially looked as if photography was a threat to them. They are associated with the privileging of certain kinds of attention in the museum. I want to suggest how our contemporary image culture can offer a different aesthetic model for museums, or more precisely, to use the French philosopher Jacques Rancière's terminology, a different "distribution of the sensible" – that is, a different distribution of the sensory capacities associated with the different social classes, and with activity or passivity, work or leisure, criticism and consumption (Rancière 2009).

Photography is particularly important in this narrative, not least because many writers have argued that the use of photographs, both analogue and digital, to reproduce and disseminate art has produced new understandings of the original in relation to the reproduction, and distinctive ways of talking about, curating, and presenting art in the museum and outside. Photographic reproduction, in short, has been instrumental in the transformation of the art museum, in the development

The International Handbooks of Museum Studies: Museum Media, First Edition.
Edited by Michelle Henning.
© 2015 John Wiley & Sons Ltd. Published 2020 by John Wiley & Sons Ltd.

of art history, and in ongoing changes in the ways in which audiences encounter art. But perhaps too much weight has been given to photographic reproduction. Is it really photography that has produced or even facilitated these changes? A number of writers have shown how other kinds of art reproduction, including wood engraving and lithography, continued to exist, and to flourish, well after the invention of photography in and around 1839. Between then and the distribution of photographically illustrated books in the late 1860s, "it was not photographs but wood-engravings that filled the pages of the illustrated magazines; intaglio work and lithography that crammed the print shop windows" (Fawcett 1986, 194). These other processes were increasingly mechanized. Wood-engraved reproductions of artworks were circulated internationally between publishers using the electrotyping process, which was invented between 1836 and 1838, very close to the invention of photography (Von Lintel 2012, 539). In 1839 new reducing machinery for bronze casting was introduced, which was so accurate that it "led to immediate comparison with the exactly contemporary daguerreotype" (Haskell and Penny 1981, 124).

Indeed, the notion that there is a technique for the reproduction and circulation of artworks that we could simply describe as photographic is questionable. Photography did not become a means for the wide circulation of prints until it could be combined with mechanical printing methods. It was only in the 1860s that photographically illustrated art books began to be published, although by then the market for photographs of artworks was an international business (Hamber 1995, 91–92). Photography lagged behind older print methods such as engraving and lithography until the invention of a series of new photomechanical processes in the 1870s and 1880s.[1] But photographic methods also transformed older techniques, being incorporated into lithography and as part of the process by which engraving or woodcuts could be duplicated, allowing for multiple blocks and longer print runs.

Painting and photography became entangled right from the start. Not only did nineteenth-century painters use the new medium as part of their process, but painting became integral to the production of the photographic print, which frequently involved retouching with inks by hand, correcting, manipulating, coloring, and generally making the photograph "print-ready." Today, digital photography and digital painting have become almost indistinguishable: manual skills are used to move and alter pixels, "painting" and "retouching" using a mouse or stylus and applications like Adobe Photoshop; and high-end facsimile reproduction involves a combination of the manual and mechanical application of paint. Bruno Latour and Adam Lowe have described the facsimile of Veronese's *Nozze di Cana* produced by Factum Arte in Madrid as "a painting, albeit produced through the intermediary of digital techniques" (2011, 276). The Veronese painting in the Louvre was scanned using a large-format CCD (i.e., the same kind of sensor that a digital camera uses) that responded to light that the device itself produced (much like a scanner, only with LED lights to reduce heat and ultraviolet), but more conventional photography was also used, via a digital Hasselblad and ambient light. After the large number of images produced were combined and manipulated to produce a copy of the entire painting, the facsimile was printed "in pigment on gesso-coated canvas," the canvas stitched together, and the joins "retouched by hand by a team of trained conservators" (Latour and Lowe 2011, 289–296). Though the technology used, and the specific combination of techniques, are very new and innovative, the hybrid painting-photograph is as old as photography itself.

And yet, in the early to mid-twentieth century, critics, curators, and academics identified photography, in particular, as having dramatically affected the art museum, and drew a sharp distinction between the (photographic) copy and the original (usually a painting). The most famous texts are Walter Benjamin's essay "The Work of Art in the Age of Mechanical Reproduction,"[2] written and rewritten in the mid- to late 1930s, and Andre Malraux's *Museum without Walls*, which was first published in 1947 (Benjamin (1936) 1992; Malraux (1947) 1967). Already, members of the early twentieth-century avant-garde combined painting and photography, but their advocates emphasized avant-garde photography's potential as art on the grounds that it did not imitate painting, but "opposed" it (Brik [1926] 1989, 216–217). For instance, the Dada poet Tristan Tzara's essay, which accompanied the publication of Man Ray's "Rayographs" in the winter of 1922, argued that the cameraless photograph (photogram) had superseded painting, a now sterile and compromised medium:

> Everything that bore the name of art had succumbed to paralysis; at which point the photographer lit his thousand-candlepower lamp, and gradually the light-sensitive paper absorbed the blackness of a few utilitarian objects. (Tzara [1924] 2002, 484)

During the late 1920s and early 1930s, in various art and culture journals, European photographers, writers, and curators debated the impact of photography on art, and especially painting (Phillips 1989; Benson and Forgács 2002). In the pages of the Hamburg journal *Der Kreis*, museum directors and curators initiated a debate about the difference between the experience of the original work of art and the experience of a reproduction or facsimile. What did this difference consist of, if the viewer was unable to distinguish one from the other?

Although the telegraphic transmission of photographs had been practiced by news organizations since around 1900, and the mass dissemination of photographs via photomechanical printing had existed since the 1860s, the preoccupation with the distinction between (static) original and (mobile) copy seems to have hindered the recognition that many of the "original" paintings in museums were born into, and inseparable from, the world of the mass copy. The French historian Michel Foucault has beautifully characterized the pervasive image culture that had emerged with technical reproduction and flourished in the late nineteenth century. In 1975 Foucault wrote a catalog essay for the painter Gérard Fromanger's exhibition *Desire Is Everywhere*, in which he described "a new frenzy for images, which circulated rapidly between camera and easel, between canvas and plate and paper," from about 1860 until 1880. Technical reproduction enabled "a new freedom of transposition, displacement, and transformation, of resemblance and dissimulation, of reproduction, duplication and trickery of effect" (Foucault [1975] 1999, 83–84).

Foucault's ability to vividly reimagine this late nineteenth-century culture of images was facilitated by his interest in heterogeneity, madness, prisons, and sexual transgression. In his account, media attempt to imprison images, which slip away. He writes:

> In those days images travelled the world under false identities. To them there was nothing more hateful than to remain captive, self-identical, in *one* painting, *one* photograph, *one* engraving, under the aegis of *one* author. No medium, no language, no syntax could contain them; from birth to last resting place they could always escape through new techniques of transposition. (Foucault [1975] 1999, 84–85)

The mobility of images ca. 1860 to 1880 has something in common with the mobility, diversity, and lack of fixity of sexual identities, "with their migration and perversion, their transvestitism, their disguised difference" (83–84). Foucault abolishes distinctions between original and copy, along with the old conception of a medium as something that merely delivered images to a receptive audience.

The cult of originality

To understand the post-photographic museum means situating museums in the play of images. We can start by questioning the idea that museums are the resting places of the originals from which reproductions emanate, since it disregards the role that facsimiles and reproductions have played in the history of museums. The idea of the museum as a place where you went to encounter "the thing itself" has not always held sway. If, as some claim, the "museum age" really only begins with the inauguration of the Louvre in the late eighteenth century, then the fascination with the facsimile and the reproduction precedes it. In the eighteenth century, casts and replicas in a wide range of materials were sold as ornaments and collectables, and there were galleries of plaster-cast facsimiles of antiquities throughout Europe.[3] In Britain, Peter Walsh has argued, the Victoria and Albert Museum established itself as a prototype of a new type of museum, willing to use reproductions instead of originals to enable it to include as much as possible of the world's artworks (2007, 24). From very early on, it included a photography collection and also used photography within the museum. The museum's photographer, Thurston Thompson, photographed the famous Raphael cartoons, and these photographs were described as "all but as valuable as the originals" in the *Athenaeum* literary magazine of 1859, which concluded that "Great works of Art are now, when once photographed, imperishable" (quoted in Fawcett 1986, 192). In the

United States, some museums modeled themselves on the South Kensington Museum, happily exhibiting reproductions where the originals were too expensive or rare (Walsh 2007, 28). Reproductions were also reproducible: in 1914 a catalog of photographs of Brucciani's Covent Garden collection of plaster casts of Byzantine, Gothic, and Renaissance works was published for use in schools (Haskell and Penny 1981, 117).

The flipside of this was that the original was effectively devalued. In exactly the same year as the *Athenaeum* described art as "imperishable," American essayist and poet Oliver Wendell Holmes had anticipated what would happen if a viewing public felt that reproductions were an adequate or satisfactory substitute, and he quipped: "Give us a few negatives of a thing worth seeing, taken from different points of view, and that is all we want of it. Pull it down or burn it up, if you please" (Holmes 1859).

To participants in the 1920s and 1930s discussions of photographic reproduction in European journals such as *Der Kreis*, *Der Stijl*, and *internationale revue*, photomechanical reproduction appeared as a threat, because it effaced the labor of the photographer so effectively that it was difficult to tell the difference between a copy and an original art object. In 1929 Max Sauerlandt, director of the Art and Craft Museum in Hamburg, launched an attack in *Der Kreis* on the collection of plaster casts put together by Carl G. Heise, director of St. Annen-Kloster in Lübeck (and responsible for one of the first major exhibitions of photography in that year). The discussion soon turned to photography because Alexander Dorner, director of the Landesmuseum in Hanover, had exhibited 35 artworks on paper alongside their printed facsimiles in May 1929. Dorner challenged viewers to identify the difference, and over 100 laypeople and experts were equally confounded (Márkus 2007, 357).

Some writers in *Der Kreis* were appalled by the notion that the reproduction might take the place of the artwork. In November 1929 Kurt Karl Eberlein, an art historian and onetime director of the Kunsthalle in Karlsruhe, wrote that all facsimiles were forgeries and that, even if 99 percent of the viewing public could not tell the difference between them and the original artwork, this did not make them the same. Eberlein argued that technical reproduction provided only "falsifying surrogates" for art (Eberlein [1929] 1989, 146). In his view, mechanical reproductions were imposters, unable to substitute for the experience of the original, since each original is "a unique, intellectually shaped physical expression of art's essence" (149). The photomechanical reproduction of an artwork was supposed to complement and promote the artwork itself, but instead, for Eberlein, it followed what Jacques Derrida described, half a century later, as the "logic of the supplement":

> The supplement adds itself, it is a surplus, a plenitude enriching another plenitude, the fullest measure of presence … But the supplement supplements. It adds only to replace. It intervenes or insinuates itself in-the-place-of; if it fills, it is as if one fills a void. (Derrida 1976, 145)

According to Eberlein,

> Every explanation of why the mysterious, magical, biological "aura" of a work of art cannot be forged – even though 99 percent of the viewers don't notice the difference – is an offence against the sovereignty of art. (Eberlein [1929] 1989, 148)

Today we tend to associate the concept of aura with Benjamin's essay, written six years later, but Eberlein's comment suggests that in 1929 it was already being used to characterize the "essence" of art. Dorner responded by pointing out that there would never be agreement between the advocates of facsimile reproduction and its detractors, because people like Eberlein felt that

> ancient works of art can only be experienced at first hand, with a fingertip sense of the cracks in the surface. Indeed, for them the arduous pilgrimage to the work of art is part of the artistic experience; they want the old work of art to stand isolated from contemporary life. (Dorner [1930] 1989, 153)

By contrast, the advocates wanted to put the past to use in the present. So the dispute also involved competing understandings of museums – one view took the museum to be the place you would go to experience the work of art in its full "presence"; the other saw the role of the museum as bringing museums into "the stream of contemporary life." Yet, as Dorner noted, museums had already torn paintings and sculptures and other works of art from their original contexts and in the process entirely transformed them. Museums and facsimiles serve similar functions, "generated by the interests and needs of the present" and are "incomprehensible apart from those interests and needs" (Dorner [1930] 1989, 152). The present absorbed the past, circulated its images, and put them to new uses for a modern mass audience.

   The art museum's act of detaching objects from their context is something that we find in all kinds of museums. It is something Barbara Kirshenblatt-Gimblett describes as key to ethnographic museums, "an essentially surgical issue … Where do we make the cut?" (1998, 18). She argues that all ethnographic objects are fragments, pieces of the world produced by active choices about where to cut, which are guided by ideas about the singularity of the object and its separability from its place in the world. The art museum makes the most radical cut since, as Hilde Hein pithily describes it, "aesthetic interest inducts an object into a realm of privileged inutility" (2000, 128). Yet, if art museums produce the original as singular by detaching it, they can never quite rid themselves of the possibility that by making the cut they have damaged the object. Latour and Lowe compare their elaborate facsimile of Veronese's *Nozze di Cana*, mentioned earlier, *in situ* in Palladio's refectory on the island of San Giorgio where the Veronese painting had first hung, to the painting that Napoleon had stolen from there and taken as booty to the Louvre. In the Louvre the painting is inappropriately framed, hung too low, the meaning changed and the balance of the composition altered (Latour and Lowe 2011, 276–277). For Latour and Lowe the recontextualizing of paintings by the museum undermines the concept of a pure "original," but to argue this they simply replace one notion of authenticity (the thing itself), with another (the original situation, prior to the cut).

The concept of the museum as a place in which we encounter the "original" is also complicated by the fact that the material object is not frozen in time but is always in a process of subtle, slow transformation. The museum actively intervenes in this process through restoration, conservation, and climate control. Latour and Lowe begin their essay with a viewer who encounters Hans Holbein's *Ambassadors* at the National Gallery in London (Figure 25.1), but finds it too "garish" and "exaggerated": restored, it takes on the appearance of a "cheap copy" (2011, 275–276). Holbein's painting is a good example since its restoration history has been documented – it had been altered in the eighteenth century, again in the 1890s, then again in the 1990s (with minor repairs in the intervening century). Martin Wyld wrote in the *National Gallery Technical Bulletin* after the 1990s restoration: "the image of the picture which is so familiar today is not that which was seen by the gallery's visitors in 1890" (1998, 9). The implicit distinction between the "image of the picture" and the picture itself is very telling. What is "the original" if not the thing we see before us? Does each restoration produce a new "image of

FIGURE 25.1   Hans Holbein the Younger, *The Ambassadors*, 1533. Note the famous distorted skull in the foreground of the picture. (For a color version of this figure, please see the color plate section.)

By permission of the National Gallery, London.

the picture" in the eyes or minds of the visitors? If so, what is the distinction between this "image" and a copy?

The 1990s restoration involved cleaning off varnish from 1891 but also removing nineteenth-century painting and then repainting areas. The restoration process incorporated reproductive imaging technologies: x-rays and digital imaging. The nose bone of the famous distorted (anamorphic) skull presented particular problems because the x-rays revealed Holbein's own paint as missing beneath the nineteenth-century paint. Digital imaging techniques were used to convert the anamorphic image to a conventional one, and this, along with various images of different skulls, was used as guidance for "a tentative reconstruction of the nose bone and the end of the lower jaw" despite "ethical reservations" and bearing in mind the "question of how the Gallery's visitor's might react if an image as famous as Holbein's skull were to be displayed incomplete" (Wyld 1998, 25). The "image" – as remembered by visitors and circulated through reproductions – determines the production of a new nose bone, a copy, not simply of Holbein's painting, but of other, actual, skulls. Only through this arduous process can the museum attempt to isolate the picture from the flow of contemporary experience, and yet, at the same time, it is the images circulating in the minds and reproductions of contemporary society that shape the restoration.

Forms of attention

Benjamin saw, as Dorner did, the facsimile reproduction as the next stage in the democratization of art begun by the public art museum. Unlike Eberlein (who wanted art to remain an elite experience), Benjamin sees this as a necessary and politicized process but, like Eberlein, he does not see facsimiles as harmless to the "aura" of the original. Benjamin argues in "The Work of Art in the Age of Mechanical Reproduction" that photomechanical reproduction gives art back an active social and political role which it had lost when it entered the museum. But Eberlein and Benjamin have one thing in common: they disagree with the advocates of facsimile reproduction who believe it will leave intact the "aura" of the work of art. Today we use "aura" to refer to some kind of ineffable aesthetic value. Benjamin sees it more precisely, as an effect of a certain social convention, a certain way of looking at art that had become the norm among a certain class of people in the nineteenth-century museum. For Benjamin, technical reproduction didn't simply damage the value or mystique of the artwork; it attacked the social norm of receptive contemplation that was associated with the encounter with the original art object in the museum, so that seeing the "original" would never be the same again. The post-photographic museum is a museum in which a certain kind of aesthetic contemplation has started to decay.

The kind of contemplation Benjamin had in mind was rooted in the idea of communion with the artwork and institutionalized in the art museum, which provided a secular substitute for religious experience in front of paintings that were once altarpieces, statues that were once gods. This is the kind of aesthetic experience expected and experienced by, for instance, the painter and physician Carl Gustav Carus in 1857. Carus had seen Raphael's Sistine Madonna in its new chapel-like installation at the Royal Gallery of Paintings in Dresden and effused that the painting "presented itself ever more radiantly and in its full significance to my soul" (quoted in Belting 2001, 61). This quasi-religious experience of the artwork in the museum is particularly associated with the Romantic belief in the autonomy of art. The Romantics conceived of both art and nature in terms of a reciprocated gaze. From this perspective, artworks were not mute objects or merely expressive of the artist and the culture, but autonomous and able to generate their own meanings to the receptive and sensitive viewer (see Stoljar 1997, 10–11).

"Insofar as the age of technical reproduction separated art from its basis in cult, all semblance of art's autonomy disappeared forever" (Benjamin [1936] 2002, 109). The effect of this is to let loose the artwork, sending it spinning into the hands of the mass audience. This audience grasps at the image, with the hand as much as the eye, because it has been trained, by cinema and mass culture, toward a new kind of attention. Like other German writers of the period, Benjamin characterizes this as "distraction" (*Zerstreuung* – sometimes also translated as "diversion"); unlike them, he represents this new kind of receptiveness as active, not passive. Frederic Schwartz summarizes it like this:

> Distraction is a hypothetical mode of visual attention, one described as routine, active and not absorbed, one representing a mode of technical problem-solving and not aesthetic enjoyment, one addressing bits and pieces from the inside and not unified wholes from a distance. (2005, 62)

Traditional aesthetic enjoyment was overturned, but in its place were new pleasures. As Schwartz points out, Benjamin was very familiar with Moholy-Nagy's book *Painting, Photography, Film*, which spoke of meditation and immersion being replaced by participation, by art forms in which the observer is able "to participate, to seize instantly upon new moments of vital insight" (Moholy-Nagy, quoted in Schwartz 2005, 54). The new form of attention is grasping, tactile, instantaneous, urgent, and active but also habitual and almost automatic – and it belongs principally to the working class; it is very different from the older attention "of the savoring bourgeoisie" (Tschichold, quoted in Schwartz 2005, 55). For Benjamin and these artists of the avant-garde, these debates were political, and their aspirations were that photographic technology could be put to use in overturning the class system. Although the larger political claims they made for this new kind of attention do not stand up to scrutiny in retrospect, the notion that the technology of mass reproduction might be associated with a change in the museum audience and a transformation of the experience of "original" works of art is crucial for understanding the practices and potential of art museums today.

We have seen how Foucault connected the technologically facilitated circulation of images with a kind of playfulness. Benjamin, too, connected the new technologies of mass image production with an increase in play (in the double sense of extension and amusement). In the early versions of the "Work of Art" essay, he argued that the origin of the technology of the machine age "lies … in play" (Benjamin [1936] 2002, 107). In the footnotes he wrote that the machine age, by liberating people from drudgery, increased the "scope for play [*Spielraum*]." This means, not just increased leisure time, but an expanded "field of action" (124). Art had always involved play, but in traditional aesthetics emphasis had been placed on "beautiful semblance" at the expense of play. Now, as new mechanical reproductive technologies take precedence, the possibilities for play increase: "that which is lost in the withering of semblance and the decay of the aura in works of art is matched by a huge gain in the scope for play" (127). One kind of pleasure (critical, contemplative) was replaced by another (playful, irreverent), and it belonged to the mass audience.

The invention of facture

Just as much as photography and technical reproduction can be said to have contributed to the decline of aura, they can also, simultaneously, be said to have been necessary both to the development of the cult of originality and to an increased interest in certain kinds of detail and texture in the art object. The value attached to the original, as against the copy, is largely post-photographic. The sociologist Gordon Fyfe makes this point in a discussion of engraving. Line engraving was a skilled craft, practiced in the eighteenth century by craftsmen organized into guilds, who commanded a near monopoly over the trade in reproductions. As Fyfe summarizes:

> In the service of patrons they reproduced the material culture of patrimonial power; they disseminated images of antiquity and they serviced the trade in reproductions of antiquities. Engravings spread news of royal, aristocratic and institutional collections and formed a part of the visual propaganda machines of European states and their rulers. (2004, 57)

In Fyfe's account, the hegemony of engraving was destroyed both by the maneuvers of art institutions, and transformations in the organization of labor during the industrial revolution, in which the guilds were replaced by capitalist relations of employment, and engravers cast as either employers or laborers (2004, 58). In capitalist society, culture is part of the market, and the destruction of the craft workshop and the guild was part of the process of creating a free flow of cultural capital.

The "visual propaganda" of the eighteenth-century engraving was the means by which aristocratic and bourgeois individuals were educated about art objects and antiquities which they had not seen in the original, but it also produced them as an audience that was discerning about the quality of the engraver's interpretation. In this period, the production of copies was not an anonymous and invisible practice. On the contrary, the skill and style of the master engraver was supposed to be evident and legible in the print. Engravers saw their task as to communicate certain classical ideals such as those of harmony and proportion. Line engraving emphasized composition and iconography, and engravers transposed paintings and statuary using a set of very specific conventions developed in the seventeenth century, a "syntax" or repertoire of cross-hatching, lines, and dots (Fyfe 2004, 54).[4] As William M. Ivins, Jr., print curator at the Metropolitan Museum of Art in New York in the mid-twentieth century, had noted, the suitability of an artwork for translation into the engraving's "net of rationality" was a criterion for its selection for reproduction (Ivins 1953; Pinson 1998, 155).

Engraving was undermined by photomechanical reproduction, not simply because the new technology was more efficient or effective than the older one, but because it accompanied and reinforced a new set of values: "Engravers fought to retain a place within the cultural apparatus, but the fight was conducted on a terrain that was increasingly defined by a photographic way of seeing" (Fyfe 2004, 59).[5] Just as engraving had influenced the canon, so artwork photography was shaping the public taste for art, but it was also shaping a distinctive new approach to seeing (and seeing through) reproductions. The photographic series which cataloged and documented exhibitions and collections, and which were sold throughout Europe, also transmitted a new kind of appreciation, which privileges the individual authorship of the artist and the authority of the original artwork while rendering the process of interpretation through reproduction increasingly invisible. For the new way of seeing, which emerged and developed with photography, an ideal reproduction would be one that effaced itself, which allowed the viewer to feel they simply looked through it to the artwork. The photograph's direct, chemical-mechanical reproduction of objects and lack of explicit syntax gave the impression of transparency.

By the 1860s, distinctions were being made between interpretive prints of an artist's work and "facsimiles" – surrogates or exact copies which stood in for the original. While photographs would be described as facsimiles, certain nonphotographic prints would be too, as Stephen C. Pinson has shown. An 1873 *catalogue raisonné* of Delacroix's work described Robaut's very precise manual copies of the drawings as "facsimiles." Yet, in the same catalog, other prints made "after Delacroix" were treated as original works in their own right, presumably because they were seen to demonstrate more interpretive freedom or stylistic distinctiveness (Pinson 1998, 160–163). But, increasingly, copying in general was becoming an anonymous and secondary practice, shifting toward the production of precise facsimiles.

The photographer who reproduced the paintings that illustrated books and catalogs was almost invariably anonymous. Their authorship is suppressed, not just in the absence of a photo credit, but more importantly in the absence of any evident "style" that shows the mark of an author. The photograph "created the illusion of communication without mediation; it brought the work of art and the signs of its making into the presence of the viewer whilst it suppressed the incorporated practices of print-making which made that presence possible" (Fyfe 2004, 52). The photograph seemed to be able to communicate or convey the unique handling and expression of an individual artist by reproducing tone and texture as well as line, composition, and iconography. Engraving had flourished in a world where art was still understood as largely collective, traditional, and convention-bound, but the developing modern culture of art valorized the individual and expressive mark.

One of the contributors to *Der Kreis* recognized that the value being placed on the material presence of the original – by both the supporters and detractors of photomechanical reproduction – was a peculiarly modern phenomenon. This was the art historian Erwin Panofsky, whose 1930 essay "Original and Facsimile Reproduction" pointed out that earlier conceptions of art, deriving from Aristotelian ideas and from Neoplatonism, had seen the materiality of the object as secondary, a passive carrier for ideas (Panofsky [1930] 2010). In the nineteenth century, the technology of photography appeared to realize the classical belief that the form is separate and distinct from its physical substrate, insofar as it seemed to separate images from their material place in the world. For instance, Oliver Wendell Holmes writes about photography as if it is a form of taxidermy, stripping reality of its outward "skin": "Men will hunt all curious, beautiful, grand objects, as they hunt the cattle in South America, for their skins, and leave the carcasses as of little worth" (Holmes 1859).

The increased emphasis on the handmade, the textural and material presence of paintings, both by painters and by writers on painting, was partly a response to this notion of photography as stripping away the surface appearance. Not only was photography unable to reproduce this physicality, but it had practically none of its own. In 1927 an article by Ernő Kállai in *internationale revue* argued that the difference between painting and photography is not about form and imitation, but is a difference of materiality. A painting or drawing is also "a physical substance with a tension and consistency of its own" (Kállai [1927] 2002, 685). By contrast, "photography is not capable of this degree of materiality and objecthood" and therefore an "emotional substrate" is hardly present. "There is no facture," declared Kállai, which means "no optically perceptible tension between the substance of the image and the image itself" (686).

Facture refers to the artist's expressive handling of their materials, the mark-making, and the sensuous materiality of the object evident in its texture and physical qualities: all those qualities that the reproduction could not possess. Yet, Dorner's exhibit showed how insensitive visitors, even expert ones, were to facture. People had to learn to see facture and, to do so, they had first to see paintings through photography: to see that the photograph itself did not possess facture. Panofsky concluded that the more faithful reproductions became the more viewers would become adept at seeing nuanced differences ([1930] 2010). But, also, photographs conveyed facture when other kinds of reproduction did not. Black and white photographs, in particular, reinforced a modern way of seeing art by drawing attention to the mark-making and texture of paintings, and by emphasizing tone and mass over line and composition.

To an extent, the museum had already begun the process of drawing attention to material presence by removing objects from their original social context. The modern Western category of art developed out of the process of divesting art objects of their representational function: as Malraux noted in *Museum without Walls*, the museum

> does away with the significance of Palladium, of saint and Savior; rules out associations of sanctity, qualities of adornment and possession, of likeness or imagination; and presents the viewer with images of things, differing from the things themselves, and drawing their raison d'être from this very difference. ([1947] 1967, 10)

Malraux, too, notices how photography contributes to this change. By beating painting at the game of illusionistic representation, it destroys the value of spectacular techniques of illusion and *trompe l'oeil*, which had dominated Baroque painting: "these spectacles ceased to be spectacle. They did not again become apparitions, but became pictures, in the sense in which we understand that word today" (Malraux [1947] 1967, 31).

The museum and photography, together, made facture conceivable. So when, in the 1920s, writers defended the handmade artifact against the mechanical facsimile, they were using a conception of the essence of art which had only relatively recently been formulated, and which had only gained prominence as reproductions and facsimiles increased their circulation.

Style

Kállai's point about the absence of facture in photography is echoed in a 1942 essay by Beaumont Newhall, the curator of a series of groundbreaking photography shows at the Museum of Modern Art, New York, during the late 1930s and 1940s. Proposing that photography be treated more widely as a topic of study within art history, Newhall acknowledged that "Art historians, accustomed to dealing with "auto-graphic" works of art, may find it difficult to evaluate photographs. Facture, draftsmanship and other marks of the individual hand are absent" (Newhall 1942, 86). Yet, while Kállai used the absence of facture to argue for the absence of emotion, Newhall emphasized the ways in which the nonmechanical and nonobjective aspects of photography enable the photograph to embody a particular vision of the world. The marks of the individual hand only get in the way of this deeper distinctiveness of style rooted in unique visual perception, so that "this apparent loss is at once a gain; it enables us to grasp the vision of an individual, of an epoch, of a people in the most direct and immediate way" (Newhall 1942, 86).

Newhall emphasized, first, the way photography gives us direct access to "vision" and, through this, style; second, human control over the medium. He distinguished the artistic control of the medium from the snapshooter who simply presses the button on a Kodak Brownie, and challenged the perception of it as a mechanical, objective medium. For Newhall, photographs have style and it is only the art historians' ignorance about photography that makes them unable to distinguish differences between photographic styles, differences that depend on technology but are driven by the photographer's unique vision. Even in the case of the photographic reproduction of paintings and sculptures (the principal use that photography had at the time for the art museum and the art historian), Newhall felt that photography was more than merely mechanical. In the best examples, Newhall argued, the photograph constitutes a piece of art criticism or interpretation:

> Too many of the photographs of paintings which are used to instruct students and to illustrate textbooks are the work of unthinking journeymen, devoid of natural taste and completely incapable of recognizing the qualities which should be brought out on the print. In the case of sculpture, photography can be a direct form of criticism. (Newhall 1942, 87)

Even reproductive photographs can be judged in terms of the quality of authorship. Yet this is the authorship of the critic. Newhall cannot restore to the photographer the status and authorial role of the engraver. For Newhall, the photographer reproducing art must still bring out what is "there" and needs to exercise connoisseurship, not to translate into a new syntax.

The idea of style allowed photographs to be admitted as artworks. But it is also possible to argue that style itself had become a dominant category for art history as a result of photographic reproduction. For example, the art historian Heinrich Wölfflin's famous distinction between the painterly (Baroque) and the linear (Renaissance) styles was based in a practice of close formal comparison between paintings – in reproduction. Late nineteenth-century art history in Germany tended toward historical surveys, but Wölfflin's lectures and books posited a different kind of art historical practice attuned to style: through comparative, formal study students should develop a "feeling" for style, an ability to recognize and distinguish styles from one another (Adler 2004, 439).

Wölfflin placed great emphasis on the experience of the artwork but this experience was conjured through the magical technology of the lantern slideshow. His lectures were deliberately populist and spectacular, using slide projections to make historically and geographically distant works of art present and immediate to the students in the lecture theater. His signature technique was to show two slides alongside one another for comparison (using two projectors), and to accompany this with a charismatic, mesmerizing presentation style. This was described by his biographer and student Landsberger in 1924: "Wölfflin considers the work in silence, draws near to it, following Schopenhauer's advice, as one draws near to a prince, waiting for the art to speak to him. His sentences come slowly, almost hesitatingly" (quoted in Nelson 2000, 419). The lecturer's performance, the darkened space, and the illuminated screen all heightened the sense of presence. As in cinema, projection served to dematerialize the image and to immerse the observer, isolating them from other distractions.

Benjamin witnessed Wölfflin's presentation style, and privately criticized it. In exalting the artwork (via the slide), Wölfflin made the student's relationship to it one of "moral obligation" (Benjamin, quoted in Foster 1996, 116). More recent commentators have argued that, indeed, Wölfflin's method was meant to inculcate certain "spiritual values"; like several other German-speaking academics at the turn of the twentieth century, he felt that the increasing secularization of education had led to a neglect of students' moral and spiritual education (Adler 2004, 433). Wölfflin emphasized the importance of students becoming "cultivated," which in the context of his formalist art history involved "a mysterious, dynamic and intuitive process of visualization" (Adler 2004, 445–456). The student experienced learning art history in terms of the transformation of their perceptual experience: "each lecture was a new adventure in 'seeing'" (Born 1945, 46). In this way, Wölfflin's interpretation seemed to be self-evident: revealed through experience and in the encounter with the essence of art.

In Germany at the time of World War I, the concept of style was linked to notions of national culture and zeitgeist, most famously in Spengler's misguided and influential *Decline of the West* (1918–1923). Wölfflin resisted simplistic attempts to see art as a straightforward expression of the mood or mentality of an age or a generation, but he did take the view that forms were connected to feeling and psychology, and that style originates in changing ideas about the human body and different kinds of movement and deportment. In his early writing this allowed him to connect the form of the Gothic three-pointed shoe to the architecture of the Gothic cathedral (Schwartz 2005, 1–18).

Wölfflin did not recognize his concept of style as dependent on reproduction. In fact, he argued that style was primarily a premodern phenomenon, something much more significant than the rapid changes of contemporary fashion (Schwartz 2005, 27). André Malraux drew on Wölfflin's theory of style but recognized more explicitly that this was something made perceptible by photographic reproduction. He famously noted how reproductions of art created relationships of equivalence – affinities – between disparate objects, by rendering objects of different sizes at the same scale, and by making them monochrome. Malraux was clear that the affinities that appear between objects in the museum without walls are actually products of photography itself:

> Black and white photography imparts a family likeness to objects that have actually but slight affinity. When reproduced on the same page, such widely differing objects as a tapestry, an illuminated manuscript, a painting, a statue, or a medieval

stained-glass window lose their colors, their textures and dimensions (the sculpture also loses something of its volume), and it is their common style that benefits. (Malraux [1947] 1967, 84)

He saw how small and ancient objects, such as belt buckles and amulets, coins and seals, appeared surprisingly modern in reproduction, because their minute scale necessitated a simplicity of form: "The unfinished quality of the execution, resulting from the very small scale of these objects, now becomes a style, free and modern in its accent" (Malraux [1947] 1967, 86). He also noticed how the faces of sculptures were lit for photographs using the same techniques as the lighting of film stars' faces, with the result that a new expressiveness and vivacity became apparent (82).

Malraux imagined a relatively benign world of reproductions, which expands human capacities and accelerates artistic progress. In the stylistic equivalences it produced between objects of very different scale, photography played a key role in changing the hierarchy of the arts, enabling the "minor arts" to rival the major ones and producing a great expansion of the canon (Malraux [1947] 1967, 79, 94). Photographic reproduction enlarged the range of historical artworks to which artists and audiences could refer, transforming not only the perception of individual artifacts, but also the canon of art itself. In a sense, this was not new. It is only since the advent of photographic reproduction that we have been able to see more clearly how the practice of engraving had played a role in producing the existing canon of masterpieces. The discipline of art history produced and maintained the canon in a process that relied on reproductions, whether engraved or photographic. To enter or to remain within the canon of great works, art objects have to be circulated through reproduction, but they also need to be repeatedly subject to new interpretations, to reframing and recontextualizations, those practices that seem to bring new life to old works. Latour and Lowe argue that "a work of art grows in originality in proportion to the quality and abundance of its copies" (2011, 279). However, as feminist art historians have shown, the selection criteria for canonicity are not reducible either to notions of aesthetic value or to the pragmatics of reproducibility, and are part and parcel of the reproduction of existing social hierarchies (Parker and Pollock 1981; Pollock 1988). Malraux ignored the way in which museums as powerful institutions work to produce and reinforce ideologies of genius and greatness. For him, the museum acted as a resource of great culture, and the museum without walls expanded this out into the world, producing a rich repertoire of images and styles. The French title of *Museum without Walls* is *Musée imaginaire*, and Malraux's originality lay in the way he conceived of mass reproduction as shaping the imaginations and image repertoires of artists and museum visitors, expanding the range of art that was familiar to them, and enabling new qualities of that art to become perceptible for the first time. For Malraux, photography made visible the definitive or essential core of a body of work:

In art every resurrection has a way of beginning step by step. Reproduction, because of the mass of works it sets before us, frees us from the necessity of this tentative approach; by revealing a style in its entirety – just as it displays an artist's work in its entirety – it forces each to rely on its basic significance. (Malraux [1947] 1967, 77)

In Malraux's hands, as in Wölfflin's, style gains a moral force. According to John Darzins, an early reviewer of the English edition of Malraux's *Voices of Silence* (of which *Museum without Walls* was one volume), Malraux's emphasis on style was grounded in his vision of the artist as a demonic figure on a quest to "reshape the world," an urge which "ensures the perpetual metamorphosis of styles and establishes a dialogue between exemplary creations" (Darzins 1957, 108). The imaginary museum accelerates this process of metamorphosis and heightens this dialogue, by giving the modern artist the ability to perceive the modern qualities in historical or non-Western art.

Like Dorner and Benjamin, Malraux saw the museum without walls as continuing a process begun by the museum. By enabling comparison between artworks, the museum made it possible to engage with art as something more than simple visual pleasure, developing "an awareness of art's impassioned quest, of a re-creation of the universe, confronting the Creation" (Malraux [1947] 1967, 10, 82). As Darzins (1957) indicates, Malraux saw art in terms of a masculine human sovereignty. He envisaged the artist as a tragic-heroic and solitary figure, working against the grain of mass society, pitting his art against a declining West and a sham mass culture, and asserting art's autonomy. Ironically, this is made possible, first, by the museum and then by mass reproduction, which enables and accelerates the metamorphosis of style crucial to artistic progress and development.

The play of images

In 1980 the American art historian Douglas Crimp read Malraux's *Museum without Walls* as an unconscious parody, which treats style as "the ultimate homogenizing principle" in which photography "reduces the now even vaster heterogeneity [of art objects] to a single perfect similitude" (Crimp 1980, 50). Malraux does not celebrate a multiple, diverse visual culture in the form of the imaginary museum, but reduces it to a repetitive sameness via the concept of style. It is also possible that repeated copying empties the object of significance by rendering it ubiquitous: is it possible to even see the *Mona Lisa* or the Eiffel Tower anymore? They have become reduced to ciphers. Or, pulled out of the canon by their ubiquity, they have become toys. For Latour and Lowe, originality grows in relation to the number and *quality* of copies, but what happens when the copies are poor, trash, kitsch even, as in the many copies of the *Mona Lisa* collected by Robert A. Baron (1999)? Is the "original" under threat? Or did she disappear a long time ago, as exhibition designer Calum Storrie writes in his book *The Delirious Museum*. Storrie uses the theft and return of the *Mona Lisa* in 1911 to think about the nomadism of the work of art. The painting, initially thought to have been taken to be photographed, when it was stolen, was recovered and returned to Paris after being displayed in

FIGURE 25.2   Officials gather around Leonardo da Vinci's *Mona Lisa* on its return to Paris, January 4, 1914. It was stolen from the Musée du Louvre by Vincenzo Peruggia in 1911, and has only just been recovered.
Photo: Paul Thompson/FPG/Archive Photos/Getty Images.

various Italian cities (Figure 25.2), but, Storrie suggests, it was never the same *Mona Lisa* again:

> In a sense it was "removed for photography" to be endlessly reproduced mechanically. "Mona Lisa" was packed up and concealed and instead of being an object fixed in place both on the wall and in the imagination, it became nomadic. It may never have returned. Now the painting is impossible to see. The space that "Mona Lisa" occupied on the morning of 22 August 1911 is taken up by a glass box and a crowd of people ... How many photographs taken by these museum visitors show nothing but the reflection of the photographer or the camera's white flash? (Storrie 2006, 15)

Mona Lisa is missing and in her place there are "poor images." The artist Hito Steyerl uses this term to describe degraded, substandard, heavily compressed digital copies "in motion" (2009, 1). Steyerl argues that poor images, often circulated illicitly, are the by-products of "the rampant privatization of intellectual content, along with online marketing and commodification" (6). Poor images include "former masterpieces of cinema and video art":

> After being kicked out of the protected and often protectionist arena of national culture, discarded from commercial circulation, these works have become travelers

in a digital no-man's land, constantly shifting their resolution and format, speed and media, sometimes even losing names and credits along the way ... [the poor image] is about defiance and appropriation just as it is about conformism and exploitation. (Steyerl 2009, 8)

It is possible to conceive of a different *musée imaginaire* which encompasses high-quality copies, "poor images" and half-remembered ones, parodies and tourist souvenirs; and which builds on Malraux's recognition that, after the museum dislocates objects and pictures from their original context, photography (and now networked digital technology) releases images into the world to such an extent that the resource of mental images (as well as reproductions) is greatly expanded. According to the art historian Hans Belting, when we see pictures we transform them into

remembered images that henceforth become part of the archive of our memory. When external pictures are re-embodied as our own images, we substitute for their fabricated medium our own body, which, when it serves this capacity, turns into a living or natural medium. (2011, 16)

Belting understands the medium as "that which conveys or hosts an image, making it visible, turning it into a picture" (2011, 18). The images held in minds and memory are ephemeral, but we pass them on to one another, and they become part of a shared cultural memory that is "the common storehouse in which images lead their own lives" (39). Our bodies become the media through which we experience mental images, and images are nomadic: "they migrate across the boundaries that separate one culture from another, taking up residence in the media of one historical place and time and then moving on to the next, like desert-wanderers setting up temporary camps" (21).

This anthropomorphic account is reminiscent of the way in which Foucault describes the transgressively plural and wandering image. It is also reminiscent of recent anthropological writing in which the "social life of things" has been used to understand the values and commodity exchange practices of cultures (Appadurai 1986). Latour and Lowe use this notion too, to challenge the distinction between an original and a copy: "A work of art – no matter the material of which it is made – has a trajectory or, to use another expression popularized by anthropologists, a career" (2011, 278). This model is more linear than Foucault's free play of images though, and retains the idea of one-way traffic, from the original to the multiple copies it spawns.

For Foucault, however, the promiscuous circulation of the image between paintings and photographs, to print and lantern slide, belongs specifically to the early period of 1860 to 1880. Foucault senses the loss of this in his own period, and his essay is on one level a rejection of the dominance of abstraction in painting which destroys the image "while claiming to have freed itself from it" (Foucault [1975] 1999, 88). Foucault wanted to "recover the games of the past," to set free the sheer pleasure of playing with images, "to put images into circulation, to convey them, disguise them, deform them, heat them red hot, freeze them, multiply them" (89). As Adrian Rifkin suggests, "Read afresh today, it [Foucault's essay] evokes as much the present and future world of electronic communication as the aporias of modernism in the 1970s" (1999, 41).

Foucault and Belting are describing the movements of the "virtual" image. As several writers have argued, the "virtual" is not specifically a property of digital or electronic media, but is a term used since the seventeenth century to understand images seen through lenses or in mirrors which, although they do have materiality, appear to us as immaterial and able to be transferred from one surface or support to another (Friedberg 2006, 8–12). Belting writes:

> In the modern age, the museum has become a refuge for pictures that have lost their locus in the world and exchanged it for a locus in the world of art. But this secondary link to a place is now also dissolving, giving up its physicality as images enter the world of high speed, ephemeral, pictorial media. (2011, 40)

With digital photographic reproduction, storage, and retrieval of images, the movement from artifact to virtual image is facilitated, so that "technological images have shifted the relationship between artifact and imagination in favor of imagination, creating fluid transitions for the free play of the mental images of their beholders" (Belting 2011, 41).

Twenty years ago, writers and curators anticipated the impact of the combination of computers and telephone technology for the dissemination of images, but they could not foresee the ways in which mobile phones equipped with cameras and apps such as Instagram, Flickr, and Facebook would contribute to making image sharing such a common cultural practice. Only recently has the discussion of the digital image shifted toward an interest in the cultural and philosophical consequences of practices of transmitting, sharing, and transforming images as they pass between different kinds of devices and from one medium to another. These practices even affect the act of spectatorship in the museum as people take out their camera phones, take pictures, and post them online. These images go to their Flickr stream, to Instagram and Tumblr: some of the brand names evoke a kind of play – tumbling, simultaneous, spontaneous, instant.

It is tempting to imagine the post-photographic museum as the playful museum, as the alternative to the museum as the house of originals. Against the doomsayers who cite the short amount of time spent in front of each painting at the Louvre as some sign of cultural decline, we could see this fleeting attention as part of the flickering, active, and yet distracted attention which early twentieth-century commentators posited as a radical and collective substitute for bourgeois individualist attention. Mobile handheld media enable the variously reverent and irreverent ways in which people take and share souvenirs of their visits. Increasingly museums feel unable to prevent the use of camera phones, despite concerns regarding the impact of this on visitor attention (on the change in policy at the National

FIGURE 25.3   Matti Braun's *Gost Log* at Arnolfini, Bristol, UK, 2012.
Mobile phone photo: Michelle Henning. Reproduced by permission of Arnolfini.

Gallery, London, see Bland 2014; Malvern 2014; Williams 2014). While many museums and galleries discourage, or at best tolerate, visitor photography, some encourage it – for example, in 2012, Arnolfini, in Bristol in the United Kingdom, encouraged visitors to take personal photographs of their Matti Braun exhibition *Gost Log* (Figure 25.3), inviting them to share them via Twitter, Facebook, and Instagram. There are also activist interventions using networked art, augmented reality, and mobile handheld media. These activities set the image into unruly circulation again and permit us to see playful possibilities in the art museum. Peter Samis (2008), associate curator of interpretation at San Francisco Museum of Modern Art describes this in terms of the "exploded museum," and Haidee Wasson (in Chapter 26 in this volume) in terms of "elasticity". The space for play – *Spielraum* – is also the expanded and networked field of action.

Samis uses the example of students visiting the Museum of Modern Art, New York, in 2005 with digital recorders and creating irreverent "guerrilla podcasts." In Chapter 20 in this volume, Beryl Graham writes of augmented reality media art projects that use visitor's mobile phones to undercut the official narrative of the museum. Storrie's "delirious museum" develops from the argument that "museums should be a continuation of the street," resisting their tendency to order and control. Storrie is attracted to museums that have a "messy vitality," that spill over into the everyday (2006, 2–3).

However, the history of the art museum is to a great extent the history of the institutionalization of an idea of private, contemplative aesthetic experience that is at odds with the collective, participatory, communicative but also commodified aesthetic pleasures that underpin these new practices (Hein 2000, 132; Klonk 2009, 16, 129). As numerous blockbuster exhibitions demonstrate, we are still in thrall to the thing itself, to the original artwork as an expression of individual genius, even in cases where the artworks themselves seem to militate against such a reading. Here is the Tate Modern website on its Roy Lichtenstein retrospective: "Room after room will pay tribute to his extraordinary oeuvre, celebrating the visual power and intellectual rigour of Roy Lichtenstein's work" (Tate 2013). Even video art, developed from a tradition which set out to challenge the ways in which museums separate art from everyday life, can end up reproducing or reinforcing the isolation of the individual spectator from collective experience. While other commentators see new media as damaging the private contemplative space of the gallery (see, e.g., Bland 2014), the art historian Charlotte Klonk sees new media installations, particularly video art, as on the whole reinforcing it with dark cinematic spaces:

> The introduction of the bodiless, lost-to-the-world cinema spectator into the art gallery does away with the last public space in which cultural reception can take place as an engaged process together with others … Unlike Boris Groys (and many others), I do not fear the introduction of new media into the art gallery because they represent a threat to the gallery as a space of contemplation. Rather, it is the disappearance of what is – potentially at least – a space of public interaction and communication that I would regret. (Klonk 2009, 223)

We might also want to question the model that proposes digital, computer-based, and mobile media as harmlessly "playful" and the skittish, superficial, glancing attention associated with computing as a viable alternative to deep contemplation. Parallel processing – the computer's ability to keep several programs running at the same time – trained computer users to hop between tasks, something that is glossed as a superior ability via the term "multitasking" but which can equally be understood in terms of "the increased expectations of 24/7 productivity" and increasingly targeted marketing (Friedberg 2006, 235). In this context, close, sustained attention, with an eye for nuance and detail, might be a luxury with a critical edge, and the social, collective experience of new media may not be so sociable after all (Turkle 2011). In this context, solitary contemplation can be associated with freedom: to lose oneself in a work of art or have it "speak to your soul" is something to treasure. Producing this possibility can be a political practice, as Rancière suggests: "Constructing a place for solitude, an 'aesthetic' place, appears to be a task for committed art" (2009, 53).

On the other hand, the possibility that play can become labor, that attention can be harnessed economically, should not force us to abandon it as a model for thinking about the art museum in a culture of digital and electronic reproduction.

Digital media offer possibilities for control, but also for relinquishing control. This is not about the "gamification" of museums (i.e., the use of games and the harnessing of the pleasures of play to engage visitors and increase visitor numbers). It is about a model of play that involves aesthetic pleasure, participation, and collective engagement, a "delirious" loss of control and uncontainability – extending endlessly beyond the walls of the museum, into everyday experience, across media and bodies, and back again.

Notes

1   The lead Woodburytype, the Stannotype, and the collotype are examples of processes used in the late 1870s. In the 1880s came the introduction of the mechanical halftone process which translated the continuous tone of the photograph into dots with the use of a screen.

2   This is the title by which the essay tends to be known to English speakers, as it is that of the first English translation, by Harry Zohn, which was published in 1969 in Arendt's collection of Benjamin's writings, *Illuminations*. However, in this chapter I quote from the translation published in the *Selected Writings* under the less elegant title "The Work of Art in the Age of Its Technological Reproducibility" (Benjamin [1936] 2002).

3   There were cast galleries at the French Academy and the Palazzo Sacchetti in Rome, the Palazzo Farsetti in Venice, at Mannheim and Charlottenburg, and in Peter the Great's Imperial Academy of Fine Arts in Russia – to name just a few of those listed in Haskell and Penny (1981).

4   The term is Ivins's: "painstakingly as Durer might copy a real rabbit … in his own syntax, when it came to copying a print by Mantegna he refused to follow Mantegna's syntax, and retold the story, as he thought, in his own syntax" (Ivins 1953, 61, quoted in Fyfe 2004, 54). The syntax developed by engravers was systematic and linear, a "net of rationality" as Ivins termed it, into which the visual language of the work of art was translated (Ivins 1953; Pinson 1998).

5   Amy Von Lintel (2012) has argued that wood engraving, in particular, not only survived after photomechanical reproduction but was a more popular (because it was less expensive) way in which reproductions of art circulated to nonacademic audiences, general readers, and for self-instruction. In formal education contexts, however, photomechanical reproduction was being used, for instance, in the "picture study" of nineteenth-century American schools (Stankiewicz 1985).

References

Adler, Daniel. 2004. "Painterly Politics: Wölfflin, Formalism and German Academic Culture 1885–1915." *Art History* 27(3): 431–456.

Appadurai, Arjun. 1986. *The Social Lives of Things: Commodities in Cultural Perspective.* Cambridge: Cambridge University Press.

Baron, Robert. A. 1999. "From Romance to Ritual: Mona Lisa Images for the Modern World." *Visual Resources: An International Journal of Documentation* 15: 217–234.

Belting, Hans. 2001. *The Invisible Masterpiece*. Chicago: University of Chicago Press.

Belting, Hans. 2011. *An Anthropology of Images: Picture, Medium, Body*. Princeton: Princeton University Press.

Benjamin, Walter. (1936) 2002. "The Work of Art in the Age of Its Technological Reproducibility," 2nd version. In *Selected Writings*, vol. 3, *1935–1938*, edited by Harold Eiland and Michael W. Jennings, translated by Edmund Jephacott et al. Cambridge, MA: Harvard University Press.

Benjamin, Walter. (1936) 1992. "The Work of Art in the Age of Mechanical Reproduction." In *Illuminations*, edited by Hannah Arendt, 211–244. London: Fontana.

Benson, Timothy, and Eva Forgács. 2002. *Between Worlds: A Sourcebook of Central European Avant-Gardes 1910–30*. Cambridge, MA: MIT Press.

Bland, Archie. 2014. "Camera Phones at the National Gallery Stoke Fears that Technology Is Leaving Us Incapable of Deep Engagement with Anything." *Independent on Sunday*, August 17.

Born, W. 1945. "Heinrich Wölfflin, 1864–1945." *College Art Journal* 5(1): 44–47.

Brik, Ossip. (1926) 1989. "The Photograph versus the Painting." In *Photography in the Modern Era: European Documents and Critical Writings, 1913–1940*, edited by Christopher Phillips, 213–218. New York: Metropolitan Museum of Art/Aperture.

Crimp, Douglas. 1980. "On The Museum's Ruins." *October* 13: 41–57.

Darzins, John. 1957. "Malraux and the Destruction of Aesthetics." *Yale French Studies* 18: 107–113.

Derrida, Jacques. 1976. *Of Grammatology*. Baltimore: Johns Hopkins University Press.

Dorner, Alexander. (1930) 1989. "Original and Facsimile." In *Photography in the Modern Era: European Documents and Critical Writings, 1913–1940*, edited by Christopher Phillips, 151–154. New York: Metropolitan Museum of Art/Aperture.

Eberlein, Kurt Karl. (1929) 1989. "On the Question: Original or Facsimile Reproduction?" In *Photography in the Modern Era: European Documents and Critical Writings, 1913–1940*, edited by Christopher Phillips, 145–150. New York: Metropolitan Museum of Art/Aperture.

Fawcett, Trevor. 1986. "Graphic versus Photographic in the Nineteenth-Century Reproduction." *Art History* 9(2): 185–212.

Foster, Hal. 1996. "The Archive without Museums." *October* 77: 97–119.

Foucault, Michel. (1975) 1999. "Photogenic Painting." In *Gérard Fromanger: Photogenic Painting*, by Gilles Deleuze and Michel Foucault, 81–108. London: Black Dog.

Friedberg, Anne. 2006. *The Virtual Window: From Alberti to Microsoft*. Cambridge MA: MIT Press.

Fyfe, Gordon. 2004. "Reproductions, Cultural Capital and Museums: Aspects of the Culture of Copies." *Museum and Society* 2: 47–67.

Hamber, Anthony. 1995. "The Use of Photography by Nineteenth-Century Art Historians." In *Art History through the Camera's Lens*, edited by Helene E. Roberts, 89–121. London: Routledge.

Haskell, Francis, and Nicholas Penny. 1981. *Taste and the Antique: The Lure of Classical Sculpture 1500–1900*. New Haven: Yale University Press.

Hein, Hilde. 2000. *The Museum in Transition*. Washington, DC: Smithsonian Institution.

Holmes, Oliver Wendell. 1859. "The Stereoscope and the Stereograph." *Atlantic Magazine*, June. Accessed August 29, 2014. http://www.theatlantic.com/magazine/archive/1859/06/the-stereoscope-and-the-stereograph/303361/.

Ivins, William M. 1953. *Prints and Visual Communication*. London: Routledge & Kegan Paul.

Kállai, Ernő. (1927) 2002. "Painting and Photography." In *Between Worlds: A Sourcebook of Central European Avant-Gardes, 1910–1930*, edited by Timothy Benson and Eva Forgács, 684–689. Cambridge, MA: MIT Press.

Kirshenblatt-Gimblett, Barbara. 1998. *Destination Culture: Tourism, Museums and Heritage*. Berkeley: University of California Press.

Klonk, Charlotte. 2009. *Spaces of Experience: Art Gallery Interiors from 1800–2000*. New Haven: Yale University Press.

Latour, Bruno, and Adam Lowe. 2011. "The Migration of the Aura; or, How to Explore the Original through its Facsimiles." In *Switching Codes: Thinking through Digital Technology in the Humanities and the Arts*, edited by Thomas Bartscherer and Roderick Coover, 275–297. Chicago: University of Chicago Press.

Malraux, André. (1947) 1967. *Museum without Walls*. London: Secker & Warburg.

Malvern, Jack. 2014. "National Gallery Admits Defeat on Camera Phone Ban." *Times*, August 13.

Márkus, György. 2007. "Walter Benjamin and the German 'Reproduction Debate.'" In *Moderne begreifen: Zur Paradoxie eines sozio-ästhetischen Deutungsmusters* [Modern understandings: On the paradox of a socio-aesthetic pattern of interpretation], edited by C. Magerski, R. I. Savage, and C. Weller, 351–364. Wiesbaden, Germany: Deutscher Universitäts-Verlag

Nelson, Robert S. 2000. "The Slide Lecture; or, The Work of Art History in the Age of Mechanical Reproduction." *Critical Inquiry* 26(3): 414–434.

Newhall, Beaumont. 1942. "Photography as a Branch of Art History." *College Art Journal* 1: 86–90.

Panofsky, Erwin. (1930) 2010. "Original and Facsimile Reproduction." Translated by Timothy Grundy. *Res: Anthropology and Aesthetics* 57–58: 331–338.

Parker, Roszika, and Griselda Pollock. 1981. *Old Mistresses: Women, Art and Ideology*. London: Routledge & Kegan Paul.

Phillips, Christopher. 1989. *Photography in the Modern Era: European Documents and Critical Writings, 1913–1940*. New York: Metropolitan Museum of Art/Aperture.

Pinson, Stephen C. 1998. "Reproducing Delacroix." *Visual Resources: An International Journal of Documentation* 14: 155–187.

Pollock, Griselda. 1988. *Vision and Difference: Femininity, Feminism and Histories of Art*. London: Routledge.

Rancière, Jacques. 2009. *The Emancipated Spectator*. London: Verso.

Rifkin, Adrian. 1999. "A Space Between: On Gérard Fromanger, Gilles Deleuze, Michel Foucault and Some Others." In *Gérard Fromanger: Photogenic Painting*, by Gilles Deleuze and Michel Foucault, 21–60. London: Black Dog.

Samis, Peter. 2008. "The Exploded Museum." In *Digital Technologies and the Museum Experience: Handheld Guides and Other Media*, edited by Loïc Tallon and Kevin Walker, 3–17. Lanham, MD: AltaMira.

Schwartz, Frederic J. 2005. *Blind Spots: Critical Theory and the History of Art in Twentieth-Century Germany*. New Haven: Yale University Press.

Stankiewicz, Mary Ann. 1985. "A Picture Age: Reproductions in Picture Study." *Studies in Art Education* 26(2): 86–92.

Steyerl, Hito. 2009. "In Defense of the Poor Image." *e-flux journal* 10. Accessed August 29, 2014. http://worker01.e-flux.com/pdf/article_94.pdf.

Stoljar, M. M. 1997. "Introduction." In *Novalis: Philosophical Writings*, edited by Margaret Mahony Stoljar. New York: SUNY Press.

Storrie, Calum. 2006. *The Delirious Museum: A Journey from the Louvre to Las Vegas*. London: I. B. Tauris.

Tate. 2013. "What's On: Lichtenstein: A Retrospective." Accessed August 29, 2014. http://www.tate.org.uk/whats-on/tate-modern/exhibition/lichtenstein.

Turkle, Sherry. 2011. *Alone Together: Why We Expect More from Technology and Less from Each Other*. New York: Basic Books.

Tzara, Tristan. (1924) 2002. "Photography in Reverse." In *Between Worlds: A Sourcebook of Central European Avant-Gardes, 1910–1930*, edited by Timothy and Eva Forgács, 483–484. Cambridge, MA: MIT Press.

Von Lintel, Amy M. 2012. "Wood Engravings, the 'Marvellous Spread of Illustrated Publications,' and the History of Art." *Modernism/Modernity* 19: 515–542.

Walsh, Peter. 2007. "Rise and Fall of the Post-Photographic Museum: Technology and the Transformation of Art." In *Theorizing Digital Cultural Heritage*, edited by Fiona Cameron and Sarah Kenderdine, 19–34. Cambridge, MA: MIT Press.

Williams, Zoe. 2014. "Selfie-Portrait of the Artist: National Gallery Surrenders to the Internet." *Guardian*, August 15.

Wyld, Martin. 1998. "The Restoration History of Holbein's Ambassadors." *National Gallery Technical Bulletin* 19: 4–25.

Michelle Henning is Senior Lecturer in Photography and Visual Culture in the Media Department, College of Arts and Humanities at the University of Brighton. She is also a Visiting Senior Research Fellow in the Digital Cultures Research Centre at the University of the West of England, Bristol. Prior to this she was Associate Professor of Media and Culture at the University of the West of England, Bristol. She is a practicing photographer and designer and has written widely on museums, media, and display techniques in her book *Museums, Media and Cultural Theory* (Open University Press, 2006), as well as in numerous collections.

26 THE ELASTIC MUSEUM
Cinema Within and Beyond

Haidee Wasson

The museum has an enduring relationship with moving image technologies. Indeed, the museum has a long and sustained relationship with many technologies often understood as integral to the modern age: not only cinema but also photography, lithography, radio, and television. Through disposable dailies, framable reproductions, lickable stamps, ephemeral sounds, and more, museums have for the better part of a century expanded their reach far beyond their brick-and-mortar sites to include monthly magazines, newspapers, book clubs, Sunday radio shows, subway trains, television series, and film programs. These technological capacities have created a kind of subgenre of curatorial activity, leading museum curators, educators, and publicity officers to innovate display techniques not just in museum halls and galleries but also through a variety of sometimes enduring but often ephemeral media, effectively participating in a vast media ecology.

Just as the modern museum has spiraled outward, it has also brought media inward: live radio broadcasts in the 1920s, audio guides in the 1950s, podcasts in the 2010s. Museum auditoriums have also served as veritable multimedia laboratories, architecturally inscribed in museum spaces for well over 100 years. Neither the white box nor the black, museum auditoriums present what you might call a "gray space," with their artificially lit, often windowless, spaces, enlivened by projection booths, wired audio setups, and live performances. In such spaces, individual viewers of a museum's wares have become seated spectators and audience members, witness to expert lectures and highly choreographed performances, spectacular images, and reproduced, amplified sounds.

Museums have enthusiastically availed themselves of technologies we often think of as belonging to the reviled mass media in order to disseminate their holdings and also to display, present, and perform their authority. Yet, for too long,

The International Handbooks of Museum Studies: Museum Media, First Edition.
Edited by Michelle Henning.
© 2015 John Wiley & Sons Ltd. Published 2020 by John Wiley & Sons Ltd.

museums have been seen as somehow anathema to media, as phenomena and rituals fundamentally opposed to the amorphous mass and repetitive sameness of film or television. The case of projected moving images in the museum provides an interesting example. The former is easily positioned as ephemeral and disposable, the latter as permanent and enduring. This basic opposition frames many of the foundational texts we have for thinking about media and museums (Henning 2006, 71). And, while the broad-stroke differences between, say, a museum and a movie are plain and obvious, it is equally true that lingering too long on the most obvious differences between these two media or their most prominent institutions tends to distract from the ways in which they have worked in happy consort. Museums produce television programming and provide settings for independent and also blockbuster films. Celluloid, electronic, and digital imagery are often highlighted elements of visits to contemporary museums, beginning in entryways and leading us through the galleries and learning centers, cafeterias and gift shops. And this state of mutual imbrication is by no means recent. Reframing, though drawing substantially on my previously published research (especially Wasson 2006; 2011), this chapter demonstrates another path into the history of what I contend is a complex but not essentially contradictory set of relationships between the museum and its media.

The case of museums and cinema will provide a through line, a pairing wherein it is rather easy to find a reasonably harmonious and mutually interdependent history of experiment and collaboration. By way of two approaches to one case study, I will propose several research directions that provide some productive avenues for future historical inquiry into relations between museums and movies, and museums and media, more generally. I will argue that these two seemingly very different modes of display, with their very distinct institutions, can be understood less as opposites and more as enduring and integral interlocutors. I will position film as a technology that has been fundamentally useful to the museum, long appropriated by and ultimately congruent with museum operations, one among many elements of not just basic display techniques but a more nimble way of imagining museum infrastructure. In short, I will argue that assessing film technologies within and beyond the museum requires us to think more fully about what constitutes museum space (auditoriums, museum mobiles, traveling shows) and what constitutes the pace and rhythm of a museum visit: that is, how to understand the speed and density of what we look at and for how long we look when wandering the gallery. What are the spatial and temporal dynamics of the modern mediated museum more generally?

To be sure, cinema can be thought of as a display device, a performative technology, and an infrastructural mode of museum work. And this insight can be comfortably applied to the ways that museums have similarly deep and complex relationships with modern media and their animating technologies more generally. American museums have for the better part of the twentieth century been quick, and even eager, to avail themselves of media technologies for a range of reproduction, display, and dissemination purposes. Thinking about media in the context of museums not just as content but as infrastructure, and in certain cases as architectural elements of the museum, helps us to understand more fully the ways in which the museum has long worked to extend its reach and transform its spaces. Thinking of museums and media in these ways also suggests that the museum should not be thought of solely as a permanent, unmoving, physical structure but as a kind of tentacular hub for a range of circulating things and ways of presenting those things.

In what follows, I will take two contrasting approaches that illustrate what I am calling the elastic mediated museum. I will focus on one prominent institution: the Metropolitan Museum of Art (the Met), New York City. First, I will outline what I call the *expanded museum*. By this I mean to name a museum enabled by media, with an extended reach and increased pathways to dissemination and influence beyond a unique physical site. Second, I will examine what might be called the *condensed museum*, which names the museum transformed by efforts to dynamize displays and performance techniques within the museum. The focus of this section will be based on activities that took place predominantly before World War II. Cinema provides a thread through both foci. So too does the question of scale. If film and other media helped to transform the museum infrastructurally, they did so in part by fundamentally furthering the museum's extant plays on scale. With film and a wider embrace of other media, museums obtained access to a wider range of operational, illustrative, and presentational techniques that freed curators and educators from fidelity to the original object and the relatively inelastic and occasionally palatial spaces of the museum. With films, for instance, a viewer of a 4×5 foot film screen might view an otherwise expansive museum by way of a condensed, shrunken filmed tour of its halls. This film might be watched while inside, nearby, or outside of the museum itself. With films, a small vase might be enlarged and shown in close-up to fundamentally stretch and expand an otherwise miniscule thing. Through the basic film techniques of framing, shot length, and editing you can further direct and control what might otherwise be the more organic biological movements of the human eye or perambulating legs. With cinema's machine techniques you can speed up or slow down a distracted museum wanderer or rectify his/her misdirected attention. You might ask the viewer of a museum film to look at many things more quickly, or fewer things more slowly. The museum's embrace of film and its cognate media requires us to tend to vectors outward and inward, thinking about the scale and pace of the institution.

The expanded museum

Lantern slides, motion-picture films, even projectors are lent, and portable art and science exhibits are prepared for classroom use. No doubt the time will come when collections of the Field Museum of Natural History in Chicago, the American

Museum of Natural History in New York, the Metropolitan Museum of Art and similar great institutions will ramble over whole states in special railway trains.

Kaempffert 1932

The American art museum has a constitutive tension at its core, one that is endemic to privately funded yet publicly mandated – as opposed to princely – museums (Hooper-Greenhill 1992).[1] It has been tasked with managing the dual tendencies of, on the one hand, functioning as an adaptive site of public education and democratic access and, on the other, serving as an enduring and sacral repository for precious objects. Or, as Lawrence Levine (1988) has phrased it, American art museums have from the beginning enacted a contest between the "didactic and the ideal." The balance of this contest has shifted significantly throughout the public art museum's long life, with a strong current that runs from nineteenth-century curiosity to twenty-first-century spectacle. Inside and outside the museum, debates have persisted about the institution's goals, as well as the methods it should adopt to realize them. Like all institutional debates, these must be understood in relation to the historical, social, aesthetic, and political forces that provide the context in which such institutions function. Some art museums have clung tightly to their elite remit and others have worked toward more populist aims. Within this spectrum, one fact remains clear: the American art museum itself has long been – to greater and lesser degrees – a mediated museum, integrated with a range of media technologies and systems, occupying a complicated and not simply antagonistic relationship to popular and consumer culture.

As I have argued elsewhere (Wasson 2006), the art museum's expanded reach involves a predictable impulse toward what is conventionally termed within professional literature "museum education" and "museum extension," including educational programs that take place either at the museum using lecturers, slides, and other forms of augmentation, or at other locations such as schools, galleries, colleges, and art societies. Linked to this are efforts to publicize and merchandize the museum, using contemporaneous technologies frequently fueled by consumerism. To be sure, the late nineteenth century provided a stage wherein, as Lawrence Levine (1988) has argued, the art museum was discursively distinguished from more populist and polyglot museums, refashioned as a sacral space. Yet, during this same period, this newly sanctioned art museum was simultaneously if slowly finding ways to stay relevant and visible within the new modes of leisure afforded by rapid urbanization, immigration, consumer capitalism, and so-called mass media.

Around 1900, I have shown, that part of the battle for relevance and efficacy was waged under the banner of education. Museums of art as well as science, natural history, and technology began to formalize their role as active and engaged public educators (Wasson 2006). They coined the term "docent" to designate a new role for museum guides, conceived as both students and teachers. Additionally, traveling educators with lantern slides and elaborate lectures animated museum auditoriums, built to augment museum galleries and hallways and to ensure the institutions' civic function. Visitors of all ages encountered regular presentations illuminated by projected slides, film, and also recorded sounds. Such performances were held in the evenings, on Saturdays, and, in the late 1910s and 1920s, increasingly on Sundays to facilitate the attendance of working people and encourage family participation. Other standard activities included classes, formal gallery talks, group tours, and discussion groups. Dedicated children's clubs, rooms, and galleries, as well as after-school classes, all became regularized elements of museum programming. Other groups also used museum resources: YMCAs, YWCAs, 4-H clubs, Boys and Girl Scout groups encountered lectures, but more often games, quizzes, and treasure. These activities transpired in science, nature, and art museums (Ramsey 1938, 111).

The difficulty of travel to museums and the constraints of the museum's physical immobility soon gave way to the institutionalization of extension programs. In the first decade of the twentieth century, museums such as the Met and the American Museum of Natural History (AMNH) actively assembled traveling exhibitions composed of printed matter, lantern slides, mounted objects, and sometimes films, film stills, and film strips (Stevens 1916; Ramsey 1938; 1940). Andrew McClellan gives the example of the comparatively small Boston Museum of Fine Arts, which by 1916 had 30 trained docents serving 4300 annual visitors, with an additional 8000 student attendees. The museum circulated 25,000 reproductions for classroom use (McClellan 2003, 19). At the Met, the extensions programs grew rapidly and, by 1925, there were as many as 3427 different loans made, consisting of 115,954 individual items (Metropolitan Museum of Art 1925, 44). Ten years later these numbers had increased to 4369 and 179,239 respectively (Metropolitan Museum of Art 1935a, 51). During the 1920s, attendance at the museum itself was well over a million visitors per year. Yet the number of those exposed to its art and its discourses about art increased significantly when we consider the growth of its presence in other media forms: films, newspapers, magazines, and radio.

Historian Neil Harris (1990) has observed that, during the early part of the twentieth century, museums competed successfully with other urban attractions, world's fairs, and department stores as authoritative articulations of the newest and most appealing modes of visual display. By the 1920s, however, despite such efforts as traced above, museums were nonetheless criticized for their reluctance to further adapt to the mediated modes of display and dissemination that were transforming American culture. These critiques were particularly evident in middle-brow literature and urban newspapers. While some commentators celebrated the museum's efforts to appeal to "the living," just as many decried the museum's utter failure to keep pace (Harris 1990). Radio, cinema, advertising, and department stores all seemed more vital and accessible platforms for cultural engagement.

Eager to continue adapting to the modes of display and curation that held sway with the public, Met curators and educators established a surprisingly wide range of strategies to enliven their art and improve museum status. (Alison Griffiths (2007) addresses similar attempts at the AMNH.) With magazine sales exploding, radios proliferating, and film audiences growing, fulfilling the museum's educational mission required responding to and accommodating the rapidly changing environments in which the museum's public encountered the world. One telling and unexpected example arises in the museum's use of film. The Met organized a film library as early as 1922 in order to augment its growing collection of educational loan items. And, in 1925, it inaugurated "a series of cinema films relating to various phases of art and illustrating the objects in its galleries" (*Metropolitan Museum of Art Bulletin* 1925). In other words, the Met produced, distributed, and exhibited movies.[2] In the spring of 1926, these films appeared twice weekly in museum galleries, gradually expanding to four regular showings: two during the week and two on weekends. These films also circulated to other museums, art schools, and societies.[3] Subjects included travel, history, architecture, and – of course – art appreciation. Noteworthy among them were numerous tours of particular collections or museum wings, designed to augment views of museum space and also to make this same space mobile. Galleries and collections appeared on screen – this made them available, or at least visible, to an otherwise dispersed public.

The Met films reflect the size and scope of museum activities. For instance, some films commissioned by the museum emphasized the highly gendered and feminized link between museum and home. Views of old American furniture and pottery marked points on a tour of the museum's American Wing. Other titles plainly announced the unsettling relations of the Met to the history of imperialism. *Firearms of Our Forefathers* (1923) provided a sweeping overview of weaponry owned by the museum, "from the Indian's Bow and Arrow to the Modern Machine Gun." Some of these films were undisguised documents of museum-sanctioned excavations (and colonialist thievery), shot on location and then fashioned as exotic tours of, for example, Egyptian ruins; some were highly fictionalized shorts which told stories based on or embodied in museum objects (i.e., Greek myths told by markings on a museum vase). The museum's long-standing role as an educator in art-making appeared in films about making pottery or crafting bronze statues. The number of titles increased throughout the 1920s and 1930s. Educational titles made outside the museum filled out the collection; cinema catalogs were published in 1930, 1932, 1935, and 1940 (Metropolitan Museum of Art 1930; 1932; 1935b; 1940).[4]

The internal discussion conducted by museum officials confirms that their film work was neither random nor ad hoc but one element of a clearly articulated strategy to further mediate the museum. By 1926, a select group of museum officials and educators credited motion pictures with being a key strategy for modernizing museum activities. The Met's publications celebrated cinema as a means to enliven art and expand the museum's audience. Education staff at the Met prophesied that "the motion picture screen can do for art as much as it has done for the drama, and even more" (Elliott 1926, 216). Much like the natural history museum across the park, film was imbued with the ability to spectacularize science, to dramatize nature, and to enliven art. But, above all, cinema was rhetorically crafted as elemental to the museum's most foundational purpose. Further, the reduction of these films from 35 mm to 16 mm in 1928 signaled an early attempt to make use of a young but growing network of portable film projection devices. In this instance, the Met was what we would call today an early adapter of new technology. It is worth mentioning that it was not primarily the wonders and attractions of cinema as a kind of modern magical device that were invoked but more cinema's evolving languages that were of interest, including the short film, the didactic film, and the fantasy film, along with basic techniques of framing and editing.

As these films traveled beyond the museum's walls, museum officials announced a clear mission. In addition to bringing motion and an afterlife to ostensibly dead art objects, these films also brought the same to the museum, broadening the reach of its collections and curatorial practices to "places heretofore untouched" (Elliott 1926, 216). In short, through film, it was imagined that the art museum would live again, film serving as a dynamic delivery system not just for painting and sculpture, but also for the museum itself.[5] These films constituted prepackaged lessons in art interpretation designed and orchestrated by the museum. Each film made both the art and the lesson mechanically reproducible, and therefore mobile. As a modern medium, film seemed to provide a relevant and contemporary method of art instruction through which the museum might reaffirm and extend its museological influence. The Met circulated its films not to movie theaters but to the growing network of 16 mm projectors that could increasingly be found in affluent homes, museums, libraries, colleges, and universities. Museum officials sought to carve out uses for cinema that had been overlooked or simply ignored by the dominant American entertainment industry. To them, film was not necessarily one thing or another but a malleable tool that could be adapted to suit its purposes; this included new kinds of films but also new methods of display.

An important thread in the museum's dialogue with cinema did indeed pivot on understanding the ways in which movie theaters and museums could be understood as sufficiently similar as to require not just a response by museum officials but also adaptation. The museum's standing committee on cinema, established alongside its film library, issued statements during this period not just advocating for the utility of the motion picture to art education at the museum but also acknowledging cinema's general and sizable influence on the recreational habits of all potential museum-goers. In other words, movie theaters served as what Andreas Huyssen (1986, 3) would call a "hidden dialectic" in the museum's film projects, an animating force against which and with which a range of so-called respectable film discourses were being generated. George C. Pratt, chair of the cinema committee, confirmed that the Met's incorporation of film was indeed a reasoned concession to the educational utility of the medium, as well as acknowledgment of "its place among recreational plans" of the people (quoted in *Time* 1924). Museum administrators sought to design a distinct and edifying form of cinema, transforming film into a carefully controlled museological form of exhibition. Poised as a complement and correction to Hollywood, the Met sought to continue distinguishing itself from populist cultural forms. Yet this was not a crass generalized dismissal of all aspects of popular commercial cinema. While Hollywood might rely on sensationalism and formula, hope prevailed nonetheless. Huger Elliott, head of museum education, declared in 1926:

> Thousands of people are looking for motion pictures which have artistic, instructive, and entertaining value, but the average motion picture producer does not show such films. He has overlooked his latent public and has sought to please only those who enjoy the type of pictures now generally shown, with their cheap love scenes and impossible plots. (1926, 216)

While Elliott and Pratt may have officially derided popular melodrama and Hollywood formula, it is also clear that, in preaching against a caricature of commercial cinema, hope remained in the audience itself: movie crowds were less ignorant than they were simply ignored. And so they proposed instead a good or *useful cinema* (in Tony Bennett's sense of useful culture; see Bennett 1992; Acland and Wasson 2011), carving out a space for the museum within the technological apparatus so often dismissed by the cultural elite.

The appeal here was not just about respectable content but also respectable spaces. One of the most interesting questions raised by the Met's early film program was the way it functioned to extend the reach of the museum. Sent out like mobile, mechanical docents, sanctioned with the museum's imprimatur, these films helped to create satellite museums out of ad hoc, often impromptu, spaces. This impulse served to supplant a long tradition of educational and itinerant projection and facilitated the gradual emergence of an institutionally based, 16 mm network of self-operated projectors. So the museum became an enduring site of film exhibition, with its in-house ability to show films throughout its varied spaces. The Met also made films and so, together with its exhibition program, which included lending and circulating its films, offered an example of what Tony Bennett (1992) has called the museum's "exhibitionary complex." Through the museum's film program, the museum rendered its art and its now dispersed publics more visible as film audiences. Both art and public were framed and in a sense brought into being by the logics of the authoritative institution, which encouraged particular reasons to gather and ways of watching and, ultimately, of behaving while viewing movies.

Film was but one of the many modes by which the Met made itself visible to an expanding audience. Much in the way that literature became an early subject for quality radio programming, so too did art. The museum supplied radio content for the ascendant form, with radio rapidly becoming a standard element of museum outreach thereafter (for more on this, see Rubin 1992). By 1928, this included weekly evening radio talks about art and museum activities. Within a year the Met's Department of Educational Work had delivered 55 talks on topics ranging from "Egyptian Art" to "Art in Daily Life" (*Metropolitan Museum of Art Bulletin* 1929, 217). Radio was also used as a way to instruct patrons on how to be a good visitor at the museum, with titles such as "The Collections and How They May Be Studied" (*Metropolitan Museum of Art Bulletin* 1928a, 59). Radio may have democratized institutions of high culture, but it also promulgated its values and worked to shape media listeners into particular kinds of museum visitors. In other words, the Met embraced media in order to expand the museum. They did so by experimenting with media as a form of out-of-museum curation. For instance, in 1929 the museum sent lantern slides to local high schools. A local radio station broadcast information about the slides to coordinate with their projection. The Met effectively entered the classroom by air (*Metropolitan Museum of Art Bulletin* 1929, 218).

Museums also embraced the world of newspaper publishing. While museums of science and art held an ample supply of inexpensively reproduced images, newspapers had a comparably vast, dispersed public which daily sought out word of what was new in the immediate and wider world. Relationships of mutual benefit developed. In my writings I have given a number of examples of the attempts, during the 1920s, to coordinate newspaper schedules with radio and museum programming (Wasson 2006). For instance, Chicago's *Daily News* called these "radio photologues" and Buffalo's *Courier Express* called them "Roto-Radio Talks." Listeners were directed to look at particular images in the Sunday paper while the radio broadcast unfolded; and sound effects, as well as educational lectures, augmented and transformed the otherwise blurry images. For instance, jungle noises were added to images of wild animals (Ramsey 1938, 195–197; see also *Museum News* 1924; 1929a; 1929b; 1931; Bach 1938). I describe this as a new form of virtual museological curation, which coordinated airwaves, newspapers, museums, and a geographically expanded audience relocated to urban, and an increasing number of suburban, homes.

These experiments were dependent on the frequent reproduction of artworks on special photo pages in newspapers. Sometimes these art images filled an entire page especially devoted to a particular exhibition or theme. Other times they shared space with pictures of fashion contestants, bathing beauties, coronations, and presidential speeches. The Met frequently collaborated with newspapers; images from its collection appeared regularly in the *New York Times*. These might appear under the guise of an announcement about a new acquisition or an upcoming exhibit. Survey exhibits were also attempted. In 1924 Edward Robinson, then director of the Met, selected a series of images under the title "From the Renaissance to the Present." In advertisements for the serialized museo-newspaper exhibit, the paintings were described as representative of the Met's collection, "all varying in theme, but all bearing the mark of genius." These images, billed as masterpieces, were published in order to be "suitable for framing," a nod to yet another museum frontier: the American home (*New York Times* 1924). During the 1930s, it was also not uncommon to find newspapers and magazines that published art reproductions and also sold higher-quality versions of the reproductions it featured. The *New York Times* made the photos published in its picture pages available for purchase "for framing or other private use," advertising its service in the paper itself.[6] Women's magazines and department stores offered similar services.

Museum–media collaborations also include early experiments with television, which began as early as television itself. In the year of television's debut at the 1939 World's Fair, the Museum of Modern Art (MoMA) broadcast the grand opening of its signature building on West 53rd Street (see Spigel 2004; Wasson 2005). The Met followed shortly thereafter with didactic art programming, beginning as early as 1941 and then resuming in 1944 (Schoener and Wurlitzer 1956, 76). Early tourism programs that featured museums, such as "Treasures of New York," provided live televisual tours of New York area museums during the 1951 season (Carson 1951). As Lynn Spigel has shown, MoMA actively engaged the potential of television during the whole of the 1950s, orchestrating and planning new genres of art/museum curation (Spigel 2004; 2008). Throughout the late 1940s and 1950s, museums across the United States participated in television programming: Art Institute of Chicago, Brooklyn Museum, Philadelphia Museum, Cleveland Museum of Art, Albright Knox Art Gallery (Buffalo), Detroit Institute of Art, and Baltimore Museum of Art, among others (Schoener and Wurlitzer 1956, 77). Indeed, museums were at the forefront of several television innovations. For instance, in 1954 the National Broadcasting Company (NBC) conducted its first color-compatible broadcast. The show was titled *A Visit to the Metropolitan Museum of Art*, and featured its newly renovated building (Spigel 2004, 367). Collectively, these ventures into reconceiving the museum as a distinct genre of cultural programming, fully integrated around mass media and the American home, represent the genealogy of what is now a common sense aspect of contemporary art institutions. Museum publicity events, spiraling websites, satellite museums, mall-based retail outlets, television series, and countless coffee table books now punctuate this foundational fact of museum authority and identity. Each of these, in one way or another, reorient museum address away from an abstract idea of "the public" and toward the individualized and mobilized consumer.

Speaking of consumerism, the Met also had considerable relationships with department stores throughout the 1920s and 1930s, offering classes in art history and design to store clerks. The museum also published articles about the importance of art education in women's magazines such as the aforementioned *Ladies' Home Journal*, *House Beautiful*, *Ladies Home Companion*, and *Country Life*, as well as more specialized home, decorating, and design magazines including *Magazine of Art*, *Arts and Decoration*, and *Architectural Record*. As I have argued in a more in-depth discussion of the museum's relationship to retail and consumerism (Wasson 2006, 174), the Met addressed the American home as if it were a de facto museum satellite (Townsend 1921; Bach 1923; Davis Seal 1925; *House Beautiful* 1925; Kent 1929; *Arts and Decoration* 1934).

Let me provide a final example of the Met's search for retail influence and the use of media. In May 1927 the museum sponsored an exposition of modern design held by Macy's, the well-known department store. The collaboration satisfied the museum's determination to spread its influence as well as Macy's interest to exercise its own authority as a tastemaker. Macy's provided valuable retail space to museum-like exhibits of design objects. It also offered a lecture hall in which art experts – including those employed by the Met – delivered talks on the history of art and design. The museum supplied selected objects from its collection, and retained visibility in all advertising for the week-long event (Friedman 2003, 18–19). Thirty thousand catalogs were printed, with the Met's name prominently featured on each and every cover (Macy's 1927). WJZ, a local radio station, broadcast the daily lectures that were given at Macy's as part of the regular *Metropolitan Museum of Art Show*. Fifty thousand visitors attended during the one-week run, an audience many times that which entered the museum's primary site just up the street. Through a highly coordinated and purposeful media event the Met made friends with a range of media forms, successfully fulfilling the show's stated purpose: to link "art with everyday household life." Such collaborations became a widely emulated model both for museums and for retail (Friedman 2003, 26).[7]

As this example shows, art museums found larger audiences not just through media but through such collaborations with commercial institutions. In this way, they could expand the influence of the art institution, which increasingly rein-vented itself, as I have argued, as a producer of good taste. The technologies, insti-tutions, and language of mass media played an instrumental role in constituting this new spatially dispersed museum.

The condensed museum

Despite or perhaps because of its mediated iterations, there is something that remains formidable about the Met as a particular kind of place. The quintessential example of the American "universal survey museum," the Met has at least rhetori-cally sought to display and thus order everything (Duncan and Wallach 1980). Founded in 1870 by wealthy industrialists and urban reformers determined to establish New York as the capital of American civility, the building and the collec-tions it housed self-consciously mimicked its European predecessors. Though it has long been derided by its critics as a mausoleum, its wealthy trustees and patrons (Morgans, Rockefellers, and Vanderbilts alike), along with various museum presi-dents, have nonetheless presided over a collection that has grown to include two million objects spanning 5000 years, dispersed across two million square feet of prime Manhattan real estate.[8] The defiant majesty of the building and its commen-surate institutional ambitions have persisted alongside its mediated expansions and, as I will now show, the contraction of its spaces and sometimes its art. Presently, this latter dynamic is nowhere more clear than through the portals of a handheld smartphone, tablet, or laptop computer. Seen through the instantaneous point-and-click logics of the World Wide Web, the museum is less a monumental mausoleum than a small, quaint moving postcard; a networked, digital snow-globe wherein its endless collection of old art, its cool, quiet sanctum, its grand halls, looming columns, and endless galleries are radically diminished in size and abbreviated in time. From 40 feet to four inches, from 5000 years to five seconds, the multiplication of museum views transforms old things into manageable, bite-sized morsels and endless quick views which flash by on a desk, a lap, or in the palm of one's hand. This tendency to reproduce and hence play with museum scale is not new and has a long precedent in previous technologies of reproducibility. In this section, I turn my focus to film's role in this enduring dynamic of mediating the insides of the museum.

As I have already shown, film and other media have long been an integral element of the American museum's efforts to help visitors navigate its spaces and engage more fully in its mission. This has entailed using films to illustrate lectures, to animate museum objects (people, rocks, paintings), to spectacularize science, and to dramatize the extent of the museum's imperial reach by showing images captured from distant places and cultures (Griffiths 2002; 2008). In what follows, I will focus on specific films made by the Met. These films will be positioned less as a known genre of cinema and more as articulations of a specifically museological impulse, one that used the specificities of film to effect a particular curatorial end. By way of close analysis, I will suggest that the museum films' short length but long takes (that is, their slow pace) are intimately connected to the museum's effort to manage time and perception in its galleries. Film and its established conventions of spectatorship (seated and not moving) offered the capacity to condense, dynamically manipulate, reconfigure, and ultimately control time in an automated fashion far more than previous museum display techniques – the diorama or the lantern slide, for instance. Thus, during the period under examination, film was seen as a way to more efficiently direct the museum-goer's eye as to how to look at its art and, more precisely, how long to look. The idea of the didactic public display of art in a museum has long complicated the simple view of the museum as a mausoleum. The Met's use of film is but one symptom of this, indicating the museum's struggles to respond to changing visual technologies and also to evolving public expectations of engagement. Shown within the museum's walls, as well as beyond them, these short films worked to refigure the space and time of the museum as well. These films, exhibited to a seated audience, promised to alleviate the demands on the museum-goer of the lengthy trek down palatial museum halls, or the disordered wandering the elaborate architecture of the museum allowed. They helped to order the proliferating assemblage of things, directing the eye to one particular object for a predetermined amount of time. They instructed the spectator to look at significant fragments rather than at the overwhelming whole. Museum films offered another kind of museum experience. Shrunken, two-dimensional, often small (4 × 5 foot or 8 × 10 foot), glowing in the dark, 10, 20, or 30 minutes long – museum films provided *a particular viewing speed* as well as a *unique scale* by which to differently see the museum and its objects.

Recent work in film studies has shown the productive benefits of understanding cinema in relation to the rapidly changing visual and aural culture of which it was a part. Linking cinema to other forms of movement and other modes of temporality, we can observe the ways in which the moving image reflected and refracted a moving world (Charney and Schwartz 1995; Rabinovitz 1998; Gunning 2000; Doane 2002). But what does the modern trope of movement mean for an ostensibly static space like the museum? By the 1920s, the motionless nature of museum space was increasingly seen by museum reformers as a problem. In other words, as the universal survey museum became a fixture in the American cultural scene, and the hierarchies of class and taste that it promulgated became solidified, the very *still* aspects of its art and architecture were seen as a key impediment to engaging a larger public immersed in moving pictures and things (discussed earlier). In short, the museum's specific efforts to invoke timelessness were seen as symptom of both its elitism and its aversion to public engagement.[9]

As I have already argued, film – along with cognate media – enabled the museum to be more structurally nimble, with its art appearing and then disappearing in disposable dailies and weaving across airwaves. Yet, there remained a broadly based and substantial discussion about how to make sense of motion *within* the museum. It was during this period that members of the avant-garde began to develop challenging models for art exhibition that worked to defy the static models that dominated in established museums. Throughout the 1920s and 1930s and into the 1940s, artists such as Frederick Kiesler, László Moholy-Nagy, Herbert Bayer, and El Lissitzky reworked exhibition design to incorporate the kinetic, the quick view, and chance into the experience of exhibited art. As a result, they hung art on portable wooden structures, ribbons, and moving conveyor belts. Many incorporated photography, film, and art reproductions. Moholy-Nagy designed a room called "The Room of Our Time" (1930, Germany), in the center of which was a machine (*Light Machine*) that projected patterns of abstract light when a button was pressed. In this same room a double glass screen was mounted where two films were to be shown, one a documentary and the other an abstract experimental film (Staniszewski 1998, 22).

The avant-garde's embrace of movement and film notwithstanding, the American art museum adopted a more cautious, and at times even disciplined, approach to movement in general and the movement of images in particular. To be sure, efforts to understand and direct all manner of movement inside the museum became a centerpiece of American museum reform. This controlled movement, however, had less to do with experiments in hanging its Rembrandts across clothes lines or succumbing to the peripatetic spectator, and much more to do with actively directing the movement of people and their eyes. In other words, select museums began focusing on how *people* moved through museum spaces, and thus examining how museum-goers perceived displayed art. Beginning in 1928 – with a slew of studies to follow in the 1930s – Edward S. Robinson, a professor of psychology at Yale University, published a report entitled *The Behavior of the Museum Visitor*

(1928).[10] The report was commissioned by the American Museum Association, and endowed with funds from the Carnegie Foundation. Robinson oversaw a study of museum-goers at the Pennsylvania Museum (and Industrial School, Fairmont Park). Resonating with other Taylorist time–motion studies seeking to make factory workers and housewives more efficient, Robinson and his researchers, armed with stopwatches, measured how much time museum-goers spent looking at each piece of art as they walked through the museum. They did so with the aim of arguing how much time museum-goers *should* spend looking at art in order to maximize their appreciation of it, compared to how much time they actually *did* spend. Much to the dismay of those who cherished the ideal of the museum-goer as a committed and contemplative type, results indicated that the average museum-goer looked at each piece of art for an average of about three seconds. As a result, the Philadelphia museum adopted new strategies for hanging art, which included the now familiar chronological arrangement, in order to make it easier for museum patrons to make sense of painting more quickly and without putting undue pressure on them not just to see everything but also to find order in everything that they saw. The museum instead offered a kind of synoptic view, what was termed a "historical pageant" of art, ostensibly made easier and more familiar because it resembled the experience of walking down a nicely ordered city street. This conceptualization of the street as a safe, familiar, and manageable one, easier to make sense of than the conventional museum, clearly presents an idea of a typical Main Street that is counter to many of the contemporaneous writings that fashioned cities as overwhelming with stimulus, suitable only to rapid montage and quick viewing (*New York Times* 1927, 13). Robinson's study suggested that it was in fact the museum that overwhelmed; the city was comparatively calming.

Anxiety about attention, in this instance the attention of the museum-goer, is one echoed throughout writing that wrestles with the question of how to make sense of modernity's flurry of sensory stimulation, and how to make sense of the new forms of subjectivity, perception, and sometimes pathology these conditions enabled (Schivelbusch 1979; Crary 1990; 1999; Simmel 2005). Museum officials too sought a name for the unique experience of the modern as brokered by the magnitude and density of museum exhibitions. Named "museum fatigue" during the late 1910s, a term used frequently during the 1920s, this new condition served as a catchall to index a kind of sensory overload or exhaustion, said to be variously emotional, physical, and intellectual (you also see the condition of "eye strain" invoked). Museums, it was thought, simply overwhelmed people by offering too many objects in a vast disorienting environment. In short, the scale of viewer to things viewed was disproportionate to the ideal museum experience.

Museums – especially science museums – responded by experimenting with new and adjustable electric lighting mechanisms, new display cases, and what were termed "satisfying vistas and restful retreats," which I take to mean simply places where people can sit, like benches (*New York Times* 1930, 129). One the most common responses to the condition of museum fatigue was to argue that the museum-goer could only alleviate his/her symptoms by better training his/her eye to see properly, to teach it what to look at and how to look at it. For museum professionals committed to maintaining the museum's authority and effectiveness, museum fatigue was caused by the undisciplined eye, the eye that was always darting about from object to object, which exacerbated the condition – this wandering irrational eye being in a sense the very eye embraced by the avant-garde (see *Museum Work* 1924a).[11] Eye fatigue was also correlated with physical fatigue at the museum. One museum in Dayton, Ohio, named its new modern theater with state-of-the-art projection facilities as key in its strategy to combat museum fatigue, presumably as it allowed museum-goers to relieve their tired feet, and to watch less taxing visual forms on screen. In short, films were used here to provide a reprieve from the overwhelming demands – physical and perceptual – made by the museum and its contents.[12] Films ostensibly calmed the harried eye by providing a clear line of sight to a plainly displayed object, deciding for the viewer where to look and for how long. The wandering eye and wandering museum-goer, conceived as a problem, found their cure in this useful form of museum cinema.

While museum fatigue was a condition applied to patrons of both art and science museums, it is worth pointing out that art museums had been slowly moving away from the more muddied salon style of hanging paintings, a style in which paintings were hung according to size, shape, and the whims of the connoisseur. Instead, increasingly scientific methods dictated that paintings be hung by chronology or geography (and eventually by formal attributes, schools, or movements), in a manner that allowed such logics to be observed from painting to painting. The problem of classifying art, and then adapting display techniques that reflected more rational classification schemes, was complicated at the Met. Not only did the museum (as it does now) seek to possess and display a "universal survey" of art, but many of its objects were donated by wealthy collectors who required that their objects stay together; the display logic remained constrained by a patron's individual taste, travel routes, or habits of acquisition. The more modern and rationalized criteria for displaying art, with single works mounted in clear isolation from others – a style of exhibition that would characterize MoMA during the 1930s – were much slower to arrive at the Met. Nonetheless, the trend in American art museums was toward simplifying and rationalizing display techniques, and eliminating what some critics called the problem of "art clutter." To sum up, the trend toward simplified display techniques was both a scientific and also a pedagogical one.

The use of films and screens at the Met must be understood within the context of this dialogue about museum fatigue and changing modes of display. Films and film screens were used to simplify and further order museum art and exhibitions, providing relief to the exhausted museum visitor. For instance, the Met's filmed tour of its American Wing highlighted housing design and interior decoration as arranged chronologically by curators in its exhibition halls. A prominent feature of the museum, the American Wing opened in 1924 to much national acclaim, particularly in popular media and women's magazines (for instance, *Ladies' Home*

Journal declared the wing proof that "Americans are a home-loving race" (Davis Seal 1925, 20)). The 45 minute film (the longest of the Met's films) surveyed the halls of the wing in chronological order, emphasizing pertinent furniture and tapestry details, using close-ups and long takes to punctuate and dramatize them. Armoire and armchair participated in narratives of patriotic assent. Select objects appeared in isolation and close-up – they were thus functionally enlarged and emphasized in order to provide opportunities for more studied perusal; some objects were placed on a revolving stand in order to allow for examination from all angles. Rotating in their often enlarged state, chocolate pots or tea kettles acquired a more prominent role in the exhibit's loose historical and nationalist narrative. Larger furniture shrunk to fit the film screen became less monumental and more quaint, resembling the contents of a doll's house rather than a dame's dining set. The slow speed of the stationary but panning camera offered a panoramic view, a new kind of mechanical museum view: not too fast so as to irretrievably transform the objects or distress the spectator, but not too slow so as not to lose the interest of the cinema-habituated museum-goer. The camera here replaced the movement of a head or the motion of a crowd, becoming curator and tour guide, providing a distinct kind of museological gaze, and rendering quite differently the static objects at least some of which could just as easily be seen with the viewers' own eyes, at their own pace, down the hall (*Metropolitan Museum of Art Bulletin* 1935). The ability of film to play with the scale of found objects creates another dynamic to museum display, speeding up, slowing down, setting in motion, enlarging, and shrinking an endless assortment of objects into the new mechanical display window. Chosen items were all recast to screen size, each centered and perfectly fit within the standardized frame of the celluloid window.

This recasting of the museum's exhibitionary drama reinforces a certain density to the museum's visual fabric, and a particular response to debates about movement, perception, and overstimulus (museum fatigue). While asserting a degree of control over how some of its exhibitions and objects would be seen (very few films featured paintings, for instance) film screens also multiplied and extended previous display techniques, providing a different kind of venue for the vast views that formed the basis of the museum's spatial majesty, offering short films (usually 20 minutes) that featured 10 to 20 second slow fragments instead. And, to be sure, compared to the 3 second rapid view of the museum-goer observed by Robinson, museum films functionally slowed the museum-goer down, weaving steady shots of single (but sometimes multiple) items, ranging from 5 to 15 seconds on average, formed into a new whole through editing, and made newly digestible by their small size, comparatively long takes, and short overall length. Such techniques of visual display served to effectively address – so it was believed – not simply a more *attentive* but a more *retentive* museum-goer, that is, a museum-goer that ostensibly learned more.

Within this idea of the art museum's increasingly dense visual field was more than a multiplication of views to the selected art objects it held and exhibited.

Equally important is that these new museum display techniques also reproduced particular views of the museum itself, setting these views in motion, with particular spatial and temporal sequencing. Yet, each film did so in reasonably distinct ways. *The American Wing* (1925) film was a highly didactic, chronologically arranged inventory of items in the exhibit hall, with brief intertitles announcing the period or pedigree of what was coming next. It presented in highly ordered, rational terms an exhibit that was itself highly ordered and rational. Indeed, it would be easy to mistake this for an inventory film. But some of the museum's films pushed the limits of the fledgling visual experiment by introducing elements of fantasy. In *A Visit to the Armor Galleries of the Metropolitan Museum of Art* (1922), viewers engaged in slow tours of chain mail and gothic plate armor displayed on walls and in cases. Similar to *The American Wing*, this film provided a moving view of the galleries, with single objects isolated for more detailed exegesis. Yet, it augmented the straightforward didacticism of these segments by adding fantastical journeys. This visit to the armor gallery, for instance, included meeting an ambitious knight who "comes to life by the light of the moon." The intrepid knight wanders out of his display case, through the museum, and out into the world. While on his journey he encounters an enemy. A duel ensues, with Central Park as backdrop. The knight makes quick business of his challenger and then promptly returns to his case. A museum docent then methodically dissects each part of the knight's armored suit, explaining by intertitle and gesture its key qualities. Sustained close-ups of the suit's component parts provide an ostensibly enlightening counterbalance to the previous and comparably exciting swordplay.

These films implicate the museum and its contents in a wide range of popular discourses forwarded contemporaneously by other media. In the case of our brave knight, there is a self-conscious attempt to index a range of educational but also fantasy and adventure genres. Further, the use of reasonably familiar technologies (films and museums), combined into something more experimental (museum films and cinematic museums), is here made concrete by our fragmented knight's dissected suit and by slow camera pans of old furniture, which appear to be as much a carryover from the slide show as anything that is conventionally considered devoutly cinematic. In other words, these films are notably unspectacular and rather slow to the contemporary eye. Yet, the act of the museum turning the camera's gaze on itself, transforming the displayed objects and venerated halls into two-dimensional, black and white, silent, small, and portable moving images, proved sufficiently compelling to authorize a new genre of film – the museum film – as well as a new use for cinema, offering a museum in a can, a museum that alleviated museum fatigue by instructing the eye and also relieving the eye with these new, spatially complex screened environments.

Perhaps most interesting of all is a film entitled *Behind the Scenes at the Museum* (1928). In this film, the inner workings of the institution are revealed with a kind of privileged front-stage/back-stage structure. Museum workers are shown punching clocks, donning aprons, and tending to the inner machinations of the museum's public displays. The museum becomes a place of rationalized, methodical, Fordist work. In other words, this film spends less time on Persian pottery and Roman statuary and more time on the other sorts of operations the museum undertakes that have nothing to do with its art per se: the inventory and cataloging department, the photography and film divisions, and the publicity division. Paramount within the rhetoric of the film is the need of the museum to configure itself as an ordered but bustling hive of activity, fully engaged with the latest technologies of dissemination and display: as a place where relevant, efficiently managed things are always happening. In other words, the museum was making itself visible to its public by extending its mannered and authoritative exhibitionary impulses, linking its inner workings to the motion of the camera, the circulation of photographs, and the pulse of the press. This controlled and particular exhibitionary impulse also included the newness of the specific display techniques that brought this film to the museum-goer: an emergent network of small self-operated film screens that functioned at a clear remove from the dominant commercial movie theater.

Importantly, each of these museum films and the view to the museum they supply entirely avoids the problem of art clutter, emphasizing instead ordered operations and controlled slow views of previously still but simultaneously fast or overwhelming art. It also avoids the problem of other museum patrons, who are almost entirely absent from these museum scenes. In sum, while museum administrators understood that the museum must adapt to the moving pleasures of a moving world, they worked to develop a form of cinema – the short slow film – that satisfied the needs of the institution, and the impulse to make films *useful* within the context of an institution whose modes of display were deemed both dated or static but also overwhelming.[13]

In Alison Griffiths's important work on the use of film at the American Museum of Natural History, she argues that that museum's use of film was framed during a roughly similar period, first and foremost, by its efforts to exploit the popular and spectacular appeal of films, while balancing an institutional concern to maintain the sobriety of science and the propriety of pedagogy. Museum officials, Griffiths (2007) argues, were worried that film might too easily render the museum victim to the seductions of popular amusement and the presumed seductions of moving images. But across the park at the Met, museum movies did not seem to ruffle as many feathers, partly because the Met was making its own films and thus had more direct control over the content and style of films (the AMNH often had visiting lecturer-projectionists), and partly because of differences between the institutions. Absent from any remaining evidence at the Met is a concern about film images or museum cinema being too sensational, too populist, or too distracting. In fact, quite the opposite is true. At least for some museum educators, film was a safe respite from and an appealing alternative to the attractions of the museum.

Conclusion

So, what does this new mechanical gaze and its expanded networks tell us about the long history of museums and cinema in particular, and media more generally? First and foremost, a close examination of a particular institutional context demonstrates that at least this museum has a long and intricate relationship with a range of media forms. These relations have both expanded how the museum operates and contracted its techniques of display. Thinking about cinema in the museum indicates the importance of understanding scale as a relative term, requiring consideration of the varied standards and measures attendant throughout film and museum history as it is known, and as it is being discovered. Here I have suggested an expanded idea about what counts as both film and museum history, stretched to include other institutions that shaped particular ideas about the forms and functions of both.

Thinking of film infrastructurally offers a model for considering the ways in which the distinct institution of the museum appropriated a particular technology and made it useful in multiple ways, expanding the museological reach outward and also shaping its techniques of looking inward. Film, along with other media, has long functioned as content delivery, as curatorial device, as public relations, and as infrastructure. With the embrace of media forms, what we call the museum has clearly long existed beyond its brick-and-mortar site, spiraling outward into various media ecologies. Media technologies also challenge us to think about the interior and often cavernous spaces and display platforms within the buildings we call museums, and the ways that technological change has been persistently negotiated for the better part of the last century. This focused study indicates that scale is a key operative term in making sense of these mediated museum pasts. For instance, the categories of the short and slow film, and the small screen, acquire particular meaning in this context. The length, speed, and size of these films allowed cinema to become more useful to the spaces and temporalities of the museum. It allowed flexible programming, temporary projections and repurposable spaces, physical relief, and manageable modes or glimpses of art and objects that seemed otherwise unmanageable, particularly to cultural reformers eager to maximize the wider impact of museum exhibits. Thus, the very term, I think, invites us to think not just about the temporality of a film's whole and its parts but also about its institutional frame. By this I mean to say that we might think of the film's scale (temporal and spatial) as not just qualities intrinsic to institutions of cinema but also as irretrievably tied to those of the museum, with its own distinct approaches to scale, whether that means size or speed. That is, what informs our understanding of something as short or long, big or small, fast or slow, is also tied to the structures and institutions that undergird the context of display and of watching.

By using the term "scale" I also mean to invoke the relational aspects of the concept. As Anna McCarthy has written, concepts of scale "enable conceptual movement between argument and evidence, generality and specificity, concreteness and abstraction" (2006, 25). In other words, by investigating a specific site and its changing representational practices, those which expand and those which contract, the concept of scale becomes a productive tool in seeking to understand the concrete specificity of particular media as well as the abstract implications of their hybrid and ever evolving forms and functions as they are imbricated with the museum. At one level, then, scale allows for considerations of size and speed (absolute or relative) across, within, and beyond the screened image. For instance, examining the question of scale allows us to explore the relationships between the screen and the aesthetic, ideological, social, and material networks of which it is a part. The implications of this help to disarticulate the film screen from the film camera, and in a sense the celluloid strip, in order to think about cinema as a distinct element of a range of display and distribution apparatuses. More specifically, in the context of the Met, scale allows us to consider modes of visual presentation in specific and dialectical relation. Formally, we can see aesthetic specificities. Structurally we can see qualitatively different concerns being brought to bear both on the image and on the screened environment. The trope of scale – the expanded and the condensed – also provides a different view of the museum, allowing a more fulsome and elastic idea about the ways in which, as an institution, it has long made use of architecture, but also of varied media, to conduct its business productively. We might still visit a museum but we live with museums every day through their dispersed paper, celluloid, electronic, and digital iterations. Indeed, I would suggest that it is partly through these media that the museum itself has successfully survived as an institution, weaving its way into cultural common sense. These expansions and contractions are not new or recent but are enduring and constitutive elements of the museum's history and influence.

Notes

1 Eilean Hooper-Greenhill argues that these deeply contradictory functions are endemic to the public museum, born of the republicanism emergent with the French Revolution. These museums represent a sharp turn away from the powers of the cleric, the king, and the aristocracy and toward the functions of the modern state and its needs to manage populations (Hooper-Greenhill 1992, 167–190).

2 From 1923 onward 16 mm emerged as the standard gauge for extra-theatrical film exhibition. The Met's entry into the field is early and suggests the emerging common sense both of the 16 mm format and the idea that institutions seeking to keep current needed to respond to and integrate cinema into operations. For more on the importance of 16 mm and cultural institutions during this period, see Wasson 2005, ch. 3.

3 The Met also acted as distributor and exhibitor for films made by Yale University Press, entitled *The Chronicles of America Photoplays*. In 1925 this consisted of 15 films of a planned 33. Each covered a topic in American history, for example, "Columbus," "The Pilgrims," "The Puritans," "Alexander Hamilton," and "The Frontier Woman."

4   These catalogs are available online as part of the museum's digital collections.

5   This affirmed that "quiet contemplation of a thing of beauty" remained the keynote of aesthetic enjoyment, and that the motion picture had little in common with this task. Yet, its value to the quiet contemplation of art resided in its service to the art object, providing it with a secure vessel and thus safe passage into the world (Elliott 1926, 216).

6   *New York Times*, May 5, 1935, X7.

7   This program continued and one source estimated that, in 1928, 250,000 people had wandered through Macy's exhibit on art and industrial design (Friedman 2003, 7). For a fascinating account of other contemporaneous collaborations between department stores and the Newark Museum, as well as the related progressive ideas of that museum's director, John Cotton Dana, see Duncan 2002.

8   The two standard histories of the Met are Tompkins (1989) and Howe (1946).

9   The Met was inevitably named as a primary promulgator of the museum as a site of elite collection and overt display of wealth. The following is typical of left-leaning critics: "Instead of refracting the light of improved artistic standards into the practical affairs of their sprawling localities, they store the culture brought to them through leisure and wealth in the sterile salons of self-sufficient cliques" (T. R. Adams in 1939, quoted in Low 1942, 30).

10 Robinson went on to work at the Boston Museum of Fine Arts and then to the Met to become head of their Educational Department in the 1930s.

11 "Museum fatigue" became a general call for more museum education in general (see Elliott 1928; *New York Times* 1932).

12 The question of fatigue and gender was also important to the idea of museum fatigue. One museum in Columbus, Ohio reported attempting to increase male patronage and to create more appealing ways to engender art appreciation. "Art smokers" were initiated whereby, once a month, an evening was set aside in which men were invited to the museum. As this new male patron entered the gallery he was given a pipe filled with "well selected" tobacco. "As he stretched himself out in the easy chairs that had been provided he found himself as comfortable as in his own club. While thus at ease, officials of the gallery or others discussed in the most informal fashion the current exhibition or matters of general art interest. They stressed the relation of art to business and home ... Art was elevated to masculine standing and understanding" (*Museum Work* 1924b).

13 For instance, a learning laboratory and theater were planned which invited museum-goers to choose a film on entering, and to project the film more than once if need be, "to fix it more firmly in memory." The short film here was part of a repertory theater, sufficiently efficient in form and function to facilitate better mental retention in an otherwise crowded museum mentality (see *Metropolitan Museum of Art Bulletin* 1928b). Thus, while films were a regular part of museum activities, used precisely because they were a compelling and necessary addition to their other methods of visual display, museum officials worked hard to control the images shown at the museum, and also to balance them with erudite lectures, endless display cases, and muted dioramas.

References

Acland, Charles, and Haidee Wasson. 2011. *Useful Cinema*. Durham, NC: Duke University Press.

Arts and Decoration. 1934. "A Parade of Contemporary Achievements at the Metropolitan Museum." 42: 12–25.

Bach, Richard. 1923. "A Museum Exhibit as a Spur to Industrial Art." *Arts and Decoration* 18: 10, 62.

Bach, Richard. 1938. "Neighborhood Exhibition of the Metropolitan Museum of Art." *Museum News* 15: 7–8.

Bennett, Tony. 1992. "Useful Culture." *Cultural Studies* 6(3): 395–408.

Carson, Saul. 1951. "On the Air." *New Republic* 124: 30–31.

Charney, Leo, and Vanessa R. Schwartz, eds. 1995. *Cinema and the Invention of Modern Life*. Berkeley: University of California Press.

Crary, Jonathan. 1990. *Techniques of the Observer: On Vision and Modernity in the Nineteenth Century*. Cambridge, MA: MIT Press.

Crary, Jonathan. 1999. *Suspensions of Perception: Attention, Spectacle, and Modern Culture*. Cambridge, MA: MIT Press.

Davis Seal, Ethel. 1925. "The American Wing of the Metropolitan Museum." *Ladies' Home Journal*, May: 20–21.

Doane, Mary Anne. 2002. *The Emergence of Cinematic Time: Modernity, Contingency, the Archive*. Cambridge, MA: Harvard University Press.

Duncan, Carol. 2002. "Museums and Department Stores: Close Encounters. In *High-Pop: Making Culture into Popular Entertainment*, edited by Jim Collins, 129–154. Oxford: Blackwell.

Duncan, Carol, and Alan Wallach. 1980. "The Universal Survey Museum." *Art History* 3(4): 448–469.

Elliott, Huger. 1926. "The Educational Work of the Museum." *Metropolitan Museum of Art Bulletin* 21(9): 201–217.

Elliott, Huger. 1928. "Educational Activities: A Brief Overview." *Metropolitan Museum of Art Bulletin* 23(9): 218–220.

Friedman, Marilyn F. 2003. *Selling Good Design: Promoting the Early Modern Interior*. New York: Rizzoli.

Griffiths, Alison. 2002. *Wondrous Difference: Cinema, Anthropology, and Turn-of-the-Century Visual Culture*. New York: Columbia University Press.

Griffiths, Alison. 2007. ""Automatic Cinema" and Illustrated Radio: Multimedia in the Museum." In *Residual Media*, edited by Charles Acland, 69–96. Minneapolis: University of Minnesota Press.

Griffiths, Alison. 2008. *Shivers Down Your Spine: Cinema, Museums, and the Immersive View*. New York: Columbia University Press.

Gunning, Tom. 2000. "The Cinema of Attraction: Early Film, Its Spectator, and the Avant-Garde." In *Film and Theory: An Anthology*, edited by Robert Stam and Toby Miller, 229–235. Oxford: Blackwell.

Harris, Neil. 1990. *Cultural Excursions: Marketing Appetites and Cultural Tastes in Modern America*. Chicago: University of Chicago Press.

Henning, Michelle. 2006. *Museums, Media and Cultural Theory*. Maidenhead, UK: Open University Press.

Hooper-Greenhill, Eilean. 1992. *Museums and the Shaping of Knowledge*. London: Routledge.

House Beautiful. 1925. "The House in Good Taste." 57: 33–36.

Howe, Winifred. 1946. *A History of the Metropolitan Museum of Art, 1905–1941*. New York: Columbia University Press.

Huyssen, Andreas. 1986. *After the Great Divide: Modernism, Mass Culture, Postmodernism*. Bloomington: Indiana University Press.

Kaempffert, Waldemar. 1932. "Vital Museums of the New Era." *New York Times*, March 20, SM12.

Kent, H. W. 1929. "Modern Art Makes Itself at Home." *Woman's Home Companion* 56: 11.

Levine, Lawrence W. 1988. *Highbrow/Lowbrow: The Emergence of Cultural Hierarchy in America*. Cambridge, MA: Harvard University Press.

Low, Theodore L. 1942. *The Museum as a Social Instrument*. New York: Metropolitan Museum of Art for American Association of Museums.

Macy's. 1927. *Catalog of the Exposition of Art in Trade at Macy's*. New York: Macy's.

McCarthy, Anna. 2006. "From the Ordinary to the Concrete: Cultural Studies and the Politics of Scale." In *Questions of Method in Cultural Studies*, edited by Mimi White and James Schwoch, 21–53. Oxford: Blackwell.

McClellan, Andrew. 2003. "A Brief History of the Art Museum Public." In *Art and Its Publics: Museum Studies at the Millennium*, edited by Andrew McClellan, 1–50. Oxford: Blackwell.

Metropolitan Museum of Art. 1925. *Annual Report to the Trustees*. New York: Metropolitan Museum of Art.

Metropolitan Museum of Art. 1929a. "Accessions and Notes." *Metropolitan Museum of Art Bulletin* 24(8): 217–218.

Metropolitan Museum of Art. 1929b. *Annual Report to the Trustees*. New York: Metropolitan Museum of Art.

Metropolitan Museum of Art. 1930. *Cinema Films: A List of Museum Films and Others, with the Conditions Under Which They Are Distributed*. New York: Metropolitan Museum of Art.

Metropolitan Museum of Art. 1932. *Cinema Films: A List of Museum Films and Others, with the Conditions Under Which They Are Distributed*. New York: Metropolitan Museum of Art.

Metropolitan Museum of Art. 1935a. *Annual Report to the Trustees*. New York: Metropolitan Museum of Art.

Metropolitan Museum of Art. 1935b. *Cinema Films: A List of Museum Films and Others, with the Conditions Under Which They Are Distributed*. New York: Metropolitan Museum of Art.

Metropolitan Museum of Art. 1940. *Cinema Films: A List of Museum Films and Others, with the Conditions Under Which They Are Distributed*. New York: Metropolitan Museum of Art.

Metropolitan Museum of Art Bulletin. 1925. "Cinema Films." 20(1): 2.

Metropolitan Museum of Art Bulletin. 1928a. "Accessions and Notes." 23(2): 58–62.

Metropolitan Museum of Art Bulletin. 1928b. "Accessions and Notes." 23(9): 222.

Metropolitan Museum of Art Bulletin. 1929. "Accessions and Notes." 24(8): 217–218.

Metropolitan Museum of Art Bulletin. 1935. "Notes: A New Museum Film." 30(7): 150.

Museum News. 1924. "Illustrates Talks by Radio." 1: 2.

Museum News. 1929a. "Museums and Newspapers Co-operate in Roto-Radio Talk." 15: 1.

Museum News. 1929b. "Lantern Slides Supplement Museum Radio Talk." 6: 2.

Museum News. 1931. "New Automatic Motion Picture Projector Installed in Three Museums." 9: 4.

Museum Work. 1924a. "Museum Fatigue." 7(1): 21–22.

Museum Work. 1924b. "Art Smokers for Business Men." 6(5): n.p.

New York Times. 1924. "Masterworks Reproduced." February 24, E7.

New York Times. 1927. "Stop-Watches Held on Museum Visitors." October 9, 13.

New York Times. 1930. "Dayton's Museum." May 9, 129.

New York Times. 1932. "Art Museum Names Winlock Director." January 19, 23.

Pratt, George C. 1925. *Museum News*. New York: American Museum Association.

Rabinovitz, Lauren. 1998. *For the Love of Pleasure: Women, Movies, and Culture in Turn-of-the-Century Chicago*. New Brunswick, NJ: Rutgers University Press.

Ramsey, Grace Fisher. 1938. *Educational Work in Museums of the United States*. New York: H. W. Wilson.

Ramsey, Grace Fisher. 1940. "The Film Work of the American Museum of Natural History." *Journal of Educational Sociology* 13(5): 280–284.

Robinson, Edward S. 1928. *The Behavior of the Museum Visitor*. Washington, DC: American Association of Museums.

Rubin, Joan Shelley. 1992. *The Making of Middlebrow Culture*. Chapel Hill: University of North Carolina Press.

Schivelbusch, Wolfgang. 1979. *The Railway Journey: The Industrialization of Time and Space in the Nineteenth Century*. Oxford: Blackwell.

Schoener, Allon T., and Thekla Wurlitzer. 1956. "Television in the Art Museums." *Quarterly of Film, Radio, and Television* 11(1): 70–82.

Simmel, Georg. 2005. "The Metropolis and Mental Life." In *The Urban Sociology Reader*, edited by Jan Lin and Christopher Mele, 23–31. New York: Routledge.

Spigel, Lynn. 2004. "Television, The Housewife, and the Museum of Modern Art." In *Television After TV: Essays on a Medium in Transition*, edited by Lynn Spigel and Jan Olsson, 349–387. Durham, NC: Duke University Press.

Spigel, Lynn. 2008. *TV by Design: Modern Art and the Rise of Network Television*. Chicago: University of Chicago Press.

Staniszewski, Mary Anne. 1998. *The Power of Display: A History of Exhibition Installations at the Museum of Modern Art*. Cambridge, MA: MIT Press.

Stevens, George. 1916. "The Use of Motion Photography in Museums." *Metropolitan Museum of Art Bulletin* 11(9): 203–204.

Time. 1924. "Dove and Donkey." 3(4): 17.

Tompkins, Calvin. 1989. *Masters and Masterpieces: The Story of the Metropolitan Museum of Art*. New York: Henry Holt.

Townsend, Richard T. 1921. "The Metropolitan Museum of Art and Your Home." *Country Life* 40: 65–66.

Wasson, Haidee. 2005. *Museum Movies: The Museum of Modern Art and the Birth of Art Cinema*. Berkeley: University of California Press.

Wasson, Haidee. 2006. "Every Home an Art Museum: Towards a Genealogy of the Museum Gift Shop." In *Residual Media*, edited by Charles Acland, 301–344. Minneapolis: University of Minnesota Press.

Wasson, Haidee. 2011. "Big, Fast Museums/Small, Slow Movies: Film, Scale and the Art Museum." In *Useful Cinema*, edited by Charles Acland and Haidee Wasson, 178–204. Durham, NC: Duke University Press.

Further Reading

Seldes, Gilbert. 1944. "Television and the Museums." *Magazine of Art* 37: 178–179.
Spigel, Lynn. 2001. "High Culture in Low Places: Television and Modern Art, 1950–1970." In *Welcome to the Dreamhouse*, 265–309. Durham, NC: Duke University Press.

Haidee Wasson is Associate Professor of Cinema at Concordia University, Montreal. Her award-winning books include *Museum Movies* (University of California Press, 2005); *Inventing Film Studies*, coedited with Lee Grieveson (Duke University Press, 2008); and *Useful Cinema*, coedited with Charles Acland (Duke University Press, 2011), which was named best edited collection by the Society of Cinema and Media Studies. Her current research examines the history of portable film projectors, exploring how the ideal of a small, adaptable, self-operated model of cinema interfaced with key institutions throughout the twentieth century, including museums and galleries, world's fairs, and the military.

INDEX

Page numbers in *italics* denote figures

The International Handbooks of Museum Studies: Museum Media, First Edition.
Edited by Michelle Henning.
© 2015 John Wiley & Sons Ltd. Published 2020 by John Wiley & Sons Ltd.